Law and Modernization in the
Church of England

This House I Have Built

A Study of the Legal History of Establishment in England

Is it credible then that God should dwell with men on the earth? If heaven and the heaven of heavens do not contain thee, how much less this house which I have built?

—2 Chron. 6:18

Law and Modernization in the Church of England

Charles II to the Welfare State

Robert E. Rodes, Jr.

The University of Notre Dame Press

Notre Dame   London

Copyright © 1991 by
University of Notre Dame Press
Notre Dame, Indiana 46556

Library of Congress Cataloging-in-Publication Data

Rodes, Robert E.
    Law and modernization in the Church of England :
Charles II to the welfare state / Robert E. Rodes, Jr.
        p.   cm.
    Includes bibliographical references and index.
    ISBN 0-268-01293-8
    1. Ecclesiastical law—England—History.   2. Church and
state—Church of England—History.   3. Church of England—
Government—History.   4. England—Church history—Modern
period, 1485-
I. Title.
KD8605.R622   1991
344.42'096—dc20   91-50567
[344.20496]   CIP

Manufactured in the United States of America

Sancto
BEDAE VENERABILI
ex Voto

Contents

Introduction

This is the last of three volumes on the legal history of the peculiar church-state relationship that has prevailed in England with remarkable tenacity since the Gospel was first preached to the Anglo-Saxon kings. The first volume, *Ecclesiastical Administration in Medieval England*, dealt with the institutional patterns of Anglo-Saxon Christianity, with the reshaping of those patterns in response to the Norman Conquest and the Gregorian Reform, and with the administration of the medieval church as it emerged from the process. In the second volume, *Lay Authority and Reformation in the English Church*, I tried to show how the medieval kings and their apparatus of government set limits on the power of the clergy, and tried to maintain their own version of a Christian state, and how the medieval Commons looked to the government to redress their grievances with the clergy. I tried to show how these medieval attitudes provided a political and ideological basis for the Reformation, and resulted in a very different kind of Reformation from the one that took place on the Continent of Europe. I dealt with the administration of the reformed Church of England and its relations with the state up to the time of the Civil War.

This volume begins with the Restoration of the monarchy in 1660, and with it the restoration of the Anglican Church. The first chapter describes the relatively peaceful century and half when the spiritual aspirations (such as they were) of the nation were more closely reflected in the institutional patterns of the church than they had ever been before or were ever to be again. The next two chapters treat of the painful juridical adjustments that had to be made when the old synthesis finally came unstuck and the church had to take its place among the institutions of a modern, efficient, and pluralist state. The last chapters show the equally painful and far more tumultuous adjustments of the laws governing the church's doctrine, its liturgy, and its internal affairs to accompany its changed position in society. I am not sure whether my treatment sheds any great light on the anomaly of "establishment," as people now call the inherited church-state nexus.

But I have set forth a few thoughts on the subject when the occasion has presented itself.

In this volume, as in the other two, I have dealt from time to time with the dialectical tension between two ecclesiological emphases that I have called Erastianism and High Churchmanship. Erastianism is an emphasis on the church as one of a number of institutions through which society conforms itself as far as possible to the prevailing understanding of God's will. High Churchmanship is an emphasis on the church as an expression of the divine transcendence, and of the divine judgment under which every social order lies because it is not the Kingdom of God. Erastianism is not inherently committed to subjecting the church to the state, but it is compatible with the state exercising a good deal of control over the church, as it does over the other important institutions of society. By the same token, High Churchmanship is not inherently hostile to the higher aspirations of the state, but the rulers of the state are apt to think it is. I believe the two emphases reflect inherent tensions in the Christian Revelation, and that no version of institutional Christianity can prosper unless both emphases are present in it. Judged by that criterion, the English church-state nexus has had its ups and downs, as we shall see.

There is more statutory material in this volume than in the previous ones. As statutes are necessarily duller than cases, parts of the volume are heavier going that I would have liked them to be. I like to think that the fault is the legislators' not mine. The Pastoral Measures, 1968 and 1983, are longer and more complicated than the Statute of Provisors, but they are just as necessary to cover in a work like this.

I have tried to make myself responsible here for presenting whatever of importance can be learned from the statutes and the law reports. I have drawn on other material, whether primary or secondary, mainly to fill in necessary background for the legal materials. I have also drawn on some primary material such as the Oxford diocesan papers and the General Synod Reports to shed light on the practical workings of the institutions I take up. A good deal of this material was serendipitously encountered; I make no claim to cover it fully.

These limitations on the task I have set myself may explain some of the gaps in what I have produced. There are fascinating people everywhere in this account whose stories I have not been able to tell. There is also the deeply moving and deeply mysterious story of the spiritual journey of a great nation through a crucially important period of its history. I have not tried to address that story directly. Nor have I tried to account for the fact that the Church of England ministered to a substantial majority of the English people at the beginning of my story, but ministers to hardly more than ten percent of them now. *Spiritus ubi vult spirat.* Success in building a house for the Lord cannot always be measured by how manifestly He chooses to dwell there.

My intellectual debts have continued to pile up. The bishop of Chichester (the Rt. Rev. E.W. Kemp) has given me valuable insights into the present condition of the church, as he gave me valuable insights into earlier times when he was my Director of Studies thirty years ago. The Rev. David Hares has shared with me his experiences both as a working vicar and as a member of the General Synod. The Rev. Dr. Geoffrey Rowell, Mr. F.D. Price, Professor Thomas L. Shaffer, and the Hon. John T. Noonan, Jr. have all read the manuscript of this volume and made valuable suggestions. Professor Christopher B. Fox did the same for the chapter dealing with his period, the eighteenth century. The Ford Foundation and the University of Notre Dame have provided me with time and money at various crucial points in my research, and at one such point the Prior and Community of Blackfriars, Oxford, provided me with a place to work. Brenda Hough and Edward Pinsent of the General Synod Library were most helpful to me in an all too brief visit to their precincts. Mary Ambrose of our 1987 law school class, Bradley Benson, 1988, and Robert D. Ryan, 1990, served me as research assistants at different times. Melissa Murphy typed the text for me. My secretary, Linda Harrington, after typing and making sense of footnotes and index cards, proceeded with elegant mastery to turn the whole typescript into camera-ready pages. My wife, as usual, has been the most supportive of colleagues during the course of the project, and the most stringent of readers at the end.

One final acknowledgment is to my subject-matter itself. I have learned many things about both law and Christianity from this history — things that I have used in many different ways and hope to be able to use in many more. While I am an American and a Roman Catholic — never English and no longer Anglican — I have been writing about the nation that taught me my profession and the church that taught me my faith. I hope I have not failed to express my deep and abiding respect and affection for both.

Notre Dame, Indiana
Feast of St. Bede the Venerable, 1991

1. The Quiet Time

The Restoration settlement of the church was built on the premise that nothing had happened with juridical effect since the outbreak of the Civil War.[1] All the endeavors at a negotiated compromise between Laudians and Puritans came to naught in the face of the conceptual logic and political attractiveness of this simplified treatment of the episode just ended. Bishop Skinner of Oxford, who had spent the Interregnum in England, defying the authorities as best he could, no doubt took a grim satisfaction in dating his official documents (following his royal master's example) as if he had never been out of office. Where bishops and cathedral canons had died off, their places were rapidly filled up: people who had bought or leased their lands from the Commonwealth government were anxious to have someone with whom they could arrange to legalize their tenure.

With bishops and canons came ecclesiastical courts.[2] Charles was not seven weeks off the boat when archdeacons were appointed in Canterbury and Lincoln. Commissaries, officials, chancellors, registrars and the lot followed in their pristine profusion during late 1660 and early 1661. Before long, even the apparitor was back at his baneful trade.

The displaced Laudian clergy did not wait for these courts to operate. They resorted to the royal justices, or to simple self-help, to claim their canonical own.[3] Their more pliable colleagues, meanwhile, who had held places under all vicissitudes, and meant to go on doing so, began dusting off their Prayer Books and getting their surplices out. When Parliament in 1661 and 1662 restored to the church courts certain powers that had been taken away in 1640, and imposed a slightly modified Prayer Book on the clergy, it was doing no more than putting the finishing touches on a fait accompli.[4]

Professor R. G. Usher has perhaps gotten more criticism than he deserves for calling this situation "the church as Bancroft left it."[5] The institutional patterns which Bancroft put in final form were in fact duplicated with no small fidelity in the early days of the Restoration. The

1

differences on paper were only slight ones, or seemed so at the time. To be sure, the society on which they had to operate was a very different one, as became apparent in the ensuing years. Great changes were inevitable, but Usher's statement is not a bad starting-point for describing them.

Also, it helps to remind us that no one tried to bring back that more radical thing, the church as Laud left it. Bancroft died not in 1640, but in 1610. Almost all that Laud accomplished or tried to in the intervening time was tacitly forgotten. The High Commission, which bore the whole weight of Laud's program, was the one legal institution well and truly abolished, and forbidden by statute to come back.[6]

On this point, perhaps the church as Coke left it would be a better description. Coke's attack on the High Commission, and Coke's insistence that a defendant in a church court should not be made to incriminate himself were embodied in the first ecclesiastical legislation of the Long Parliament, and were left in force when most of the rest of that legislation was repealed.[7] Also, it was Coke's practice with his writs of prohibition and the like that formed the unquestioned basis for the relations between church and state after 1660.

This state of affairs was reflected in a general acceptance of Erastian ideology by the Restoration prelates and their allies. There was to be some close reasoning and sharp polemic about ideology all through the rest of the seventeenth century and a good part of the eighteenth, but the dominance of Erastianism in one form or another over the institutional structures of the church was not to be seriously challenged until the Benthamites and the Tractarians came along.

The story of the intervening period, which is what I want to tell in this chapter, is one of the gradual adjustment of inherited institutions to meet the needs of a different kind of society from the one in which the institutions were developed. Just how or to what extent it was a different kind of society need not concern us here. Every period of English history evinces profound changes along with (for an American at least) awesome elements of continuity. It will do for our purposes to say that the society that grew up after the Restoration was a different kind of society in that it wanted, and got, a different kind of church.

I. The Triumph Of Erastianism

A. Ideology.

Edward Stillingfleet (1635-1699), marked out in the sixties as a Bright Young Man, taken in the nineties for the most learned of bishops, set the tone of post-Restoration Erastianism with his *Irenicum — A Weapon-Salve for the Church's Wounds or the Divine Right of Particular Forms of Church Government*, first published in 1659, and put into a second edition in 1662.[8] His concrete proposal (like that of anyone else who aspired to be irenic in those days) was modified episcopacy. His route for getting there was a combination of medieval Erastianism and Hobbes's new theory of the Social Contract. The steps of the argument are these:

1. There is no divinely instituted form of church government except to the extent that a ministry is required. Whether the required ministry includes an episcopate he does not say. He evidently thought so later in life.[9] Also, earlier, when episcopacy was officially abolished under the Commonwealth, he had taken the trouble to get a bishop to ordain him. But even if he thought that divine law required that there be bishops, he did not think it required any particular bishop to have any particular powers.

2. The natural law requires people to join with their fellows for religious worship. Divine positive law requires that the religious worship in question be Christian, i.e., that it consist of the preaching of the Gospel and the administration of the sacraments.

3. A society for this purpose arises by convention. Here is where Hobbes comes in. Those who find themselves members of such a society must adhere to it unless it imposes on them something unlawful; otherwise, they are schismatics.

4. A nation, through its corporate acceptance of Christianity, becomes, *qua* nation, a society of the kind envisaged. This hypostatic union of church and state, despite its Hobbesian origin, is, of course, entirely in keeping with the medieval Erastian view — that too saw church and state as a single society.

With this understanding of the groundwork of church polity, Stillingfleet was able to accord the "civil magistrate" of Reformation doctrine the prerogatives of the Hobbesian "sovereign" in ordering all things in the society. To be sure, he was prepared to hold back from the civil magistrate a certain modicum of power that inhered in the divinely appointed ministry. As he grew older, and became more intimate with the problems of a prelatical church, he seems to have expanded somewhat his view of that inherent power.[10] He ended up thinking that the power to preach, to administer the sacraments, and even to excommunicate, was in some way attached by divine authority to the office of a bishop. But he continued to hold that the specific jurisdiction of a bishop, the conditions of its exercise, and even the power to exercise it at all within the territory of a Christian nation, were given him by the positive law of the nation.

In this way, Stillingfleet, with a little help from Hobbes, brought into the mainstream of clerical thinking the view that

> the holy Church of England was founded in the estate of prelacy by the king and his progenitors, and the earls, barons, and other nobles of his said realm . . .[11]

which, as I have tried to show in these volumes, was the view of the laity all along. Having accepted this principle, he was not slow to accept the corollary — that the various rights of the clergy, including tithe, arose not from theology, but from English positive law. This again was the traditional lay view, and became the accepted doctrine among the Restoration clergy.[12] In the prevailing legalism of the period, it gave a more effective support to church finances than any divine right learning would have done. Basically, of course, this was the same argument as the one about customary rights that the orthodox medieval Commons had raised against the Lollards, or the one about property that was to serve nineteenth-century churchmen so well against the utilitarians.

What Stillingfleet did for jurisdiction and revenues, a man named Hugh Davis did, with equal learning though with less resulting fame (he is not in the *Dictionary of National Biography*, for instance), for the liturgy, and to some extent for the doctrines of the church. His *De Jure Uniformitatis Ecclesisticae*[13] appeared (in English; only the title is Latin) in 1669. Davis was evidently more of a High Churchman than Stillingfleet. His work is punctuated all over with the kind of divine right thinking we will have to look at shortly. But his main contribution is the notion that liturgical uniformity and doctrinal uniformity (insofar as doctrine is a matter of external profession) are good in themselves. They have a value distinct from whatever edification there may be in the liturgy uniformly offered, or whatever cogency in the doctrines uniformly professed. Uniformity is good because it promotes charity and peace. It is appropriate then for the civil magistrate to frame a uniform order. This everyone should accept if he can, acquiesce in passively if he cannot.

Davis was the first of a long line. Whether later people read him, or whether they arrived independently at similar conclusions I cannot say. But all those clergy who subscribed the Prayer Book and the Articles at ordination and institution, not out of conviction but for the sake of peace, were following principles most fully elaborated in the *De Uniformitate*. When you accepted these things as "agreeable to the word of God," you did not mean that they were the tenets of your faith, you simply meant that you were willing to accept them as doctrinal formulations not unbecoming a Christian church. You were prepared to join with your fellow Christians in a body whose official formulas were worded in this way.[14]

This approach to doctrine and liturgy is in a way the capstone of an Erastian structure. It makes the whole ecclesiastical and theological enterprise an analogue of secular law. It puts your acceptance of the church on the same basis as your acceptance of the other institutions of society — as expedients to reconcile conflicting interests and enable members of the community to pursue common purposes in peace. The laity, as we have seen, always tended to accept the church in this way. From now on a good part of the clergy were to do the same.

How far all this learning was opposed to the High Church orthodoxy of the previous reign was probably not apparent at the outset. As we saw in the last volume, the High Church version of the royal supremacy was a supremacy of the king's sacred person, whereas the Erastian version was a supremacy of the whole governmental apparatus carried on in his name.[15] As between these two versions, Restoration terminology was ambiguous. When you spoke of the civil magistrate, it was not clear whether you meant any civil magistrate within his proper sphere of authority, or only the supreme civil magistrate, the king. On the other hand, when you spoke of the king, it was not clear whether you envisaged his acting in person or his acting only under the forms of law. Also, in the prevailing reactionary euphoria, the rhetoric of the martyred Carolines seems to have passed current among a good many people who did not advisedly accept their doctrines. It took the advent of James II to sort out who thought what, and to show how strong the Erastian principles had become.

James's reign made the High Church position difficult, and his overthrow made it all but impossible. It was bad enough to have your church headed up by a Lord's Anointed who refused its communion and devoted his powers to undermining it. But with William and Mary there could be no Lord's Anointed at all. These sovereigns, having no title to their places except the general submission of the civil government led by Parliament, could not be accepted as heads of the church unless the Royal Supremacy was to be accepted as the supremacy of the whole apparatus of government — was to be accepted, that is, on Erastian terms.

For the irreconcilable Carolines, this was the end. The archbishop of Canterbury, five bishops, and four hundred clergy refused the oath of allegiance to William and Mary, and were deprived. They and their successors, the Nonjurors, constituted a small and dwindling schismatic body for something over a century. To be sure, not every Nonjuror was a full-fledged Caroline. Those (all but one of the bishops involved) who signed the famous Seven Bishops' Petition thought it would be sinful to accord James power to dispense from an Act of Parliament — a position which seems to give Parliament some kind of share in the divine unction. What is important is not the exact point at which these people drew the line, but the fact that the general Caroline attitude toward the supremacy passed out of the church with them. The idea that it was a personal supremacy of the monarch was not even mooted again till the time of Victoria — a lady so respectable it was possible to forget that she too owed her title to the events of 1688.[16]

The Erastian, of course, had no trouble reconciling himself to the new state of affairs. Stillingfleet developed the necessary rationale in a couple of pamphlets entitled *The Unreasonableness of a New Separation*, and *A Vindication of Their Majesties' Authority to Fill the Sees of the Deprived Bishops*.[17] In the first, he argued that a de facto government is entitled to allegiance, and therefore to an oath of allegiance, from the people, and therefore from churchmen — all commonplace doctrine except in divine-right circles. This principle, coupled with the views on the civil magistrate which Stillingfleet had set forth in his earlier writings, provided a basis for the argument of the second pamphlet. The power to say who shall act as a bishop in the realm, or who shall occupy revenues originally provided by the state, is a power belonging to the state. Hence, a bishop deprived of his see by the government is truly deprived, and another may in good conscience take his place. The deprived bishop remains an orthodox Catholic bishop in good standing: only an ecclesiastical synod can deprive him of that status. But he ceases to be the bishop of such-and-such a place in England when the English government says he does.[18]

Despite these blows, there remained a certain amount of High Church thinking in the establishment. This thinking, with divine right monarchy a lost cause, turned toward that other Laudian tenet, divine right episcopacy. Efforts were made to systematize and exploit those inherent powers which the prevailing Erastianism admitted to exist in theory. Edmund Gibson (1669-1748, bishop of Lincoln, 1716, of London, 1720) propounded the idea that the government's authority over ecclesiastical proceedings arose from the fact that those proceedings had temporal effect — a theory that Stillingfleet had considered and rejected. On this basis, Gibson made a detailed proposal for restoring a full-scale ecclesiastical discipline with merely spiritual force.[19] The judicial offices of vicar-general and official-principal were to be separated. The vicar-general, subject only to canon law, was to concern himself with "the Government of the clergy as to Manners and Function, the Visitation of Dioceses, the Detection of Vice, the Support of Churches and Ecclesiastical Mansions, the care of all things put to Public Worship, and the right of inflicting spiritual censures to attain these spiritual ends." The official-principal, meanwhile, was to handle matrimonial and testamentary cases in accordance with secular law, along with anything else the secular authorities saw fit to entrust to the church courts. Excommunication was to be a purely spiritual censure, imposed by the vicar-general. One who disobeyed the official-principal was to be pronounced not excommunicate, but "contumacious," and subjected to the secular, but not the spiritual, sanctions formerly imposed on excommunicates.

All this was embodied in Gibson's *Codex Juris Ecclesiastici Anglicani*, a vast, erudite, and sometimes tendentious compilation of canon and statute law affecting the church, first published in 1713. Like a number of proposals of its learned and creative author, it gained more notoriety than acceptance.

I have come upon just one solid doctrinal attack on it, *An Examination of the Scheme of Church Power Laid Down in the Codex*[20] (1735), by Michael Foster, a common lawyer faithful to the Erastian traditions of his forebears. Foster (1689-1763, justice of the King's Bench from 1745) was a sound man and well thought of, though hardly in the front rank of a profession that included Mansfield and Blackstone. He began by showing (which was true enough) that Gibson's doctrine was really traditional clerical doctrine in a new form. He then showed that historically clerical control had been no better for the church than it was for the state — in Reformation times the clergy were mostly all papist; in Charles I's time, they had alienated almost everyone with their pedantic insistence on foolish ceremonial niceties. Finally, he showed (the bedrock Erastian tenet) that the things Gibson wanted the church courts to do were in fact conducive to the good of the whole community, so that the laity were as much entitled as the clergy to have a hand in them.

However the intellectual honors might have fallen between Gibson and Foster, in the political context Gibson did not have a chance. The Tories could not be pried loose from their attachment to the vestiges of temporal power, and some of them were still nostalgically committed to the fading fortunes of the House of Stuart. The Whigs were traditionally mistrustful of ecclesiastical authority, and Gibson was not the man to set their fears at rest. The aristocracy were not interested in a conception of the higher places in the church that would make their dim or unambitious relatives incompetent to fill those places. The government was not interested in putting bishops to full-time diocesan work and distracting them from their proper business of supporting the government in the House of Lords. The growing forces of Latitudinarian thought resisted being denounced for doctrinal error, even if only with spiritual effect. And no one in that permissive age was interested in having his vices detected.

Gibson's was the last attempt, and it was a foredoomed one, to give High Churchmanship any real scope in the institutional life of the church. For more than a century, the church-state nexus, articulated on Erastian lines, pursued the even tenor of its ways, more fully integrated than ever before or since, while the High Church vision of ecclesiastical autonomy and divine right episcopate slumbered in country rectories and college common rooms, waiting for Keble's Assize Sermon and a new birth.

B. Legislation.

In the prevailing Erastian framework, Convocation, the church's traditional legislature, fell into what Dean Sykes has called an "eclipse."[21] It met for the transaction of business in 1661, again in 1689, fairly regularly from 1700 to 1717, one last time in 1741, and then not until the 1850s. The rest of the time, it met when Parliament met, prepared a Loyal Address, and was duly prorogued — one of those colorful institutions like the Chiltern Hundreds or the Cinque Ports.

How this came to pass is a richly complicated story. I will give here only the bare bones of it as I have gotten them out of Sykes. It seems that the bishops agreed informally in 1662 that the clergy should be taxed with rest of the country, instead of voting their own taxes in Convocation. Why they were willing to give up this valuable, if obsolete, prerogative without a fight is not clear, but they may have been threatened with a general reassessment of the values of clerical livings. The pre-inflation value in the books of King Henry VIII had long been taken for ratable value, but there was no reason why it had to be. Not only the subsidies voted by Convocation, but also the first fruits and tenths that the Crown collected in any event, could have been charged on true value if the Crown had cared to press the point. In any event, after Convocation stopped voting subsidies, the government was interested in it only on those rare occasions when it wanted the church reformed.

So it was that William III let Convocation proceed to business once at the beginning of his reign and once at the end, hoping he could get a scheme through for the comprehension of Protestant Dissenters. Anne, who would have liked to see the needs of the church for internal reform met, made a number of tries in her reign, and George I made one try at the beginning of his. On all these occasions, the benevolent apathy of the government was turned into outright hostility by the intransigent Toryism of the Lower House.

Canterbury Convocation (York scarcely figures in these affairs; it had seldom done more than rubber-stamp decisions made at Canterbury) had then, as it has now, an Upper House consisting of the bishops of the province, and a Lower House consisting of representatives of the clergy. The Upper House, therefore, were all government appointees — generally Whigs if William appointed them; generally Tories if Anne did; but in any case men with enough political finesse to attain to high office by political appointment. Some members of the Lower House followed the bishops, to whom they owed their preferment. But a majority were spokesmen for disgruntled squires. I gather that they hoped through alliance with like-minded people in Parliament to bring back the good old days — though it is not at all clear what good old days they had in mind.

So the Lower House not only turned up its nose at comprehension of Dissenters, it tried to get Latitudinarian divines tried for heresy. When it was not about these activities, it still shirked the humdrum tasks of administrative reform; rather, it spent its time on a tumultuous assertion of its own prerogatives, first against the Crown, then against the Upper House.

In the 1690s, it was generally thought that the Submission of the Clergy under Henry VIII precluded Convocation from doing any kind of business without a royal license. But in 1697, one Francis Atterbury, a brilliant and vaguely unscrupulous High Churchman, initiated a controversy as bitter as it was erudite by contending that the royal license was needed only to make canons; anything else Convocation could do on its own. On the wording of the statute, Atterbury had the better case, and if he and his followers had been willing to cooperate with the bishops they might have prevailed.[22]

There is no more enduring problem for High Church Anglicanism than the reluctance of the bishops to play the role in which they are cast. Whoever legally controlled the Convocation agenda, no bench of bishops was minded to confront, or even greatly embarrass, the secular power. So it was not enough for the Lower House to claim that its deliberations were not subject to control by the Crown; it found it could not accomplish its purposes without cutting loose from control by the Upper House also. Here the historical claim was good deal more tenuous. Atterbury tried to analogize the relation between the two houses of Convocation to that between the two houses of Parliament, but the history of Convocation was quite different.

The merits of the controversy need not detain us, because in fact they were never decided. From 1700 on, the two houses were chronically deadlocked, and the government simply prorogued the whole Convocation when things got too bad. In 1717, when Queen Anne's zealous churchmanship was out of the picture, and when the Lower House was trying to get the Bishop of Bangor deposed for heresy, the government finally decided they had had enough.

So Parliament became the church's legislature[23] — a position which the Commons had hankered after in the Middle Ages, and were only prevented from taking on at the Reformation by the vigorous opposition of Elizabeth and James. Statutes of the period affected such varied matters as probate proceedings (1671, 1692), solemnization of marriage (1696, 1753, 1781), vicarages (1677), curacies (1713), cathedral statutes (1707), union and division of parishes (1714, 1733, 1781), and practice in the church courts

(1787, 1813, 1829). It was an age of modest legislative adjustment, and the church came in for its share.

But the reforms that the real church reformers were interested in — tightening up on pluralism and nonresidence, controlling personnel and procedures in the church courts, and in general updating the Canons of 1604 — these Parliament went into spottily or not at all. As the focus of public interest shifted gradually to secular matters, it became harder and harder to get the legislators even to take an intelligent interest in church affairs.[24]

We should not go all the way, though, with those who attribute the ensuing stagnation to the downfall of Convocation. For one thing, many of the most pressing reforms (Gibson's court proposal for one) could not have been implemented without statutes whether or not there was a Convocation at work. For another thing, if the bishops had formed a solid bloc in the House of Lords, and traded off their votes on secular matters for legislative concessions on ecclesiastical affairs, they might have put through a good deal of what they wanted — but it is hard to imagine them doing such a thing.

The long and short of it is, I think, that the Erastian adjustments of the late seventeenth century had produced a situation that no one was anxious to change. Even those who found in it a good deal to grumble at were willing to put up with it lest something worse befall. Sykes characterizes the whole situation as *"quieta non movenda,"* i.e. don't rock the boat.[25]

C. Law and Administration

The acceptance of Erastian doctrine cut more ways than one. If church polity was a creature of English positive law, it was entitled to share in the substantial respect, even veneration, that English positive law was coming to enjoy. When Stillingfleet said that ecclesiastical law was as much a part of the law of the land as equity or admiralty, or for that matter the common law itself,[26] he made a point that the laity were scarcely able to gainsay.

With the ideology agreed on in these terms, there was no great technical obstacle to making the church courts and the canon law into functional parts of a unified legal system. Professionals on both sides were soon at work adjusting the various precedents to this end. For instance, before the seventeenth century was out, it was finally recognized that a church court does not necessarily step outside its jurisdiction when it subjects a layman to an erroneous application of canon law. In the normal course of events, you appeal from an erroneous decision, rather than bringing a lay proceeding to prohibit it. In 1677, the judges, ignoring a decision of Coke's the other way, refused to prohibit a church proceeding to collect an improperly apportioned churchrate,

> for they said, if they were grieved, they might appeal; and it was proper for the Examination of that Court, for Church-Rates were not suable for at the Common Law; and they having Conusance of the Principal, might examine the Equality of the Rates as incidental.[27]

The logic of a holding like this is obvious if you recognize the church courts as a body of professional lawyers trying to do a job. This is just what Coke would not have granted them. He (and his fathers before him) were sure a layman would never have a fair break in an ecclesiastical court. The language just quoted bespeaks a new spirit on both sides.

Still more of a change of spirit is manifested by the 1702 case of a lay peace officer who entered a church to suppress a riot, and was left to make good his excuse before the spiritual court that had him up for brawling in church.[28] It would have been unthinkable in the Middle Ages, and in Coke's time also, I have no doubt, for a secular official to be charged in a church court on account of anything he did under color of his office.

At the same time, the lay courts developed more flexibility in allowing the church courts to take cognizance of matters of obvious ecclesiastical concern even when the letter of the law would forbid. So in 1682, when a parson brought a church defamation action for saying that his preaching was all lies, the church court was allowed to proceed, simply because the case was "fit to be tried" there, even though as a general matter slander of a man's professional competence was suable for only at common law.[29]

Along these lines, the most important case was *Slater v. Smalebrooke* (1665),[30] where the King's Bench, sharply limiting the effect of a 1618 decision, permitted a church court to deprive a clergyman of his benefice for an offense that it could not have handled in an ordinary correction-of-morals case. The clergyman in question had forged his letters of orders, and was contending, correctly enough, that only the lay court had jurisdiction to punish for forgery. The church proceeding that the King's Bench allowed to go forward may have been to deprive him as a layman rather than as a forger; the reports are not clear. But it was established, at least as a matter of dictum, that a temporal offense would support a deprivation proceeding. This distinction between correcting a sinner *pro salute animae* and getting rid of an unfit minister was long overdue; it was unknown to the medieval canon law.

In an age of general leniency toward unfit clergymen, the holding of *Slater v. Smalebrooke* was not immediately followed up. It lurked about in the lawbooks for more than a century until it was firmly established in *Burgoyne v. Free* (1825-1830).[31] Free, a parson who had lived up to his

name with a succession of housekeepers, defended a deprivation proceeding
by raising a 1787 Statute of Limitations which provided that an
ecclesiastical proceeding for incontinence could not be brought more than
eight months after the act complained of. Free had been incontinent for
fifteen years, but there was no specific act pleaded within the previous eight
months. Nevertheless, the highest courts in both church and state held he
could be deprived.

The handling of the case by the different courts is subtle, but it is worth
following, because it shows how attitudes toward the unified system had
developed by the end of the period we are considering. In the first place,
the Court of Arches, faithful to the canonical tradition, assumed that Free
was correct in contending that the proceeding *pro salute animae* and the
deprivation proceeding were inseparable. It endeavored to integrate the
1787 statute into that tradition by arguing that Free's specific acts of
incontinence were not being specifically punished, but were being treated as
part of a general course of conduct which, in the case of a cleric, warranted
correction. But the King's Bench, affirmed by the House of Lords, relied
on the distinction made in *Slater v. Smalebrooke*. Accordingly, it prohibited
the proceeding insofar as it was *pro salute animae*, but allowed it to go
forward insofar as it was for deprivation. Free then went back to the
ecclesiastical proceeding and argued that a deprivation suit which was not
pro salute animae could not be entertained because it was unknown to the
canon law — fair enough under the traditional canon law. The highest
church court, the Court of Delegates, did not meet this argument head-on.
It simply said that a church court could hear a case with the limitations the
lay courts had put on it, even though there was no canonical basis for such
limitations.

The businesslike relations between the two court systems in this difficult
case, ending with the church courts accepting a proceeding that had been
tailored into an uncanonical shape by the lay courts, shows how far the two
sets of professional judges had gone in the period toward achieving a sense
of common purpose. Up to the Civil War, the two systems had pursued
quite separate intellectual ways, and largely separate juridical ways. The
secular law gave effect to the canons and to ecclesiastical judgments only
on certain specific matters (mostly personal status, decedent estates and
tenure of benefices) where it was traditional to do so. The church courts
gave effect to secular law only when they were forced to. Anyone who has
followed the preceding volumes in this work will have seen a number of
situations which the two sets of judges treated in completely different ways.

The church courts had been the more doggedly consistent in this stand.
Before the Reformation, they paid no attention to either common or
statute law. They accepted writs of prohibition from the lay courts as

exercises not of legal authority but of *force majeure*. As long as no prohibition was actually issued, they went right on entertaining cases that the lay courts would have prohibited if asked. After the Reformation, they took Acts of Parliament into their system (or tried to), but they were still sluggish about doing so with the common law. Especially did they tend to resist the supervisory powers of the lay judges, fighting off writs of prohibition by political action or by evasion.

The intellectual rapprochement that accompanied post-Restoration Erastianism showed itself among the church lawyers first in their treatises.[32] Gibson (1713), Ayliffe (1726), and Burn (1760) all compiled canons, statutes, and common law precedents quite indiscriminately, regarding them as making up collectively the ecclesiastical law. By the middle of the eighteenth century, the church courts were taking the same view. In 1753, and again in 1798, the Court of Arches laid down that a suit which the common law courts would prohibit was not to be entertained.[33] It examined the reported prohibition cases to determine whether the case before it should be dismissed.

The lay courts reciprocated by giving new scope to the canons and the interpretations put on them by the church courts.[34] Thus, in 1743 they upheld a set of statutory commissioners who taxed a vicar in accordance with the canonical practice on dilapidations. To be sure, they held in 1736 that the Canons of 1604 were not binding on the laity (because the laity played no part in enacting them), but even these they imposed on the clergy. For instance, in 1741 the Court of Chancery held a clergyman in contempt for performing an uncanonical marriage of a ward of the court.

The general professional rapport indicated by these cases imparted to the church courts a rather different conception of what they were about. As adjuncts to a unified system of administering justice they could not be quite so much agencies for Christianizing the country.[35] By the 1790s they were finding it possible to handle Jewish marriage cases, with only a passing thought for the anomaly involved. In 1809, the Dean of the Arches could remark cheerfully enough in a case fraught with theological problems (whether a child of Dissenters was entitled to Anglican burial) that he was only deciding law, not theology.

The professional and secular coloration taken on by the church courts set them off more and more sharply from the everyday business of the prelates in whose name they acted.[36] In 1705, the Queen's Bench held that a bishop, in appointing a new vicar-general, could not limit the traditional powers of the office. In 1733, when the chancellor of the Oxford diocese had a dispute with the archdeacon over who was to conduct visitations and when, they referred it for arbitration not to their common superior the bishop, but to three ecclesiastical lawyers from outside the diocese. The bishop's courts had come to be almost as remote from the bishop as the king's courts were from the king.[37]

For the eighteenth century bishop, therefore, his own courts were so mysterious and frightening that he was reluctant to use them.[38] White Kennett (bishop of Peterborough, 1718-1728) complained that the difficulty of going to law was a barrier to his getting rid of unfit clergy in his diocese. A dispute between the bishops of Lincoln and Oxford over who had jurisdiction over the Oxfordshire peculiars of the Lincoln chapter dragged on for years because no one was willing to take it to court. When a clergyman was involved in a dispute or a problem which seemed to involve a serious legal question, the bishop would either wash his hands of it or send it for the opinion of counsel.

The lower clergy had the same trouble as the bishops.[39] In the early nineteenth century, a vicar saddled with a drunken curate found it easier to complain to the bishop than to make out a court case. A parson, a squire, and the bishop of Oxford all three had all they could do to keep up one another's courage in going through with a proceeding against an incestuous parishioner. A minister felt he owed the bishop an explanation of why he was taking a local farmer to court.

In the process, the judge of a bishop's consistory court became as much the bishop's legal advisor as his legal delegate.[40] In 1801 the bishop of Oxford wrote his chancellor asking how to speed up a case against a drunken incumbent. The chancellor felt it would be unjudicial to give such advice, and the bishop responded by asking where he should get legal advice if not from his chancellor. In 1803 we find the same chancellor advising the bishop on the pros and cons of a morals prosecution against a prominent adulterer.

The estrangement of the bishops and clergy from their courts was in part attributable to the integration of the latter into the unified Erastian structure. But it had roots also in Elizabethan ecclesiastical administration. The late medieval system had been outrageously legalistic in its conceptions, and both arbitrary and inefficient in the execution of them. The first generations after the Reformation naturally tended to react by making the episcopate less legal, and at the same time making the legal process more efficient and more fully routinized. Only by a certain split between the two aspects of church government could the two goals be realized at once. Laud, through the *plenitudo potestatis* of the Crown, tended to pull the two elements back together, but his work was all undone. At the Restoration the culmination of the tendencies begun at the Reformation became inevitable. The church's legal system became more legal, more efficient, more routine than ever before. At the same time, it moved sharply to the outer perimeter of the church's life.[41]

II. Loose Ends

Thus made peripheral to the church's life in the Spirit (or to her life in the nation if you prefer), many traditional legal concerns were sloughed off entirely, or at least relegated to the dusty shelves of the professionals at Doctors' Commons or the Inns of Court. By the end of the eighteenth century, unless you were a lawyer, you probably cared very little whether a case belonged in the lay or the spiritual courts. The traditional parish discipline on which the Elizabethan bishops had so set their hearts was virtually at an end. The law of patronage, and even that of simony, fell into the general mass of inherited technicalities that occasionally (but not too often) came between a Georgian squire and the full enjoyment of his property. Other problems that had set previous generations of churchmen by the ears were finding their own roads to a comparable oblivion. Here, we will take our leave of some old friends before proceeding to see what ecclesiastical administration was really concerned with in the period.

A. Jurisdiction of Courts.

1. Expansion of Lay Remedies — The process, begun in the sixteenth century, of transforming the medieval into the modern common law was gradually imparting new scope, and sometimes new rationality, to the system all through the period we are considering. There was some shift in emphasis from procedural to substantive law, so that the lay courts would often apply an old remedy to a new fact situation if they discerned the kind of substantive claim that that particular remedy was appropriate to deal with. As a result, a number of these lay remedies picked up church matters within their expanding scope. In some cases, such as defamation, they expressly displaced the church courts when they did so.[42] In more cases, they cut in on them indirectly by doing a better job. Here are the most important of the lay remedies that affected the church in this way:

1. *Actions for the protection of real property* were made available to a parish incumbent to vindicate his traditional "freehold" in his church.[43] As early as 1663, he was allowed to proceed under the forcible entry statute instead of invoking the cumbersome writ *de vi laica amovenda*. By the early nineteenth century, he was able to treat as a trespasser (trespass *quare clausum fregit*) a churchwarden who put up a monument without permission.

2. *The action on the case* became generally available against anyone who injured you by his unlawful conduct. Thus conceived, it almost entirely displaced the church's defamation proceedings, as we shall see. It was also available to an incumbent against his predecessor

for dilapidations, and to a parishioner for refusing him the sacraments, disturbing his occupation of a pew, or burying a stranger in his family vault.[44] There were some moves toward making it available against an ecclesiastical judge for a wrongful excommunication.

3. *Restitution* — A principle was gradually developing to the effect that if you had been unjustly enriched at another's expense, or if he had made a payment that you should have made, he was entitled to reimbursement from you. Actions of "quasi-contract" were created to implement this principle; the traditional action of account and the traditional bill in Chancery were given new scope to the same end.[45] In the process, the quasi-contractual action of *quantum meruit* (an action to recover the fair value of services performed with an expectation of payment but without an agreed-on wage) became available to a curate or a parish clerk. That of money had and received (available where A collected money that should have gone to B) was used by cathedral canons to litigate over the distribution of chapter funds. In certain circumstances, a pair of churchwardens were allowed to bring an action of account against their predecessors, or a bill in Chancery to make parishioners reimburse them for expenses. In all these cases, the church court proceeding, if available at all, was vague in scope, and subject to the usual difficulties of enforcement.

4. *Exchequer proceedings* — By medieval practice, if you owed money to the king, and someone else owed money to you, you could sue him in the Court of Exchequer so as to recover from him the wherewithal to pay the king. It did not matter whether your claim was legal or equitable, or even whether it was one that would otherwise have belonged exclusively to the church courts. The Exchequer would hear it and give you a judgment if you made out your claim. Somewhere along the line — I am not sure just when — the allegation that you owed money to the king became fictitious. You did not have to prove it in order to bring your case, and you did not have to pay the king anything if you collected. So the Exchequer became a good place to recover money judgments without the procedural complications that obtained in other courts. The clergy used it fairly often to collect tithes, and even Easter offerings.[46]

5. *Chancery proceedings* were becoming widely available for the specific enforcement of trusts and contracts. They were often used to adjudicate tithe settlements made in connection with parish enclosure schemes. They were used also to determine rights to

nominate clergymen to endowed chapels or lectureships, and to enforce agreements concerning the exercise of patronage rights.[47]

6. *Mandamus* was a writ that lay to compel anyone to take official action that the law required him to take. It was available to make an archdeacon swear in a properly elected churchwarden, to reinstate an ecclesiastical judge or a parish clerk improperly deprived of his office, to admit a man duly appointed to a cathedral prebend, or to make parish churchwardens hold a vestry meeting.[48] But it could not be used to control a discretionary function. Thus, a bishop could be ordered to examine a man seeking a license as a curate, lecturer, or schoolmaster, but not to issue the license after he had examined the man and found him in any way unfit.[49]

7. *Feigned issues* — As contracts became generally enforceable, so did wagering contracts. Accordingly, it became possible to get virtually any issue of law or fact tried in a common law court by alleging fictitiously that you had a bet on the outcome. This device was used both by the Court of Chancery and by the church courts to send specific issues for trial at common law. For the church courts, it was one way of escaping the writs of prohibition that awaited them if they tried an issue that belonged in the common law courts.[50]

2. Control of Ecclesiastical Courts — The thinking that made the lay judges more respectful to their ecclesiastical colleagues did not always make them more permissive. Seeing the church courts as part of a rational and integrated system, they found a number of new occasions for intervening in church proceedings to keep the whole system running in the way they thought it should. For instance, because the question whether an executor had paid a legacy or not was like a question of debt, the church courts were made to accept the testimony of a single witness on it, as a common law court would, instead of following their own two witness rule.[51] Or, since the parson had a freehold in his church and anyone interfering with it was a trespasser, the lay courts would prohibit a church proceeding to let a preacher preach there without the parson's permission: the church court was being asked to condone a trespass.[52]

For comparable reasons (none of them set out at all clearly in the reports, but all of them related to the right to enjoy property or the duty to pay money) the lay courts in the late seventeenth and early eighteenth centuries scrutinized in one way or another the form or outcome of ecclesiastical proceedings concerning pews, burial fees, court offices, interpretation of cathedral statutes, and dissolution of marriages.[53]

A couple of Acts of Parliament added to the grounds of lay intervention.[54] It had been held since the Reformation that the interpretation of Acts of Parliament belonged to the lay courts even if the acts themselves dealt with ecclesiastical matters. Accordingly, when an act was passed in 1671 regulating the administration of intestate estates, the lay courts found themselves reviewing ecclesiastical determinations about who might administer such estates. There was also an act of Henry VIII limiting the cases where a marriage was invalid for consanguinity to those where the parties were related within the "Levitical degrees." The pre-Civil-War lay courts had applied this act once or twice, but they generally avoided the thankless task of delimiting the precise scope of Leviticus 18 through writs of prohibition. The King's Bench in the 1670s was not so inhibited.

In other cases respect prevailed over supervisory zeal. Take, for instance, *Sir Oliver Butler's Case* (1673).[55] Sir Oliver was sued by his lady for alimony, when he had already made her a £300 settlement. He thought the spiritual court should not be allowed to hear the case, but he was told in the King's Bench that it was all right, because the spiritual court would take the settlement into account in fixing the amount of the alimony. Sir Oliver's case for a prohibition was just as plausible as some of the cases in the same period where prohibitions were granted. So was the case of the parson who thought he should not have to pay his successor for dilapidations because there had been a third man in the benefice between him and the one who was suing him. He too was left to make out his case in the church court and appeal if he lost.[56] What these cases indicate, taken in conjunction with those going the other way, is a certain ambiguity in the practical meaning of the new rapport between the two sets of courts. It was all sorted out in the end, but it took a while.

There was less ambiguity in the attitude toward procedural matters. The church courts were allowed almost complete control over their organization and processes.[57] They controlled admission and discipline of proctors and advocates (but not suits to collect their fees). They were allowed to use customary forms of pleading which the common lawyers would have considered too vague to answer. They were allowed to foreclose common law or statutory rights if these were not presented in proper procedural form. They were even allowed to interpret for themselves the statute forbidding self-incrimination and *ex officio* proceedings. In short, the procedural rights of a litigant were considered as safe in the hands of an ecclesiastical judge as in those of a lay judge.

The old law, both before and after the Reformation, had been very confusing as to the effect of an ecclesiastical judgment in the lay courts. Now it was finally established that such a judgment was conclusive as to anything it purported to decide within the jurisdiction of the court that rendered it.[58] In 1734, for instance, it was held that a church court's refusal to enforce a marriage contract barred a common law proceeding for breach of the same contract. The principles of *res judicata* and collateral estoppel applied to church courts in the same way as to any other courts.

Direct enforcement of ecclesiastical judgments was still through the old process of excommunicating the violator, then suing out a writ *de excommunicato capiendo*, whereby the sheriff would jail him until he gave bond to comply. The scandal of invoking the highest censure known to the Christian religion in what were often trivial cases had been pointed out from the first years of the Reformation, but nothing was done about it until 1813. The solution adopted in that year was so simple that it is hard to see why it took so long. For violation of the order of a church court the status of an excommunicate was replaced by that of a contumacious person, who suffered no spiritual disabilities, but could be put in jail by the old process, with the writ renamed *de contumace capiendo*. Everything else remained as it was before.[59]

The main problem (aside from general inefficiency) under the process, by either name, was how specific the church court had to be in explaining why it had excommunicated the offender or declared him contumacious. As far as I can see, before the Civil War no reason had to be given; Coke's opinion to the contrary is made up out of whole cloth.[60] But after the Restoration Coke's view (which was logical enough, despite its lack of precedent) prevailed, and we get a spate of cases on just what must be alleged for the writ to be good.[61] A compromise was reached between Coke's *méfiance* and the latter-day respect for the church courts. the request for the writ (a document called a signification) had to state clearly that the contumacy occurred in a proceeding within the spiritual jurisdiction, but did not have to show why the proceeding was in the spiritual jurisdiction. For instance, "a cause of defamation" would not do, because there were some causes of defamation which a church court could not hear. But "a cause of defamation merely spiritual" was acceptable.

As far as I can see, the prohibition proceeding, which was the main device for controlling the church courts, had undergone no significant change since Coke's time. I tried to show in the last volume how the old process, as restructured in the 1590s, would have been a fairly sensitive device for reviewing church courts if the common law judges had been more sympathetic in the way they used it.[62] It involved a preliminary writ of prohibition, temporarily stopping the church proceeding, on the basis of the original pleading (the libel) in the church court, or on a factual assertion (the surmise) showing that the church court lacked jurisdiction over all or part of the case. There would then (after further procedural steps that need not concern us) be a full-fledged hearing on the law or trial of the relevant facts. After this, either the prohibition would stand, putting an end to the church proceeding, or a writ called "consultation" would issue, allowing the church proceeding to go forward. Or there could be a "special consultation," allowing the church court to deal with certain aspects of the case, but not others.

This process gave the common law judges a great deal of flexibility in deciding when and with what effect they would intervene. First, they could, if they chose, stop a church proceeding cold at any stage, even after it had gone to judgment.[63] They could even stop a successful defendant from recovering his costs. Second, they could use the process as a form of appellate review, allowing the church courts to decide a matter in the first instance, and intervening only if the church courts decided it wrong.[64] Finally, they could take to themselves the trial of a particular issue, allowing everything else to be tried in the church court.[65] This they would do by trying a surmise based on that issue, and granting a consultation based on the result of the trial. The following hypothetical cases will illustrate the three alternative approaches:

1. A, a parish clerk, sues in the spiritual court for his wages. As his office is a lay office, and his wages the subject of a lay contract, the spiritual court has no jurisdiction, and either party can have a prohibition at any time. For instance, if A loses, he can have a prohibition to keep B from recovering his costs.

2. C, a parson, sues D, a parishioner, for tithes — a suit clearly within the ecclesiastical jurisdiction. D claims he has already paid the tithes, and shows a document purporting to be a release. The effect of this document depends on the common law. But as it raises a collateral matter in an ecclesiastical suit, D cannot have a prohibition until the church court has had a chance to pass on its effect. Afterward, he can have a prohibition by showing (a) that the church court rejected the release out of hand without passing on it, or (b) that it rejected the release for failure to meet canonical standards of authenticity, where these differed from those of the common law, or (c) that it misunderstood the legal effect of the release. If the church court gives the release its common law effect, there can be no prohibition.

3. E, a parson, sues F, a parishioner, for the tithes due under a *modus decimandi*, a customary manner of paying tithe that E claims prevails in the particular parish. Although tithe suits are for the church courts, trying the existence and validity of a custom belongs to the lay courts. Accordingly, F can have a prohibition against such a suit as this. But if E pleads and proves in the lay court that there is in fact such a custom as he claims, a consultation will issue.

The lay court having tried the question it was entitled to try, the
church proceeding can now go forward.

Examples of cases in all these categories can be found from before the
Civil War, but they look a bit haphazard: it is hard to be sure why a
particular case was put in a particular category. After the Restoration, the
judges began imposing an orderly and rational pattern on the whole system.
Finally, Mansfield tied it all up in a neat package in 1776.[66]

Along with this ordering and rationalization, there went a certain
modification of the procedures in the direction of allowing the church
courts more chance to police themselves. This was all part of the new
rapprochement between the two systems. The lay courts now seemed
interested in getting cases expeditiously determined in the courts they
belonged in, rather than in checking the pretensions of an alien and
overweening body of churchmen. They became a little more careful not to
set the prohibition process in motion unless they were sure it was invoked
in good faith. We find them throwing out proceedings that seem to be
brought for purposes of delay, or on a surmise notoriously false.[67] On
occasion, they might require the surmise to be supported by affidavits
before they would make the opposite party answer it.

They were a little more careful also, it seems to me, to see that a church
court got to hear as much of a case as it was entitled to.[68] Where the
proceeding covered a number of matters, they might go over the libel
paragraph by paragraph, awarding a consultation on any paragraphs that
were proper for a church court to hear. Ultimately (1836; a 1734 case is
contrary), they even decided that you could not have a prohibition after
judgment where the libel showed some matters that belonged in the church
court and some that did not. By waiting till after judgment, you had
deprived the courts of a chance to treat different parts of the libel in
different ways. So they would uphold the whole proceeding rather than set
the whole proceeding aside.

For rather similar reasons, it was decided that where the trial of an issue
belonged in the lay court (the usual, if not the only, case was an issue as to
the existence or legality of a custom), if you once allowed the issue to be
tried in a church court you were bound by the result.[69] The church
courts, as we have seen, responded to this principle by trying such issues
when they had occasion to in accordance with common law rather than
canonical rules.

There was some departure from the precedents laid down in Coke's time
regarding the treatment of issues involving statutes.[70] In the earlier
period, the interpretation and application of a statute tended to be treated
in the same way as the existence and validity of a custom. They were
issues for the lay courts to try. A church proceeding would generally be
stopped until the lay court had determined any statutory issue involved in

it: i.e., such issues were treated in accordance with the third of the hypothetical cases stated above. But from the Restoration on they were more apt to be treated like the second, so that a prohibition would issue only on a showing that the church court had already considered the statutory issue and decided it wrong. This made for a considerable shift in balance. It meant that in perhaps the majority of cases that concerned both systems the lay court sat as a forum for appellate review rather than as a forum of first impression.

In just one area, the desire for an integrated approach seems to have limited church jurisdiction, rather than expanding it. That was the area of secular crime — a growing one as Parliament undertook to punish more and more matters that earlier generations had left to the church to correct. The lay courts established that facts amounting to a temporal felony could not be the subject of an ecclesiastical proceeding for moral correction.[71] For instance, a man could not be had up for solicitation of chastity where the facts amounted to attempted rape. However, the church courts could attach collateral consequences to felonious conduct. For instance, if your wife married another husband, you could have a separation for adultery even though she was also guilty of the felony of bigamy. Similarly, when the performance of clandestine marriages was made a felony in 1753, it was still possible to deprive a clergyman for performing one.

As to petty offenses, cognizable by the justices of the peace, the church courts were generally allowed to act independently, but they had to take the justices' determinations into account. They could not punish A for begetting a bastard if the justices had already declared B the father.[72] I suspect also, though I can find no case on the point, that they could not put the mother to penance if the justices had already had her whipped.

Burn, writing of the state of all this learning in the mid-eighteenth century, is not entirely satisfied that the church courts are given the scope they deserve. But he is at least grateful that the time is past

> wherein the contests between the two jurisdictions were violent, and carried on with obstinacy on both sides.

"It is the glory of the present age," he continues,

> that these ferments have at length subsided. Learned men can now differ in opinion, without bitterness and mutual reproaches; and the several discordant parties have been instructed to live together in a mutual intercourse and communication of good offices. Persecution hath departed to its native hell; and fair benevolence hath come down from heaven. The distinctions which were introduced during the plenitude of papal power have fallen away by degrees; and we shall naturally recur to the state wherein popery took us up, in which there was no thwarting

between the two jurisdictions, but they were amicably conjoined, affording mutual help and ornament to each other.[73]

B. Lay Morals.

When the ecclesiastical apparatus was set back in motion in 1660, there was evidently every intention of putting it firmly to its old work of ferreting out sinners and standing them in white sheets.[74] Bishop King of Chichester, in his visitation of 1662, put to his parish churchwardens — and moreover got them to answer — a set of articles as full in this regard as any the Elizabethans had used. Edmund Gibson, as archdeacon of Surrey in 1712, was still trying to get churchwardens to present common drunkards and swearers, sabbath breakers, and notorious sexual offenders. Indeed, printed forms inquiring after such matters persisted into the mid-nineteenth century. But the élan had gone out of the system by the 1670s, and it was scarcely possible to take it seriously beyond the early eighteenth century.

The steps in this process of obsolescence can be traced out fairly well, although the available records are spotty.[75] A set of churchwardens' presentments from the Archdeaconry of Chichester in the 1660s shows a sprinkling of sexual offenders, both general fornicators and parents of bastards, whereas a comparable set from Kent shows none at all. A visitation book of the bishop of Oxford from 1685, in which recent presentments were compiled for the bishop's use, shows a number of "scandalous" people, who were probably guilty of some kind of moral offense. Surveys taken by the bishop of Lincoln between 1718 and 1721 show that about one parish priest in five or six could remember a public penance performed or commuted in his parish in the previous few years. The bishop's chancellor and the archdeacon of Oxford both held regular courts through the mid-eighteenth century, at which a number of sexual offenders were cited — though most of them seem not to have shown up in court. After that, the court sessions became very sporadic. Parson Woodforde, in his famous diary, covering the last quarter of the century, recorded one public penance, and seemed to consider it a fairly remarkable event. By the beginning of the nineteenth century, the bishop of Oxford was being advised by his chancellor that trying to set the process in motion would simply hold the whole church court system up to scorn:

The penance of publick exposure in a white dress is obsolete or nearly so, and I submit to your Lordship whether it would be prudent to attempt that which would probably not only be insignificant in itself at best, but would possibly be converted into a sort of triumph by such a man as you describe. The power of the Ecclesiastical Court is too weak for any great utility; but such as it is we must manage it as we can so as not to expose it to contempt, where we cannot enforce it to good effect.[76]

One of the latest recorded penances, in the nineteenth century, after people had begun building railroads, was called off because of the influx of sightseers.

Just what brought the venerable institution of moral correction to this ignominious pass is a bit of a puzzle. To be sure, it was not very congenial to eighteenth century society ("a Discipline too wholesome to be digested," Gibson called it).[77] But it was not all that congenial to Elizabethan society either; nor did the eighteenth century stand out in its capacity for getting rid of uncongenial institutions. A variety of more specific causes can be suggested, but with each of them there is the question why it took so long to operate. Putting a number of different elements together, one can give a coherent account of what happened, but I am not really satisfied that it tells the whole story.

The first, and probably the most important, specific cause was a change in the rules of the game by the Restoration Parliament. The 1661 legislation, restoring the status quo of 1640, contained the following proviso:

> . . . it shall not be lawful for any . . . person having or exercising spiritual or ecclesiastical jurisdiction, to tender or administer to any person whatsoever, the oath usually called the oath ex officio, or any other oath, whereby such person to whom the same is tendered or administered, may be charged or compelled to confess or accuse or to purge him or herself of any criminal matter or thing, whereby he or she may be liable to censure or punishment.[78]

The main purpose of this language was to prevent a revival of the inquisitorial process used in the defunct High Commission, whereby a person could be questioned under oath before he was accused of anything, and then punished for any wrongdoing his answers disclosed.

But it affected also the normal canonical process for correcting offenders. That process involved a specific accusation, usually by the churchwardens of the offender's parish. If he denied the accusation, and (as was usually the case) no one came forward with evidence for a formal trial, the accused had to clear himself by a canonical "purgation." This was a formal denial under oath, supported by a specified number of "compurgators" who would swear that the accused's oath was worthy of belief. If he failed to support his denial in this way, he could be put to penance, just as if he had admitted the charge, or been found guilty in a formal trial.

Under the proviso just quoted, an accused could no longer be made to answer a charge under oath, as accuseds had often, if not always, been in the past. More important, if he denied the charge, he could not be required to make a canonical purgation. So unless he admitted the charge on account of a personal desire to stand in a white sheet for it, there was no way of reaching him without bringing forth formal proof.

One other possibility was suggested by the ever resourceful Gibson.[79] He pointed out that if a person had a bad reputation with regard to a given offense, he could be censured, or at least admonished, even if he cleared himself of the actual offense, on account of whatever he had done to get the bad reputation. This could still be done to him, Gibson suggested. An offense which could not be proved could be treated like one of which the accused had cleared himself. The trouble with this is of course that under the new rules the reputation itself would have to be formally proved.

But a formal canonical trial cost a good deal of money.[80] You probably had to hire a proctor to prepare articles. You had to examine witnesses before a notary. He had to be paid for taking the testimony down, and the register of the court had to be paid for filing it. After 1694, all the material was subject to stamp duties of sixpence (later raised to a shilling) a page. The question was who was to lay all this money out in order to drape white sheets around a couple of village lovers. In the old days, when the churchwardens had once made a presentment, it was up to the court officials to process it. The latter called in offenders in batches, and put them to their answers or purgations at a shilling or sixpence a time, and thereby made a decent, though by no means princely, income out of their offices. But if they were going to prepare articles and examine witnesses, they needed more money than that out of a given case. Their fees were their only means of livelihood, and they had no funds to pay for a prosecution that did not pay for itself.

So by the early eighteenth century, complaints were coming in that the court officials would not process a presentment unless the offender was rich.[81] It was not worthwhile proceeding unless he could pay substantial costs, or better still, commute his penance for three or four pounds.

Commutation of penances was an old story.[82] The canons required a good reason, related to the spiritual welfare of the offender or of the congregation. They required also the personal permission of the bishop. Finally, they required that the money be put to charitable uses in the offender's parish, and that the fact of commutation be made public so the congregation would know that the offender had not gone scot free. In the old days, general corruption had often led the court officials to violate these rules. Now, with the number of cases decreasing and the cost of each rising, it was probably stark financial necessity that led them to do so. There are traces of high-minded officials who tried to bring genuine fruits of repentance out of the system, by imposing true penances, and, on occasion, waiving their fees;[83] but high-mindedness to the point of economic destitution can hardly be in sufficient supply to keep a court system running.

As the parish had a claim to any sums received in commutation of a penance, the courts often preferred for the parishioners not to hear when one of their neighbors commuted.[84] Accordingly, when an offender was presented, that was apt to be the last anyone in his parish heard of the case. If the offender was poor, there would in fact be nothing done about him. If he was rich, he would probably be allowed to commute, without telling the parish — though in some cases a rumor would filter through that he had bought off the processes of the church.

Some effort was made to get the churchwardens to do the work of prosecuting the offenders they presented.[85] But they were generally not about to commit parish funds for this purpose — much less their own. Sometimes they were told that it was their duty to follow through on their presentments. But unless there was a question of recovering money for the parish (as in a presentment for not paying a churchrate), they did not see their duty this way. Even if they were sufficiently incensed to start a case moving, they were apt to get discouraged as the processes and payments wore on.

As the system decayed, it became harder and harder to get people to respond to its processes.[86] Contumacy had always been a problem with proceedings of this kind because of the cost of getting the necessary writs from the lay courts to impose temporal sanctions on those who disobeyed the processes of the church. Without the aid of the secular arm, the church court could only excommunicate — a sanction that lost more and more of its terrors as the hold of the church on the people became less and less. And even this sanction was expensive for the people prosecuting the case. After they had paid for the necessary citations, they would have to come into court and get an excommunication pronounced. Then they would have to take out a "schedule of excommunication," and move for "letters denunciatory" to issue. Then they would have to take these out and deliver them to the parish priest. Each of these steps had a fee attached. In the end, it was easy to think it was not worthwhile to go on.

Let us take a look at the system at work in the time of full decay. On Saturday, October 17, 1741, twenty-four persons were introduced to the bishop of Oxford's Consistory Court for sexual offenses. Here is what happened to them:[87]

First, there were Edward Pawling, and his wife Hannah, accused of premarital incontinence. Edward came in and confessed. He said Hannah was not well enough to come. He was ordered to submit to a private penance (in the presence of ministers and churchwardens only, instead of the whole congregation — the usual treatment when the guilty couple had married before being brought to book). He was also told to pay costs. His wife's case was postponed. On November 28, it was noted that he had not yet taken out the "schedule" that described his penance and instructed his parish minister to have him perform it. This is the last entry in the case, except for a series of nonappearances and postponements, until November 6, 1742, when the case was finally dismissed. The reasons for the dismissal were not specified. There is no indication that Pawling either did his penance or paid his costs, but perhaps he did.

Then there was John Cozier, presented on fame (i.e., reputation) of adultery.[88] He did not show up in court, but on December 12, he appeared in the home of the official's surrogate, waived his objection to its not being a regular court session, and denied the accusation. He was told to come to court and receive a set of articles setting forth his offense. He showed up in court on February 20, 1742. He was then offered a chance to bring a certificate from his minister and churchwardens that they believed him innocent (a process that looks a bit like the old purgation, without the oath). He was given until May 8 to bring in such a certificate, or else receive articles. On May 28, he brought in the certificate, and his case was dismissed.

Richard Sandelands was the only one of the lot out of whom the process got a definite sum of money. He was accused of getting his servant girl with child; he denied it. He was given a day to come in and receive articles. One Edward Bilstone was appointed "promoter" of the case, and told to prepare these articles. Bilstone was one of two proctors who seem to have constituted the practicing bar of the Oxford church courts. Most of their work was done in probate cases in the archdeacon's court.[89]

Six weeks later, on November 28, 1741, Sandelands came in again, and found there were still no articles. Bilstone was told to get them up promptly or the case would be dismissed. On January 23, 1742, another postponement was granted, because Bilstone was ill. The articles finally came through on February 20, 1742. At this point, Sandelands put in a document called a "protest," the tenor of which does not appear. This the judge refused to receive because it was not on stamped paper. The case was postponed again. On November 6, 1742, Sandelands failed to appear. There was another postponement, although Bilstone wanted him excommunicated. He showed up on the thirteenth, and was postponed to December 11. He failed to come in on the eleventh, and the case was postponed to February 5, 1743. On that date it was postponed another fortnight to the nineteenth. On the nineteenth, Bilstone was ill, and the case was put off until March 19.

Finally on March 19, 1743, there was a confrontation of sorts. Sandelands tried to get off by showing that the churchwardens had disavowed the presentment on which his original accusation was based. But the judge asked him straight out whether he was guilty or not. Despite not being under oath, he admitted that he was. He was given until May 14 to receive Bilstone's bill for costs. There was no mention of penance.

The court itself put off its May 14 session until June 18, and then from June 18 until July 16 — perhaps it was a good summer for fishing. On July 16, Sandelands did not show up. Bilstone was given till the next court day to bring in his bill. He brought it on October 29 (which was in fact the next court day), but Sandelands still was not there. Finally, Sandelands came in on November 12, 1743, and received Bilstone's bill. It was for £ 4/2/6. The court struck off the change, and Sandelands paid in £ 4. The case was over, a little more than two years after it had begun. Sandelands had made eight court appearances in the case, Bilstone nine. Three times Sandelands had found Bilstone absent or unprepared; four times Bilstone had found Sandelands missing; five times they were both there.

These were the most active cases of the lot. We can take up the other twenty offenders in a batch. They were eleven women accused of being the mothers of bastards, two men accused of being the fathers of other bastards, two unmarried couples accused of living together and having children, two women accused of fornication, and one man accused of adultery. One of the mothers was dismissed on the spot on account of a letter she had brought from her minister. One of the fathers was dismissed because the apparitor said he had gone for a soldier. Three of the accused denied the charges, and were given a day to receive articles. These and the girl with the letter from the minister were apparently the only ones that showed up. Bilstone was appointed promoter in ten cases (two of the three denials, and eight others).

One of the cases entered on October 17 simply disappeared from the records after the original entry. So at the session of November 28, 1741, there were seventeen left. One of these was dismissed as the woman involved had married and left the jurisdiction. Eight of the remaining sixteen were postponed. As to the other eight, the additional citations (*viis et modis*) decreed at the October 17 session had not yet gone forth.

By January 23, 1742, one further case had disappeared without explanation. In seven others, the citation had still not gone forth, so it was ordered that nothing more be done till further order of the court. Two of these seven were dismissed for no stated reason on November 6, 1742; in the others, no further entry appears. That leaves eight. On January 23, three of these were postponed due to Bilstone's illness; three were postponed for no stated reason; in the remaining two the accused were excommunicated.

On February 20, it was noted that the schedule of excommunication had not been taken out for the two excommunicated in January. Two others were excommunicated. The other four were postponed. At this point, then, there remained eight of the original twenty accused, four of these being excommunicated. Of the latter four, there is no further entry on three.

On November 6, 1742, one of the four postponed in February was dismissed. The reason does not appear, but he had denied his guilt in the first place, and no promoter had been appointed for his case, so perhaps it was want of prosecution that led to his dismissal. As to the remaining four accused, no action was taken on the one that had been excommunicated in February. The other three were postponed, although Bilstone had wanted them excommunicated for not showing up. They were finally excommunicated on November 13. That left four accused, all of them excommunicated. Two of them had come into court at the introduction of their cases a little over a year before. The other two had never come in. All four were among the cases Bilstone had been assigned to promote.

The next step was to get from the court a "schedule of excommunication." The exact purpose of this document eludes me, but I gather it served to promulgate the sentence of excommunication, and so make it official. Thereafter, the court could order "letters denunciatory" to issue, on the strength of which the offender could be denounced in his parish church. It was not until forty days after this denunciation that the secular arm could be invoked with a writ of *significavit*. In initiating this process, Bilstone skipped the court sessions of November 20 and December 11, 1742. It was not until February 5, 1743 that he took out schedules of excommunication in his four cases. Then on March 19, the court ordered letters denunciatory to issue.

At this point, Bilstone seems to have given up. He never took out the letters denunciatory. Every court day for the next two years, the four cases were duly entered with a notation that the letters had not issued. Finally, on December 7, 1745 the judge cleared his docket by ordering these and a number of other cases to stand as they were on the previous court day (November 16).

So the twenty-four persons accused on October 17, 1741, were finally all disposed of in a little over four years. None had done penance, none had been brought to trial. One had admitted his guilt and paid costs; one had established his innocence after a fashion. Seven had come into court at least once, two of these oftener. Ten cases were formally dismissed; fourteen simply disappeared. Bilstone, in nine court appearances, netted four pounds less the stamp duties and court fees on one set of articles, one bill of costs, and four schedules of excommunication. We can see where this system was heading.

As the game became more and more costly and futile, the churchwardens on whom it depended became less and less interested in playing it. Early in the eighteenth century, the clergy were complaining that as matters stood there seemed to be no point in making presentments:

> My Lord, as things are carried on by Ecclesiastical Officers, I see no encouragement given either to Us to present nor any Necessity even for ye Churchwardens so solemnly to oblige themselves to do it. In my parish, both Incest and Polygamy, tho' duly presented, have pass'd to all appearance unpunished.[90]

Added to this procedural discouragement was, I suspect, a change in attitude toward the work of policing morals in the first place. This may be attributable to a general increase in permissiveness and perhaps in licentiousness during the period. The several Declarations of Indulgence, followed by the Toleration Act of 1689 may have had some effect also. The anomaly of having a church impose moral correction on people who did not attend its services or accept its ministrations may have been more apparent to parish churchwardens than it was to ecclesiastical lawyers. In some cases, the creation of new temporal offenses may have persuaded the churchwardens that correcting offenders was no longer their business. At any rate, by the mid-nineteenth century, churchwardens were responding to printed forms asking about moral offenses with a firm statement that it was "no part of their duty" to deal with such matters.[91]

There was no way to get them to make presentments unless they wanted to.[92] They could be reminded of their oath, and exhorted to live up to it. In theory, if they failed to present an offender they knew about, their successors could turn around and present them. But the lay courts would prohibit (it is not clear to me on what ground) an archdeacon from ordering a set of churchwardens to present so-and-so on pain of excommunication.

Of course, if a churchwarden was conscientious about his oath, the court had a certain hold on him. He could be given a set of articles, and made to swear to answer them truthfully.[93] However, the ecclesiastical lawyers, in their zeal for avoiding any conflict with the lay courts, took most of the teeth out of the churchwarden's oath. A couple of cases in the King's Bench in 1672 had held that if a set of articles was so general it might conceivably include offenses over which the church courts had no jurisdiction, the churchwardens did not have to answer it under oath. So it became the custom (much to Gibson's disgust) to have them swear simply to present whatever was presentable under the ecclesiastical laws of the realm. This oath would cover their answers to specific articles only by implication, or not at all, depending on how they interpreted the law. They interpreted it as giving them a good deal of discretion as to whom not to present.

Under the Canons of 1604, the minister was supposed to present anyone the churchwardens left out.[94] But he too knew how futile the whole process was. Also, since the Act of Toleration made attendance at his church to all intents and purposes voluntary, he was often reluctant to clash with his parishioners over such matters. I doubt if he presented anyone the churchwardens wanted to spare.

It was possible in theory for a private person to promote a case out of mere zeal for the correction of morals.[95] But he would probably have to pay for it out his own pocket, and he might be liable in a defamation suit if he lost. So unless you seriously offended a wealthy man, you were probably fairly safe from being proceeded against in this way.

This moribund apparatus may have been given a modest extension of life by some kind of connection with the secular bastardy laws.[96] When a woman of a parish produced a bastard, it was of the utmost importance for the churchwardens and overseers of the poor to make some man responsible for the child's support; otherwise the parish would be responsible. This vital purpose could be accomplished either by dragooning the father (or bribing some other man if it came to that) into marrying the mother, or by proving paternity before the justices of the peace, who would then enter a support order and enforce it. Which alternative the parish officers preferred varied a good deal from parish to parish. The father, I suppose, would be apt to prefer marriage, because the justices of the peace could be pretty rough. If the parish was one in which the officers thought marriage was better for the poor rates, they were not apt to take no for an answer. In one case, the Bishop of Oxford had to intervene to stop them from making a man marry the mother of his child when he already had a wife.

What I suspect is that there was some way the ecclesiastical proceeding could be used to get people to marry, or else could be used to get the mother to name the father. In view of what we have seen of the system at work, it is doubtful that the possibility of being stood in a white sheet would accomplish much, but it is possible that the church proceeding might have served as an earnest of the more formidable one before the justices. Or it may have been that a sheaf of official documents, coupled with persuasions by minister and churchwardens, could bring people round without further proceedings. Many a bill collector works on comparable principles today.

Another possibility is this. There is a certain amount of canonical authority for excluding persons of bad character from matrimony in the same way as from Communion. Once in a while, a minister would bring this up, to the consternation of parish officials intent on a shotgun wedding.[97] It may be that penances were sometimes imposed to restore the mother's character, and so overcome objections of this kind.

In any event, there appear in the records of the Oxford Consistory Court in the 1740s a number (about three a year) of cases where mothers of bastards admit their guilt, and are assigned penances at rather cozy court sessions, not regular ones.[98] Evidently, these women came forward voluntarily, without any formal presentment or citation. And in each case the father of the bastard was named. Some of these women may just have had guilty consciences — a woman of this mind is mentioned in a letter from her parish priest to the bishop in 1757 — but in most cases it seems likely that the parish officers arranged the affair.

We need not speculate further about these matters. Whatever use the system was to the parish was not sufficient to keep it alive beyond the mid-eighteenth century. I suppose it exists in theory even today. But it has been officially characterized as obsolete.[99]

The passing of the church's jurisdiction over morals did not of course mean an end of its concern with marriage. The church authorities ceased to investigate invalid marriages on their own initiative, but they did continue to try them in their courts on the initiative of one of the parties; this jurisdiction they kept until 1857. The also tried to deal with clandestine marriages, generally by punishing clergy who performed them. The primary concern of the church with this offense was taken away, as we have seen, by an act of 1753 making it a felony. The ceremony itself remained pretty well under exclusive church control until 1836. Before that, a ceremony in a Dissenting chapel would get you out of a prosecution for fornication, but it would not get you a share of your wife's estate when she died.[100]

One other aspect of the old moral discipline that survived after a fashion was the proceeding for defamation. As time went by, this was more and more hemmed in by the increasingly available lay proceeding, but it was not in fact abolished until 1855. The last public penance Tate records in his general review of parish records is one for defamation in 1846.[101]

C. Lay Conformity and Attendance.

Until the 1689 Toleration Act, the old penalties for not going to church, or for attending "conventicles," were still in force, supplemented with some stringent new ones brought in by the triumphant royalist churchmen. In fact, in the first years, the old apparatus of presentment was fairly active in turning offenders up.[102] There were "sectaries" and papists who did not come to church. There were Anabaptists and Quakers who did not have their children baptized. There were even some old-style puritans who came to church and sat with their hats on, or tried to receive Communion sitting down. There were some who were simply "negligent," preferring the alehouse of a Sunday.

But Laud's fiery zeal for there being one flock and one shepherd was no longer moving the system from the top. The justices of the peace were apt to look the other way.[103] The common lawyers found ingenious technicalities to block prosecutions. The churchwardens had the problems just discussed in getting presentments processed if they made them. As for the bishops, they were making their main attack on Dissent — as they continued to do throughout the eighteenth century and part of the nineteenth — by compiling statistics and urging their clergy to bring round the erring brethren by learned discourse and pious example.[104] So, while a few conventicles were suppressed, and a few twelvepenny fines imposed or at least threatened, the serious Dissenter had come to be pretty safe from anything worse than the importunity of the parish incumbent long before the Toleration Act made his situation official.

I will defer to another chapter the further history of the statutory disabilities of Dissent — how the handful of Roman Catholics continued to be subject in theory to the old laws, how the more numerous Protestant Dissenters gradually escaped from a swarm of petty harassments, what efforts were made to remodel the Church of England to bring in more people, and what conceptual difficulties were encountered in reconciling total national commitment to one church with total freedom and equality for other churches. What I want to consider here is the situation of the majority who continued to adhere in some sense to the Church of England.

On paper, the Toleration Act did not affect them at all. to take advantage of it, you had to be a "person dissenting from the Church of England." Further, to avoid the penalties for not attending your parish church on a given Sunday, you had to attend a properly registered congregation of Dissenters that Sunday. So the statute did you no good if you were one of the alehouse and bowling people, the "negligent" ones. Further — a subtlety developed by Chief Justice Holt — it did you no good if you were an ecumenical type who went sometimes to the Anglican services, sometimes to Dissenting ones. Your attendance at the Anglican services showed that you were no Dissenter from the Church of England; hence, your attendance at a Dissenting conventicle was subject to all the traditional penalties.[105]

This, then, was how the law read on paper. In practice, it did not work out that way at all. Many churchwardens, constables, justices of the peace and the like seem to have supposed that it did away entirely with the penalties for nonattendance, as the earlier royal declarations had tried to do.[106] Others simply could not be bothered chasing down the people who stayed away from the local church to find out whether they had gone somewhere else. Prideaux, in his handbook for churchwardens (1701),

tried to persuade them that they should present all absentees they were not
sure about, and let those who qualified under the act make their defense in
court.[107] But the churchwardens, sensibly enough, were unwilling to put
their neighbors to all this trouble. The law reports show a couple of
prosecutions for nonattendance as late as the mid-eighteenth century,[108]
but on the whole compulsory church attendance went out with the
Toleration Act.

It was mainly the negligent ones who got the benefit. The real
Dissenters, as I say, had usually been left alone anyhow. Further, the
penalties as administered were often enough to turn a person out of the
alehouse without weakening another person in a serious religious resolve.
So, when the persecution came to an end, attendance in some Anglican
parishes was halved, while the Dissenters hardly picked up anyone at
all.[109]

D. Patronage, Simony, Etc.

The conditions of clerical life had improved by the eighteenth century to
the point that a good many livings provided respectable support for a
gentleman.[110] It became economically feasible, and socially acceptable, to
bestow these on the younger sons of the gentry, or on the distant relatives
and hangers-on of the nobility. If you had such a benefice in your gift, you
could use it to discharge a family obligation or a debt of gratitude, or to
enhance your political influence in the countryside. If you had no interests
of this kind, you could (subject to a couple of restrictions which we will
take up shortly) transfer your rights for cash to someone who had.

The new conditions produced a few new developments in the ancient and
convoluted law of advowsons.[111] A brisk market made it possible to
mortgage them, and the courts had to decide on occasion whether
mortgagor or mortgagee should present to the benefice. The use of
advowsons to provide for relatives meant that they figured on occasion in
private trusts; this raised some pretty questions for the Court of Chancery.
Also, some streamlining of the litigation process was undertaken. A statute
of 1708 made it possible to use the standard writ of *quare impedit* in cases
where you would formerly have had to use the obsolescent writ of right of
advowson, if, indeed, you had any remedy at all. By 1733, the courts of
equity had developed procedures for making the bishop honor equitable
interests in advowsons as the common law courts made him honor legal
ones.

Now that there was a customary and legitimate way of turning advowsons
to account — something there had not been since the employment of clerics
as bureaucrats went out at the close of the Middle Ages — it became

possible to bring the cruder forms of simony under some kind of control. Taking cash to present a man to a benefice, exacting from him a favorable lease of the glebe or making him promise to accept less than full tithe became aberrations once more, instead of the fairly common practices they seem to have been in the late sixteenth and early seventeenth centuries. The measures developed in those days, strengthened a bit by one or two post-Restoration decisions,[112] were now sufficient, evidently, to keep such practices in hand. At least, they no longer had a prominent place in the catalogues of abuses.

There were only a few rules relating to simony that troubled the typical eighteenth century patron making use of his rights. The most important was the rule that you could not buy or sell the right to present to a vacant benefice. Naturally, the sooner the incumbent was apt to die off, the better the price an advowson would bring on the market.[113] Still more was this true of the "next presentation," a right that could be sold separately, and often was. But once the incumbent did die, or otherwise leave the benefice, there could be no sale until a new presentment was made. The advowson would be a dead loss to the patron for that incumbency unless he had a friend or relative of his own that he wanted to provide for.

This rule was interpreted no more broadly than its letter required.[114] It was all right to sell when the incumbent was on his deathbed: we need a definite rule, and being almost dead but not quite is too vague. It was all right to sell when the incumbent had been instituted but not inducted into another benefice: by long tradition, institution (canonical admission by the bishop) concerns only the church authorities; induction (putting into physical possession by the archdeacon) is the only act of which the lay courts take notice.

With advowsons and next presentations going on the open market, it was natural that a minister with a little money should want to buy one and be his own patron. The medieval canon law had forbidden a cleric to present himself to a benefice, but it was generally felt that this rule was not received in England. A statute of 1713 made it illegal for a cleric to buy a next presentation and present himself, but he could still buy the whole advowson and do so.[115]

Another old canonical rule that interfered with a completely free use of the family living was the one that forbade a son to occupy his father's benefice unless there had been a third person in between. A dispensation could be had from this rule from the Archbishop of Canterbury, and Burn says that no less than three hundred such dispensations were issued between 1660 and 1710. But he points out that the dispensation is probably unnecessary, because the rule has not been enforced since the Reformation.[116] We may suppose that by the late eighteenth century people were no longer bothering to get dispensations of this kind.

The only serious problem a patron encountered in using his rights to support his relatives and friends was in having the living available when it was needed. Suppose you are the squire of Blackcurrent Parva, and own the advowson of the local church. Your eldest son, William, will inherit your land when you die. You have bought a commission in the army for your second son, George. That leaves Harry, a bright lad, now seventeen. The living is occupied by your cousin Arthur, now fifty-eight, who was presented by your father some years ago. You have it all arranged that Harry will pursue his studies, matriculate in due course at Oxford, and take orders when he reaches the canonical age of twenty-three. Arthur, who will then be sixty-four, and ready for a little help with his pastoral work,[117] will make Harry his curate and pay him a reasonable stipend. When Arthur dies, you (or William, if he has succeeded you by then) will present Harry to the living, and he will live happily ever after.

But suppose Arthur dies unexpectedly when he is fifty-nine and Harry eighteen. Now you are in trouble. The living is vacant. If you do not present someone to it in the next six months, the bishop will fill it himself on account of a "lapse." But if you do present someone, he may stay in the benefice for years and years, leaving Harry unprovided for. Even the oldest and most decrepit of clergymen is apt to show a disconcerting longevity when someone is anxiously waiting to step into his shoes.

Fortunately, the solution to your problem is not far to seek.[118] Your solicitor will explain to you, if you do not already know, how you can present someone to "hold the living" until Harry is old enough. You do this by means of a "resignation bond." It is all perfectly legal; in a case like yours, not even the bishop will mind. The resignation bond is a sealed instrument which you make a clergyman execute when you present him to the benefice; it obligates him to pay you a large sum of money if he does not resign when you tell him to. You will have no trouble finding a clergyman willing to execute such a document. A short time in even a mediocre living is worth more than a long time in a bad one. And it is far better than languishing in any of the numerous curacies that afford neither security of tenure nor good pay. You will probably want to bestow this temporary good fortune on someone to whom you owe a favor, or someone who can do you a favor in return. But you must not take cash from him or make him promise to remit your tithes: that would be simony, and you could lose your presentment for it.

Logically, the execution of a resignation bond should also be simony. It is something of value to the patron, and it is given him for the sake of the presentment. This argument was put to the common law judges in the early seventeenth century, and rejected for rather complicated reasons which I tried to sort out in the last volume. It was put again in the eighteenth century, and rejected on the basis of the earlier precedents.[119]

A number of bishops and canonists continued to accept the argument in theory, and to hint that a cleric could not in good conscience take the canonical oath against simony if he had subjected himself to a resignation bond. But they too were aware of the value of family livings in cementing the alliance between the landholding class and the church. In practice, they would make no difficulty if the bond was used to "hold the living" as in the situation I just described.

Not that there was much they could have done about it. The standard procedure for the ecclesiastical authorities in a case of simony was refusing to institute the guilty cleric into the benefice involved, or depriving him if he had been instituted already. I have found no case before 1783 in which either of these steps was taken on account of the execution of a resignation bond. If there had been such a case, the lay courts would certainly have intervened to uphold the validity of the bond. What the bishops did try from time to time was refusing to accept a resignation brought about by the patron through the use of a bond.[120] But the standard bond was so worded that if the bishop refused to accept the resignation the cleric would have to pay the penalty sum provided for, just as if he had not resigned at all. Presumably, the bishop would usually relent rather than subject the cleric to this liabilty.

But if the bond was put to a bad use, that was another story.[121] Besides making the cleric resign to make room for one of your friends or relatives, the only thing you could legitimately do with his bond was to hold it over his head in order to make him reside, serve the cure, and keep himself sober and chaste. If you tried to extort money, or to make him take less tithe that he was entitled to, the bishop would refuse to accept his resignation, and the courts of equity would enjoin you from enforcing the bond. If you had already collected money from him, he could probably get it back in an action at law. I should imagine that these remedies kept these forms of outright extortion fairly well in hand. Resignation bonds played their part, to be sure, in the general subordination of the eighteenth century clergy to their patrons, but that was an altogether more subtle affair.

In 1783, the House of Lords, which had not dealt with resignation bonds until then, altered the situation radically in the case of *Bishop of London v. Ffytche*.[122] The bishop, on finding that Ffytche's presentee had executed a resignation bond, refused to institute him, and Ffytche brought *quare impedit*. The bishop urged two defenses: first, the giving of the bond was simony; second, it made the presentee so dependent on his patron as not to be a fit pastor. The common law judges found the first point well settled against the bishop, and the second too vague to be sound. The House of Lords reversed without opinion, eighteen bishops and Lord Chancellor

Thurlow voting for reversal, eighteen lay peers for affirmance. Thurlow
was the only reputable lawyer on the prevailing side; the fact that his
brother was a bishop may have been relevant. The bishops were a good
deal blamed for using their votes to overrule the lawyers on a clear point of
law. But it seems to me that even as a matter of strict law the bishops
were right. The House of Lords is not bound by the precedents of inferior
courts, and there was nothing but such precedents to support the lawyers'
view.

What the *Ffytche* case invalidated was a *general* resignation bond — one
that in terms required the incumbent to resign when the patron said to.
The lower courts held that it was still permissible for a legitimate purpose
to exact a *special* resignation bond — one which specified the circumstances
under which resignation might be required.[123] Thus, if the incumbent
undertook to resign when so-and-so was ready to take the living, or to
resign if he ceased to reside and personally serve the cure, the bond would
still be enforced.

In the 1826 case of *Fletcher v. Sondes*,[124] the House of Lords
invalidated special resignation bonds as well. The Lords finally accepted
the argument the bishops had been making since James I's time: since the
execution of the bond was a valuable consideration for the presentment, it
made the presentment simoniacal. Lords who voted the other way pointed
to the desirability of providing benefices for the relatives of patrons, in
order to keep "the landholding interest" attached to the church. Their
arguments were so persuasive that the Lords proceeded to undo as a
legislative body what they had done as a court. It was enacted (and
remained the law for the rest of the century) that a resignation bond was
valid if it specified by name one or at most two relatives of the patron in
whose favor the resignation could be exacted, if it was registered in the
diocesan registry, and if one of the named persons was presented within six
months after the resignation took place. The basic concept of the family
living was saved.

That special kind of patron the lay impropriator figured in a number of
cases and a few statutes during the period we are considering. His
relations and litigations with his vicar had not changed too much since
earlier times. He was, though, given new encouragement to turn over
some of his church revenue to better the vicar's lot; in a number of cases,
he in fact did so.[125] I have the impression that the incessant propaganda
about the anomaly of his receiving ecclesiastical revenues had gradually
made a small dent in public opinion. His obligations in a parish where
there was no vicar were a good deal modified.[126] He had always been
obliged to hire a curate to hold services. Now occasions were found to give
that curate a secure position. For one thing, it was held that if permanent

sources of revenue were settled on him, either by the impropriator himself
or by Queen Anne's Bounty (a scheme for increasing clerical incomes which
we will take up in due course), he would have tenure in his position from
then on. Moreover, it was held in 1683 that the Crown, at the behest of
the Attorney General, could require the impropriator to settle part of his
revenues on the curate as a perpetual endowment, thus making him
virtually the same as a vicar.

The impropriator's other main duty, repairing the chancel, was less
satisfactorily dealt with. In 1677, a bishop tried to enforce this duty by
sequestering the impropriate rectory, but he was not allowed to.[127] I
suppose this holding was an inevitable consequence of Henry VIII's statute
making the rectory a lay hereditament, but it was hard on bishops trying to
get chancels repaired. One can think of a number of alternative
procedures that might have worked, but I find no indication that any of
them was tried. This particular obligation seems to have remained easy to
evade and hard to enforce as long as it existed.

In the late eighteenth and early nineteenth centuries, a certain number of
impropriators began to take their titular rectorship seriously, and to interest
themselves in the religious affairs of their churches. Fortunately, the courts
did not encourage them in these concerns.[128] A lay rector, like any other
patron, had the right to prevent a wastage of church property; patrons had
had that right since the Middle Ages. But he had no special standing to
prevent unauthorized preaching in his church. That was a matter between
the bishop and the incumbent, though the impropriator could be received
as an ordinary parishioner to promote a suit. Nor could the impropriator,
by means of his theoretical freehold in the chancel, move seats and
monuments about or dig out a burial vault for himself and his family. He
had to get a "faculty" from the bishop's court, just as anyone else did.

All in all, we can say that for most of the eighteenth century the law of
patronage did not raise any serious problems for the church. This general
mellowing of the situation seems to be part of the overall success of the
Erastian settlement. The basic tension in the institution of patronage had
been between various secular interests and the interest of the clergy in their
cohesiveness as a distinct order in society. This notion of a distinct order
was hardly raised in the eighteenth century. The clergyman had his
responsibilities, as anyone else did, but he did not feel himself entitled to
any greater status than his income and his background afforded, and this
much the whole society was willing to concede him. Careerism and
dependence on personal and family connections were no different and no
less respectable among the clergy than among other men. The law of
patronage fitted so neatly into the prevailing scheme of things that there
was very little to argue about.

E. Parish Institutions

The English parish had combined secular and ecclesiastical functions and interests time out of mind. Between the Reformation and the Civil War, several forces had operated to bring its primordial ambiguity into sharp relief. The Tudor state and the Elizabethan episcopate had both laid on new functions and supervised more rigorously the performance of old ones. The common law courts had moved with more zeal than sensitivity to vindicate the powers of the laity, and the prevalence of customs over canons. At the same time, the church courts had tried to push their traditional powers to their full extent in order to keep control over institutions that played a vital part in the work of the church. The Erastian rapprochement that followed the Restoration required the courts to sort out these conflicting interests, and make as much sense of the situation as they could.

1. *Churchwardens* were the most important parish officials.[129] Historically they were the representatives of the parish community in its dealings with ecclesiastical authority; they had accumulated a number of temporal functions as well. On the ecclesiastical side, their main duties were to handle certain funds, property, and records, to keep the church in repair, to maintain order during services, and to report to the bishop and the archdeacon on the state of the parish. Each parish had two of them. Under the Canons of 1604, one was chosen by the minister, one by the parishioners.[130] The common law courts had established that a custom of the parishioners choosing both would prevail over the canon. At first, it was also held that both would be chosen by the parishioners if there was no evidence of a custom one way or the other. The idea espoused by the judges until about 1700 was that the canon as such could have no effect because the churchwardenship was a lay office: if the minister got to choose one churchwarden, it was because there was a custom in the parish for him to do so. But in 1746 it was held, in a good deal of disregard of the precedents, it seems to me, that the canon would be followed unless a custom was shown of doing something else.

The churchwardens had to be sworn in before the archdeacon. But the archdeacon was supposed to swear in anyone who applied.[131] He would be subject to a writ of mandamus if he tried to determine whether the candidate was fit for the post (the parishioners who chose him and have to live with their choice are the best judges of that), whether those who chose him were entitled to do so (a question of custom triable at common law), or even whether he was elected by the parishioners as he claimed to be. If two candidates showed up, both claiming to have been elected, the archdeacon was evidently expected to swear them both in and let them litigate in the lay courts on a feigned issue.

In fact, the church authorities exercised more discretion than the lay courts allowed.[132] If a man was obviously ineligible (e.g., an alien), or obviously not properly elected, he would probably not go to the expense of initiating lay proceedings that he would ultimately lose, so the archdeacon felt free not to swear him in. On the other hand, where it was a matter of deciding between the minister's candidate and the parishioners' we may suppose that the church courts trod warily if they trod at all.

Churchwardens did not have to be churchmen. To be sure, in 1682, the Bishop of Oxford fired a churchwarden for not receiving the Sacrament, but I doubt if the lay courts would have supported him in such an action even then. Anyhow, it was clear after the Toleration Act that a Dissenter could be a churchwarden.[133] He had a statutory right to appoint a deputy if he had scruples against doing the job himself, but there was nothing to stop him from doing it himself if he wanted to. As a result, churchwardens who were hostile or apathetic to the church's work became one of the perennial problems of administration.

As the churchwardens were parish officers, their accounts were made to the parishioners, and not to the ecclesiastical authorities.[134] One 1691 case made an exception when it came to accounting for funds spent on duties imposed by church law, but that seems to have been an aberration. The rule imposed over and over during the eighteenth century was that a church court could order the churchwardens to deliver up their accounts to the parish, but could not itself examine the accounts if the parishioners failed to do so. It is not clear what the parishioners were to do if they examined the accounts and disapproved them. The church courts did entertain proceedings in such cases, but there is language in the common law cases to indicate that they were not supposed to. Perhaps the parishioners could have sued in the lay courts, in the same way as a ward could sue his guardian or a beneficiary his trustee.

2. *Parish Clerks* were supposed to clean the church and make appropriate responses during the services. Their fees were purely customary, and in some parishes were worth arguing about. The canons provided that the incumbent was to appoint the clerk because he served a fundmentally ecclesiastical function; the parishioners often claimed the appointment, probably because they put up the money.[135] The resulting argument goes back to the Middle Ages. The courts dealt with the clerkship about as they did with the churchwardenship. It was a lay office. Who got to appoint to it was a matter of custom, triable in the lay court (there is no case on what happened where there was no showing of a custom either way). The ordinary could swear in the clerk, but not determine his right to the office.

If two candidates showed up, he was to swear them both and let them litigate on a feigned issue. Furthermore, if the clerk cared to appoint a deputy, the ordinary had to let him in too.

Nor could the church court determine an action by the clerk for his fees.[136] Either because the fees were all customary or because the clerkship was a lay office — it is not clear which — the lay courts said he had to bring a contractual action to collect.

The church authorities had a little better — though by no means spectacular — luck in enforcing some kind of discipline on the parish clerk.[137] A couple of Jacobean cases had completely denied them jurisdiction to deprive a clerk of his lay office, even if he performed the services all wrong. But in 1726, after a considerable period without a case, there appeared a clerk who had just been put in the pillory for attempted sodomy. The court refused a prohibition on an ecclesiastical proceeding to deprive him. The judges said that his office was spiritual except as regards appointment to it. To be sure, in 1733, they characterized this as a "hasty opinion in which they were transported by the enormity of the case," but they had in fact followed it in a case of less enormity in 1731. In 1753, the Court of Arches tried to reconcile the cases from the lay courts by suggesting that there was one rule where the clerk was appointed by the incumbent, another were he was elected by the parishioners. This distinction seems rather a *deus ex machina*; there is nothing said about it in the cases referred to.

The problem was finally more or less solved by a 1776 case that gave the incumbent — not the church court — the power to fire the parish clerk for misconduct, subject to a review of his reasons in a mandamus proceeding by the clerk seeking reinstatement. If the lay court was satisfied with the reasons (a large "if": in the particular case, the fact that the clerk was bankrupt and in jail, and had appointed a totally unfit deputy was held insufficient), no mandamus would issue. The church courts would not have allowed the minister to fire the clerk without preparing articles and proving them in a proper criminal proceeding, but that did not matter, because under the lay office concept the church court could no more reinstate the clerk than it could deprive him.

The last step in this development came in 1844,[138] when the lay court required the minister to give the clerk a hearing before firing him. But in the same year a statute was enacted turning over the whole process to the archdeacon or the bishop.

3. *The Vestry* was a general meeting of the parishioners to conduct their affairs. It was of relatively ancient origin, perhaps the same institution as the one that regulated the course of agriculture in the common fields. It was called the vestry because it met in that part of the church. The church

authorities were concerned with it because it elected at least one
churchwarden, passed on the churchwardens' accounts, and, most important
of all, made rates for the repair of the church fabric. The only real success
the church authorities had in controlling this powerful body was in gaining
for the parish incumbent a right to preside.[139] But they could not make
the vestry act if the churchwardens refused to summon it. They could not
control what went on at a meeting once it assembled (except to prosecute
for brawling in church if it ended in a riot). Nor could they appoint
churchwardens or pass on accounts if the vestry failed to do its work. All
these things they tried to do and were rebuffed by writs of prohibition.
Stultifying parish vestries became a standard tactic, as we shall see, for
Dissenters who wished to avoid contributing funds to support the church.

F. Miscellaneous

Here is a catena of matters, once of some moment, that require only
brief mention for the period we are now considering.
   1. Freehold Offices[140] — The feudal idea of an office as a specific
piece of property with fixed sources of income attached maintained a firm
and baneful hold as regards any offices carried over from the old days. In
1691, the common law judges overruled an earlier case to hold that a
bishop could not fire his chancellor for being too ignorant to do the job.
In 1705, they said he could not alter the traditional powers of his vicar
general when he made a new grant of the office. In 1757, no less an
authority than Mansfield rejected the doctrine laid down by Coke that an
office had to be "necessary" as well as "ancient" before it was exempted from
the Elizabethan statute against alienating the possessions of a bishopric.
One Trelawney, Great and Chief Steward of the Bishop of Winchester, was
allowed to go on drawing down £ 100 a year for doing absolutely nothing
in that capacity, as he had done when his father was bishop, and as "the
greatest men in the kingdom or the nearest relations of the bishops" had
done successively for generations. It was not until the mid-nineteenth
century that the bishops regained some right to supervise their courts,
recruited a new type of administrative assistants who did a day's work for a
day's pay, and stopped giving out unnecessary offices.
   2. Peculiars[141] — A peculiar was an enclave of A's jurisdiction in B's
diocese. These were maintained with great exuberance in the Middle Ages,
especially by monasteries. Those that remained when the monasteries were
done away with were run fairly soberly after the Reformation. But now,
with church courts everywhere moribund, these enclaves made a modest
but important contribution to the general decay. Someone like the
archbishop of Canterbury could probably keep a court system going in his

peculiars, but the average bishop had enough trouble running his own diocese without worrying about a couple of distant parishes in someone else's, while the colleges, cathedral chapters, and private persons who held most of the peculiars were neither willing nor able to set up adequate courts. So an eighteenth century peculiar provided the patron, incumbent, and parishioners with a firm base for resisting the exercise of any jurisdiction at all. Responsible ecclesiastics who had peculiars seem to have been a bit embarrassed by them, but still unwilling to give up something that was part of the ancient heritage of their various positions. There was talk as early as 1800 of making a clean sweep of all peculiars by Act of Parliament, but nothing came of it until the reforms of the 1830s.

3. *Cathedrals and Colleges* — For some reason, perhaps the weakening of central authority in the church, disputes over the running of cathedrals and colleges took on a new verve in the eighteenth century.[142] Some were pursued with a pertinacity and gusto that had scarcely been seen since the great jurisdictional battles of the early Middle Ages. In one case, Exeter College, Oxford, closed its gates against a visitation by the bishop of Exeter. In another, the master of Trinity College, Cambridge, brought off a series of maneuvers that held his position for over thirty years against all that a majority of the fellows, backed on occasion by the bishop of Ely and the vice-chancellor of the University, could do to throw him out. While all this was going on, the lay courts were determining when they would use mandamus to reinstate a man put out by a college visitor, or ejectment to give him back his lodging. And Parliament in 1707 resolved a technical question about the validity of cathedral statutes adopted by Henry VIII with an act so ambiguous that it kept the courts busy off and on for the rest of the century.

We need not go into all these legal complexities. The disputes seem finally to have been exhausted rather than resolved, just as the earlier ones were by the fifteenth century. We may suppose, though, that they contributed to the general moss-grown impression both colleges and cathedrals give us when we look at them in the early nineteenth century.

4. *Privileges and Restraints of the Clergy* — In theory, if you hit a clergyman, he could have you up in a church court. In practice, though, the church courts being what they were, and a perfectly good lay remedy being available, he would probably not bother with the church proceeding. I have found some examples in this period of ministers complaining of defamation, but not of their complaining of physical violence.

As regards defamation, a minister had broader protection than a layman in both sets of courts.[143] If you cast aspersions on his fitness for his job, he could sue in either court, whereas anyone else was limited to the lay court. Also, he could complain in either court about reflections on his

sobriety, his sexual morals, and the like, because they went to his fitness for
his job. To this day, a beneficed clergyman is the only male who can
maintain an action for slander of chastity without showing special damages.

"Benefit of clergy," which had been gradually transmuted from a privilege
of being proceeded against in the church courts into a privilege of
committing certain crimes with impunity, was available any number of
times to a genuine minister, whereas a layman could have it only once.
This distinction, the product, it seems of some bad drafting in Edward VI's
time, endured until 1825, just two years before the whole institution was
abolished for everyone.[144]

It was still the law that a clergyman could not have his benefice seized
for his debts. The bishop sequestered the revenues in response to a writ
from the lay court, and paid over to the creditors whatever he did not need
to provide for the service of the cure. This system was developed as early
as the fourteenth century, and evidently still worked.[145]

The canonical strictures on clerical recreations and businesses had
gradually dropped out of the picture by this time. Bishops still tried to
discourage the clergy from undue indulgence in hunting and carousing, and
there was a good deal of discussion about whether it was appropriate for
them to serve as justices of the peace.[146] In 1830, Bishop Bagot of
Oxford refused to license a curate who had just gone through bankruptcy
as a horse dealer. But it was contemporary good sense, not traditional
canon law, that the bishops applied in these cases.

There was also a statute of Henry VIII that forbade "spiritual persons" to
take farm leases, or to engage in certain kinds of trade.[147] A clergyman
was not allowed to escape debts incurred in violation of this statute, but
leases made in violation of it were sometimes held void. The statute made
enough exceptions (for instance, a clergyman might take a lease of
farmland if he had not enough glebe) so that the country clergy could often
improve their financial lot by working an extra field or two, or trading up
an occasional horse, and their neighbors thought all the better of them for
doing so. The statute was modified in 1803 to allow many of the activities
in question with the prior permission of the bishop.

"After all," says Burn, summing up his article on these matters,

these distinctions of the clergy are shadows rather than substance; being
most of them about matters which are obsolete and of no significance.
The *restraints*, as to the scope and purport of them, are such as the
clergy for the most part would chuse to put upon themselves: and the
privileges, such as they are, seem to be scarcely worth claiming; and some
of them one would almost imagine to bring a disgrace upon the clergy,
rather than to be of any real benefit to them; for why should a clergyman
be protected from paying his just debts more than any other person, or

be saved from punishment for a crime for which another person ought to be hanged?[148]

5. *Fees, Abuses of Authority, etc.* — What I have said about the disciplinary processes of the church is probably enough to explain why extortionate use of them was no great problem any more. As well might one try to rob banks with a water pistol. People actually found guilty of offenses may have commuted their penances for a pound or two, but I doubt if anyone would have been willing to buy off an apparitor to avoid being cited. Gibson in his days as an archdeacon checked up on the suppression of presentments, but I suspect it was inertia and not venality that he had in mind.[149]

But as the church courts handled some kinds of private litigation (marriage and probate being the most important), excessive fees for their services were still a problem.[150] Court fees had last been officially fixed by Archbishop Whitgift late in Elizabeth's reign. By the Canons of 1604, no other fees than those Whitgift provided for could be lawfully charged. But the decline in the value of money over the ensuing century and more had made these totally unrealistic. In some dioceses new schedules were adopted despite the canon; in others, I suspect, the officials charged what the traffic would bear. It was not until 1829 that Parliament arranged for a new official fixing of court fees.

Surplice fees — payments to a minister for ministering on a given occasion — raised new difficulties with the legalization of Dissent. These were customary payments; the minister could sue for them in the church court, but the proceeding would be brought over to a lay court on a prohibition if the existence or validity of the custom was denied. A number of ministers tried to establish customs of collecting the fee for a given ministration whenever the occasion for it arose, even if the ministration was not actually performed. If you had your child baptized by a Dissenting minister, or if you were married in a neighboring parish, your parish incumbent might claim the same fees as if he had performed the baptism or the marriage himself. The lay courts, however, following a line of cases developed in Coke's time, held to a strict no-work-no-pay principle: a custom of paying for a ministration that was not in fact performed was unreasonable and therefore invalid.[151] In 1753, the church courts follwed suit.

6. *Mortmain*[152] — As we saw in the last volume, by the latter part of Elizabeth's reign, the mortmain laws were not doing much to inhibit anyone's charitable purposes. To give land to a corporate body, you needed a royal license, but for an ordinary charitable trust you could do as you pleased. A law of Charles II did away with the necessity of a license if you wanted to give an impropriated rectory to the vicar, or buy lands of any

kind to augment a poor living. Later, the people in charge of Queen Anne's Bounty were given statutory carte blanche to take all the land they could get. The royal power to license donations in cases not provided for in these statutes suffered a temporary setback at the overthrow of James II. Despite the antiquity of mortmain licenses, they were not specifically provided for in the relevant statutes, so they fell under the ban on all royal dispensations that was enacted by Parliament when William and Mary came in. A few years later, however, they were specifically and fully revived by Parliament.

In 1736, an access of Whig anticlericalism led to a new legislative assault on charitable gifts.[153] It took the form of a law invalidating any charitable trust set up by will or by grant executed less than a year before the death of the grantor. It applied only to real property. This peculiar law, which lingered through most of the nineteenth century in England, and which has some descendants on American statute books even today, seems quite unrelated to either the history or the purpose of mortmain laws. The underlying notion of priests preying on the credulity of the dying seems more appropriate to anti-papist propaganda than to the realites of mid-eighteenth century Anglicanism. But the authors of the law evidently felt that a Georgian squire would hold onto his land unless he was unmanned by the fear of death; no doubt they knew with whom they were dealing. It was considered a great benefit to Queen Anne's Bounty, and to the cause of building new churches, when both were exempted from the operation of this act in 1803.

7. *Secular Functions* — There is not much in this period on the secular use of church buildings — though there is one instance as late as 1800 of an attempt to hold Quarter Sessions in a church. (The bishop told the churchwardens to prevent it.)[154] There were one or two statutes still that the minister was supposed to read off to the congregation, and there were various public notices that had to be put up in the church porch — as indeed there still are.

The power of the church over physicians, surgeons, and midwives had pretty well lapsed by the end of the seventeenth century, though some of the applicable statutes remained on the books until Victorian times.[155] Occasionally, a surgeon's license was still taken out, but secular forms of professional qualification (university degrees, approval by professional societies) were more usual. Proceedings for unlicensed practice, meanwhile, were among the first to go of the various disciplinary proceedings against the laity.

The church had been entrusted since Henry VIII's time with the keeping of records of baptisms, marriages, and burials.[156] These were public records, and people had a right to inspect them for legitimate secular purposes (e.g., the establishment of heirship). When Toleration came in, there was a problem of keeping up the registers to show the vital statistics of Dissenters. A number of ministers made register entries on reports by their Dissenting colleagues, a practice that was discouraged by the church authorities, but finally made statutory in 1812.

The registers were used after 1694 for the collection of a tax on births, marriages, and burials.[157] They were also used to implement a statute of 1666 to encourage sheep raising by requiring all corpses to be buried in woollen. Until the act was repealed in 1814, all burials were supposed to be noted by a certificate of compliance. Tate finds that the parish clergy were not very efficient in supporting government policy in any of these ways, or, indeed, in keeping up their registers at all.

They would have been still less efficient, I suspect, in taking a census of crops, as proposed by the government in 1801.[158] It appears that the bishops tactfully declined to saddle them with this task, saying that there was no way to make them do it.

III. Ecclesiastical Administration

A. Resources.

The declining emphasis on juridical forms left the bishop and the archdeacon looking less like government officials and more like the field supervisors of a large business. Deploying personnel and resources, keeping up plant and equipment, handling complaints, looking after the staff — most of their work could be described in such terms as these.

For the bishops, this field work was mainly done in the summer. The development of regular sessions of Parliament kept bishops out of their dioceses in the same way government service had done in the Middle Ages.[159] A bishop's first duty was felt to be faithful attendance and voting in the House of Lords for the party that had made him a bishop, and that might one day translate him to a better see. By the beginning of the eighteenth century, this duty was keeping him in the capital from autumn through spring every year. If he was both conscientious and in good health (a majority, but not a vast majority, were) he might be expected to spend from three to five months in his diocese, no more. In this time, he had to do all his visiting, and hold all his confirmations. The rest of the year he could only write letters, and hold an occasional ordination in London.

The reversion of the bishop to part time status seems to have enhanced the position of the archdeacon.[160] There were no suffragan bishops in those days, and no more than nominal rural deans. So the archdeacon was in a unique position to travel about the parishes, look over the fabric of the churches, and get to know the local clergy. If he was good at his job, he could render invaluable advice to the bishop (the ancient epithet *oculus episcopi* came into vogue), or even do much of the supervisory work in the bishop's stead. It is interesting in this respect how much Gibson the archdeacon addressing his clergy looks like Gibson the bishop doing the same.

Besides the archdeacons (generally one to a county), the main officers of diocesan administration were the bishop's chancellor, his secretary, and his one or two chaplains.[161] The chancellor headed up his court system, and stood in for him on some of his visitations. The secretary, probably trained as a solicitor (i.e., in civil rather than ecclesiastical law) advised the bishop on miscellaneous legal matters — leases, sequestrations, parish enclosure agreements submitted by the incumbent for approval, augmentations of benefices, and what have you. He and the chancellor between them advised the bishop on disciplinary matters; how they shared out the work depended no doubt on their own inclinations and abilities, the predilections of the bishop, and the circumstances of the case. The chaplains examined applicants for ordination, or clerics who sought institution to benefices or licenses as curates, lecturers, or preachers. They probably gave advice on other aspects of clerical placement as well.

Bishops and archdeacons kept up in attenuated form the traditional visitations of earlier times.[162] The clergy of one or more deaneries (probably more) would assemble in a central location on two or three weeks' notice passed around by an apparitor. The visitor who met them might be the bishop or the archdeacon in person, the archdeacon or the chancellor standing in for the bishop, or a senior clergyman standing in for the archdeacon. It did not really matter except that if the bishop said he was going to come in person and failed to do so, the clergy would be put out, because they would have brought great numbers of their parishioners for confirmation, and would have to send them home without it.

If it was the bishop's visitation, and he came in person, he would spend the morning delivering an address ("charge") to the clergy, setting forth appropriate pastoral exhortations, together with his views of current ecclesiastical affairs, and his plans for running his diocese.[163] In the afternoon, he would confirm. As these confirmation sessions were apt to be few and far between (due oftener to illness and poor roads than to outright neglect of duty), there might be some hundreds of people of all ages assembled for the rite. The resulting confusion would generally make the whole affair less edifying than it should have been.

The archdeacon might deliver a charge as the bishop did.[164] A substitute, if he was a clergyman, might preach a sermon, but that would be a different matter. The chancellor, of course, being a layman, could do neither, though he might have someone else preach a sermon. Perhaps whoever stood in for the visitor could read a charge prepared by his principal.

Meanwhile, there were documents to examine and money to pay.[165] The visitor was entitled to look at each incumbents's letters of orders, along with the records of his institution and induction, and of any dispensations he held. There was a fee of sixpence or a shilling on each such document, and another shilling for the apparitor general, presumably for having summoned the incumbent to the visitation. There were also "procurations" to pay. These were medieval cash commutations of the duty of the local clergy to put up the visitor and his retinue for a specified number of nights. By the seventeenth century they had generally become ordinary taxes, payable whether there was a visitation or not; still, the visitation was a good time for collecting them.

The churchwardens would submit bills of presentment, also accompanied with a modest fee.[166] These were usually on printed forms, making fairly detailed inquiries, but less detailed than they had been in the seventeenth century. The visitor sometimes made up one of his own and had it printed; sometimes he bought a stack printed up with a blank to fill in the diocese and year. Often, regardless of what information the forms required, the churchwardens would simply scrawl "all well" across the bottom. Sometimes, though, they answered the questions specifically. My impression is that they were faithful enough in letting the visitor know if there was anything wrong with the church building or furniture, or if the minister failed to live up to the unexacting standards of service and conduct that prevailed. About moral lapses of their neighbors, they were sometimes evasive:

> that all are at all times exempt from suspicion with regard to every one of these improprieties we cannot aver, or say that any are notoriously guilty.

No doubt their purpose was to discharge their oath without exposing the parish to the expense of prosecuting anyone.

As time went on, the bishop came to rely more and more on questionnaires submitted to the clergy, supplementing those the churchwardens filled in.[167] As far as I can see, this practice of canvassing the clergy came in with the Restoration; its first use was to get information on the number of Dissenters in the different parishes. It became a regular feature of visitations, and was used on other occasions as well. The information most commonly sought was on the number of Dissenters, the conduct of services, the teaching of the Catechism, the operation of charities, and the income of incumbents and curates. This information, and such other data as seemed relevant found its way generally into a notebook which the bishop kept parish by parish.[168] He used it to keep himself generally informed, rather than to take any specific official action.

When the papers were handed in and the charge delivered, the clergy and the visitor would dine together at the latter's expense, probably at a local inn.[169] It is characteristic of the eighteenth century that this part of the process seems to overshadow the rest of the agenda in the clergy's minds.

Much of the work of administration was done informally. The correspondence files of the bishops of Oxford (there is a set in the Oxfordshire Record Office running from 1635 to 1844) show a great variety of problems dealt with in this way.[170] A parish minister wants to know if a woman can marry whose husband was sentenced to death but the sentence commuted to transportation for life (no). A minister accused of keeping low company in pubs assures the bishop that he goes home early (he is not to do it at all). One hundred and twenty parishioners complain of a vicar whose reading of services "was so wild, disjointed, and unbecoming that the gravest persons in the Church could not refrain from laughing." Could the bishop persuade him to hire a curate? (no reply recorded). A rector wants to know what to do about a set of parishioners who claim a custom of eating at his expense on certain days (they may go to court if they wish). The owner of a family vault wants to know if the incumbent has been overcharging him for burying people there (the bishop checks with the archdeacon, with counsel, and with the incumbent himself). A clergyman complains about the closeness with which the last visitor inquired into his moral character, and wants to know what the bishop has heard to make him suspect (the bishop did not mean for the visitor to inquire so closely as to give scandal; he will not say why he ordered the inquiry, but this is not the first clergyman so inquired into nor probably the last). Then there are excuses for not residing to be considered, curates to be put in and taken out, stipends to be fixed, new churches and rectories to be built, quarrels and even fist fights to be patched up. In most cases, firmness, tact, and the prestige of the episcopal office solve the problems. Occasionally, as in one of the cases just mentioned, the parties are put to the law.

Although ecclesiastical administration was no longer the chief task of the church courts, there were three areas in which they had to be used. One was clerical discipline. A curate could have his license lifted rather summarily (if he had one), but an incumbent could not be put out without a full disciplinary proceeding. There were not a lot of these necessary, but there were some. Then there were cases involving church buildings. You needed a document called a faculty to put up a pew or a monument in church, and you had to go through a court proceeding to get one. The court also had to be invoked to build a new building or tear down the old one. For this, the chancellor would appoint a commission to make suitable inquiries and report on plans or expense.[171] Finally, there were financial matters. Payment of tithes and churchrates was generally enforced in the church courts, although there were cases in which the justices of the peace had been given jurisdiction by statute. Also, commutations of tithe and redistribution of church land (both of which were often involved in parish enclosures) had to be approved through the church court. Here again, a commission would be appointed to inquire and report.[172]

A handful of judicial processes, then, a visitation devoted more to conviviality and the gathering of information than to any administrative purpose, and a great deal of informal supervision and guidance — these were the resources available to an ecclesiastical administrator in the period. Let us see what he tried to accomplish with them.

B. Functions.

1. Recruitment and Placement of the Clergy — There was no significant change in this period in the laws relating to ordination, though the manner of their enforcement had its ups and downs. As had always been the case, a bishop held ordinations when he could or would, and ordained anyone with the requisite qualifications who showed up.[173] These qualifications included a baptismal certificate (which served also no doubt as proof of canonical age), a degree (in theory, other intellectual qualifications would do, but it was not customary at this time to ordain non-graduates), certificates of good character and orthodoxy from the candidate's home clergy and his college, and a "title" — the promise of a clerical job in the diocese of the ordaining bishop.[174] His intellectual qualifications would be inquired into further by the bishop's chaplains when he came for ordination. There was no necessity that his degree be in theology, though by the 1790s some candidates thought fit to present certificates that they had attended lectures on the subject. If the canons were followed, the chaplains would exact some knowledge of Latin, of Scripture, and of the major doctrines of the church, but I do not find that they drew up systematic written examinations before the 1820s. The title was probably required with some fidelity right along, though it was not regularly set forth in the ordination records till the middle of the eighteenth century.

If the bishop of the diocese where a man was to serve did not plan to hold an ordination at a convenient time, he could issue "letters dimissory" authorizing some other bishop to ordain the man. It was the responsibility of the bishop issuing these letters to satisfy himself as to the age and moral character of the ordinand; the ordaining bishop would check his learning.

A statute enacted at the Restoration required a man to take orders before being put into a benefice.[175] Its purpose was to keep Presbyterians out, but it created problems for a young Anglican destined for a good church living. When his living fell vacant, he had six months to get his orders and be presented to the living; otherwise the presentment would lapse, and the bishop could put in his own man. A bishop might be persuaded to be lenient about enforcing his rights,[176] but it was safer to persuade him to be lenient about conferring orders. Accordingly, he might be under a good deal of pressure to accept testimonials without checking on who had signed them, to overlook a man's lack of full canonical age or full mastery of Latin, and to go through the whole screening process with unseemly haste: "In fact these galloping Candidates who think nothing of their profession till their expected preferment is vacant, are among the Causes of Mischief."[177]

On the other hand, if a man sought orders before his preferment was vacant, he might try to get by with a spurious title. He had to show that he was going to be employed immediately on ordination, not merely after Old So-and-So died. So he would get a friendly incumbent to promise to have him for a curate. A careful bishop would check up on such titles as this by determining why the incumbent needed a curate and how much he was planning to pay.[178]

As had been the case since the Middle Ages, however, a careful bishop was at the mercy of his negligent colleagues in the matter of ordinations. A young man, particularly a well-connected young man, who shopped around enough would be sure to find some bishop willing to stretch a point. Habitual carelessness or indifference was not widespread, but there were always one or two hacks on the bench, or men of advanced senility, and even the good men nodded on occasion.

In theory, even if a man had been ordained, the bishop could still keep him out of the diocese if he was bad enough.[179] There was a case in 1693 and another in 1720 holding that a bishop who examined a presentee to a benefice and found him disqualified could reject him without proving the grounds of disqualification before a lay court. These cases, virtually overruling an important Elizabethan decision, gave bishops more scope for keeping unfit men out of benefices than they had had since the Reformation.

As to curates and lecturers (a lecturer held a position involving the preaching of sermons in a given church), the bishop had even more discretion than he had with presentees to benefices. He could evidently refuse a license for any reason that appealed to him, though the courts might intervene if he refused for no reason at all, or did not take reasonable steps to inform himself of the man's qualifications.[180]

In practice, it does not seem that the bishops made much use of the discretion allowed them. Sykes tells us that they seldom examined presentees to benefices, and even if they examined them and found them wanting, were more apt to put them in on a promise of improvement than to leave them out.[181] Nor does it seem that they made any systematic examination of men seeking licenses; the license probably issued automatically if the terms were satisfactory, and no specific objection came to light. In fact, a great number of curates did not even bother getting licensed. All the license did for the curate was give him a little more security in his job (we will take this up shortly). He was not supposed to officiate without it, but most bishops would ignore his doing so unless someone complained.

The eighteenth century was a golden age of pluralism and nonresidence.[182] These vices, of course, had always flourished in the church, but now the range of socially (and to some extent legally) acceptable excuses was so great that the practices were hardly considered vices any more.[183] Leaving out of account the sinecures — cathedral prebends mainly reserved for the aristocracy, or for bishops who occupied poor sees — it was considered quite appropriate for a man who had a benefice with cure to add on another in order to make up a decent support for his family. And reasons of health, family, business, the lack of appropriate housing, or the need of residing somewhere else were all accepted as excuses for his not residing.

There were a certain number of somewhat motheaten legal rules that stood in the way of being either a pluralist or a nonresident. Each had its own particular provisions, and its own particular loopholes. They presented no serious obstacle to a determined man with the right connections and the right advice, but each had to be gotten around in its turn.

First, there was the canon law on pluralities. It made one benefice void if you took another, and its origins went as far back as 1215. It was in fact applied on occasion:[184] the patron of the first benefice might present a new incumbent, displacing you. Less likely, but always possible, the bishop in charge of the old benefice might give the patron notice that you had vacated it, thereby requiring him to present a new man within six months or suffer a lapse. Or the bishop in charge of the new benefice might refuse to put you in until you had resigned the old one.

This canonical rule could, like any canonical rule, be dispensed from.[185] The Canons of 1604 provided that no such dispensation could issue unless the benefices were no more than thirty miles apart, unless the would-be pluralist was a Master of Arts and a licensed preacher, unless he gave bond to reside for a reasonable time on each cure (Burn says keeping hospitality for two months will do), and unless he put a fully qualified curate into the benefice on which he did not habitually reside. I suppose that in theory these conditions could themselves be dispensed from, but I do not find that they were. It does appear, however, that the conditions did duty for any stricter standards that the authorities might have liked to impose. Dispensations seem to have emerged routinely from the archbishop of Canterbury's Faculty Office whenever a man met the conditions and paid the fees. By no means every pluralist actually got such a dispensation: the rest presumably contented themselves with making sure that their bishops and patrons would not object.

The other potential obstacle was a statute of Henry VIII.[186] Like the canon, it made your first benefice void if you took another; unlike the canon, it could not be dispensed from. Also, unlike the canon, it could be enforced by the bishop without prior notice to the patron. It afforded, however, a number of helpful exceptions. In the first place, it did not apply unless the first benefice was valued at £ 8 or more in the King's Books, a 1534 survey of ecclesiastical revenues. Some benefices had not become valuable until after 1534; others had not existed then. If you held one of these, the statute would not stop you from taking another. There were also personal exemptions. Sons and brothers of nobles or knights could hold two benefices; so could holders of degrees in divinity. Members of the royal family could appoint any number of chaplains who could then hold three benefices. Nobles, archbishops, bishops, and great officers of state could appoint chaplains (from one to eight, depending on the rank of the magnate in question) who could then hold two benefices each. The exception for chaplains was drafted, of course, when great men employed chaplains about their secular business. In this period, when nobody needed a chaplain except perhaps one to read prayers in his house, the status was purely honorary. If an eligible person put you on his list, you were ready to take your second benefice when it came up. You were ready, that is, when you had come to terms with the canon referred to above. Canon and statute were cumulative; you had to comply with both.

As to residence, there were also ancient canons. They permitted the bishop to admonish a man to reside, and to bring proceedings to deprive him if he disobeyed. There was some talk in the lay courts about the power to deprive being superseded,[187] but most people seemed to think it was in effect. Here again, a dispensation was possible, but if your excuse persuaded the bishop to let you alone, you did not need one.

There was also legislation of Henry VIII, part of the statute whose provisions on pluralism we just took up.[188] By it the nonresident forfeited £ 10 a month, half to the king, and half to whoever cared to sue. An exception was made for a pluralist residing in one of his other cures or preferments. There were also exceptions for students, lecturers, and professors in universities, for certain bureaucrats and court personnel, and for many different chaplains. The chaplaincies were not as useful to a would-be nonresident as they were to a would-be pluralist, since chaplains were exempted from residence only while they were in daily attendance on the persons whose chaplains they were. There was also some learning to the effect that they had to be performing religious duties: serving their masters in some secular capacity would not do. The great way of getting around this statute was through its reference to "wilful" absence. Burn suggested, to most people's satisfaction, it seems, that if your excuse was good enough your absence was not wilful.

Through most of the eighteenth century, this statute was a sleeping dog. Late in the century, the Evangelical movement awakened it. Certain people began systematically bringing the litigations provided for, and were so successful that Parliament had to modify the statute drastically.[189] A law was passed in 1803 and revised in 1817, expanding somewhat the categories of exempted officials and chaplains, providing for discretionary exemptions outside the enumerated categories, and spelling out the power of the bishop to compel residence. The private action to recover penalties was not abolished under this law, but it was severely restricted. No more than a year's penalty could be recovered at a time. Suit could be brought only during May through December of the year following the offense, and only after laying all the evidence before the bishop, who had thirty days to stop the litigation by bringing a proceeding of his own.

One other statute that stood in the nonresident's way was that of 1571 that made his leases void.[190] This seems to have operated regardless of his reason for not residing. The lay courts even allowed him to plead it against his own lessee, despite the contention that he should not take advantage of his own wrongdoing. I suppose the reason this statute was not more effective against nonresidence was that neither the incumbent nor the lessee had any motive to make use of it. The nonresident incumbent could hardly work the land himself, and he would have no reason to expect a higher rent from someone else if he put his present lessee out. The lessee, for his part, probably had a profitable arrangement; most lessees of church land did.

A bishop who tried hard enough to prevent pluralism or nonresidence would probably have succeeded. The law, while equivocal, was more on his side than not, and the archbishop of Canterbury would probably not give the requisite dispensations if the local bishop objected loudly enough. In any event, the typical cleric, in the interest of his future career, would probably avoid an all-out legal confrontation with his bishop.

But generally a bishop would not push too hard. He was part of the same social milieu as the upper-class clergy. He was apt to be receptive to the kind of excuses they were apt to advance. Besides, nonresidence was not all loss to the service of the cure. A young and ambitious curate might well do the job more successfully than an old and gouty rector with a fashionable and discontented wife. Also, the tithepayers of the parish might prefer not to have the incumbent standing by to see how much they paid. We find churchwardens on occasion seconding their incumbent's plea not to reside. So the matter was apt to be settled in a polite exchange of letters, in which the bishop's main concern was not with the excuses advanced by the nonresident but with the status and compensation of the man he put in to serve in his place.[191]

Here is a letter that will show how the system worked.[192] John Marshall, rector of Swyncombe, Oxon., is writing to the bishop in 1800 for permission to accept another benefice. He has taken himself out of the statute of Henry VIII by showing that he is a chaplain to the Prince of Wales. The bishop has replied to his first letter by asking for more information about the condition of the curate of Swyncombe, one Mr. Armstrong. Marshall replies:

My Lord,

I am very thankful to your Lordship for being pleased to inform me that you will not withhold your consent to my taking another Living with that I now hold. & the *condition* on which your Lordship grants it I think so Just and proper that whenever a fair opportunity offers I shall certainly embrace it. but My Lord, I request your Permission to trouble you with a short detail how I am really at present circumstanced. when I first was presented to Swincombe, which I owe to my kind & noble Friends the Duke & Duchess of Devonshire, I fully intended Residence. as there is no Land nor any accommodation for a large Family & that the necessaries of Life could not be procured nearer than Nettlebed or Henley — I endeavored to rent some ground convenient — but my Endeavors were fruitless; it has always been the Policy in that Parish to keep the Rector at a Distance. could I have taken the Management of my Tythes into my own Hands I should have found my account in it — but without the means of drawing them, Barns to store them or ground to build upon, this was impossible. I therefore was obliged to submit to the Terms of the Farmers themselves — since which time there has not been made by me the slightest advance, tho' the World has undergone material Changes. when Mr. Armstrong was licensed to my cure (which he is *conditionally* unless I myself should serve it) a Stipend of Forty Pounds a year was deemed by the late Bishop adequate to the value of the Living — & indeed my Lord, it is in reality so, being, after the Deductions which I am subject to are made, of Land Tax, Income Tax incidental expenses & the Repairs of the Chancel & Parsonage, which owing to its not being inhabited are almost annually very heavy, & particularly so the present year, I believe it will be found to be full a *third* part of the real Issues and Profits of the Living.

with respect to what I am now offered, my Lord, by the Bristol family,
I accept it rather as a mark of my Respect for them, & in compliance
with their kind Zeal to benefit me, which I believe will eventually be the
case, than from any *present* imolument or advantage. the Living is a
discharged one [i.e., exempted from payment of first fruits and tenths
under Queen Anne's legislation relieving benefices worth less than £ 50 a
year at that time], the Vicarage of *Chesterford* Magna in Essex of the
yearly value of £ 40. a gentleman who married a Relation of the Family
& who has the adjoining Living but no House undertakes the Duties of
the Cure for the Parsonage. I sincerely wish, my Lord, it was agreeable
to Mr. Armstrong, for whom I have a great regard, to occupy My
Parsonage of Swincombe I do not mean on the same terms, I will most
cheerfully grant it to him with whatever Surplice Fees [fees payable on
performance of specific ministerial services; before the Reformation, they
were called stole fees] may arise with the Cure & think myself obliged by
his Acceptance. The Curate of Swincombe is certainly a more
independent man than its Rector at present; he has no Children to think
of. I have six grown up & whose Education has been very expensive.
My Eldest, your Lordship may recollect something of at Ch. Ch. [Christ
Church, Oxford] — as you, my Lord, was chiefly instrumental in snatching
him from Ruin. I have the comfort however of now knowing that he is a
steady & most respectable character — he accompanied his excellent
Friend Frederick North to Ceylon, who is Governor there, & who is
extremely attached to him — about a year since he married the only
Daughter of Governor Brook & is happily settled. I have two in the
King's Service one in the army the other in the navy, & three girls who
are all Expensive.

    I beg your Lordship will pardon my trespassing so far on your
Patience; I judged it right to be explicit, & to submit myself entirely to
your Lordship's Consideration.

    I have the Honour to be my Lord with all Duty & Respect your
Lordship's obliged and obedient humble servant.
                John Marshall

The bishop did not keep copies of his own letters, but he noted on the
back of this one that he had "answered that the Curate's Salary ought to be
£ 50 pr. an." Marshall replied agreeing with the raise

tho I myself am not likely to receive any immediate Benefit. The Living
I have been presented to by the Bristol Family has lately lapsed to the
Bishop of London in whose Diocese it is, who with great liberality &
Politeness has also presented Me. but should I accept it as I should
deem it my Duty to reside [there is no indication what happened to the

relative's husband who served the cure for the parsonage; perhaps the liberality and politeness of the Bishop of London did not extend to this arrangement], & that it would remove me to too great a distance from my kindest & best Friends the Duke & Duchess of Devonshire on whom my chief dependence rests, unless the matter is otherwise arranged, I shall be obliged to decline it.

Note that from Swyncombe to Great Chesterford is a good deal more than thirty miles.[193]

Note also how well it was understood on all sides that what was good enough for Armstrong was by no means good enough for Marshall. The whole social basis for pluralism and nonresidence in the period (or in any other period for that matter) was that the incumbent was a gentleman and the curate something less. If the climate was unhealthy, the parsonage in disrepair, the necessities of life not procurable, they were as much so for the curate as for the incumbent. In all logic, the more miserable the situation was, the stronger the case was for giving the emoluments to the man who in fact put up with it. But in that stratified society, no one thought along such lines as these. If a place was not fit for a high-class cleric, he moved out and put in a low-class cleric for whom it was fit.

The bishop's concern, as I say, was with getting the job done, and with securing reasonable treatment for the man who did it. There was supposed to be morning and evening prayer every Sunday and holy day (neglect of holy days was taken a good deal less seriously than neglect of Sundays), though one service a Sunday was acceptable if the living was poor. The children were supposed to be taught the Catechism, but a few sessions during Lent were generally considered enough.[194] The bishops were not apt to accept excuses for failing to keep up this modicum, such as it was. Bishop Secker of Oxford, for instance, was not at all sympathetic to a pluralist vicar who could not find a man to come oftener than once a month to serve his extra cure at the customary fee of a crown a time:

I wrote him a sharp letter on this and he hath since been with me & promised to have service every Sunday.[195]

Of course, a man with a good horse could do what was required in more places than one. In the more poverty-stricken livings, there was quite a game of musical chairs developed in this way.[196] The incumbent of A, say, might do better to hire the neighboring incumbent of B to serve his cure, while he himself moved off entirely to serve as curate of C. Marshall's reference to the man with a benefice but no house, who served the cure of Chesterford Magna in exchange for the use of the parsonage, shows another kind of arrangement that might be made. In the vicinity of Oxford, it was particularly easy to serve cures with commuters; there was always someone in orders at the University who would take on the duty of a Sunday for a few shillings. Parishioners were remarkably patient with arrangements of this kind. They did not complain until the man who did the work got so busy that he held the services sporadically or at unseasonable hours. The bishop was called in, for instance, and put his foot down when a man tried to serve four cures at once.

Unless a living was terribly poor, a bishop would try to have it served with a full time curate.[197] He had the right to make a nonresident hire a curate on pain of being called back to residence. Where there was a chapel of ease in the parish, he could make even a resident incumbent hire a curate for it, rather than pocket the revenues and serve the chapel himself. Whether the bishop could also impose a curate on a resident incumbent who neglected his responsibility was a moot point. In the Oxford correspondence, the possibility was mentioned. Certainly the power existed in the medieval canon law, but it had no clear basis in this period until it was embodied in a statute of 1817.

Besides putting in curates, bishops also tried to get them fairly paid.[198] The Marshall correspondence quoted above shows one bishop using his powers to this end. In the case of a nonresident, a statute of 1713 specifically authorized the bishop to fix a stipend of between £ 20 and £ 50. The upper limit was raised to £ 75 in 1796; a sliding scale based on population was substituted in 1817. There was trouble over how the statutes applied where more than one curate was required — whether the limit was so much a curate or so much for the lot. There was also trouble over how the use of the parsonage fitted in. A nonresident incumbent was apt to include the parsonage in his lease of the revenues to a lay farmer, and so leave his curate no place to stay. The bishop would sometimes try to get the house for the curate — whether in addition to the statutory stipend or in lieu of part of it is not clear. Finally, there was trouble if a spendthrift incumbent assigned or mortgaged his income. It was not at all clear that the bishop's right to fix the curate's stipend prevailed over the right of the mortgagee or assignee to collect.

The statutes gave the bishop no power to fix the salary of a curate hired to help out a resident incumbent. Whether he had such power under the canon law is doubtful. The common law courts regarded the relation between an incumbent and his curate as a secular contract, so they would not allow the bishop's order to supersede a specific agreement unless there was a statute.[199] But the bishop could always refuse a license if he was dissatisfied with the terms. Hence, he could be a powerful third party in the preliminary negotiations if he cared to be.

A curate's main problem, aside from his pay, was job security. How much of this he had depended on several circumstances.[200] If your curacy had been augmented by Queen Anne's Bounty, it was a benefice by statute, and you had as good a tenure as a rector or vicar. If it was a "perpetual curacy" for some other reason (say it had been privately endowed), the incumbent probably could not throw you out, but the bishop probably could. For any other kind of curacy, you could no doubt make a contract which the common law courts would enforce, but a "nomination" by the incumbent, even if it purported to be for life, was not such a contract. If the curacy had been your title for ordination — i.e., if the bishop had ordained you on the strength of the incumbent's promise to make you his curate — the incumbent could not fire you without getting you another job. But if the incumbent moved on to a new benefice, he did not have to take you with him, nor did his successor have to keep you on where you were.

In ordinary circumstances, a curate's best protection was probably a license from the bishop. It was generally felt (whether correctly or not I am not sure) that a licensed curate could not be gotten rid of unless the bishop could be persuaded to lift his license.[201] One vicar told his bishop quite frankly that he preferred for this reason not to have his curate licensed (the canons did not give him a choice, but the bishop sometimes did). A bishop might well not unlicense a curate unless he could be shown a good reason — sometimes he refused to displace a curate even to enable the incumbent to come back and reside. It was no doubt for this reason that Marshall took the precaution of getting Armstrong a conditional license.

Even if the curate had no license, it is not clear that the incumbent could fire him at will.[202] There was a medieval canon that required a reason, and Burn felt that the reason had to be judged by the bishop. Of course, under the Canons of 1604, the curate had no right to be there in the first place without the license, so it is hard to see how the medieval canon could apply. Actually, though, questions like this did not often come up. When there was a quarrel between an incumbent and his curate, it was usually settled without anyone going to the strict letter of the law. The bishop would probably try to patch things up one way or another, and, as I have pointed out, none of the clergy, whether incumbent or curate, was apt to want to confront the bishop in court.

2. *Guidance and Discipline of the Clergy* — I have referred to the variety of matters a bishop handled through informal correspondence. For the clergy ministering in his diocese, this aspect of a bishop's work afforded a freely available source of guidance in all kinds of perplexities, financial, liturgical, and pastoral.[203] How can incumbent A get his tenant out of his vicarage so he can reside? Should Vicar B seek an augmentation from Queen Anne's Bounty, or should he fight with his parishioners to collect more tithes? Rector C wants to exchange part of his glebe land for some other land in the parish. Vicar D wants to remit a year's rent for a tenant

who has had a run of bad luck. Incumbents E and F want the bishop to
arbitrate a dispute they have been having. Rector G wants to know who is
going to pay for the decoration of his chancel now that the parishioners
who promised to do so have moved. Incumbent H has put up a new
baptismal font and wants to know what to do with the stones from the old
one. Vicar I is worried about a Methodist meeting house about to be built
in his parish. Rector J refuses to bury Dissenters in church and wonders if
he is doing the right thing. Each of these people expected, and apparently
got, a thoughtful and courteous answer from his ordinary.

The occasions for treating the clergy more sternly were not as numerous
as they had been in the past. The old forms of roistering and pub-crawling
seem to have gone out of style as the clergy worked their way into the
middle class. Despite the charges of the satirists, there does not seem to
have been a great deal of clerical incontinence. There was a bit more
drunkenness, but again not a lot — as judged, of course, by the standards of
that hard-drinking age. Nor was there much in the way of liturgical
violations. The conscientious nonconformist was put out of the Church of
England at the Restoration, and the Anglican so negligent as to leave out
chunks of the service seems to have faded out. The minister in this period
may have said the Prayer Book services perfunctorily, but he apparently
said them the way they were written, and said them in his surplice. Also,
as far as I can see, he preached regularly; he was accused of boring or
mystifying his congregation, but not of being a "dumb dog" as his pre-Civil-
War counterpart often was. There were liturgical controversies in this
period, but most of them involved matters like congregational singing
versus singing by choirs.[204] This kind of thing the officiating clergy had
the right to determine, though the bishop might intervene if they went too
far in alienating their parishioners.

The performance of clandestine marriages continued to be a disciplinary
problem, but it was dealt with increasingly by the state rather than the
church.[205] In any event, the main offenders in this regard were not the
regularly officiating clergy with whom the bishop was concerned, but the
hedge priests, men with no fixed positions, who took on odd jobs when the
chance arose.

A new problem that came up occasionally, but still not often, was that of
the minister who got into such financial trouble as to impair his
ministry.[206] We find a vicar who had left his benefice and gone off as a
service chaplain for this reason; a would-be curate who had gone through
bankruptcy as a horse-dealer; a man £ 600 in debt who made £ 130 a year
from two benefices and a curacy, and was applying for a position as a
schoolmaster to make ends meet; even a man claiming a poor law
settlement by reason of his service as a curate.

These different disciplinary matters came to the bishop's attention sometimes through an incumbent complaining of his curate or vice versa, sometimes through letters from parishioners, and sometimes through formal presentments by churchwardens.[207] However the information came in, the bishop would have it quietly looked into, and would handle it informally if he could. He might send the person complained of a copy of the complaint; he might keep his sources secret and send on the gist of the charge; or he might investigate more at large without stating the grounds of complaint at all. In any event, he would try to straighten things out by exhorting his clergy to more circumspect behavior, by finding new jobs for curates who could not get along where they were, or by issuing specific reprimands and exacting promises of improvement.

The only cases I find in the eighteenth century where a bishop went on to bring formal proceedings against a clergyman involved incontinence, drunkenness, or failure to obey a monition to reside.[208] Incontinence seems to be the only offense for which a man was deprived on his first conviction. A cathedral prebendary who claimed that the statutes entitled him to a warning did not get much sympathy. A man who could plead a general pardon did better, but there were no such pardons issued after 1747. There was some debate over whether a man could be deprived for neglect of duty as well as for moral offenses. A majority of the Court of Delegates, the highest appellate tribunal in church causes, said that he could, but I find no evidence of such deprivations taking place. One other ground of deprivation was simony. Here, the bishop had not much discretion, as the statute made the incumbency void. But as we have seen, there were not many cases of strict simony in this period.

The general falling off of disciplinary problems seems to be due as much to a change in standards as to an improvement in clerical character. We may say that the two changes went hand in hand. The medieval church had attempted to impose on the clergy standards of self-dedication that cut across both economic and social realities. The church in the century after the Reformation maintained many of the medieval standards, and added standards of worship and belief that many people could not accept. In both periods, as a result, the church failed to impose its standards on great numbers of the clergy, and great numbers of the clergy were in the demoralizing position of knowing that they were not living up to what was expected of them. The eighteenth century church, by contrast, asked nothing of the clergy that ordinary working Christians were not willing to give. The average clergyman was prepared to do what he was supposed to, and to take ordinary satisfaction in doing it. The disciplinary process had only the occasional deviant to cope with, as other disciplinary processes do.

3. Irregular Ministry — The bishops were given the leading part in
enforcing the decision taken at the Restoration to make a clean break
between Anglicans and Presbyterians. The Act of Uniformity of 1662 gave
them new powers, and the lay courts interpreted their traditional powers
more broadly. The statutory requirement of episcopal ordination to hold a
benefice was made enforceable in the church courts through assimilation to
the traditional power to deprive *quia mere laicus* (the two things were not
really the same: under the medieval law a man with first tonsure was not
mere laicus, and if he once got into a benefice he could not be deprived
unless he failed to take orders after being admonished to do so).[209] The
power to reject an unfit presentee to a benefice was broadened, as we have
seen.

As to the rest of the clergy, the Act of Uniformity required an episcopal
license (a license by the bishop's chancellor, or by a chapter in their
peculiar jurisdiction would not do) for parish lecturers, who had provided a
focus for nonconformity in the old days. Licensing of curates and other
officiating clergy went back to the canons of 1604 and their Elizabethan
predecessors; that of preachers to the fifteenth century. A bishop could not
use these licensing powers to determine who was lawfully chosen to a
specific position, but there was virtually no limit on his power to reject a
man he considered unfit.[210]

In fact, very few bishops saw fit to establish this system of across-the-
board licensing as it was first envisaged. The general requirement of
licenses to preach was in abeyance.[211] Probably most people with specific
lectureships had the appropriate licenses, but I doubt if as many as half the
regular curates did, or any appreciable fraction of those who officiated only
occasionally in any one place.

But if a particular unlicensed person came to the bishop's attention as
one who should not be allowed to officiate in the diocese, the bishop
certainly had sufficient power to stop him.[212] Even a man occupying a
donative (a benefice which the patron could fill without resort to the
bishop) could be proceeded against for officiating without a license; so
could a man preaching in a parish church at the invitation of the
incumbent. The offender could be ordered not to do it again, and
excommunicated and imprisoned by the secular arm if he disobeyed. Or
the bishop could send people to remove him from the pulpit by force. Nor
could he use the Act of Toleration to escape these sanctions: to have the
benefit of that act, he had to declare himself a dissenter from the Church
of England; even then, he could not minister in an Anglican church.

A series of cases beginning in 1700 gave the parish incumbent as much
control over the exercise of the ministry in his parish as the bishop had in
his diocese.[213] I have already mentioned the first case in the series; it

held that a man elected to a lectureship was still a trespasser if he tried to preach in the parish church without the incumbent's permission. Whether courts later in the century would have kept up the trespass rationale is debateable. They did, though, hold that a bishop could not be made to license a lecturer elected without the incumbent's consent, because the license would be futile. The bishops, for their part, evidently accepted the doctrine of the lay courts, and would not license a lecturer without the incumbent's consent. Bishop Secker, however, held that a lecturer once licensed with the incumbent's permission was entitled to stay on even if he and the incumbent fell out later — a view that was never passed on by the lay courts.

Other decisions supplemented the incumbent's freehold in the parish church with a monopoly on the holding of Anglican services elsewhere in his parish.[214] If you built your own chapel, whether alone or with a consortium of wealthy friends, you could not hire a man to hold services there unless he got the incumbent's permission. Even then, he could not hold any services but morning and evening prayer and Holy Communion (i.e., he could not bury, christen, or marry), and he had to turn the Communion offerings over to the incumbent as the Prayer Book rubric required. If you built a chapel for the public, dedicated it to God, and had the bishop consecrate it, it became a "chapel of ease" and a charity which the Attorney General would enforce. This kept the incumbent from taking the revenues and holding the services himself, but he still got to nominate the curate who was to serve there.

To get around any of these rights of the incumbent, you had to show either an immemorial custom or a deed supported by an adequate consideration, and signed by patron, incumbent and ordinary all three (just what was required for the alienation of any other piece of church property).[215] The immemorial custom was no help except in the case of chapels in old manor houses, and some traditional chapels of ease. No lectureship could show an immemorial custom, as there had been none before the Reformation. The chapels founded by seventeenth century puritans, reserving to their descendants the choice of a suitable curate, were in no better case; in one of these the vicar was given the power to nominate after the inhabitants of the area had been exercising it for ninety years. The men who built proprietary chapels in fashionable resorts, and supported them by the pew rents of their rich congregations, had to buy off each successive incumbent to carry on. As for founding chapels and lectureships with the three necessary consents, it was evidently hard to get all tree at once. Besides, in the seventeenth century when a good many of them were founded people probably did not consider all these consents necessary.

I have great trouble seeing where the courts got their decisions on all these points.[216] The medieval precedents show great, indeed excessive, tenderness for the financial claims of the incumbent, but I cannot see that he had an absolute veto either over the establishment of chantries (the equivalent of lectureships, with a mass instead of a sermon) in his own church or over the establishment of chapels elsewhere. As for proprietary chapels, it would seem that a medieval man could have such services as he pleased as long as he had a consecrated altar (or a priest with a papal indult to carry a portable one), and a priest in good standing, and as long as he attended mass in his parish church on Sundays and holy days. The bishop could license him to attend his own chapel instead of the parish church. He would have to do something for the incumbent or the bishop would not give this permission, but again it does not seem that the incumbent (still less the patron) had a veto. The canons of 1604 and their Elizabethan predecessors, in order to suppress nonconforming worship, had forbidden services in private houses except in a "chapel allowed by the ecclesiastical laws of this realm." This prohibition was still in force for anyone who did not qualify under the Toleration Act, but again there is no indication that patron or incumbent had a proprietary interest in its enforcement. In short, the eighteenth century doctrines on the rights of the incumbent were in accord with the traditional ethos of the parish system, but there was no direct precedent for them. As we shall see, they had a baneful effect on the expansion of the parish system to meet shifts in population.

4. *Buildings and Grounds* — The ecclesiastical authorities retained their traditional jurisdiction over the consecrated ground of church and churchyard.[217] They had occasionally to deal with traditional abuses of the former — as late as 1800, the magistrates proposed to hold their Quarter Sessions in Banbury church. They could also prevent encroachments on the latter, though the lay courts took over if the offender claimed the land as his own. In matters of furnishing and laying out the church, the ordinary, under him the incumbent, and under both the churchwardens had a general say, subject to a number of rules which we will consider.

Another aspect of the church's authority over the sacred precincts was presented by a number of cases involving the old offense of "brawling" in church or churchyard.[218] A statute of Edward VI, which addressed itself to this offense, was held in 1702 to be cumulative with, rather than exclusive of, the ancient jurisdiction of the church *ratione loci*: the church court was not limited by either the penalties or the process provided in the statute. The procedure established on these terms, until it was done away with in 1860, enabled the church courts to keep a good deal of control over the conduct of vestry meetings, to insure respect for officials during visitations, to check the more flagrant abuses of the pulpit, and to maintain decorum during services.

The aspect of their control over the church premises that kept the authorities busiest was checking the exuberance of the upper classes in filling the place with their status symbols — their lofty pews in the body of the church, their storied urns and animated busts about the walls, and under the floor the bodies of their dead. Of all these, the most prevalent, and in many ways the most obnoxious, were the pews. The problem of private pews was not a new one; it had been discussed extensively in Coke's time.[219] But the difficulties were increased, especially toward the end of our period, by the growth in many places of populations who could not all be comfortably seated in the local churches; by the increase in numbers and importance of people anxious to mark their social position with appropriate seating and willing to pay for the privilege of doing so; and by a growing need for the money that could be had by affording such persons what they sought. By the early nineteenth century, the rental of pews had become a recognized source of church revenue, and one that was relied on heavily in legislation for the building of new churches. Later generations were to blame the system for the prevailing notion that the church was only for the rich: "Pew rents are to Protestantism what the sale of indulgences was to the Papacy."[220]

Except for a general recognition of class distinctions, the law did very little to encourage abuses in seating. The general principle was that everyone in the parish had the right to a seat, and the churchwardens were to assign him one located in accordance with his station in life.[221] Once a seat was assigned him, he had the right to occupy it and could bring common law or ecclesiastical proceedings against anyone who disturbed him (the cases of self-help that make such lively reading in the Elizabethan records do not appear in this period). But his right was subject to that of the churchwardens to make new arrangements when the needs of the parish required; this they could not grant away.

The churchwardens in their turn were subject to the ordinary, who had the general power to supervise the conduct of worship in his diocese. It followed that a person with a faculty (i.e., a grant out of the bishop's court relating to the fabric of the church) assigning him a particular pew could not be put out of it by the churchwardens. Through the early eighteenth century, faculties of this kind were issued rather freely — probably to anyone who took the trouble to build a pew. Later on, they were issued much more sparingly, generally only to people who contributed substantially to building or repairing the whole church.

A faculty could legally do either of two things. It could attach a pew permanently to a particular house, for the inhabitants to sit in, whoever they were, or it could give a pew to a particular person or persons, to sit in as long as they lived and remained in the parish. No faculty could entitle a person to buy, sell, or inherit a seat except in connection with a house, and no faculty could entitle a non-parishioner to a seat.

A sufficient custom could attach a seat to a house, just as a faculty could; if such a custom was shown, the common law courts would keep either the churchwardens or the ordinary from dislodging the inhabitants of the house.[222] But a custom could stand you in no better stead than a faculty: it could not give a general claim unconnected with a house, and it could not give a personal claim to a non-parishioner. Nor could a custom give the parishioners as a group power to dispose of seats independently of the ordinary. Gibson (and Burn on his authority) was afraid the ordinary could lose his powers by not exercising them, but the common law courts, which had the last word on matters of custom, were clear that he could not.

The seating process was evidently a good deal more venal in practice than it was on paper. Churchwardens tended to abandon their responsibilities, and allow pews to be freely sold, rented, or lent. One pair seem to have been genuinely surprised when the bishop of London's Consistory Court told them they could not allow a pewholder's lessee to prevail over a parishioner in need of a seat.[223] Also, the proprietary chapels that came into vogue in the last half of the eighteenth century were apt to be supported by the pew rents of the people who came to hear the fashionable services. Such buildings were not subject to the general law. The people who put one up could dispose of the seats in any way they wished, unless either the ordinary or the incumbent cared to require a certain number of free seats as a condition for allowing services to be held in the place.[224] There is no indication that any of them did.

People have always been buried and memorialized in church, as anyone can see who walks round a few old churches. But people in this period seem to have been particularly zealous for putting the departed under the paving stones, and devoting great reaches of wall space to remembering them. The power to supervise this form of devotion was divided between the incumbent and the ordinary.[225] Sometimes, the churchwardens took a hand, though I do not see where they had a legal basis for doing so.

The incumbent's consent would evidently suffice for burying someone in church, or for putting up a monument in the first instance. But you needed a faculty to keep a vault for the exclusive use of your family, or otherwise to reserve burial space for someone not yet dead. In the case of a monument, you would need a faculty if the incumbent refused to consent to your putting it up (he could be heard in opposition to the faculty, but he did not have a veto on granting it), or if you wanted to be sure that the ordinary would not bring proceedings to take it down.

Like the incumbent, the ordinary had no general veto power. If a
monument was put up without his consent, he had to bring a formal
proceeding and show that it was unsuitable before his court would order it
taken down. By the same token, if anyone asked for a faculty, it was not
the ordinary but his court, presided over by his chancellor, that decided
whether the faculty was to be issued. In either case, the whole process was
subject to the regular course of ecclesiastical appeals. I gather most of the
monuments one sees from this period were put up without faculties. The
relation between the typical incumbent and the substantial householders of
his parish being what it was, his consent was probably not hard to come by,
and the relation between the bishop and his courts being what it was, the
bishop was not apt to set proceedings in motion to undo what was done
with the incumbent's consent.

For some reason, the problem of keeping churches in repair seems to
have been less acute than in earlier times.[226] Churchwardens reported
cases of disrepair, and archdeacons turned them up on their visitations, but
the statistics were by no means as disheartening as they used to be. Why
this was the case is hard to say. The procedures for getting repairs made
were if anything less effective than they had been in earlier times. To
collect money from parishioners to repair the nave, a churchrate had to be
made — a difficult task, as we shall see. To get the rector to repair the
chancel was possible if he was a clergyman and had a substantial benefice,
but if he was a lay impropriator the process was pretty unwieldy, and if he
was poor it would do no good. Nor could any great amount be realized by
taking up a voluntary collection. What probably happened was that in most
places a few wealthy parishioners were persuaded to take responsibility for
doing what was required, and were perhaps compensated with pews or
memorials for doing so.

What really gave trouble was keeping parsonage houses in repair.[227]
These buildings had been much neglected during the Civil War and the
Interregnum; indeed, many had been wrecked by religionists opposed to the
occupant of the moment. This state of affairs presented especial difficulties
for the bishops, because it afforded the most common and the most
acceptable of the various excuses incumbents offered for not residing.
Improvement was slow during most of the eighteenth century. The bishop
could order the incumbent to make repairs, and could sequester the living
if he failed to do so. The incumbent himself could sue his predecessor at
common law. There was even a procedure for appointing commissioners
to arrange for the erection of a new building where the old one had
deteriorated beyond repair. But none of these measures was very effective
to raise the necessary funds for the work. A zealous bishop would no
doubt prod a nonresident incumbent gently to put aside some of his money
for this purpose, but, as we have seen, the substantial and irreducible needs

of a middle class family came first, and after them came the stipend for the curate.

The modest pace of repair and rebuilding provided in these ways picked up gradually with increased prosperity. There came to be livings, as we have seen, which squires and even noblemen regarded as suitable for their younger sons. A man who intended to put his son in the local parish might well fix up the house for him to live in. Then too, men who went to great expense to expand their manor houses — there were a lot of such men in this period — might include some help for the local incumbent, either out of a sense of noblesse oblige or out of a desire to make the village a fit setting for the manor house.

Finally, a series of Acts of Parliament, beginning in 1777, enabled the incumbent, with the consent of the patron and the ordinary, to borrow money on the credit of his revenues for the purpose of rebuilding or repairing his parsonage. The loan was to be paid off at five percent per annum over a period of twenty-five years, rising to ten percent if the incumbent did not reside twenty weeks a year in the house provided. Further, if the incumbent was nonresident and the living worth more than £ 100 a year, the ordinary and the patron could make the arrangements without his consent, thus cutting out his excuse for nonresidence. The governing bodies of Queen Anne's Bounty and of all colleges were authorized to lend money under these acts. A good deal of progress was made under them, though there was still a problem as late as the 1830s.

5. Education, Charity, etc. — The church still had a great deal to do with the work of education and poor relief, though in a less formal way than in earlier times.[228] The parish incumbent or his curate would often teach school, sometimes in the aisle of the church. The incumbent was apt to be named a trustee of local legacies for the poor, and even if he had no express powers given him, he was expected to look over the shoulders of the churchwardens when they administered such funds. A statute of 1709 empowered him to administer a parish library.

While the judicial enforcement of charities, even those with religious objects, had been pretty well taken over by the Attorney General, proceeding in Chancery, the ecclesiastical authorities gave the subject a good deal of informal attention, matching that of the parish clergy. They checked up in their visitations on what schools, almshouses, and legacies for religious worship or poor relief there were in each parish, and how the institutions were conducted or the funds applied. They wrote and answered letters when anything seemed to be going wrong. As far as I can see, they were active and conscientious in this work, but they were probably not terribly efficient. The more systematic investigations of the mid-nineteenth century turned up a good many abuses that they had missed.

There survived from the old canon law (supported by a number of statutes) a certain amount of ecclesiastical control over schoolmasters.[229] The lay courts whittled down the bishop's power in various ways. As it had traditionally extended only to grammar schools, it could not now be applied to primary schools any more than to dancing schools or to universities. The 1604 canon requiring the schoolmaster to bring the children to church could not be enforced against a lay schoolmaster because the 1604 canons did not bind the laity. Where the school had statutes given by the founder, they limited the bishop's authority over the masters to an undetermined extent. But the bishop could still require the ordinary schoolmaster to have a license, could proceed against him in the church court for teaching without it, and could examine both his moral and his intellectual qualifications before licensing him.

Until the Toleration Act, the bishop's licensing authority tied in with various provisions intended to keep Dissenters from teaching school. These provisions, like others for the suppression of Dissent, were probably not fully enforced. The Toleration Act was ambiguously worded as regards schoolmasters. A case could be made for saying Dissenters could still not teach school, or for saying that they needed a license but could not be denied one on account of their religion. But Burn says that in practice they were regarded as not needing a license at all. This principle was made explicit in a statute of 1779. But an Anglican still needed a license, and could still be denied it if he was not of sound religion.

IV. Finance and Deployment

The period we are considering was characterized by tentative shifts in the patterns of church finance and deployment. The fixed sources of endowment characteristic of the Middle Ages were becoming less fixed in the face of new economic patterns, new attitudes toward capital and land use, and new attitudes toward the church. The free enterprise puritan lectureships, supported by subscriptions, collections, and grants as often as by endowments, had been discouraged after the Restoration, but they lingered in many places. The proprietary chapels of eighteenth century provenance were typically supported by pew rents, and remained so as long as they continued in style. The centralized financial institutions that became so prominent in the mid-nineteenth century were making a beginning, but had not yet come into their own. New churches were rising slowly to meet new needs, but the arrangements for them were as conservative as possible. On the whole, there is little to be said about these matters that is not a coda to something that has been said already, or a prelude to something that will be said further on.

The landed endowments of the church were still subject to the restrictions on leases and alienations that were set up in Queen Elizabeth's time. A few statutes in the late eighteenth and early nineteenth centuries let up on these rules in one or two details, without seriously modifying them.[230] The main inconvenience in this situation was its hampering of parish enclosures. Not until 1815 did a minister, even with the consent of his patron and ordinary, have a statutory power to effect a permanent exchange of scattered glebe lands for new and more compact holdings. Sometimes private Acts of Parliament were arranged to validate transactions of this kind. Also, Burn tells us,

> it hath been sometimes practised . . . for the incumbent to make an exchange during his own time, in which his successors will find the same advantage; until by length of time all remembrances where the lands formerly lay shall be worn out: which altho' it doth not operate to effect a legal title, yet no person being grieved thereby, will probably never be inquired into and disannulled.[231]

However such arrangements were validated before the secular law, the ecclesiastical authorities evidently took an interest in them.[232] The Oxford diocesan records for the late seventeenth and early eighteenth centuries show several elaborate proceedings by the bishop's chancellor for confirming exchanges of glebe on parish enclosures, after having them investigated by commissions made up of local parishioners and neighboring clergy. But not all alienations were so carefully supervised. Eighteenth century prelates were constantly bewailing lost endowments, mounting antiquarian projects to bring them back, and calling for new "terriers" lest any more be lost. (A terrier is a list of landholdings made up for a permanent record; under the Canons of 1604, every parish was supposed to have one and record a copy with the bishop.)

Tithes were even more apt to slip away than lands were.[233] Strictly speaking, tithe was not a landed endowment, it was a personal obligation of the landholder to the clergyman to whom it was due (for instance, the titheholder was not entitled to compensation if a piece of land was put to unproductive use, or flooded in connection with a drainage scheme). But tithe was apt to be readjusted along with glebe in an enclosure, or to be lost through prolonged acceptance of less than full value.

To be legal, a permanent readjustment of the tithe obligation, a *modus decimandi* (or a "composition real;" I will leave the difference to a footnote), had to be supported either by an immemorial custom or by an agreement. An agreement, to be binding, had to have the consent of the patron and the ordinary and had to date from before the 1571 statute that limited alienations of church property.[234] The immemorial custom was the more usual claim. By the common law reckoning, a custom was not immemorial if anyone could show that it had a beginning later than 1189. But this beginning had to be shown: a custom would be allowed if its beginning was entirely forgotten. In matters of this kind, it did not take very long for forgetfulness to set in. There was one exception to the rule that a beginning must be shown. It operated strongly against the clergy. If the custom involved a cash payment nearly equal to the value of the tithe, it would be disallowed as "too rank." Because of the great increase in the value of money, the payment could not possibly have been made in 1189.

So a custom of not paying full value for tithe could set in rather quickly, whereas a custom of paying full value could not. As a result, the clergy were continually being exhorted by their superiors to collect all they were entitled to lest they disinherit their successors.[235] The law was not too unfavorable to their doing so. A statute enacted in 1696 gave them a summary proceeding before two justices of the peace to collect small and uncontested claims without going through the difficult and decrepit ecclesiastical coercive process. For larger claims or contested ones, there was also the process in the Exchequer. Bishop Secker of Oxford, addressing his clergy in 1750, pointed out that their colleagues had won 600 out of 700 such proceedings between 1660 and 1713.

The practical obstacles were more formidable than the legal ones. John Marshall, rector of Swyncombe, alluded to some of them in his letter, quoted above. To send somebody around with a wagon, field by field, loading on sheaves of wheat, to collect every tenth lamb and calf in the parish, then transport the lot to market for a profitable sale, might be more than an ordinary scholar was up to, especially in an uncooperative parish. It was easier to accept what was amicably offered, while looking for an augmentation, or for a better benefice.[236]

Both landed endowments and tithes were regularly leased out. The leases were restricted as follows by the old statutes:[237]

1. No lease could run longer than three lives (till the death of the last survivor of three named persons living when the lease was made) or twenty-one years.
2. Lands had to be leased in customary parcels, and at no less than the customary rent. By a statute of 1800, such parcels could be broken up, and the rent apportioned among the pieces.
3. Lands of a benefice with cure could not be leased beyond the incumbency of the lessor, unless both the patron and the ordinary consented. Even then, the lease could be avoided if the lessor did not reside.
4. Until a statute of 1765, no one could lease tithes beyond his own time. Afterward, tithes could be leased on the same terms as land.

Nothing in these rules kept the lessor from raising the rent when a lease ran out. But most of the properties involved had been leased for so long at the same rental that a clergyman was under a good deal of pressure not to ask for more. Lump sum payments, called entry fines, for renewing leases on the old terms, were more flexible — and also more interesting to a lessor, who could pocket the whole sum immediately, rather than prorate it over the life of the lease. Even here, though, a clergyman was considered more avaricious than became his cloth if he tried to charge what the traffic would bear. In short, with a few notable (and generally odious) exceptions, the clergy were exploiting their old sources of revenue in the old ways, and were holding aloof from the more enterprising forms of property management that were beginning to come in.

There remained also a certain amount of the small change of clerical income, left over from the Middle Ages.[238] In addition to voluntary offerings, which the law dealt with only to the extent of seeing that the parish incumbent got certain of them instead of others ministering in his parish, there were customary amounts payable on certain occasions. All of these were originally fees for the performance of ministerial acts; I took up in the first volume the rather convoluted history of why they were not considered simoniacal. More recent practice had divided them into two classes. In the first class fell those due "of common right." These were no longer attached to a particular ministerial service, and were payable when the occasion arose unless there was a local custom of not paying them. This class included mortuaries, payable on the death of a parishioner, regardless of where or how he was buried; Easter offerings (4d a house in London; 2d a head elsewhere), payable every Easter regardless of whether you came to church; and procurations, payable to bishops and archdeacons at their traditional visitation times, regardless of whether the visitation took place. All of these could be sued for in the church courts, or, under the 1696 act, before two justices of the peace like small sums of tithe. A custom of not paying would be pleaded in the lay courts like a *modus decimandi*.

Other offerings a minister could have only if there was a custom of paying them; those for marriages, christenings, and burials were the most usual. Suits for these offerings were evidently like suits for tithe where the plaintiff's case was based on a *modus*: the custom had to be established in a lay court. The lay courts (and by the mid-century the church courts were following them) were strict about not allowing any such custom unless the service was actually performed. A custom of paying the minister so much whenever and wherever his parishioner was married, christened, or buried was a bad custom.

It is not very clear what happened to all these petty payments. In theory, it was not possible to extinguish them legally before the reform legislation of the 1830s. Most of them probably died out in the meantime because they were not worth the trouble of collecting. But at least through the middle of the eighteenth century they were still being litigated over in some places.

Churchrates, assessed pro rata on lands of the parish for building or repairing the church, were not a real problem until the 1830s, but the legal principles that made them a problem had already developed.[239] These rates were voted by the parish vestry, and were collectible in the ecclesiastical court (after 1813, before the justices of the peace if the liability was less than ten pounds and uncontested). A lay court intervened in one case where the repair of the chancel was among the objects of the rate, because that was the rector's responsibility; otherwise, the lay courts left the whole process alone. The fact that the rate was too heavy (£ 6000 in 1681), or that it called for a more splendid reconstruction than the particular ratepayer wanted, was no objection as long as a majority vote of the parish vestry had set it up.

But if the majority of the parish were willing to let the church fall down, there was really very little anyone could do. It was established in 1676 that the bishop could not make rates himself if the parishioners failed. If he could show that the repairs were in fact necessary, he could probably excommunicate everyone who voted against the rate, but this expedient was too cumbersome to be tried. The churchwardens could do a little better than the bishop. They could keep calling meetings till those opposed to the rate got tired of coming; if no one at all came, they could probably make the rate themselves. These powers also were never put to the test — probably because the dissident parishioners had as much staying power as the churchwardens: as long as a majority of those at the meeting voted no, the churchwardens were powerless. Also, the churchwardens themselves might be against the rate.

Why this state of the law did not create more trouble than it did is hard to say. My impression is that few rates were wanted, rather than that many were willingly voted. A certain tolerance for ramshackle churches seems rather in the spirit of the times.

The wave of the future in ecclesiastical financing, though it can scarcely have appeared so at the time, was the central fund, assembling revenue from many sources, and distributing it to meet many needs. The movement in this direction followed a similar movement in secular government whereby the self-financing operations of the Middle Ages were gradually replaced by operations financed out of the Exchequer.

The augmentation of poor livings was the first ecclesiastical object aimed at by a fund of this kind, and the first fund for the purpose was that of the

Feoffees for Impropriations of the 1630s.[240] The Feoffees were private
persons of puritan leanings, and they managed to accumulate a great
number of impropriated rectories, whose proceeds they bestowed in the
form of stipends for ministers of their choice. Laud broke up their fund,
rightly supposing that it threatened royal and episcopal authority by
concentrating the pursestrings in different, and generally hostile, hands.
But the attractiveness of the idea was indicated by the success it had.
Another attempt in the same direction was made in the Commonwealth
period by transferring confiscated ecclesiastical revenues to a set of
Trustees for Augmentations. The capital for this body, of course, was
made up of property that had to be given back to its former owners at the
Restoration.

The idea of a central fund for augmentations remained attractive. It was
finally made a reality with the establishment of Queen Anne's Bounty in
1704.[241] This fund was launched with the first fruits and tenths of
ecclesiastical livings that had been a royal tax for general purposes since
Henry VIII's time. This tax imposed on every benefice listed in Henry's
valuation survey (the King's Books) one entire year's value as set down in
that survey for the first year of each incumbency, and one tenth of that
value for every subsequent year. Benefices worth less than £ 50 (current
value, not value in the King's Books) were exempted by an act of 1707.
The sums in question were of course far less than they would have been if
they had been taken on current value; still, they made up between £ 17,000
and £ 20,000 a year. Provision was made to encourage the channeling of
private benefactions into the same fund. Also, it received eleven annual
grants of £ 100,000 out of the national treasury, beginning in 1809.

Once the scheme got going, it operated by bestowing capital sums on
particular benefices, the poorest ones through selection by lot, the slightly
richer on a basis of matching gifts from private benefactors. The capital
sums were supposed to be laid out in land, but the procedure for buying
land was so cumbersome that the money was often left with the Bounty
Office for long periods at interest. We need not go further into the exact
workings of the program. They are complicated, and G.F.A. Best has
untangled them nicely. An overall verdict on operations in the first century
should be that they were a modest success. For instance, in 1745, the
bishop of Oxford reported that the Bounty had augmented all the livings
under £ 10 in his diocese.[242]

The device of centralized funding was also used in the work of church
and chapel building that went on at a gradually increasing pace (though
with considerably less urgency than the situation required) as the period
progressed.[243] Queen Anne's Bounty itself was involved in the legislation
for borrowing money to build parsonage houses (1777, 1803, 1824).
Legislation adopted late in Anne's reign and reactivated at the beginning of

George I's established a duty on coal to be put into a special fund in the
Exchequer for building fifty new churches in the London area.
Commissioners were appointed to decide where the new churches were to
go; then they were set up one by one through local acts of Parliament
appropriating specific amounts from the fund for each.

A more comprehensive system was adopted in 1818.[244] A commission
was set up, authorized to issue up to £ 1,000,000 in Exchequer bills
(increased by £ 500,000 in 1824), and empowered to put up new churches
where they were needed. The commission could meet the full cost of
building and endowing the new church if the parish was poor and populous
enough; otherwise, it could marshal the available resources of voluntary
offerings, churchrates, and pew rents, and supplement them from its own
funds. It had put up six hundred-some-odd new churches by the time it
was superseded by more efficient measures in Victoria's time.

Providing adequate parochial status for churches built and endowed in
these different ways was rather more of a problem than providing money
for them. What made all the trouble was the vested interest an incumbent
and his patron had in the cure of souls throughout the territory of an
existing parish.[245] Short of an Act of Parliament, nothing whatever could
create a new parish within the boundaries of an old one. As we have seen,
the ordinary, the patron, and the incumbent, if they all three agreed, could
erect a chapel of ease in a parish, served by a perpetual curate, but even
then they had to provide some permanent compensation to the existing
("mother") church if their arrangement was to be legal. Queen Anne's
Bounty, under legislation of 1714, could turn a perpetual curacy into a full-
fledged benefice by augmenting it, and could negotiate for a transfer of the
patronage of the curacy from the parish incumbent to one or more of the
private benefactors who put up the chapel — but it could not put up a
chapel where there had not been one before unless the ordinary, the
patron, and the incumbent of the mother church agreed.

Parliament had the power to bestow greater rights on a new church, but
was very chary of using it. Certain private bills, to be sure, allowed persons
endowing a new church to have the advowson of it, or allowed the
incumbent of a new church to be free of the incumbent of the old, but it
seems likely that the consent of those whose interests were affected had
been obtained before these acts were introduced.[246] The acts
implementing the scheme for fifty churches in the London area did create
new parishes, but they made substantial annual cash payments to the
incumbents of the old ones, and gave the advowson of each new church to
the patron of the old.

The 1818 legislation, the first to allow new parishes to be made by
administrative order, was still extremely tender toward existing rights. The
patron of the mother church could prevent a new parish being established;

if he did permit it to be established, he was to have the advowson of it.
The incumbent could not stop the new parish permanently, but he could
keep it a chapel of ease during his own time — thereby getting to nominate
the curate. Also, the commissioners were empowered to compensate both
the incumbent and his successors for their loss of revenue. Without the
patron's consent, all the commissioners could do was set up a chapel with a
perpetual curate nominated by the incumbent of the mother church, and
excluded from any share in the latter's revenues.

The patron's veto was partially mitigated by an act of 1824, which enabled
persons paying the entire cost of a new chapel to appoint the curates for
forty years, after which time the patronage would revert to the old patron
or the old incumbent in accordance with arrangements made under the
1818 act. It was not until 1831 that a statute provided for giving a new
church full parochial rights without the consent of the patron of the old
one, or for allowing persons who built and endowed a new church to have
the full advowson of it.[247]

It was high time. In the preceding half century or more, the established
church had suffered a radical disadvantage in competing with Dissenters,
who could cope with shifts of population by setting up new congregations in
new buildings when and where they chose.

V. Conclusion

The eighteenth century church, with its prayer book liturgy, whose
intrinsic dignity and beauty were now crowned with venerable historical
associations; with its parishes and parish vestries that served all purposes of
local government, both religious and secular; with its fancy pews and
monuments for the rich, its benches and humble stones for the poor, its
somnolent congregations, its moss-grown churchyards where even those
who stayed away in their lives were content to be buried; with its rectors
who sat on commissions of the peace and drank and hunted with the
squires, and its hard-riding curates who labored on the edges of the middle
class; with its musty law books, its superfluous officials, its convivial
visitations, and its amiable letter-writing bishops; with its whitewashed
interiors and its sober and unambitious piety, probably achieved a fuller
integration of institutional, social, and religious forms than the English
Church has had at any other time before or since. The legal and
institutional forms taken up in this chapter have a good deal more to do
with Parson Woodforde than Laud's High Commission has with George
Herbert, or Archbishop Chichele's Register with Chaucer's Parson.

The very vices of the system played their part in the overall rapport.
Remote, mysterious, and obsolete legalities offered a respectable livelihood

to those who understood them, an easy conscience to those who got around them, a sense of fitness to those who benefitted from them, while affording a supple acquiescence in the real demands of the society. The decadence of the disciplinary system allowed for true supervision where it was truly wanted, and a tacit withdrawal of supervision were it was not. In general, the abandonment of any serious attempt to make things or people over allowed the church to preserve a substantial impress on things and people as they were.

The administrative structure, despite the fading out of traditional controls, was well able to do the things the society really wanted done — or at least the things the society was willing to pay for having done. The society wanted a conformable liturgy performed by a decent Christian with reasonable regularity in as many parishes as possible. This the bishops had ample authority to secure, and this on the whole they did secure. The society wanted a homiletic and artistic statement of the baroque harmony underlying its distinctions of status and degree. The laws of faculties, pews, monuments, and proprietary chapels provided this. The society wanted a clerical presence distributed among its several ranks, reconciling both rich and poor to the respective states to which God had been pleased to call them, cementing the alliance between church and state, God and man, setting the seal of a quiet sanctity on the whole order. Through the structure of patronage and revenues, it got this too.

The ultimate downfall of this pleasant and peaceful state of things was a product of its very success in implementing the Erastian ideology I took up at the beginning of this account. Institutional Christianity, through its total integration with the overall society, had subjected itself to the inevitable changes to which the overall society was exposed. Underneath the placid surface of this singularly static century and a half, new forms of religious experience were developing that could not be given adequate institutional expression within the existing framework, and new forms of secular experience were developing that could not find a religious expression within the existing patterns of divine sanction and liturgical form. The Erastian church-state nexus had fixed on an accidental conjunction of elements that existed at a point of time, and could not be arrested.

2. The Rise of Religious Pluralism

Of all the forces, economic, social, and intellectual, that went to undermine the comfortable Erastianism of the eighteenth century establishment, none is more difficult to put into perspective than religious pluralism. At the same time, none is more important for a just perception of what happened to the church — to say nothing of the spiritual life of the nation — during the nineteenth century. It is this development that I will try to sort out in the present chapter.

The problem with it is its very familiarity. We are so used to the experience of some people belonging to one church, others to another, that we forget how long it took to establish the principle, and how persuasive an alternative is available. At the Reformation, no Englishman had belonged to a different religious body from any other Englishman since 1290, when the Jews were expelled from the country. It took something more than a century to show that this could now no longer be the case.

Note that religious pluralism, the recognition that the civil community contains more than one church, is not the same as religious freedom — although that too was a slow growth in the period following the Reformation. If everyone belongs to the same church, that church may be either permissive or coercive as to the beliefs and practices of its members. It may have heretics burned and Sabbath breakers put in the pillory, or it may run bingo games on Sunday evenings and make its most heterodox members into bishops and theology professors. Conversely, if there are a multiplicity of churches, they may all be favored, they may all be persecuted, or the members of one may be subjected to anything from petty harassment to the rack to get them to leave it and join another.

Freedom and persecution alike may be either pluralist or not as the occasion serves.

On the other hand, freedom in a pluralist context takes a different form from freedom in the context of a single church. If pluralism prevails, then churches are assemblies of like minded people, and religious freedom is the ability of a person who disapproves of the teaching or practice of one church to leave it and join another. But if pluralism is not the rule, then one church embodies for good or ill the entire spiritual life of the civil community, and a person's religious freedom depends on there being room for him in that one church. With the decline of zeal for persecution toward the end of the seventeenth century, the question of pluralism *vel non* became intertwined with the question of which of these forms religious freedom should take. It is a peculiarity (and perhaps a strength) of the Anglican settlement that the question never got a clearcut answer one way or the other.

I. Identity

A. Roman Catholics.[1]

It does not seem that a self-conscious English Roman Catholic body distinct from the Church of England can be discerned much earlier than 1570. That was the year the pope excommunicated Elizabeth for taking the nation into schism. Not long afterward, priests trained on the Continent began coming into the country and teaching that Catholics must stay away from the Anglican services and attend their own despite the penalties for doing so.

Until then, the matter was in doubt. I cannot find any evidence that anyone cut himself off from the Church of England because of the schism under Henry VIII. Even with the introduction of a new liturgy of questionable (at best) orthodoxy under Edward VI, there is no indication that a systematic alternative was maintained anywhere except in the household of Mary, the future queen. Indeed, what evidence there is suggests that Catholic minded people gave effect to their views by performing the new services with the vestments, the ceremonies, and the intonations of the old.[2]

As the new forms became more and more firmly settled in place during the first decade of Elizabeth's reign, Catholics again acted more like disgruntled parishioners than like members of another church.[3] Some priests elevated the Host at the Prayer Book Eucharist. Others said the Latin mass in their rectories after saying Prayer Book services in their

churches. Some laypeople took their rosaries to church. Others
participated in matins and evensong, but not in the Eucharist. Still others
sat with their hats on or resolutely thought about something else while the
service was going on.

When the Roman authorities set out to organize this passive resistance
into an alternative church, they had a fairly solid canonical foundation on
which to build. A Christian of orthodox faith who denies the authority of
the Roman see is a schismatic. A Christian who denies a tenet of the
orthodox faith is a heretic. In either case, he sins gravely, and is subject to
specific canonical penalties. But unless he is denounced by name, you need
not avoid his company. You can eat and drink with him (though some
aloofness might be seemly), pass the time of day with him, even pray with
him privately. On the other hand, you must do nothing to encourage him
in his sinful behavior. You may not participate in his liturgy because it is
not the liturgy of the church. You may not receive the sacraments from
him because he has no authority to administer them. You may let him
come to your mass because there is no canonical rule that excludes him,
but you may not give him Communion because he is in a state of sin. In a
pinch, you may allow him to suppose that you are of his persuasion, but
you must not profess to be, because that would be denying your own faith.

From these principles, the English College at Rome developed whole
books of casuistry for their new-minted priests to use in learning to instruct
their flocks. The treatment of the problems was urbane, learned, and
coldly rational, with only occasional glimpses of the life and death issues
that were at stake.

These books trace out a transformation of the applicable rules from a
system for dealing with religious deviants into a system for being religious
deviants. They tell the Catholic how to conduct himself in a group of
Anglicans when they rail against the church or the pope (if his silence gives
scandal, he must speak up even in fear of his life; otherwise, it is better to
keep quiet); when they kneel down to pray (assuming these are private, not
public, prayers, he may participate if they contain no heresy, may take his
hat off and kneel even if they do); when they go off to church (if he will
otherwise get in trouble, he may join them unless he knows from
experience that doing so will endanger his faith).

The books also teach the Catholic how to treat the church institution
formerly his own. He may pay tithes because they are compulsory and it is
lawful to buy off persecution. But it would be better to cheat on them and
give the proceeds to the Catholic Church or the poor. He may contribute
to the upkeep of a church building, because churches do not cease to be
Catholic when heretics take them over, but he may not contribute to the
purchase of Prayer Books or other apparatus of heretical worship. If he
holds an advowson, he may not present an Anglican clergyman; to do so is

to cooperate in heretical worship and set up a ravening wolf where a shepherd should be. But if in spite of these strictures he makes the presentment, it is lawful, indeed commendable, to take a kickback from the presentee and use it for Catholic priests. Trafficking in heretical offices is not simony.

The touchiest issue the books deal with is attendance at church. It is not to be done, first, because the pope has forbidden it, second, because it is often taken for a profession of heresy or schism, and, third, because for some people it is a danger to their faith. The difficulty in applying the prohibition arises because of the different reasons for it: how rigorously you must comply depends on which reason applies in your case.

The third reason can usually be written off. Anyone who has gone to the trouble to become or remain a Catholic is not likely to change his mind on account of anything he hears in a parish church:

> By and large, those who are physically present in these churches will not pay attention to what is said, or if they do pay attention, they will often be more strongly confirmed in the faith by hearing the nonsense of the heretics.[4]

So, while not endangering your faith is a divine command that admits of no dispensation or excuse, there are very few to whom it applies in this situation.

The pope's prohibition, of course, applies to everyone who aspires to be a Catholic. On the other hand, it is only human law. Grave fear or even severe inconvenience will excuse compliance. The penalty for not coming to church is a shilling a week under one statute, twenty pounds a month under another. Arguably, these are not severe enough to provide an excuse. But if your nonattendance draws the attention of the queen's pursuivant, the authorities may find out that you have been hearing mass (£ 100 fine and a year in jail), or that you have been converted since 1581 (high treason: hanging, drawing, and quartering). A law merely ecclesiastical cannot oblige you to undergo such dangers as these.

But the law against professing heresy or schism is another matter. Ever since the apostle Peter came to grief in the high priest's courtyard, Christians have recognized that you cannot disown your faith even to save your life. This is divine law, and admits of neither dispensation nor excuse. The only question it raises is how far the laws and customs of the country have made church attendance a true criterion of adherence to the national church. On this, the casuists are neither unanimous nor altogether consistent.[5] One of them — possibly Gregory Martin, the Bible translator — is fairly complacent:

But you say by way of objection that a man shows himself to be a heretic by going to their churches. I reply in the negative, for a Catholic can go to their churches and sermons in order to ridicule what they say and do.

And in another place:

[T]hey do not show themselves to be heretics by going into these churches, but simply do not reveal themselves to be Catholics, as they are not bound to do, except in cases of necessity.

But according to another set of responses (possibly attributable to Cardinal Allen and the Jesuit Robert Persons):

Catholics were never allowed to join heretics in their public or private prayers. Nor is it allowed in England at the moment, for it is a means of distinguishing Catholics from heretics.

But even this set will grudgingly allow a servant to accompany his master to church:

It seems that it is not always mortal sin if such servants do not give scandal by coming to church, but it would be better for them to look for other masters or to refuse this sort of service entirely.

Both sets agree that it is permissible for a nobleman to attend the queen in church, although he should beg off if he can. They part company again on whether a Catholic may avoid persecution by allowing his child to be baptized in the Anglican church. One says yes if the rite contains no heretical doctrine; the other says not at all. They differ also on whether Catholics may marry in the Anglican church to avoid bastardizing their children.[6] The first response is:

The resolution of this case seems most difficult to me and needs further consideration and further information.

The second is:

that it does not seem lawful for Catholics to take that sacrament from heretics for any reason nor to celebrate matrimony in a heretic church, even if they suffer great damage to their property or reputation by not doing so.

The more lenient view in these matters may go with some hope of a political change:

[I]t is important to keep noble and rich families in their former positions of honour and dignity, so that, after the death of the Queen, they can stand up for the faith with full authority and protect it with their strength and power against the audacity of heretics.

Allen and Persons were either less hopeful or more prudent about expressing their hope. But, whatever might happen when the queen died, these books show that the Roman Catholics in England had become by the end of the reign a self-conscious, self-confident, and disciplined body distinct from the national church.

B. *Protestant Dissenters.*

It was a good deal longer before most Protestant Dissenters recognized themselves as belonging to separate churches. We may suppose that some of them had arrived at that recognition by 1604, for two of the canons promulgated by the Church of England in that year seem to refer to them. Canon 10 excommunicates

> Whoever shall affirm, that such ministers as refuse to subscribe to the form and manner of god's worship in the church of England prescribed in the communion book, and their adherents, may truly take unto them the name of another church not established by law; and dare to presume to publish it, that this their pretended church hath of long time groaned, under the burden of certain grievances imposed upon it and upon the members thereof before mentioned, by the church of England and the orders and constitutions therein by law established . . . .

And Canon 11 excommunicates

> Whoever shall affirm or maintain, that there are within this realm other meetings assemblies or congregations of the king's born subjects, than such as by the laws of this land are held and allowed, which may rightly challenge to themselves the name of true and lawful churches . . . .

Arguably, these canons were made for Roman Catholics, but I am inclined to think not. In the first place, Roman Catholics seem adequately dealt with by other canons in the series.[7] Moreover, the offenses described in Canons 10 and 11 do not seem to correspond very well to the Anglican understanding of what Roman Catholics were doing wrong. Papists were not adherents of non-subscribing ministers, they were adherents of the pope. Their allegiance was not to a pretended church, but to a foreign one. Nor was it for any individual congregation that they challenged the name of a true and lawful church.

But if Canons 10 and 11 referred to Protestant Dissenters, they referred to only a few of them. In 1604 and for a long time after, most Dissenters were still hoping to take possession of the national church, or at least to

make a place for themselves within it. As a result, they did not develop
what the Roman Catholics had had from the 1570s on, that is, a continuing
structure that potential adherents could seek out and join. Some of them
were Independents, forerunners of today's Congregationalists. These
developed a few congregations with some degree of continuity, though
more seem to have broken up when particular ministers died, were
arrested, or moved on. In any case, their polity required no structures
beyond the individual congregation, and the times were not suitable for
setting up anything that was not required.

The oldest, and probably the largest, faction of Dissenters was
committed to the Calvinist polity of elders and presbyteries.[8] The elders
were laymen elected to assist the minister in parish affairs. The
presbyteries were assemblies of ministers and elders from all the parishes
in a designated territory. It was considered appropriate, but not necessary,
to group the presbyteries into larger areas governed by representative
synods. It was the presbyteries that gave the English and Scottish
Calvinists the name, Presbyterian, by which they generally went. As we saw
in the last volume, they attempted during Elizabeth's reign to set up the
institutions their polity required on a more or less clandestine basis within
the national church. They had only sporadic local successes in doing this.

Under the Commonwealth, Parliament provided for setting up the
Presbyterian polity nationwide.[9] But the law was never fully implemented.
The Presbyterian polity was a clerical initiative. It had not much grass-
roots popular support in England, and after Cromwell took power into his
own hands in 1653, it had not much governmental support either. It was
too elaborate to be established without one support or the other. There
were only bits and pieces of it in place when the Commonwealth came to
an end, and these disintegrated rapidly under the new conditions.

The Commonwealth, by abolishing the episcopal polity and failing to
erect the Presbyterian in its place, left ministers pretty much on their
own.[10] In 1654, Cromwell set up a commission to pass on the fitness of
anyone seeking admission to a benefice or an endowed lectureship, and
another to eject "scandalous" ministers from their posts. But anyone who
avoided popery, prelacy (i.e., adherence to the abolished episcopate),
unbecoming conduct (a broad category, to be sure, embracing card playing,
morris dancing, and the like, along with traditional categories), or political
disaffection would probably be safe from running afoul of either
commission. Also, neither commission exercised any kind of day-to-day
supervision. The one was *functus officio* once the minister was in place,
and the other could do nothing with him until he was bad enough to be
fired. Nor did either of them have jurisdiction over a minister who was

supported by the voluntary offerings of his adherents rather than occupying a benefice or an endowed lectureship.

The result was that a minister, once in place, could preach (if he kept off politics) and conduct public worship (if he did not use the Book of Common Prayer) in just about whatever way he pleased. If his parishioners disliked what he was doing, there was no way they could get rid of him. On the other hand, if they found a minister more to their liking, they could set up a competing congregation.

At the Restoration, any minister who held a benefice from which the incumbent had been put out for conformity to the Prayer Book or loyalty to the king was made to withdraw in favor of the man he had supplanted. Others, however, were left in place while a series of negotiations, conferences, and political maneuverings were undertaken in the hope of producing a scheme by which Anglicans and Presbyterians could live together in one national church. Various proposals for a polity of "modified episcopacy" — i.e., presbyteries with permanent presiding officers — and miscellaneous changes in objectionable liturgical elements were put forward and rejected until Parliament finally passed a new Act of Uniformity, putting affairs just about where they had been left in 1640, and giving all beneficed clergy until St. Bartholomew's Day, 1662, to conform.[11]

The clergy expelled under this act, the "Bartholomew Men," having failed to organize while they were in power, were in no condition to organize now.[12] Those who continued in the ministry — as most of them seem to have done — tended to work as itinerant preachers, sometimes in fields or houses, sometimes in Anglican churches whose incumbents were either sympathetic or absent. A few became connected with settled congregations, but more of them avoided persecution by keeping on the move. Their followers, meanwhile, attended the Anglican services, or else found nonconforming services wherever they could.

Denominational identity for the laity was even more confusing than for the clergy. By the 1660s, the Quaker meetings and at least some Baptist congregations had definite membership and rigorous discipline that members could be admonished, excommunicated, or expelled for violating.[13] These two denominations also had practices that tended to define them. The Baptists insisted on adult baptism, and required anyone who joined them to be baptized anew. The Quakers refused to take oaths, to tip their hats, or to use titles of honor. The Quakers, like the Roman Catholics, were strict in their refusal to attend Anglican services. It was their belief that only interior worship is acceptable to God. Some Baptists were steady recusants also. Following their principle that infant baptism is no baptism at all, they concluded that they could not in good conscience go to hear an unbaptized minister preach.

The majority of Dissenters, nominally Presbyterians or Independents, were much more tenuously defined than the Baptists or Quakers.[14] The Presbyterian polity called for laymen to occupy important places in church government, but even where the governing bodies were set up, the lay places in them could not be kept filled. Most laypeople limited themselves to expressing their convictions by attending or not attending services. In this, they tended to be eclectic. Most of them, whatever their doctrinal or liturgical reservations, did not scruple to attend Anglican services from time to time. There were, to be sure, individual hard core recusants. A survey taken by the bishop of Oxford in 1682[15] has in one parish:

> Mr. William Stafford a Great Olivarian, & in those dayes an officer: & to this time a great promoter of separating principles: in Church affaires holds that every One that worships God in the Publick place is a Barbarian to him, and he to them — . . . .

There were also in the parish some wishy-washy recusants such as Christopher Cook, who

> answers in the General that he cannot come, and sometimes adds some of the old Empty reasons, because of the Mixture of good & bad in our congregation & at our Ordinances & c.

or

> John North junr, whose Father hath bin long a stubborn & Resolute seperatist & is still living but so weake that he is never likely to go out of doors; and his son haveing a wife and children & expecting a Considerable Estate from his Father, saith, it may be he may come to Church if it please God to take his Father, but he is not willing to be under the obligation of a promise.

But it seems that rather more Dissenters were like the four women and one man in another parish who

> doe commonly come to our church in the morning & go to the Conventicle in Banbury in the afternoon.

Having no central denominational authority to guide him, the typical Dissenter evidently found his own individual sticking place. For instance, some of those who disapproved of the Prayer Book offices walked into church when the sermon started, and walked out again when it was over.[16]

The Act of Toleration of 1689, by which Dissenting worship was finally made legal, tended to sharpen the distinction between Anglicans and Dissenters by making its benefits available only to the latter. It applied in terms to "persons dissenting from the Church of England," and to

Dissenting congregations registered as such. Chief Justice Holt established very early that it offered no encouragement to an ecumenical spirit among Anglicans:

> If a man be a professed churchman, and his conscience will permit him sometimes to go to meeting instead of coming to church, the Act of Toleration will not excuse him, for it was not made for such sort of people.[17]

This passage comes from a 1704 case interpreting the compulsory attendance laws, which were already pretty much a dead letter. But similar principles were invoked all through the eighteenth century and into the nineteenth against any efforts of the clergy to cross denominational lines.[18] The Act would not protect an Anglican minister who violated the doctrinal or liturgical formulas of his own church. It would not authorize him to preach or hold services without the proper permission from the local incumbent. Still less would it protect him if he ministered in a Dissenting congregation. By the same token, it would not protect a Dissenting minister who tried to preach or officiate in an Anglican church, or an Anglican who permitted him to do so. In short, the prevailing interpretation of the Act was such as to drive people — and especially ministers — to make up their minds whether they were Anglicans or Dissenters.

Another way in which the Act of Toleration contributed to denominational identity was through the pattern of land tenure it introduced. Registration under the Act made it possible for Dissenting congregations to conduct regular services openly and without penalty. They naturally wished to have buildings in which to do so. But registration did not confer corporate status on a congregation or enable it to hold property. Accordingly, if you wanted to build a chapel for a Dissenting congregation, you had to put the land in the hands of trustees. These trustees would then be subject to supervision not by the congregation, the minister, or the higher denominational authorities if there were any, but by the Court of Chancery.[19] That court would enforce a trust for lawful Dissenting worship in the same manner as any other charitable trust — that is, by requiring the trustees to follow any instructions contained in the document by which the trust was established. If that document called clearly for carrying out the wishes of the congregation or of some denominational authority, then the wishes of the congregation or authority would be imposed on the trustees by the court. But if the document was indefinite or ambiguous, the court might prefer a presumed intention of the founders to the present practice of the congregation or denomination. Or it might allow the trustees to do as they pleased on the ground that there was nothing in the foundation document to warrant interfering.

This state of the law put a premium on a congregation either having clear criteria for voting membership or having a clear affiliation with a central authority. Only by subjecting the trustees unambiguously to a vote of the members or to the mandates of higher authority could the draftsman of a trust document be sure the property would not go astray. The question is too complicated to be gone into here, but it appears that the decay of the early Presbyterian and Independent congregations during the eighteenth century, the disappearance of many of them, and the shifting of others into Unitarianism or other doctrines that their founders would have repudiated were due in great part to the failure of their trust documents to set up adequate control over the trustees, and that that failure in turn was due to the lack of sharply defined authorities in whom the appropriate control could be vested.[20] The Baptists and Quakers, who not only had clear standards of membership but also had set up central or regional authorities or both as early as the 1660s, fared rather better. So did the Presbyterian congregations that were set up under Scottish auspices after the Presbyterian polity became official in Scotland in 1689. These had trust deeds affiliating them to the National Synod of the Church of Scotland, which deeds the Court of Chancery was prepared to enforce.[21]

The final stage in the denominational definition of English Protestants was initiated by John Wesley, whose Methodist movement began coming into prominence shortly before the middle of the eighteenth century, and became somewhat precariously identified as a separate denomination by the end of that century.[22] Wesley's governing idea since his days as a young clergyman at Oxford had been to develop a society through which members of the Church of England could be offered a deeper spiritual life than the conventional pieties and practices of the church afforded them. A rigorous regime of Bible study, frequent prayer, Communion, good works, and mutual correction and encouragement was to be provided for those who chose to come together in such a society. It appears that Wesley's friend George Whitefield led him to include open-air preaching in his plan.[23] By the 1740s, there were a number of societies about the country, operating on this plan with supervision and preaching from Wesley himself and his personal surrogates. The surrogates, generally called preachers after their principal function, were not attached to any one society; they rode circuit. A few of them were ordained, but most were not.[24] Subordinate to these itinerant leaders were local leaders and preachers in the different societies, democratic in their outlook and in their relations with the membership, but actually appointed from above. The structure was completed by regional meetings and a national Conference, entirely subordinate to Wesley during his lifetime, but set up to take over on his death.

Law and circumstance worked together against Wesley's tenacious desire to keep this elaborate enterprise within the Church of England.[25] We

have looked at the legal dispositions that prevented irregular ministries
from taking root in the established church. The most important of these,
the one against preaching without a license, and the one against holding
services outside a proper church or chapel, were derived from the Canons
of 1604, and therefore were not binding on the laity — although the clergy
could be suspended, excommunicated, and finally imprisoned for violating
them. But the Conventicle Act, one of a series of Restoration statutes
adopted for the purpose of suppressing Dissent, forbade gatherings of more
than five people for religious worship other than the Prayer Book services.
The penalty could be as much as £ 10 for anyone present, £ 20 for the
owner of the house where the gathering took place, £ 100 for the minister.
The Act of Toleration did not free anyone from the burdens of this
Conventicle Act unless he professed himself a Dissenter and took
appropriate oaths. To be sure, the Conventicle Act was not systematically
enforced, but it could be, and if the local magistrates were sufficiently
aroused against Methodism, it would be. Furthermore, while a trust for
lawful Dissenting worship was enforceable in Chancery, a trust for unlawful
conventicles would probably not be. This may have been the reason why
Wesley, toward the end of his life, finally adopted a policy of registering all
the meeting houses of his organization as Dissenting chapels.[26] Trustees
of some of the individual meeting houses had already taken this step long
before.

The people who were particularly attracted by Methodism were apt to be
people who had become alienated from the established church by the
formalism of its services and the worldliness of many of its clergy. Many of
them found it a hard saying of Wesley's that they had to attend the Prayer
Book services in their parish churches, and receive the sacraments from
their parish ministers. Nor, in many places, did the church or the minister
encourage them to follow Wesley in this. Some of the most effective
Methodist preaching and organizing was done in towns that had gained
population in the incipient industrial expansion of the time, and had room
for only a fraction of their people in their parish churches. Furthermore,
many Anglicans, clergy and laity alike, regarded the Methodists as
dangerous fanatics, and tended to expel them, or worse, if they showed up
at church.[27]

Nor did Wesley do much to impress his followers with the reason for his
insistence on their frequenting these uncongenial and unwelcoming
congregations. Ecclesiology was never his strong point as a theologian,
and, because he was not founding a church, he felt no need to instruct his
followers in his doctrines on the subject, such as they were. It was not
apparent to them why they could not receive the sacraments where they
prayed. Nor was it apparent to them how the ceremony by which their

itinerant preachers were commissioned differed from the ordination that enabled a priest of the established church to administer the sacraments.

The concessions Wesley made to these concerns during his lifetime tended to obfuscate the situation rather than resolve it. In a few places, where the parish church was especially inconvenient or the parish minister especially scandalous, he allowed his societies to meet at the same time as the parish services were held, or to have Communion in their own meeting houses. He eventually ordained a few men (he had decided as early as 1745 that a priest has the same power to ordain as a bishop), but not enough to keep his followers from wanting their unordained preachers to administer Communion.

Matters reached a crisis when Wesley died in 1791. To keep from totally fragmenting the organization, the Conference, to which had passed such of Wesley's authority as did not die with him, adopted a system of local option. Individual societies, with the approval of the circuit meetings, could decide to hold meetings during service time, to administer sacraments (whether or not the preacher was ordained), or both. Most of them eventually took up the option, although in a few places with sympathetic Anglican incumbents, the local Methodists attended Anglican services and received Communion in the Anglican church well into the nineteenth century. Indeed, it appears that some people in some places regularly attend both churches even today.[28]

While both the Act of Toleration and the Conventicle Act tended to sharpen denominational lines, there were two pieces of seventeenth century legislation that had the opposite effect. These were the Corporation Act (1661) and the Test Act (1673).[29] Between them, they prevented anyone from occupying a post in municipal or national government, the royal household, or the military unless he received Communion in the Church of England. The picture sometimes painted of whole congregations communicating hypocritically in order to qualify for office under one or the other of these acts seems exaggerated. One Communion after all was all it took to qualify an officeholder for as long as he held the office. A man could make a career by receiving Communion only when he changed jobs. But what the acts did do was favor Dissenters who had no conscientious objection to receiving Anglican sacraments over Dissenters who had such objections. Accordingly, they encouraged people to keep up a rudimentary tie with the established church who might not otherwise have done so.

Part of the Tory agenda in Queen Anne's time was an Occasional Conformity Act, which penalized anyone who attended Dissenting worship after qualifying for office by receiving the Sacrament in the Church of England. After a couple of other attempts to enact this law were turned back by the House of Lords, it finally made its way into the statute books toward the end of the reign (1711), only to be repealed again in 1719. So the Corporation and Test Acts continued to support a certain amount of ecclesiastical fence straddling, especially among Methodists, until they themselves were repealed in 1828.

By the end of the eighteenth century, the organization and legal status of the main Protestant Dissenting bodies had become fairly clear. But the vicissitudes of the past two centuries had left them with a continuing ambiguous attitude toward their own ecclesial identity, as well as toward the national church. Many Dissenters saw no inconsistency between their membership in their own churches and their continued participation in the affairs of the Church of England. Dissenting Members of Parliament did not hesitate to vote on church questions. Dissenting parishioners (except Quakers) accepted office as churchwardens, and involved themselves in liturgical disputes in that capacity. Dissenters occasionally prosecuted ritualist clergy in the bishops' courts. As late as 1917, some Dissenters considered it a grievance that the newly established church electoral rolls were to be limited to people who not only claimed to be members of the Church of England, but also disclaimed membership in any other church.[30]

In addition — though this point is a little harder to pin down — I have the impression that most Dissenters remained content to leave to the Anglicans the task of providing such ministrations as were required by the nominal Christians who made up a large part of the population. It seems to have been universally understood that it was the Anglican, not the Dissenting, minister who would give the Invocation on public occasions, and that people who sought religious observances only for baptisms, marriages, and burials would seek them from the established church. I believe this understanding played a major part in the later history of the establishment.

II. From Toleration To Pluralism

A. Disabilities.

By the end of the eighteenth century, it had become fairly difficult for an Englishman to get in trouble with the law by either practicing or not practicing a religion.[31] The Methodists, as we have seen, had joined other Protestant Dissenters under the shelter of the 1689 Toleration Act. An act of 1791 put Roman Catholics in nearly the same position as Protestant Dissenters, except that for another thirty-eight years they were not allowed to have bells or steeples on their churches. A cynical move by the London authorities to mulct Dissenters by appointing them to offices for which they were ineligible and then fining them for not accepting was stopped by Lord

Mansfield in 1767. An act of 1696 permitted Quakers to take an affirmation instead of an oath in most cases where an oath was required, a privilege extended to the Moravian Brethren in 1749.

In theory, anyone who did not attend some lawful place of worship every Sunday was subject to a shilling's fine for each omission.[32] This old penalty remained on the books till 1846, but no one enforced it. More formidable, but also fortunately not enforced, was a 1697 act against blasphemy, carrying up to three years in prison for denying the Trinity, the Christian religion, or the divine authority of the Old and New Testaments. This act covered Unitarians until they were exempted from it in 1813, and atheists until it was repealed in 1967. As it applied only to people who had been brought up Christian or who had professed Christianity within the realm, Jews were not subject to it. As far as I can see, though, the Conventicle Act applied to a Jewish congregation as well as to any other. So attendance at a synagogue was theoretically subject to penalties until that act was repealed in 1812. Even then, Jewish worship was not strictly lawful. Not until 1846 did Parliament put Jewish congregations on the same footing as Catholic and Protestant.

While these penal laws were not directly enforced, they did affect the disposition of property.[33] A trust for a form of worship permitted by the Act of Toleration would be enforced in Chancery; a trust for another religion would not. In the famous case of *Da Costa* v. *De Pas* (1754) a legacy for the establishment of a yeshiva was diverted on this ground to the support of a Christian foundling hospital. Other cases went the same way, and trusts for Jewish worship remained unenforceable until the 1846 legislation just referred to. As for Roman Catholics, the 1791 act made it possible for them to endow churches and schools, but trusts for private masses or religious orders remained illegal until 1926.

Oddly enough, Unitarians did not start losing their property on account of illegality until after they had stopped being illegal.[34] Most Unitarian congregations had been formed by Presbyterians or Independents in the late seventeenth or early eighteenth century, and had gradually shifted their doctrine over the years. Their property was held on trusts that imposed no doctrinal requirements. In the case of *Attorney General* v. *Pearson* (1817-35) the court took the property of such a congregation and put it into Trinitarian hands on the ground that the founders of the congregation cannot have intended Unitarians to enjoy their benefactions because at the time Unitarianism was illegal. This may have been what the founders would have said if asked, but it was certainly not what they did say. Parliament rescued the Unitarians in 1844 by giving them a prescriptive right to their property.

Persons of attentuated religion or no religion at all had a few theoretical dangers that continued into the 1840s. Of course, the Conventicle Act was not a problem for them because they did not meet for religious worship. But the penalties for not going to church applied to them on paper until 1846. Also, if they expressed their views too forcefully, they could be had up for the common law offense of blasphemy, which was not superseded by the 1697 act.[35] It is still possible to commit this offense; the House of Lords affirmed a conviction in 1979. By the 1840s, however, the courts were holding that you could say what you pleased about religious questions as long as you did not say it in an offensive way. In 1917, the courts even upheld a bequest for the promotion of secularism, holding that rational argument against the Christian religion was not blasphemy.

Turning from private to public life, we find that in the first decades of the nineteenth century non-Anglicans were still being systematically excluded. As we have seen, the Test and Corporation Acts barred from most public offices anyone who would not receive the Sacrament in the Church of England at least once per appointment. These acts did not apply to Parliament — nor could they as long as some members of Parliament came from Scotland, where Presbyterianism was established. But both Roman Catholics and Jews were excluded from Parliament by oaths that they could not take.

An act of 1828 amended the Test and Corporation Acts to eliminate the requirement of receiving the Sacrament.[36] Instead, it provided for an oath that the officeholder would not use his office to the detriment of the established church. As this oath had to be taken "upon the true faith of a Christian," Jews were no better off than before. Neither were Roman Catholics: besides the reception of the Sacrament, the acts imposed two other requirements that remained in effect. Both acts required an oath that no foreign prelate has any jurisdiction in England. The Test Act also required a declaration of disbelief in transubstantiation. Insofar as these provisions affected Roman Catholics, they were taken away in the following year by the Roman Catholic Relief Act of 1829. Jews had to wait until 1858 to be relieved from the language about the true faith of a Christian.

Most of the legislation relieving non-Anglicans of their legal burdens was enacted for the benefit of specific groups. It remained possible, therefore, to be excluded from the benefit by not being a member of one of the groups in question. Charles Bradlaugh, the atheist propagandist, found in 1881 that there was still no way he could qualify himself for the seat in Parliament to which he had been elected.[37] He scrupled to take an oath, and was ineligible to take an affirmation. Not until 1888 was his case finally provided for.

B. Taxation.

When the first Parliament elected under the reformed franchise began its work in 1833, the personal and political emancipation of non-Anglicans was not complete, but it was far enough along for the triumphant reformers to turn their attention to other religious questions. Establishment as such came in for some hostile rhetoric in this period, but it seems not to have been in any serious danger. Disestablishment was more a threat with which to intimidate supporters of the status quo than a serious item on anyone's political agenda. Evidently, one did not have to be a strong churchman to believe that the lower orders in society needed more Christianity than could be paid for out of the collection plate, or that there were important public advantages in having bishops appointed by the government.

The forms of religious inequality that were seriously addressed in the period fell under two main heads. One was financial. There were still ways in which the established church was supported out of general public funds, or out of particular levies to which non-members had to contribute. The other was administrative — or perhaps I should say governmental. Important functions that a modern government generally performs for its citizens were still committed to agencies of the church, and often administered in such a way that a Dissenter could not, or could not comfortably, accept them.

1. Grants — As we saw in the last chapter, Parliament in 1818 created a fund of a million pounds for the building of new churches, and supplemented it with another half million in 1824. This appropriation, conceived as a national thank offering for the favorable conclusion of the Napoleonic Wars, was the last major subvention out of the national treasury for church purposes within England. In 1833, the Church Building Commissioners set up to administer this fund were still at work, and were still issuing Exchequer bills to finance their undertakings. They had not yet spent all their money, but their project was so far along that no one was for stopping it. On the other hand, no one was for giving them any more money either. The subject was mooted when a Tory majority was returned in 1841, but Sir Robert Peel, the embattled Tory prime minister, was not willing to brave the political consequences of giving the Scots, the Irish, and the English Dissenters ground for making common cause against the establishment. The Church Building Commissioners were to have nothing more from the Treasury but their expenses until they were abolished in 1856.[38]

Local churches in 1833 were still getting a good deal of support from municipal funds. Certain patterns of churchmanship and of church finance had been associated with towns and townspeople since the seventeenth century, and these were often effectuated through the governing bodies of the various towns. Many of these bodies had a longstanding custom of paying stipends to certain lecturers and curates out of their general revenues. Many of them held endowments that had been given for church purposes. Many of them were patrons of benefices.

I do not find that this situation was directly attacked. Rather, it was swept away by a general rationalization of municipal affairs.[39] The Municipal Corporations Act of 1835 replaced the bizarre and restrictive franchises that had developed under medieval borough charters by electoral rolls including all the taxpaying householders of each municipality. To remedy the arbitrary and often corrupt stewardship of charitable funds by the old corporations, the act provided for putting all such funds into the hands of trustees distinct from the reorganized governing bodies. Church endowments were transferred along with the rest. Other provisions of the act restricted the purposes to which general revenues could be put. Customary stipends were secured to their present holders, but further contributions to the church were not included among the permitted purposes. All rights of patronage were to be sold off for cash. Proposals to leave them in municipal hands and proposals to turn them over to church authorities were alike rejected. Independent of any express language in the act, the Court of Chancery found this whole scheme inconsistent with any further municipal support for the church.[40] Furthermore, Dissenters were so numerous on the new voting rolls as to make such support politically unlikely even if it had been legal.

There remained a provision of the 1818 Church Building Act that authorized municipal corporations, along with private corporations and government departments, to donate land for the building of churches and parsonages. I find no indication of how much use this provision got. It was supplemented in 1873 with an act that put non-Anglican places of worship and residences on the same footing as Anglican.[41]

2. *Tithe* — The most important compulsory payment for church purposes was tithe. It was never clear philosophically whether this exaction was properly understood as a form of tax and therefore to be deplored or as a form of endowed income and therefore to be protected. By the newly prevailing liberalism of the time, taxing people to support a church they did not believe in was unacceptable, whereas all forms of property were to be respected.[42] All taxation must be rationally ordered to a public end. On the other hand, if either merit or rationality were to be a requirement for keeping property, no magnate in the kingdom would be safe.

Tithe had something of the nature of property because it issued out of land. Whoever occupied the land was responsible for counting off every tenth sheaf at the harvest, and leaving it in the field for the parson or other tithe owner to pick up.[43] The parson had to come on the land and fetch it, and, within reasonable limits, the landowner could tell him what path to use. Tithe was a share of the crop, not a share of the profit: no expenses could be deducted before it was set out. As a legal institution, tithe had a certain resemblance to an easement or similar right of one person in another's land.

Its original status as a personal obligation of each Christian had been eroded by a medieval decision to collect it from the lands of Jews, and by the virtual disappearance of "personal" tithes on the wages or profits of labor.[44] On the other hand, some elements of the original status as a personal obligation persisted. The normal method of enforcement was still the venerable ecclesiastical process for the correction of sinners. Also, the tithe owner fell short of having a tangible interest in anything in particular. He had no complaint if a landowner stopped using his land for agriculture. Nor was he entitled to compensation if a piece of land was flooded pursuant to an exercise of eminent domain.

The situation was further complicated by the fact that something like one-third of the tithes in England had been in lay hands since the dissolution of the monasteries under Henry VIII.[45] As payments to local magnates on whose ancestors Henry had bestowed them, these tithes looked very like a number of other payments, all as sacrosanct as they were antiquated that the landed aristocracy collected from the people who worked their land. But the manner in which these laypeople held and collected their tithes was precisely the same — even to the use of church courts — as the manner in which churchmen held and collected theirs. Whatever tithe was in the hands of lay owners, it had to be the same in the hands of churchmen.

With tithe in this ambiguous situation, the Elizabethan Roman Catholic casuists had called it a charge on land rather than a contribution to the church, and had allowed Catholics to pay it.[46] The Quakers, on the other hand, had seen it from the outset as a church tax, and had refused to pay it. A series of statutes, beginning in 1696, had responded to their refusal by providing special procedures to seize their property rather than trying to coerce them into delivering it. The only other resistance to tithe on overtly religious grounds was that of the Irish Roman Catholics. Their objection was less to the nature than to the amount of the payment. It seemed to them unfair that so much money should go to the support of a church that served so few people. This objection was finally to result in the Irish Anglican church losing not only its tithes but its landed endowments as well. But it was not nearly so cogent in England, where most of the people had some kind of tie with the church.

The attack in England was mainly in the interest of agricultural efficiency.[47] There had been considerable innovation in agricultural practice during the preceding century or so, involving new patterns of landholding, new methods of growing, and often new crops. Often these changes did not lend themselves well to the old practice of dividing a crop into ten parts and leaving one of them in the field for the tithe owner to come and collect. One Member of Parliament in 1835 regaled the House with the following story. A constituent laid out an acre of his ground in cabbages. Instead of going through the field every day or so, picking the cabbages that appeared to be at their best, and sending them off to the market, he had to pick the whole field at once so that he could divide the crop into ten piles and leave one for the parson. Having done this, he sent for the parson. The parson seems to have been anxious to pick a quarrel. I suspect that his real complaint was that the land was in cabbages instead of good Christian cereal grains, but what he argued was that the ten piles were not equal. The grower told him to choose whichever pile he thought was the biggest, but the parson — evidently out of sheer orneriness — refused. So the grower chose one pile for the parson and took away the other nine. The next step in the grower's plan for exploiting his land was for him to let his lambs feed on the remains of his cabbage plants. But the parson's cabbages were still in a pile in the field. After demanding in vain that the parson come and take them away, he went ahead and let the lambs into the field, where, sure enough, the first thing they ate was the parson's cabbages. The parson then went to a church court, claiming seven shillings as the value of the cabbages to which he was entitled. Despite what seems like a good defense, and despite his claim that the cabbages were worth no more than tenpence, the grower paid up, and paid £ 15 costs into the bargain. His lawyers had advised him that a successful defense would cost more than that.

Even a devout churchman could see that neither growers nor parsons were well served by a system that produced such results as this. Furthermore, those farmers and landowners who improved the yield of their land with innovative techniques or crops felt that it was unfair for them to have to give one-tenth of the improved income to the tithe owner, who had done nothing to earn it. Also, since tithe was on the gross, not the net, return from the land, it could be a disincentive to any improved technique that cost money to use. Note that this complaint posed a conceptual dilemma for supporters of the status quo. If tithe was a form of traditional charge on land, it should not take account of new improvements in the course of agriculture. On the other hand, if it was an ad valorem tax, it should not be going to support the church.

This was the situation that was dealt with by the Tithe Commutation Act of 1836.[48] The basic idea of this measure was to make tithe more acceptable and less vexatious by making it more like a rentcharge. It provided for the replacement of the traditional tithes in kind by a cash payment varying with the going price of the main cereal grains. The commutation was to be carried out parish by parish under the supervision of a commission appointed for the purpose. It was to be done by agreement if possible: if the holders of two-thirds of the tithes agreed with the owners of two-thirds of the land, the commission could impose their agreement on the whole parish. If no such agreement was reached, the commission could make an order on the request of any parishioner.

Whether by agreement or by order, the commutation was to be computed in the same way. The cash values of the parish tithes for the years 1829-1835 were to be averaged. It was then to be determined how much grain the cash amount thus arrived at would have purchased if laid out one-third in wheat, one-third in barley, and one-third in oats at the average market price for the same years. From then on, the "tithe rentcharge" every year for the parish would be the average market price of that amount of wheat, barley, and oats over the seven years next preceding the year in question. The Comptroller of Corn Returns, an official charged with assembling information of that kind, was to determine and publish the applicable averages every year. Special provisions were made for market gardens, orchards, coppices, and hopyards, and for land that had not been cultivated during the base years or had not paid tithe.

When the tithe rentcharge was properly computed for a whole parish, it was to be apportioned among the lands in the parish, and among the tithe owners if there were more than one.[49] This too was to be accomplished by agreement with the approval of the commission, or, if the parties could not agree, by the commission on its own. If a tenant disapproved of the arrangement, his landlord would have to pay the tithe rentcharge, and collect the traditional tithes in kind from the tenant.

The rentcharge established in this way and assigned to particular fields was collectible not in the ecclesiastical courts, but by the same kind of distress (i.e., seizure of chattels found on the premises) as rents and other payments issuing out of land. If there was nothing to distrain, the land itself could be seized and occupied until the arrears were levied or paid. But the freehold could not be sold as it could be for some such payments.[50]

This scheme met the serious objections to tithe as they had been raised by English farmers and landowners. The rentcharge was shorn of the incidents that made it look like a personal obligation or an ad valorem tax. It rose and fell with the price of the main cereal grains, so it could not destroy a farmer in a bad year or two. At the same time it did not vary with the use to which the land was put, so it did not discourage innovative agriculture. Nor did it get in the grower's way by requiring him to harvest his crops in a particular manner, stack them in a particular place, or give the parson and his wagons access to his fields.

With the old tithes in kind, there disappeared the old reciprocal obligations of the parson, such as holding a party for the tithepaying parishioners, or maintaining a bull and a boar for the parishioners to breed their stock.[51] Some of the more radical reformers argued that there had also been an obligation to use tithes for the relief of the poor — an excuse for now confiscating some or all of them for that purpose. It was often argued in response that the tithes that originally went for that purpose were mainly those of the monasteries, which had already been confiscated. This argument never achieved a major place in the polemics of the day: the historical evidence was too tenuous to give much support to either side.

The agitation over tithes had its ups and downs in the century following this act.[52] Generally, when the whole English agricultural enterprise was prosperous, things went smoothly enough, but when farmers had trouble making ends meet, they tended to feel the new tithe rentcharge as an injustice little different from the old tithes in kind. An act of 1891 made some difference by putting the burden of the rentcharge on the landowner instead of the farmer: landowners tended to be from a different social class from the farmers, and one better disposed to the established church. But after the First World War a number of farmers bought the land they were cultivating, and the objections multiplied once more.

In 1936, after trying a couple of other expedients with indifferent success, Parliament adopted a plan to amortize all tithe rentcharges over the ensuing sixty years, and, during those sixty years, to keep farmers and parsons from each other's throats by interposing between them the cool and inexorable ministrations of the Board of Inland Revenue. Under the Tithe Act of that year,[53] tithe owners were given Treasury "stock" (the nearest American equivalent is government bonds) instead of their rentcharges. The stock is marketable and bears three percent interest. Each tithe owner received an amount calculated to yield interest equal to his former rentcharge, less certain deductions to reflect the fact that he would have an easier time collecting his money, and would not have to pay local rates on it.

Meanwhile, the Act provided for the former tithepayer to pay the Inland Revenue a yearly "annuity" equal to the same annual value, but without the deductions. The annuities, along with an annual contribution from the Treasury, were to be put into a special account. Out of this account, the interest was to be paid on the stock, local authorities were to be given sums to make up for their lost rates, and one or two other obligations formerly met out of tithes were to be bought off. The rest of the account was to be saved up. It was expected to be enough to redeem the stock at face value on October 2, 1996. As originally planned, the annuities were to cease when the stock was redeemed. Actually, though, they were abolished in 1977.[54] The stock, or some of it at least, is still awaiting the 1996 redemption date.

Both the transition from tithes in kind to rentcharges and the transition from rentcharges to stock resulted in a drop in the actual monetary return to the tithe owner. The 1836 legislation deprived him of his share of any improvement in the yield from land subject to his tithe. The 1936 legislation deprived him of the benefit of any increase in the price of grain, and took away his hedge against inflation. In short, while the tithe owner's property right was respected in principle, it was roughly handled in practice. The reason, it seems to me, is that both measures came out of the political process as compromises between people who thought tithe should be paid in kind down to the last sprig of mint and rue and people who thought it should not be paid at all. The ancient institution of tithe remained ambiguous and controversial to the end.

If the alignment of parties on the subject was not quite the same in 1936 or 1836 as it was in 1336, the lines of descent can still be traced. On the one hand, the fourteenth century Commons thought of tithe as a customary public subvention for the church. They were willing to pay it because they believed in the church, and this was the expedient their ancestors had hit upon for supporting it. But the logic of their position would not call for continuing to pay tithe if they stopped believing in the church or if they found a better way to support it. Many of their nineteenth century descendants did one or both of these things. The medieval churchmen, on the other hand, thought of tithe as a radical tenth of the gross national product that belonged to God for the benefit of His church because He had so commanded. Nineteenth century churchmen could not take so high a view of the matter as that, but they were willing to insist that their rights were at least as sacred as Lord Whiffleberry's right to shoot rabbits or Mrs. Higginbottom's trust fund for the Quaker meeting house.

The anonymous editor of *Crockford's Clerical Directory* was still seeing the argument in the traditional terms in his prefaces for 1936 and 1937.[55] He referred to a witness before the Royal Commission preceding the 1936 Act who said "that the complete abolition of tithe in the interest of English justice 'might save the Church from being utterly discredited . . . . ' " and asked how she proposed to pay for the church's ministrations in her locality "when 'English justice' had stripped the Church of property which it held by a title longer than her own." Referring to the redemption stock, he said:

> One thing we think certain. Before many years are out attempts will be made to represent the £ 70,000,000 worth of stock which the Church has received as a lavish endowment out of public funds . . . . It will be necessary to say very often and very plainly in the most public fashion

possible that the money is nothing but payment for property which the Church was not anxious to part with, which the Government compelled it to sell for about four-fifths of its real value.

Fortunately, the prediction of further controversy seems to have been mistaken. As far as I can see, the whole subject has been fairly quiet since 1936, and the final redemption day bids fair to come off without anyone but historians paying much heed.

A lay responsibility for the church that shared some of the history of the tithe rentcharge was the responsibility of lay rectors to repair the chancels of their churches. The beneficiaries of King Henry's confiscation of religious houses took on this burden with the appropriated rectorial tithes that the former houses had held. The burden went with the tithes and with the rentcharges that replaced them in 1836. The 1936 Act provided in most cases for abolishing the obligation and compensating the parish with a payment out of the annuity fund. But there was an exception. In certain cases, the rectorial tithes and the titheable lands had fallen into the same hands. Under these circumstances, the tithe rentcharge could be extinguished by being "merged" into the land at the behest of the owner. When that happened, the obligation to repair the chancel would attach to the land, even though the land paid no tithe. Thus, in 1936, it would no longer be an obligation that went with tithe rentcharge, so it would not be abolished as part of the statutory scheme. In the few places that have gone through this evolution, it persists to this day, and an unsuspecting landowner is still occasionally hit with a bill.[56] He is apt to react as one who has been arbitrarily singled out to be a victim of religious persecution.

The 1836 act did not affect the money payments in lieu of tithe that had been established in London by an act of Henry VIII, and in other cities by custom.[57] A series of acts beginning in 1671, after the London fire, and ending in 1879, changed the London payments into fixed amounts to be collected like rates for other local government purposes. These survived a number of vicissitudes until they were finally redeemed under a local act of 1947. Outside London, agreements or local acts did away with a number of payments in lieu of tithes, or transformed them into rentcharges of the kind disposed of in 1936. Other such payments survived, and perhaps still do. A 1963 act provides for redeeming any that remain, but only with the consent of the person who will have to pay.

The 1836 Act permitted but did not require the inclusion of mortuaries and Easter offerings in the package of payments replaced by tithe rentcharge. To the extent such payments were customary, and were not commuted under the 1836 Act, they remained in force.[58] Mortuaries were abolished by the Church Assembly in 1963, but Easter offerings, if the custom of paying them has not died out, are in force still, collectible from

Anglican and non-Anglican alike. They are mentioned in the current
edition of *Halsbury's Laws of England* as part of the current law, but, aside
from two cases from the 1860s, neither Halsbury nor I has any evidence of
any place where there is still a custom of paying them.

3. *Churchrates* — Except for tithes, no compulsory church payments were
more controversial than churchrates, the ad valorem real property taxes
that parishioners were supposed to adopt whenever money was needed to
repair the fabric (except the chancel) or provide the necessities for worship.
As the nineteenth century progressed, new standards of piety and decorum
provided more occasions for making these rates. At the same time,
Dissenters, freed from their legal disabilities, began concerning themselves
more with financial liabilities, and at least some Anglicans, in keeping with
the spirit of the age, were ready to concede that the Dissenters' grievance
was a just one. Parishioners were becoming reluctant, sometimes militantly
so, to vote the necessary funds.

Since churchrates had to be voted on every time, they could not be made
to look like property rights. Sometimes, however, they could be turned into
contract rights — almost as good under the prevailing ideology. Under a
statute of 1819, the vestry, with the concurrence of the incumbent and the
bishop, could authorize repairs on credit, and meet the cost, plus interest,
out of churchrates levied over the next ten years.[59] Once the obligation
was incurred, the vestry would be required to vote the necessary rates. A
writ of mandamus would be available out of the royal courts if they failed
to do so.

But the courts would not allow the vestry to be put under the pressure of
a *fait accompli*.[60] The churchwardens could not spend money and then
reimburse themselves with a rate. Except as provided in the 1819 statute, a
"retrospective" rate, i.e., one to pay for work already done or money
already borrowed, was illegal even if the vestry adopted it. Nor could the
statute be relied on after the event. A rate made under it could not be
enforced unless the necessary consents had been obtained before the work
was done or the debt incurred.

Accordingly, the parish vestries had pretty nearly complete control over
the levying of churchrates — either direct control through their power to
vote or not vote a rate or indirect control through their power to grant or
withhold one of the consents required under the 1819 statute.

These bodies were differently constituted in different parishes.[61] The
traditional or open vestry consisted of whatever parishioners showed up in
response to a notice posted on the church door. But rich parishioners had
up to six times as many votes as poor parishioners under an 1818 act that
applied to most parishes outside London. This difference was felt to be

helpful in getting churchrates voted, since rich people were apt to be more favorable to the church than poorer people were.

Instead of open vestries, many parishes had select vestries, either by statute or by immemorial custom. The customary ones tended to be self-perpetuating: when a member died or resigned, the others chose a replacement. Other self-perpetuating vestries were appointed by commissioners under various church building acts or under local acts. Two statutes provided for select vestries elected by the parishioners. One, from 1831, was optional for urban parishes and large (800 or more ratepayers) rural ones. The other, from 1855, was compulsory for parishes in and around London.

Not all select vestries had power to vote churchrates. It was specifically provided in 1856 that those created under the 1855 act had no such power. If a churchrate was needed, the old vestry had to be convened in the old form, even though all its other powers had passed to the new one. An 1831 case reached the same result with respect to a select vestry created under one of the church building acts. The rationale was that an Act of Parliament should not be construed as taking away an existing right unless it did so expressly, and the right of the whole body of parishioners to make or not make churchrates was an existing right. There were no cases raising the question under the 1831 act, but the same rationale might well have applied.

In addition to the 1819 act authorizing repairs on credit, there were a few other statutes, mostly local, that required the making of a churchrate. Where one of these applied, the writ of mandamus was available to see that the rate was levied — just as it would be available if the vestry did not raise the necessary funds to discharge its civil obligations such as repair of bridges or relief of the poor.[62] But in the absence of a statute, the courts would not issue the writ to compel a churchrate. While they recognized the ancient canonical obligation of the parishioners to keep the church in repair, they insisted that that obligation was of exclusively ecclesiastical cognizance.

The ecclesiastical authorities had no success enforcing this obligation on their own. The two possible alternatives were to coerce the recalcitrant vestries or to bypass them. Both were tried in the 1830s and 40s, and both eventually failed.

The medieval canonists were clear that the parishioners were to be coerced if they failed to make the necessary repairs, but not at all clear on how the coercion was to be accomplished.[63] It was suggested in the nineteenth century, on tenuous evidence, that the medieval remedy of choice had been to lay the parish under interdict — obviously a futile expedient where the people blocking the rate were Dissenters. A dictum of Lord North in 1675 indicated that all the parishioners could be excommunicated, and then absolved one by one as they gave security to vote for a rate at the next vestry meeting. But when this procedure was actually tried, the practical and conceptual obstacles proved insuperable.

In the first place, the ecclesiastical courts were very strict about the conditions that had to be met before the principle could be invoked.[64] Where the rate voted by the vestry was only half enough to meet the estimated cost of the necessary repairs, the only remedy was to spend the money, leave the job half done, and go back to the vestry for more. An inadequate rate was still a rate. Conversely, where a churchwarden joined in a vestry resolution that churchrates were "at all times bad in principle and particularly unjust in practice, and quite uncalled for at the present time," it was held that he was not guilty of anything absent a showing that the church was coming to harm for lack of the necessary funds.

Finally, in 1843, a proceeding got through the church courts successfully.[65] There were sufficient allegations both that the vestry had refused any rate whatever and that the church was in need of repairs. But if the church courts were satisfied, Lord Denman in the Queen's Bench was not. He issued writs of prohibition to stop proceedings against the recalcitrant parishioners. In the first place, he could not get over the conceptual barrier presented by the fact that the offense if any was corporate, whereas the church's power of correction was individual:

> We are by no means satisfied that the refusal to join in making a church rate can be an offence in a parishioner, because it cannot be necessary for all the parishioners to join in making it: a majority may do this act; and if it is done, what offence can there be in refusing to concur in it? If no rate is made, it can hardly be conceived that that default should be produced by the refusal of a single parishioner to concur in imposing one.

Beyond this, Lord Denman found a policy objection. It was against the nature of a deliberative assembly to coerce the members in their deliberations:

> A parish meeting being convened to consider the granting of such rate ... the parishioners go to the meeting to take part in its deliberations and exercise their judgment on the question raised. Must they not examine it with freedom? Are they bound to vote one way? On the contrary, the law permits them to object to the grant proposed; to argue that it ought not to be made; to vote for refusing it.

So much for trying to coerce the vestry.

The effort to bypass them instead gave rise to one of the great ecclesiastical litigations of the nineteenth century, the famous Braintree case.[66] The case is rich in philosophy, technicality, and rhetoric, and deserves to be taken up in some detail. It began in December of 1836, when the parishioners of Braintree in Essex, who had evidently laid out £ 35 two years previously to repair their church, were summoned to a vestry meeting and asked to levy another £ 105. But the parishioners had been converted to the voluntary principle, and had read up on their rights:

Resolved, that it appears to this meeting that the existing law which authorizes churchwardens to convene a parish meeting for the purpose of levying a church-rate does also recognize what is to be called the voluntary principle, to this extent, that by it no church-rate can be laid but by the free consent of the majority of the parishioners duly assembled in vestry to determine upon it; that the parishioners of Braintree are fully prepared to vindicate this redeeming feature of the law as it now stands, by freely exercising the just rights that the law secures to them, and determining for themselves whether a church-rate shall now be laid or not; that having accordingly well considered the proposition to levy a church-rate on the present occasion, and the principles involved in that proposition, it is their matured conviction that, so long as the parochial churches are exclusively devoted to the use of the established sect, all expenses of repairs should be defrayed out of the ample revenues of that richly endowed sect, or if there be no ecclesiastical funds available for such purposes, that all expenses of repairs should be defrayed by the voluntary contributions of those who exclusively enjoy the use of the buildings; and, finally, that the consideration of a church-rate be postponed to this day twelve months.

By the summer of 1837, the estimate for repairs had risen to £ 538/12/ and the churchwardens tried again. A meeting was duly summoned for June 2. The parishioners were as articulate as before, and indignant at being summoned:

That as little more that six months have elapsed since the parishioners of this parish in vestry assembled resolved, by a large majority, that the consideration of the church rate be adjourned for twelve months; the churchwardens have shown themselves to be greatly wanting in that respect to the parishioners, as a body, which is due to them from every parochial officer, in assembling the parish again to agitate the question of church-rate before the expiration of the time to which the consideration of that question had been postponed, and that this meeting cannot but deeply regret that the clergyman of the parish should have given his sanction to a proceeding at once so frivolous and vexatious as that which now calls this numerous assembly of rate-payers from their several occupations; that, thus conveying to the vicar of the parish, and to the churchwardens, the expression of their grave disapprobation for the

uncalled for and improper agitation of the parish, this meeting will give
to the demand of the churchwardens no other answer than that which
they have already within six months received, and which will be found on
the minutes of the vestry, signed by the vicar as chairman (the resolution
of December), — "resolved, that the consideration of a church-rate be
postponed to this day twelve months."

After this resolution was passed by a show of hands, a poll was demanded
and taken — i.e., provision was made for eligible voters, whether or not
they were at the meeting, to come in when they could and vote on the
resolution. When the poll was closed on June 6, the vote was 207 for the
resolution, 70 against.

On June 10, the churchwardens got together and made the rate
themselves at three shillings on the pound of annual value of the ratable
lands. Their attempt to collect it produced the first three of eight reported
decisions stemming from the deterioration of the Braintree church.

The churchwardens' main argument in these cases was provided by the
principle *ubi jus ibi remedium*. It was very clear, and had been since the
fourteenth century, that if the church was in need of repairs the
parishioners were obliged to make a rate. Since ecclesiastical censures
were of little effect and mandamus was not available, the action taken by
the churchwardens should be upheld by process of elimination.

The precedents did very little for this argument one way or the other.
The great eighteenth century commentators were clear that the
churchwardens could act alone if they called a meeting and nobody came,
but not at all clear as to what could be done if the parishioners came and
refused the rate. Sir Simon Degge, whose 1676 treatise on parsons and
their problems was being reissued as late as 1820, "conceived" that the
churchwardens could act alone in such a case, but admitted that others
thought the opposite. One case, *Gaudern* v. *Selby*, decided in the Court of
Arches in 1799, was evidently dug up from manuscript sources for the
occasion. It held that an allegation that a majority of the parishioners had
voted against a rate was not a sufficient defense in a proceeding to collect
the amount due. It was peculiarly worded, and the dates it gave were
impossible. Stephen Lushington, the judge of the London Consistory
Court, had been thirty years in that court without ever hearing of the case.
Since it appeared authentic, however, and came from a higher court than
his own, he felt bound to follow it. But he made pretty clear that he would
have rejected it if he had been free to exercise an independent judgment on
the question.

Lord Denman in the Queen's Bench issued a prohibition against the
enforcement of Lushington's decision in favor or the rate. Needless to say,
he made short work of *Gaudern*. He made almost equally short work of

the *ubi jus* argument. The remedies of excommunication and interdict had worked well enough before the Reformation, and were the exclusive remedies at the time. The fact that they had lost their terror in more recent times did not suffice to create new remedies to take their place. (Like most nineteenth century Protestants, Denman overestimated the terror that ecclesiastical censures had inspired in medieval Catholics.) His decision was unanimously affirmed in 1841 in the Exchequer Chamber, and the proceeding was at an end.

In the summer of 1841, the repairs had still not been made, the estimate had risen to £ 713, and the same churchwardens were still in office. These churchwardens, incidentally, were more zealous for churchrates than most of their confreres were. Since at least one of them must have been elected by the same vestry that kept refusing the rates, it is hard to see how they continued so long in office. In many churchrate cases, one or both of the churchwardens appeared among the defendants.

The churchwardens summoned a meeting in May of 1841, with no success. The vicar then got a monition out of the London Consistory Court ordering the parishioners to assemble for the purpose of making a rate. On July 15, they assembled pursuant to the monition. The estimates were read without objection, but the majority of the vestry was as recalcitrant and as articulate as ever:

> That all compulsory payments for the support of the religious services of any sect or people appear to the majority of this vestry to be unsanctioned by any portion of the New Testament Scriptures, and altogether opposed to, and subversive of, the pure and spiritual character of the religion of Christ. But that for any one religious sect to compel others, which disapprove their forms of worship or system of church government, or which dissent from their religious principles and creeds, to nevertheless submit to, support, and extend them, appears to this vestry to be a yet more obvious invasion of religious freedom and violation of the rights of conscience; while also it appears to be a gross injustice to Dissenters, as citizens, to compel them to pay for the religious services of others, in which they have no part, while they build their own chapels, support their own ministers, and defray the charges of their own worship. That compulsory church-rates, and more especially such rates upon Dissenters, thus appearing to be, as a tax, unjust, and as an ecclesiastical imposition, adverse to religious liberty, and contrary to the spirit of Christianity, this vestry feels bound, by the highest obligations of social justice and of religious principle, to refuse to make a rate, and does refuse accordingly.

This resolution was passed by a show of hands, no poll being demanded.

The churchwardens then proposed that those parishioners who were willing to obey the court's monition should concur in a rate of two shillings in the pound. They did so, over the objections of the majority, and the churchwardens began litigating to collect.

The argument against the rate was obvious. A rate cannot be adopted except by majority vote of the vestry, and there was no majority of the vestry voting for this one. In response, the proponents of the rate came up with an ingenious analogy. If a group of electors meet to choose someone for an office — say a town official or a representative in Parliament — any vote cast for an ineligible candidate is "thrown away," i.e. treated as no vote at all. So if a majority vote for an ineligible candidate, the minority's candidate, if eligible, will be declared the winner, having received the greatest number of the votes effectively cast. Since the law requires the vestry to make a rate, the resolution not to make one is ineligible to be a resolution in the same way a child or a lunatic is ineligible to be a Member of Parliament. So the votes for such a resolution are thrown away, and the remaining voters constitute an effective majority.

The English judiciary split almost evenly on this argument. Lushington in the London Consistory rejected it, but he was reversed by Sir Herbert Jenner Fust in the Court of Arches. Lord Denman, who had granted the prohibition in the previous case, denied it in this one. His decision was affirmed 4-3 in the Exchequer Chamber. From there the case went to the House of Lords, where five judges advised the Lords to affirm it and five to reverse it. Of the Lords themselves, only Lord Truro, who had just stepped down as Lord Chancellor, delivered an opinion on the merits. He was for granting the prohibition, and the House went with him. So in 1853, twelve years after the meeting of the Braintree vestry, it was established as the law of England that a minority of a parish vestry cannot make a churchrate if the majority refuse.

Fortunately, the Braintree church did not fall down.[67] The vicar raised a subscription which was "handsomely responded to," and the restoration of the building went on steadily from 1852 to 1879. Perhaps the contributors were attracted by all the publicity, or perhaps the local ratepayers, having made their point, were willing to contribute. The church is mentioned in several modern guidebooks as well as the *Encyclopedia Britannica* as a good example of Early English.

This completes the roster of attempts to coerce or bypass the vestry. Two other possibilities were mooted but, as far as I know, never tried. One was for the incumbent as ex officio chairman of the vestry to refuse to put an anti-churchrate resolution to a vote. Whatever effect this might have had as a parliamentary maneuver, it would not have produced a majority vote in favor of a rate. The other possibility was for the

churchwardens to call a meeting every night until the opponents of the rate
got tired of coming. But the opponents seem to have been high principled
Dissenters. Their rhetoric bespeaks a good deal of staying power. And in
Braintree there were enough of them so they could take turns coming one
night in three and still be sure of a majority. In short, it was clear from
1853 on that there was no way a churchrate could be made unless a
majority of the parishioners wanted it.

While these things were going on in courts and vestries, the philosophical
issues were being mooted in press and Parliament.[68] The arguments for
making Dissenters pay churchrates were pretty much the same as the ones
that persuade us today that there is no injustice in making Christian
Scientists pay taxes for public hospitals or making Amish parents pay taxes
for public schools. The services benefit the whole community, so it is only
right that the whole community should pay for them. A person may choose
not to take advantage of them, but that does not affect his obligation to pay
his share of the community expense.

If we find this reasoning less persuasive when applied to churches than it
is when applied to hospitals and schools, it is because religious pluralism,
which was a debated principle in the nineteenth century, is a commonplace
today. But note that many dissenters from our arrangements for health
care or education are just as religiously motivated as were nineteenth
century Dissenters from the established church. Nor are they any more
misguided in the eyes of mainstream doctors and educators than nineteenth
century Dissenters were in the eyes of mainstream churchmen. In context,
then, the philosophical arguments in favor of churchrates, while they were
not irresistible, were far from frivolous.

One or two compromises were suggested. For instance, an 1859
pamphleteer proposed letting Dissenters apply their share of the rates to
their own churches.[69] He thought that in this way the vestry might come
to represent all the Christianity of the parish rather than only the
established church. This experiment in grass roots ecumenism was never
tried, so its inventor did not have to deal with hard questions like whether
Dissenters would rate themselves for superfluous ornaments to their own
churches so that Anglicans could be made to pay for necessary repairs to
theirs, or whether if the vestry took responsibility for all the churches in the
parish the one the majority belonged to would not be more sumptuously
provided for than the others.

In 1834 and again in 1837, bills were put forward in Parliament that
would have abolished churchrates and given the newly created Ecclesiastical
Commissioners an equivalent amount — £ 250,000 a year — with which to
finance the necessary repairs.[70] Under the 1834 bill, this sum was to
come out of the general revenues of the state. Naturally, people who
thought Dissenters should not have to pay taxes to repair Anglican

churches did not see this proposal as improving matters. Furthermore, the Land Tax, out of which the funds in question were to come, was inequitably assessed and any increase in its yield would enhance the inequity. So, although the bill was supported by leaders of both parties, it was voted down. The 1837 bill proposed to raise the £ 250,000 by improved management of episcopal and capitular estates. Now it was the churchmen's turn to object. Episcopal and capitular revenues, whether actual or potential, belonged to the church already. They could not be compensation for another source of revenue that was being taken away. The bill was accordingly allowed to die.

For two more decades, the church beat back attacks on churchrates. But with the difficulty of getting vestries to make them and ratepayers to pay them, the game seemed less and less worth the candle. In 1868 the churchmen (or enough of them to get a bill through Parliament) accepted a moderately face-saving solution that made churchrates voluntary instead of abolishing them outright.[71] The vestry could still make them, but no one had to pay them. The voluntary churchrates provided for in this way endured for some time in rural parishes, but by now they are pretty well a thing of the past. It has evidently turned out to be less cumbersome and just as effective to take up a collection as other churches do.

The 1868 legislation preserved compulsory church rates in cases where money had been borrowed on the strength of them and in certain parishes where they were provided for by statute as a substitute for tithe.[72] In these cases, the vestry could still be compelled by mandamus to levy the rates and property owners could still be compelled to pay them. There was a case imposing such a rate as late as 1914.

A suitably ironic conclusion to the churchrate controversy was provided by the 1878 case of *Regina* v. *Lee*.[73] The case involved a church in Lambeth that was in such disrepair that the Metropolitan Board of Works took action against it as a dangerous building. Using their powers under the Metropolitan Buildings Act of 1855, they called on the incumbent to make the necessary repairs, and when he failed to do so, made them themselves and sent the incumbent a bill. But the court said that he was not liable. An incumbent is not the "owner" of a church within the meaning of the statutory provision making the owner of a dangerous building liable for repairs. In fact, nobody is liable for repairs to a church except the parishioners, and under the 1868 act they cannot be made to discharge their liability. So there was no way the Board of Works could be reimbursed for the repairs, and the church was repaired out of public funds after all.

C. Secularization of Functions.

1. Local Government — The separation of church and state at the local level was taking place gradually during most of the nineteenth century, although it was not made fully explicit until the nineties. Outside municipal boundaries, and for some purposes within them, the primordial unit of local government for both secular and ecclesiastical purposes was the parish.[74] Some historians think that in the Middle Ages there was a formal distinction between the secular "vill" and the ecclesiastical parish. I am more persuaded, however, by the alternative view that there was not even a formal distinction before the nineteenth century. On this view, the civil community, whatever its name, became the parish simply by including church affairs among its other concerns.

As we have seen, the traditional parish was governed by a vestry that met in the robing room of the church with the parish incumbent presiding. Its chief officers were called churchwardens, and in most parishes one of them was appointed by the incumbent. Despite these ties with the church, the parish dealt with secular affairs as freely as with ecclesiastical. While most of its functions were fixed by custom or statute, it probably had the power to make bylaws and levy rates for any purpose that commended itself to a majority of the vestry.

Legislation during the nineteenth century operated in several ways to dismantle this venerable hybrid.[75] For one thing, the new parishes that were created under gradually broadening statutory authority beginning with the Church Building Act of 1818 were all parishes for ecclesiastical purposes only. The secular purposes continued to be discharged by the churchwardens and vestry of the original parish. So a substantial number of people became accustomed — not without some false starts to be sure — to taking their secular business to one agency of local government and their ecclesiastical business to another.

Also, a good deal of the innovative legislation that followed the reformist triumph of the 1830s was administered locally by agencies set up for the purpose — highway districts, sanitary districts, and the like — rather than by the traditional parishes. The ancient parish function of poor relief, which had long had its own officials, devolved upon larger units under a series of statutes beginning in 1834. In the process, the residual role of churchwardens and vestry was for the most part eliminated — together, it was said, with the personal concern of the parish clergy for the poor.

With the loss of the poor relief function, followed by the abolition of compulsory churchrates, most parish vestries had no regularly occurring function except the election of churchwardens. Thus, they were not in session regularly enough to exercise a continuing supervision over local affairs, and whatever power they had to take on new functions for the common good lapsed.

The evolution was somewhat different in the London metropolitan area. The Metropolis Management Act, 1855,[76] refurbished the metropolitan parishes — except the ones that existed for ecclesiastical purposes only — provided them with elected vestries, and gave them a variety of municipal functions under the supervision of the newly created Metropolitan Board of Works. These parishes and their vestries retained ecclesiastical functions along with the paving and lighting of streets and the digging of sewers. But a great many new ecclesiastical parishes had been created in the metropolitan area, so that the ecclesiastical jurisdiction of a typical vestry under the 1855 act extended over only a fraction of its secular territory.

The definitive separation between secular and ecclesiastical functions was mainly brought about in the process of organizing local government more effectively for secular purposes.[77] The Local Government Act, 1894, provided rural parishes with parish meetings and parish councils to which were transferred all the powers of vestries and churchwardens except those relating to ecclesiastical affairs. The London Government Act, 1899, abolished all the vestries created under the 1855 act, turned all their secular functions over to the newly created London boroughs, and provided for the creation of an ecclesiastical vestry in any parish that did not already have one.

These laws did not provide for urban parishes outside London. Vestries and churchwardens in such parishes retained a residue of secular functions until 1934, and discharged them along with their ecclesiastical functions until the latter were turned over to parochial church councils in 1921.

2. Courts — In the 1830s, the church courts still retained an extensive jurisdiction over the whole population in matters which according to nineteenth and twentieth century ideas should be dealt with in a secular court or in a court of some religious body to which the litigants belong. Most of this jurisdiction was transferred or abolished in the course of the ensuing reforms.

The most important part of this jurisdiction, the part that kept a whole separate bench and bar at work, was that over decedent estates and marriages. The jurisdiction over decedent estates was peculiar to England even in the Middle Ages. The rationale was evidently that if the testator declared his will orally on his deathbed (the so-called "nuncupative" will) instead of writing it down in advance, the attending clergyman would be in the best position to supervise the proceedings and authenticate the result, and his ecclesiastical superiors would be in the best position to hold him accountable for doing so.[78] This rationale lost much of whatever force it had when auricular confession fell into disuse (some say was abolished) at the Reformation. It became totally anachronistic when nuncupative wills were virtually abolished in 1837.

The matrimonial jurisdiction was of course founded on the religious character of the marriage relation itself. But it was incongruous (as well as uncanonical) for Anglican judges to exercise it when the parties belonged to some other religion or no religion at all. Sir William Scott in the London Consistory Court did a creditable job deciding whether the formalities of Jewish marriage law had been properly observed by a Jewish couple,[79] but it seems an odd assignment for someone whose authority came from an Anglican bishop.

In 1857, the church's probate and matrimonial jurisdictions were transferred to newly created secular courts, which later merged into the Probate, Divorce, and Admiralty Division of the High Court of Justice.[80] The canonical and other principles that the ecclesiastical courts had been applying became, with some statutory modifications (mainly the introduction of divorce *a vinculo*, formerly available only by private bill in Parliament), the secular law on the subject of marriage and probate. The specialized ecclesiastical and admiralty bar was abolished, and its advocates and proctors became ordinary barristers and solicitors. Doctors' Commons, which had served the advocates as an Inn of Court served the barristers, was abolished and its property divided among its current members.

As late as 1835, the church was still collecting most of its own revenues in its own courts.[81] The justices of the peace had been given exclusive jurisdiction over most cases where the claim was uncontested and amounted to less than ten pounds. There were also special provisions for Quakers; they would sooner go to jail than pay money to the church, and the church courts could not levy on their property as the justices could. But otherwise, if you owed money to the church, it was the church courts that made you pay.

This power, rather than being done away with, disappeared with the revenues to which it applied. The rentcharge that replaced tithe in 1836 was collectible by distress rather than by ecclesiastical proceedings. After 1868 most churchrates were not collectible at all. But those churchrates that were not abolished because money had been borrowed or tithes extinguished on the strength of them were still collectible in the church courts unless they were small enough to fall within the exclusive jurisdiction of the justices. So were mortuaries and other compulsory offerings wherever they still existed. As we have seen, mortuaries have now been expressly abolished, and the rest of the payments have become obsolete.

Until 1932, it was the church courts that made lay rectors repair chancels.[82] They could do this only by monition, followed by imprisonment if the monition was disobeyed. The churchwardens could not make the repairs and then collect from the rector, because the church court's jurisdiction extended no farther than was necessary to see to the repairs. Under the Chancel Repairs Act, 1932, the parish was allowed to recover a money judgment in the county court.

The disciplinary power of the church courts over the laity was already moribund, as we have seen. The only survivors into the 1830s were the defamation action, and the action to punish "brawling," i.e., untoward behavior in church or churchyard. The defamation jurisdiction was taken away in 1855.[83] By then, the secular tort proceeding was covering nearly all the ground. The only gap created by the abolition of the church proceeding was in the case of slander of chastity. Until 1891, a woman had to show a pecuniary loss to recover in a lay court when her chastity was impugned. It appears that a man whose chastity is impugned (except a beneficed clergyman) still has no remedy without such a showing.

The church's jurisdiction over brawling was generally invoked only when services were disturbed. Occasionally, though, a vestry meeting would get out of hand, and some of the participants would be subject to discipline because the meeting was held in church.[84] It was held that words in a vestry meeting could not amount to brawling because vestry business required full discussion. But the court drew the line at blows. An act of 1850 provided for moving the vestries of larger parishes into secular quarters. Presumably vestrymen could then belabor each other with the same consequences as befell anyone else doing the same.

Ecclesiastical jurisdiction over brawling by the laity was abolished in 1860.[85] Instead, disturbing religious worship or acting riotously, indecently, or violently in any place of worship or burial of any denomination was made a secular offense. Any constable or churchwarden could arrest the offender and bring him before the justices of the peace, who could fine him up to five pounds or imprison him up to two months. Brawling clergy, however, were still subject to church proceedings — as some of them found out during the ritual controversies.

3. Marriage and Vital Statistics — At the beginning of the reform period, only Quakers or Jews could be legally married in England without going through an Anglican ceremony. This ecclesiastical monopoly was a relatively late development, the result, as far as I can see, of a combination of misapprehension and inadvertence. To understand the effect of the reform legislation, we shall have to trace this development briefly.

During the first half of the eighteenth century, a marriage was uncanonical if it was celebrated without banns or, in the alternative, a license from the local ordinary, and if it was not celebrated in a parish church between the hours of 8:00 A.M. and noon. But it was not invalid. Neither the Canons of 1604 that imposed these requirements nor the statutes of 1696 and 1711 that reiterated some of them purported to make it so.[86]

Whether it was invalid in the absence of an episcopally ordained clergyman is another question.[87] Burn seems to have thought so, although he is cryptic on the point. The seventeenth and eighteenth century authorities cut both ways, and the significance of any one of them is exquisitely debateable. Modern historians, looking at the whole range of evidence, tend to believe that a clergyman may have been required for some of the legal effects of a marriage, but not for mere validity.

Rightly or wrongly, however, enough people in the eighteenth century were convinced that a marriage was not valid without an episcopally ordained clergyman in attendance for a number of down-at-heels clergymen to eke out gin and beer money by performing irregular marriages.[88] Unemployed and often unfrocked, these men were too abject to be vulnerable either to canonical censure or to statutory penalties. Indeed, so many of them were in debtors' prison that the kind of marriages they performed were popularly referred to as Fleet marriages. Note that the requirement or supposed requirement could be fulfilled by any priest or deacon ordained by a bishop. He did not have to have any particular cure of souls. He did not have to be in good standing with the church. A rake, a gambler, a drunkard, or a bankrupt would do so long as he had been ordained by a bishop. More important for our present purposes, a Roman Catholic clergyman would do, although a Presbyterian or a Baptist would not.

In 1753, Lord Hardwicke as chancellor put through a bill to solve the problem of secret and irregular weddings.[89] It made marriages invalid for all purposes unless they met the requirements of banns or license and celebration in church between 8:00 A.M. and noon. The only exceptions were Jews, Quakers, and couples with a special license from the archbishop of Canterbury. The penalty for purporting to solemnize a marriage without meeting these requirements was raised to fourteen years transportation, but the effective sanction was the invalidity of the marriage. It was no longer possible for an heiress to run off and marry a footman or an heir to get drunk and marry a whore. It was also no longer possible for non-Anglicans other than Jews and Quakers to marry in their own places of worship.

The debates on Lord Hardwicke's Act show no thought whatever for the effect of its provisions on Dissenters.[90] Egalitarians argued that the imprudent marriages of the aristocracy played an indispensable part in the redistribution of wealth and power. Justices of the peace argued that waiting for banns would give village swains a chance to run out on their pregnant sweethearts, and public nuptials would allow village gossips to count the months to the birth of the first child. The theologically minded argued that Parliament had no power to make a marriage invalid. But no one mentioned that Dissenters would have to change their marriage practices.

Perhaps the reason was that most Dissenters, when they were not running off to be married in jails and taverns like their Anglican neighbors, were content to be married in the Anglican church. Presumably the legislators who made an exception for Quakers would have been willing to make one for Baptists and Presbyterians if they had been asked. And if Baptists or Presbyterians had been in the habit of marrying before their own ministers, the validity of such marriages could not have been as doubtful as it was. The question would have been decided one way or the other.

Roman Catholics were in a different case from other Dissenters. Having episcopal orders, they could marry validly before their own priests, and until Lord Hardwicke's Act they generally did so. Perhaps the reason no one in Parliament took their practice into account is that they were not numerous and they kept a low profile. Furthermore, simply being a Roman Catholic was illegal at the time, and was to remain so for another twenty-five years. This illegality may have kept them from pressing their claims, or it may have kept others from taking them into account.

The Roman Catholic hierarchy responded to the new legislation by encouraging the faithful to have both Anglican and Roman Catholic ceremonies.[91] Not all the faithful complied. The canon law of their own church did not require any particular form for validity — the decree of the Council of Trent on the subject had not been promulgated in England. So the Anglican ceremony would suffice for both civil and religious validity. On the other hand, people who were led by custom or piety to marry before a priest of their own church could safely omit the Anglican ceremony unless they had a stake in the civil validity of their marriage — which they probably would not have unless they were landowners. It was theoretically possible that the couple could be stood in white sheets for fornication and the priest sent to spend fourteen years in Australia, but neither was very likely. We have seen what was happening to the processes for punishing fornication, and the laws against priests had long been too severe for serious enforcement. It appears that two ceremonies were customary among the gentry, whereas a majority of the humbler folk were content with one or the other.

It is not quite accurate, by the way, to say that Lord Hardwicke's Act required an Anglican ceremony or an Anglican minister. All it required was solemnization in an Anglican church during the specified hours. It was theoretically possible for the couple to walk in with their own minister (as long as he was ordained by a bishop) and have their own service — though I know of no case of its being done.

As matters stood at the beginning of the 1830s, then, only Jews or Quakers could be validly married without going through an Anglican ceremony. On the other hand, it does not appear that the Anglican ceremony was imposed on anyone who could not in conscience accept it, or on anyone whose own religious discipline required an additional ceremony for validity. There was, therefore, a certain plausibility in the argument of some conservatives that the Dissenters' claim to a change in the law was not for the discharge of their consciences, but for an equality of treatment that could only be a prelude to disestablishment.[92]

But there were no such ungenerous views expressed on the floor of Parliament.[93] It was conceded on all sides that the system set up by Lord Hardwicke's Act was an affront to the consciences of Dissenters, even if not formally incompatible with them. Furthermore, it was pointed out that a conscientious Anglican minister might well be affronted by having to perform the ceremony for a couple who regarded it as odious, or even took the occasion to protest publicly against it.

The question was how to meet this grievance without unduly disrupting a system that had worked well enough for a substantial majority of the population. Several expedients were suggested, each with its own objections. The simplest would have been to set up a civil ceremony and require it of everybody for validity. People could then fill in whatever religious ceremony they pleased. This was the system that had been in effect in France since Napoleon's time, and the Roman Catholics of that country — who could scarcely be accused of failing to take seriously the religious aspect of marriage — managed to live with it even if they did not like it. But most Anglicans and many Dissenters were not prepared to follow the French in this regard. So rigid a dichotomy between the civil and the religious spheres was foreign to the English experience. Indeed, I suspect that the success of the French accommodation depended on canonical rules that made the civil ceremony as invalid for religious purposes as the religious ceremony was for civil purposes. Anglicans had no such rules. Many of them could be expected to neglect the religious ceremony entirely if a civil ceremony were to be made compulsory. And even if they were to seek the religious ceremony, some Anglicans wondered if that ceremony could properly be used for a couple that was already married.

Another alternative was to establish a civil ceremony for Dissenters only. Peel introduced a bill to this effect in 1835. But the Dissenters were virtually unanimous in rejecting it. They felt it would indicate that they took a less religious view of marriage than Anglicans did.

Then how about allowing Dissenters to solemnize marriages in their own churches before their own ministers just as Anglicans did? The problem here was how to assure adequate records and provide against clandestinity.

Anglican marriages could be performed only in specific churches, and only after banns or a license. Anglican parishes had to keep registers and record marriages in them. There was no problem with allowing marriages to be performed and recorded in respectable Dissenting congregations, but not all Dissenting congregations were respectable. To form one, a person need only register and take an oath. To let people marry validly in every congregation so formed would be tantamount to bringing back Fleet marriages.

Lord John Russell in 1834 introduced a bill that would have allowed Dissenters to be married in their own churches. It did not quite manage to get around the difficulties. It provided against fly-by-night congregations by not allowing a building to be used for marriages until twenty householders certified that it had been their usual place of worship for at least a year. It provided against clandestinity by leaving the existing system of banns and licenses intact. So, while the bill would have allowed a Dissenting couple to marry in their own church, it would have required them to have their banns read in an Anglican church, or else get a license from an Anglican bishop or his surrogate. This arrangement too was unacceptable to Dissenters. It was also incongruous, and tended to defeat the purpose of the banns. Particularly in an urban parish, the couple involved might be total strangers to everyone who heard the banns.

In 1836, Russell tried again, this time successfully.[94] Legislation adopted in that year set up a network of registrars based on the newly established machinery for administering the poor law. Notice to a local superintendent registrar was provided for in lieu of banns, and a license from the superintendent registrar in lieu of one from the bishop. Twenty-one days after notice or seven days after a license, a couple could be married in the place specified in the notice. This could be either an Anglican church or a building licensed by the superintendent registrar for the purpose. As under the previous bill, a building could be licensed on petition of the owner plus twenty householders who had worshipped there for at least a year. Every marriage in such a building had to take place with the doors open between 8:00 A.M. and noon. There had to be a registrar and two witnesses in attendance, and certain statutory language had to be included in the service. The congregation did not have to keep a register: the attendant registrar would bring a book with him. Couples who did not want to be married in church at all could repeat their vows before the superintendent registrar himself.

For Anglican marriages, the new procedure was optional. Banns and episcopal licenses were still available on the same terms as before. Quaker and Jewish marriages were partially integrated into the new system. Couples did not have to have a registrar in attendance, but they did have to give advance notice to the superintendent registrar. Anglican churches,

Quaker meetings, and synagogues were all provided with register books that they could turn over to the superintendent registrar to complete his files. The registration requirements, incidentally, seem to have taken the courts out of the business of applying the formal requirements of Jewish marriage law. The synagogue official before allowing a marriage to be registered had to satisfy himself that those requirements had been met,[95] and I find no case of a court allowing his determination to be collaterally attacked.

Not everyone entitled to take advantage of the new system did so. Laying the Registrar General's annual report for 1851 alongside the results of the famous Census of Religious Worship taken on Sunday, March 30, of that year,[96] we find that at mid-century 29.5% of the population chose to worship in the Church of England, while 84.9% chose to be married there. 29.2% worshipped in Dissenting churches, but only 6.2% married in them. 39.2% stayed home on Sunday, but only 4.4% married in registry offices. Among non-Anglicans, only Roman Catholics show a larger percentage of marriages (4.2%) than of Sunday worshippers (2.1% of the population).

The cost of the new procedures may have had something to do with the continuing popularity of the old ones. The 1836 act gave a shilling to the superintendent registrar for receiving the statutory notice, and another shilling for issuing the certificate at the end of twenty-one days so that the marriage could take place. The registrar got another five shillings for coming to the wedding with his book. In the Anglican church, the fees for both banns and ceremony were fixed by custom, and generally fixed low before inflation set in.[97] Furthermore, the new procedure required two personal appearances before the superintendent registrar. The registry districts generally comprised several parishes, so that a worker might lose the better part of a day's wages getting there and back. An Anglican marriage, by contrast, required only a visit to the local incumbent to set a date and arrange to have banns read. This could be done in one's own parish, and probably outside of working hours.

The Roman Catholic hierarchy, responding to a Royal Commission in 1866, complained of these extra costs, and also of a few other difficulties.[98] I will leave the details to a footnote. Many of them reflect the poverty of the Catholic working class and the financial precariousness of pastoral work among them. Others bespeak a feeling on the part of the clergy that their own careful procedures are denigrated by the imposition of any additional requirements at all. I have not found any comparable statement of grievances by Protestant Dissenters.

The main grievance was met in 1898 with a statute making it possible to marry in a non-Anglican church without a registrar in attendance.[99] The proprietors or people in charge of a registered building were to designate people by name to perform marriages in that building. Then, if the registrar general was satisfied that marriages would be properly registered and registry books safely kept, the building would be provided with its own book, and the designated persons left on their own. Other grievances, such as they were, remained until shifts in economics or demography deprived them of their force.

A companion bill to the 1836 Marriage Act took the main work of civil registration away from the church.[100] Church registration of christenings, marriages, and burials had been introduced by Thomas Cromwell in 1538, and had been the rule ever since. Statutes of 1694 and 1695 had called for every parish incumbent to be informed of these events and to register them even if they did not happen in his church. These statutes also provided for registering births in families that did not believe in infant baptism. But the main object of the statutes was to tax the events in question, not to assure accurate recording of them. There was a good deal of tolerance for leaving people out of the record — so much so that Burn, without mentioning the statutes at all, assures incumbents that it "seemeth incongruous and unjustifiable" for them to record events occurring outside their churches.

The 1836 Registration Act, leaving baptisms and burials where they were, provided for the registration of births and deaths, using the same registrars as were used in the Marriage Act. As for marriage, Anglican churches, and other congregations that kept their own registers (Quakers and Jews until 1898, most non-Anglicans thereafter) were given duplicate books, and required to forward one copy to the superintendent registrar.

The most vigorous proponents of establishment attacked this measure because it made it possible to have a name and a status in society without being baptized.[101] Together with the secular alternative to church marriage, it effectively cut a substantial part of the population off from their main points of contact with the church. These views were so earnestly presented and in such high quarters (including the archbishop of Canterbury in the House of Lords) that they cannot be written off as merely frivolous. The only concession made to them in the legislation, however, was a provision for adding a baptismal name to the registry entry of birth if the child was baptized within six months. My impression is that the dire predictions of the opponents of the act were not verified — that most people continued to have their children baptized as they continued to be married in church.

4. Education and Charity — Through the first decades of the nineteenth century, most of the educational and charitable enterprise of the nation was still bound up with the established church. The bonds owed more to habit than to doctrine. They dated from times when everyone thought of education and charity as religious matters, and most people thought of religious matters as church matters. As we have seen, most educational and charitable funds were in the hands of lay corporations or lay trustees, and all of them were subject to lay control. But it was still considered fitting for bishops and clergy to be involved, as their medieval predecessors had been.

In most parishes, there were odds and ends of benefactions collected and distributed by the incumbent and the churchwardens.[102] Lists of them are still set up in many churches. Often, too, it was the incumbent or the curate who took the responsibility for what education there was in a parish without an endowed school. A churchman still needed the ordinary's license to teach school, and the Canons of 1604 still offered the parish curate a preference for such a license.

In many cases also, the piety of earlier times had set up elaborate educational and charitable foundations with statutes providing for teachers or governors ("warden" or "master" was the usual title for the latter) to be in holy orders, and pupils or beneficiaries to study catechism or attend church or both. The clerical supervisors were expected to see to the moral and spiritual welfare of their charges, as well as to lead them in the prescribed liturgical observances. Reformed theology had done away with the prayers for the dead that figured so prominently in medieval foundations, but the view that the poor should be more religious than other people continued to flourish among the rich.

Foundations of this kind included the Universities of Oxford and Cambridge, as well as their constituent colleges: until the University of London was founded in 1827, you could not study in an English university without subscribing the Thirty-Nine Articles or teach in one without taking orders.

But most foundations were less prominent than the universities and colleges. The archetypal case is the one described by Trollope in *The Warden*.[103] Here is Trollope's account of Hiram's Hospital as it existed sometime during the 1840s:

> In the year 1434 there died at Barchester one John Hiram, who had made money in the town as a woolstapler, and in his will he left the house in which he died and certain meadows and closes near the town, still called Hiram's Butts, and Hiram's Patch, for the support of twelve superannuated wool-carders, all of whom should have been born and bred and spent their days in Barchester; he also appointed that an alms-house should be built for their abode, with a fitting residence for a warden, which warden was also to receive a certain sum annually out of the rents of the said butts and patches. He, moreover, willed, having had a soul alive to harmony, that the precentor of the cathedral should have the option of being also warden of the alms-houses, if the bishop in each case approved.

From that day to this the charity has gone on and prospered — at least the charity had gone on and the estates had prospered. Wool-carding in Barchester there was no longer any; so the bishop, dean, and warden, who took it in turn to put in the old men, generally appointed some hangers-on of their own; worn-out gardeners, decrepit gravediggers, or octogeneraian sextons, who thankfully received a comfortable lodging and one shilling and fourpence a day, such being the stipend to which, under the will of John Hiram, they were declared to be entitled. Formerly, indeed, — that is, till within some fifty years of the present time, — they received but sixpence a day, and their breakfast and dinner was found them at a common table by the warden, such an arrangement being in stricter conformity with the absolute wording of old Hiram's will: but this was thought to be inconvenient, and to suit the tastes of neither warden nor bedesmen, and the daily one shilling and fourpence was substituted with the common consent of all parties, including the bishop and the corporation of Barchester.

Such was the condition of Hiram's twelve old men when Mr. Harding was appointed warden; but if they may be considered to have been well-to-do in the world according to their condition, the happy warden was much more so. The patches and butts which, in John Hiram's time, produced hay or fed cows, were now covered with rows of houses; the value of the property had gradually increased from year to year, and century to century, and was now presumed by those who knew anything about it, to bring in a very nice income; and by some who knew nothing about it, to have increased to an almost fabulous extent . . . .

For many, many years, — records hardly tell how many, probably from the time when Hiram's wishes had been first fully carried out, — the proceeds of the estate had been paid by the steward or farmer to the warden, and by him divided among the bedesmen; after which division he paid himself such sums as became his due. Times had been when the poor warden got nothing but his bare house, for the patches had been subject to floods, and the land of Barchester butts was said to be unproductive; and in these hard times the warden was hardly able to make out the daily dole for his twelve dependents. But by degrees things mended; the patches were drained, and cottages began to rise upon the butts, and the wardens, with fairness enough, repaid themselves for the evil days gone by. In bad times the poor men had had their due, and therefore in good times they could expect no more. In this manner the income of the warden had increased; the picturesque house attached to the hospital had been enlarged and adorned, and the office had become one of the most coveted of the snug clerical sinecures attached to our church.

Hiram's Hospital had many real life examples to match. The common element in all of them was an endowment for the support of a certain number of scholars or pensioners ("bedesmen" in Trollope's account, "almspeople" in many of the law reports) or both, plus one or more clergymen to take care of them. The combined forces of inflation and economic development would tend to give such an endowment a money income far in excess of what the founder had envisaged.

The founding documents almost invited the clergy to pocket the increase as Hiram's warden did.[104] It had been held as early as 1609 that if the foundation bespoke a general charitable intent (as most but not all did), the increased revenues had to go to beneficiaries of the charity: the trustees or the founder's heir could not have them. But the way most foundations were set up, the master or warden was as much a beneficiary of the charity as were the scholars or pensioners. The foundation was generally not specific about how the avails were to be distributed. In some cases, a fixed sum in shillings and pence was provided for each scholar or pensioner; this made it fairly easy for the master or warden to suppose that the rest was for him. Even if nothing was said either way, a poor person should be content to be fed, sheltered, and clothed, while a clergyman should expect to live as became his cloth. Here is Archdeacon Grantley, the warden's son-in-law, defending the status quo in Hiram's Hospital. First, supported by the opinion of an eminent lawyer, Sir Abraham Haphazard, he explains the situation to the warden and the bishop:

> Under Hiram's will two paid guardians have been selected for the hospital; the law will say two paid servants, and you and I won't quarrel with the name . . . . In point of fact, it being necessary to select such servants for the use of the hospital, the pay to be given to them must depend on the rate of pay for such services, according to their market value at the period in question; and those who manage the hospital must be the only judges of this.

The last point evokes misgivings in the warden, who notes that he himself is the one who mainly manages the hospital. But the archdeacon is not worried:

> Oh well, that's nothing to the question; the question is, whether this intruding fellow, and a lot of cheating attorneys and pestilent dissenters, are to interfere with an arrangement which everyone knows is essentially just and serviceable to the church.

When the archdeacon goes to address the pensioners themselves, both he
and Trollope grow more eloquent:

> As the archdeacon stood up to make his speech, erect in the middle of
> that little square, he looked like an ecclesiastical statue placed there, as a
> fitting impersonation of the church militant here on earth; his shovel hat,
> large, new, and well-pronounced, a churchman's hat in every inch,
> declared the profession as plainly as does the Quaker's broad brim; his
> heavy eyebrows, large open eyes, and full mouth and chin expressed the
> solidity of his order; the broad chest, amply covered with fine cloth, told
> how well to do was its estate; one hand ensconced within his pocket,
> evinced the practical hold which our mother church keeps on her
> temporal possessions; and the other, loose for action, was ready to fight
> if need be in her defence; and below these the decorous breeches, and
> neat black gaiters showing so admirably that well-turned leg, betokened
> the decency, the outward beauty and grace of our church establishment.

From this stance, he begins castigating the old men for asking for more
than they have been receiving:

> When John Hiram built a hospital for worn-out old men, worn-out old
> labouring men, infirm old men past their work, cripples, blind, bed-
> ridden, and such like, do you think he meant to make gentlemen of
> them? Do you think John Hiram intended to give a hundred a year to
> old single men, who earned perhaps two shillings or half-a-crown a day
> for themselves and families in the best of their time? No, my men, I'll
> tell you what John Hiram meant; he meant that twelve poor old worn-
> out labourers, men who could no longer support themselves, who had no
> friends to support them, who must starve and perish miserably if not
> protected by the hand of charity; he meant that twelve such men as these
> should come in here in their poverty and wretchedness, and find within
> these walls shelter and food before their death, and a little leisure to
> make their peace with God . . . .
>
> Now let me ask you, . . . do you think you are worse off than John
> Hiram intended to make you? Have you not shelter, and food, and
> leisure? Have you not much more? Have you not every indulgence
> which you are capable of enjoying? Have you not twice better food,
> twice a better bed, ten times more money in your pocket than you were
> ever able to earn for yourselves before you were lucky enough to get into
> this place?

In Trollope's novel, this reasoning was deployed in support of a warden who
took in eight hundred pounds a year, while his twelve poor charges made
twenty-four pounds, six shillings, and eightpence each. In real life, the

same reasoning was making clergymen entirely comfortable receiving upwards of a thousand pounds while supporting their charges at less than ten.[105] Many charities were set up in such a way as to limit the number of beneficiaries. The founder generally said how many pensioners were to be supported (though the managers often kept fewer). The number of scholars was apt to be more flexible, but it was commonly limited by restrictions on the area from which they were to be drawn or the type of education they were to receive. Lord Eldon had decided some years previously that a seventeenth century foundation was bound to a seventeenth century curriculum.[106]

The resulting education — mostly Latin and Greek — was still customary among the aristocracy, but it was of little use to people who expected to work for a living. A schoolmaster in Brentwood, Essex went from six or seven scholars up to a hundred when he substituted reading, writing, and arithmetic for the traditional curriculum, and then went back to six or seven when Lord Eldon's strictures were imposed on him. Here, as elsewhere, the restrictions on the scope of the charity meant more money and less work for the clergyman in charge.

To cope with all this obsolete and misappropriated charity, the law had but one weapon — the doctrine of cy-près. Under this doctrine, where a testator or settlor indicated a general charitable intent, but his benefaction could not be applied to the specific object he ordered, it was lawful to apply it to a related charitable object instead. Unfortunately, this doctrine could not be invoked where the original object was merely useless instead of impossible — another of Lord Eldon's contributions to the law on the subject.[107]

Sir John Leach, Master of the Rolls from 1827 to 1834, devised a principle that would have made cy-près effective in bringing many old foundations up to date.[108] In the *Brentwood School* case (1833), he reasoned that the clergyman in charge of such a foundation is entitled to no more than the fair value of his services. Any income that is not needed to pay him that, and is not needed to meet specific benefactions provided for by the founder, can be applied cy-près to related charitable objects chosen by the court. But Leach's initiative was not to be followed. The Chancellor, Lord Brougham, reversed a decision of his in a rather similar case, also in 1833. It appeared that the two cases could not be reconciled, and the authority of the higher judge was naturally regarded as superseding the good sense of the lower. In any event, Leach appears to have had the reputation of an eccentric despite (or perhaps because of) his good sense on this subject.

The enforcement of charities was in an even worse way procedurally than it was substantively.[109] The 1601 act discussed in the last volume had

fallen into disuse by the middle of the eighteenth century, for reasons not
altogether clear. It was partly that commissions under the act were issued
ad hoc, and local magnates became less and less willing to serve on them.
The complexity of Chancery proceedings on appeal from the commissioners
was also a factor. So, probably, was a general hardening in the attitude of
the upper classes toward the poor, a phenomenon noted by social historians
of the eighteenth century. In any event, the last commission under the
1601 act was issued in 1787, worked its way to Lord Eldon's bench in 1803,
and was not disposed of until 1818.

Enforcement by the Attorney General was available and used. But the
Attorney General did not usually move on his own initiative. He acted at
the behest of a relator, and the relator had to pay the costs if the Attorney
General lost the case. The prospect deterred so many people from
becoming relators that there were never enough to enforce all the charities
that needed enforcing.

Reform of this situation impinged on so many vested interests and so
many ideological presuppositions that it was a long time coming.[110]
Commissions were investigating and reporting all through the 1820s and
'30s. But, except for a very gingerly permission to expand the curriculum
of grammar schools, no legislation ensued until the adoption of the
Charitable Trusts Act, 1853 and the Endowed Schools Act, 1869.

The 1853 act created a body called the Charity Commissioners,
empowered to investigate the affairs of charities and bring appropriate
proceedings for reforming them. With respect to smaller charities, whose
funds could be eaten up by Chancery proceedings, an 1860 amendment
allowed the Commissioners to take action without resorting to court. But
none of this legislation changed the substantive law. Neither the
Commissioners nor any court could do more than develop a scheme for
carrying out the founder's original purpose, or, if that was not possible, for
applying the funds according to the doctrine of cy-près. If more needed to
be done, the Commissioners had power to submit a scheme to Parliament.
But Parliament proved so chary of enacting such schemes as to discourage
the Commissioners from submitting them.

The 1869 act was much more sweeping. It applied only to educational
foundations, and not to all of them, but where it applied, it authorized the
commissioners (new ones were provided for in this act, but they were
abolished in 1874, and their functions turned over to the ones appointed
under the 1853 act) to depart as far as necessary from the founders'
intentions in order to develop a rational scheme for applying the funds.

Whether charities were reformed by the courts, by the Commissioners,
or by the legislature, the reform was apt to include elimination of any
preference for churchmen among the administrators or the beneficiaries. It
was held as early as 1837, when municipal governing bodies were being

replaced as trustees under the provisions of the 1835 Municipal Corporations Act, that no such preference would be given unless the founder had expressly provided for it.[111] The 1853 act provided that preferences enjoyed by the Church of England under existing law or court order should be preserved. But the provision did not protect a customary preference unless there was a legal basis for it, and the courts generally did not find a legal basis unless they had to.[112] The 1869 act forbade requiring trustees, masters, or pupils to be of a particular religion unless the school was endowed out of church funds, or unless instruction in the tenets of a particular religion was expressly provided for by the founder.

Applying the exceptions often involved a subtle analysis. Was a foundation set up in the 1400s with provision for its inmates to attend mass and pray for the dead turned into a Church of England charity by the Reformation? Can we infer that a Jacobean founder intended to benefit Anglicans from the fact that no other religion was legal at the time? The fact that a person is a Dissenter does not mean that he can be excluded from Communion in the Church of England. Does it follow that a provision that beneficiaries receive Communion does not make the charity one limited to Anglicans? All of these questions had to be decided by the courts.[113]

In 1857, in the case of *Attorney General* v. *Calvert*,[114] Sir John Romilly as Master of the Rolls laid down a set of ground rules that made good sense, and were generally accepted. He divided charities into three categories, religious, educational, and purely eleemosynary. He reasoned that the founder of a religious charity would naturally have his own religion in mind. Accordingly, both trustees and beneficiaries should be of the founder's religion. On the other hand, if a charity is purely eleemosynary, it is not to be supposed without "a clear and distinct expression of unequivocal import" that the founder intended to impose any kind of religious test:

> No doctrine of law, no precept of religion, establishes, that the act of relieving a fellow creature from the privations or calamities which have befallen him ought to be preceded by ascertaining that he holds opinions in accordance with the true doctrine of Christ, as promulgated in the Gospel, or with those which the donor believes to be such. The duty of relieving his fellow creature in distress is imposed on the Christian irrespective of religious doctrines and tenets, and notwithstanding that the object of charity may worship God in an erroneous manner, but in that which he believes to be most acceptable to his Creator.

Educational charities are in an intermediate case. Here, in the absence of contrary evidence, it will be presumed that the founder intended to make secular education available to anyone who might benefit from it. Since religion is necessarily a part of a complete educational program, and religious instruction is necessarily instruction in some particular religion, it is appropriate to include instruction in the founder's religion as part of the program.[115] But unless the founder has clearly provided otherwise, dissenters from his religion will be permitted to take the secular instruction and get their religious instruction elsewhere.

These categories were the beginning, not the end, of analysis. There was first the matter of deciding which one of them to apply.[116] Founders tended to mix religious and secular objects with great abandon, and to impose extraneous pieties on the recipients of their secular aims. One case involved a 1614 donation to support a school, a set of almshouses, and a preacher — all three categories in one. A particularly celebrated case, *Baker* v. *Lee*, in the House of Lords involved a provision for instructing the local youth in godly learning, and using the rest of the funds to repair the local highways and bridges. The Master of the Rolls was prepared to allow three trustees of this charity (out of twenty) to be Dissenters. The Lords Justices of Appeal in Chancery overruled him, and were affirmed by an equal division of the House of Lords. This case was interpreted in a later Chancery case as holding that the classification of the whole charity will depend in every case on which of the three purposes is the predominant one.

There was also a problem determining what a founder's religion was. If there was no evidence on the point, Romilly would presume that it was "the established religion of the country." Since, as we have seen, the differentiation of religious bodies came about only gradually, this presumption made most founders before the eighteenth century into Anglicans. It was ingeniously argued in *Baker* v. *Lee* that the same presumption made contemporary Dissenters into Anglicans as well:

> The law knows no distinction between Churchman and dissenter. All parishioners have a right to seats in the Church, all may be buried in the churchyard, and all may be compelled to be churchwardens; nor is there any rule of law which supplies a test to distinguish them.[117]

It might have been added that all, barring "notorious evil livers," were entitled to receive Communion in the parish church. Lord Campbell gave this argument shorter shrift than it deserved:

> Nonconformists, as a class having serious disabilities and some privileges, have long been recognized by Acts of Parliament and in judicial proceedings. The distinction is reasoned upon by both sides in this suit, and the three gentlemen whose appointment as trustees is in controversy are admitted not to be members of the Church of England.[118]

Another of Romilly's presumptions turned pre-Reformation Catholics into Anglicans.[119] Accepting that the Church of England was the same church before and after being reformed, he held that the important thing about a pre-Reformation founder was not that he adhered to the jurisdiction of the pope or to Catholic doctrines concerning the Eucharist or prayers for the dead, but that he adhered to the established religion of the country. When that was reformed by Edward VI or Elizabeth, his foundation was reformed with it. But such of his religious intentions as remained legal remained in force.

There was yet another problem deciding what those intentions were. All of Romilly's presumptions were open to refutation by evidence to the contrary, and there was a good deal of question whether a given piece of evidence was to the contrary or not. In the *Calvert* case itself, Romilly had to decide whether a provision for the almspeople to attend church made it impossible for Dissenters to be included among them. He decided that it did not:

> I am unable to see anything in this will which should exclude any Dissenters from obtaining the benefit of the charity created by it, who can conscientiously comply with the directions laid down by the founder, modified as they are, by the change produced by the Reformation and the statutes which have since passed. Whether the Dissenter can do so or not is an affair between God and his own conscience, but, as I conceive the duties imposed upon the trustees, it is not an affair on which they are called upon to judge.[120]

Later in the century, an attempt was made to apply this reasoning to a case where the foundress of a set of almshouses had required the beneficiaries of her charity to receive Communion as well as to attend church. There was good authority for saying that Dissent, as such, was not a ground for repelling anyone from the Sacrament if he was willing to receive it, and the Charity Commissioners made use of this authority to argue that Dissenters were eligible for accommodation in these almshouses if they were willing to fulfill the condition. But Stirling, J., was not persuaded. He noted that the rubrics in the Prayer Book provided that no one was to be admitted to Communion who was not either confirmed or ready and desirous to be confirmed. He suggested that a person who received Communion in the same spirit as a Georgian officeholder subject to the Test Act would lack some of the moral and spiritual qualities that the foundress hoped to find in her almspeople.[121]

This case arose not under the 1853 act and its amendments, but under the Local Government Act, 1894, one of the laws, already taken up, that split the ecclesiastical from the secular functions of local government.[122]

Implementing these laws required the division of parochial charities between ecclesiastical and secular, so that the latter could be turned over to the new agencies of secular government. In making this division, the Charity Commissioners and the courts continued to use the classification developed by Romilly in the *Calvert* case.

The acts we have been considering did not apply to the universities or their colleges: these were dealt with under acts of their own.[123] The first relaxation of religious restrictions was inserted almost as an afterthought in a bill making sweeping reforms at Oxford in 1854. The companion bill for Cambridge, adopted in 1856, provided the same relaxations, presumably for symmetry. What these bills did was abolish any oaths, declarations, or subscriptions required for matriculation, or for any bachelor's degree except in divinity. These abolitions turned out not to be very controversial. Their acceptance evidently owed as much to Anglicans as to Dissenters. Even if one accepted the Thirty-Nine Articles, one might think that subscribing them was too heavy a burden for the conscience of a young man who had not studied theology.[124]

While these acts made it possible for Dissenters to take degrees, they maintained the ecclesiastical character of the faculty and administration by providing that no one could occupy a position for which a degree was required without taking the oaths and making the declarations and subscriptions formerly required for the degree. Nor did the acts touch any requirement of chapel attendance and the like that might be imposed by an individual college, or the pervasive requirement that college fellows be ordained. The colleges were empowered to relax the standards of eligibility for their fellows, but it does not appear that they were in a hurry to relax this one. The chief concern was with geographical restrictions — more founders than not had chosen to bestow their bounty on people from particular parts of the country.[125]

On paper, faculty and administration were opened to Dissenters by the Universities Tests Act, 1871. It provided that no religious test of any kind could be required for eligibility for any office or teaching position in any college, or for any degree except in divinity (the previous acts had covered only the baccalaureate). Nor could any person be required to attend lectures to which he (or his parents if he was a minor) objected on religious grounds, or public worship in any church to which he did not belong.

There were some qualifications. The act was not to interfere with existing provisions for religious education or for chapel services, except to the extent of exempting objectors from the former and non-Anglicans from the latter. Indeed, every existing college was obliged to keep up the services, and to provide religious instruction for all Anglican students *in statu pupillari* (i.e., persons below the degree of M.A.). It was also provided that the act should not affect eligibility for offices outside the universities, and that it should not make laymen eligible for positions reserved to the clergy.

Since the college fellowships were in fact still reserved to the clergy, it took another act to complete the work of the 1871 act. The Oxford and Cambridge Act, 1877, set up a body of commissioners for each university, with power during the ensuing four years to make sweeping financial, organizational, and pedagogical reforms, including a complete overhaul of all the college statutes. Their enactments were subject to the approval of the Privy Council, and could be vetoed by either house of Parliament, but they did not require any consent from the college affected. There had been similar commissions under the 1854 Oxford act and the 1856 Cambridge act, but their statutes could be thrown out on two-thirds vote of the governing body of the college. This time, the college could send three commissioners to sit with the main body (though there had to be four of the latter for a quorum), but it could not block a proposed statute. After the commissioners went out of existence, the colleges could amend or repeal the resulting statutes, but only with the approval of the Privy Council, again subject to veto by either house.

The commissioners made a pretty clean sweep of requirements that fellows be in orders.[126] They allowed each college at least one clerical fellow or chaplain to carry out the program of religious education mandated by the 1871 act; they annexed a few fellowships to professorships of divinity whose holders had to be clergymen; and they allowed for special situations such as that of Christ Church, Oxford, which was a cathedral as well as a college. Otherwise, they opened fellowships to anyone with the intellectual qualifications. Of course, since the requirement of orders was the only religious requirement preserved by the 1871 act, opening a position to laymen automatically opened it to Dissenters.

This course of legislation affected only colleges in existence at the time.[127] It was possible, therefore, for religious groups to set up new foundations limited to their own members. Anglicans took up the option within the next few years, founding Keble College in Oxford and Selwyn College in Cambridge.

The educational endowments rescued and updated by the measures we have been considering were far from sufficient to meet the full need of a nineteenth century industrial society. It seems to have been widely supposed that the social unrest of the first half of the century could have been avoided by suitable moral and religious instruction of the lower classes. Further into the century, it became apparent also that an increasingly complex technology was going to require a better educated

workforce than was presently available: there was real danger that the
Germans, educated with ruthless efficiency for a generation or more, would
gain a competitive edge. Finally, with successive extensions of the
franchise, it became possible to foresee a time when the country would be
ruled over by illiterates. Provision of more and better schools was an item
on many agendas throughout the century.[128]

The Church of England had a considerable advantage in the enterprise.
It was usually considered appropriate, even if not obligatory, for the parish
clergy to interest themselves in education,[129] so the parochial and
diocesan structure offered a framework around which further efforts could
be organized. These efforts met with a good deal of success. The National
Society for Promoting the Education of the Poor in the Principles of the
Established Church (National Society for short), founded in 1811, quickly
outstripped the nondenominational British and Foreign School Society,
founded in 1804. By the 1830s, about a quarter of the school age children
in England were in Church of England schools, with only a fraction of that
number in Dissenting or Roman Catholic schools. Some of the schools in
question were modest, conducted in a spare room by the parson, the parish
clerk, or a farmer's wife. Others, though, were in capable hands, supervised
by the National Society, a diocesan school board, or both.

Some of the children who were not in full time schools attended Sunday
schools, where they picked up a modicum of literacy along with their
religious education. Others were in factory schools, maintained by their
employers to comply with ill-enforced statutory requirements. But a
substantial majority of school age children were still receiving no education
at all, and it did not appear that existing arrangements could be expected to
fill the gap.

So it seemed that the state would have to involve itself in some
systematic way. But each of the ways proposed ran afoul of one or another
of the political and religious constituencies with a stake in the matter. The
Benthamite liberals, who were behind so many of the reform initiatives of
the period, favored a uniform nationwide system of secular education on
the American or the Prussian model. This approach was opposed by the
numerous opponents of centralization in general, and by religionists of
every persuasion, who were convinced that secular education could not be
separated from its theological foundation. In 1835, in the first flush of
reformist enthusiasm, Bentham's disciple J.A. Roebuck presented a bill
embodying his party's approach. It was withdrawn in the face of all but
universal opposition.

On the other hand, any approach that involved a privileged position for
the Church of England was opposed by Dissenters even more vigorously
than by Benthamites. The Dissenters, still in the process of fighting off
tithes and churchrates, were prepared to see an invasion of their rights in

any use of public funds to support any function of the established church. When it came to education, their attitude was further hardened by the progress of the Anglo-Catholic movement in the 1830s and '40s. The Wesleyans, who had previously sided with Anglicans on a number of issues, were particularly affected by this development:

It has been publicly stated that *one* ground of our strenuous opposition to the lately-projected measure of public education was, its obvious tendency to give the Clergy of the established Church, an unfair and undue control over the religious teaching in the schools which it would have established. We think it right to confirm this statement, not out of any hostile feeling to the Established Church as such, for this has never been the feeling of our Body, but with a view to bear our distinct and solemn testimony against those grievous errors which are now tolerated within her pale. We have been hitherto accustomed to regard her as one of the main bulwarks of the Protestant faith; but her title to be so regarded has of late been grievously shaken.[130]

The "lately projected measure" referred to in this passage was a part of Sir James Graham's Factory Bill, presented to Parliament in 1843. Its object was to implement more effectively the requirement, introduced by the Factory Act of 1833, that children working in factories attend school. In every place where there were not sufficient schools certified by the National Society, the British and Foreign Society, or the Roman Catholic authorities, the bill would have provided for a new school governed by seven trustees — one Anglican clergyman, two churchwardens, two ratepayers, and two mill owners. These provisions were at first well received by the Commons, but they evoked so much objection around the country that they were finally withdrawn. No further attempt was made to give the Church of England special status in any general program of education.

The Dissenters would evidently have been content to leave education to private philanthropy as they did religious worship — a position which Macaulay likened to leaving the defense of the realm to private philanthropy.[131] Many of them continued to protest the injustice of using their tax money for the support of teaching that they did not believe in, but most of them were finally willing to settle for getting their share of whatever money was being spent.

The government began spending money in 1833, solving the religious problems involved by dividing its first grant, £ 20,000, between the National Society and the British and Foreign Society. The government hit on various expedients for allocating the grants fairly. The most usual was making them proportional to funds raised from private or denominational sources. Making them proportional to number of pupils and examination success was tried instead for a few years, but it was objected to as impairing the quality of the education offered — especially in subjects, including religion, that were not examined on.

In 1839, the government set up an agency to administer its grants and inspect the schools receiving them. Not caring to move so delicate a matter through Parliament, it resorted to an Order in Council, empowering a committee of the Privy Council (the "Committee of Council on Education") to provide for the actual inspection of the schools and distribution of the funds. The standards for government funding were set by the Minutes of this committee until 1870.

The church authorities at first resisted the government's program. While they recognized that funds could not be distributed without some idea of how they were being spent, they objected on principle to submitting church schools to state inspectors. Fortunately, in 1840, before the dispute got out of hand, a compromise was reached. It was agreed that the two archbishops should have a continuing veto over the appointment and retention of inspectors assigned to Church of England schools in their respective provinces, that their instructions with respect to religious education should form a part of the official instructions to inspectors assigned to their schools, and that copies of all reports concerning Church of England schools should be sent to the archbishop of the province and the bishop of the diocese affected.[132] Similar arrangements were made with the Dissenters' British and Foreign Society in 1843. Further battles were fought and further compromises reached over the adoption by the Committee of Council of "management clauses" requiring lay representation on the governing bodies of state-aided church schools, and a "conscience clause" requiring such schools to exempt the children of Dissenters from religious instruction and worship.

It was not until 1870 that a comprehensive statutory program was finally adopted. The Elementary Education Act of that year[133] was drafted to affect as little as possible the subsidized voluntary arrangements that were already in place. It denominated each city and each rural parish a "school district," and provided that if any such district did not have enough schools to accommodate all its children, the Committee of Council (newly named the Department of Education) would give it six months to make suitable arrangements to repair the deficiency. Failing such arrangements, the Department would set up a school board elected by the statutory voters in the city, the ratepayers in the country. This board would then provide the necessary schools, drawing on the local rates for whatever money was needed and not available from other sources.

Parliamentary grants were continued on about the same terms as before to schools meeting the standards laid down in departmental minutes. But no school could be given a grant greater than its income from other sources — contributions and fees in the case of schools not provided by a board, those plus rates in the case of a board school. No distinction was to be made between schools provided and schools not provided by school boards. However, in the case of a board school, a further grant was provided for if a rate of threepence in the pound failed to yield the greater of twenty pounds or seven shillings sixpence per pupil.

New schools were to be included in the grant system on the same terms as old ones unless the Department found a particular school to be "unnecessary." Where there was no school board, the Department practice was to regard any school as necessary that had thirty pupils. But where there was a board, the Department tended to defer to its determination of the question of necessity. Roman Catholics complained of this tendency as exposing them to the danger of losing grants "either on account of the anti-Catholic feeling of the board, or the general Nonconformist dislike to denominational education of all kinds."[134] I suspect that Anglicans had the same trouble in some places. The Department became more chary of board determinations later in the century, but the problem was not fully solved until the thirty pupil rule was made statutory in 1902.

Besides parliamentary grants, the 1870 act gave non-provided schools one further source of public funds through a provision empowering school boards to pay fees in any such school for any child whose parents could not afford them. These payments were entirely discretionary with each board, and there were great local differences in them. The Manchester board used them with such good effect that it was able to put off for some years the necessity of providing any schools of its own. The Birmingham board, on the other hand, refused to make any fee payments at all. Fee payments seem to have aroused more opposition than parliamentary grants; I am not sure why.

The act forbade making any parliamentary grant "in respect of any instruction in religious subjects." Since the grants were given to the whole school rather than to any particular program, it is not clear what that prohibition accomplished. More significant was the accompanying provision that the government inspectors were no longer to inspect the religious aspects of the education offered. The people in charge of a school could arrange for denominational authorities to make their own inspection at a different time from the government inspectors.

Non-provided schools were subject to the "conscience clause," which forbade requiring pupils to be of any particular religion, permitted parents to withdraw pupils from any religious observance or instruction offered, and required that such observances or instruction be at the beginning or end of the school day, so that non-participants could avoid them by coming late or leaving early.

The board schools were also subject to this conscience clause. In addition, they were subject to the "Cowper-Temple clause" (named after the man who introduced it), which forbade the teaching of any "religious catechism or religious formulary which is distinctive of any particular denomination." Most boards provided for Bible study under this provision; a few gave no religious education at all.

The scheme laid down in the 1870 act remained in effect with only minor alterations for the rest of the century, with continuing pressure on the non-provided schools to raise enough money to keep up their end.[135] An act of 1876 gave such schools a minimum parliamentary grant of seventeen shillings sixpence per pupil even if they failed to raise that much. In 1891, another act provided ten shillings per pupil to any school that would agree to charge no fees (or to reduce its fees by ten shillings if they were formerly higher). But by 1893 the two figures together were already ten shillings short of the average per pupil cost in the Church of England schools.

Under the act, a non-provided school could be turned over to a school board. It would then be run as a provided school. However, the transfer could be conditional. Accordingly, some transferred schools were allowed to maintain a modicum of denominational education despite the Cowper-Temple clause.[136] Schools were often forced to agree to transfers when they could not otherwise make ends meet. Sometimes the transfer evoked disagreement that found its way into the courts. It was held that the National Society had no standing to challenge a transfer agreed to by the trustees of one of their schools, that intention to transfer was not an objection to a person chosen as a trustee of a Church of England school, and that the property of a school that could no longer operate as a church school had to be applied cy-près to non-denominational education in preference to non-educational church purposes.[137]

It seems to have been the financial pressure on the non-provided schools that was the chief reason for the Education Act of 1902.[138] That act abolished school boards, made every county or borough council into a "local educational authority," and required every such authority to "maintain and keep efficient" every necessary elementary school in its district. The cost of doing so was to be met partly out of the rates, and partly out of a parliamentary grant based on the number of pupils in attendance in the district. The Board of Education (a proper government agency under a minister, set up in 1899 to replace the Committee-Department set up in 1839 and renamed in 1870) had power to decide whether a non-provided school was necessary, but it could not call a subsisting school unnecessary if it had thirty pupils in attendance.

Provided schools continued to be subject to the Cowper-Temple clause in the 1870 act. Non-provided schools were to offer religious education in accordance with their founding trusts. The House of Lords held in 1907 that such religious education had to be paid for along with the rest of the program of a school.[139]

In exchange for their new financial responsibilities, the public authorities got new powers over the non-provided schools.[140] They appointed one-third (normally two out of six) of the governing body. They had power to make binding directions concerning secular instruction. They could "on educational grounds" veto the appointment of any teacher or require the dismissal of any teacher once appointed. They could also veto the dismissal of any teacher by the governing body unless the dismissal was "on grounds connected with the giving of religious instruction." In a case where an Anglican teacher was fired for becoming a Methodist, it was held that the personal convictions or practices of a teacher did not constitute a ground connected with the giving of religious instruction.

The 1902 act authorized, but did not require, the local authority to support secondary education as well as elementary. Support, if undertaken, was not to be conditioned on the giving or not giving of denominational education in a non-provided school. A provided school was to have no denominational education unless the parents arranged for it at private expense.

The system established in 1902 endured with only minor changes until 1944.[141] The scheme set up in that year, applicable to both elementary and secondary schools, is still pretty well in place. It divides the non-provided (now called "voluntary") schools into "aided" and "controlled." The aided schools retain about the measure of autonomy afforded under the 1902 act, but to maintain that status they have to pick up a fraction (50% under the original act, reduced to 15% by 1975) of the cost of keeping their buildings and equipment up to government standards. Any school that cannot support this burden has to become a controlled school. In a controlled school, the public authorities appoint two-thirds (raised to four-fifths in 1980) of the governing body, and all the teachers. The rest of the governing body (called "foundation managers" or "foundation governors" because they represent the original founders of the school) are authorized to arrange for two periods a week of religious instruction in accordance with the trust deed or traditional practice of the school, and to demand that twenty percent of the teaching positions be reserved for people they find qualified to give such instruction.

Under the 1944 act, every school must have collective worship, and every school must have some kind of religious instruction, subject in both cases to the right of parents to have individual pupils excused. The voluntary schools, both controlled and aided, are evidently free to worship according to the uses of the denomination that set them up, whereas the provided schools must have non-denominational worship. Similarly, the instruction in the provided schools is still subject to the Cowper-Temple clause.

An innovation is the provision for an agreed syllabus of non-denominational instruction. Each authority has to set up a committee to develop such a syllabus. The committee must have representatives of the Church of England and of such other bodies as local circumstances make appropriate. It appears that ecumenism has progressed to the point that committees constituted in this way are in fact able to develop the necessary syllabi, or to agree on syllabi developed elsewhere.[142] If they fail to do so, however, the central government will impose a syllabus.

From an Anglican standpoint, there is much food for rueful reflection in this account of the progress of state supported education. The church fought long and hard for its own schools because churchmen felt that Christianity was a whole way of looking at the world. They believed that secular education could not be separated from denominational education.[143] The utilitarian goal of a religiously neutral secular education and the Dissenting goal of a nondenominational religious education were for them as unacceptable intellectually as they were morally.

But there was no way the state could support an educational enterprise conceived in such terms as these. Even conceding the theoretical dependence of every branch of knowledge on theology, utilitarians could not be expected to trust clergy and bishops to supervise the imparting of the practical skills required for daily living in an increasingly complex society. Indeed, the clergy and bishops were slow to make up their minds that there was anything besides Bible and catechism that the lower classes needed to know.[144] As for the Dissenters, whatever their views of the relation between revealed truth and secular knowledge, they could not be expected to accept any arrangement that paid their tax money into the established church.

The result was a standoff. Every party had enough power to block the others' agendas, but not enough power to implement its own. Compromise was imperative, and the obvious basis for compromise was for the state to take control of secular education, and leave religious education to the church. The resulting compartmentalization became more rigorous with every new measure that was adopted. The theoretical inseparability of temporal and spiritual branches of knowledge could not stand up against the political realities of a pluralist society.

5. *Burial* — It appears that at common law the survivors (sometimes the executors, sometimes the next of kin, sometimes merely the people who happened to have the corpse on their hands) were obliged to make some decent disposition of the body of a deceased person, but were not bound to

any particular way of doing so.[145] Every baptized person who was neither a suicide nor an excommunicate had a theoretical right to be buried in the churchyard of his own parish or in that of the parish where he died. But there was no way this right could be enforced if those who made the arrangements chose to bury him somewhere else. There was no law against burial on private property unless it constituted a nuisance, and the corpse once buried could not be dug up without authority, even for the purpose of burial in a churchyard. In 1884, it was even held lawful to burn a corpse if it was not done in such a way as to offend the neighbors or to frustrate the coroner.

There was accordingly no obstacle to Dissenters having their own burial grounds, and many of them did.[146] However, most mainstream Dissenting congregations continued to use the churchyard. Also, even if a congregation had its own burial ground, individual members might be buried in the churchyard, either to keep families together or because the fees were less. Dissenters, as such, were not barred from Anglican burial.[147] It was argued in a couple of cases that they were unbaptized because the ministers who baptized them were not validly ordained, but the courts, following the more common theological opinion, held that lay baptism is valid. There was also a rubric excluding excommunicates, which could be put together with certain provisions of the Canons of 1604 that seemed to excommunicate all Dissenters. On the other hand, it was not clear that the rubric survived the 1813 statute limiting the civil disabilities and incapacities consequent upon excommunication. In any event, under the decision in *Middleton* v. *Crofts* (1736), the Canons of 1604 did not bind the laity. And even if they did, their provisions penalizing Dissent would probably be superseded by the Toleration Act.

Although Dissenters could be buried in the churchyard, they had to be buried with Anglican services rather than their own. Dissenters could hold funeral services in their own church before coming to the graveside, but the Anglican incumbent had both the right and the duty to read the Prayer Book office at the grave, and he and the churchwardens and the sexton were entitled to customary fees.[148] Dissenters naturally found this situation to be a grievance. Some Anglicans also objected to it. The Prayer Book office expresses more confidence in the eternal salvation of the deceased than some of the stricter clergy thought appropriate in some cases.

There was occasional friction between Anglicans and Dissenters over monuments. Control over tombstones and other monuments, like control over everything else erected in church or churchyard, belonged in theory to the ordinary, but in most cases if the incumbent was satisfied nobody complained. On the other hand, if the incumbent was not satisfied, a

proposed monument could not be erected without a faculty out of the
bishop's court. Incumbents from time to time objected to inscriptions, and
court proceedings ensued.[149] The general rule was that no inscription
could be allowed that violated official Anglican doctrine, but otherwise the
courts would permit any decent sentiments to be expressed. They
overruled an incumbent who objected to referring to a Wesleyan minister
as "Reverend," and another who objected to a general request to pray for the
soul of the deceased. But it appears that an incumbent was within his
rights in not allowing a Roman Catholic to inscribe "Jesus, mercy, Mary,
help" on a tombstone.

These accommodations, such as they were, were subjected to a number
of pressures as the nineteenth century progressed. The easygoing theology
of the eighteenth century gave way to stricter doctrines on all sides, and the
development of Anglo-Catholicism accentuated the mistrust of Dissenters
for the established church. Furthermore, as the more serious grievances of
the Dissenters were met, they were ready to turn their attention to others.
At the same time, the growth of urban populations with a high death rate
made it necessary in many places to replace or supplement the traditional
churchyards if health and decency were to be maintained.

A series of statutes, mostly adopted in the 1850s, met this situation with
the typical expedients of the time.[150] The Queen in Council, on grounds
of public health, was empowered to order burials to be discontinued in any
existing churchyard or burial ground, and to designate areas in which no
burial ground could be opened without permission from the Home
Secretary. Parish vestries, and certain other local government bodies, were
empowered to set up "burial boards" to lay out and maintain new burial
grounds under the Secretary's supervision. The new ground did not have to
be in the parish it served. Two or more parishes could agree to set up a
combined board to lay out a combined burial ground, which did not have
to be in any of the parishes served.

The board was required to divide its burial ground into consecrated and
unconsecrated portions — calling on the bishop to consecrate the former.
With the approval of the bishop, the board could build an Anglican chapel
on the consecrated ground. If it did so, it had to build a
nondenominational chapel on the unconsecrated ground unless the
Secretary, on the request of three-fourths of the vestry, decided such a
chapel was unnecessary.

The board could allocate the unconsecrated portion in any way it saw fit.
It could, if it chose, make a permanent allocation to a particular
denomination. Such an allocation would be irrevocable, but only the
Attorney General would have standing to enforce it. It was not a trust,
and, except in the enforcement of trusts, denominational authorities had no
official recognition in the law.[151]

The consecrated portion was supposed to have the same legal status as the churchyard or churchyards that it replaced.[152] The minister, churchwardens, clerk, and sexton of the parish (that of the deceased if the burial ground served more than one) were entitled to perform the same services and receive the same fees as if the burial had been in their churchyard. Nevertheless, important rights of theirs were displaced by the power of the burial board to manage the whole ground. In the churchyard, the incumbent (or the churchwardens: it was never clear which) could assign any extra space to non-parishioners, and charge whatever the traffic would bear. In the new burial ground, that right belonged to the board. The board also had the right to assign exclusive or permanent space, authorize the construction of vaults and the like, and pass on the suitability of monuments, subject to the approval of the bishop as to consecrated ground. The board could set the fees for any such privilege. If there was a customary fee, that part of the board's fee would have to be passed on to the incumbent or churchwardens but in the churchyard the incumbent or churchwardens could charge a reasonable fee whether it was customary or not.

The board had no right to displace the incumbent with its own chaplains or the sexton with its own gravediggers, but it had no duty actually to enforce the rights of either, or even to warn them of a proposed funeral so that they could be there to claim their own rights. While they were entitled to perform their respective services and collect their respective fees, they were not entitled to fees unless they performed the services or at least showed up prepared to do so. Since the burial ground might be miles from the parish church, having no right to notice could well be tantamount to having no right to fees.

It is not at all clear what would happen if the family and friends of the deceased brought along their own clergyman to officiate, and the incumbent was not on hand to take his place. It was a violation of ecclesiastical law for anyone but an Anglican clergyman in good standing to officiate on consecrated ground, or for an Anglican clergyman to officiate anywhere without permission of the incumbent of the parish within whose boundaries the act was done. Since the burial board did not have to locate its ground within any of the parishes it served, the incumbent whose permission was required was not necessarily the one who was himself entitled to officiate. The burial board was expected to prevent any violation of these principles that came to its attention, but was evidently not expected to go out of its way to ferret such violations out.

The situation was further complicated by the Burial Laws Amendment Act, 1880,[153] an act whose main purpose was to give Dissenters rights in rural churchyards where there was no burial board. It provided that on suitable notice to the incumbent otherwise entitled to officiate, a person could be buried in consecrated ground with any "Christian and orderly service" or with no service at all. For symmetry, it was also provided that any Anglican clergyman in good standing could read the Prayer Book service at a burial in unconsecrated ground.

In the case of a burial in consecrated ground under this act, the fees otherwise payable were expressly preserved. This time, the person entitled to the fees was also entitled to notice so he could claim them. But there was still a problem in a board burial ground: it was the person arranging the funeral, not the board, that had to give the statutory notice. If he failed to do so, it would be hard to track him down.

As regards burial with Anglican services in unconsecrated ground, the act seems to do away with the veto of the parish incumbent over services in his parish, by entitling the person arranging the funeral "to have such burial performed therein according to the rites of the Church of England by any minister of the said church who may be willing to perform the same."

Unlike the burial boards, certain cemetery companies chartered under private bills, and certain local authorities setting up burial grounds as a public health measure, could retain their own chaplains to perform Anglican services in consecrated ground.[154] Some private bills provided for compensation to the parish incumbent; others did not.

The situation developed by this course of legislation took care of the major grievances of non-Anglicans, but it left residual grievances on all sides. Dissenters and other advocates of religious liberty were dissatisfied with the provisions requiring burial boards to build Anglican chapels at public expense, and with the preservation of customary fees for Anglican clergy even when they performed no services. Anglicans, on the other hand, along with others sentimentally attached to the idea of burial in consecrated ground, were unhappy with the financial disincentives to such burial on account of the extra fees to parish clergy and officers, and with the fact that a burial board could lawfully choose not to provide any consecrated ground at all.

In response to a report of a select committee setting forth these grievances, Parliament adopted the Burial Act, 1900.[155] This act provided for the Home Secretary to arrange for consecration of a portion of a burial ground if the burial authority (a term introduced to designate a board or another agency with similar powers) in charge of it failed to do so. The provision for putting up Anglican chapels was repealed. The authority could put up a non-denominational chapel at its own cost, or any number of denominational chapels at the cost of the members of the respective denominations.

The act abolished all rights to collect fees except for services rendered.[156] The burial authority could do as it pleased about gravediggers and the like. As for ministers, each authority was to adopt, subject to approval by the Home Secretary, a table of fees — the same for all ministers of whatever denomination. The authority would then collect the specified fee and turn it over to the minister performing the service. Anglican ministers were forbidden to charge more. Others could presumably make what separate arrangements they pleased, or whatever ones the rules of their particular denomination allowed. Vested rights were preserved for fifteen years or the existing incumbency, whichever was longer, but they could be commuted by agreement for a lump sum. Public health cemeteries were assimilated to other public burial grounds, and local authorities were no longer permitted to hire chaplains. It continued to be the duty of the parish incumbent to read the Prayer Book service at burials in the consecrated part of a public burial ground as well as in the churchyard. Whether he had the right to read the service if it was to be read at all is not clear. Presumably the general principle of ecclesiastical law that one minister is not to officiate in another's parish remained in effect.

The 1900 act was repealed by the Local Government Act, 1972,[157] and its provisions replaced by administrative regulations. But the provisions for burial remain about the same, except that the burial authority no longer collects fees for ministers. Non-Anglicans may make what arrangements they please, and Anglicans are subject to a church enactment fixing their fees.

When a churchyard was closed for burials by Order in Council, the churchwardens remained responsible for keeping it in decent order. But in most parishes, the closure would abolish the funds available for the purpose. The parish fees payable when a parishioner was buried in a board burial ground generally went to the incumbent or the sexton, and the fees for extras — vaults, monuments, etc. — or for burial of non-parishioners went to the board. Accordingly, it was provided in an 1855 statute that the churchwardens could draw their expenses from the local poor rates if there was no other legally chargeable fund.[158] If public health required, further orders could be made, calling on the churchwardens to seal vaults, or even remove bodies to other consecrated ground. The church courts had jurisdiction to issue faculties authorizing any such measures, but without an Order in Council, there was no authority for reimbursing the churchwardens out of the rates. Even with the Order in Council, it was evidently a good idea for the churchwardens to seek a faculty, because that would tell them what to do with the remains.

In built up areas, the disused churchyards became important sources of open space, and there was interest in landscaping them to use them better for that purpose. Also, with urban expansion, there was often need to widen a street by a churchyard, or to put sewer lines through one. The ecclesiastical courts split over whether they had authority to authorize such works.[159]   The general rule was that they could issue faculties for any alterations in church or churchyard that comported with their sacred character, but that neither could be secularized except by Act of Parliament. Thomas Tristram, one of the most eminent church lawyers of the period, sitting in the London Consistory Court, held that recreation or transit did not secularize a churchyard. His doctrine involved some departure from earlier precedent, which he justified by invoking a general principle of flexibility and common sense, together with the high cost of putting through a private Act of Parliament. Lewis Dibdin, a younger man who was to become equally eminent in his time, held that such flexibility was not appropriate. It was Tristram's view that ultimately prevailed.

All modification of burial grounds required care for the reverent treatment of any human remains encountered in the process, and their return to consecrated ground. As far as possible, even the earth into which the bodies of Christians had dissolved was to be retained in its consecrated location. All faculties contained provisions to maintain this principle, and anyone who acted without a faculty could get into trouble for violating it. A churchwarden who dumped a load of dirt and bone fragments on a neighboring field in the course of altering a footpath through the churchyard was required to put all the bones back, and, as far as possible, the dirt.[160]

The Disused Burial Grounds Act, 1884 forbade the erection of structures of any kind on disused burial grounds, whether Anglican or not, except for the enlargement of a church.[161]   This not only forbade development of the site, it forbade such standard park fixtures as bandstands, large monuments, and restrooms — although it permitted tool sheds. It is still in force except where specific legislation (notably, the Town and Country Planning Act, 1944 and its successors, and the Pastoral Measures, 1968 and 1983) authorizes development after appropriate transfer of remains. Where the ground is not taken for development, a series of Open Spaces Acts (1881 through 1906 — the 1906 act is still in force) authorize local government agencies to take possession, title, or both and hold the ground as an open space for recreational use. In the case of consecrated ground, development under the Open Spaces Act requires a faculty from the bishop. The bishop's permission is also required for sports or games to be allowed. Under the Town and Country Planning Acts, no faculty is required either to transfer the remains or to develop the site, but if the bishop lays down reasonable conditions on the transfer of remains, they must be complied with.

Non-Anglican church authorities are not recognized as such in any of the applicable statutes, but whoever gives up land under the Open Spaces Acts can impose conditions on his gift, and can also grant or withhold permission for sports or games. Regulations under the Town and Country

Planning Acts call for consulting "appropriate denominational authorities" as to reburial;[162] in doing so, they go beyond the governing statutes.

The functions we have been considering were originally assigned to the church because they were closely connected with religion. They still are. They have been assumed by the state because they are of great public concern. They always were. Through the first quarter of the nineteenth century, the English had in their established church an institution in which religious connection and public concern could be harmoniously combined. But it turned out that the harmony was purchased at a price of depriving Dissenters from the national church of any but an attenuated place in the national life. Churchmen kept hoping that the price could be eliminated and the harmony preserved, but it was not to be. In the nature of things, people could not be expected to feel entirely at home in a society that required them to look for major social amenities to the ministrations of a church in which they did not believe.

The expedients developed to deal with this situation were in great part results of the way in which the situation arose. English pluralism was not ancient like that of the Ottoman Empire. It was not a negotiated settlement like that of Germany, or, with some qualifications, France. It was not a foundation principle of a new country, like that in most of the United States. Rather, English pluralism was the result of a gradual wearing away of a unitary system through concessions made because it seemed right to make them.

So England could not do as the Ottoman Empire did, and allow each religious group to administer social amenities to its own members through its own institutions. Most Dissenting groups had not the resources, the organization, or the inclination to play such a part. The institutional diversity among religious groups in the Ottoman Empire bespoke deep-rooted cultural as well as theological differences. There was nothing of the kind in England.

England had too many different groups too widely distributed on the ground to maintain a system of coordinate establishments like that in Germany. Before the Irish church was disestablished in 1869, there had been modest government grants to the Presbyterians and the Roman Catholics in Ireland,[163] but it would have been impractical to extend those grants far enough to put even those two groups on an equal footing with the Anglicans.

And it was too late to adopt the American expedient of offering amenities across the board on a religiously neutral basis, and leaving the religious dimension to free enterprise. By the time the state was ready to enter the field of education, there was already an enormous educational enterprise in place under church auspices. Similarly, since everyone in the country was entitled to an Anglican burial and an Anglican marriage service, and the majority of the people wanted both, it would have been bad economics, as well as bad politics, to increase the cost of these in order to make nonsectarian burials and marriages available to everyone.

Accordingly, except in the case of probate and matrimonial courts, the state set up its institutions to be either supplements or alternatives to those of the church. The commissions and councils of local government reform never quite superseded the parish vestry. The state registered births while the church went on registering baptisms as it had always done. Marriage before a deputy registrar was an alternative to church marriage, and notice to a registrar was an alternative to banns. Board schools were set up only where church schools were inadequate, and board burial grounds with consecrated and non-consecrated sections were set up only in places where the churchyard was full.

Free enterprise — the voluntary principle as Dissenters called it — was never a major element in these arrangements, but it was provided for when it appeared. Non-Anglican churches were eventually allowed to hold their own marriage ceremonies without having the deputy registrar in attendance — although they were never allowed their own banns. Schools under Dissenting auspices were given the same access to public support as those under Anglican auspices, and, where they existed, were recognized as possible alternatives to board schools. Denominations were allowed their own sections of board burial grounds, and the friends of the deceased were eventually allowed to use any graveside ministrations they chose.

The availability of alternatives did not supersede the duty of the established church to go on making its ministrations available across the board. Except in cases of remarriage after divorce and marriage with the sister of a deceased wife, where there were statutory accommodations to the consciences of individual clergymen, anyone entitled to marry at all was (and is) entitled to marry in the Church of England. Dissenters continued to have free access to Anglican schools, and Parliament reinforced their rights by exempting them from Anglican instruction and worship. Most of the population were entitled to bury their dead with Anglican rites in consecrated ground, or, after 1880, with their own rites if they preferred.

By and large, the Church of England has acquiesced in this continuing definition of its role. A few High Churchmen protested at particular points, but there was never any systematic effort to limit the ministrations of the church to its own members. Conversely, there was no systematic effort to institutionalize forms of discipline for church members that would not be appropriate for the wider society. It is particularly interesting how little effort has been made to provide separate marriage regulations for church members as those of the state move farther and farther from church teaching, or to exercise as to church members the matrimonial jurisdiction that was taken away as to the wider society in 1857. The prevailing view seems still to be that expressed by Sir Lewis Dibdin in 1932:

> There is obvious difficulty, so long as the Church and State are united, in allowing a marriage to be valid *qua* State and invalid *qua* Church.[164]

Faced with the morally irrefutable claims of pluralism, Anglicans struggled long and hard to maintain the place of their church in a unified national life. They refused to accept cultural isolation as the price of religious commitment — a price the Roman Catholics seemed willing to pay even before it was exacted of them. They rejected the liberal view of religion as an idiosyncratic element in a homogeneous culture, and the Protestant view of denomination as an idiosyncratic element in a homogeneous Christianity. They never ceased to insist that even according the fullest respect to other persuasions, England is still a Christian nation, and theirs is the national church.

In the end, they were neither politically nor intellectually capable of giving institutional content to their vision. The obstacles to giving preferential treatment to one church while giving equal treatment to all are more than political, and more than temporary. It was inevitable that the state should found its administrative reforms on either religious or denominational neutrality — the registry of births, with the child then to be baptized where the parents chose or not at all; the public gravedigger for the private funeral; the few hours of religious instruction spliced into the secular curriculum.

But these institutional transformations did nothing to deprive the Church of England of its historical associations, or its preeminent place in the hearts, the minds, and the imaginations of the people. There remained an important sense in which it was still true that England is a Christian nation and the Church of England is its national church.

This unique position presented the church with another problem. To set standards of discipline for its members and to deploy personal and material resources for an effective witness to the Gospel in a society more and more resistant to it is a problem for any church. But it has been a unique problem for the Church of England with its unique weight of history and sentiment. It is this problem that we have now to consider.

3. Value for Money

All these measures for making Englishmen equal before the law regardless of their religion or lack of it, for rationalizing tithe and abolishing churchrates, and for assigning secular functions to secular agencies, did no more than whittle at the edges of the ancient juridical and economic preeminence of the Church of England. Other churches had the legal status of voluntary associations, and drew their economic support from their adherents, whereas the Church of England was an estate of the realm, endowed by kings, magnates, and forefathers time out of mind. "Disestablishment," i.e., reduction of the Church of England to the status of other churches, was an item on many political agendas from the 1830s on, but, as I have already pointed out, it was never a serious threat.

The continuing vitality of an established church in a pluralist society is not altogether easy to explain.[1] To be sure, once specific grievances were met, the church could draw on the general vague benevolence of the English people for venerable institutions and traditional ways. Also, there were arguments for investing church endowments with the new-found sanctity of private property; such arguments were not irresistibly compelling, but many found them persuasive. Moreover, the establishment of the church was often seen as embodying the longstanding corporate commitment of the English nation to Christianity as such. That commitment might in theory be embodied in other ways, but it was not likely to be if this one were to be abandoned.

At the same time, the political forces pressing for disestablishment tended to cancel each other out. Many Protestant Dissenters were frightened away from the cause by the enthusiasm it evoked among secularists on the one hand and Irish papists on the other. Then a fringe group of High Churchmen began flirting with disestablishment as a way of avoiding state interference with their doctrinal and liturgical idiosyncrasies. The more they did so, the more their numerous opponents came to feel that establishment was not so bad after all.

150

But neither ideology nor politics would have saved the establishment if there had not been a solid utilitarian argument available in its support.The church as endowed and established was making the ministrations of religion available on a scale that private enterprise could not be expected to replace. This argument persuaded even so staunch a liberal and proponent of religious equality as Macaulay:

> If I would keep up the Established Church of England, it is not for the sake of lords, and baronets, and country gentlemen of five thousand pounds a-year, and rich bankers in the city. I know that such people will always have churches, aye, and cathedrals, and organs and rich communion plate. The person about whom I am uneasy is the working man; the man who would find it difficult to pay even five shillings or ten shillings a-year out of his small earnings for the ministrations of religion. What is to become of him under the voluntary system? Is he to go without religious instruction altogether? That we should think a great evil to himself, and a great evil to society. Is he to pay for it out of his slender means? That would be a heavy tax. Is he to be dependent on the liberality of others? That is a somewhat precarious and a somewhat humiliating dependence. I prefer, I own, that system under which there is, in the rudest and most secluded district, a house of God where public worship is performed after a fashion acceptable to the great majority of the community, and where the poorest may partake of the ordinances of religion, not as an alms, but as a right.[2]

This utilitarian argument is another manifestation of the lay Erastianism to which I have alluded so often in these volumes. Macaulay, speaking in the House of Commons in 1845, was voicing the same expectations of the established church that his predecessors in the same house had voiced in 1307:

> to inform them and the people of the law of God, and to make hospitalities, alms, and other works of charity in the places where the churches were founded.[3]

But if these were old expectations, the circumstances under which they had to be met were quite new. There was no longer any consensus — although there were strong opinions — among the people, or even among church leaders, as to what laws of God (if any) were to be taught, or what works of charity to be made. The challenge presented by this new situation was to dominate the institutional life of the church from the 1830s on.

I. Redistribution of Funds

A. *Episcopal and Capitular Estates.*

1. Redistribution — Utilitarian arguments for the church suffered, naturally, from the extreme inutility with which its wealth was distributed.[4] The net income of the bishops averaged £ 6,683 each. But no one got the average. The Archbishop of Canterbury made £ 22,305, and the Bishop of Llandaff only £ 1,043. Nor did the income relate to the duties. Ely, with 126,000 people and 149 benefices, was worth £ 9,597, whereas Chester, with 1,902,000 people and 554 benefices was worth £ 3,022. A few hundred cathedral clergy and denizens of collegiate churches divided among them a net income of £ 272,828, some for performing modest tasks in the cathedral liturgy or the diocesan administration, others for doing nothing at all. Out of 10,496 benefices with cure, 186 paid better than £ 1,000, while 1,915 paid less than £ 100. 5,282 stipendiary curates were averaging £ 80 apiece.

These statistics or others like them had been in circulation for some time. In 1820, the anonymous Benthamite author of *The Black Book or Corruption Unmasked* concluded that the whole clerical estate had an income of £ 5,509,000, of which £ 4,609,000 went to people who did no work. He was for diverting the whole surplus to secular purposes. There was little support for so radical a move, but it was widely conceded that the funds had to be put to more effective church uses if the church was to retain them.

The defense of the status quo was spirited, and not lacking in learning or wit — though perhaps a bit deficient in realism.[5] The funds in issue did not belong to "the Church;" they were income from the endowments of particular corporations aggregate or sole, corporations as fully entitled to their income and property as anyone else. One anonymous pamphleteer insisted that there was no more excuse for equalizing the incomes of bishops than for equalizing the incomes of peers. Another contingent, led by Sydney Smith, brought out utilitarian arguments of their own. The possibility of great wealth would attract better men to the clerical state than would the certainty of a modest competence. Equalizing the incomes of bishops would put too great a space between the lower reaches of the episcopate and the higher reaches of the lower clergy. It would knock too many rungs from the ladder of success, and turn the heads of those who managed to leap the gap. Finally, there were men such as Archdeacon Manning, the future cardinal, who had no objection to the redistribution of church funds, but insisted that it was an invasion of the liberty of the church for Parliament to do the redistributing.

It was all in vain. A commission was appointed in 1832 and another in 1835, and bills began emanating from Parliament in 1836.[6] The Ecclesiastical Commissioners Act, 1836, turned the second commission into a permanent body, authorized to implement its own recommendations as to the episcopate. These recommendations included a substantial rationalization of diocesan boundaries, the creation of new sees at Manchester and Ripon in York Province, the combination of Gloucester with Bristol and Bangor with St. Asaph (so as to keep the two new sees from increasing the episcopal vote in the House of Lords), and a collection of annual payments from the richer sees for the benefit of the poorer ones. Each see was to have a specified income (£ 15,000 for Canterbury, £ 10,000 for York, intermediate amounts for the richer sees, and £ 4,000 for the poorest). The Commissioners were to lay schemes before the Privy Council for carrying all this into effect, and were to collect and distribute the resulting funds.

In 1840, it was the turn of the cathedrals and collegiate churches to have their funds redistributed.[7] These churches showed both variety and profusion. Christ Church, Oxford, was a constituent college of the University: nothing much could be done with it until the universities were overhauled. The clergy of Durham had just founded a university of their own — evidently as a protection against the approaching nemesis. Their foundation presented special problems with which the Commissioners had to deal. The collegiate churches included the royal foundations at Westminster and Windsor, which had to be treated pretty much like cathedrals, a batch of small churches that had really no business maintaining collegiate establishments, and that had to be reorganized into proper parish cures, and Ripon and Manchester, which were to become the cathedrals of the new dioceses to be set up under the 1836 act.

The main task, then, was to rationalize and reduce the clerical staffs of the normal cathedrals, the future cathedrals, and the cathedral-like colleges. The staffs to be so dealt with fell into four main categories:

1. The residentiary canons, headed by a dean (in a few places, the head was called a provost or something else). These were the best paid of the lot, and, next to the bishops, the best paid clergy in the kingdom. Their support came partly from endowments attached to their individual canonries, and partly from sharing out income from the common endowments of the chapter. Aside from improving the general cultural tone of the diocese, it was never quite clear what these people were supposed to do. But it was generally recognized that a certain number of them were to go on doing it.[8]

2. The nonresidentiary canons, or prebendaries. These had separately endowed prebends, were not obliged to reside in the cathedral precincts, and had no share of the common funds of the chapter.

Instead of vague duties about the cathedral, they had no duties whatever. This does not mean they were completely idle. Many of them held working positions in addition to their canonries. Some were archdeacons; some were parish incumbents; a few were even bishops eking out the revenues of impecunious sees. Since these canonries had no duties, the laws against pluralism did not take account of them. They could be held along with whatever other preferment a person had.[9]

3. Various holders of endowed offices. Some of these offices had real duties in connection with the liturgy, the cathedral school, or the management of chapter estates. Others were merely honorific.

4. The minor canons. These were originally liturgical deputies for the nonresidentiary canons, and still often went by the title of vicars choral. They were generally endowed as a group rather than individually.[10] They had liturgical functions, but not onerous enough ones to keep them from serving cures in nearby parishes. They were evidently not overpaid, since the ensuing legislation put a floor (£ 150), not a ceiling, on their income.

The Ecclesiastical Commissioners Act, 1840, dealt with these categories basically as follows:

1. The number of residentiary canons was fixed for each cathedral at four, five, or six (not counting the dean). This meant adding one canon at Lincoln and St. Paul's, London, which had only three each. In the other cathedrals, it meant suppressing from one to eight positions each as they fell vacant. In order to soften the blow to would-be canons and their patrons, and to avoid a long period with no cathedral preferment available at all, the act allowed every third vacancy to be filled until the statutory number was reached. The separate endowments of all residentiary canons and deans were transferred to the Ecclesiastical Commissioners (subject to the rights of present incumbents), while the chapters were to keep their common funds to support the remaining canons and keep up their cathedrals. The act set average annual incomes ranging from £ 3,000 for the Dean of Durham to £ 350 for a canon of St. David's or Llandaff.[11] If the chapter funds were more than enough to keep up these payments, the excess was to be paid over to the Commissioners. If the chapter funds were insufficient, the Commissioners were to supplement them. The Commissioners could authorize additional canons if new endowment was found for them.

2. The nonresidentiary canonries were all to be abolished as they fell vacant, and their revenues and endowments absorbed by the Commissioners. Provision was made for up to twenty-four honorary

canons in each cathedral. They could be given the traditional titles of suppressed prebends, but they were not to be paid.

3. Special endowments of special offices were turned over to the Commissioners, or, in a few cathedrals, to the chapters. Officeholders who did actual work were to be paid out of chapter funds.

4. Every cathedral was to have from two to six minor canons. If their corporate funds failed to provide them with £ 150 a year each, the chapter was to make up the difference.

The 1840 act also provided for enlarging the body of Ecclesiastical Commissioners. The original investigative commission, which had been perpetuated without change by the 1836 act, included the two archbishops, the bishop of London, five lay officials ex officio, and three named laymen, replaceable at will. It had been criticized for not being a church body, and for being too subject to the government. The 1840 act added the entire rest of the episcopate ex officio, three deans ex officio, six judges ex officio, and six additional laymen of whom the queen was to appoint four, the archbishop of Canterbury two. The persons appointed by name were to remain during good behavior. As the judges had tenure in their judicial posts, only the cabinet members provided for in the first commission were removable by the government. Most — though not all — criticism of the Commissioners' constitution was met by this reorganization.[12]

The course of legislation beginning with the two acts just taken up shows continuing ambivalence as to whether positions with actual duties should be separately endowed. Under the 1836 act, as we have seen, the individual bishops kept their endowments, and either gave or received annual cash payments to keep their incomes within the statutory average. In 1860, provision was made for the Commissioners to take over all episcopal endowments, and return to each bishop for the duration of his tenure such endowments (the same or others) as would secure him the statutory income.[13] The bishop could then, if he chose, let the Commissioners manage for him the endowment thus provided. This was the next thing to turning the whole endowment over to the Commissioners and putting bishops on salary — a step that was finally taken in 1943.[14]

The 1840 act exempted from suppression canonries annexed to archdeaconries, bishoprics, professorships, or the like, and even authorized the Commissioners to annex further canonries to archdeaconries instead of suppressing them. But in 1850, it was provided that the Commissioners could absorb these endowments as well (subject to a veto by the patron of the position to which the canonry was annexed), and substitute a fixed payment out of their common fund.[15]

The separate endowments of chapters, preserved under the 1840 act, were a bone of contention for some time.[16] Since the income of the chapter members was fixed by statute, they had nothing to gain from improving the management of their estates: the increase would all go to the Commissioners. The Commissioners felt that they were losing money by the chapters' inefficient management. The chapters, for their part, although they had no financial stake in their estates, cherished the rural and aristocratic associations that went with having them to manage. The dispute was eventually resolved by a series of deals between the Commissioners and the individual chapters substituting a readjustment of landed endowments for the payments back and forth. The chapters retained or were given endowments calculated to yield the statutory income for the members plus enough to keep up the fabric and services, the Commissioners kept the rest, and each side was free to manage its own property in its own way for its own benefit. This situation continued until 1931, when the cathedral endowments were pooled one more time, and provision was made for supporting cathedrals either by annual payments or by endowments other than land.

The separate endowments of corporations of minor canons were also preserved under the 1840 act. In 1864, these corporations were authorized to turn over their endowments to the Commissioners in return for annual payments.[17] In 1931, all their separate income and endowment was abolished, and provision was made for payment of minor canons out of the reconstituted chapter funds.

This backing and filling with respect to separate endowments reflected a general trend in administrative history.[18] The separately endowed office was an important medieval expedient for getting work done despite only rudimentary devices for handling and distributing money. By the eighteenth century, it had become an anachronism, albeit a cherished one, and the central government began moving away from it. George III, on coming to the throne in 1760, set a precedent, followed ever since, of turning over his traditional revenues to the government in exchange for a fixed annual payment called the Civil List. Then in 1787 the Consolidated Fund Act provided for pooling most of the revenues of the central government, and meeting most expenses out of the resulting fund. Analogous reforms were enacted at intervals all through the ensuing decades. For instance, in 1812, the fees of the clerical staff of the House of Commons were pooled in the hands of commissioners, who were empowered to reorganize the offices and set salaries for them. In 1837, the numerous emoluments of the Master of the Rolls were swept into the Consolidated Fund, and the Master put on salary.

By the time the reformed Parliament was in full spate, pooling revenues under the direction of a commission, and then disbursing them for maximum efficiency, optimum deployment of personnel, and appropriate regard for merit had become the standard Benthamite agenda for dealing with almost anything. We have seen its influence on schools, charities, and even burials, as well as on the disposition of episcopal and capitular endowments. It also entered into the reform of the poor law, the judiciary, the civil service, and the police.

But there was plenty of opposition to making this kind of centralization into a general principle for running and financing the state. Many people saw the diffusion of sources of revenue as a safeguard for the diffusion of authority that figured so importantly in the preservation of English liberties. Also, it was a source of patronage for the gentry and of advancement for their friends and relatives. As a result, centralizing agendas met with opposition whenever they were brought forward, and were generally not as fully implemented as their proponents would have wished.

This process was particularly prolonged and vigorous in the church. On the one hand, the church had more misapplied funds than the other institutions of society, and on the other hand it elicited deeper and more articulate rural and conservative sentiment than they did. It took a change in both the economic and the intellectual climate to bring about the final pooling of church revenues in the twentieth century. By the end of the First World War, the financial problem was no longer one of equitable distribution of excess funds, but one of marshalling enough resources to keep afloat. At the same time, a good many Benthamite principles had been absorbed into the main body of administrative doctrine, and most of the clergy had accepted canons of efficiency like those prevailing in other professions. At that point, misgivings about the *embourgeoisement* of the episcopate and nostalgia for a mythical race of gumbooted canons who carried spiritual consolation to their tenants in the fields gave way to perceptions that the management of investments is best left to people who know what they are doing, and that the time a clergyman spends collecting his pay is time he does not spend earning it.[19]

2. *Management*[20] — It was expected from the outset that part of the gain from placing church endowments in the hands of the Ecclesiastical Commissioners would be improved management of the landed estates. This the Commissioners undertook to accomplish, at first through the efforts of a hard-driving secretary-treasurer, Charles Knight Murray, then, after 1850, through a statutory five-man Estates Committee.[21] The 1840 act gave Murray tenure of his position under a clause that he was suspected of personally sneaking into the bill. For some years, he did all the things that the full time executive of an unwieldy body might be expected to do, and did them pretty well. Finally, however, he overreached himself, misappropriated some money, and left in disgrace for Australia. The committee that took his place consisted of two salaried Estates Commissioners, one appointed by the Crown, the other by the archbishop

of Canterbury, one unpaid Estates Commissioner appointed by the Crown, and two members appointed by the larger body from among their number. This committee was empowered to manage all the estates that fell into the hands of the Commissioners, and to exercise any power of sale, lease, or whatever that the Commissioners might have — subject only to such rules of general applicability as the parent body might adopt.

The great obstacle to managing church lands efficiently was a longstanding custom of not doing so. As we have seen, most church land was let out for long periods at rentals far less than the market would have supported. A lessee made up for the low rent by paying a lump sum called an entry fine whenever his lease was renewed. The clergy had a major stake in keeping this system intact. They could pocket their entry fines immediately, whereas much of the benefit of a higher rent would have gone to their successors. Indeed, a clergyman was apt to get in such a financial bind waiting for his predecessor's leases to fall in that even if he wanted to forego the entry fine and give his successors the benefit of a higher rent, he could not afford to do so.

The lessees, for their part, would not have minded paying out their money in even yearly amounts instead of in large blocks at long and not always predictable intervals (some leases were for lives rather than for years). But they knew that, even taking the usual entry fines into account, they were paying less than full economic rent (commonly known as "rack-rent;" the term is used pejoratively in the non-legal literature, but not in the legal)[22] for their land. They would be glad to have a more rational system introduced, but not one that was going to cost them a lot more money. They included in their number enough rich people to have influence, and enough lower middle class farmers to elicit sympathy.

In 1842, provision was made to keep newly developed lands from being leased out under the old system.[23] Church corporations, whether aggregate (chapters and colleges) or sole (bishops and parish incumbents), were authorized with the consent of the Ecclesiastical Commissioners, and, in the case of an incumbent, that of the patron, to let their land for up to ninety-nine years (as against three lives or twenty-one years under the Elizabethan statutes) to anyone who would make developments, improvements, or repairs on it. They were also empowered to lay out streets and other public facilities (which the old laws would have forbidden as a form of alienation), and to authorize the opening of mines (a form of waste, and therefore of alienation).[24] But every such lease, and every lease of the same premises forever after, had, after a six year transition period, to be at rack-rent. As an incentive to take advantage of this act, any right of the Ecclesiastical Commissioners to the increased income was postponed for the time of the original lessor.

This act, of course, did nothing for most church land, which was going to be used for agriculture as it had always been. Beginning in 1840, as canonries fell vacant, parcels of this land began to make their way into the possession of the Ecclesiastical Commissioners, with many more to follow. The intentions of the Commissioners, therefore, became a matter of great moment to many lessees.

Their intention, it soon turned out, was to let their lands at rack-rent as soon as existing leases fell in. Being a perpetual body, they had no interest in entry fines, and could afford to improve their long term prospects. Nor were they greatly moved by the longstanding expectations of lessees. If land had customarily been let at less than full value, the custom represented a dereliction of duty on the part of the clergy who allowed it to be established, and it would be a further dereliction to allow it to continue. As Roundell Palmer, the future Lord Chancellor and Earl of Selborne, put it, no one can "acquire a vested interest in the mismanagement of public property."[25]

The first few applications of this policy seem to have gone off without too much difficulty, but, as luck would have it, two thousand acres in one village came into the hands of the Commissioners in 1841 and 1842. The land was divided among some fifty lessees, one of whom was a powerful Member of Parliament named Evelyn Denison (brother of the fighting archdeacon whom we shall meet in the next chapter, and of other dignitaries in church and state).[26] When the intentions of the Commissioners with respect to this village became apparent in 1845, Denison organized a nationwide lessees' lobby that soon had six thousand members.

The ensuing agitation had something to do with the reorganization of the Commission and the addition of Estates Commissioners in 1850. It also produced the Episcopal and Capitular Estates Act, 1851.[27] Under that act, the holders of episcopal and capitular estates were authorized to sell them outright to their present lessees. Sales were subject to the approval of the Estates Commissioners "who shall pay due regard to the just and reasonable claims of the present holders of lands under lease or otherwise arising from the long continued practice of renewal." The resulting funds were to be kept by the Commissioners, who could either invest them for the benefit of the sellers, or allow the sellers to use them to buy other land. In the latter case, the new land could not be leased except at rack-rent.

In determining a fair price under this act, the Commissioners were offered a couple of parliamentary reports as a guide for their discretion, and they could agree to submit disputes to arbitration. But once they decided on a price, there was no appeal from their determination. Presumably, once Parliament had made a policy decision in favor of the claims of the lessees, the Commissioners could be trusted to implement it fairly. It appears that they did so, and that they also treated in the same way the cathedral lands that had already come into their possession — although the act did not apply to those lands.

While this act authorized bishops and chapters to sell their land outright to their lessees, they were still forbidden by the Elizabethan statutes to sell them to anyone else. Under the Ecclesiastical Leasing Act, 1858,[28] they (along with parish incumbents) were empowered, with the approval of the Ecclesiastical Commissioners, to sell to anyone they pleased. The Commissioners were required to lay out the purchase money in other lands for the seller. As under the 1851 act, land newly acquired under this act could not be leased except at rack-rent.

This 1858 act differed from the 1851 act in two important respects. First, it was administered by the whole body of Ecclesiastical Commissioners instead of by the three Church Estates Commissioners; second, it required the Commissioners to buy new lands for the seller of the old ones, instead of allowing the seller to buy with the approval of the Commissioners. I have not been able to find the reasons for these differences.[29] A couple of conjectures are possible. The 1858 act purports to be an extension of the 1842 act for development leases (the Ecclesiastical Leasing Act of 1842, not to be confused with the Ecclesiastical Leases Act of the same year, which we will take up later). That may be why it does not invoke the Estates Commissioners, who were not created until 1850. Also, like the 1842 act and unlike the 1851 one, it applies to parish incumbents as well as to bishops and chapters. Perhaps parish incumbents were not to be trusted on the real estate market.

B. Support for the Working Clergy.[30]

The Ecclesiastical Commissioners' money, beyond what was needed to maintain the statutory reduced condition of the bishops and chapters, was to be devoted to the alleviation of poverty among the working parish clergy. The governing legislation, presumably to make up for the loss of any local ties the displaced canons and prelates might have had, required the Commissioners to pay special attention to the places from which they drew their money; otherwise, they had a fairly free hand.

They shared the enterprise with the older institution of Queen Anne's Bounty. There was talk from time to time of merging the bodies, but the merger did not finally occur until 1948. The Bounty, as we have seen, was originally funded by the old Henrician first fruits and tenths. These, being fixed in amount, did not keep pace with inflation. Also, some of the money came out of benefices that were themselves candidates for grants from the Bounty, and more of it from funds that had been or were soon to be taken over by the Ecclesiastical Commissioners. By the time first fruits and tenths were abolished in 1926, collecting them had become more trouble than it was worth. The Bounty, however, by a century and more of paying out less interest on funds in its hands than it got from investing them, had accumulated a capital sum that continued to fund some of its projects. To this were added the proceeds of eleven annual grants of £ 100,000 each received from Parliament between 1809 and 1819. Once the Ecclesiastical Commissioners got off the ground, they were a much larger source of funding than the Bounty, but in their early days, while waiting for all the protected incumbents to die or resign, they were glad enough to borrow £ 600,000 from the senior agency.

There was some overlap between the two agencies, but not as much as there might have been. The Bounty dealt with the very poorest livings, wherever they might be found, while the Commissioners concerned themselves with poor livings in the population centers, even if there were poorer ones elsewhere. The Commissioners, pursuant to their mandate to consider places from which they drew their money, funded livings in those places that they would not have funded elsewhere. The Bounty had no such mandate. The Bounty had a statutory mandate to assist in the repair of dilapidations and the building of parsonages, and could make loans out of its capital for the purpose. The Commissioners were never involved in that work, and never made loans. On the other hand, the Commissioners were the only ones with power to increase the stipend of a curate who assisted an incumbent in his own church rather than officiating in an outlying chapel. Both agencies went beyond their general funding criteria in order to match private benefactions. But here too the Bounty looked for levels of abjection, while the Commissioners looked for levels of potential usefulness.

The Bounty's charter from Queen Anne required it to do its funding "by the way of purchase and not by the way of pension." All through the eighteenth century, its governors considered this principle to require buying land and turning it over to the favored benefice. Such a policy created problems, because there was not always suitable land on the market, and the interest the Bounty paid on capital grants waiting to be laid out in land was less than a good portfolio of securities would provide. In 1829, the Bounty started allowing grants out of its parliamentary appropriations — but not out of its other funds — to be invested in securities rather than in land. The Commissioners, meanwhile, made all their grants in the form either of a specified annual payment out of their income or of the income from a specified amount of their capital.

Redistribution of parish incumbents' income and endowment was not a serious option in England. What stood in the way was patronage. An advowson is a form of property, as much so as a field or a barn or the right to shoot pheasants. Its value is obviously a function of the value of the living its owner can bestow. Therefore, to take away some of the income or endowments of one benefice and attach them to another is all of a piece with taking Squire A's meadow and giving it to Squire B. Given the prevailing attitude toward private property, such a step was politically impossible; indeed very few even suggested it. There was some modification of the endowments of benefices in Crown or ecclesiastical patronage, and the Ecclesiastical Commissioners were empowered to shift endowments between benefices in the same patronage. But nothing that would reduce the overall income of benefices in the gift of a lay patron was authorized to be done without that patron's permission. It was also true, of course, that any augmentation of a benefice out of Bounty or Commissioners' funds constituted a windfall for the patron. But that too fell under the aegis of private property, and nothing could be done about it.

Estate management was less of a problem for parish incumbents than for the higher clergy. The parson's or vicar's tithes almost always arose in his own parish, and since 1836 there was no difficulty in determining how much they were or how he was to collect them. His glebe lands were also usually in his own parish. If he chose, he could work them himself, and it was widely felt that his ministry to the rural community would be strengthened if he did so.[31] On the other hand, if he chose to make leases, he could not make them beyond his own time without the consent of the patron and the ordinary, who would not be anxious to have him impoverish his successors. My impression is that it was not customary to seek such permission, and that the usual lease was expressly limited to the lessor's incumbency.

The leasing of incumbents' glebe land was affected by two statutes adopted in 1842.[32] The Ecclesiastical Leasing Act of that year we have already looked at. Under it, incumbents, like other ecclesiastics, were authorized to make mineral leases, to lay out streets, and to make ninety-nine year leases to people who would develop their land. All leases required the consent of the Ecclesiastical Commissioners; a lease by a parish incumbent also required the consent of the patron, but not of the ordinary.

The Ecclesiastical Leases Act of 1842 applied only to parish incumbents. It permitted leases of up to fourteen years, or twenty if an expensive and innovative program of husbandry was contemplated. The lessee was required to use the best husbandry current in the vicinity, and to pay the best rent the land could reasonably be expected to fetch. As under the common law and the Elizabethan statutes, the consent of both patron and ordinary was required. The Ecclesiastical Commissioners' consent was not necessary. It is not clear what this act added to the Elizabethan statute on the same subject. It was worded as a further enabling act, not as a restrictive act. Accordingly, the courts held that a lease valid under the Elizabethan statute was not invalid for failure to meet the conditions laid down in this one.[33] But I have found only one suggestion as to what this act permitted that the old act forbade. Since the old act required that the customary rental be reserved, it arguably did not permit the leasing of land that had not customarily been leased. The 1842 act may, then, have been part of a general trend to encourage more innovative and more efficient agriculture.

As we have seen, incumbents were empowered in 1858, along with prelates and chapters, to sell their land outright. They needed permission from their patrons, and from the Ecclesiastical Commissioners, who were then to buy them new land with the proceeds. A more radical authority to sell, this time applicable only to parish incumbents, was adopted with the Glebe Lands Act, 1888.[34] This act was administered not by the Ecclesiastical Commissioners (although they were to invest the proceeds on behalf of the seller), but by the Land Commissioners. That body was produced by an amalgamation of the one appointed in 1836 to administer the transformation of tithe into a rentcharge with other commissioners appointed to deal with copyholds and enclosures. They also had some powers with respect to settled land. In short, they had a broad and expanding assignment to supervise the transition from medieval to modern conceptions of land use. By a series of statutory metamorphoses over the ensuing decades, they were to become the Ministry of Agriculture. Their role evidently responded to a perception that land was no longer a suitable investment for the church, and should be phased out. Any incumbent could sell his land with their permission. Parliament departed from ancient tradition by allowing them to overrule any objection made by patron or ordinary. The proceeds of the sale could not be invested in new lands (except to provide a garden for the parsonage). They could go to repair dilapidations, or to buy off charges on other landholdings; otherwise, they were to be invested in securities of the kind fiduciaries could invest in. The church's glebe was steadily but gradually liquidated under the permission afforded by this act and the 1858 act.[35] There were about 659,000 acres of glebe when the 1888 act came on the books. By the time the remaining glebe was transferred to diocesan stipends funds in 1976, there were no more than 164,000 acres left. The loss of rural contact represented by this erosion continued to be lamented right up to the end, but the perception that an effective minister is too busy to be an effective tiller of the soil, or even an effective landlord, finally won out.

The redistribution of incumbents' incomes that was prevented by ideology and politics in the nineteenth century was brought about by economics in the twentieth.[36] Between the foundation of the Ecclesiastical

Commissioners and the Second World War, a whole century of legislative and financial initiatives had operated to make benefices vulnerable to inflation by changing their primary endowment from land to fixed income securities and fixed charges on central funds. All the augmentation grants from the Ecclesiastical Commissioners were in the form of so many pounds of annual income, or the income from so many pounds of capital, which, given the Commissioners' investment policies, must have amounted to about the same thing. Until 1948 all the Commissioners' money that was not in land was in fixed income securities. In some cases, their investments were limited by statute either to government securities (funds awaiting new land purchases under the 1851 and 1858 provisions for sale of land), or to those plus corporate debentures (proceeds of sales under the Glebe Lands Act, 1888). Until 1961, other fiduciaries could not invest in ordinary shares (Americans would say common stocks) of business corporations unless their foundation documents expressly authorized them to do so. I see no reason why either the Commissioners or Queen Anne's Bounty should have been subject to this restriction, and it did not require any new legislation to enable their successors, the Church Commissioners (formed by merging them in 1948), to abandon it. Nevertheless, they seem to have adhered to it. Their policy affected not only benefices that had fixed capital allocations, but also benefices that had their own portfolios — those whose land was sold under the 1888 act, and certain of those augmented by Queen Anne's Bounty after 1829.

Meanwhile, in some cases, even if the benefice endowments were still in land, the Ecclesiastical Commissioners might have a statutory power to skim off the difference between present and past income. The Ecclesiastical Leasing Act of 1842 allowed them to do this with improvements resulting from development leases, and the 1858 extension allowed them to do it with the income from new land bought to replace old. The object of these provisions was to give the Commissioners the benefit of improved management of the endowment, but it also operated to give them the benefit of any fall in the value of money.

The last protection of endowment income against inflation was lost in 1936, when tithe rentcharge, which had been pegged to the market value of the three principal cereal grains, was replaced by stock, yielding a fixed number of pounds.[37]

As a result of these developments, the inflation that set in after the Second World War made it impossible for any but a handful of parish incumbents to live on their endowments. Augmentation out of central funds became the rule, not the exception. At the same time, the central funds, despite the Church Commissioners' belated turn to growth securities, were themselves feeling the effects of inflation, and had to be supplemented by asking churchgoers to contribute as members of other churches do.[38] The response of the churchgoers was generally good. The resulting funds were collected partly by the parochial church councils, bodies established in 1921 to take over the ecclesiastical work of the traditional vestries, and partly by diocesan stipends funds, established by general church legislation in the 1940s.

The diocesan stipends funds and the Church Commissioners (to the extent their money was not already committed) still followed the old plan of insuring that every clergyman was paid no less than a specified amount. But at this point very few clergymen were collecting any more from their endowments than the minimum thus established. So the contributions from the funds were adjusted accordingly, leaving most benefices at about the same level with a few differentials introduced on purpose to reflect differences in duties.[39] The rich benefices, with a few exceptions, differed from the poor ones not in paying more money to their incumbents, but only in getting smaller payments from the diocesan stipends fund.

Guy Mayfield, writing in 1963, lists the following sources of income for a typical parish incumbent:[40]

1. Endowment held by the Church Commissioners in the account of the benefice, probably arising from a sale of land under one of the mid-nineteenth century acts, or else from the redemption of tithe rentcharge in 1936. This endowment would be carried as so many pounds of capital in the common fund. Some separate portfolios for individual benefices were abolished in 1938, the rest in 1951.
2. Glebe.
3. A fixed annual payment from the Commissioners, probably based on a nineteenth century augmentation grant.
4. A contribution from the parochial church council, resulting from a negotiation between it and the diocesan board of finance, administrator of the diocesan stipends fund.
5. A contribution from the diocesan stipends fund, based on the same negotiation. The money in the fund would come partly from local sources, partly from block grants by the Church Commissioners.
6. Easter offerings (voluntary ones, not the anachronistic and probably defunct compulsory ones mentioned in the last chapter), and fees for weddings, funerals, and the like.

In Mayfield's typical example, the contribution from the diocesan stipends fund amounts to about one-fourth of the total; that and the contribution from the parochial church council, together make up one-third.

The Ecclesiastical Commissioners had always taken into account the need to hire a curate to assist a resident incumbent as one of the reasons for augmenting the incumbent's income. After 1928, they were authorized instead to make the curate a direct annual grant to supplement what the incumbent was able to pay him.[41]

In 1976, the sources of remuneration for the working clergy were redistributed one more time. Under the Endowments and Glebe Measure adopted in that year:[42]

1. All benefice endowments except glebe became the property of the Church Commissioners if they were not so already, and all separate capital accounts for individual benefices were abolished. The Commissioners' general fund was charged with an annual payment in the amount of the former endowment income or £ 1,000, whichever was less. A clergyman currently receiving more than £ 1,000 of endowment income was to be paid the excess out of the general fund as long as he held the benefice.

2. All glebe became the property of the diocesan board of finance for the diocese where the benefice was located, to be used for the benefit of the diocesan stipends fund.

3. All unendowed grants, whether of capital or of income, were abolished if they were for incumbents. If they were for curates or lay workers, they were made the responsibility of the diocesan stipends fund, fed by a block grant from the Commissioners.

Except for a few provisions for the protection of existing rights, the measure says nothing about what is to be done with the money it frees up.[43] The Commissioners' money is presumably still governed by the 1840 requirement that it be used to support the cure of souls. I gather that whatever of it goes to support the parish ministry now takes the form of block grants into diocesan stipends funds. Those funds were mandated in 1949 to support the cure of souls in their respective dioceses, limited in 1953 to the support of clergy engaged in the cure of souls in the diocese, expanded in 1976 to cover lay workers as well.

The 1976 measure was a partial implementation of a series of proposals beginning with the famous report, *The Deployment and Payment of The Clergy*, prepared by Leslie Paul for the Church Assembly, and published in 1964.[44] Paul was for pooling all church revenues, and putting the entire clergy on salary. They should all have a uniform base salary, with family allowances, and increments for longevity or especially demanding posts. A commission appointed by the Assembly to consider the Paul Report came up with similar recommendations in 1967. Against this background, the 1976 measure must be seen as a compromise. It continues to give the typical parish incumbent a certain quantum of income that goes with his office rather than his person. But the maximum endowment income is set at a figure that no clergyman can live on unless he is independently wealthy, and the managers of the central funds are free to use any criterion they wish for supplementation. There is scope enough to rationalize the distribution of clerical incomes in any way that seems appropriate.

C. Social Responsibility.

The centralization of church endowments in a single agency has provided an obvious target for people concerned with the social responsibilities of property owners.[45] By the 1880s, the Ecclesiastical Commissioners had begun taking heat for being the owners of great blocks of slum housing, as well as an embarrassing number of gin mills and whorehouses. Much of the blame they did not deserve: the most offensive holdings were held by other people under long leases made by bishops and canons before the Commissioners took over. As the leases fell in, the Commissioners gradually developed sound, humane, and sometimes creative policies for dealing with their property. Their successors the Church Commissioners are still among the largest landowners in England, and the only complaint I have seen about their management concerns a tendency to support gentrification in the Metropolis:

> There must surely be some atrophy of the imagination in intelligent men who fail to see that . . . .no agency for the Church can devote considerable resources to very expensive, very luxurious housing, without some damage to our Christian witness . . . .A man walking the streets frantically searching for a home for his wife and children won't be impressed, as he sees offices and luxury flats absorbing land and money and building resources, when told that all these exciting developments pay the curate's wages.

This, from an undated pamphlet, circa 1968, presents an interesting contrast with the earlier complaints about rundown conditions.

With the investment of church funds in commercial stocks beginning in the late 1940s, other problems of social responsibility have arisen. The Church Commissioners have considered the problem of South African investments, taking a fairly conservative position on it. I do not find that they have concerned themselves in other ways with the social policies of the businesses in which they invest. Certainly, they have made no general effort to coordinate either their investment policy or their exercise of the corporate franchise with the church's developing witness to the duties of employers toward workers or the duties of multi-national corporations toward the Third World. They have this failing in common with a good many other institutional investors.

II. Redistribution of the Ministry

A. The Parochial System.

1. Church Building and New Parishes — Needless to say, improved support for the parish ministry would not have solved many of the church's problems if the parishes themselves had continued to be distributed on the ground in accordance with the demographic exigencies of the eleventh century. We have seen that the assignment of parochial status to new churches was a slow growth in the late eighteenth and early nineteenth centuries because of tenderness for the rights of mother churches and their patrons. Two sets of statutes put together between 1831 and 1856 gradually made it possible for new parishes to be established on almost the same footing as old ones.

We have already followed the course of the Church Building Acts from 1818 through 1831. In the latter year, the Church Building Commissioners were empowered, with no permission except that of the local bishop, to confer limited parochial status on certain of their churches, and assign the patronage to those who contributed to the building of the church or the endowment of the minister.[46] The patron had no veto unless he wanted to undertake the project himself. A parish could not be divided under this authority unless it met certain criteria regarding the inadequacy of existing arrangements: either there had to be two thousand or more parishioners and room for no more than a third of them in the existing church or chapels, or else there had to be at least three hundred parishioners living more than two miles from any existing church or chapel and less than one mile from the one to be put up. This restriction was abandoned in 1851.

Where the Church Building Acts authorized the Church Building Commissioners to build a church, endow a minister for it, and then assign it a parochial district, the New Parishes Acts, beginning in 1843,[47] authorized the Ecclesiastical Commissioners to create a parochial district (called a "Peel District" after the Prime Minister), and then build a church and endow a minister for it. Like so many of the Ecclesiastical Commissioners' projects, these were set in motion by a "scheme" prepared by the Commissioners, and approved by Order in Council. The approval of the bishop was required, but the patron and the incumbent of the mother church had only the right to comment.

The advantage of the New Parishes Acts was that the minister, being assigned to the district before the church was built, could participate in the fund raising. The district did not become a full-fledged parish until the minister was endowed and the church built. The money came from the Commissioners' common fund, from their £ 600,000 loan from Queen

Anne's Bounty, and from private benefactions. Pew rents, an invidious creation of the eighteenth century, were not allowed at first, but in 1856 they were permitted as a last resort.[48] As under the Church Building Acts, private contributors could be given patronage rights in the new church.

Neither set of acts allowed any of the endowment of the mother church to be diverted to a new parish without the consent of the patron. As a result, the clergy of some new parishes were substantially poorer than their neighbors in old ones.[49] In other cases, however, the original parish had been supported in considerable part by fees and offerings, so that the subtraction of a large group of parishioners impoverished the mother church. Both sets of statutes allowed the incumbent of the mother church, and, if appropriate, his successors to be compensated for this loss out of the income of the new parish.

Although the Church Building Commissioners were absorbed by the Ecclesiastical Commissioners in 1856, the two sets of statutes were not combined until 1943.[50] But by the time all the funds were in and the building built, a parish created under one set was in about the same case as one created under the other. Chapels of ease, perpetual curacies augmented by Queen Anne's Bounty in the eighteenth century, and, to some extent, proprietary chapels were mostly brought under the same system over the years, so that by the last quarter of the nineteenth century the parish system was pretty well up to date, pretty well uniform, and capable of further updating as required.

The only remaining difference between new and old parishes was in terminology. Until 1868, the incumbent of a new parish was called a perpetual curate, a term coined in 1714 to designate a curate who could not be arbitrarily dismissed because his position had been augmented by Queen Anne's Bounty. As a curate, he was "nominated" by his patron, rather than "presented," and "licensed" by the bishop, rather than "instituted" and "inducted." But his benefice, unlike the earlier perpetual curacies, was subject to the laws against pluralism, and the right to nominate could be litigated over like an ordinary advowson. Under the Incumbents Act, 1868, any perpetual curate who could perform weddings and funerals was given the title of a vicar, although he was still nominated and licensed rather than presented, instituted, and inducted.[51]

2. Union of Benefices — In some cases, pastoral efficiency called for putting old parishes together rather than creating new ones. It had always been competent for a bishop to unite two benefices with the permission of the patrons (who would agree to take turns presenting to the united benefice), provided the churches were close enough together for one clergyman to serve them both, or for both sets of parishioners to worship in one of them, and provided at least one of the benefices was too poor to afford decent support to a clergyman of its own. There were two statutes (1545 and 1665) that supported this practice in specified circumstances, and several cases upholding it even when the statutes did not apply.[52] But some bishops went farther and purported to unite non-contiguous and non-poor benefices so that a favored clergyman might avoid the laws against pluralism by claiming that his two benefices were one. This practice was as disreputable as it was legally tenuous, and the Ecclesiastical Commissioners sought to bring it under control in the legislation that they put through Parliament as the Pluralities Act, 1838.[53]

That act provided that contiguous benefices with an aggregate value of no more than £ 500, serving cures with not more than 1,500 people between them, could be united by Order in Council on the representation of the archbishop of the province. The archbishop, in turn, was to act on the certification of the local ordinary that the proposal would be advantageous to the interests of religion. The consent of both patrons was required, and the order uniting the benefices was to indicate how they were to take turns making presentments. The £ 500 limitation was taken away in 1850,[54] but the population limit remained. It was forbidden to unite benefices except under the provisions of this act.

The next step in the development of machinery for uniting benefices was taken for the London metropolitan area in 1860.[55] An ad hoc commission was provided for to prepare a scheme for submission to the Ecclesiastical Commissioners, and by them to the Privy Council. The process was set in motion by the bishop, who appointed two clergymen to the commission. The other three members were a clergyman appointed by the Dean and Chapter of St. Paul's, and two laymen appointed by parish vestries or municipal governments, depending on where the affected benefices were. All the affected patrons, and the vestries of all the affected parishes, had to approve the scheme before the Commissioners could present it to the Council. Other interested persons could appeal to the Council's Judicial Committee.

If the revenues of the benefices being united were more than enough when pooled to support the remaining clergyman, the scheme could provide for diverting the excess to any other metropolitan benefice the Commissioners thought should have it. And if the combined parish was not going to need two churches, the scheme could provide for making a school out of the redundant church, or even for tearing it down and selling the site.

The main features of this 1860 legislation, both procedural — development of schemes by a local body, input from patrons and parishioners, presentation to the Privy Council by the Ecclesiastical Commissioners, and appeal to the Judicial Committee — and substantive —

diversion of excess revenues from the united benefice, and secularization or demolition of redundant churches — were to be picked up over and over in the far more elaborate legislative packages developed in the twentieth century.

The first of these was the Union of Benefices Act, 1919.[56] This, unlike the 1860 act, applied nationwide. Unlike either of the previous acts, it permitted a scheme to be implemented without the consent of the patrons of the affected benefices. Both the patrons and the parishioners (through the churchwardens) were represented on the ad hoc commission that prepared a scheme under this act, but neither had a veto.

This act was replaced in 1923 by a measure of the recently formed Church Assembly.[57] This measure preserved the ad hoc commission, now consisting of one member appointed by the bishop, one by the Ecclesiastical Commissioners, and one jointly by the patron and the parochial church council of each affected parish. There was also to be a diocesan committee to supervise the whole process, and to be represented on the ad hoc commission if there were more than two parishes involved. There was specific provision for a scheme to regulate the patronage rights in the united benefice. Taking turns making the presentment was still to be the usual way of maintaining the rights of the different patrons, but it was not mandatory if some other approach seemed better. Another innovation was authority to include in the scheme a specific provision for curates or lay workers to be endowed with part of the endowment of the united benefice.

The measure required the framers and approvers of a scheme to take into account both the needs of the parishes being united and the wider needs of the church. This requirement gave rise to a couple of cases in which the Judicial Committee of the Privy Council overruled the Ecclesiastical Commissioners.[58] I will describe the second one; the facts of the first are almost identical. Westoe and South Shields, St. Hilda, were two urban parishes side by side, both well endowed and supported, both flourishing. In each of them, the endowment was adequate to support the incumbent, the services were well attended by the standards of the day, and there was an active congregation ready to contribute both time and money. On the other hand, either church would more than accommodate all the worshippers in both parishes, and everyone in either parish was within easy walking distance of either church. Meanwhile, on the other side of town, there was an area with a large and growing population of poor working people who lived some miles from any church at all. It was readily apparent both to the bishop and to the Ecclesiastical Commissioners that if the two parishes just described could be united, the entire endowment of one of them, plus the money brought in by selling the site of one of the

churches, could be used to put up and fund a new church for the empty
space.

The scheme to do this went through the ad hoc commission, three to
two, with the representatives of both affected parishes dissenting (by this
time the measure had been amended to add a fifth member, representing
the diocese).[59] It breezed through the bishop and the Ecclesiastical
Commissioners, and came before the Judicial Committee on a parishioner's
appeal. The Committee expressed — as it always does — its profound
respect for the superior wisdom of bishops and Ecclesiastical
Commissioners in deciding how best to serve the church. But it pointed
out that the proposed scheme would not be of the slightest benefit to either
of the parishes involved. Under the applicable language, there was no
power to make such a scheme. In other words, a measure for the union of
benefices that needed uniting was not a general measure to redistribute
parish endowments for the benefit of the whole church.

3. *Pastoral Reorganization* — The first opportunity for a more general
redistribution came with the air raids during the Second World War.
Churches, like other buildings, got damaged, and, like other buildings, they
had the benefit of government payments to compensate for the damage.
But rebuilding a church in a place where a church was no longer needed
made no more sense than rebuilding a slum in its original form. The
Reorganization Areas Measure, 1944,[60] was patterned on the Town and
Country Planning Act of the same year (and more remotely, the Artizans
and Labourers Dwelling Improvement Act, 1875). A parish whose church
had suffered war damage (or whose population had shifted as a result of
war or urban renewal), together with any adjoining parish, could be
declared part of a reorganization area. Within that area, schemes
developed by a diocesan reorganization committee and approved by the
Ecclesiastical Commissioners, could provide for changing parish boundaries
in any way that seemed appropriate, shifting the sites of churches or
parsonages, and abolishing any benefices that seemed to need abolishing.
The incumbent of an abolished benefice was to be given, if possible,
another benefice created by the same scheme; otherwise, he was to be
compensated. Regard was to be paid to the interest of the patron of the
abolished benefice, but what regard was not spelled out. If a new benefice
was created, he could presumably be given a share in its patronage (he
could evidently not be allowed to displace the patron of an old benefice not
abolished), but there was no requirement that he be given anything at all
except a chance to object. The endowments of all the benefices in the
reorganization area could be pooled, and both incumbents and curates put
on stipends. A couple of diocesan funds were to be set up to collect and
distribute the pooled funds. Government war damage payments were also

to go into one of these funds. To the extent that the damaged property was not to be restored, the money could be put to any pastoral purpose the diocesan reorganization committee desired.

The diocesan reorganization committee administering this measure consisted of the bishop and all the archdeacons plus a combination of lay and clerical representatives provided for by the diocesan conference (a body of elected lay and clerical representatives established as part of the movement for ecclesiastical self-government that set in during the latter part of the nineteenth century).[61] In 1949, provision was made for this committee, or another one similarly constituted, to be the "pastoral committee" of the diocese. As such, it was to administer the Union of Benefices Measure for the whole diocese, replacing the ad hoc commissions provided for in 1923.

The Pastoral Reorganization Measure, 1949,[62] also modified the language about taking diocesan and parochial needs into account. I do not find the change very significant, but the Judicial Committee used it to alter the criteria laid down in the *Westoe* case just discussed. The 1949 measure also contained a controversial provision authorizing the Commissioners (the *Church* Commissioners since their reorganization in 1948), at the request of the bishop with the concurrence of the pastoral committee, to divert excess endowment income from any benefice to the diocesan stipends fund. This provision evoked some objections in Parliament, and was not repeated in any later legislation until all the endowments were centralized in 1976.

All the different devices for putting parishes together and pulling them apart were combined into a single program under the Pastoral Measure, 1968.[63] This elaborate enactment continues basically to govern changes in the parochial system. Formally, it has been replaced by the Pastoral Measure, 1983, but the two measures differ only in minor details. Under either measure, the diocesan pastoral committee has power to draw up schemes or orders for making new parishes, combining old ones, or otherwise shifting parish arrangements anywhere in the diocese. If the bishop approves, the draft will then go before the Church Commissioners. A scheme must then be sent to the Privy Council, with provision for the Judicial Committee to hear appeals from it, as under the previous laws.[64] An "order" (as opposed to a "scheme"), an innovation, can deal with certain minor matters on the Commissioners' own authority, without resort to the Council. The language affecting the balance between parochial and diocesan interests has again been changed, probably with no significant effect. Clergymen displaced by any scheme (a clergyman with tenure in his position cannot be displaced by an order) are to be compensated under an elaborate procedure set forth in a schedule to the measure. A patron gets nothing for the abolition of a benefice in his gift, except that he can be given a share in the patronage of any new benefices, unless there are practical or pastoral obstacles standing in the way. Patrons and incumbents, along with archdeacons, rural deans, parochial church councils, and local government agencies in charge of land use planning, are entitled to have input before the committee and the Commissioners and to appeal to the Judicial Committee.

Another innovation under this legislation is the provision for team and group ministries. Where there is a team ministry, the cure of souls is exercised by a group of clergy appointed for a fixed term rather than for life. The head of the group is called a rector, and the rest are called vicars. They can divide the duties in any way they or the bishop see fit. In a group ministry, all the incumbents in a group of parishes assume joint responsibility for the cure of souls in the combined parishes, without affecting either their tenure of their individual benefices or the status of the constituent parishes. They are supposed to "meet as a chapter for the purposes of discussion and reaching a common mind on all matters of general concern or special interest to the group ministry." These provisions picked up expedients that had been tried successfully in several places during the years between the Second World War and the enactment of the measure.[65]

The provisions for redundant churches were also updated in this measure. A general provision was made for the deconsecration of any site or building put to a secular use under a pastoral scheme.[66] The former laws evidently allowed the site of a demolished church to be secularized (in the leading case a brewery was to be put up on the site, and we cannot suppose a consecrated brewery was envisaged), but if the building was left standing and made into a school or library, the law was not clear. It had been held in the eighteenth century that a monastic chapel used as a cowshed since the Reformation could be restored to liturgical use without a new consecration. In any event, the 1968 measure set this question at rest. There are theological objections to secularizing a consecrated building, but they were evidently no more persuasive in 1968 than they were in King Henry's Time.

The measure also provided for the first time that disused burial grounds (as distinguished from sites of demolished churches) could be built on. It was provided that the Disused Burial Grounds Act, 1884,[67] would not apply if nobody had been buried in the ground for fifty years, or if no relative of a more recently buried person objected. Since the 1884 act owed as much to the desire for open space in the cities as it did to piety, it is not clear what effect this new provision will have on the amenities of urban life. Presumably, it will not apply to burial grounds already disposed of in some other way. Also, of course, it will not prevent the need for planning permission for any development of the site. It is interesting, by the way, that this provision gives the Church of England a privilege that other denominations do not have: the 1884 act applies to disused burial grounds of all kinds, and those of other denominations are still subject to it in its original form.

Among redundant churches were naturally included many old ones. The policy of keeping up with demographic changes could easily clash with the policy of preserving historic buildings.[68] Provision was made in the Reorganization Areas Measure, 1944, for consultation with the Royal Fine Arts Commission before a building of archaeological, historical, or artistic interest was taken down. Parliament took a hand in 1952 by providing arrangements for making London churches with no parishioners into "guild" churches, holding weekday services for city workers.[69] But the proliferation of pastoral schemes plus the growing concern for the environment required more complex provisions. The 1968 measure set up the Redundant Churches Fund to take title to such redundant churches as ought to be preserved and cannot be put to a secular use. The Fund keeps up these churches partly with money received by the Church Commissioners from selling the sites of other churches, and partly from a parliamentary grant. In addition, the Fund has the same powers as other owners of historic buildings to make arrangements for the Secretary of State for the Environment or the Historic Buildings and Monuments Commission to take over and manage its buildings.

It appears that the powers under the Pastoral Measure have been put to extensive use. Welsby, writing in 1983, reported that the number of pastoral schemes had reached as high as 300 a year, and that nearly 500 churches were declared redundant between 1969 and 1979. Of these, some 200 were demolished, and some 150 preserved by the Redundant Churches Fund.[70]

There appears to be no statutory obstacle to the government making grants to preserve historic churches even though they are still used for worship: it makes grants for other kinds of buildings that remain in normal use. In the late 1970s, the government expressed willingness in principle to make such grants.[71]

4. *Stipendiary Curates* — Most of the arrangements we have already considered for stipendiary curates remained intact into the last half of the present century, and some of them are still intact. The great compendium of the Pluralities Act, 1838, clarified some of the earlier material, and made a few changes in detail.[72] It required a commission of inquiry before a bishop could impose a curate on an incumbent who was not doing his job. It gave a newly installed incumbent six months to get rid of his predecessor's curate, and made clear that in all other cases an incumbent could not fire his curate without the bishop's permission. It required every

curate's license to specify the stipend, and carry a written declaration that
the incumbent intended to pay the specified amount and the curate to
receive it without any deduction. It made any agreement to take less or
any release for less void and not pleadable in court. It provided that any
dispute over the stipend should be heard by the bishop and not taken to
court. The reason these provisions were so forcefully stated was evidently
that many people (Sydney Smith for one) believed that a curate who had
agreed to take less than the law allowed would, and should, consider
himself honor bound to live up to his agreement. Anyone with so active a
sense of honor would presumably be caught out by the statutory
declaration.

The bishop, unlike the incumbent, could lift a curate's license at any time
and for any cause that seemed to him good and reasonable.[73] He did,
however, have under the statute to give the curate "sufficient opportunity of
showing reason to the contrary." The curate was allowed to appeal to the
archbishop, who was to do whatever he thought just and proper about the
case. The courts held that these provisions required both the bishop and
the archbishop to hear the curate in person, but did not make the
archbishop's order a judicial determination of a kind that could be appealed
to the Privy Council. Other cases held that a man with a license to
minister in a proprietary chapel was not entitled to these statutory
procedures because he was not strictly a curate, and that an institutional
chaplain, despite his license from the bishop, could be fired by the people
in charge of the institution in the same way as any other employee.

An important innovation brought in by the 1838 act was the power to
require an overworked incumbent to take on help that he needed and could
pay for, even though he was doing his best to serve the cure himself.[74]
The bishop was authorized to make the incumbent appoint a curate in any
benefice worth £ 500 or more if there were 3,000 inhabitants or a chapel of
ease with 400 people in its district. Furthermore, if a commission of
inquiry appointed under the act found that the cure was being inadequately
served, the bishop could impose a curate on a resident incumbent
regardless of either income or population, and regardless of negligence.
The only limit was that the curate could not be assigned more than half the
total income of the benefice unless the inadequate service was due to the
incumbent's negligence. It followed, of course, that unless the benefice
could support two clergymen the bishop could not put in a curate.

The relation between an incumbent and a curate involuntarily imposed
upon him remained ambiguous until it was clarified by a series of further
enactments.[75] The Sequestration Act, 1871, authorized (but did not
require) a bishop to inhibit a sequestered incumbent from interfering with
his curate. An 1885 amendment to the Pluralities Act forbade a
nonresident to interfere with his curate, or to return to residence without

the bishop's permission until his license for nonresidence expired. The Benefice Act, 1898, authorized a bishop to inhibit an incumbent from any further participation in the service of his cure when a curate had been imposed on account of his neglect of duty. Finally, the Benefices (Ecclesiastical Duties) Measure, 1926, provided for permanently ousting an incumbent when such an inhibition had been in effect for five years.

The 1926 measure, although it looks much more complicated than the nineteenth century legislation, added very little of importance except the provision for ousting the incumbent. Its enactment so outraged the anonymous editor of *Crockford* that we may suppose that the earlier enactments had not been much invoked.[76] All the provisions he was most worried about had been the same or worse since 1817. He seems to have been generally knowledgeable about what went on among the working clergy. If he did not know that proceedings could have been taken for inadequate service before 1926, we may presume that no such proceedings were in fact being taken. And if they were not being taken before 1926, there is little reason to suppose that they were being taken afterward. The Law Reports bear these speculations out. They show that the appellate procedure established in 1898 and retained in 1926 was invoked only twice — once in 1917, once in 1930.[77]

After the Second World War, the 1926 measure was replaced by the Incumbents (Disability) Measure, 1945, and the Incumbents (Discipline) Measure, 1947.[78] I will take these up later. Their provisions for curates are ancillary to other ways for dealing with inadequate performance by the incumbent. Since one of these measures applies only to disability and the other only to negligence or misconduct, there is no longer a general provision for making a resident, able, and conscientious incumbent hire a curate because the work is too much for one man to handle. The 1838 provision about parishes with three thousand inhabitants or chapelries with four hundred is still in force, but the general authorization was restated in the 1898 act and the 1926 measure, and repealed with the latter. As far as I know, the authority thus eliminated has never been missed.

Of course there is another way to get a curate into a parish with a hard-working resident incumbent, and that is to provide separate funding for the purpose. The Church Pastoral Aid Society was founded in 1836 under Evangelical auspices to make such funding available, and other societies followed. There was some complaint at first about the standards of churchmanship that these societies imposed on their beneficiaries, but the argument that he who pays the piper calls the tune came to be generally accepted.[79]

As we have seen, the Ecclesiastical Commissioners had always made some grants for the purpose of enabling incumbents to hire curates to help

with their work. They began making such grants more frequently in the
late nineteenth century. A measure of 1928 enabled them to make
payments direct to the curates involved instead of going through the
incumbents.[80] In 1976, all these grants were centralized, and responsibility
for paying the curates was assigned to the diocesan stipends funds of the
various dioceses. Also, a scheme under the Union of Benefices Measure,
1923, or the Pastoral Measure, 1968, could provide for using a specified
part of the revenues or endowments of a benefice to support a curate.
Now that the curate's pay does not have to come out of the incumbent's
pocket, we may suppose that getting a conscientious but overburdened
incumbent to accept a curate is no longer a serious problem.

B. Diocesan Organization.

   1. New Dioceses — Redistribution of dioceses was only slightly less urgent
in the 1830s than redistribution of parishes. As we have seen, the
Ecclesiastical Commissioners Act, 1836, provided for some alteration in
boundaries, and also authorized the combination of two pairs of existing
sees to make room for new ones at Manchester and Ripon in the rapidly
growing north country. But what was really needed was an increase in the
total number of dioceses. This was long prevented by the political
impossibility of increasing episcopal representation in the House of Lords.
The difficulty was not overcome until 1847, when the establishment of the
see of Manchester had been put off for more than a decade by obstacles to
the projected combination of Bangor with St. Asaph. (The incumbent
bishops, who were protected for their own time, had displayed unexpected
longevity, and by the time one of them had died, the beleaguered Welsh
Anglicans had built up a formidable opposition to having one less bishop in
their midst.)[81]
   The solution, when it came, was so simple that one wonders why it took
so long.[82] It was provided that Manchester could be set up as an
additional see, but that its bishop would not assume a place in the House
of Lords until some other bishop died or resigned. In the future, five sees
— Canterbury, York, London, Durham, and Winchester — were always to
carry seats in the Lords, while the remaining twenty-one places were to be
allotted to the remaining diocesan bishops on the basis of seniority. The
arrangement is perhaps typical of political compromises in that it accords
neither with the view that bishops as such should sit in Parliament nor with
the view that they should not. But it has maintained a Christian presence
in the legislative process without subjecting rearrangement of church
institutions to considerations of secular politics. Now that the powers of
the House of Lords are so attenuated, there would seem to be no harm in

giving seats to the whole bench of bishops — as was done with the peers of Scotland in 1963. But no one seems to be interested in doing so.

After the House of Lords problem had been disposed of, the main barrier to the increase of the episcopate was lack of money. When the Ecclesiastical Commissioners were first set up, the money they got from episcopal sources was put into a special fund, and there was some hope of using it for setting up more sees. But the people who supported the taking over of excess episcopal revenues were evidently as unwilling to have the money spent on new bishops as on old ones. The Ecclesiastical Commissioners Act, 1850, absorbed the episcopal fund into the common fund.[83]

Finally, in the mid-seventies, a decision was made to expand the episcopate by seeking new funds. An act was adopted in 1875 providing in this way for a new diocese of St. Alban's.[84] The Ecclesiastical Commissioners were to open an endowment fund for it, and when a specified income had been secured, they were to prepare an Order in Council to set it up. The act established the boundaries of the new diocese, specified what church was to become the cathedral, provided for dividing the income between the bishop and the chapter, authorized the queen to appoint the bishop by letters patent until there was a chapter to carry out the normal election procedure, adopted the expedient just described concerning the House of Lords, specified certain contributions — mainly buildings — that neighboring bishops had agreed to make to their new colleague, and provided for a modest contribution from the Commissioners. But the Commissioners were forbidden to make any contribution from their common fund beyond what was expressly authorized. The plan was evidently a success, for the new diocese was established less than two years after the bill became law.

A similar act was adopted for Truro in 1876. The see was funded and established in the same year. Then, in 1878, an act was adopted for four additional sees. The 1878 act put all the general provisions in the body of the act, and the provisions peculiar to individual dioceses in a schedule at the end. It was therefore possible to adopt the general principles by reference, and all future legislation did so. In this way, Parliament created eight additional bishoprics before the Church Assembly was established in 1920, and the Assembly created five more in the next few years. In all, eighteen new dioceses were established between 1875 and 1927, with the average time between the enabling act or measure and the Order in Council implementing it being about two and a half years.

2. *Suffragan Bishops* — Diocesan bishops have traditionally had episcopal helpers to hold some of their confirmations and ordinations, and to perform other pastoral and liturgical functions for which a bishop is

appropriate, even if not required.[85]   All the powers of such an auxiliary bishop depended on an ad hoc commission from the diocesan.   The bishops recruited for this office before the Reformation were sometimes Irish or foreign bishops set wandering by poverty or politics, sometimes local clergymen appointed by the pope to sees *in partibus infidelium*, i.e., ancient bishoprics that no longer required resident bishops because their territory was occupied by Moslems.   In the Roman Catholic Church, auxiliary bishops are still appointed to these sees (now called titular so as not offend the Moslems and the remaining Christians who live there). In English practice, these auxiliary bishops have been called "suffragans" since at least the fourteenth century. (Since the term properly designates the relation between a diocesan bishop and the archbishop of his province, I cannot explain this usage.)   When Henry VIII broke with the pope, he broke with his source of titles for suffragan bishops. Accordingly, he had an act passed in 1534 naming certain English towns that he could use for the purpose.[86]

The office of suffragan bishop fell out of use in the late sixteenth century, and no one was appointed to it from 1592 until 1870.[87]   Charles II spoke of reviving it, but never did. The reasons for this long abeyance are obscure, but it seems likely that Gibson was on the right track when he suggested that the increasingly onerous parliamentary duties of a diocesan bishop had made his connection with his diocese so tenuous that it might dissolve altogether if he could get someone else to do his ordaining and confirming for him. In any event, the 1534 act remained on the books, ready to be drawn on when the pastoral and demographic changes of the nineteenth century gave new cogency to the need for more bishops.   After a few tries at filling in the gap with superannuated colonial bishops, the practice of appointing suffragans was revived in 1870, and has continued ever since.

Under the 1534 act, any bishop who needs a suffragan may nominate two priests to the sovereign, who will choose one, and name him bishop of one of the specified towns.   In this capacity, his connection with the town is merely nominal, and his powers are only those listed in his commission from the diocesan. His office is not specifically funded, although the Church Commissioners have authority under a 1943 measure to pay him a stipend out of episcopal revenues pooled in their hands.[88]   Otherwise, he is paid by whatever other preferment he holds. Since his duties as a suffragan bishop do not occupy him full time, he is probably also an archdeacon, a cathedral canon, or a parish priest.

The 1534 act established twenty-five see cities for the suffragans. Power was given in 1888 to establish more by Order in Council, and it has been used fairly regularly.[89]   On the other hand, some towns have dropped out either because they have become full-fledged diocesan sees or because they are in Wales. As of 1985, there are sixty-two suffragan bishops in office in thirty-seven dioceses. London, with five, has the most. The towns from which the suffragans take their titles are customarily in the diocese they serve, although the statute does not require them to be.

Since the last new diocese was created in 1927, the administrative tasks of bishops have multiplied to the point that they have trouble keeping up with them. At the same time, dividing dioceses to the extent necessary to give adequate relief would distribute diocesan bishops so thick on the ground as seriously to impair the significance of their office. Also, many of the more burdensome jobs have to be done by any diocesan, whatever the size of his diocese. It has therefore occurred to a number of people, both bishops and commentators, that suffragans could be put to better use than they were in the past. Here is Bishop Kirk of Oxford,[90] writing in his diocesan magazine in 1942:

> It cannot be too emphatically stated that there are two very different conceptions of the functions of a suffragan bishop. The first may be called that of the 'assistant-suffragan,' the second that of the 'administrative-suffragan.' By an 'assistant- suffragan' I mean a bishop who may fairly be described as the under-study of the diocesan bishop. He will take such ordinations, confirmations, institutions or consecrations, and preside over such meetings, in all parts of the diocese indiscriminately, as may be assigned to him from time to time by the bishop of the diocese. Apart from such *ad hoc* assignments he has in effect no duties. The case of the 'administrative-suffragan' is very different. To him is committed as a permanency a particular area of the diocese (indicated to some extent by his suffragan title), and so far as the law allows he is responsible both for the administrative and for the pastoral oversight of the area — subject of course to the right of the diocesan bishop to perform whatever functions within that area he may choose for himself. To secure some degree of legal recognition for the suffragan's position, the area committed to his charge is usually at least an archdeaconry, and he may very suitably hold the office of archdeacon as well as that of suffragan. This, however, is not essential.

Despite the last sentence, Kirk wanted all three of his archdeacons to be suffragan bishops. One already was. To provide for the others, Kirk filled a second see that had been vacant for some years, and put through an Order in Council creating a third.

3. The Dioceses Measure, 1978 — In the early 1970s, the General Synod of the church concerned itself with updating the diocesan structure. It turned out that there was more sentiment in favor of giving fuller territorial responsibility to suffragans than in favor of creating more and smaller dioceses. The Dioceses Measure, 1978, ended by making it possible to do either.[91]

This measure generally does for the diocesan structure what the Pastoral Measure, 1968/1983, does for the parish structure. That is, it authorizes a centralized administrative process for developing schemes to distribute pastoral responsibilities in new ways. It establishes a Dioceses Commission to make recommendations and process schemes. It provides for reorganization schemes, by which dioceses may be split, joined, or otherwise altered, and for episcopal oversight schemes by which a diocese may be divided into areas in each of which a suffragan bishop will exercise some of all of the functions of the diocesan. Schemes are initiated by the bishop of the diocese affected, or by the bishops jointly if several dioceses are involved. The commission then takes input from interested persons, and, if it decides to go ahead with the scheme, puts it in final form and lays it before the diocesan synod of each affected diocese. If it is approved at that level, it goes before the church's highest legislative body, the General Synod. Then, if it is a reorganization scheme, it must be approved by the Synod and sent to the Privy Council for implementation. If it is an episcopal oversight scheme, the bishop can implement it unless the General Synod passes a resolution disapproving it. Other provisions of the measure authorize schemes creating area synods for episcopal oversight areas, and for combining the diocesan committees of two or more dioceses. Welsby reports that the diocese of London has been divided under this measure into five episcopal areas, each with its own synod.

For a bishop who does not want to go so far as to put through a scheme, the measure provides new ways of increasing the authority of his suffragans. The traditional sealed commission from the bishop to the suffragan is abolished in favor of a signed "instrument" setting forth the suffragan's powers. It is not clear what is accomplished by the change in terminology or by the abolition of the seal. The new document answers to the dictionary definition of a commission just as well as the old one did, and, as far as I can see, the old one required a seal only because the 1534 statute said it did. It may be that the old term carries some historical baggage that the framers of the measure wished to unload, but I have not been able to find what it is.[92]

The measure introduces legislative oversight into a bishop's use of suffragans. If the bishop's instrument to the suffragan empowers him to do anything besides confirm and ordain, it must be approved by the diocesan synod. And before the bishop can petition the Privy Council to create a new suffragan see or the queen to fill an old one that has been vacant for five years, he must get the approval of both the diocesan synod and the General Synod.

C. Patronage.

The pursuit of efficiency in the mid-nineteenth century had an ambivalent effect on the law of patronage. Measures for the redistribution of church endowments generally envisaged using the available patronage not for financial return but for pastoral efficiency and for the placement of deserving but unbefriended clergymen. To this end, the Ecclesiastical Commissioners Act, 1840, put all the patronage attached to individual canonries into the hands of the local bishop, and imposed severe restrictions on the exercise by chapters of their corporate patronage.[93] Where the Commissioners had discretion, they worked to the same end by trying to insure that every bishop, including the new ones, had substantial preferment in his gift. The bishop, after all, they reasoned, was the one who could be expected to know most about the needs of his diocese and the merits of his clergy.

But there was a good deal of other legislation that aimed at commercial rather than pastoral efficiency in its treatment of patronage. Advowsons could be sold for cash, and some statutes envisaged selling them and applying the cash where it would do the most good.[94] We have seen that the framers of the Municipal Corporations Act of 1835 rejected all the pastoral alternatives and directed municipal advowsons to be sold on the open market, and that the various Church Building Acts called for raising funds by giving the advowsons of new churches to contributors. An act of 1863 authorized the Lord Chancellor to sell the advowsons of over three hundred benefices in his gift, and use the proceeds to augment the incomes of the respective incumbents. An 1856 act authorized parishioners and other large groups with collective patronage rights to do the same.

Given this ambivalent attitude, assigning patronage to diocesan bishops did not insure that it would be regarded as an administrative responsibility rather than as a piece of the bishop's property. Bishops certainly did on occasion use their patronage for friends and relatives rather than for the humble and deserving clergy that the Commissioners had in mind.[95] Parliament, for its part, showed some mistrust of the bishop's administrative commitment by depriving him of his part in the processes of clerical discipline whenever the accused held preferment in his gift. Thus, the same patronage that was meant to enhance the bishop's administrative control over his diocese became a reason for limiting it.

On the private side, the pastoral conception of patronage was reflected in the development of patronage trusts, mostly under the auspices of the Evangelical party in the church.[96] These trusts would buy or be given advowsons for the trustees to use to place clergy of their persuasion. They are reminiscent of the Feoffees for Impropriations that Laud found so threatening in his day. Now, though, there was neither Laud nor the Star

Chamber to stop them. To be sure, the *imperium in imperio* that Laud feared was beyond both the means and the inclinations of the nineteenth century Evangelical party. The trusts probably did no more than secure representation in the parochial ministry for a school of churchmanship that patrons as a class tended to undervalue.

Around the turn of the century, patronage trusts ran afoul of a curious legal technicality that deprived them of some benefactions that they were intended to have.[97] Under general principles of trust law, only a charitable trust can be allowed to continue indefinitely without a specific beneficiary, and no trust is charitable unless the trustees are given specific charitable purposes to carry out. Of course, a patronage trust has no specific beneficiary. If the trustees are expressly charged to present clergymen of the Evangelical school, then the trust is charitable, because it is to promote a lawful form of religion. But simply filling benefices with suitable clergymen is not a charitable purpose, because it is no more than the legal obligation of everyone who owns an advowson. Therefore, if the founder of a patronage trust gave directions about the churchmanship of the persons to be presented, the trust was good. But if, as was more often the case, he gave directions about the people to be chosen as trustees, relying on them to see to the people presented to benefices, the trust failed for lack of a charitable purpose.

It would seem, though, that this principle did the patronage trusts less harm than might have been expected. Only the heirs of a benefactor had standing to bring it up, and they only with respect to the particular benefaction. We may suppose, therefore, that most of the patronage trusts were repaired in some way before they lost all their advowsons. Some of them are still in existence.

Private interests in the commercial efficiency of advowsons tended to call for increasing their liquidity. Where professional advancement in an earlier period had depended on the patronage of some highly placed friend or relative, there were many men for whom it now involved a cash investment. A man who looked to a patron for advancement might be expected to make do with whatever preferment that patron had in his gift, but a man who had, or whose father or uncle had, so many hundred pounds to spend on his career had to be careful to spend it wisely. If a young man wanted to be an army officer, the available funds could be spent on buying him a commission. If he wanted to be doctor, they could be spent on buying him a practice, if a barrister or solicitor, on placing him in a good office. If he wanted to be a clergyman, it seemed natural that the same funds should be spent on buying him a living.

The obstacle, of course, was the law of simony, which, as we have seen, made it illegal to pay the owner of an advowson for presenting a particular person to the benefice. Ancillary to this ancient rule were others that had been adopted over the years to plug loopholes. Several related to the sale of next presentations.[98] Such a sale gave the buyer the right to fill the next vacancy that came up in the benefice, but left the advowson itself in the hands of the seller. For the owner of the advowson, it was a way of realizing upon his property without diminishing his capital; for the buyer, it was a way of placing a particular clergyman without making an expensive long-term investment. Once the benefice had fallen vacant, such a sale could not lawfully be made, although it could be made while the incumbent was on his deathbed, and a contract for such a sale could be executed after vacancy if it had been made before. There was a statute of Queen Anne that made it unlawful for a clergyman to buy a next presentation and present himself. On the other hand, there was nothing to stop a clergyman's father from buying a next presentation and presenting his son. Nor was there anything to stop a clergyman, if he could afford it, from buying the whole advowson and presenting himself. A bishop in 1875 tried to revive the medieval canonical rule against self-presentation, but the lay courts would have none of it.

To get your son or yourself into a benefice, it was not enough to buy the advowson or the next presentation; you also had to get rid of the present incumbent. Generally, there was no problem getting him to resign as part of the transaction. Often he or some member of his family would be the seller, and the sale would be part of a carefully orchestrated step in his career. In any event, he would be apt to feel honor bound to fall in with the best interests of the patron.

But pinning him down legally was more difficult. Paying an incumbent to resign was just as illegal as paying a patron to present. In fact, an incumbent could not even retire on a pension until a statutory procedure was adopted in 1871 — the pension was considered a payment for giving up the benefice.[99] So if a contract for sale of the advowson or the next presentation spelled out the understanding of the parties that the incumbent was to resign, the whole transaction would be illegal. It was legal, however, for the seller to agree to pay an exorbitant interest on the purchase price until a vacancy occurred.[100] It may also have been legal — though this was not tested in the courts — to postpone the payment of the purchase price or even the consummation of the sale until vacancy. If the buyer was not content with a tacit understanding, one of these expedients would probably be invoked.

More disreputable, but also legal, was having the incumbent resign before putting the patronage up for sale, and then filling the benefice with an aged or terminally ill clergyman, so that the buyer could be safely promised a quick vacancy. One witness before an 1874 select committee of the House of Lords described a presentee who needed two men to support him walking up the aisle to be installed.[101] The bishops were advised by their lawyers (erroneously, I suspect) that they had no power to exclude a morally and intellectually acceptable presentee on the ground that he was too infirm to do the job.

Most of the questionable transactions involved the same set of advowsons, ones that had become detached from their traditional connections with local landowners, and were in the hands of clergymen or their relatives. Archbishop Benson, speaking in the House of Lords in 1886, estimated that these floating advowsons accounted for about one tenth of the livings in the country, although others had put the figure as high as one third.[102]

Many of these passed through the hands of professional agents, who acted as intermediaries in their purchase and sale. These agents evidently did not always abide by such legal restraints as there were, though they were probably not all as bad as the Reverend Murray Richard Workman (1827-80), the only one of their number whose misconduct is documented in the law reports.[103] Workman came to the attention of the authorities when one of his customers was convicted at the Worcester assizes of trying to blackmail him.

There is a reference to what seems to be the same blackmail incident in the testimony of the all-purpose reformer, the Reverend Lord Sydney Godolphin Osborne, before the 1874 committee already referred to. I assume, therefore, that Workman was the person Osborne described, although the committee reports mention no names. If so, he was an ex-convict living under an assumed name — although his claim to be a clergyman was evidently legitimate, and he had been heard to preach acceptably a time or two. In any event, he operated a publication called the *Church and School Gazette*, which carried notices of advowsons and next presentations available for purchase, and of benefices available for exchange. He performed a thorough and largely clandestine service for his customers:

> As all the smaller livings are very dear in proportion, and your capital not sufficient to obtain one with possession, I propose getting some assistance for you, but in doing this I act without your knowledge, or my endeavors might be abortive. Hence I am silent for your sake, and you must be the same.

At the time of this letter, he was evidently negotiating for a payment from the customer's uncle. Such a payment would be illegal whether the affected clergyman knew about it or not, but, as we shall see, it would be easier to set aside if he knew.

Part of Workman's service was evidently drafting letters for his customer to send to the bishop — for what purpose, I cannot tell:

> I enclose a copy of another letter for the bishop, which please send at once. The whole affair has been so far conducted very cleverly, and I am anxious for you not to spoil it by the least injudicious act or word.

Both of the above quotations are from letters that Workman sent to the Reverend J.J. Merest in November and December of 1867. Thereafter, in February of 1868, Workman bought the advowson of Upton-Snodsbury near Worcester for £ 400 from one O'Donnell, who was both patron and incumbent. In March O'Donnell resigned the incumbency, and in May Workman presented Merest, who was instituted in August. Meanwhile, in June, Workman sued Merest for an alleged debt of £ 350, and recovered judgment by agreement of the parties. A judgment, of course, could be enforced by sequestration of the benefice, without any further intervention of a court that might be told about the illegality of the underlying debt.

The figures in this story raise some problems. In one of his letters, Workman reports the income of Upton-Snodsbury as £ 120 a year, capable of improvement. Since it was stated in the House of Lords in 1886 that advowsons were fetching between five and ten years purchase,[104] it is not clear how Workman was able to get this one for £ 400. Also, unless he got some kind of down payment from Merest or his uncle that does not figure in the correspondence, he did not recoup his whole investment from this transaction. It would have to have taken some time to collect his whole £ 350 judgment from the revenues of the benefice, and even then there would be £ 50 to recoup in some other way, along with whatever profit he hoped to realize. Perhaps his plan was to sell the advowson on the market: even with a young and healthy Merest in possession, it would probably have brought him better than £ 50. Or perhaps he meant to hold it for a long-term investment.

Although this affair came to light because Merest tried to blackmail Workman, it was only Merest who got into trouble. He was fined £ 250 at the assize for the blackmail, deprived of Upton-Snodsbury under the simony laws, and unfrocked as a convicted blackmailer. Workman, who appeared as an accuser in the blackmail proceeding, and a witness in the church disciplinary proceeding, admitted the authorship of the letters, made no attempt to explain anything, and walked away none the worse for the whole affair, except that one presentment to Upton-Snodsbury was forfeited to the Crown.

The church authorities did not have adequate tools to cope with this systematic traffic in advowsons.[105] A bishop could sometimes keep a scheme from going through by refusing to accept the resignation of an incumbent. But instead of resigning, the incumbent could always give up his benefice by accepting another. The vacancy would then occur by operation of law, and there would be nothing the bishop could do about it. Arguably, the bishop with jurisdiction over the new benefice could block the scheme by turning down the presentment, but in the ordinary course of events he would not know about the scheme. Furthermore, some benefices were "donatives," into which a clergyman could be put without the intervention of any bishop at all.

On the other end of the transaction, a clergyman who actually paid to be presented to a benefice could be put out again as Merest was. But where the corrupt transaction was entered into by the clergyman's friends and relatives without his knowledge it is not clear what the church authorities could do about it (note the language in Workman's letter to Merest about acting without Merest's knowledge). Such a clergyman was *simoniace promotus*, a status created by a 1589 statute, rather than *simoniacus*, a status known to the canon law. He could not be subjected to a church disciplinary proceeding because he had not done anything wrong.[106] It was suggested that he might be put out in some kind of non-criminal church proceeding — a reasonable supposition, since the statute made the presentment "utterly void, frustrate and of none effect in law" — but I have found no case in which such a proceeding actually occurred.

The usual way of enforcing the 1589 act was by way of its provision for displacing the guilty patron for that turn and allowing the Crown to present. The presentment being void, the incumbency was equally so, so the Crown presentee could be put into the benefice without regard to the claims of the man whom the patron had put in. But the government in the nineteenth century had less need of ecclesiastical preferment than it had had in earlier times. When the Queen's Proctor was informed of a benefice in her gift — as he was by court order in Merest's case — he no doubt saw to filling it. But there was no longer anyone hard at work running down such cases in order to support clergymen in the royal service.

Presumably, a bishop who was fully informed when a presentment came before him that violated the 1589 statute could have refused the presentee. But the normal investigation on a presentment involved the fitness of the presentee and the title of the patron. A corrupt bargain involving the patron and a third party but not the presentee would normally not come to the bishop's attention. Nor is it altogether clear that the courts would have sustained a bishop in turning down a presentment on such a ground. He would have had in his favor the plain language of the statute about the presentment being void, but he would have had against him the ancient rule that bishop cannot raise patronage questions in litigation where he claims only as ordinary.[107] In any event, there is no case on the books.

In 1866, the House of Lords imposed several restrictions on a bishop's right to reject a presentee to a benefice.[108] They held that the ground of rejection was subject to review in a lay court, and had to be stated in such a way that the lay court could decide on it. They added that a disqualification created by the Canons of 1604 could not be used against the presentee of a lay patron, because those canons do not bind the laity. These holdings are surprising, as they seem to contradict a precedent going back to 1693. It was evidently this case that led the lawyers to tell the bishops they could not reject a person as too old or infirm to do the work.

Bills imposing less and less radical solutions to these problems were introduced in the House of Lords between 1874, when the first select committee on the subject reported, and 1898, when a bill was finally passed.[109] The 1874 bill would have created a patronage commission in each diocese, with the queen, the bishop, the clergy, and the landed laity choosing three members each. It would have forbidden any sale of a next presentation. As for the whole advowson, if it was appurtenant to a landed estate, it could still have been sold with the estate. Otherwise, no advowson could have been transferred, except by will or as part of a family land settlement, unless the transfer had been approved by both the bishop and the diocesan commission. No such transfer could have been approved unless the transferee was a substantial landowner in the parish, or a trust without power of sale — i.e., a patronage trust of the kind we have just considered.

A patron who wanted to sell his advowson, but could not find a qualified buyer could have required the diocesan commission to buy it from him at an arbitrated price. The price would then have been charged on the benefice in the same way as a loan from Queen Anne's Bounty. If the benefice was worth from £ 300 to £ 500, the queen, the bishop, and the commission would have taken turns presenting; otherwise, the commission would have had the same rights as any other patron. There would have been authority to lend public funds to the commissions to start the program in operation.

The bill would also have required at least three years experience as a curate before a man was eligible for a benefice — although the bishop could waive the requirement. Nor would a presentee have been entitled to institution unless the bishop certified to the patronage commission that he was qualified not merely for preferment in general, but for this particular benefice. The bishop's refusal of the certificate would have been appealable to the archbishop.

This 1874 bill was dropped without reported debate. More moderate bills introduced in 1886 and 1896 got a little farther, but not much. The bill that was finally adopted, the Benefices Act, 1898, contained only the most essential of the reforms originally proposed. It forbade sale of less than the seller's whole interest in an advowson (except that the settlor in a family settlement could reserve a life estate, and a mortgagor could reserve a right of redemption), but it made no restriction as to who the buyer could be. It forbade selling an advowson at auction, except together with 100 or more acres of land: a public auction made overly explicit to the parishioners that the seller was more concerned with money than with their spiritual welfare. It forbade a sale within a year after a presentment, or a presentment within a year after a sale "unless it be proved that the transfer was not effected in view of the probability of a vacancy within such year." It forbade any sale where payment was deferred or interest payable for more than three months, or where any payment depended on the occurrence of a vacancy. It required all transfers to be registered.

It did not give the bishop the sweeping powers of rejection the 1874 bill would have done, but it did allow him to turn down a presentee less than three years ordained, as well as a presentee too infirm to do the work, or one in serious financial difficulties. But the bishop was still not authorized to demand a certificate from the diocese where the presentee had worked before — an issue in the 1866 case referred to above. Nor, as far as I can see, was he authorized to turn down a presentee on account of a corrupt transaction to which the presentee was not himself a party.

Where the rejection was not based on a matter of doctrine or ritual, the bishop's refusal was made appealable to a newly created court consisting of one judge from the civil courts, who would try all questions of law or fact, and one archbishop (the provincial on appeal from a bishop, the other archbishop on appeal from an archbishop), who would decide any questions of pastoral discretion. A bishop was forbidden to institute a presentee until he had given one month's notice to the churchwardens, who were to inform the parishioners. Giving parishioners either a veto or a chance to remonstrate with the bishop had been talked about in connection with some of the earlier bills. This provision gave them no official standing, but it offered an opportunity to approach the bishop with any ground of refusal they knew of.

Further developments had to await the social changes after the First World War, and the establishment of the Church Assembly in 1919. With fewer people entering the clergy than were needed, and with the reduction in the relative value of benefice endowments, it was no longer obvious that the opportunity to place a clergyman in a benefice was a valuable property right entitled to the protection of the law. In any event, people were becoming less impressed with property rights as such. It was also coming to be generally expected that a professional man would advance his career through merit, not through the investment of capital. The system of patronage was coming to be seen less as a way of getting jobs for the friends and relatives of patrons, and more as a way of assuring variety in the parish clergy, supporting valuable bits of idiosyncracy (not to say eccentricity), and insuring that all schools of churchmanship were represented.[110] The time was ripe for imposing new limitations on patronage rights — even, some said, for doing away with them entirely.

In 1923, therefore, it was provided that after two more vacancies an advowson could not be sold unless it was appurtenant to land and sold with the land.[111] The owner, if he chose, could make it incapable of sale before the two vacancies occurred. The same measure dealt with a couple of other old problems by repealing the limited authority for resignation bonds adopted in 1828, and by providing that a clergyman who subsequently came by an advowson could not present himself.

In 1932, diocesan boards of patronage were created, with lay and clerical membership, and the bishop as ex officio chairman.[112] They differed from the commissions proposed in 1874 in not having government representatives, and in not requiring the lay members to be landholders. These boards were empowered to acquire and hold advowsons, and to make presentments. Since the 1923 measure applied only to transfers for a valuable consideration, any patron finding his diminished rights not worth the trouble could, and still can, turn his advowson over to the board.

In 1931, the parishioners were finally given an official voice in the presentation process.[113] Such a voice had been proposed for some time: a bill for the purpose had been introduced as early as 1886. That bill would have given the patron just two chances to come up with a candidate acceptable to a board of parishioners before the right to fill the benefice passed to the bishop. This stringent requirement was accompanied by other provisions that would have given the same board a veto over liturgical innovations by the incumbent. We may suspect, therefore, that the bill was intended more as a brickbat in the liturgical battles of the time than as a serious effort to deal with patronage rights.[114]

In any event, it was not easy to devise a plan that would give the parishioners powers that were neither illusory nor destructive of the patron's rights. As Bishop Stubbs, the great ecclesiastical historian, pointed out to his clergy in 1886, if the parishioners have an unlimited veto, they can pick a man and veto everyone else, whereas if they have a limited number of rejections, the patron can secure an unfettered choice by nominating patently unacceptable people until the number is used up.[115]

The 1931 measure navigated fairly well between the Scylla and Charybdis that Stubbs envisaged. It provided in the first place that upon being informed of a vacancy present or impending, the parochial church council might make written representations to the patron concerning the conditions, needs, and traditions of the parish, but without mentioning the name of any particular clergyman. If the parochial church council desired more input than this, it could pass a resolution calling for a conference

between the patron or his representative and the churchwardens as
representatives of the council. If the churchwardens then did not accept
the person proposed by the patron, that person could not be put in unless
the bishop approved of him as suitable for that particular cure. If the
bishop's decision was unfavorable, either the presentee or the patron could
bring it before the archbishop for review. Note that this was the first time
a bishop was allowed to reject a generally acceptable presentee on the
ground that he was not suitable for the particular position to which he had
been presented.

It was held that neither the bishop nor the archbishop acted judicially in
this process.[116] There was nothing to stop either of them from acting on
confidential information without giving the presentee or the patron any
chance to explain or refute it — or, for that matter, even to know what it
was. Earlier versions of the measure were objected to on this ground, and
one was withdrawn due to objections by the Ecclesiastical Committee of
Parliament after it had been passed by the Church Assembly. How
persuasive you find such objections depends on how you strike the balance
between the property right of the patron and the administrative function of
the bishop. After all, no one objects when the regional manager of a chain
store decides for reasons he does not care to explain that Smith is not the
person to manage the store in East Oshkosh. The objection in the case of
the church is part of a more general complaint voiced from time to time
that the church is in the process of being assimilated to a business
enterprise.[117]

A measure adopted in 1986, to go into effect at the beginning of 1989,
strengthens and elaborates the process of taking parishioners' input.[118]
The parochial church council still prepares a statement describing the
conditions, needs, and traditions of the parish. They can now ask the
bishop to respond with a statement describing in relation to the benefice
the needs of the diocese and the wider interests of the church. The council
is now required to appoint two representatives, who need not be the
churchwardens. The patron may not present anyone who has not been
approved both by these representatives and by the bishop, unless their veto
is overturned by the archbishop. But the bishop or the parish
representatives must give reasons for their rejection — which they did not
have to under the 1931 measure.

The council can still request a meeting before the patron makes his
choice. Under the new measure the whole council, except for the outgoing
incumbent and his wife, are entitled to attend the meeting, and at least a
third of them must attend for it to be valid. The bishop must also come or
send a representative and the rural dean and the lay chairman of the
deanery synod must be invited (unless the dean is the outgoing incumbent).
This meeting is evidently intended only for an exchange of views. No

binding resolution is provided for, and the veto powers of the parish representatives and the bishop are the same whether or not a meeting has been called for.

The 1986 measure makes a number of other changes in the law of patronage. The most important is in providing that patronage rights can be exercised in person only by communicant members of the church. Any patron who cannot declare himself to be such a member must appoint a representative who can. This requirement applies to all non-Anglican patrons, and the special disabilities of Roman Catholics and Jews are done away with.

The measure attenuates considerably the traditional status of an advowson as a piece of real property. It severs advowsons from other real property to which they may have been appendant. It forbids all sales, even for benefices, if there are any, that have not yet had two vacancies since 1923. Even gratuitous transfers cannot be effected without giving the bishop and the parochial church council a chance to object. All advowsons must be registered, and registration is conclusive as to who is the patron. The right to be registered is determined in the first instance by the diocesan registrar, with a right of appeal to a Patronage (Appeals) Committee consisting of two ecclesiastical judges, one diocesan registrar, and two other people. There is no express abolition of the jurisdiction of the lay courts to try patronage cases, but the conclusiveness of the registration process would seem to have that effect. It is interesting that the church has gained by this measure a jurisdiction that Innocent III at the height of his power could not touch.

The measure also reduces the rights of a patron regarding alienation of property and modification of buildings belonging to the benefice. These rights were justified mainly on the ground that such changes might reduce the value of the benefice in the patron's gift. The financial changes in recent years have made this justification obsolete.

With this measure, the patronage system appears to have survived a particularly precarious period of its existence.[119] A measure to abolish it entirely failed to pass the church's General Synod in 1973 only because of a tie vote in the House of Bishops. A measure to allow individual parishes to abolish or retain it as they chose was put before the Synod in 1978. The 1986 measure seems to be among the more conservative of the proposals mooted in recent years.

Patronage, like other institutions such as the House of Lords, seems to continue in great part because nobody is sure what to put in its place. Bishops, parochial church councils, and diocesan boards are the main possibilities, and all have drawbacks. The parochial church council is not in a very good position to know who is available. It is significant that in the one reported case involving a candidate rejected by the council under the

1931 measure the candidate was a former incumbent who had gone off on the missions and wished to return.[120] The bishop and the diocesan board probably know the clergy of the diocese pretty well, but they probably have little contact with the rest of the clergy. Leslie Paul, in his 1964 report, proposed supplementing them with a national Clergy Staff Board.[121] For those who worry about the bureaucratization of the church, such proposals of course only make matters worse:

> The abolition of patronage in its present form and the substitution of staffing boards would quickly obliterate those sanctifying tensions which mark and safeguard the spirituality of the Church of England. The traditions of the Church of England have so developed that one cannot be a mere Anglican, faceless and indistinguishable from another. He belongs to one of these traditions, be it Evangelical, Central, Catholic, or a blend of these. The traditions are of the essence of the Church of England, which is not a sect of episcopalians. The spirituality of the Church, which Anglicans have struggled to preserve throughout its history, proclaims this truth in a unique way. The substitution of appointment by committees and boards for the patronage system would obliterate this spirituality. The clergy acceptable to a bureaucratic system of appointment would need to be colourless men with convenient views.[122]

In view of the experience of other Christian bodies, and of Anglicans in other countries, these strictures cannot be fully accepted. But there is enough to them to give pause to the advocates of across the board centralization of the placement process.

Meanwhile, it is not very clear what the private owner of an advowson is supposed to do with it. There is no way he can turn it to personal account. He cannot sell it, and if he could, there would probably be no one interested in buying it. If he has a clergyman among his friends or relatives, it would be mere coincidence if the benefice in his gift turned out to be more suitable to that clergyman than one the clergyman could come by in some other way. As we have seen, clerical incomes have been largely equalized, and clergymen are in short supply. It is pastoral opportunity or personal taste that leads a clergyman to take one position rather than another.

So the advowson is for the patron a responsibility rather than a source of benefit, pecuniary or otherwise. If he is of a particular school of churchmanship, he can discharge that responsibility in favor of his school — though he might do better to turn it over to a patronage trust of his persuasion. If he is himself a parishioner, he can have the advantage of securing for himself and his neighbors the ministrations of a person he likes or at least approves of. But there is a high probability that he will be a person who takes no interest in ecclesiastical affairs. He may be a passive worshipper, he may belong to some other religious body, or he may be one of the eighty-some-odd percent of the population who, even if they profess to belong to the Church of England, do not regularly attend any church at all. In such a case, he may or may not have a friend who is a communicant, who is concerned with how the benefice is filled, and who is willing to go through all the inquiries and conferences called for by the 1986 measure.

Many patrons, therefore, feel the weight of a responsibility that they have no personal stake in discharging in a particular way, and not enough information to discharge well. They have tended to turn their advowsons over to bishops or diocesan patronage boards, usually bishops. The 1986 measure allows them instead to choose any of a number of bodies (chapters, patronage boards, universities, or colleges) to act for them with respect to particular vacancies. It remains to be seen how many of them will choose this alternative.

When Paul wrote in 1964,[123] somewhat less than a quarter of the advowsons in the country were in private hands; there will probably be less by now. The rest were distributed as follows:

Crown and government Officials: 6-7%
Colleges: 7%
Bishops: 30-35%
Cathedral chapters: 5-6%
Diocesan patronage boards: 2-3%
Parish clergy of mother churches: 8-10%
Patronage trusts: 14-16%

The percentages differ because they were produced by different people counting approximately 12,000 benefices one by one.

What the figures seem to show is that private patronage, for good or ill, is on the way out, but that non-private patronage will probably go on being widely enough distributed so that neither the loss of variety feared on the one hand nor the full rationalization hoped for on the other is likely to come to pass.

III. Clerical Discipline and Service of Cures

The early reform period saw two major statutes dealing with the traditional vices of the clergy along more or less traditional lines.[124] The Pluralities Act, 1838, covered pluralism, nonresidence, neglect of duty, and unsuitable occupations. The Church Discipline Act, 1840, covered lapses in morals and deportment. The reworking and strengthening of the earlier material in these statutes endured with minor changes until quite recently, and some of it is still in force.

A. Pluralism.

The traditional reason for letting a clergyman hold more benefices than one was that he deserved a higher income than a single benefice could provide.[125] The decree of the Fourth Lateran Council (1215) forbidding pluralities authorized dispensations for "sublime and literate persons who ought to be honored with greater benefices." The statute (1529) by which Henry VIII hoped to make up for the lax enforcement of the Lateran decree contained broad exceptions for university graduates, for government officials, and for the chaplains and relatives of the aristocracy. The tightening of standards in the Elizabethan and Jacobean canons was addressed in great part to insuring the learning and piety of the would-be pluralist. In this canonical and statutory climate, pluralism had supported the civil service through most of the Middle Ages, and had supported major scholarly achievements during the seventeenth century, including the King James Bible.

But by the nineteenth century, most pluralists were distinguished for their connections rather than for their accomplishments.[126] Diana McClatchey lists all the pluralists holding preferment in Oxfordshire in 1825. There were eight with cures aggregating £ 1,000 or more a year, and twenty-three more with between £ 500 and £ 1,000. Aside from accumulating benefices, I do not find that any of them did anything more noteworthy than occasional service as a justice of the peace. Needless to say, people who thought bishops and canons were overpaid could not be expected to countenance such pluralists as these making nearly as much.

So the traditional reason for pluralism held no attraction for the reformers of the 1830s. On the other hand, there was another reason that was becoming more and more cogent as people became more and more concerned with support for the working clergy.[127] If a benefice was too poor to support a full time incumbent, letting someone hold it together with a neighboring cure, dividing his time between them, might well be the best way of making sure that services would be maintained. At least, it was apt to be better than any of the other available expedients.

Accordingly, the 1838 act aimed at limiting pluralities to benefices near enough to be served by one man, and at least one of which was so poor as not to give adequate support to a full time incumbent of its own. The churches could not be more than ten miles apart. If one benefice had a population of more than three thousand, the other could not have more than five hundred, and the two between them could not pay more than £ 1,000 a year. However, if one benefice had a population of more than two thousand and paid less than £ 150, the bishop could allow it to be held with any other benefice regardless of size and income, as long as the churches were not more than ten miles apart.

While this act was under consideration, it was stated on the floor of the House of Commons that there were 412 clergymen with three livings each, 57 with four, and three with five.[128] The act provided that no one could hold more than two benefices, or even (except in emergencies) serve more than two cures in a day, whether as incumbent or as curate.

Earlier legislation, whether statutory or canonical, had not applied to cathedral preferment without cure of souls. This act, presumably to spread the benefit of these lucrative and undemanding positions, provided that no one could hold preferment in more than one cathedral, could hold more than one piece of cathedral preferment together with a benefice with cure, or could hold more than one benefice with cure along with cathedral preferment. The only exception was for archdeacons. An archdeacon could hold his archdeaconry along with anything else he could lawfully hold, as long as his cathedral preferment, and at least one of his benefices with cure, was in the same diocese as his archdeaconry. As we saw in connection with the redistribution of cathedral revenues in 1840, the reformers of this period were not quite sure how archdeacons ought to be supported.

As was the case under earlier legislation, even if a person fulfilled the statutory conditions for holding two benefices, he still had to have a dispensation to do so. The exclusive power to grant such dispensations was left in the hands of the archbishop of Canterbury, where it had been since the Reformation. The reason one archbishop had this power and the other did not is that it was originally a power of the pope, and all the pope's routine dispensing powers were transferred to the archbishop of Canterbury by the statutes of Henry VIII. The archbishop still had a good deal of discretion. The act required him to satisfy himself "as well of the Fitness of the Person as of the Expediency of allowing such Two Benefices to be holden together . . . ." However, his denial could be appealed to the Privy Council. The 1604 canons had required a bond to reside part time on each benefice before a dispensation for plurality could be granted. This requirement was expressly abolished. Anyone who was lawfully a pluralist could now reside on either benefice, as we shall see.

The sanction provided for unlawful pluralities was the traditional one: the old living became void upon acceptance of the new. Or if a person entitled to hold two livings accepted a third, both of the first two became void unless he filed a declaration in the diocesan registry showing which one he planned to retain. The distinction between benefices absolutely void under King Henry's statute and benefices voidable under the general canon law was done away with. In every case, the old living was to "be and become ipso facto void, as if he had died or had resigned the same." Since the old benefice was automatically vacated on acceptance of the new, the courts held that the acceptance of the new did not violate the act, and that possession of an incompatible benefice was not a ground for a bishop to refuse institution into a new one.[129]

I have often wondered why vacation of the first benefice was originally chosen as the main sanction for enforcing the laws against pluralism. It would seem that refusing institution into the second until the first had been at least conditionally resigned would have been more effective. Routine inquiries on presentment to the second benefice should disclose the existence of the first, whereas it would be pure happenstance if the bishop responsible for the first benefice were to find out about the second. There is a case in the books involving a man who took one benefice in 1821 and another in 1825, and was not put out of the first until 1848.[130] The framers of the 1838 act evidently hoped to improve the situation by careful record keeping. They provided an annual questionnaire that every incumbent had to fill out and return to his bishop. It is not clear whether this expedient did any good. McClatchey's Oxfordshire compilations indicate that the overall number of pluralists fell off substantially after the 1838 act, but that the percentage who lacked the proper dispensation fell off only a little.[131] In 1825, fifty-seven out of eighty-two, 70.7 percent, had no dispensations; in 1866, the figure was fifteen out of twenty-three, 65.2 percent. It does not appear that these undispensed pluralists escaped detection by being underhanded or sneaky; McClatchey evidently found a number of them simply by checking *Crockford* and other earlier directories. They were probably not caught simply because nobody was systematically engaged in catching them. There were fewer of them not because there was a better enforcement machinery, but because the church was developing a class of clergy more serious about their pastoral responsibilities, and less willing to violate the law.

The limitations as to population under the 1838 act lasted until 1930. But the rules concerning income and distance were tightened and simplified in 1850.[132] It was provided that no two benefices with cure could be held together unless the churches were no more than three miles apart, and unless one of them had an income of £ 100 or less. The figures were changed to four miles and £ 200 in 1885, four miles and £ 400 in 1930.

The change from limiting aggregate income to limiting the income of the poorer of the benefices held together was debated in Parliament.[133] Some members thought it was outrageous for a man with a rich benefice to gobble up a nearby poor one. But others pointed out that it was unlikely that anyone other than a neighboring incumbent could be gotten to take full responsibility for the cure of souls in a parish worth less than a hundred pounds. One member referred to a parish worth eighty pounds, which was held in plurality by a neighboring incumbent who paid fifty to the curate who actually served it, and pocketed the other thirty. But this situation cannot be taken as showing a serious defect in the law. The local bishop had ample power to prevent it by fixing the curate's stipend at the full value of the benefice.[134]

The same 1930 measure that made minor changes in the prescribed values and distances introduced an alternative approach to pluralism that was later to displace the old one. It provided that the machinery set up by the Union of Benefices Measure, 1923 — which we have already looked at — could be used, instead of uniting two benefices, to provide that they could be held in plurality. When that was done, the limitations as to value and distance would no longer apply to the two benefices in question. The Pastoral Measures, 1968 and 1983, adopted the same approach, and repealed all the earlier provisions.[135] So, as the law now stands, benefices with cure can be held in plurality only in accordance with a pastoral scheme or order, and if the scheme or order provides for holding them in plurality, they cannot be held separately. It is still provided that no one can hold cathedral preferment in more than one cathedral. He can hold one cathedral preferment plus one benefice with cure only if the cathedral statutes so provide. Where a plurality is not allowed, the acceptance of a new benefice or preferment still automatically voids the old one.

B. Nonresidence.

As we have seen, Parliament adopted a major statute on nonresidence in 1803, and revised it in 1817.[136] The 1838 act used the structure and much of the language of the earlier legislation, but reduced the acceptable grounds for not residing. There were three classes of legitimate nonresident incumbents:

1. Those exempted without the need of a license because they were performing specified duties elsewhere. The Georgian acts had preserved and even expanded the broad range of academics, bureaucrats, and household chaplains exempted under Henry VIII's statute (1529). The 1838 act limited such exemptions to lawful pluralists while residing on their other benefices, canons while keeping obligatory residence in their cathedrals, dons while lecturing in the universities, heads of certain public schools, and chaplains to the royal family, Parliament, or the Inns of Court, while in residence and performing duties as such.
2. Those holding licenses which the bishop (or the archbishop on appeal from the bishop's refusal) was authorized to issue on being satisfied that certain specified conditions obtained. The conditions

provided for in the earlier statutes included illness of the incumbent
or a member of his family, unfitness of the residence house, low
income requiring the incumbent to serve as a curate elsewhere, and
compliance with the requirements of an office legitimately held but
not listed among the specific exemptions. The 1838 act eliminated
the last two of these grounds, and severely qualified the others.

3. Those holding discretionary licenses issued by the bishop with the
approval of the archbishop where none of the statutory
requirements was met. The provisions for these licenses were not
significantly changed in the 1838 act. No doubt they were invoked
in more cases with the narrowing of the other categories.

The traditional power of a bishop to enforce residence by monition was
given statutory form in 1803. If a nonresident had neither a license nor a
ground of exemption, the bishop could issue a monition requiring him to
reside within thirty days. If he failed to do so (or failed to pay the cost of
preparing and serving the monition) the bishop could sequester the fruits of
the benefice, apply the proceeds to the upkeep of the fabric and the service
of the cure, and turn over what remained to Queen Anne's Bounty. If a
benefice was sequestered for three years running (reduced to two years in
1817), or three different times within that period, it became void as if the
incumbent had died or resigned. The patron could fill it immediately, but
not with the same man. The 1838 act made no major changes in this
procedure, except to make the benefice void after only one year of
continuous sequestration or two sequestrations within two years, and to
require the patron to be notified of the voidance before the bishop could
start counting six months to declare a lapse and fill the benefice himself.

The 1838 act finally did away with the private action to collect penalties
from the nonresident. The penalties were retained as they had been set in
1803 (from one-third to three-fourths of the annual income depending on
how long the incumbent was away) to replace the ten pounds a month
provided for by the act of Henry VIII. But they were now collectible only
in the bishop's court by a person authorized by the bishop to sue for them,
and the proceeds went not to the informer or to the Crown, but to the
augmentation of the benefice, the repair of the church or parsonage, or the
general purposes of Queen Anne's Bounty.

The bishops' statutory power to deal with nonresidence was of course
subject to supervision by the lay courts. With the proliferation of
government agencies and functions in the middle decades of the nineteenth
century, these courts were in the process of developing the principles that
became the foundation of modern administrative law. Several of their
decisions applied such principles to nonresidence cases. Some applications
favored the bishops, others the nonresidents.

The good news for the bishops was that they had virtually complete discretion in deciding whether an excuse for not residing was good enough. The governing legislation allowed a bishop to issue his monition whenever it appeared to him that an incumbent was not keeping sufficient residence, and to proceed to sequestration unless the incumbent either returned or stated "such reasons for . . . nonresidence . . . as shall be deemed satisfactory by the bishop." The courts in this period were prepared to give literal effect to a provision such as this: when a statute attached consequences to the satisfaction or dissatisfaction of a specified official, or to a state of affairs as it appeared to such an official, they would not consider a claim that he ought to have been satisfied or ought to have seen things differently.

Accordingly, when the Reverend Josiah Bartlett was convicted of libel at the Hereford Assizes, and was sentenced to two years imprisonment, the courts made no trouble about his bishop ordering him to reside, sequestering the benefice when he failed to do so, and declaring the benefice vacant when the sequestration had continued for a year.[137] Bartlett's repeated claim that the law does not demand the impossible was held to be a matter within the exclusive discretion of the bishop.

But if the courts were more willing to let the bishop go his own way substantively, they were also more willing to fault his procedures. In 1832, the redoubtable Bishop Blomfield of London came a cropper when he tried to impose a curate on a negligent incumbent without first hearing the incumbent in his defense.[138] Although the governing statute (1817) allowed the bishop to act if he was satisfied "either of his own Knowledge, or upon Proof" that the cure was being inadequately served, the court read into it a requirement that the party adversely affected be heard. *Audi alteram partem* is an ancient principle of British justice, and if Parliament wishes to exclude it, it must do so expressly. Later cases were to hold the same thing with regard to a variety of statutory powers, including the power of the Wandsworth Board of Works to demolish a house put up without proper notice, the power of the justices of the peace to levy execution on the property of a Liverpool resident who failed to pay his gas bill, and the power of the Archbishop of Canterbury to approve or disapprove the action of a diocesan bishop in unlicensing a curate.

The requirement of hearing the party adversely affected was not a requirement of a full judicial proceeding, or even of an administrative trial of the modern kind. It was simply that the person affected be confronted with the proposed official action and the reasons for it, and be given the opportunity to bring forward reasons for doing differently. But even though the necessary procedures were rudimentary, according them was not

as simple as some bishops might have supposed. The case of *Bonaker* v.
Evans (1850) shows how easy it was for a bishop to get in trouble.[139]
Bonaker had lived for some years in a neighboring town five miles from
his church. He had had a license to do so, evidently on account of the
condition of the vicarage house. But this time when the license ran out (as
under the statute it did at the end of the calendar year following the year it
was issued), the bishop did not see fit to renew it. Accordingly, Bonaker
became an unlicensed nonresident, and in due course he was served with a
monition to reside. He responded with a communication reporting that he
had just moved into his "damp, uncomfortable hole of a vicarage," and
reproaching the bishop in terms more plaintive than convincing for not
continuing his license to reside in better quarters. The bishop was
evidently not fully reassured by this statement, for arrangements were
made, presumably at his behest, to check up on whether Bonaker was in
fact residing. At the end of six months, a report was made — by whom
does not appear — listing the nights in which Bonaker had slept at the
vicarage. They amounted to thirty-eight all told for the six months.

The bishop's secretary wrote confronting Bonaker with this report.
Bonaker responded that it was a lie, but he did not offer any alternative
version of the truth. The bishop then served him with a new monition, and
after hearing nothing further for the statutory period of thirty days,
sequestered the benefice. Bonaker got his money back from the
sequestrator because he had not had an adequate hearing before the
sequestration was ordered. The court was not altogether clear on what the
bishop did wrong or failed to do right. Under the teaching in Bartlett's
various lawsuits, it would seem that the bishop had full power to decide
both whether it was true that Bonaker stayed at the vicarage only thirty-
eight nights, and whether staying that many nights constituted a sufficient
residence. It would also seem that Bonaker should have known he was in
trouble unless he persuaded the bishop to see one question or the other his
way. But the bishop had not told him specifically that a sequestration was
in the offing unless he met the accusation. It was significant to the court
that the bishop's last communication was a second monition rather than a
threat to sequester. It was suggested that Bonaker might have supposed he
was being offered a *locus penitentiae*.

When the report of Bonaker's case came out, Bartlett, who was now out
of prison, but whose benefice had already been given to another, sued to
get his benefice back on the ground that he had not been heard before his
bishop proceeded from monition to sequestration.[140] He lost. The court
had no trouble distinguishing his case from Bonaker's. Bartlett, who, unlike
his colleague, had had good legal advice throughout, had responded to the
monition with an affidavit setting forth his inability to reside on his benefice

on account of his confinement in prison. The court found that that affidavit constituted the presentation he was entitled to make, and that the bishop, by issuing the sequestration, had rejected it. We are left unsure whether Bonaker did better than Bartlett because he wrote a letter instead of an affidavit or because the bishop issued a second monition instead of a sequestration.

The courts' main device for securing the regularity of administrative proceedings was allowing collateral attack on irregular ones. Thus, in the secular cases referred to above, the Wandsworth Board of Works was held liable as a common trespasser when it tore down a house without holding a hearing, and the Liverpool Gas Company was held liable for conversion when it took property under a warrant issued without a hearing. Judges and sheriffs were protected against personal liability, but their immunity did not necessarily extend to the people who set their processes in motion.

So it is not surprising that sequestrations for non-residence were open to collateral attack. In 1847, a particularly litigious (and particularly well-paid) nonresident named Bluck succeeded on this ground in collecting from a parishioner £ 28/4/2 of tithe rentcharge which the parishioner had already paid to the bishop's sequestrator.[141] The Sequestration Act, 1849, perhaps passed with this case in mind, seems to protect anyone who pays a sequestrator against liability to the incumbent. But the incumbent could still sue the sequestrator himself and recover his receipts; this is what Bonaker did.

Bonaker's case exemplified another important aspect of the problem of nonresidence. Besides nonresidents who actually absented themselves from their cures, there were numerous nonresidents who lived in the vicinity and served their cures, but for one reason or another did not live in their official residences. It had been the law at least since Coke's time that it was not enough for an incumbent to reside in the neighborhood or even in the parish. He must reside in the actual residence house.[142] The theory was that he had a duty to keep the house up for his successors, and would be more apt to do so if he lived in it. Bonaker had been out of his vicarage for nearly thirty years when he called it a damp uncomfortable hole. Whether its condition was originally a cause or an effect of his absence is a moot point.

Under the 1817 act, if there was no house of residence, the incumbent could live where he pleased, as long as it was within the boundaries of the parish and not unreasonably far from the church.[143] But if there was a house, however unsuitable, he had to be licensed as a nonresident unless he lived in it. The 1838 act modified these provisions in two directions. It extended them to a case where there was no fit house as well as to a case where there was no house at all. At the same time, it required in either case that the incumbent take out a license from the bishop specifying the house in which he was to live, and that the house so specified be no more than three (or in a city or market town, two) miles from the church. But the license issued under these provisions was not a license for nonresidence. As long as it was in effect, the house was treated as a proper residence house and the incumbent as a proper resident.

If the incumbent was to live farther away than that, or if his house was not unfit — it sometimes made financial sense for him to let out his house and take lodgings — he had to be licensed as a nonresident. And once he was so licensed, the bishop had unlimited discretion as to whether to let him go on serving the cure, or whether instead to appoint a resident curate. In short, it was possible for an incumbent such as Bonaker to serve his cure personally while living five miles away, but it was entirely up to the bishop whether to permit him to do so.

Letting the residence to tenants was not forbidden if the incumbent had the necessary permission to live somewhere else. But he was required to include in the lease a provision that the tenant would vacate if the bishop either ordered the incumbent back into residence or required him to put in a resident curate. A tenant who retained possession against the bishop's order was liable to a penalty of two pounds a day as well as to summary eviction. If the incumbent failed to put the statutory provision in the lease, the tenant could still be put out on the bishop's order, but he could then sue the incumbent for damages.[144] The authority to evict a tenant under these provisions is still in effect, and has been held to supersede the various statutory protections for tenants that have been adopted since World War II.

The 1838 act strengthened the 1777 provisions for borrowing money on the security of benefice revenues in order to repair or improve the residence house. Some of the bishop's powers under the earlier act were turned into duties, and he was provided with the beginnings of an administrative machinery for exercising them. Whenever a benefice fell vacant, he was to commission four beneficed clergymen to find out if there was a fit residence on the premises, and whether the benefice was worth £ 100 a year. If the answer to the first question was no and the answer to the second was yes, the bishop was to order the necessary construction or repairs, and mortgage the benefice revenues (generally to Queen Anne's Bounty) to pay for them. The patron and the incoming incumbent were entitled to be consulted about this process, but not to veto it.

It was not always dilapidation or neglect that made a residence house unfit. Standards of domestic comfort were on the rise for the clergy as they were for the rest of the middle class. As a judge put it in 1859, upholding a mortgage to support substantial additions:

[T]he rectory house was of the following character. [describing it as it was before the improvements] Now, no doubt, in times happily now long gone by, a clergyman might have been expected to be contented with such a residence. But things have much changed since then, and a clergyman is now expected to occupy the position of a gentleman, and requires a residence that should at least possess the decent comforts of a gentleman's house.[145]

Most of the law on residence is still about where it was in 1838, but the provisions on upkeep of houses have undergone a number of revisions. The first came in 1871, applicable to dilapidations in the strict sense, but not to improvements of the kind envisaged in the passage just quoted. The Ecclesiastical Dilapidations Act, 1871[146] provided for the appointment of official surveyors of dilapidations in every diocese. On vacancy or in response to a complaint to the bishop, a surveyor was to inspect for dilapidations, and report on the work necessary to make them good, with the probable cost of having it done. The incumbent was then required to have the necessary work done; otherwise, the bishop would have it done at the incumbent's expense.

If the dilapidation had occurred during a previous incumbency, the present incumbent could recover from his predecessor the sum specified in the surveyor's report: both present and former incumbent could present objections to the report, but neither could attack it collaterally. The present incumbent was liable for the repairs whether or not the previous incumbent or his estate was good for the money. This of course was harsh treatment of the incumbent, who might be entirely blameless in the matter. But it meant that buildings could be repaired without abiding the vicissitudes of a lawsuit.

Pending completion of repairs, the incumbent was required in most cases to deposit the necessary funds with Queen Anne's Bounty in a special Dilapidation Account for his benefice. If the Bounty lent him money on the security of his revenues and potential recovery from his predecessor — as they were authorized to do with the permission of the bishop and the patron — that money would go into the same account. The Bounty would then pay contractors direct.

The system set up in 1871 was revamped and strengthened in 1923.[147] Every diocese was provided with a Dilapidations Board to appoint and supervise surveyors. Surveys were to be made every five years, rather than on complaint or voidance, and the incumbent was to make annual payments calculated to amortize over a period set by the Board the repairs called for in the surveys. The payments were held by Queen Anne's Bounty in long and short term Repair Accounts for each benefice. If repairs became necessary before the money for them accumulated in the accounts, the Dilapidations Board could request Queen Anne's Bounty to advance the necessary funds and charge the future revenues. If any dilapidations were due to gross negligence or misconduct on the part of a present or former incumbent, he or his estate would be immediately liable to Queen Anne's Bounty for the cost. Otherwise, no incumbent was to be held liable beyond the annual assessments.

The editor of *Crockford* was unhappy about the provision in this measure for having contractors paid direct by Queen Anne's Bounty. He felt it made the clergy look wealthier than they were — a concern that evoked his elegant polemics on other occasions as well.

> When repairs have been done, and the barriers which interpose between the Incumbent and the use of his own money for his own purposes have been surmounted, the Governors of Queen Anne's Bounty send him a cheque. This is drawn, not to his order (he might misappropriate it), but to that of the tradesman who has been employed. The payee marks the image and superscription, and not unnaturally concludes that some benevolent fairy has intervened to relieve the Incumbent of all liability. It is not inconceivable that he resolves to charge her at a higher rate next time he gets an opportunity, and tolerably certain that he does not keep the information to himself: at any rate in a village. It is difficult to convince him that the Royal Bounty is merely disbursing part of what it has extracted from the rightful owner's pocket some time previously. We can see no reason for assuming that the clergy are not on a level of intelligence and probity sufficiently high to be allowed to handle their own money in the ordinary way in common with all other classes of His Majesty's subjects, not being certified lunatics or undischarged bankrupts.[148]

It is not clear whether the editor realized that the 1871 legislation was open to the same objection.

Oddly enough, the 1871 and 1923 provisions did not repeal the 1777 and 1838 ones. It is hard to believe, though, that bishops appointed four commissioners on every vacancy to survey the residence house under the 1838 act when there was a surveyor required to do the same thing under the 1871 act. Phillimore, writing in 1895, describes the 1777 and 1838 acts in a chapter called "Residence Houses" and the 1871 act in a chapter called "Waste and Dilapidations," paying no attention to the possible overlap.[149] What I suspect is that the incumbent himself used the 1777-1838 provisions when he wanted to borrow money to enhance his own comfort, while the authorities used the 1871 act to redress the incumbent's negligence and enforce repairs that the incumbent did not care to make.

The two sets of laws have now been replaced by the Repair of Benefice Buildings Measure, 1972.[150] That measure turned the whole responsibility for residences and other buildings over to a Diocesan Parsonages Board. Each Board has taken over all the repair accounts for all the benefices in its diocese. Using those funds, plus contributions from parishioners and general diocesan funds, the Board provides at least quinquennial surveys, makes all necessary repairs, buys all necessary insurance, and even, if it chooses, reimburses the incumbent for taxes. Only in case of a deliberate act or omission is an incumbent or former incumbent liable for repairs. If it appears from a surveyor's report that he is so liable, the Board can sue him, but the report, unlike reports under the earlier legislation, is open to collateral attack in such a suit.

C. Debt.

Another way a clergyman could impair the service of his cure was by running up debts. From at least as early as the mid-thirteenth century, there was a procedure by which the holder of a judgment against a beneficed clergyman could collect it out of the clergyman's ecclesiastical revenues. The bishop would sequester the benefice in response to a royal writ, and the sequestrator would pay the proceeds to the judgment creditor, after deducting whatever sums the bishop ordered to provide for the service of the cure, and to keep the incumbent — and after the Reformation, his family — from starving.[151] By the mid-eighteenth century, this procedure could not be used until the sheriff had attempted a conventional execution of the judgment and found no secular property to apply to it. By the 1830s, the sheriff had to name the benefice in his return before the bishop could be given a writ to sequester it. By 1848, the sequestrator had to account to the lay court as well as to the bishop for what he did with the money he collected — although expenses for purely ecclesiastical purposes could not be questioned in the accounting.

It took some work to correlate this procedure with the developing law of bankruptcy.[152] The future revenues of a benefice were not assignable by an incumbent, and therefore were not reachable by his trustee or assignee in bankruptcy without a special provision for reaching them. Nor was it consistent with the rights of the parishioners and the church for the trustee to take possession of a benefice as he would of a farm. But the trustee could not get a writ to the bishop to sequester the benefice because the trustee was not a judgment creditor. The situation was provided for in 1826 by a statutory provision that the order appointing the trustee was to serve the bishop in lieu of a writ. He was to sequester the benefice and have the sequestrator pay the trustee as he would a judgment creditor. The sequestration was not affected by the discharge of the debtor in the bankruptcy proceedings.[153] Its availability was treated as an asset of the estate to be applied to the debts. It would continue until all of them were paid off.

The sequestration affected the income but not the status of the incumbent debtor.[154] He was still responsible for the service of the cure, still entitled, and required, to live in the residence house, still entitled to appoint the parish clerk, and perform whatever other functions belonged to his office. It was provided in 1871 that if after six months the bishop considered that this situation was causing a scandal in the parish, he could inhibit the incumbent from residing or serving the cure, and appoint a curate to take his place until the sequestration was ended.

Until the mid-nineteenth century, the bishop's good faith was evidently the only limit on how much of the sequestered income he diverted to pay a curate or to support the incumbent. The 1861 Bankruptcy Act specified that if the incumbent continued to serve the cure, the bishop could assign him only the statutory stipend that would go to a curate if the incumbent did not reside.[155] The 1871 act provided the same figure where the bishop appointed a curate.

There were various laws that provided disciplinary sequestrations that might overlap sequestrations for debt.[156] The 1838 Pluralities Act was explicit in making a sequestration for nonresidence take precedence over one for debt. Other provisions were not explicit, but the courts gave them precedence also. On a disciplinary suspension, the bishop was entitled to all of the income that was not allocated by statute or needed to keep up services. The debts of the misbehaving incumbent could not deprive him of this right. Nor would the disciplinary measure be fully effective if the incumbent could have his debts paid off while it was in force.

Until 1898, there was no limit to the time a benefice could be sequestered to pay the incumbent's debts, except, of course, that if the incumbent ceased to hold the benefice his creditors had no further rights in it. The Benefices Act, 1898, provided that any future incumbency would be terminated if the benefice was sequestered within twelve months of the incumbent taking possession, was sequestered for more than a year , or was sequestered twice in a two year period.[157] In this way sequestrations for debt were assimilated to sequestrations for nonresidence under the 1838 act.

This ancient procedure with these few modifications is still in place, although we may suppose it is no longer of much importance. It presumably applies only to endowment income, and, as we have seen, endowment income is not usually enough to support a clergyman and his family without supplementation from other sources. In the normal course, a clergyman's creditors today are probably better off using whatever devices are available to collect from other wage earners.[158] It is likely also that today's clergymen do not run up debts as exuberantly as their predecessors did. They cannot afford to.

D. Clerical Avocations and Amusements.

The 1838 act updated the earlier restrictions on clergymen engaging in business.[159] The Henrician rules against buying and selling for profit — themselves based on ancient canonical rules — had been rewritten in 1817 with language perhaps broader than its framers had intended. A few months before the 1838 act was adopted, the Court of Exchequer had thrown out a suit by a bank on a bill of exchange because two of the partners in the banking company were clergymen. In vain did the bank argue that the language of the 1817 act should be interpreted in the light of the less restrictive Henrician statute it had replaced, and that banking should not be considered an unbecoming occupation for a clergyman.

The ink was scarcely dry on the opinion in this case when Parliament adopted a retroactive change in the law, validating the transaction that had just been declared invalid and any others open to the same objection. Our main 1838 act was adopted some months later with provisions to rectify the situation for the future. It was provided that a clergyman could be interested in any business undertaking as long as there were at least five other people involved, and as long as he did not participate in the management or do the trading in person. An act of 1841 inserted similar provisions into the main body of business association law. It was also made clear that violation of those restrictions that continued in force, although it might subject a clergyman to ecclesiastical censures, would no longer invalidate a contract.

The law on farm leases continued to reflect the prevailing ambivalence concerning the agrarian pursuits of the clergy. I have referred to the widespread feeling that the rural clergyman gains rapport with his flock by working in the fields as they do. However, the work could also give rise to accusations of neglect. In 1917, a set of such accusations found its way into the law reports.[160] The Reverend William Rice, was complained of for being too busy in his fields and pastures to catechize or prepare his sermons, for driving his sheep through the village on a Sunday morning, and for coming to church dirty for services. The last accusation, incidentally, was made nearly five centuries earlier against a convent chaplain who gave further scandal by riding in from haying on the same horse with one of the nuns. We must set against accusations of this kind Rice's claim that his glebe was too poor to attract a tenant, and that the rest of his income was too meager for him not to make the most of his glebe. Add also the fact that incumbents often opposed restrictions on clerical farming, because they were letting their curates farm the glebe to supplement inadequate stipends.

As we have seen, King Henry's statute, reworking traditional canonical strictures, forbade clergy to take agricultural leases. It contained a number of loopholes, however, and in 1803 bishops were given a plenary power to dispense from it. An 1817 act — the same one we have already considered in connection with pluralism and nonresidence — replaced the earlier statute, left out the loopholes, and restricted the bishop's dispensing power to seven years at a time. However, it allowed a clergyman to lease up to eighty acres without asking leave of the bishop at all. These 1817 provisions were picked up almost verbatim in the 1838 act.[161] Note that none of the statutes interfered with a clergyman working his own glebe, or with an incumbent turning his glebe over to his curate as long as he did not reserve a rent.

The 1838 provisions as to both business and farming are still in force. However, their effect has been greatly diminished by the dispensing power given the bishop under the Clergy (Ordination and Miscellaneous Provisions) Measure, 1964.[162] The bishop can authorize any trade or business whatever, even if it is forbidden under the earlier legislation. He must, however, consult the parochial church council of the parish where the clergyman officiates before he either grants or denies the permission requested. His denial is appealable to the archbishop of the province. This measure appears to be cumulative with the 1838 provisions. It would seem, therefore, that anything permitted in 1838 (e.g., joining a partnership with six or more members, or leasing eighty acres of land) does not require the bishop's permission, and that anything the bishop could have authorized in 1838 (e.g., leasing more than eighty acres) he can still authorize without consulting the parochial church council.

Turning from business to pleasure, we find that canonical tradition barred the clergy from four categories of recreation that were not generally regarded as immoral for the laity. These were hunting, attendance at shows and dances, gambling, and visiting taverns or alehouses.[163] Only the last two were specifically forbidden by the Canons of 1604, but those canons did not purport to be a complete compilation, and the other two categories were also generally regarded as forbidden. As we have seen, none of these prohibitions was much enforced during the eighteenth century and the first quarter of the nineteenth.

The revival of these strictures is generally attributed to the Evangelical movement. The Tractarians, however, were not far behind. If their standards of clerical decorum were less rigorous than the Evangelicals', their zeal for canonical niceties was greater. By the sixties or seventies, the two factions between them had not only made it unusual for clergymen to hunt, dance, gamble, and frequent theaters or pubs, but even made it

questionable for them to smoke cigars or participate in village cricket
matches.[164]

How much the canons, or even the authority of the bishops, had to do
with this development is hard to say. It is fairly clear that canonical rules
of this kind were not enforced in court. All the court cases I have found
involve sexual misconduct, drinking well beyond the bounds of conviviality,
or other conduct that would be as objectionable for a layman as for a
clergyman.

There was probably a generation or so in which bishops did some hard
work on clergymen who followed the easy ways of their Georgian
forebears.[165] Matthieson reports a bishop in 1825 who was refusing to
license curates unless they promised not to hunt. The literature has some
choice anecdotes about encounters between the redoubtable Bishop
Phillpotts of Exeter and the equally redoubtable fox hunting parsons of his
diocese. There is a notebook of Bishop Wilberforce of Oxford covering the
years 1845-1850 containing a list of those present at a ball, with the names
of clergy underlined; a handwritten list of clerical hunters in Oxfordshire; a
newspaper list of all the hunting licenses issued in Berkshire for 1847, with
the names of the clergy ticked off in ink; and a newspaper clipping from
Buckinghamshire that deserves to be quoted in full:

GAME HUNTING MISSIONARIES

It will no doubt be of the very highest service to the interests of
humanity that we should give publicity to the fact that the county of
Buckingham can this year boast of having twenty-nine reverend and
learned clergymen to wage war against the vermin which infest the
farmer's crops. The names of these philanthropic worthies deserve to be
handed down to futurity, seeing their "feet are beautiful upon the
mountains" because they "publish peace" to the turnips. We therefore
cannot do less than give their names in rank and file, and in alphabetical
order, having some difficulty to single out the best of them for the head
of the list:

[followed by a list of names]

Presumably the people whose names were on these different lists heard
from the bishop about it. Presumably also, heavy sarcasm from the local
press would have an effect quite independent of episcopal displeasure.
Also, the professional ethos of the clergy themselves must have changed a
good deal as Victorian sensibility developed.

Ultimately, a reaction set in against barring the clergy from the innocent
recreations of the rest of the population. W.S. Gilbert in the *Bab Ballads*
traces the change of heart of a bishop who

Sought to make of human pleasures clearances
And form his priests on that much-lauded plan
That pays undue attention to appearances . . . .

Enraged to find a deacon at a dance
Or catch a curate at some mild frivolity,
He sought by open censure to enhance
Their dread of joining harmless social jollity.

His opposition evidently extended to pantomimes, Punch and Judy shows,
singing in amateur operatic quartets, and even playing croquet. But after
being followed about in his own social life by a Phantom Curate, who
showed up whenever he was doing something he did not allow his clergy to
do,

At length he gave a charge and spake this word:
"Vicars, your curates to enjoyment urge ye may;
To check their harmless pleasuring's absurd;
What laymen do without reproach the clergy may."

The bishop's word seems to be the standard embodied in the new canons
adopted in Canterbury in 1964 and in York in 1969. Unlike the 1604
canons, these have no specific prohibitions of clerical recreations. They
merely tell a minister not to "give himself to such occupations, habits, or
recreations as do not befit his sacred calling, or may be detrimental to the
performance of the duties of his office, or tend to be a just cause of
offence to others."[166] This language officially supersedes the prohibitions
of gambling and alehouses in the 1604 canon. Whether it also supersedes
the pre-Reformation canonical rules against hunting or attendance at shows
and dances is less clear, but I would be surprised if anyone tried to enforce
the old rules today in a case where the language of the new canon did not
apply.

E. Vice, Scandal, and Neglect.

The Church Discipline Act, 1840,[167] covered all offenses against
ecclesiastical law, although it was not used for mere failures to live up to
traditional or puritanical notions of what becomes the cloth. Aside from
doctrinal and liturgical cases, which I will take up in the next chapter, the
main cases under it involved sexual immorality, drunkenness, or crime. It
simplified both the jurisdictions and the procedures that had dealt with
such matters in the past.

Proceedings under this act could be set in motion in either of two ways.
The bishop of the diocese in which the alleged offense took place could

appoint a five-man commission to hear evidence and report on whether there was a prima facie case or not. Alternatively, that bishop, or any other bishop in whose diocese the accused held preferment could issue "letters of request," sending the case direct to the provincial court for trial.

If the bishop chose the commission alternative, and the commission reported a prima facie case, and if either the accused or the complainant (if there was one) did not want the bishop to handle the case by himself, the bishop had another choice to make.[168] He had a second chance to send the case to the provincial court by letters of request. If he chose not to do this, he was obliged to have articles drawn up, setting forth the specific charges, and try the case himself with three assessors (one barrister, one archdeacon, dean, or chancellor of his diocese, one person of unspecified qualifications). There was an appeal to the same provincial court that he could have requested to try the case in the first place. Whatever way the provincial court got the case, there was a further appeal to the Judicial Committee of the Privy Council, which had been made the church's court of last resort in 1833.

The bishop's option to send cases to the provincial court instead of trying them himself was not new.[169] Letters of request were mentioned in a statute of 1532, and mentioned as an existing practice. The bishop obviously kept more control over a situation if he dealt with it at home. He did not have to initiate proceedings even if there was a complainant urging him to do so. On the other hand, if a commission was once convened, the bishop could not drop the case if either a complainant or a fellow bishop in whose diocese the accused held preferment wanted him to go on. Bishops sometimes kept additional control by having their secretaries act as complainants. This practice was upheld by the lay courts against the contention that it impaired the impartiality of the bishop.

Sending the case to the provincial court had the advantage of providing a more experienced tribunal. This must have had great appeal to a bishop who felt that there were no major pastoral considerations involved in a case. There was also the advantage that the provincial court could deal with offenses covering more than one diocese, or with offenses committed in one diocese by a clergyman from another.[170] It had been held as early as 1845 that a commission could consider only offenses within its own diocese. Accordingly, when a Lincolnshire rector was accused of misbehaving with a woman in London, the bishop of Lincoln had to use letters of request; otherwise, he could not have dealt with the matter at all.

The bishop's control over the commission alternative was diminished by a provision that substituted the archbishop for the bishop whenever the accused held preferment in the bishop's gift.[171] Because of this provision, G.A. Denison, the redoubtable archdeacon of Taunton, was prosecuted by

Archbishop Sumner after two successive bishops of the diocese had decided
not to issue letters of request. Under the provision in question, the
archbishop acted not as archbishop, but as the bishop's surrogate. He had
to hear the case within the bishop's diocese, and his judgment was
appealable to his own provincial court, just as if the bishop had delivered it.

The act contained a two-year statute of limitations. What had to be
done within the two years was the filing and service of articles.[172] It was
not enough to convene a commission within the time. This requirement
put a certain amount of pressure on the commission proceedings. In
Denison's case the preliminaries ate up the statutory period and Denison
got off after all.

Where the proceeding was based on a criminal conviction in a lay court,
it could be brought within six months of the conviction even if that was
more than two years after the actual misconduct. Earlier acts could also be
brought forward to support a more severe treatment of later ones (it is one
thing to be drunk on one occasion, another to have been drunk once a
month for three years), or to inculpate an otherwise ambiguous situation
(for a man to be seen kissing a woman seems less innocent if they were
found in bed together on an earlier occasion).[173] Misconduct more than
two years old could also be used by a bishop as a ground for refusing a
presentee to a benefice. Such a refusal did not depend on the 1840 act,
and was therefore not subject to the limitations of that act.

There were two recurrent questions that the 1840 act failed to resolve
satisfactorily. One was whether the giving of scandal was an offense in its
own right, or merely a basis for inquiring whether some other offense had
been committed. The other was how to treat conduct that was at once an
ecclesiastical offense and a secular crime. Both these questions were
historically obscure, and both called for difficult policy decisions.

Under the canon law as it stood before 1640, the giving of scandal was
punished as part of a proceeding addressed to whatever substantive offense
the scandal involved.[174] If a person was widely suspected of doing
something wrong, but there was no hard evidence to prove he had done it,
he could be cited into court and made to clear himself by means of a
canonical purgation. As we have seen, this consisted of a formal
exculpatory oath, supported by compurgators, who swore that the oath was
worthy of belief. If, as was often enough the case, a person succeeded in
this way in clearing himself of the substantive offense, but could not deny
having a bad reputation in the matter, he could be ordered to stop
whatever he had been doing to establish the reputation. In some cases, it
appears, he could be put to penance as well, or at least made to apologize
for the scandal.

The 1661 statute forbidding the church courts to require anyone to clear
himself by oath made it impossible to deal with scandal in the traditional

way.[175] Since the necessity of the oath had arisen from the existence of the bad reputation, there had been no occasion for censuring the reputation without requiring the oath. There was, therefore, no precedent for doing so. Gibson, as we saw, proposed doing it even without the precedent, but the temper of the times was no kinder to this than to his other suggestions for tightening church discipline. I have found one case (1703) in which a man was tried and convicted on a regular canonical accusation for having the reputation of an adulterer. He was ordered to apologize for the scandal, and refused to do so. His excommunication went through two levels of courts before it was thrown out by the Court of Delegates.

When the *Free* case, which we looked at earlier, established that a church court had more power to get rid of a scandalous minister than it had to punish a layman, it became possible to take a new look at scandal. A couple of cases in the 1840s — one just before, one just after the new act took effect — established that a clergyman who consorted with young men under suspicious circumstances could be deprived of his office without being found guilty of sodomy — either because he had violated the canons requiring him to set a good example to other Christians or because his pastoral usefulness was destroyed by the suspicion that he had permitted to arise.[176]

But when cases involving scandal came to trial, it was not clear just what issue was to be tried. In each of the cases just referred to, the issue seems finally to have been not what reputation the accused had, but what his relation was with the young men in question. In another case, a minister was deprived because of the scandal arising from his conviction of being drunk and disorderly.[177] He was not allowed to show that the conviction was had on perjured testimony, because the conviction created scandal whether or not he had actually committed the offense. But he was also not allowed to show that there had been no scandal because all the parishioners knew that the testimony was perjured. In short, the relation between the scandal and the substantive offense remained ambiguous. The courts claimed a power to punish behavior calculated to give scandal, but they required no proof that scandal was actually given.

The 1840 act did nothing to resolve this ambiguity. It could be set in motion either by a complaint that the accused had committed an offense against the ecclesiastical laws or by the existence of scandal or evil report as to such an offense. But when the statutory commission reported, it was not supposed to say whether there was scandal or not: it was supposed to say whether there was sufficient prima facie ground to proceed further. If so, the accused was to be tried not for having a bad reputation, but for having committed some specific offense.[178] The act did not purport to make anything an offense that was not one already.

The ambiguity as to scandal heightened the difficulty with acts that offended against secular as well as ecclesiastical law. Until 1576, such acts were treated as they had been before the Reformation.[179] The ecclesiastical authorities could bring what canonical proceedings they pleased, and impose whatever penalties the proceedings made appropriate. The lay authorities, for their part, could also bring what proceedings they pleased, but a convicted clergyman was handed over to his ordinary instead of undergoing the punishment prescribed for lay offenders. The ordinary would treat the lay conviction not as a conviction (under the medieval canon law, lay courts had no power to try clergymen), but as the equivalent of a bad reputation. Unless the lay court had ordered him kept in prison, the offender would be put to a canonical purgation, and released if he made it successfully.

In the late medieval period, this "benefit of clergy" was gradually transformed into a general mitigation of the criminal law, most of whose beneficiaries were not genuine clerics. As a result, the ordinary's part in the process became useless, burdensome, and sometimes embarrassing. It was therefore a practical reform to provide, as was done in 1576, that persons claiming this benefit should no longer be turned over to the ordinary, but should be let go — after up to a year in prison if the judges so ordered.

This was the state of the law in 1618, when Sir Henry Hobart, Chief Justice of the Court of Common Pleas, decided the case of *Searle* v. *Williams*.[180] Searle was a parson convicted of manslaughter at the Assizes, and let go on his claim to benefit of clergy. A canonical proceeding was then brought to put him out of his benefice on account of the manslaughter. It is not clear whether the proceeding was based on violation of prevailing standards of clerical deportment or on the ancient canonical irregularity attached to homicide as such; I suspect the latter. Before the proceeding was completed, Hobart and his companions issued a prohibition at Searle's request. Searle "ought not to be questioned now in the Spiritual Court for this manslaughter . . . ."

Hobart's reasoning is difficult to follow, and it invokes some bad history as it proceeds. The general idea seems to be that but for the 1576 statute a clergyman who escaped temporal punishment by benefit of clergy could then escape canonical punishment by making a purgation. Since the statute was meant to do away with a meaningless formality rather than to change the outcome of any case, a clergyman who successfully invoked benefit of clergy in the lay court would have to be treated as if he had also successfully purged himself in the church court.

The basic holding of the *Searle* case applied only to clergyable felonies, and became obsolete when benefit of clergy was abolished in 1826.[181]

But in the course of his opinion, Hobart delivered himself of a dictum that lasted a good deal longer. That was that a clergyman could not be deprived or censured for an act that was also a lay offense until he had been tried and convicted in the lay court. This principle was reiterated, with a reasonably persuasive rationale, as late as 1886.[182] Lord Penzance (a good enough judge as far as I can see; his role in the ritual prosecutions has brought him more obloquy than he deserves) pointed out that if the accused were to be acquitted in a church trial, his acquittal would not protect him against a secular prosecution, but it would prevent his being deprived if the secular trial resulted in a conviction. So, if the church could try the case before the state did, the two proceedings might end with a parish in charge of a convicted criminal whom there was no way of displacing. For serious offenses, therefore, there had to be only one trial, and that had of necessity to be the secular one.

The problem, of course, was prosecutorial discretion. Not every act that qualified on paper as a crime was one the lay authorities wanted to spend their time and resources punishing. Particularly in the case of sexual irregularities, the church might have a great interest in weeding out clergymen guilty of conduct that the state had little interest in prosecuting. It is one thing not to impose on an active homosexual the life imprisonment to which he was theoretically subject until 1967;[183] it is quite another to leave him in charge of a parish.

To some extent, the problem might have been met by prosecuting the offending clergyman for causing scandal instead of for actual immoral acts. I have already referred to two sodomy cases in the 1840s in which such prosecutions were allowed. But this expedient would have been conceptually messy, and it would not always have worked. For instance, a bishop might well have wanted to prosecute a clergyman who wrote obscene letters not only before his conduct came to the attention of the public prosecutor, but also before it caused scandal by becoming public.[184]

It was partly to meet this difficulty that Parliament took a new approach to secular crimes in the Clergy Discipline Act, 1892.[185] That act provided that any conviction carrying a sentence of imprisonment with hard labor — as well as any bastardy order, or any adverse judgment in a matrimonial litigation — would result without further process of any kind in the vacancy of any preferment held by the clergyman involved, and in his inability to hold new preferment without specific permission of the bishop and the archbishop affected. In addition, the bishop could, if he chose, depose him from the ministry entirely.

If a clergyman was convicted in a lay court of any act constituting an ecclesiastical offense, but was not sentenced to imprisonment with hard labor, or if he was accused of an immoral act, immoral habit, or

ecclesiastical offense (except one involving doctrine or ritual) for which no
lay proceeding had been brought, he was to be tried in an ecclesiastical
court, and sentenced to deprivation by the bishop or lesser punishment by
the judge. If there was a lay conviction it was to be conclusive as to the
commission of the act constituting the offense. Any other fact question was
to be tried by the ecclesiastical judge with five assessors, three clergymen
and two justices of the peace. Appeal could be taken to the provincial
court or the Privy Council at the option of the appellant, but not from one
to the other.[186]

It was held that a person brought to trial under this act could not defend
by showing that his conduct constituted a secular crime of which he had not
yet been convicted.[187] Getting rid of the old restriction was one of the
purposes of the new legislation. Also, the act contained a provision that
proceedings under it would not bar subsequent lay proceedings for the
same conduct. This provision would have been superfluous if there could
be no proceedings under the act unless the lay proceeding had already
taken place. Lord Penzance's concern about the effect of a church acquittal
followed by a lay conviction was presumably met by the provisions
concerning the conclusiveness of the latter. If the lay conviction carried a
prison sentence, it resulted in deprivation without any proceeding in which
the earlier acquittal could be brought up. Even if it did not carry a prison
sentence, it was conclusive as to the conduct involved, and therefore would
not admit of the accused bringing up a previous trial in which he was found
not to have done it.

The provision for cases not involving automatic deprivation gave a
certain amount of trouble as to just what it covered.[188] The operative
language reads as follows:

> If a clergyman either is convicted by a temporal court of having
> committed an act constituting an ecclesiastical offence, and the foregoing
> section [as to automatic deprivation] does not apply to him, or is alleged
> to have been guilty of any immoral act, immoral conduct, or immoral
> habit, or of any offence against the laws ecclesiastical, being an offence
> against morality and not being a question of doctrine or ritual, he may
> be prosecuted . . . .

Later, the act defines immoral acts, conduct, and habits as including any
acts, conduct, or habits proscribed by the two 1604 canons denouncing
general unbecoming behavior and requiring the clergy to set a good
example.

A few cases will indicate the difficulties encountered in interpreting this
language.[189] Most of them were resolved in favor of getting rid of
unsuitable clergymen. *Young* was a clergyman who was found sitting in a

dancing room with a prostitute on his knee, swapping jokes with those present. He admitted that what he had been doing was inappropriate, but insisted it was not immoral. The court found him guilty under the definition referring to the canons: that definition made almost anything immoral if it was inappropriate. *Fitzmaurice* was convicted at the Petty Sessions of soliciting alms under false pretenses, and of being a rogue and vagabond. He was evidently not subject to automatic deprivation because he was not sentenced to imprisonment with hard labor. He argued that the first branch of the above language did not apply to him because neither soliciting alms under false pretenses nor being a rogue and vagabond was an ecclesiastical offense, and that the second branch did not apply to him because they were not immoral, not being within the canons by which that term was defined. The court made short work of him, evidently on the theory that immoral acts were not limited to acts within the canons referred to, although they included such acts. *Moore* was found to have used, on several occasions over the course of three years "language . . . which certainly could not be defended, and the use of which would be disgraceful to anybody, whether clergyman or layman." But Lord Halsbury in the Privy Council was not willing to say that using such language on any given occasion amounted to an "immoral act" within the meaning of the statute. He then went on to say that "immoral conduct and immoral habit are probably the same thing," and that three or four occasions in three years cannot amount to a habit.

A significant and probably unexpected result of the 1892 act was the elimination of scandal as in independent ground of complaint. Sir Lewis Dibdin brought that result about in two cases seventeen years apart.[190] The *Harris* case (1893) was a proceeding under the new act before Dibdin as chancellor of the Rochester diocese, sitting with five assessors. The charge contained, along with several accusations of drunkenness, an allegation of scandal, which Dibdin struck out. He pointed out that, although the 1840 act referred to scandal, the 1892 act did not. It followed that scandal had to be prosecuted under the old act and not under the new one (the 1840 act was repealed as to any case covered by the 1892 act, but retained for any other case).

In the *Lax* case (1910), the prosecutor took Dibdin at his word and proceeded under the 1840 act. Lax (like Free, a century earlier, aptly named) was a married clergyman accused of associating with a certain young woman of his parish in a manner that caused grave scandal to the church. While no evidence of adultery could be brought forward, they had been seen strolling in a meadow arm in arm, and sitting in a pub with her head on his shoulder. Dibdin, now promoted to judge of both provincial courts, threw the case out. He argued that with the abolition of compulsory purgation in 1661 it was no longer possible to make a person answer for scandal unless the scandal arose because of blameworthy conduct on his part. But if the blameworthy conduct came within the 1892 act, that act was exclusive and the 1840 one could not be used. In view of the reference to canons about setting a good example, what Lax was accused of could be dealt with under the 1892 act, and therefore this proceeding under the 1840 act must be dismissed. This is persuasive enough, but hard to reconcile with the earlier decision in *Harris*. Dibdin did not try. It was cited to him in argument, but not mentioned in his opinion.

A further weapon against clerical misconduct was provided by the Incumbents (Discipline) Measure, 1947.[191] We looked at that measure in connection with the appointment of curates for incumbents who are not adequately serving their cures. As we saw, it replaced the provisions of the Benefices (Ecclesiastical Duties) Measure, 1926, insofar as they dealt with neglect of duty. Where the 1926 measure, like its predecessors since 1817, had covered all situations in which the cure was inadequately served, cases of illness or superannuation were now to be dealt with under the Incumbents (Disability) Measure, 1945, cases of misconduct under the 1947 measure, cases of mere overwork not at all.

The new measure tinkered a little with the machinery. Instead of the ad hoc commission provided for in 1926, it referred preliminary inquiries to a standing Ministerial Committee set up in each diocese under the companion measure of 1945. Instead of the court provided for in 1898 and continued in 1926 — one civil judge to decide the law and the facts, one archbishop to decide the sentence — it provided a Special Court consisting of the regular diocesan judge sitting with two lay and two clerical assessors chosen from a standing panel.

The disciplinary thrust of the 1947 measure was enhanced by a specific reference to "conduct unbecoming the character of a clerk in Holy Orders." The 1926 measure and the lone case interpreting the 1898 act[192] had subsumed such conduct under the head of neglect of duty — doing, it seems to me, some violence to the usual understanding of the term. The new disciplinary emphasis was also reflected in the sanctions available. The 1926 measure had aimed primarily at providing for a curate where the incumbent was not adequately serving the cure. The provision for vacating the benefice after five years seems an addendum rather than an integral part of the scheme. In the 1947 measure, on the other hand, the appointment of a curate seems ancillary to the disciplining of the incumbent. It is one of a number of actions available to the bishop, ranging from mere censure to immediate deprivation.

Anglican clergymen have long been on the whole a well-behaved lot, and are even more so now that there is so little non-religious incentive for becoming or remaining one. There have been very few cases under the acts and measures we have been considering.[193] Phillimore, writing in 1895, lists twenty-four reported cases, and I have found only dozen or so since. Of these, one involves the appointment of a curate under the 1838 and 1898 provisions regarding neglect of duty and another a similar appointment under the 1926 measure. The others all arise under the 1892 act. I find no reported cases under the 1947 measure. As for unreported cases, *Crockford* for 1933 refers to two under the 1926 measure. A 1972 case says that there were "only a few" under the 1947 measure. We may assume that there were not many more under the others.

It seems to have been a desire to rationalize the whole court system, rather than any dissatisfaction with this particular aspect of it, that led to the material being reworked one more time in the Ecclesiastical Jurisdiction Measure, 1963.[194]

That measure is modestly innovative. It keeps the grounds for automatic deprivation as they were in the 1892 act, with such changes as were required by developments in the criminal and matrimonial proceedings referred to.[195] A 1974 amendment authorized an archbishop, after submissions from the offending clergyman and his bishop, to forego deprivation and leave the clergyman in possession. It appears that this clemency must be exercised across the board if at all. There is no provision for depriving a clergyman of some of his preferment and leaving him in possession of the rest. On the other hand, if he holds preferment in both provinces, there would seem to be nothing to prevent the two archbishops reaching opposite results as to whether to deprive him or not. If he holds preferment in two dioceses of the same province, the measure is not clear as to whether the archbishop acts separately on reference from each bishop or once on recommendations from both. If the former, presumably he could act one way as to one diocese, the other as to the other.

As under the 1892 act, a criminal conviction, even when it does not result in automatic deprivation, is still conclusive as to the commission of the act charged.

Where there is no ground for automatic deprivation, the measure sets up a procedure for doctrinal and liturgical offenses, which we will consider in the next chapter, and then goes on to provide for proceedings charging:

any other offence against the laws ecclesiastical, including —
  (i) conduct unbecoming the office and work of a clerk in Holy
      Orders, or
  (ii) serious, persistent, or continuous neglect of duty:

> Provided that no proceedings in respect of unbecoming conduct shall be taken in respect of the political opinions or activities of such person; And provided further that no proceedings in respect of neglect of duty shall be taken in respect of the political opinions of such person.[196]

This language probably covers anything that the 1840 act, the 1892 act, or the 1947 measure would have covered. The provisions for conduct unbecoming and neglect of duty were taken almost verbatim from the 1947 measure.

"Conduct unbecoming" is not defined anywhere.[197] The one case on it seems to give it a fairly broad sweep, and the analysis in *Halsbury's Laws of England* suggests that it includes anything that has been found objectionable under earlier laws, as well as any violation of current canonical standards (which are about as vague as this language is). The 1947 language referred to "conduct unbecoming the *character* of a clerk in Holy Orders," whereas the 1963 language speaks of "conduct unbecoming the *office and work* . . . " There are no cases from which we can learn the significance of this change. Arguably, bookmaking, check-kiting, prizefighting, and streaking are unbecoming to the character of a clergyman, but not necessarily to his office and work. During the debates on the 1892 act, a clergyman was reported to have said that if he was sober on Sunday morning he could do his job perfectly well even if he was drunk the rest of the week.[198] This is too narrow an understanding of office and work, but if office and work is a narrower concept than character, it is hard to know just what it encompasses.

The exception for political opinions appears in the 1947 measure, but that for political activities is new. Presumably, it protects clergymen against either bishops or parishioners who believe that they should not be participating in election campaigns, anti-nuclear demonstrations, or meetings in support of striking workers. It offers partial, but not complete, protection in the event of a clash with the lay authorities through a course of civil disobedience. Assume, for instance, that a clergyman is arrested and tried for either trespassing on a nuclear weapons base or fire-bombing an abortion clinic. If he is sentenced to imprisonment, even if the sentence is suspended, he will be automatically deprived unless the archbishop chooses to rescue him: the political exception does not apply to the automatic deprivation section. But if he is merely fined, there would seem to be no way to reach him under church law. His political motivation shields him from any accusation of conduct unbecoming, and there is no other ecclesiastical law that he violates. Of course, if he is too busy demonstrating to take care of his parish, he can be proceeded against for neglect. The measure protects political opinions but not political activities against that charge.

The procedures for these offenses combine and simplify those under the 1840 and 1892 acts. The bishop has a veto, as he had under the 1840 act but not under the 1892 one. If he chooses not to exercise his veto, he puts the case in the hands of an "examiner" chosen from a panel of barristers and solicitors. If the examiner finds a case to answer, the bishop must appoint a promoter. The case will then be tried before the judge of the diocesan court, sitting with two lay and two clerical assessors, appointed from other panels. Procedure is assimilated to that of the lay courts in criminal cases, with the assessors acting the part of the jury. There is an appeal to the provincial court (still called the Court of Arches in Canterbury and the Chancery Court in York), and from there to the Privy Council.

It was nine years before all this machinery gave rise to a reported case, and when it did, it did not work at all well.[199] The offending clergyman, one Bland, less aptly named than Mr. Free or Mr. Lax, fell out with his parishioners for unspecified reasons, at least partly relating to his unwillingness to perform rites of passage for people only tenuously connected with the church. He refused to baptize a child whose parents never came to services, he wrote letters that the court characterized as rude, and he berated people verbally in various ways. The prosecution was based on specific incidents, but the incidents bespoke a longstanding and widespread clash.

The promoters of the case chose to prosecute the refusal to baptize as neglect of duty, and the letters and beratings as conduct unbecoming. Bland tried to have the baptism charge treated as one concerning doctrine, since his refusal was based on a theological objection to baptizing children whose parents could not be relied on to bring them up as Christians. The court rejected this contention. However, the conviction of neglect of duty was rejected on appeal because of a misdirection of the assessors as to the facts. The appellate court added that as a general matter violation of a specific duty on a specific occasion should be charged specifically rather than as neglect.

The trial court also found several charges of conduct unbecoming made out, and on one of them the appellate court agreed. There was therefore a sentence to be imposed. The trial court had ordered Bland deprived of his position, pointing out that the situation in the parish made it pastorally imperative that Bland and his parishioners be parted, and that there was no other way to effectuate the separation. The appellate court, however, held that the measure gave the trial court no warrant for considering anything but the gravity of the offense in determining what sentence to impose. Bland was accordingly rebuked and left in possession. After an elaborate and closely reasoned opinion reaching this result, the appellate judge ended by stating that the 1963 measure was incapable of dealing with the kind of pastoral problem that had given rise to this case, and by exhorting everyone concerned to find some other way to handle such problems.

The criticisms expressed by the court in the *Bland* case had a good deal to do with the adoption of the Incumbents (Vacation of Benefices) Measure, 1977.[200] The procedures laid down in this measure did not replace the 1963 ones, but they offered a more pastoral alternative based on earlier models. At the same time, they replaced the procedures adopted in 1945 for the compulsory retirement of a clergyman too aged or infirm to do his job. Thus, the provisions for neglectful and obnoxious clergy and the provisions for superannuated or disabled clergy, separated in 1945-47, were put back together again as they had been in 1926. The two lines of inquiry provided for are stated as:

> whether . . . there has been a serious breakdown of the pastoral relationship between the incumbent concerned and his parishioners and whether . . . . the breakdown is one to which the conduct of the incumbent or of his parishioners has contributed over a substantial period,

and,

> whether . . . the incumbent . . . is unable by reason of age or infirmity of mind or body to discharge adequately the duties attaching to his benefice.

The language about breakdown of the pastoral relation was perhaps suggested by the court in the *Bland* case. I suspect that it owes something also to the no-fault divorce law that had been adopted a few years previously, authorizing divorce where there has been an "irretrievable breakdown of the marriage."[201]

The inquiry into breakdown of the pastoral relation may be initiated by the archdeacon, by the incumbent himself, or by a two-thirds majority of the parochial church council. Allowing the incumbent to set the process in motion is new, and goes with recognition elsewhere in the measure (including the language just quoted) that the parishioners, rather than the incumbent, may be at fault. Indeed, if any of them are found to be at fault, the bishop is expressly empowered to administer them an official rebuke.

The first step in dealing with an alleged breakdown of the pastoral relation is an intervention by the archdeacon, who is to try to patch things up, and then to report to the bishop whether further proceedings are required. If he recommends further proceedings, the bishop must set them in motion. Even without such a recommendation, the bishop must proceed further on the request of the incumbent, and may do so on the request of the parishioners. The essentially pastoral role of the archdeacon in this process seems a good deal of an innovation — his office is usually concerned with temporal matters.[202] Perhaps the modern tendency to combine the office with that of a suffragan bishop has led to a changed conception of the archdeacon's role.

If further proceedings are to be had, the incumbent has a choice between a diocesan committee and a provincial tribunal. The diocesan committee, which is also used in disability cases, consists of three clergymen and two laymen appointed from standing panels set up by the diocesan synod. The members need not have legal training, but they may call in a barrister or solicitor to advise them. The provincial tribunal consists of five members appointed ad hoc from outside the diocese in which the parish is situated. Two must be clergymen and two must be laypersons. The fifth, who is to preside, must be either a Queen's Counsel or a judge of a diocesan court.

If the committee or tribunal finds that the pastoral relation has broken down, the bishop may rebuke anyone found to be at fault, may restrict the incumbent if he is at fault and turn over his functions to someone else, or if four out of five committee or tribunal members so recommend, may put the incumbent out of the parish no matter who is at fault. The committee or tribunal may also find that the breakdown is due to the age or infirmity of the incumbent in which case the bishop may proceed as in a disability case.

An incumbent who is put out for disability is pensioned off as if he had voluntarily retired. One who is put out on account of breakdown of the pastoral relation is compensated as if his benefice had been abolished under a pastoral scheme. Compensation comes out of the diocesan stipends fund, and may be made either in periodic payments or in a lump sum. If the ex-incumbent accepts other employment, turns down suitable preferment, or leaves the ministry, his compensation may be reduced or terminated. The provision for compensation obviously makes the whole approach less punitive than it would otherwise be — the absence of such a provision was one of the objections to an earlier version of this measure that was rejected by the Commons in 1975.[203] If an incumbent is so bad that there is no further use for him in the ministry, and, at the same time, he is unwilling to take up another line of work, there will be a financial incentive to proceed under the 1963 measure instead of this one. Otherwise, it would seem that an incumbent could be replaced without unduly taxing diocesan resources.

IV. Lay Offices and Officers

As we have seen, the unreformed church of the eighteenth and early nineteenth centuries had lay officers at provincial, diocesan, and parochial levels. Many of them had lifetime tenure of their positions. Some of them did useful work commensurate with their pay; some did a little useful work for a lot of money, and some did nothing at all. Their compensation was generally fixed by custom. Part of it came from fees paid by people who used their services, part from general funds, and some from endowment. One way or another, these offices have either disappeared or turned into ordinary jobs.

At the provincial and diocesan levels, most of the offices in question were in the courts, although some were in cathedrals and others were attached to the person of a bishop or archbishop. The cathedral offices were reorganized with the rest of the cathedral establishments in 1840. Endowments were taken over by the Ecclesiastical Commissioners, and such officers as had work to do were paid out of chapter funds.[204] The bishops' secretaries and other personal assistants were sometimes entitled to fees for particular services, but they were generally paid out of the bishops' own revenues until 1943. They are now, like the bishops themselves, paid salaries by the Church Commissioners.[205] Under modern practice, other people can be hired at need for administrative tasks, and paid out the regular diocesan budget, or out of the budget of the General Synod.

Court personnel were, and still are, compensated mainly out of fees paid by litigants and others requiring their services. A series of acts and measures beginning in 1829 provided for these fees to be officially set, and forbade any others to be taken.[206] The power to set the fees has been variously assigned to archbishops, bishops, judges, and lawyers. The measure presently in force (1962) gives it to a Fees Committee consisting of one judge or former judge appointed by the Lord Chancellor, one barrister appointed by the chairman of the Bar Council, and one solicitor appointed by the president of the Law Society. The committee is set up ad hoc when the archbishops ask for it, and disbanded when it has either made an order or reported that none is necessary.

There is not much direct evidence to show what became of the traditional officeholder who had a freehold in an ancient office, drew the customary emoluments, and spent a fraction of them hiring a deputy to do the actual work. There were a number of forces at work that must have contributed to his disappearance. In the first place, the bishops of the mid-nineteenth century tended to be more concerned about administrative efficiency than their predecessors were. In the prevailing climate of opinion, even people who were far from accepting a utilitarian philosophy were apt to be sensitive to utilitarian practical concerns. Then, too, the 1836 reforms reduced episcopal revenues to the point where there was not a lot to spare for friends, relatives, and hangers-on. Finally, where fees were set by statute, they were presumably set at no more than a reasonable compensation for a person doing the work. If so, they would have provided no surplus for an officeholder who hired a deputy.

None of these changes directly affected an officeholder's freehold in his office. There was no change in the law that a properly confirmed grant of an ancient office with the customary emoluments is binding on the successors of the grantor. An 1847 statute[207] provided that all future grants were subject to alteration by Parliament — an important provision, as the reformers were always very tender of any vested rights that arose before such a caveat was enacted. But the legislative reforms that might have been expected to follow never came about.

Meanwhile, the courts provided the bishops with a couple of weapons against useless officeholders left over from their predecessors' time.[208] One case held that a bishop need not give a reason for rejecting the deputy through whom an officeholder proposed to do his work. This holding gave considerable scope for a bishop to satisfy himself that the work of his diocese would be competently done. It must also have increased the cost of hiring a deputy. Another case held that a person who customarily performed a task for a bishop at piece rates had no complaint if the bishop assigned the task to someone else. This meant that an officeholder could be sure of nothing but his flat salary. The man involved in the case, the Receiver General of the Bishop of Ely, was entitled to ten pounds a year plus so much a lease for drawing up leases. The bishop had his secretary (not an ancient office, therefore held on whatever terms and emoluments the bishop contracted for) draw up all the leases, leaving the Receiver General with nothing but the ten pounds.

At the parochial level,[209] the traditional officers were the churchwardens and the parish clerk. The sexton had a traditional position also, though it might be stretching a point to call him an officer. In some parishes there were "sidesmen" to assist the churchwardens. Their original function was to accompany the churchwardens to visitations and the like; now, they helped to keep order in church. In some parishes, there was also on organist, but his position was not traditional, and carried only such rights and duties as were contracted for.

We have already taken up the way in which churchwardens were elected. It did not change materially until parish vestries were replaced for ecclesiastical purposes by parochial church councils in 1921.[210] At that time, the vestry's responsibility for electing churchwardens was turned over to a newly devised hybrid meeting. All the voters resident in the parish are eligible to attend whether they are Anglicans or not. So are all the people on the church electoral roll (generally, Anglicans who worship in the parish church), whether they live in the parish or not. This body has no other purpose; its existence reflects a continuing ambivalence as to whether the church serves the whole population or only the active members of its congregations. As formerly with the vestry, if the meeting and the incumbent cannot agree on two churchwardens, each chooses one. The legislation adopting this system would seem to supersede any local custom of choosing churchwardens in some other way.

Until 1964, Dissenters were eligible to be churchwardens, although they could refuse the office if they had conscientious scruples against executing it.[211] During the nineteenth century, they were actually chosen often enough to play a somewhat bewildered part in some of the ritual cases. A non-Anglican can still be chosen with the permission of the bishop; it would no doubt be an unusual case in which such permission was either asked or given.

As we have seen, the responsibility of the churchwardens for policing lay morals became obsolete with the rest of the apparatus of moral correction. Most of their financial responsibilities were turned over to the parochial church councils in 1921.[212] They are still responsible for keeping order in church, and for reporting to the bishop or archdeacon when there is a visitation. They still pass the collection plate in church and have a residual responsibility for the vestments and other objects necessary for the liturgy. It is not their place, however, to remove illegal ornaments put in by the incumbent, or to change the interior design without a faculty from a court.

Until 1921, the parish clerk was chosen by the minister, and the sexton by the vestry, unless there was a custom of choosing them in some other way. Both generally held their positions for life, and collected whatever fees or emoluments were customary in the parish.[213] In a few cases, the clerk's position was endowed. The Lecturers and Parish Clerks Act, 1844, in addition to requiring endowed lecturers (i.e., clergymen who preached sermons) to assume pastoral and liturgical duties, authorized the appointment of ordained clergymen to parish clerks' positions. A clergyman so appointed would be licensed like a curate, and would have the same security in his position. I do not know how often this permission was used. Presumably, there would be occasion for using it in any parish where the clerk's pay was up to the going rate for curates.

The 1921 measure setting up parochial church councils authorized them, jointly with the incumbent, to assign the duties of parish clerk and sexton to whatever people they wished on whatever terms they could arrange.[214] But if they pass a resolution simply appointing a person to be parish clerk or sexton without specifying the terms, they have probably appointed him for life with the customary fees and emoluments. In most places, it is now usual not to appoint to the traditional offices, but rather to appoint a "verger," who cannot appeal to any customary prerogatives.

Before the 1921 measure, the organist, if there was one, was generally hired and paid by the vestry, although it was up to the incumbent to tell him what to play.[215] The powers of the vestry concerning him were of course among those given to the parochial church council in 1921. The incumbent is still responsible for choosing the music, but the new canons require him to "pay due heed" to the organist's advice.

In recent years, there has developed a broader range of lay ministries licensed by the bishop.[216] Deaconesses (juridically, and perhaps theologically, distinct from the women deacons authorized in 1986) have generally the same status as lay workers, although they are "ordained" rather than licensed. Many lay workers are volunteers, but there is provision in the law for making them a regular part of team ministries, and for paying them out of diocesan funds. Their functions are curiously reminiscent of the ones originally attached to the minor orders that were abolished by the Church of England at the Reformation and by the Roman Catholic Church in 1983.

V. Church and Churchyard

The general law concerning seats in the church remained throughout the nineteenth century, and remains today, about as I described it in the first chapter.[217] It is up to the churchwardens (subject to the directions of the ordinary, but not those of the incumbent or the parishioners) to assign people seats, or to tell them where to sit if they have no seats assigned. A resident of the parish must be allowed to enter and sit down if there is a seat available, and must be allowed to enter and stand if there is not. A parishioner with a regularly assigned seat may occupy it at any regular service, and may exclude others from it. But unless he has a faculty out of a diocesan court, or a comparable right by prescription, the churchwardens may move him if they see fit. Faculties were given with considerable freedom in the eighteenth century, but became harder to get as the nineteenth century progressed.

In churches or parts of churches subject to the general law, the churchwardens were never allowed to rent out pews, although they often did so if nobody complained.[218] Most of the teeth were extracted from this principle by an 1898 dictum of Thomas Tristram, the leading ecclesiastical judge of the time, that although churchwardens could not rent out the seats, they could exercise their discretion by assigning the best seats to people who contributed to parish funds. Tristram's reasoning on this point is obscure, but what I believe he had in mind is this: Churchwardens had always been expected to assign seats in accordance with social distinctions. Accordingly, the best seats had always gone to the landowners in the parish. The real justification for this favorable treatment was that the landowners were the ones who paid the rates for the upkeep of the building in which they sat. With the abolition of compulsory churchrates, the voluntary contributors were the ones who paid the bills. It was only fair, therefore, that they should be the ones who got the favorable treatment. This argument is far from explicit in Tristram's opinion, but he pays so much attention to the abolition of compulsory churchrates that I think I am on the right track when I interpret him in this way.

As we have seen, there were two sets of nineteenth century statutes for building new churches.[219] Under the Church Building Acts, a church could be built and a parish assigned it. Under the New Parishes Acts, a new parish ("Peel District") could be created and a church built for it. The Church Building Act churches could be financed by pew rents, although twenty percent of the seats had to be free. The Church Building Commissioners set up a scale of rentals for the different parts of the church. The churchwardens could then let the pews to parishioners for the amount specified (or to capital contributors rent-free). If not enough parishioners came forward to take all the rentable pews, residents of adjoining parishes could rent the rest. The free seats had to be plainly marked — whether to encourage the poor to sit in them or to discourage the rich from doing so does not appear.

Until 1856, there was no provision for renting pews in the churches of the Peel Districts. However, if such a church received a grant under one of the Church Building Acts, it became subject to those acts and the pews could be rented. Long after the bulk of their funds was exhausted, the Church Building Commissioners continued to make nominal grants for the purpose of enabling Peel District churches to rent out pews.[220]

Provision for pew rents was eliminated when the two sets of acts were combined in 1943, and has not been revived in the Pastoral Measures now in place. Accordingly, any church built after 1943 is subject to the general law. But where pew rents were established under the earlier legislation, they can still be collected unless they have been done away with under provisions adopted in 1851 and 1856 for replacing them with endowment.

Around the middle of the nineteenth century, there began to develop a serious opposition to the practice of renting pews.[221] A good deal of controversy ensued. The Free and Open Churches Association was founded in 1866, and began putting out pamphlets. Some incumbents, including the hymn writer John Mason Neale, personally chopped down the pews in their churches. In one case, the churchwardens and the pewholder broke into a locked church to put up a pew that the minister had just taken down; the minister won the ensuing litigation. In another case, the bishop sent a man to sit in someone else's pew, and then sue the pewholder for putting him out; that man won also.

In this controversy, the argument on one side was that the renting of pews introduced an invidious distinction among Christians, one condemned by Christian teaching in general, and by a passage in the Epistle of James

(2:2-4) in particular, and that the practice did nothing for church finances that a system of offertory envelopes would not do just as well. On the other side was the traditional willingness to have the church reflect the social gradations of the secular community, along with some reluctance on the part of the well dressed and well scrubbed middle class to mingle too closely with the scruffy and unwashed poor. Chadwick points out that although the Roman Catholic church maintained a firm policy against renting out seats, Newman advised Faber to make some compromises in order to keep his upper class English converts from abandoning the Brompton Oratory to their working class Irish coreligionists.[222] I have the impression that by the end of the century improved standards of dress and sanitation had deprived this particular point of whatever effectiveness it had had earlier on. In any event, the renting of pews had ceased to be a common practice by the turn of the century, and has become a good deal of a rarity today.

There are still faculty pews attached to houses, and in a few churches there are pews owned outright under private acts. In either case, the rights of a pewholder cannot be taken away, even by a new faculty. It appears that there is room for flexibility when a church is remodelled.[223] The pewholder must be given comparable seating under as good a title as he had before, but he cannot insist on leaving his old pew in place to destroy the effect of the new design. On the other hand, it was held in a recent case that he cannot be required to content himself with chairs to be set up during service time on the site of his former pew.

Questions regarding church furnishing and architecture have arisen more frequently and more acrimoniously since the 1830s than they did before. Changes in demography, lifestyle, taste, economics, and liturgy have all played their part in disputes over how churches and churchyards should be laid out, and how they should be furnished.

To all such questions the same legal principles apply.[224] The general rule is that any alteration in the structure of the church or the landscaping of the churchyard, or the introduction or removal of any item of furniture, any decoration, or any monument requires a faculty from the diocesan court. The issuance of the faculty is discretionary with the court, subject to a canonical requirement that certain things be on hand. The provincial court on appeal may substitute its discretion for that of the diocesan court. There is a further appeal to the Judicial Committee of the Privy Council, which generally limits itself to passing on legal questions. It has power to exercise an independent discretion, but even in its most activist period during the nineteenth century it was extremely reluctant to do so.

Any parishioner has standing either to initiate or to oppose a petition for a faculty.[225] The understanding of who is a parishioner has been broad. For instance, it was held that any Member of Parliament is a parishioner of

St. Margaret's, the parish church adjoining Westminster Abbey. In one case, a man who had rented a room in the parish for the sole purpose of bringing a faculty proceeding was held to be as much a parishioner as one who lived there from some other reason. A 1938 measure extended the standing of parishioners to nonresidents on the church voting roll. It appears also that people with an interest can be given standing even if they are not parishioners at all. Thus, in one case a faculty was issued to the Air Minister to take down a spire that presented a hazard to aircraft landing at a nearby field.

The 1938 measure just referred to provided for participation in the process by the archdeacon and by an advisory committee to be set up in every diocese. The court was empowered to depute the archdeacon to supervise the execution of the works authorized in the faculty, or, if necessary, to do them himself. The archdeacon was also given standing to appear as a party. A 1964 revision allowed him to recover his legal fees out of diocesan funds, and the Court of Arches has suggested that he should use his powers to see that all the witnesses in a difficult case are professionally cross-examined.

The diocesan advisory committee gives advice to the archdeacon, to the court, or to people involved in proposed alterations. The 1938 measure said nothing about who were to be members, but the 1964 one required all the archdeacons in the diocese to be included. I gather the remaining members are apt to include both architects practicing in the diocese and some of the antiquarians and local historians that no English county is without. With the concurrence of this committee, the archdeacon may authorize work that is agreed on by the incumbent, the churchwardens, and the parochial church council, and that does not alter the structure or appearance of the church. The judge in his discretion may divert other non-controversial petitions to the archdeacon to be dealt with in the same way. The order issued by the archdeacon under this procedure is called a certificate rather than a faculty, but it has the same effect.

It is a peculiarity of this body of law that what is done without a faculty cannot be undone without one.[226] The rule takes the church exactly as it finds it and starts from there. Accordingly, many changes are made without faculties, and, if no one complains, they are as firmly established as the original condition was. There is provision, however, for making anyone who introduces a change without a faculty pay the cost of restoring the status quo if the court issues a faculty to restore it.

Once a faculty issues, departure from its terms may be punished as a contempt of the court that issued it.[227] But the church court cannot prevent alterations being made with no faculty at all. In one case (1861), the Court of Chancery used its general equity powers to enjoin an incumbent from making changes until he had received a faculty for them. I have not found any later exercise of the jurisdiction assumed in that case. Phillimore (1895) refers to it as a thing of the past, while the third edition of *Halsbury's Laws of England* (1955) treats it as currently existing, and the fourth edition of the same work (1975) does not mention it at all.

The faculty jurisdiction has been invoked for a variety of purposes since the mid-nineteenth century. It played a part in many of the great ritual cases — generally when some parishioner sought a faculty to remove popish trappings introduced by a Tractarian incumbent. I will defer consideration of these cases to the next chapter. We looked in the last chapter at some faculty cases involving the wording of inscriptions on tombstones and the landscaping of churchyards. There are still tombstone cases, but these days they tend to involve questions of taste rather than questions of doctrine.[228] Sometimes the court has to restrain the zeal of the incumbent or the parochial church council for uniform design. Other times it must restrain the exuberance or idiosyncrasy of the bereaved. One recent case held that a color photograph of the deceased and another of the car in which he met his end were not appropriate adornments of a tombstone. Another forbade a list of mourners that omitted the widow but included the woman whose "loving but not adulterous" relationship with the deceased had led her husband to kill him.

The small change of church decoration and furnishing has produced a number of faculty cases with no particular doctrinal content.[229] An incumbent puts up a box to collect offerings for altar flowers. The churchwardens want it taken down because it intercepts offerings for the poor (they win). Everyone concerned wants to put up a plaque over the baptismal font showing Baby Jesus in the bath. The court makes them put it somewhere else because putting it over the font could lead people to think Jesus was baptized as a baby. A group of veterans want to put up their regimental colors in church (they may). An arrogant and abrasive incumbent, with the concurrence of the churchwardens and most of the parochial church council, has replaced a painting of Our Lady with a reproduction of the Black Madonna of Czestochowa and a stand to hold candles before it. The arrogance and abrasiveness of the incumbent are irrelevant, since the churchwardens and the majority of the council are with him this time. But the old painting is a memorial. He must put it back and put the new one somewhere else. A family whose members are all commemorated by tablets on the church wall wants to commemorate the last two in the same way. They may: times have changed and landowning families are no longer memorialized as a matter of course, but these men were distinguished naval officers, their memorial will round out a historical record on the church wall, and we are promised there will be no more of them. A parish wishes to install electric votive candles. Generally, no.

Cases involving the more general remodelling of churches come mainly from two periods. One is that of the nineteenth century Gothic revival,[230] the other that of the pastoral and liturgical changes following the Second Vatican Council. In the first period, some of the controversies related to the strict legality of certain architectural elements and the liturgical practices associated with them; these I will defer to the next chapter. But other controversies related to such questions as rearranging the seating to accommodate a choir. Still others evidently arose out of the zeal of some restorers for replacing genuine English Gothic with spurious French Gothic.

> The Church's Restoration
> In eighteen-eighty-three
> Has left for contemplation
> Not what there used to be.

It is to this movement that we presumably owe the proposal rejected by Dr. Tristram in the London Consistory Court, to raise the roof of the Tottenham church and install clerestory windows. In the same category belong an assortment of chancel screens, reredoses and the like that seem to respond more to secular medievalism than to any doctrinal or liturgical consideration. In 1873, the parishioners of St. Barnabas, Pimlico, tried to put up a marble baldachino with three gables over their main altar, claiming, perhaps disingenuously, that it was a mere architectural embellishment without doctrinal or liturgical significance. Dr. Tristram disagreed.

In exercising the discretion committed to them, the nineteenth century courts took into account the opinions of the parishioners, the judgment of the bishop, and their own opinion of the likelihood of anyone, justly taking offense. They considered any architects' affidavits that were brought before them. They also relied a good deal on their own common sense, and, I suspect, on their own canons of taste.

Consulting parishioners brought forward a tension that had been building for some time, and was to become crucial — the tension between the worshipping congregation and the geographical parish. In the clerestory case just referred to, a majority of the parish vestry opposed the change, whereas a majority of the churchgoing vestrymen favored it. Tristram held, sensibly enough, that the churchmen's wishes would be given greater weight concerning the interior of the church, but that the external appearance was of concern to everyone who had to look at it. In another case, involving the seating of the choir, it appeared that a great number of worshippers from outside the parish favored the change, while the numerous parishioners who opposed it went to church elsewhere or not at all. Tristram held that the views of non-parishioners should not be taken into account even though they attended the church. As for non-attending parishioners, there was some evidence that they had been driven away by the choral services that the rector was facilitating by the change. So it would not be fair to deprive them of their voice in the matter.

As for the bishop's judgment, the court acted in the bishop's name, but it was no more bound by his opinion than the Court of Queen's Bench was by the opinion of the queen. On the other hand, if the change resulted in a pastoral disaster the bishop would have to cope with it. It was only prudent to see what he thought before acting. There was evidently some tendency among the clergy to approach the bishop informally with proposed alterations and bypass the faculty procedure entirely. Bishop Stubbs, addressing the Oxford clergy in 1890, attempted to discourage this practice, mainly because it did not allow the opposition to be heard and evaluated:

> It is extremely unadvisable that the clergy or the Church laity of any parish should, by introducing changes in the church, seem to try to steal a march on the parishioners in general.[231]

Note the distinction between the "Church laity" and the "parishioners in general."

Barring doctrinal or esthetic eccentricities, the people who put up the money for church restoration in the nineteenth century must have been able in most cases to carry it out about as they pleased. A century and more of benign neglect had left many churches in a ramshackle condition that someone had to do something about, and the abolition of compulsory churchrates meant that neither the incumbent nor the vestry had much power to see that something was done. Also, in many country parishes the local squire was patron of the church and landlord of most of the parishioners, so that no one cared to dispute whatever he wanted done and could pay for. In such parishes, the renovations were probably carried out without faculties in many cases. If a faculty was sought, there would be so little opposition that it would issue as a matter of course. On the other hand, where the owner of two parishes took down one church and restored the other for the use of both sets of parishioners, the court found he had gone too far.[232]

Most of the recent remodelling cases have involved changes to accommodate new approaches to the liturgy, alternative uses of the building, or both.[233] Remodelling for liturgical purposes generally involves a more central location for the altar (Communion table), and a rearrangement of the seating to match. The courts, with the experience behind them of the replacement of altars by tables under Elizabeth I, controversies under Charles I over where to put the tables, and controversies under Victoria over whether tables can be made out of stone and called altars, have wisely decided that these matters are without doctrinal significance, and that whatever commands a consensus in the parish may be done. The prevailing judicial mood seems to be that this too will pass. In one or two cases, the court has required the parish to make the proposed change in a temporary form and live with it for six months before they pour the concrete or bolt down the wood.

Alternative uses generally involve plays, films, or concerts in the body of the church, and various forms of socializing in attached structures. The current canons are generally favorable to these uses as long as

> the words, music, and pictures are such as befit the House of God, are consonant with sound doctrine, and make for the edifying of the people.[234]

It is felt that allowing the church to be used in this way provides a bridge to the non-churchgoing majority of the population. It also brings in a certain amount of needed money. Faculties are necessary to remove pews for more flexible seating arrangements, to provide additional restrooms and the like, and sometimes to add on additional space. In passing on these proposals, the courts pay a good deal of attention to professional architects both on and off the diocesan advisory committee. As regards non-professionals, they continue to give the whole community a say about the external appearance of the church, while the members of the worshipping congregation have most of the say about the interior. The nineteenth-century holding that people from outside the parish are not entitled to a say even if they worship in the church is presumably superseded by the provisions for including them on the electoral roll.

The tensions between the worshipping congregation and the local community cropped up in an interesting way in the 1980 case of *St. Thomas, Lymington*.[235] The incumbent and the parishioners wanted to replace the existing church hall with an addition to the church itself. The main purpose of the change was evidently to allow the congregation to socialize as an extension of their participation in the Eucharist. Townspeople who objected to the encroachment on the open space in the churchyard were heard respectfully, but the professional architects who felt that the encroachment was not serious were given more weight. Other opposition came from non-churchgoers who participated in various secular activities in the church hall. They felt that some of the activities in question would be inhibited by the location of the new facility on consecrated ground, and by its status as a part of the church. The court puzzled a good deal over what to do with this objection. It finally worked around the problem by pointing out that it had no jurisdiction over the hall, since it was not on consecrated ground, and that if the parish had a duty to maintain a social center for the secular community that duty was not one for the church court to enforce.

A couple of interesting cases, nearly a century apart, involve the introduction of newfangled heating devices into old cold churches.[236] The churchwardens of Pontesbury in Hereford hired a contractor in 1887 to put in a patent stove. Without consulting them, he cut out a piece of the wall holding up the church tower, dug up some of the ground without properly disposing of the bones turned up in the process, and put the stove so near the floor of the vestry that the rector was afraid the building would catch fire. After hearing conflicting evidence from architects, Dr. Tristram let the churchwardens off with a scolding, plus payment of costs, plus an order to reinter the remains displaced by the contractor and take the necessary measures to reinforce the tower and fireproof the vestry floor. He did not specify whether they could pay for all this out of parish funds, but I presume they could. It is interesting that no proceedings were taken against the contractor.

The churchwardens who put central heating into the church of St. Agnes, Toxteth Park, in 1984 came to the attention of the court when they wanted a faculty to sell a valuable altar cloth in order to pay the bill. As they had proceeded without a faculty, they would have had to pay out of their own pockets if the vicar and the parochial church council had not come to their rescue. As it was, the court felt obliged to allow the sale, and these churchwardens also escaped with a scolding.

The faculty for selling the altar cloth is an example of a new set of cases that have been engaging the attention of the courts in recent years.[237] A church that has been around long enough is apt to have odds and ends of furniture and decoration that would fetch very tidy sums if they were turned over to Sotheby's and placed on the current inflated art market. The resulting funds could be used not only for heating the church, but also for making much needed repairs, or, if the church is in good repair already, for such pastoral purposes as an expanded inner-city ministry. Also, if, as is often the case, the valuable object is in an accessible position in a church open for prayer or sightseeing, the insurance cost may well be an unacceptable drain on parish funds.

The courts are on the whole reluctant to liquidate the church's art holdings. But they tend to grant faculties if the parish is urgently in need of funds. They are more willing to have something sold if it is presently reposing in a bank vault (as most old Communion plate is) than if it is a subsisting feature of the church. If it requires restoration or preservation that the parish cannot undertake, that need will be taken into account.

If the courts do allow an object to be sold, they may set a reserve price, but they are not willing to require the parish to find a purchaser who will not turn it to a secular use, or even to require a museum instead of a private purchaser. There are laws against shipping antiques out of the country, and they apply to the church's antiques, but it is not for the church courts to enforce them.

The faculty may specify which parish expenses are to be met from the proceeds of the sale, and may require some of them to be spent on a suitable memorial to the donor of the original object, or on a replica of the object to be set up on the original site. It appears, though, that the court has no authority to order part of the proceeds of a sale to be spent for church purposes outside the parish. Since the object belongs to the parish, so do the proceeds, and the faculty jurisdiction is not an expedient for the redistribution of church funds.

The ownership of churches, churchyards, and objects devoted to worship has only a limited effect on their treatment by the church courts. As a general rule, the land and buildings belong to the incumbent and the movable property to the churchwardens, but the rule is subject to a few exceptions.[238] In the first place, a lay rector may have a freehold in the chancel and even the churchyard. As we have seen, this gives him no right to control the chancel. It may, however, entitle him to pasture sheep in the churchyard. On the other hand, the incumbent is not enough of an owner to be held under laws imposing responsibility on the owners of dangerous buildings, although he is enough of an owner to pay rates on his fees for allowing non-parishioners to be buried in the churchyard.

In some churches, the vicissitudes of history have left lay landowners with freehold ownership of various galleries, chapels, or aisles.[239] Either ownership interests were reserved when land was given to build the church, or they were in the hands of guild chantries whose assets were confiscated at the Reformation and granted out wholesale to lay magnates. It appears that if an aisle or chapel was secularized at the Reformation, the owner has been free ever since to do whatever he pleases with it. He can wall it off, he can keep his garden tools in it, and, since the Roman Catholic Relief Acts, he can bring a Roman Catholic priest to say mass in it. But if it has been used for Anglican worship since the Reformation, whether by holding services in it or by sitting in it to follow services in the main church, the case is different. It remains a consecrated place, and it cannot be used either for secular purposes or for non-Anglican worship. The same, by the way, is true of consecrated institutional chapels, even if consecrated in error: if the proprietors of a school or hospital want an ecumenical chapel, they must see that no one invites the bishop to consecrate it.

The question whether such places are subject to the full scope of the faculty jurisdiction remains in some doubt.[240] The authors of the third edition of *Halsbury's Laws of England* (1955) argue that it does, and cite a 1937 case in which the London Consistory Court took jurisdiction over a petition for a faculty to demolish a consecrated institutional chapel, and imposed some onerous conditions on granting it. On the other hand, a number of cases show that proprietors of aisles and chapels have habitually put up monuments and coats of arms in them, buried their dead in them (subject to the Burial Acts), sat in them, and excluded others from them, all without asking faculties, and that the lay courts have generally protected them in doing so. The fourth edition of Halsbury (1975) is content to say that "there has been uncertainty" on the subject.

There is much less uncertainty as to movable property. If the building is subject to the faculty jurisdiction, so is everything in it. Whatever is brought into the church for its beautification or for use in the services becomes the property of the churchwardens without any formal donation unless ownership is expressly reserved for someone else. The reservation probably entitles the owner to a faculty to take his property away, but it does not entitle him to take it without one. The principle figured in an 1861 case involving the unpaid seller of an organ, and in a 1979 case involving a painting claimed as a loan.[241] Both cases were decided on other grounds, but the principle was not challenged.

The same principle is applied to accouterments of tombs.[242] These remain the property of the person who set them up until that person dies. From then on, they belong to the heirs of the person commemorated. But they still cannot be removed from the church without a faculty. The rule as to their ownership is an old one. It appeared first in a Year Book case in which a widow sued a parson for stealing a sword and some coat armor from her husband's tomb. It was reiterated in a couple of Jacobean cases, probably to keep Protestant iconoclasts from defacing family memorials along with the trappings of popery and superstition. There ensued a long period in which no one was much interested in taking down monuments, and it was thought that changes in the law of succession might have affected the old rule. But in recent years when parish fund raisers have started eying the available antiquities, the law has turned out to be just as Coke stated it in 1612.

But the courts will probably not respect the descendant of a crusader trying to turn his heritage into cash as they would the manufacturer of an organ trying to collect a fair price for his work. We may suppose that faculty cases involving monuments and accouterments will be decided in accordance with the economic versus the artistic concerns of the parish rather than any right the owner may have to realize on his property. On the other hand, the parish, however needy, cannot sell what it does not own. It would seem, then, that if the incumbent and the parishioners want to turn Sir Eglamore's battle ax into new restrooms for the Sunday school, Sir Eglamore's heirs can figure in the proceedings as a dog in the manger, even if not as a rival claimant to the funds. In the one case of this kind where there was an identifiable heir, he expressly disclaimed his rights, and allowed the sale to proceed for the benefit of the parish.[243]

The whole range of private rights in churches is now covered under the Faculty Jurisdiction Measure, 1964.[244] Under this measure, unless there is an objection from someone with a reasonable claim to ownership, a faculty may issue vesting a private aisle or chapel in whoever owns the rest of the church. A faculty may issue "for the moving, demolition, alteration, or execution of other work to any monument" regardless of the owner's objections, unless the owner is willing to take the monument away with him. The bishop is authorized to extend faculty jurisdiction to any building licensed for Anglican worship, even if not consecrated, and provision is made for terminating exclusive burial rights after a hundred years unless a faculty is issued renewing them.

If the claimant to an aisle or chapel or the owner of a monument cannot be found after reasonable effort, the faculty may issue without him. The requirement of reasonable effort is not perfunctory: if the court is not satisfied from evidence before it that the effort has been made, it will disclaim jurisdiction to issue the faculty.[245] The wording of the Administration of Estates Act, 1925, is such that the devolution of a monument remains subject to common law principles of primogeniture, whereas that of an aisle or chapel is probably subject to the same rules as other property. So if both have been neglected for several generations it will be easier to find the owner of the monument than the owner of the aisle or chapel. One case proved particularly easy because the person commemorated had a title, and the title is still in existence. Like the monument, the title passes by primogeniture, and is unaffected by the 1925 act.

It is apparent that this measure does nothing to cure the possibility of a standoff between the parish authorities and the owner of a monument. The owner can block a faculty simply by offering to take the monument away with him (and once he has taken it away, he can sell it on his own account if he pleases), but he cannot take it away without a faculty which the court will probably not grant unless the parish authorities ask for it.

VI. Conclusion

With the election under the reformed franchise in 1832, a new set of utilitarian concerns came to dominate the church. Such churchmen as were not utilitarians themselves found it politically expedient to support reforms calculated to meet utilitarian criticisms, or at least to tax their ingenuity thinking up utilitarian justifications for the status quo. Of course, utilitarian concerns were not new to the church. I have tried in these volumes to show just how old they are. But the goals were newly stated and embraced with new urgency and new resourcefulness. The ministrations of the Church of England were to be made available to everyone in the country. They were to be offered everywhere in a decent building by an adequately trained and adequately supported minister, and the whole enterprise was to have the central intellectual and administrative backing it needed to accomplish its task. The fact that many of the people chose alternative ministrations or none at all, and the fact that political considerations made it impossible to fund the project except through existing endowments or voluntary contributions complicated the situation without in any way affecting the goals.

On the whole, these goals were successfully achieved in the half century or so following the reform Parliament, even if they were not achieved with administrative elegance or logical symmetry. A floor was put under clerical incomes and a roof over clerical heads. Churches were built within walking distance of the people who were supposed to go to them, whether they in fact went or not. Income producing property was managed in income producing ways, and any funds that did not support the parish clergy supported the piety, learning, and administrative efficiency, rather than the indolence, of their superiors.

By and large, these remain the goals of the church, and by and large they are still being achieved. It has taken some shifting of boundaries, buildings, people, and funds. Villages that used to have their own clergy must now be content with someone coming in on Sundays from a few miles away. Some churches are vacant and some are secularized. But the ministrations of the church are still available to everyone in the country. The buildings are still in repair, and the clergy are still trained and still supported, although they have more trouble making ends meet than they used to have. They still have a good deal of intellectual backing, and perhaps more administrative backing than they need.

The price of this achievement has often been seen as an attenuation or neglect of other qualities that a Christian might like to see exhibited in the church. It involves maintaining a traditional liturgy week in and week out for a largely indifferent population most of whom are moved only occasionally by nostalgia or personal crisis to attend. It involves exchanging countless secular amenities so that people will know where to come in their rare moments of spiritual concern. Could not the time and energy be better spent proclaiming the Gospel on a take-it-or-leave-it basis, and ministering to people who wanted to be ministered to? It involves a deployment of clergy such that forty-two percent of them minister to eleven percent of the population.[246] Could they not do more good deployed in some other way? It involves diluting the apostolic presence of the bishops with a multiplicity of boards and committees. Can the message of Christ be effectively presented through a bureaucratic veil? These questions and others like them were being asked in 1832, and they are being asked today.

Guy Mayfield, the late archdeacon of Hastings, says toward the end of a ruefully polemical little book written in 1965: "The Church of England is called by God to make saints of the English."[247] Whether you consider this a utilitarian goal depends I suppose on what you think saints are and how you think they are made. If it is utilitarian, it represents a deeper utility than Macaulay proposed in the language I quoted at the beginning of this chapter, or than the 1307 Parliament proposed in language I also quoted. But in a crucial point Mayfield's vision of the Church of England is the same as Macaulay's, the same as the 1307 Parliament's, the same as Pope Gregory's in 596. It is that the mission of the Church of England is to the whole English nation. It is not like other bodies that minister only to that fraction of the population that becomes identified with them by doctrine or practice. The character of the church's ministry and the character of its administration are inevitably affected by this aspiration to universality, and by its manifestation over the years. The Church of England is the custodian of much of the history, the tradition, and the literature of the English people — their ancient buildings, the language of their prayers, their monuments, their battle flags, and the bodies of their dead. It embodies clusters of sentiment in some sense religious, but too deep for articulation and too confused for doctrinal analysis. If it is to continue this ministry — and it probably is — it must do so in some tension with its status as a community of committed Christians living out their faith. It is this tension that we must explore in our final two chapters.

4. Sion's War

I. The New High Churchmanship

As the nineteenth century progressed, antiquarians and people with a stake in the status quo were not the only ones to be dismayed at the inexorable process that was turning their old, comfortable, and divinely approved church-state nexus into an uneasy alliance between a utilitarian church and a secular state. There were many serious churchmen who believed that God's utility was not Jeremy Bentham's utility, and that a secular state could no more hope to flourish than could a secular man. Some were traditional High Churchmen who followed old principles into a new political context. Others came out of the Evangelical movement, or out of older traditions of Anglican piety, and were driven in a High Church direction by the tendencies to personal and corporate infidelity that seemed to be developing all around them. Starting in Oxford, these new High Churchmen became a force to be reckoned with first in the intellectual life of the church, then in its pastorate, and, finally, in its government. Their story has been told often, well, and from many standpoints favorable and unfavorable. I will tell here only as much of it as is needed to understand their encounter with the legal system, and what happened to the legal system as a result.

A. Sources of Discontent.

High Church discontent embraced some of the same objections everyone else had to existing conditions, and extended also to most of the remedies everyone else proposed. Taken as a whole, it was very broad and not altogether specific. It included elements of spiritual awakening, elements of political malaise, and elements of juridical frustration.

The spiritual awakening probably owed most to the Evangelical reaction against the dry theology and perfunctory worship that had been so common in the previous century. By the 1820s, the reaction had gone far beyond the confines of the Evangelical movement, so that churchmen of many different kinds were feeling their way toward a deeper level of devotion. In an academic setting, it was natural that such churchmen should seek a solid intellectual foundation for their piety, and equally natural that their quest for such a foundation should expose them to the Caroline divines, and to the witness of Christian antiquity. These studies, in turn, led them to see traditional Catholic beliefs and practices in a more favorable light, and, accordingly, to take a new interest in such of those beliefs and practices as were retained, at least on paper, in the Church of England.

These developments were reinforced by the romanticism and medievalism that had come to play a prominent part in art and culture. People who read the novels of Sir Walter Scott and put up imitations of fifteenth century buildings were not apt to condemn medieval religious practices out of hand. Some of the medievalism of the period was no doubt a mere recreational respite from the relentless practicality of industrial, commercial, and political life. But in the late 1830s, a group of Cambridge students set out with real spiritual motivations to recover the religious heritage of their ancestors by studying the churches in which their ancestors worshipped. It has been suggested that Cambridge did for Catholic liturgy in the Church of England what Oxford did for Catholic doctrine.[1]

The political malaise of the High Churchmen grew out of a combination of circumstances. The old view that the state's agencies constituted the voice of the Anglican laity became harder and harder to sustain as one measure after another was adopted making Dissenters eligible for public office. It became next to impossible when Roman Catholics were given the vote in 1829. The demographic reform of the franchise in 1832 did still more to change the political identification of church and state: the newly enfranchised boroughs tended to be dominated by Dissenters. The Tories, traditional allies of the High Church party, lost the first election under the new franchise in 1832. They were not to return to power until 1841, and were to prove unreliable allies when they did. The country had made a permanent shift in the direction of religious pluralism, and the Tories could not hope to win elections except by going along.

These events were accompanied by a certain marginalization of religious concerns. We have seen how one function after another — the registration of births, the solemnization of marriages, the education of children, the burial of the dead — was taken out of the exclusive control of the Church of England and given either to the state or to all religious bodies on an equal footing. The process had an inevitable tendency to make the religious concerns on which people differed peripheral to the secular concerns they had in common. If all births must be registered in one place, but baptisms may be had wherever the parents choose, or not had at all, it is easy to suppose — however erroneously — that the powers that be consider registration more important than baptism. If I may exempt my children from religious instruction, but not from arithmetic or history, it is natural for me to suppose that the people running the school think it is more important to learn arithmetic and history than to learn religion.

Even in dealing with religious matters, the political authorities often seemed oblivious of High Church concerns. In 1841, the government agreed with the Prussian government to take turns appointing a bishop to serve all the Protestants in the Holy Land. The object was evidently to counter the influence that the French exercised in the area by appointing a bishop for the Roman Catholics, and the Russians by appointing one for the Orthodox. Neither Palmerston for the Whigs nor Peel for the Tories seems to have been concerned about the fact — of the utmost importance to High Churchmen — that their arrangement was putting the Church of England on an equal footing with the Lutheran Church of Germany. The relation of the Church of England to the Continental Protestant churches had been a matter of theological debate for more than two centuries. The government was ignoring the issue for the sake of a petty political advantage.

In 1848, Lord John Russell, when he was Prime Minister, appointed to the see of Hereford a theologian, R.D. Hampden, whose doctrine had been officially condemned by the University of Oxford a few years before. Russell seems to have made it a point of honor not to take the condemnation into account. Worse, when the dean of Hereford, in an agonized and carefully argued letter, informed him that he could not in conscience vote for the appointee as the customary procedure required, Russell responded in a famous letter, as quotable as it was callous:

Sir, I have had the honour to receive your letter of the 22nd instant, in which you intimate to me your intention of violating the law. I have the honour to be your obedient servant,
J. Russell[2]

Here, of course, was the basis for the High Churchmen's juridical frustration. The law placed every aspect of church affairs firmly under the control of the civil power, a power that was intervening in more and more aspects of life as one government succeeded another, and a power whose lack of concern for things spiritual was becoming more and more apparent. There was no requirement that the people who exercised this power be churchmen or even serious Christians. Even when they were well disposed toward the church, they were often too busy to provide the legal measures the church required. From the High Church standpoint, the legal authorities were fairly evenly divided between objectionable action and objectionable inaction.

Frustration with this state of the law was enhanced by reflection on the nature of the church and what its law ought to be. The church was supposed to teach authoritatively, and to drive out strange and erroneous doctrines. Indeed, its bishops and priests at their ordination made (and still make unless the Alternative Service Book, 1980, is used) a solemn undertaking to do just that. Legislative and judicial bodies in the church were to assist them in the responsible discharge of their God-given function. But the legal structures actually in place seemed rather to throw up obstacles than to assist. They assured the appointment of a bench of bishops less interested in orthodoxy than in peace. They protected heterodox clergymen against those few bishops who were minded to do something about them. They assured that professing erroneous doctrine or even joining a schismatic church could not render a person ineligible for the sacraments and other ministrations of the Church of England. It is not surprising that High Churchmen saw the whole apparatus as an alien presence imposed on the church by the state, and basically hostile to the church's mission.

B. The High Church Agenda.

These grievances did not immediately give rise to a coherent agenda for meeting them. The early controversial literature, including the *Tracts for the Times* (1833-41), was devoted mainly to broad protest and doctrinal elaboration — what modern activists would call consciousness raising. And much of the later literature was devoted to specific narrow issues — mostly ephemeral ones as it turned out, though the whole fate of English Christianity seemed to depend on each of them while it was under debate.

But underneath all the polemic it is possible to discern an orderly development of High Church theory and practice, with specific proposals for new or restored ways to worship God, to spread the Gospel, and to run the church. I see four stages in this development, each emerging fairly logically from the previous one.

The first stage was characterized by a turning to Catholic tradition and apostolic authority to counter the loss or feared loss of temporal advantage. Whatever course the state might take, the Church of England was still the traditional vessel of English Christianity, and (except for the corrupt and alien papists) the only English church with episcopal orders and valid sacraments. Newman, in the first *Tract for the Times*, put it this way:

Should the Government and Country so far forget their GOD as to cast off the Church, to deprive it of its temporal honors and substance, *on what* will you rest the claim of respect and attention which you make upon your flocks? Hitherto you have been upheld by your birth, your education, your wealth, your connexions; should these secular advantages cease, on what must CHRIST's Ministers depend? Is not this a serious practical question? We know how miserable is the state of religious bodies not supported by the State. Look at the Dissenters on all sides of you and you will see at once that their Ministers, depending simply upon the people, become the *creatures* of the people. Are you content that this should be your case? Alas! can a greater evil befal Christians, than for their teachers to be guided by them, instead of guiding? How can we "hold fast the form of sound words," and "keep that which is committed to our trust," if our influence is to depend simply on our popularity? Is it not our very office to *oppose* the world, can we then allow ourselves to *court* it? to preach smooth things and prophesy deceits? to make the way of life easy to the rich and indolent, and to bribe the humbler classes by excitements and strong intoxicating doctrine? Surely it must not be so; — and the question recurs, on *what* are we to rest our authority, when the State deserts us?

CHRIST has not left His Church without claim of its own upon the attention of men. Surely not. Hard Master He cannot be, to bid us oppose the world, yet give us no credentials for so doing. There are some who rest their divine mission on their own unsupported assertion; others, who rest it upon their popularity; others, on their success; and others, who rest it upon their temporal distinctions. This last case has, perhaps, been too much our own; I fear we have neglected the real ground on which our authority is built, — OUR APOSTOLIC DESCENT . . . .[3]

The emphasis on apostolic descent bespoke a role for the episcopate which the bishops currently in place could scarcely be expected to fill. Appointed by the government, usually for political reasons, and generally by ministers hostile to the High Church movement, these prelates were quite content to be upheld by their birth, their education, their wealth, and their connections, believed that by sacrificing some part of their secular advantages under the guidance of the Ecclesiastical Commissioners they had a good hope of preserving the rest, and, if they believed in Apostolic Succession, were willing to be quiet about it in a church whose royal head was married to a German Lutheran.

The High Churchmen accordingly looked elsewhere for manifestations of apostolic authority. The first place they looked was in the written formularies of their own church. The Book of Common Prayer was adopted with varying degrees of episcopal participation in 1549, 1552, 1559, and 1662, but it was possible if you overlooked the political context to see it as an emanation of episcopal authority. The Canons of 1604 were genuine products of the bishops and clergy in Convocation. Even the Thirty-Nine Articles could be regarded as a canonical product if the 1562 Convocation, newly purged of all members who refused to accept the royal supremacy, could be regarded as a true Convocation.

High Churchmen found in these formularies a "higher" — i.e., more Catholic — doctrine of sacraments and ministry than had been usual in the church since the days of the Nonjurors (although both Keble and Denison professed to have learned such a doctrine from their fathers).[4] More important, they found what might be called a minimalist understanding of the Reformation. As I tried to show in the previous volume, the Calvinist, and therefore the English puritan view was that the Reformation had returned the church to first principles, whereas the prevailing Anglican view was that it had changed things only where they had been specifically found in need of change. Accordingly, the Prayer Book and the Canons of 1604 contained a good deal of language that could be read as establishing that whatever was in force before the Reformation was still in force unless it had been expressly abolished. it also contained language encouraging the High Church initiatives for studying Christian antiquity and recovering traditional doctrine.

In this way, the High Churchmen arrived at the second stage in the development of their agenda — the recovery of traditional Catholic doctrine. By the 1840s, they were claiming a broad liberty to hold and teach such doctrine within the Anglican Church, and making some moves to exclude alternative doctrines.

This stage brought them into much conflict with public opinion, and some conflict with the law.[5] Newman and Pusey published a posthumous volume of the works of their friend Hurrell Froude, who thought the Reformation was a disaster that could be overcome by paying as little attention to it as possible. Newman put out the notorious Tract Ninety, in which he argued that Catholic doctrine and practice, rightly understood, were not condemned by the Thirty-Nine Articles. His disciples Frederick Oakeley and W.G. Ward went on to argue that an Anglican could, and probably should, accept the entire teaching of the Roman church without ceasing to be Anglican. Froude's polemics evidently outraged almost everyone who had not known and loved him when he was alive. Most people who were not dedicated partisans of Newman thought Tract Ninety was disingenuous. Ward was stripped of his degrees by solemn act of Oxford University, and Oakeley was inhibited from the ministry by a court. But the crisis passed. Newman, Ward, and Oakeley became Roman Catholics, and Pusey became the leader of a polemically more circumspect but doctrinally unrepentant Anglo-Catholicism that ultimately found a solid and respected place in the church.

As Catholic doctrine worked its way out of the universities and into the midst of the working clergy, the High Church agenda moved into its third stage, the adoption of Catholic pastoral and liturgical practices. Stone altars, reredoses with statues, crucifixes, candles, and even rood screens began appearing in the new Gothic Revival churches that were being put up under the Church Building Acts, and reappearing in some of the churches from which they had been removed at the Reformation. Priests began celebrating Communion with their backs to the congregation, elevating the consecrated elements, putting on chasubles, using incense, and referring to the service as the mass. Other ceremonies were adopted from research into medieval precedent, observation of demotic Roman Catholic worship at Continental holiday resorts, or mere imagination. Priests also began hearing confessions — a practice for which the Prayer Book makes gingerly provision in its Office for the Visitation of the Sick — and encouraging their congregations to confess regularly, sick or well. Religious communities and other forms of special discipline made their appearance. A few priests tried to police the doctrines of the laity by repelling people from Communion who put forth heterodox beliefs or who attended non-Anglican worship.

There has been a good deal of debate as to why all these innovations (revivals, if you prefer) were undertaken and what they accomplished.[6] One view attributes them to antiquarian pedantry, and holds that they consummated the alienation of ordinary people from the church. Another holds that they were brought in by popular demand, and had special appeal to working people because of the drabness of the rest of their lives. Owen Chadwick is persuasive in taking a position between these views. He argues that the "Ritualist" clergy commended themselves to the urban poor more by the dedication of their lives than by the richness of their liturgy, and that they kept their churches full not because their parishioners loved ceremonial, but because non-parishioners who loved it came from all over to participate. He finds a good deal of merit in having the church offer a variety of liturgical styles so that people can choose the one that best suits them.

Chadwick's permissiveness was ultimately established as the norm, as we shall see. But it ran counter to the original Reformation settlement, which was based on doctrinal diversity offset by liturgical uniformity. The courts were still prepared to enforce the settlement on those terms, and it is here that the High Churchmen engaged in the epic legal battles that we will take up shortly. It is out of those legal battles that the fourth and final stage of the High Church agenda arose — the provision of institutions of self-government for the church. Under this head came the restoration of the ancient provincial Convocations, the establishment of diocesan synods, and, ultimately, the establishment of the National Assembly and its successor the

General Synod, whose measures have the force of Acts of Parliament. All of these we will examine in due course.

II. The Battle in the Courts

At least from the publication of Froude's *Remains* in 1838, the authorities in both church and state were generally unfavorable, often downright hostile, to the High Church agenda in each of its successive manifestations. Some of the disapproval was theological. For Evangelicals, who were becoming more numerous in the episcopate because Whig prime ministers tended to appoint them, the High Churchmen were betraying the basic principles of the Reformation. For liberal churchmen, intent on having the church keep pace with the breadth and tolerance of the times, the High Churchmen seemed pedants and obscurantists bent on reviving the Dark Ages. There was also a strong line of disapproval on political grounds. The structures of the church had been set up with great care to accommodate a variety of believers within a national religious consensus. The High Churchmen seemed determined to repeal the accommodation and break the consensus apart.

As a result, the High Churchmen were constantly running afoul of one authority or another, ecclesiastical or secular. To all forms of authoritative opposition, they responded with equal insouciance that they had to obey God rather than men. With the sides drawn up in this way, court battles were inevitable. The Reformation settlement of the Church of England was relentlessly juridical. In Elizabeth's time, and again in Charles II's, Acts of Parliament had set it up, and courts and judges had enforced it. Acts of Parliament were still supporting it, and courts and judges were still ready to enforce it. The stage was set for some of the oddest litigations in English history.

A. The Law.

1. General — The applicable law continued to reflect the original decision for doctrinal accommodation and liturgical uniformity. It had always been pretty permissive in matters of doctrine, and had become more so over the years. The act setting up Elizabeth's High Commission had provided that that body was to regard nothing as heresy that was not expressly denounced as such in the plain words of Scripture, by the first four general councils, or by Parliament with the concurrence of the two Convocations.[7] The plain words of Scripture do not expressly define any heresies, and neither Parliament nor either Convocation has ever done so, so there remain only the traditional heresies — Arianism, Nestorianism, Donatism, and the like — denounced by the four general councils. The act applies only in terms to the High Commission, but Coke and his colleagues held that other ecclesiastical courts would do well to accept the same limitation. The only other provision on heresy is the act of Charles II abolishing the burning of heretics, but leaving the powers of the ecclesiastical courts as they were. Whatever were the powers in question, I find no evidence of their being invoked after James I's time. An eccentric mathematician named Whiston was had up for heresy in the Canterbury Convocation in Queen Anne's time, but the members of that body were so doubtful of their powers that they ended by condemning his book rather than his person, and even that condemnation was not confirmed by the queen.[8] In 1717, as we have seen, Convocation was more or less permanently prorogued lest it undertake another heresy proceeding. No other tribunal attempted to fill the gap.

Until the reforms that we took up in a previous chapter, the universities of Oxford and Cambridge had some authority to monitor the orthodoxy of their resident members.[9] Various university tribunals could censure their works, deprive them of their positions, and even strip them of their degrees and forbid them access to the library. The doctrinal standards to be enforced by the exercise of these powers were generally formulated in medieval or Caroline times, in such vague language as "sound religion" or "the Catholic faith." These powers had not often been invoked, but Whiston, whom I just mentioned, lost his professorship under them in the early eighteenth century, and a layman named Frend lost his degrees and his library privileges under them toward the end of the same century. Newman's eccentric disciple W.G. Ward was to suffer the same fate in 1845.

The procedure for confirming the election of a bishop includes a place where objectors are invited to come forward and state their objections. When Hampden was elected to the see of Hereford in 1848, and on a couple of later occasions, people attempted to take advantage of this invitation by raising the doctrinal failings of the bishop-elect. In no case were they successful. The ecclesiastical judges consistently refused to hear any objector, and the lay court (by a split vote in 1848, and unanimously in 1902) refused a writ of mandamus to make them do so.[10] The statutes requiring the speedy election and confirmation of the person chosen by the Crown were held to vest the question of fitness in the ministers who advise the appointment. The argument that the call for objectors to come forward could not have been intended as a meaningless gesture had to give way before the logic of the statutory scheme of Crown appointments — especially as there was no statutory basis for the confirmation proceeding.

There is in the ordination service a place where the members of the congregation are invited to come forward if they know of any "Impediment or notable Crime" making the ordinand unfit. This presumably could have been used for doctrinal objections, but I do not find that it was. An objection was made in St. Paul's Cathedral in 1905 on account of the liturgical practices of the ordinands, but the bishop, on legal advice, ruled that such practices were neither an impediment nor a notable crime. When the objector (J. A. Kensit, a vigorous Protestant agitator of whom we shall see more later) persisted in reading his objection, he was taken before the magistrates and convicted of disrupting a religious service.[11] An objector on doctrinal grounds would presumably have fared no better.

There were (and continued to be until 1969) statutory provisions for fining and imprisoning anyone who spoke disrespectfully of the Eucharist or the Book of Common Prayer.[12] These strictures dated from 1548, and there was obviously no longer any thought of subjecting anyone to the punishments prescribed. But Coke had held in 1606 that the ecclesiastical authorities could punish clergymen for violating statutes of this kind without limiting themselves to the statutory punishments. So the 1548 statutes could still be regarded as setting doctrinal standards for the clergy.

Another explicit doctrinal standard was provided by the Thirty-Nine Articles. There was an Elizabethan statute punishing any clergyman who "advisedly maintained or affirmed" a doctrine contrary to any of them.[13] This provision remained on the books until 1963.

Both the Thirty-Nine Articles and the Prayer Book were further binding on the clergy because of statutes requiring them at various points in their careers to express some form of assent or approbation of them.[14] Until 1865, a clergyman had on several occasions to subscribe the Articles verbatim. On other occasions a declaration of assent would do. From 1865 to 1974, the following declaration was required on various occasions of every clergyman:

> I assent to the Thirty-Nine Articles of Religion, and to the Book of Common Prayer and of the ordering of bishops, priests, and deacons. I believe the doctrine of the Church of England as therein set forth, to be agreeable to the Word of God; and in public prayer and administration of the sacraments I will use the form in the said book prescribed, and none other, except so far as I shall be ordered by lawful authority.

Presumably, then, it was and continued to be forbidden for a clergyman to maintain doctrines clearly inconsistent with either the Articles or the Prayer Book.

Oddly enough, it was less clear that he was forbidden to maintain doctrines inconsistent with the Bible. The Sixth of the Articles, and the rite of ordination in the Prayer Book hold that Scripture contains all doctrines necessary to salvation, and forbid imposing as necessary any doctrine that cannot be proved from Scripture. Denying the divine inspiration of either the Old or New Testament would be a violation of the 1697 statute taken up in an earlier chapter, and denying the canonicity of one of the books would be inconsistent with Article Six, for they are listed there. But teaching a doctrine inconsistent with some scriptural passage (as long as you did not claim that the doctrine was necessary to salvation) or denying that one or another of the events narrated in the historical passages actually took place was nowhere explicitly forbidden. Until new developments in German criticism made their way to England in the 1840s, there was hardly a problem.[15]

Liturgy and administration of the sacraments were governed by a series of Acts of Uniformity (1548, 1559, 1662), which required all public services in the Church of England to be strictly conformable to the Prayer Book. This requirement did not leave much room for debate as to the words used in the services, but it gave little guidance on gestures, vestments, or physical surroundings. On these matters, previous generations had been content to follow custom, but the new High Churchmen often preferred to recover lost Catholic traditions.[16]

One source of guidance, such as it was, was the Ornaments Rubric, included in the 1662 Prayer Book, and, with slightly different wording, in the 1558 one:

> Such Ornaments of the Church and of the Ministers thereof, at all times of their Ministration, shall be retained, and be in use, as were in this Church of England, by the authority of Parliament, in the second Year of the reign of King Edward the Sixth.

Since the traditional Catholic Eucharistic vestments were evidently not abolished until the fifth year of Edward VI, there was a good case to be made for saying that they were still required, even though they had not been used for some centuries, and even though the Canons of 1604 made a different provision. The rubric was part of the Prayer Book, and the Prayer Book was enjoined by statute; hence, the rubric had a status which neither custom nor canon could impair.

The 1604 canons called for the Eucharist to be celebrated at a "holy table." How nearly a structure could resemble a medieval altar and still be a table became a serious question with the Gothic Revival, and remained one as late as 1987. The Elizabethan prelates and Cromwellian soldiers who worked so hard to replace altars with tables were presumably convinced that they were two different things. Later generations were not so sure.

The authoritative sources, Articles, Prayer Book, and canons, offered similarly ambiguous, tenuous, or debatable provisions on other Catholic practices. A Prayer Book rubric provides that for the Eucharist "it shall suffice that the bread be such as is usual to be eaten." Are the words "it shall suffice" to be taken literally, or does the rubric forbid bread that is not such as is usual to be eaten? Another rubric says that if any of the consecrated bread and wine remain after everyone has communicated, "it shall not be carried out of the church, but the priest and such other of the communicants as he shall then call unto him shall immediately after the blessing reverently eat and drink the same." This rubric was probably adopted to keep the clergy from taking the consecrated elements home for their dinner. Does it also forbid keeping some on hand for the sick? And if the consecrated elements may be kept on hand, what reverence should be given them? Article 28 says: "The Sacrament of the Lord's Supper was not by Christ's ordinance reserved, carried about, lifted up, or worshipped." Does that mean that Christ said *not* to do any of these things, or only that He left the question open?

Both in the Office for the Visitation of the Sick and in the Exhortation appended to the Communion service, the Prayer Book provides for confessing one's sins to a priest and receiving absolution. The Canons of 1604 complement these provisions by forbidding a clergyman to reveal the sins confessed. But the invitations are so worded as to suggest that the ministry is provided for overscrupulous people, and that a person of robust faith ought to do without it. What is to be said, then, of a clergyman who exhorts people to make a regular practice of going to confession?

Until 1874, the normal procedures for dealing with doctrinal and liturgical matters were the same as those for dealing with other matters. A clergyman accused of heterodox teaching or unconformable services could be proceeded against under the Church Discipline Act, 1840, in exactly the same way as a clergyman accused of fornication or simony. Alternatively, the bishop could refuse him institution to a benefice or deny or withdraw his license as a curate, in which case both he and his patron had the same remedies as they would have had if the bishop had found he knew too little Latin. Altars, crucifixes, and statues of Our Lady were subject to the same faculty jurisdiction as pews, heating stoves, and memorials to the local squire.

We have had occasion to look at all these procedures with one exception. That is a proceeding called *duplex querela* or double quarrel, whereby a clergyman refused institution to a benefice can call the bishop to answer in the archbishop's court.[17] The origin of this proceeding is obscure. It is mentioned in the Canons of 1585 and 1604, and there is a trace of it in a Jacobean report. The eighteenth century commentators mention it, sometimes with fairly elaborate descriptions, but have no contemporary examples of its use. By 1849, it was said to have been dormant for "upwards of a century." It was to have a moment of glory (or notoriety) in that year, and to be sporadically useful from then on.

Although the proceeding appears never to have been used except by a clergyman denied admission to a benefice, it evidently started out as an exercise of the general power of a metropolitan to take over a matter from a suffragan who failed to act on it. This power is amply documented in both medieval and modern Roman Catholic material, although I have not been able to find the name *duplex querela* in either. Burn suggests that the Latin should be translated "double complaint" rather than the customary "double quarrel." He traces the name to a custom (for which I have no evidence) of citing the person who stops the suffragan from acting along with the suffragan himself. My own speculation, for what it is worth, is that the name should be translated "duplicate process," and comes from the fact that a proceeding is initiated in the metropolitan court while a parallel proceeding is still going on before the suffragan.

The aggrieved clergyman begins the proceeding by getting a monition out of the metropolitan court. This document issues without a hearing, and requires all clerks and literate persons to admonish the suffragan (with due regard for his reverence and dignity) to take the specified official action, or come into court and show why he has not done so. If he fails to do one or the other, or if he comes into court and fails to show a legally sufficient cause, the court will itself take the necessary action on the archbishop's behalf.

The clergyman's remedy of *duplex querela* existed side by side with the patron's traditional remedy of *quare impedit*, an action in the lay courts to obtain a writ ordering the bishop to admit the patron's presentee. It was held in 1874 that a clerical patron who presented himself had to use one remedy or the other; he could not bring both at once.[18]

2. The 1874 Act — It was in the midst of the series of litigations we are about to consider that Parliament adopted the Public Worship Regulation Act, 1874,[19] in an ill-fated attempt to simplify procedures in liturgical cases. This act covered unauthorized alterations or illegal decorations of the church, use of unlawful ornaments or vesture, failure to use prescribed ones, changing, dropping, or expanding the Prayer Book offices, or failing to follow the rubrics. The remedy it provided was cumulative; it did not supersede any remedy previously available. It was expected to be attractive to people aggrieved by liturgical violations because it was expected to be quicker and surer than the alternatives.

Proceedings could be set in motion by the archdeacon with jurisdiction over the parish where the violations were taking place, by any churchwarden of that parish, or by any three male persons who had lived in the parish for a year, and who were willing to certify to the bishop that they were members of the Church of England. These provisions excluded most Dissenters (but not all — some were willing to claim membership in more than one church) and people who moved into the parish in order to litigate. Both had been allowed to bring suit under other acts. It was decided not to require the promoter of the suit to be a person who actually attended worship in the parish, because it was felt that people who were driven away by illegal liturgical innovations were still entitled to have them abolished.

Upon receiving a "representation" from someone authorized to complain, the bishop had to consider all the circumstances of the case, and decide whether to proceed further. If he decided not to proceed, he had to state his reasons in writing. This provision giving the bishop a veto over proceedings was controversial. There had to be some room for discretion, because, while the act was aimed at High Church innovations, no church party was in strict compliance with the law. Evangelicals ("Low" Churchmen) tended to slight the saints' days and to leave off their surplices when preaching. Latitudinarians ("Broad" Churchmen) often refused to recite the Athanasian Creed with its consignment to perdition of anyone who did not accept the full equality of the three Persons of the Blessed Trinity. Parish clergy of many different persuasions sometimes had occasion to bury people for whom they did not want to express a "sure and certain hope of resurrection to eternal life." Many of them also lacked the time or the inclination to say the morning and evening prayers every day as the rubrics required. Accordingly, there was a problem bringing High Churchmen ("Ritualists") to book without making trouble for anyone else. Giving the bishop an unrestricted discretion was probably not the best possible solution. Many proponents of the act had wanted to make the bishop's refusal to proceed reviewable by the archbishop. An amendment to that effect passed the Commons by a large margin, but was defeated in the Lords.

As under the 1840 act, the bishop's powers passed into the archbishop's hands if the accused held preferment in the bishop's gift. This happened very seldom, probably because the bishops of the time did not bestow their preferment on Ritualists.

If the bishop chose to proceed on the representation, he had first to find whether the parties were willing to submit to his personal judgment, without appeal. In the wildly unlikely event that both parties were so willing, the bishop could hear the matter any way he thought fit, and enter a binding judgment. His judgment, however, was not to be taken as finally deciding any question of law. I know of no case in which the parties chose this route.

If either party was unwilling to submit to the bishop, the bishop was to forward the representation to the archbishop, who was to turn it over to a judge newly provided for, and instruct the judge to hear it somewhere within the diocese or province, or in London or Westminster. The archbishop could impose narrower limits than the statute provided — as Archbishop Tait was to learn when the Queen's Bench issued a prohibition on one of the first prosecutions under the act.[20] Tait had ordered the case heard within the diocese of Rochester or in London or Westminster, and the court had sat at Lambeth Palace because no other place had been assigned it. The Queen's Bench held that "London" did not mean the whole metropolis, because if it did the word "Westminster" would be superfluous. As Lambeth Palace was not in London, Westminster, or the diocese of Rochester, the archbishop's order had not been followed, and the proceeding was void. It was argued that the word "province" had been left out of the order only by inadvertence, but the court refused to correct what the archbishop had written.

The status of the judge provided for in this act was ambiguous. The two archbishops were to appoint a person by agreement, subject to the approval of the government. The judge so appointed was to become ex officio judge of each provincial court (the Arches Court of Canterbury and the Chancery Court of York) when the respective judgeships next fell vacant. He was also to become ex officio Master of the Faculties to the Archbishop of Canterbury when that ancient, well paid, and undemanding office fell vacant. After he took over the provincial judgeships (which happened soon after the act took effect) his proceedings were to be deemed to be taken in the traditional court of whichever province was involved. Nevertheless, in the Lambeth Palace case just referred to, the Queen's Bench held that he was exercising a new jurisdiction, and could not rely on the traditional power of the Court of Arches to sit anywhere in the province. This holding was to give both pleasure and ammunition to those who resisted the authority of the new proceedings on the ground that they were not in an ecclesiastical court.

Lord Penzance, the first judge appointed under the act, made matters worse by refusing to take the customary oaths and execute the canonical subscriptions that had been required for the offices now being merged into his.[21] Since an Act of Parliament made him ex officio occupant of these offices, he reasoned, he could not be required to fulfill any further conditions for them. His logic was irrefutable, but it did nothing to commend the legitimacy of his judgments to people who felt that only an ecclesiastical court could decide liturgical questions.

Trials under the act were to follow the newly reformed procedure of the lay courts rather than the leisurely pace of traditional canonical proceedings. Appeals were to be taken to the Judicial Committee of the Privy Council, which was to decide each case on the record from the trial court, without being allowed to take additional evidence as appellate courts could do in other canonical proceedings.

Judgments emerging from this process took the form of monitions to remove the offending objects or cease the offending practices. In the case of an alteration to the building, the monition could be obeyed without a faculty. Alternatively, if the alteration was legal, although unauthorized, the court could issue a faculty to leave it in place. A clergyman who disobeyed a monition was subject to inhibition (temporary exclusion from the ministry) after three months, deprivation after three years. These sanctions proved inadequate against determined opposition, as we shall see, and had to be supplemented by the traditional writ *de contumace capiendo*, by which people who defied the ecclesiastical courts could be put into secular jails.

3. *The Court of Last Resort* — The Judicial Committee of the Privy Council heard all ecclesiastical appeals. It was created in 1833 to perform various appellate tasks outside the regular court system, whose appeals fed into the House of Lords.[22] Its jurisdiction extended to all the colonies and dependencies, the Isle of Man, the Channel Islands, and the church. Its judgments took the form of advice to the sovereign as to how she should exercise her general prerogative of doing justice where no one else was assigned to do it. As regards the church, the Judicial Committee took the place of the Court of Delegates that had exercised the final appellate authority of the sovereign ever since the sovereign had taken it from the pope. In 1833, no one had thought of its having doctrinal or liturgical questions to decide.[23] Most ecclesiastical appeals had involved the probate and matrimonial jurisdiction (abolished in 1857) with a few drunk or incontinent clergymen for variety. Only a handful had had anything to do with doctrine or liturgy.

The Judicial Committee, like the lower court, was easy to regard as a merely secular tribunal. It consisted of certain designated judicial officials plus whatever other judges or ex-judges happened to be Privy Councillors. Until 1876, bishops also participated in cases arising under the Church Discipline Act, 1840. In other ecclesiastical appeals, bishops were brought in to sit as "assessors." An assessor in the Roman and canonical systems occupies a position somewhere between a juror and an expert witness. The court has every reason to take him seriously, but no obligation to follow his decision on any question. In 1876, the practice of appointing bishoips as assessors was made statutory, and the number of episcopal assessors was fixed at five.[24] At the same time, the 1840 provision for making bishops full members of the tribunal was repealed.

In cases under the 1874 act, some objection was made to the presence of the archbisahop of the affected province among the assessors, since it was his duty to set the whole process in motion. In the abstract, this objection was not persuasive, since the act gave the archbishop no discretionary or judicial role in the earlier stages. But it had a certain cogency during the crucial first few years when the archbishop of Canterbury was Tait, who had put the bill through Parliament in the first place in order to put down Ritualism.

B. The Cases.

In a series of cases beginning in the early 1840s, the Judicial Committee, with some help from other courts, used the available laws and procedures to elucidate what a clergyman of the Church of England could lawfully say or do in the way of doctrine or liturgy. History has not been kind to these decisions. Although it is over forty years since I was an Anglican, my outrage at some of them is still vivid in my mind. But looking at them as a lawyer rather than as a former Anglo-Catholic, I find myself taking a more balanced view. The hope to produce religious harmony by judicial decision was no doubt doomed from the start, but it was not an ignoble hope. The enterprise of maintaining peace through making and enforcing laws often appears unpromising, but it has successes to record.

1. Doctrine — In its approach to doctrine, the Judicial Committee was very clear that its role was not to bear witness to any particular truth, but simply to set the limits of what was permissible. On more than one occasion, they had to scold the Dean of the Arches (judge of the Canterbury provincial court) for purporting to set forth the official teaching of the Church of England on a point in issue. That was to be done, if at all, by a church synod. The court sat simply to determine whether particular doctrines, be they true or be they false, were such as a clergyman was forbidden to hold or teach. A doctrine, to be prohibited, had to contravene either the Thirty-Nine Articles or the Prayer Book. Those were the official formularies of the Church of England. Where they were silent, liberty prevailed.

Furthermore, these formularies were to be construed like other legislative enactments, not like conciliar pronouncements on disputed points of doctrine. Since they were being invoked to punish doctrinal deviance, they were subject to the rule that penal enactments must be strictly construed. The usual arguments from legislative history were also applicable. For instance, the fact that a doctrine was explicitly imposed by the language of an earlier version of the Articles or the Prayer Book would support an argument that it was not implicitly imposed by a later version that had dropped the explicit language. By the same token, a formula that emerged from a controversy between two schools of thought would be treated in the same way as a statute emerging from a hard-fought legislative battle — as a compromise or a modus vivendi, not as a resolution of the issue in favor of one or the other of the contending parties. It followed that the writings of sixteenth and seventeenth century Anglican divines could be looked at to show what was permissible, but not what was compulsory.

The approach raised a couple of questions that were never fully resolved. The thirty-fifth Article refers to the two Books of Homilies that were set forth in the early years of the Reformation to be read in church by ministers who had no license to preach their own sermons. It says they "contain a godly and wholesome doctrine, and necessary for these times." Does it follow that any doctrine inconsistent with the Homilies is inconsistent with the Articles? Fortunately, the person against whom this argument was urged was sufficiently convicted on other grounds, so the question never had to be decided. The other question was more serious. It was how and to what extent doctrinal principles could be deduced from the liturgical texts in the Prayer Book. There is an old maxim *lex orandi lex credendi*, but it cannot be applied with complete literalism. Lord Langdale, speaking for the Judicial Committee in the famous *Gorham* case, pointed out that everyone who dies baptized and not excommunicated is put into the ground with the words:

> Forasmuch as it hath pleased Almighty God, of his great mercy, to take unto himself the soul of our dear brother here departed, we therefore commit his body to the ground . . . in sure and certain hope of the resurrection to eternal life.

and yet the Church of England does not teach that all such persons without exception are saved, i.e. that God takes them "unto himself."[25] Langdale offered a distinction between "instructional" and "devotional" parts of the Prayer Book, but there are certainly some passages in the Prayer Book that would be hard to put definitively in one category or the other (for instance, "Those whom God hath joined together let no man put asunder."). But no such passages figured in the cases.

On the whole, the principles adopted by the Judicial Committee made deciding doctrinal cases a fairly straightforward task. What you had to do was take some passage from the writings of the accused, lay it alongside some Article or Prayer Book passage, and decide whether they were inconsistent. The first two cases in which this was done were easy ones. *Henry Erskine Head* (1843),[26] a Protestant minded rector in the diocese of that most pugnacious of High Church bishops, Henry Phillpotts, responded to the announcement of an upcoming confirmation by publishing an attack on the whole system of Christian initiation, of which confirmation was a part. He insisted that the confirmation service, the catechism by which children were prepared for confirmation, and even the baptismal service were full of "strange and erroneous doctrine," evidently of a popish kind. Since all these offices were contained in the Prayer Book, Head's claim was obviously inconsistent with the Prayer Book, and the court had no difficulty finding it so.

Frederick Oakeley (1845)[27] was as definite on the Catholic side as Head was on the Protestant. When his friend W.G. Ward was dismissed from Oxford for Romanizing, Oakeley came to his support by writing and publishing a letter to the bishop of London claiming that it was acceptable for a clergyman of the Church of England to hold the entire doctrine of the church of Rome, and that he, Oakeley, in fact did so. With this invitation, Sir Herbert Jenner Fust in the Court of Arches had carte blanche to range through the entire corpus of the Council of Trent looking for formulas that contradicted one or another of the Thirty-Nine Articles. Naturally, he had no trouble finding them, and condemning Oakeley accordingly.

Oakeley had evidently supposed himself to be following the teaching of Newman in Tract Ninety. Newman had indeed argued that the Thirty-Nine Articles could be taken in a "Catholic" sense, but he did not go so far as to insist on the full Tridentine package. In any event, Jenner Fust was not required to confront Tract Ninety directly, because Oakeley did not present any argument in the case, although he appeared and participated in some of the preliminary phases.

In a way, though, Jenner Fust is answering Tract Ninety when he says:

> In pursuing this inquiry the course which I am inclined to take is to confine myself to the plain and grammatical construction of our articles, and not to seek the opinion of others; for to do otherwise would, I conceive, tend to weaken their authority.

While Tract Ninety speaks of interpreting the Articles literally, its basic approach is to interpret them as rejecting vulgar errors prevalent in the late medieval church, and then to show that true Catholic teaching also rejects those errors. Newman draws on a considerable store of historical and theological scholarship to support these points. He is doing this because he has a stake in making the Articles consistent with Catholic doctrine. He has such a stake because he believes in Catholic doctrine, and is obliged to adhere to the Articles. In short, he is interpreting a legal enactment by resorting to a normative criterion extraneous to it. Despite the furor, there is nothing dishonest in doing this: lawyers and judges do it all the time. But it is entirely inconsistent with the criteria laid down by the courts for use in doctrine cases.

I have no doubt that the Judicial Committee would have approved Jenner Fust's reading of both the Articles and the Tridentine decrees, and would have affirmed his judgment. Oakeley did not stay to find out. Some months after the judgment came down, he took himself and his Roman doctrines into the Roman Catholic Church, where he lived happily ever after. He spent the last thirty years of his life as a canon of Westminster Cathedral.

Two other cases involved exuberantly heterodox clergymen who proved more difficult to bring to book because it took some work to extract from their writings specific propositions to measure against the Articles and Prayer Book.[28] *Dunbar Isidore Heath* (1862) and *Charles Voysey* (1871) were both evidently believers in a religion of general benevolence that made them uncomfortable with such doctrines as original sin and atonement. Voysey was also unhappy with the divinity of Christ, and rejected such parts of the Gospel of John as seemed to support that divinity. Dr. Lushington, Dean of the Arches at the time, accepted a set of articles (i.e. statements of charges) against Heath that quoted long passages from his writings and alleged in general terms that they were incompatible with official church formularies. On an interlocutory appeal, the Judicial Committee reformed the articles so that they alleged specific propositions as deducible from the writings in question, and referred to specific formularies with which those propositions were inconsistent. The prosecution in Voysey's case followed this approach from the start.

Heath appears not to have denied that his doctrine was correctly stated. He claimed that his views when fairly construed did not contravene the formularies referred to in the articles against him. He also claimed that he had not intentionally contravened any of the Thirty-Nine Articles, and that he was therefore not liable under the statute that penalizes "advisedly" maintaining a doctrine contrary to those Articles. But both the Arches and the Judicial Committee found that his doctrines — or most of them — were contrary to the Articles, and that advisedly maintaining such doctrines means maintaining them on purpose, not necessarily maintaining them with knowledge that they contravene the Articles. On failing to make a satisfactory retraction, Heath was deprived of his preferment.

Voysey, in addition to arguing that his doctrines were not contrary to the formularies, insisted that many of them were not correctly stated. The courts had, therefore, to examine his writings to show that the views he was charged with holding were in fact contained in them. This they did, and Voysey was also deprived of his preferment.

Most of the points meticulously made in these two cases are straightforward enough. The claim that Christ's blood was not shed to propitiate the Father or to reconcile man to Him is obviously inconsistent with Article 31, which speaks of propitiation, and Article 2, which speaks of reconciliation. The claim that forgiveness of sin has nothing to do with the Gospel is inconsistent with the Creeds (contained in the Prayer Book, and also adopted by Article 8), and with Articles 16 and 27, all of which speak of forgiveness. The claim that children are not by nature under God's wrath is inconsistent with the assertion in Article 9 that in everyone born original sin is deserving of God's wrath and damnation. But some questions are more puzzling. Is the claim that it is idolatrous to worship Christ inconsistent with the various formularies that proclaim Him divine? (Yes, according to the court.) Is denying the immortality of the soul and the propriety of speaking of people as "going to heaven" or "going to hell" inconsistent with belief in the life everlasting proclaimed in the Apostles' Creed? (Not necessarily.)

Particularly difficult was Voysey's wholesale rejection of parts of the Bible, for which he appealed to the acceptance of contemporary critical approaches in the *Essays and Reviews* case (which we will look at shortly). The Articles are clear that nothing is to be taught as necessary to salvation unless it can be proved from Scripture, but they say nothing about how such proof is to be mounted, nor do they say that *everything* that can be proved from Scripture must be believed. The Judicial Committee met Voysey's argument by distinguishing a critical approach from mere captiousness. Article 6 lists the canonical Books of the Bible and says that their authority has never been doubted. But if they can be rejected for no better reason than that they are inconsistent with the doctrine that one wishes to hold, they cannot be said to have any authority at all. Also, to the extent that Voysey rejects passages on the ground that they are contrary to other passages, he violates Article 20, which says the church may not "so expound one place of Scripture, that it be repugnant to another." What is forbidden to the whole church should be forbidden *a fortiori* to a country vicar.

Catholic Eucharistic doctrine was involved in two major cases, and came off fairly well, all things considered. *George Anthony Denison,*[29] archdeacon of Taunton and uncompromising controversialist, held that

> To all who come to the Lord's Table, whether worthy or unworthy, the Body and Blood of Christ are given, and by them received.

This was good Catholic doctrine:

> Sumunt boni, sumunt mali,
> Sorte tamen inaequali
>   Vitae vel interitus
> Mors est malis, vita bonis;
> Vide, paris sumptionis
>   Quam sit dispar exitus.

But it was hard to reconcile with Article 29, "Of the Wicked, which eat not the Body of Christ in the use of the Lord's Supper." The usual High Church response was to interpret "eat" in a spiritual sense. Their interpretation was supported by the text of the Article, which says nothing about not eating, and speaks only of not being "partakers of Christ." Denison also put considerable weight on his own use of the term "receive." Article 25 speaks of those who receive unworthily, and is therefore inconsistent with saying that the unworthy do not receive at all.

As an examining chaplain, Denison caused a flap by telling ordinands that he expected them to adhere to his Eucharistic doctrine. He was shortly brought to the point of resigning his chaplainship. He then determined to test the legality of his doctrine by preaching it in Wells cathedral and daring all and sundry to prosecute him. In the ensuing litigation, his doctrine was condemned, but he himself escaped in a series of procedural tangles, of which he was willing to take advantage

> because it is not to be disputed that a man, who is a member of a Church established by Law, must be tried and convicted, if tried and convicted at all, according to Law.[30]

Shortly after the offending sermons, Richard Bagot, bishop of Oxford in Newman's time, now bishop of Bath and Wells, called Denison in, got him to undertake to stop unchurching those who disagreed with him, and then let him go as holding a view within the range of permissible teachings. Bagot died and a successor also refused to prosecute. But it turned out that Denison held preferment in the gift of the diocesan bishop, so John Bird Sumner, the Evangelical archbishop of Canterbury, had power to appoint a commission under the Church Discipline Act, 1840, and elected to do so. The Queen's Bench rejected Denison's claim that his encounter with Bagot was res judicata on the matter: Bagot had not acted judicially.

The commission reported a prima facie case, but the archbishop by then had thought the better of the whole proceeding, and decided to stop it. This time, the prosecution resorted to the Queen's Bench. That court held that once the commission had reported there was no option not to proceed, and issued a mandamus to the archbishop to try the case. The archbishop then summoned Denison to appear before him in Doctors' Commons in London, the Inn of Court for the ecclesiastical and admiralty bar. Denison blocked that move by persuading the Queen's Bench that even though the archbishop was hearing the case, it still had to be heard within the diocese of Bath and Wells. Finally, the archbishop and two assessors heard the case at Bath, condemned Denison's doctrine, and when he would not retract, ordered him deprived of his preferment. Denison appealed to the Court of Arches, which held that since it was the archbishop's own court it had no jurisdiction to hear an appeal from the archbishop. Back to the Queen's Bench for another mandamus. Since under the statute the archbishop was acting in place of the diocesan bishop, his court must be treated as the bishop's court, and therefore the Arches must hear the appeal. On hearing it, the Arches decided that the proceeding was barred by the two year time limit for proceedings under the act. The sermons had been preached in the summer and fall of 1853, and Denison had not been served with an effective citation until June, 1856. For purposes of the act, a proceeding is commenced when a citation is served for a formal proceeding, not when a commission makes its preliminary inquiry. This decision was affirmed by the Judicial Committee, and Denison was still Archdeacon of Taunton when he died at ninety in 1896, intransigent to the end:

> English Churchmen seem to me, not to be defenders of ALL which GOD has given them to defend, but to be givers-up of one part of it after another, in the vain hope of saving the rest by some art or contrivance of man's device. This may be Conservative, but it is not Catholic: it may be Policy, but it is not FAITH.[31]

Among those proclaiming solidarity with Denison in this affair was *W. J. E. Bennett*.[32] Until 1851, Bennett had been in charge of a parish in a poor neighborhood in the metropolis. He had become a scapegoat when the London populace decided that Anglican Ritualists were responsible for the pope's decision to restore the Roman Catholic hierarchy in England. Holding riots at Bennett's church became a Sunday amusement for a good many people (encouraged, I suspect, by some who opposed other forms of Sunday amusement), and remained so for some weeks until Bennett was persuaded to resign. He then became vicar of Frome in Somerset, where he was accused of dropping the first letter of the name. He used the Eucharistic vestments and other Catholic liturgical practices, but insisted that he introduced no such practices until his parishioners were ready to accept them. He thought it was desirable to have variety in the liturgy to meet the needs and desires of different congregations, and had an amicable arrangement with neighboring incumbents to encourage parishioners to attend whichever services they liked best.

In 1867, he published *A Plea for Toleration in the Church of England*. Its basic thrust was as the name implied, but in the course of it he set forth his own Eucharistic doctrine to support the liturgical practices for which he claimed toleration. In the same year, he published *Some Results of the Tractarian Movement of 1833*, in the course of which he recounted the story of Denison's trial, including his own support for Denison. These two publications gave rise to a prosecution claiming four types of doctrinal error:

1. By expressing support for Denison, he adopted Denison's teaching, condemned by Article 29, that the wicked receive the Body and Blood of Christ.

2. He maintained that there is a real, actual, and objective presence of the Body and Blood of Christ in the consecrated elements (in an earlier edition, he had said "visible presence," but the correction in a later edition was held to be a sufficient retraction). This was alleged to be contrary to various provisions of Article 28, especially the statement that "The Body of Christ is given, taken, and eaten, in the Supper, only after an heavenly and spiritual manner."

3. He maintained that adoration is due to Christ present in the consecrated elements (corrected from a statement in an earlier edition that the elements themselves were to be adored). There is a Declaration on Kneeling in the Prayer Book that says that although people are to receive Communion kneeling, "thereby no adoration is intended, or ought to be done, either unto the Sacramental Bread or Wine there bodily received, or unto any Corporal Presence of Christ's natural Flesh and Blood." It also says in Article 28 that "The Sacrament of the Lord's Supper was not by Christ's ordinance reserved, carried about, lifted up, or worshipped." Also, particular acts of adoration, some of which Bennett in his publication admitted doing, had already been specifically condemned in one or another of the liturgical cases.

4. He maintained that the priest in the Eucharist is offering a sacrifice, whereas Article 31 says that "the sacrifices of masses, in the which it was commonly said, that the Priest did offer Christ . . . were blasphemous fables and dangerous deceits."

Bennett did not appear in response to these charges. Presumably, he was following what had become common High Church practice — spurning the courts for their secular provenance. Despite his absence, he was acquitted on all charges, both in the Arches and in the Judicial Committee. The reasoning was about the same in both courts, although the lower court addressed the questions at greater length, and was castigated by the Judicial Committee for deciding more than was necessary or appropriate.

1. The charge of adopting Denison's errors was thrown out. To turn a general expression of support for a person into a wholesale adoption of all that person's doctrines would be inconsistent with the specificity required for these punitive proceedings.

2. The court did not find the doctrine of the Real Presence to be excluded by Article 28, since "it does not appear to affirm, expressly or by implication, a Presence other than spiritual." Note was taken also of the rejection of any "corporal presence" in the Declaration on Kneeling. Where the current version, adopted in 1662, referred to corporal presence, an earlier version (1552) rejected "any real and essential presence." It followed that the framers of the current version wished to leave room for a person to affirm a real and

essential presence that is was not corporal. It was not clear that Bennett affirmed any more than this.

3. Adoring Christ present in the consecrated elements was found not necessarily to imply adoring the elements themselves or any corporal presence in them. Therefore, it was not clear that Bennett's views on adoration were inconsistent with the Declaration on Kneeling or with Article 28. As for the liturgical cases, they certainly made any act of outward adoration illegal, but Bennett was not charged with liturgical violations. And "even if the Respondent's words are a confession of an unlawful act, it is questionable whether such a confession would amount to false doctrine."

4. "The distinction between an act by which a satisfaction for sin is made, and a devotional rite by which the satisfaction so made is represented and pleaded before God, is clear, though it is liable to be obscured . . . ." The use of the word "sacrifice" to denote the latter rite was considered unfortunate, but there was enough precedent for it among Anglican divines of good repute so that it could not be condemned out of hand. It was not clear that Bennett had used the word in any sense other than this acceptable one.

Bennett was vicar of Frome for the rest of his life. He was a good — perhaps a great — pastor, but he was no theologian. It was Pusey's doctrine that he was attempting, not altogether successfully, to set forth in his publications, and it was Pusey who got him to put out a new edition with the corrections that saved him from being condemned.[33] The prosecution was mounted by an organization called the Church Association, formed in 1865 to carry on litigations of this kind. It was the Low Church answer to the English Church Union, formed in 1860 to litigate on the High Church side. Pusey realized that he was the real target of the prosecution, and tried to get the Church Association to include him as a defendant so he could respond. Bennett's decision not to appear in the case left Pusey in an exposed position with no way of protecting himself. Sir Robert Phillimore was aware of this situation when he decided the case in the Arches court:

> I cannot shut my eyes to the fact that I am not trying Mr. Bennett alone, but also divines eminent for piety, learning, and eloquence, whose opinions Mr. Bennett has borrowed, and in some respects caricatured, but does not allow, by the course which he has taken, to be vindicated or explained.

It is for this reason that Phillimore deployed such vast (and in the opinion of the Judicial Committee superfluous) erudition in his opinion. He hoped to supply the Judicial Committee with the authorities that Pusey would have used if he had been a party.

There are two more doctrine cases to be discussed. Both of them were gall and wormwood to the High Church party, although they rest on pretty much the same principles that were used to condemn Oakeley, Heath, and Voysey, and to let Bennett off.

George Cornelius Gorham[34] held a doctrine on the subject of baptism that was evidently idiosyncratic, but nearer to the Calvinist mainstream than to Catholic tradition. It was his claim that baptism does not of itself confer grace. It has a good effect on one who receives it worthily, but not on one who does not. He accepted infant baptism, as Article 27 required him to do, even though Article 9 says that all children are born unworthy. He supposed that God makes them worthy recipients through a prevenient grace based on the faith of the parents and godparents.

In 1847, Gorham was presented to a vicarage in the diocese of Henry Phillpotts, bishop of Exeter. Phillpotts, a vigorous and pugnacious prelate of the school of High Churchmanship commonly referred to as high and dry, did not by any means hold with all the Catholic practices that younger High Churchmen were bent on restoring. But on this point he was solidly in the Catholic tradition. Anyone who is baptized receives grace through the sacrament, and that grace will be effective unless the recipient does something to prevent it. His doctrine was clearly incompatible with Gorham's. After he had spent eight days examining Gorham (orally, with questions and answers written down by a chaplain), he refused to put him into the benefice on the ground that he held doctrines contrary to the "true Christian faith" as well as to the official teachings of the church.

Gorham thereupon instituted a proceeding of *duplex querela*, the first for upward of century, as we have seen. He began with a claim that the searching examination to which the bishop had subjected him was illegal. But Jenner Fust in the Arches held that only the bishop could say how much of an examination was necessary, and the Judicial Committee held that any objection Gorham might have had was waived by his continuing to participate. Therefore, the question was squarely before both courts whether Gorham's doctrine was compatible with the Articles and the Prayer Book.

Jenner Fust held that it was not. The liturgy proclaims immediately after the minister has finished baptizing a child that "this child is regenerate," and the confirmation office has a collect saying that God has previously "vouchsafed to regenerate these Thy servants by water and the Holy Ghost . . . ." The Prayer Book catechism teaches every child to refer to "my Baptism; wherein I was made a member of Christ, the child of God, and an inheritor of the Kingdom of Heaven." Finally, a rubric in the baptismal service says:

It is certain, by God's word, that Children which are baptised, dying before they commit actual sin, are undoubtedly saved.

For Jenner Fust, these formulas commit the church to a doctrine that baptism necessarily regenerates anyone who does not pose an obstacle, and since infants cannot pose an obstacle, baptism necessarily regenerates infants.

He made light of Gorham's argument from the Articles. Granted that Article 25 says that the sacraments have their effect only on a worthy recipient, it says nothing about what makes a recipient worthy. The best Gorham could do to fill in the gap was to say that since infants are inherently unworthy (Article 9 on original sin), they must be made worthy by an act of prevenient grace called forth by the promises entered into by parents and godparents. But the Prayer Book contains an office for private baptism in emergencies. In that office the baptism takes place without any promises at all, and the child is still said to be regenerate. Gorham suggested that in that case the promises are implied — pointing out that the confirmation office and the catechism both call for the child to adopt the promises made at his baptism, making no distinction between public and private baptism. Jenner Fust did not really address this point. In the end, all he said about the Articles was that they shed no light on the question before him, so he must look to the Prayer Book alone.

Gorham offered one other line of argument. It was that his was basically a Calvinist doctrine, and that the authors of the Articles and Prayer Book, many of whom were themselves Calvinists, could not have meant to exclude a Calvinist option. Jenner Fust expressed some doubt as to how Calvinist the authors in question were, or how Calvinist Gorham was for that matter. Actually, though, it made no difference. A doctrine inconsistent with Gorham's was so clearly laid down in the Prayer Book, without contradiction from the Articles, that no private opinion could avail against it.

The Judicial Committee reversed. Lord Langdale for the Committee was charier than Jenner Fust of deriving doctrines from liturgical formulas: I have already referred to his use of the burial service analogy on this point. Also, he found the liturgical formulas more ambiguous than Jenner Fust did. While the office of baptism proclaims the child regenerate as soon as the baptism takes place, there is leading up to the act of baptism a series of invocations and exhortations that might well be interpreted as petitions for prevenient grace and expressions of confidence that the prevenient grace will be forthcoming as requested. Furthermore, the catechism contains the following sequence:

Q. What is required of persons to be baptized?

A. Repentance, whereby they forsake sin; and Faith, whereby
   they stedfastly believe the promises of GOD made to them
   in that Sacrament.

Q. Why then are Infants baptized, when by reason of their
   tender age they cannot perform them?

A. Because they promise them both by their Sureties; which
   promise, when they come to age, themselves are bound to
   perform.

Langdale found this language to support Gorham's view that baptismal
regeneration is not unconditional, but that the promises of the godparents
fulfil the conditions that the infant cannot personally fulfil. To allow the
provisions for emergency baptism to prove the contrary would be a tail
wagging a dog. It would be more consistent with the general tendency of
the formularies to suppose that the promises are implied where they are
not expressed.

It followed that the Prayer Book, like the Articles, is ambiguous, and
therefore that it could not be said that Gorham's doctrine was excluded by
any official formulary of the church. Langdale bolstered this argument with
a certain amount of reference to theological writings. While he agreed
with Jenner Fust that no theological writing could be normative, he argued
that any doctrine that notable Anglican divines taught with impunity would
be difficult to regard as officially condemned.

The case was remanded to Jenner Fust, who instituted Gorham into the
vicarage on authority from the archbishop. Phillpotts wrote a protest, and
a letter to the churchwardens expressing his objections.[35] Someone
suggested that he license someone else to minister in the parish in
competition with Gorham, but he wisely decided not to. Gorham spent the
remaining six years of his life in undisputed and relatively uneventful
possession of his parish.

The Judicial Committee's decision was concurred in by all the judges but
one. The majority included Stephen Lushington, the only member of the
panel trained in ecclesiastical law. He was judge of the London diocesan
court, where we have already encountered him in connection with the great
Braintree churchrate litigation. He was eventually to become Dean of the
Arches. The two archbishops sat as assessors, along with Charles James
Blomfield, bishop of London and leader of the episcopate in most of their
temporal affairs. The archbishops concurred in the judgment, although
Blomfield did not. There was some complaint that Langdale, as son and
brother of prominent Evangelical clergymen, was biased. In my opinion,
though, he was right. If you set out to interpret the Articles and Prayer

Book without any prior commitment to Catholic tradition, Gorham's explanation will look about as good as the traditional one. It was prior commitment to Catholic tradition that produced all the outcry about the case.

Oddly enough, one argument that figured prominently in the subsequent protests seems not to have figured at all in either the examination or the court cases. That is that Gorham's doctrine is inconsistent with the language of the Nicene Creed, "I acknowledge one baptism for the remission of sins." This appears in the Communion service in the Prayer Book, and is made mandatory by Article 8. Also, as opponents of the judgment were not slow to point out, it is worse for a church to permit departure from one of the ancient creeds of Christendom than from some other aspect of orthodoxy. Had the point been brought up, I suppose the answer would have been that remission of sins need not be any more unconditional than regeneration is. The catechism still imposes a condition that is fulfilled by the promises of the godparents.

It is not altogether apparent why people who were content that Catholic Eucharistic doctrine should be tolerated within the Church of England were insistent that Catholic baptismal doctrine should be required. To be sure, the Gorham case came some years before the Bennett case, but I cannot believe that the passage of time had led the High Churchmen to lower their sights. Tract Ninety, published in 1841, put the case for Catholic Eucharistic doctrine no more strongly than it was put in Bennett's time. Its claim was only that the Articles admitted of a Catholic interpretation, certainly not that they required one.

The High Churchmen (with a number of exceptions, most of whom became Roman Catholics) reconciled themselves to the Gorham decision by arguing that the official formularies were so clear that their disregard by what was after all a secular tribunal could not be said to compromise the witness of the church to Catholic truth. As Pusey put it, the judgment impaired the discipline of the church, but not its doctrine.[36]

The *Essays and Reviews* case (1863)[37] brought before the Judicial Committee the critical Biblical scholarship that had been for some years appearing out of Germany to the unsettlement of English minds. The case was precipitated by a book of a kind that has played an important part in Anglican history on several occasions, one in which contributions from individual churchmen are put together around a common theme. The common theme in this case was emancipation from over-literal readings of the Bible, and, it would seem, from some traditional doctrines thought to be connected with such readings. The proponents of literal reading and traditional doctrine reacted. Pusey tried to get the Vice-Chancellor of Oxford to move against Benjamin Jowett, the famous Greek scholar and

author of one of the essays. The Vice-Chancellor doubted if he had
jurisdiction, and was sure that he should decline to exercise whatever
jurisdiction he had. Prosecutions were initiated in the Arches court by
letters of request under the Church Discipline Act, 1840, against two of the
essayists, Rowland Williams and Henry Bristow Wilson, who had in
common that they were beneficed in dioceses whose bishops were willing to
allow prosecutions, and that their essays lent themselves better than the
others to the process of extracting short passages for comparison with the
Articles and the Prayer Book.

Stephen Lushington was now Dean of the Arches, responsible for
deciding this case in the first instance. He rejected most of the charges by
holding that he had nothing to do with whether a given interpretation of
Scripture was right or wrong as long as it was not officially condemned,
that to deny the traditional authorship of a book of the Bible was not to
deny its canonicity or inspiration, and that treating a narrative account as
figurative or allegorical was a way of interpreting it, not a way of denying
its authority. Some of the accused writing he rescued by giving it a more
favorable reading than would be justified anywhere but in such a
proceeding as this:

> I do not think that I am justified in holding that Mr. Wilson, in
> representing our Lord as a moral teacher, meant to represent Him as
> that and nothing more.

> Without saying this impression of this passage is false, I cannot say it is
> necessarily the true one, especially considering this is a criminal case.

When Lushington had finished, there remained only three charges against
Williams and three against Wilson. These he was not able to get around,
and on them he imposed on each of the defendants the relatively mild
penalty of a year's suspension and costs.

The Judicial Committee reversed. They dealt with the charges that had
gotten by Lushington in just about the same way as Lushington had dealt
with the others. The charges in question were:

1. Williams had declared the Bible to be "devout reason" and the "written
   voice of the congregation." Lushington found this claim inconsistent
   with the assertion in Article 6 that "Holy Scripture containeth all
   things necessary for salvation," with reference to the Bible in Article
   20 as "God's word written," and with Article 7, which says that
   everlasting life is offered to man by Christ in both the Old and the
   New Testaments. The prosecution argued to the same effect from
   similar language in the ordination services in the Prayer Book, and
   from the statement in the Nicene Creed that the Holy Spirit spoke
   through the prophets. But elsewhere in his essay Williams had

referred to the Holy Spirit as dwelling in the church and the sacred writers. The Judicial Committee reasoned therefore that attributing the Scriptures either to the church or to the writers was not denying their inspiration.

2. Wilson also denied the plenary and literal inspiration of Scripture, using formulations less sophisticated than Williams's. The same Articles and formularies were brought forward against him. Lushington insisted that the averment that the Bible contains all things necessary to salvation necessarily implies that at least those passages which deal with salvation were written under a special divine interposition. This is what he understood Wilson to deny, and condemned him for denying. The Judicial Committee, however, read him as denying only that the Scriptures were inspired *throughout*, "upon any subject whatever, however unconnected with religious faith or moral duty." On that understanding, he could not be condemned, and Lushington would not have condemned him.

3. Williams in several passages equated "propitiation" and "justification" with peace of mind coming from consciousness of forgiveness and acceptance by God. Lushington found the passages on propitiation inconsistent with Article 31 on the Atonement, and those on justification inconsistent with Article 11 on justification by faith. The two charges were combined in some way at the appellate level, so that the one on justification did duty for both. Williams argued that when he said justification was peace of mind, he did not mean it was peace of mind and nothing else. The prosecution had placed a reductive interpretation on his language by inserting the word "only" into a paraphrase of it; this they had no right to do. The Judicial Committee agreed.

4. Wilson argued for the salvation of the generality of unbelievers. Lushington was prepared to accept that Article 9, which says that everyone born into the world deserves God's wrath and condemnation, does not require insisting that God will in fact condemn every such person. Nor does Article 11 on justification by faith demand that God condemn all the people who lack faith in Christ because they have never heard of Him. But Wilson went on to say that the difference between convenanted and uncovenanted mercies "seems either to be a distinction without a difference, or to amount to a denial of the broad and equal justice of the Supreme Being." The distinction had become popular as a way of reconciling hope for the salvation of unbelievers with the fact that salvation is promised only to believers. Lushington felt that abolishing it was inconsistent with Article 18, which condemns the claim "that every

man shall be saved by the Law or Sect which he professeth." I do not understand Lushington's reasoning here. It seems to me that the question of whom God wishes to save can be addressed quite independently of the question of what means He wishes to use in saving them. Whether for this or for some other reason, the prosecution abandoned this charge when it came before the Judicial Committee.

5. Wilson had pointed out that some people when they die seem not yet ready for either heaven or hell. He expressed hope that there would be some place where such people could continue the process of spiritual development, and that ultimately everyone could be found in the Kingdom of God. This was attacked as inconsistent with various passages in the Prayer Book that seem to refer to a final judgment in which everyone's condition will be fixed one way or the other for all time. I am not sure why it was not also attacked under Article 22, condemning the Romish doctrine of Purgatory. Lushington found Wilson's doctrine inconsistent with Prayer Book references to "everlasting fire." But the Judicial Committee accepted Wilson's argument that eminent divines had placed a more limited interpretation on the word "everlasting" and on the terms translated by that word. They also pointed out that the 1552 version of the Articles contained an express condemnation of the doctrine "that al menne, be thei never so ungodlie, shall at lengtht bee saved," and that this condemnation was omitted when the current version was adopted in 1562.

The *Essays and Reviews* judgment was a blow to High and Low Churchmen alike. The two archbishops (under the Church Discipline Act, 1840, they were full members of the tribunal and not mere assessors) dissented from the holding as to the inspiration of Scripture. The other bishop on the panel, Tait of London, soon to be archbishop of Canterbury himself, joined in the judgment (he was to cast one of two dissenting votes when the book was later condemned by the bishops in Convocation). The Committee tried to soften the blow by putting the following disclaimer at the beginning of their decision:

These appeals do not give to this Tribunal the power, and, therefore, it is not part of its duty, to pronounce any opinion on the character, effect, or tendency of the publications known by the name of "Essays and Reviews." Nor are we at liberty to take into consideration, for the purposes of the prosecution, the whole of the Essay of Dr. Williams or of the Essay of Mr. Wilson. A few short extracts only are before us, and our judgment must by law be confined to the matter which is therein contained. If, therefore, the Book, or these two Essays, or either of them as a whole, be of a mischievous and baneful tendency, as weakening the foundation of Christian belief, and likely to cause many to offend, they will retain that character, and be liable to that condemnation, notwithstanding this our judgment.[38]

They seem to have had about the same perception of their role in all the doctrine cases.

Voysey's case, which we have already considered, was decided two years after this one, and perhaps clarified it a bit. With it, the series of doctrine cases comes to an end. Never again was a clergyman of the Church of England to be required to answer for his doctrines in an English court. When Frederick Temple, who wrote the Introduction to *Essays and Reviews*, was made a bishop, the courts refused to consider objections to his doctrine.[39] Doctrinal objections were again raised in court when Charles Gore, who, after much bitter debate, made modern Biblical criticism respectable among Anglo-Catholics with his contribution to *Lux Mundi* in 1889, was made a bishop. Again the courts refused to consider them. Michael Bland, whose case we looked at in the previous chapter, contended that prosecution for refusal to baptize a child whose parents did not attend church was prosecution for doctrine, since it was doctrine that led him to refuse. But the court rejected his claim: he was prosecuted for what he failed to do, not for what he believed or taught.

The formularies under which doctrinal standards were imposed have been watered down in recent years.[40] On the various occasions when a clergyman was formerly required to declare his assent to the Articles and the Prayer Book, he has now only to affirm his loyalty to the inheritance of faith of which they are a part and his belief in the faith to which they bear witness. On the other hand, there is still a canon that says the doctrine of the Church of England "is to be found" in them. The Elizabethan statute against advisedly maintaining any doctrine contrary to the Articles was repealed in 1963, but the repealing measure contains the following language:

> The repeal by this Measure of any statutory provision under which proceedings could have been taken for an offence against the laws ecclesiastical shall not prevent the taking of any proceedings under this Measure in respect of any such offence.

I gather that the purpose of this language is to keep the repeal of earlier procedural statutes from affecting the substantive scope of clerical discipline, but it seems to have left open the theoretical possibility of prosecution for teaching contrary to the Articles.

But as the Church of England has developed, there seems to be little likelihood of anyone being taken to court for any doctrinal deviation. The cases just discussed illustrate the frustration inherent in trying to decide current theological controversies by resort to judicial interpretation of sixteenth century formularies; at the same time, no one seems interested in developing a new set of doctrinal standards to replace the old.[41] As a result, canons of scholarship have tended to take the place of canons of orthodoxy in establishing the doctrinal commitments of the church. Anglican controversialists no longer look for official condemnation of opposing doctrines. They look for such doctrines to fare in the church as the Baconian theory has fared among Shakespeare scholars, or the flat earth theory among geographers. They are not always disappointed.

2. *Liturgy* — The liturgy cases were mostly either disciplinary proceedings against clergymen accused of unlawful worship, or faculty proceedings to remove the accouterments of such worship from churches where they had been introduced. Since the High Church defendants ("Ritualists") were not prepared to take no for an answer, there were often several cases covering the same ground. So, rather than looking at individual cases, let us take up the main contentious practices one by one, and see why and with what justice they were objected to.

Stone altars[42] were built in some of the Gothic Revival churches, and introduced into some medieval ones as part of the same revival. The first to be litigated over was the one the antiquarian Cambridge Camden Society put into the Norman Church of the Holy Sepulchre in Cambridge in 1842. It was declared illegal, as were such other stone altars as came before the courts until the Holy Table Measure, 1964, authorized them.

The Canons of 1604 (c. 82) and the applicable Prayer Book rubric both speak of a "table" and say where it is to stand at Communion time. The courts reasoned, plausibly enough, that the word table implied an object that would not be totally incongruous in your dining room, and that a provision as to where it should stand at Communion time implied that it might stand somewhere else the rest of the time. On both counts, therefore, "a stone structure of amazing weight and dimensions immovably fixed" was excluded.

Sixteenth and seventeenth century history provided a *contemporanea expositio* that supported the courts in their interpretation of the canon and the rubric. There is ample evidence that the Elizabethan prelates had deliberately set out to reinforce their Eucharistic doctrine by taking down the altars and replacing them with tables that could be set up in the middle of the chancel or in the body of the church at Communion time. It was evidently envisaged that during other services the table would be kept out of the way at the far end of the chancel where the altar used to be, but that it would stand there perpendicular to the wall (table-wise) instead of along it (altar-wise). The whole idea was to stress the discontinuity between the popish sacrifice and the Protestant meal. For the purpose, it was essential that the table look like something people eat at, and that it be capable of being moved from the end of the chancel into the body of the church and back.

To be sure, by the time the current Prayer Book was adopted in 1662, it had become pretty well customary to leave the table altar-wise at the far end of the chancel, and to separate it by a rail from the rest of the church. This was evidently Laud's doing, a response to the general sloppiness that had set in by his time. He found that in many parishes the table was left in the body of the church all the time instead of being moved back and forth. There was a tendency for parishioners to toss their hats and coats on it, for children to play under it, and for dogs to use it as modern dogs use fire hydrants. After the vicissitudes of the Civil War and the Interregnum, the table returned at the Restoration to the place Laud had left it.

Placed in this way, and with a rich cloth hanging in front of it, it was hard to tell from an altar. Indeed, two pieces of nineteenth century legislation actually referred to it by that name. The Church Building Acts, 1819 and 1832, both provided that a consolidated chapelry should be under the jurisdiction of the bishop in whose diocese the "altar" of the chapel stood.[43] The mistake, if it was a mistake, was not corrected until 1845, the year Jenner Fust ordered the stone altar out of Holy Sepulchre, Cambridge. These statutes taken together argued that the terms table and altar were interchangeable, so that something being an altar did not keep it from being a table. They also argued that the law did not envisage a movable table, since it attached important consequences to its exact location. Besides, since the custom of putting rails around the table made it impractical to move it, its theoretical movability seemed not to be very important. The proponents of the stone altar at Holy Sepulchre pointed out for that matter that with strong enough machinery they could move their altar too.

The courts had two reasons for rejecting arguments based on practice since the Restoration. The most important was that there had been no change since that time in the applicable law. If contemporaneous exposition has fixed the meaning of a term, later practice will not change it, and irrelevance or superfluity do not dispense a court from the duty of enforcing the law as it is written. This seems persuasive. It is unfortunate that the Judicial Committee in one of its opinions added a second reason — that the difference between an altar and a table is inherent in the difference between Roman and reformed Eucharistic doctrine.[44] This argument, besides being offensive to High Churchmen, was too theological to comport with the courts' claim to be enforcing law rather than imposing doctrine.

Legislation since 1964 has specifically authorized the Communion table
to be either movable or immovable, and to be made of wood, stone, or any
other suitable material.[45] But it still has to be a "table." Accordingly, when
a plan was made to put a ten ton circular marble altar by Henry Moore
into the Wren church of St. Stephen, Walbrook in 1985, the chancellor of
the London diocese refused a faculty. Applying the old learning, he did not
see how this structure could be a table. The Court of Ecclesiastical Causes
Reserved (formed in 1963 to displace the Judicial Committee in doctrinal
and liturgical cases) held one of its rare sittings and reversed.[46] The
chancellor, it said, had exaggerated the difference between Roman and
reformed Eucharistic doctrine, as had the nineteenth century judges on
whose decisions he had relied:

> The Chancellor's argument appears to be as follows. To call the holy
> table an altar means that it is a place of sacrifice, and to speak of
> sacrifice in relation to the Eucharist means "a repetition at every Mass of
> the sacrifice of our Lord at Calvary." But no Anglican theologian of
> whatever churchmanship would maintain that the celebration of the
> Eucharist is a repetition of the sacrifice of Calvary, and it is highly
> improbable that any Roman Catholic would do so either.

The decision appears to be correct, but from a strictly legal standpoint I
find it unsatisfactory. It does not sufficiently refute the best legal argument
for the other side, which is that by contemporaneous exposition a "table" is
where people eat their dinner. At the same time, it does not sufficiently
deploy the best legal argument on its own side, which is that the Holy
Table Measure, 1964, despite its continued use of the word table, was
obviously intended to abolish the previous learning root and branch, and
should be interpreted as doing so. This may not be a legitimate criticism,
however. The Court of Ecclesiastical Causes Reserved was created to
provide a more theological and less legal resolution of doctrinal and
liturgical questions. In this case, that is what it appears to have done.

Crosses, images, and other furnishings were subject to one rule if they
were "ornaments," another if they were images, and a third if they were
neither.[47] Generally, anything used in the liturgy was held to be an
ornament, and governed by the rubric, already quoted, that retains such
ornaments as were in use by authority of Parliament in 1549. The Judicial
Committee held that "by authority of Parliament" covered only ornaments
expressly mentioned in the 1549 Prayer Book, rather than including
everything used without objection at that time. Thus narrowly construed, it
covered mainly books and Communion plate. Its effect on vestments we
will take up shortly.

Images, if they were not ornaments, were legal or illegal depending on whether they had been or could be objects of "superstitious" veneration. This was the criterion adopted at the Reformation for taking them down, and, as it had never been changed, it was still in effect. Stained glass windows were generally acceptable under this criterion, as were many, but not all, sculptured reredoses and the like. It was held in 1876 by Lord Penzance with the approval of the Judicial Committee that superstition as used by the reformers included orthodox Roman Catholic veneration of images as well as the heterodox devotions of the medieval populace. On this ground, crucifixes, Stations of the Cross, and statues of Our Lady were condemned more often than not, especially when they were first introduced. If an object had a familiar devotional use in Roman Catholic churches, those who introduced it into Anglican churches would be presumed to have the same use in mind.

Objects of beauty or utility that were neither ornaments nor images were generally acceptable unless they were, or appeared to be, attached to the altar in such a way as to keep it from being a table. A credence table on which the bread and wine for Communion could be kept during the first part of the service was legal on this principle. So were vases of flowers. So, in most cases, were crosses and candlesticks.

Candles had a checkered career in the courts.[48] As long as they were just there in case it got dark, there was no objection to them. But if you lit them during the service, the lighting was a "ceremony" not permitted by the Prayer Book, and therefore illegal. But suppose you lit them before the service and left them lit throughout, even though it was broad daylight? The Judicial Committee held that lit candles were an ornament, illegal because not mentioned in the 1549 Prayer Book. But an archbishop of Canterbury held that they were a decoration, legal because the reformers had found nothing superstitious about them and because they had been in regular use through most of the seventeenth century.

Here is a case that may show how these principles worked.[49] In 1873, the vicar and congregation of St. Barnabas, Pimlico (from which a stone altar had been removed by order of the Judicial Committee in 1857) sought a faculty to put a marble baldachino or canopy over their Communion table. Dr. Tristram in the London Consistory Court turned them down. Using an extensive body of historical evidence, he established that the original purpose of such a structure wdas to do honor to the Sacrament. That being the case, the structure could not be a mere decoration. It had to be either part of the Communion table or an ornament. On the first alternative it was illegal because it made the whole combination into something other than a table. On the second alternative it was illegal because it was not mentioned in the 1549 Prayer Book. Either way, it was illegal.

The law on these matters of ornaments, images, and decorations remains on paper as I have just stated it. It has been rather consistently disregarded over the years. Through the 1950s, however, an occasional litigation would occur to remind High Churchmen that their architecture and furnishings were not altogether safe.[50] Such flexibility as there was in concepts like superstition or decoration was drawn on, but courts still found themselves occasionally compelled to results that they did not like. There has been no such case since the establishment of the Court of Ecclesiastical Causes Reserved in 1963. I believe that that court, if the question were to come before it, would decline to follow Lord Penzance in holding orthodox Roman Catholic practice to be "superstitious." If so, it would produce a considerable expansion of what can legally be put into a church.

Eucharistic vestments — the ones Roman Catholic priests have been wearing since before the Reformation — are "ornaments of the minister," covered by the same 1662 rubric whose effect on "ornaments of the church" was just discussed.[51] Since the vestments are specifically mentioned in the 1549 Prayer Book, the doctrine of the church ornament cases would seem to permit — indeed, to require — them. On the other hand, there is no convincing evidence that they were in use after the first decade or so of Elizabeth's reign. While the fact that a law had been universally disobeyed for two or three centuries was not an irresistible argument for continuing to disobey it, there was naturally great reluctance to believe that a requirement so consistently disregarded was in fact imposed by the law. Still, the meaning of the applicable language seemed very clear.

On further analysis, however, the courts found the applicable language less clear than it seemed. Elizabeth's Act of Uniformity (1559) did not unqualifiedly require the ornaments of 1549. It required them

> until other order shall be therein taken by the authority of the Queen's Majesty with the advice of her commissioners appointed and authorized under the great seal of England for ecclesiastical causes, or of the metropolitan of this realm.

The 1559 rubrics did not include this language except by reference, but they were clearly subject to it.

It appears that other order was in fact taken. The "Advertisements" adopted by Archbishop Parker in 1566 called for cathedral clergy to celebrate in copes, other clergy in surplices. To be sure, the queen never gave her formal assent to the Advertisements, probably because of this very provision. But they were vigorously enforced with her entire acquiescence, and acquiescence had been sufficient to establish royal authority for other Tudor administrative actions. There is a good deal of evidence that Elizabeth would have preferred the traditional vestments, as she would have preferred some other traditional practices that she found it politically impossible to impose. Her refusal to put her name to the Advertisements seems to have reflected her annoyance at the political necessity of letting them take effect.

In any event, the Canons of 1604 (c. 58) imposed the same standards as the Advertisements, and there was no claim that these lacked royal authority. The best the proponents of the vestments could do was point out that the Elizabethan Prayer Book had been reissued in the same year with minor revisions, but with no change in the rubric requiring the vestments. But here again, the statutory provision for other order, still in force, would seem to qualify the requirement in the rubric. Furthermore, since the 1604 canons and the reissue of the Prayer Book were contemporaneous enactments of the same authority, an elementary principle of legislative interpretation required them to be interpreted if possible as consistent. Taking the provision for cope and surplice as the "other order" envisaged in the statute would make them consistent as nothing else would.

It followed that in 1662 the vestments had not only been out of use for the better part of a century, they had been illegal since 1566, or at least since 1604. Therefore, the 1662 rubric was ambiguous when it called for *retaining* the ornaments used in 1549. The only ornaments of the minister that were in use both in 1549 and far enough into the seventeenth century to be "retained" rather than "restored" in 1662 were the cope in cathedrals and the surplice elsewhere. These had been used for all services except Communion in 1549, and for all services, Communion included, since 1566 or so.

This argument was open to the objection that it proved too much. Because of the interruption of Anglican worship during the Interregnum, no vestment could have been literally "retained" in 1662. Arguably, then, the word was merely copied from the 1559 statute, and had no different significance from what it had had in 1559. Against this argument was the political situation in 1662. The prevailing concerns at that time were moderation and legality. The hope was to pacify the country by returning to the time before

> Civil dudgeon first grew high . . . .
> When hard words, jealousies and fears
> Set folks together by the ears,
> And made them fight like mad or drunk
> For Dame Religion . . . .[52]

In this atmosphere, it would have been easy to treat something done away with by usurped authority during the Interregnum as still in force and capable of being retained. And it would have been next to impossible to gain any following for the idea that people who had been straining at the surplice for a hundred years were now to be made to swallow the chasuble.

Contemporaneous exposition bore out the historical evidence that copes and surplices rather than chasubles were intended by the 1662 rubric. The Restoration prelates did in fact require copes and surplices as their predecessors had done, whereas the chasuble was unknown until the nineteenth century.

The difficulty of making a case for the vestments in the face of all this historical evidence was enhanced by the fact that if the Ritualists were right the vestments were not merely permissible, they were compulsory. Whether the rubric referred to copes and surplices or whether it referred to chasubles, there was no way it could be interpreted as offering a choice between them. Common sense rebelled against trying to put the entire church into chasubles at this late date.

A point that I have not found discussed in connection with the vestments is the interplay of church and state in the adoption of the applicable rules.[53] It is odd that people who claimed that they were not bound by the decisions of the Judicial Committee because it was a lay tribunal should claim that Archbishop Parker's Advertisements had no effect because the queen did not sign them. It is worth noting also that one of the differences between the canon law system and the common law system is that under the former a legislative enactment can be abrogated by a contrary custom of sufficient length. Any canonical support for the vestments would have disappeared in this way long before the nineteenth century if it had not been kept in force by the same Parliament that created the Judicial Committee.

Of all the controversies of the period, that over vestments was the bitterest. Chasubles remained illegal on paper until 1964.[54] As we shall see, however, it proved impossible to stop people from wearing them. After the 1880s, hardly anyone tried. The vicissitudes of enforcement brought about what the rubric did not afford — an option.

The *eastward position*[55] is that of a priest who celebrates the Eucharist with his back to the congregation, as Roman Catholic priests did until the Second Vatican Council. The term comes from the general (though not universal) custom of building churches with the main altar at the east end. Church interiors were commonly described as if they were built that way whether or not they actually were. I do not know why standing at the west side of the table looking east is called east*ward* position instead of the west*ern* position. The alternative, standing at the north looking south, is called the north*ern* position.

Catholic tradition and esthetic good sense suggested the eastward position for the main part of the Communion service. It is logical enough that when the priest is addressing the people or reading to them he should face them; but when he is addressing the Deity on their behalf, it makes sense (*pace* the modern liturgical movement) for him to face the same way they do. The reformers who rejected this liturgical approach may have had some notion of the priest as presiding over a banquet, but I believe they were less concerned with this than modern liturgical reformers are. They had two main concerns. One was that facing the east wall to address the Lord tended in the minds of people to assign Him to a fixed location — especially when the wall addressed had a crucifix and a place for the reserved Sacrament. The other was that if the priest had his back to the people, they could not see what he was doing with his hands; they were therefore encouraged to believe that it was some magic rite he was performing.

As we have seen, the reformers' original plan when they replaced the altars with tables was to stand the table perpendicular to the east wall, and move it out from the wall when Communion was to be celebrated. If this was done, and the priest stood with respect to the table where he had formerly stood with respect to the altar, he would be at one of the long sides of the table with the congregation to one side of him unless they got up and stood around the table. This is evidently the situation envisaged in the rubrics, which called for the priest to stand at the north side of the table for the opening prayers, to stand "before the people" at the Consecration, and to "break the Bread before the people."

When it became customary to leave the table in place with its long side along the east wall, the application of these rubrics became problematical. Usually, the priest stood at the north end of the table for the whole service except when he turned to the people to read a lesson, preach a sermon, or make an announcement. This position complied with the rubrics, and enabled the congregation to see what the priest was doing, but it must have looked a bit odd,[56] and it may have squeezed the priest some if the end of the chancel was narrow.

In 1871, the Judicial Committee held that this position was the only one complying with the rubrics. It was argued that the "north side" could mean the northern part of the west side, but the court was not persuaded. In 1877, however, they modified their view on the second rubric, the one referring to the time of Consecration. Since the previous decision had not settled a property right, and since the defendant had not appeared to argue his case, they were free to reconsider. On doing so, they concluded that wherever the celebrant was standing, they could not find him guilty in a penal proceeding unless it was shown that he had broken the bread where the people could not see him. Since the prosecution had proceeded on the basis that the previous case was the law, no evidence had been introduced on that point, and the accused was let off on it.

In 1891, when the bishop of Lincoln was tried before the archbishop of Canterbury for various liturgical offenses, the archbishop disagreed with the Judicial Committee on the first rubric. He said that standing at the north part of the west side was sufficient compliance with the rubric requiring the celebrant to stand on the north side. He brought forth enough historical examples to show that there had always been a minority who celebrated in this way. The Judicial Committee on appeal accepted that the archbishop had come up with further historical evidence warranting a departure from the conclusion they had reached in 1871 and again in 1877.

So the final state of the law on the position of the celebrant was that he could stand with his back to the people at the left side of the table for the early part of the service, and could stand with his back to the people in the middle at the Consecration, so long as the people could see what he was doing with his hands. At first blush, it would not seem possible for the priest to keep his hands visible to people behind his back. William Bright, the Regius Professor of Ecclesiastical History at Oxford, suggested this solution in a letter to the bishop of Lincoln:

> You would have to raise your hands in breaking the bread so that the action should be seen. This is perfectly easy, and may be done by an elevation of the arms so that the broken parts may afterwards be seen in your two hands, and the chalice may be held first to the right and then to the left, you retaining the eastward position.[57]

The proposal looks rather like the elevation of the consecrated elements, forbidden in another case, as we shall see. But no one challenged it.

Wafer Bread, the round unleavened host used for Communion in most Catholic and some Protestant churches, was declared illegal by the Judicial Committee[58] under a rubric that says:

> And to take away all occasion of dissension and superstition, which any person hath or might have concerning the Bread and Wine, it shall suffice that the bread be such as is usual to be eaten; but the best and purest wheat bread that conveniently may be gotten.

The proponents of the wafer bread argued that "it shall suffice" should be taken literally, making common bread permissible, not compulsory. They were able to show that a number of churches did in fact use wafer bread through most of Elizabeth's reign. On the other hand, it was shown on the opposing side that Bishop Cosin had proposed in 1662 to add to the rubric an express permission of wafer bread and had been overruled. The

Judicial Committee finally decided that all occasion of dissension and superstition would not have been taken away if the use of wafer bread had been a matter of choice. I find this less persuasive than some of the Committee's other holdings. If the dissentient and superstitious ones were people who thought that only wafer bread was valid matter for the Sacrament, affording a choice would seem a sufficient refutation of them.

The defendant in one of the wafer bread cases escaped conviction by objecting to the form of the charge.[59] He claimed that common bread cut into small circular pieces could be called wafer bread and still be compatible with the rubric. The Judicial Committee reluctantly found itself unable to escape the force of this argument. As a result, the liturgical watchdogs of the Church Association prepared the next wafer bread prosecution by getting a communicant to bring in his wafer as an exhibit.[60] It was duly stamped and placed in the registry of the court before any court personnel realized that it had been consecrated. It spent some months there amid growing scandal before Archbishop Tait was able to take it away and consume it in his own chapel. The Church Association was reluctant to withdraw it as an exhibit, and Lord Penzance was not sure he had power to release it unless it was withdrawn.

Miscellaneous practices such as genuflections, the elevation of the Sacrament, the sign of the cross, and processions were all condemned on the ground that they were rites or ceremonies (rites are verbal, ceremonies physical) not provided for in the Prayer Book.[61] One of the applicable Acts of Uniformity (1559) forbade any minister to

> use any other rite ceremony order form or manner of celebrating of the Lord's Supper openly or privily, or mattins evensong administration of the sacraments or other open prayers than is mentioned and set forth in the said book (open prayer . . . is meant that prayer which is for other to come unto, or hear either in common churches or in private chapels or oratories, commonly called the Service of the Church).

The Judicial Committee, reversing a vastly learned judgment of Sir Robert Phillimore in the Arches, held that neither insignificance, prevalence in the primitive church, nor practice under Elizabeth or Charles I could permit a rite or ceremony not provided for. Hymns "taken out of the Bible" were allowed under an exception written into the 1548 act (the three acts, 1548, 1559, and 1662 were all in force together, with the later incorporating the earlier by reference). The only hymn judicially considered, the *Agnus Dei*, was upheld on this ground. What would have happened if other hymns of less clear scriptural provenance (*All Things Bright and Beautiful*, for instance, or *Greenland's Icy Mountains*) had come before the court is hard to say.

Some practices got by because technically they occurred before or after the service rather than during it. Mixing a little water with the Communion wine — evidently an ancient practice symbolic of the Incarnation — was permissible on this ground if done before the service started (against the contention that the result was not "wine" within the meaning of the rubrics), but not if done during the service. Similarly, the traditional "ablution" or rinsing of the chalice and paten was held acceptable because it was done after the prescribed Communion service was over. It was merely a more elaborate way of complying with the rubric requiring the celebrant to eat and drink any of the elements remaining.

The law as laid down in these liturgical cases did not gain the acquiescence of High Churchmen, as we shall see. Nonetheless, it remained the official law until the Holy Table Measure, 1964, the Vestures of Ministers Measure, 1964, and the Prayer Book (Alternative and Other Services) Measure, 1965. These, followed by the Church of England (Worship and Doctrine) Measure, 1974, and the canons adopted pursuant to that measure, have generally authorized the prevailing deviations from the standards laid down in the old cases, subject to a requirement that existing practice not be changed in a parish without consent of the parochial church council.[62] As the law is now written, it is also possible for the General Synod of the church to adopt new liturgical forms without running them through Parliament.

But I think it would not be fair to say that the Judicial Committee decisions were rejected because they were wrong. They were the work of English judges who were assigned the task of interpreting English legal documents, and who, to the best of their considerable ability, did just that. The enterprise of using this kind of legal material to control liturgical practices may seem ill-conceived, but whatever blame attaches to it would seem to belong more to those who set it up than to those who carried it out.

3. Non-Liturgical Practices — There was not as much legal material to attack Catholic practices that were not part of the liturgy, and therefore not subject to the Act of Uniformity. Only one such practice came before the courts directly, but some of the others did so in oblique ways.

Reservation of the Sacrament[63] seems inconsistent with the Prayer Book rubric that provides that if any of the

> consecrated Bread and Wine remain after the service, the Priest and such other of the Communicants as he shall then call unto him, shall, immediately after the Blessing, reverently eat and drink the same.

It is a little difficult also to reconcile with the provision of Article 28 that

> The Sacrament of the Lord's Supper was not by Christ's ordinance reserved, carried about, lifted up, or worshipped.

Nevertheless, the practice of reservation developed apace. There was a good deal said about the need to have the Sacrament on hand to communicate sick people, but in fact Catholic Eucharistic devotions came in about as fast as reservation did. A clergyman of the Oxford diocese was deprived by Sir Lewis Dibdin in the Arches Court in 1909 when he refused to discontinue the practice. That was the only reported disciplinary proceeding on the subject, but until the practice was finally legalized under one of the alternative liturgies adopted pursuant to the Prayer Book (Alternative and Other Services) Measure, 1965, there were a number of faculty cases to take tabernacles and aumbries out of churches (a tabernacle is a box and an aumbry is a niche in the wall).

The new Prayer Book adopted by the Church Assembly in 1928 would have authorized reservation under certain limiting conditions. When that book was rejected by Parliament, the bishops decided that they would permit reservation under those conditions nevertheless. Their stand prevented any disciplinary measures from being taken, but it obviously did not affect the courts in their administration of the legal requirements imposed by Article and rubric. Some courts, however, found that if the Sacrament was to be reserved, whether legally or illegally, it was appropriate for the court in a faculty case to see that it was reserved in a suitable place:

> The duty of a diocesan chancellor in this matter is ancillary. He is not responsible for the reservation; but if he finds that reservation is in fact practiced with the sanction of the bishop in a church within his jurisdiction, it is his duty to see that the provision made for keeping the consecrated bread and wine is both safe and seemly.[64]

In 1958, in another faculty case, the Durham Consistory Court actually decided that reservation was not illegal.[65] The chancellor dealt first with the Article, drawing on the same provision for plain grammatical interpretation that Newman had drawn on in Tract Ninety. On such an interpretation, the claim that the Sacrament "was not by Christ's ordinance reserved" was no argument against reserving it:

> Many, many other things which are perfectly proper and perfectly legal have not been ordained by Our Lord.

He then disposed of the rubric in a manner curiously reminiscent of Lord Langdale's treatment of the Prayer Book in the *Gorham* case:

> It is, in my view, of the highest importance to remember that the Book of Common Prayer is not itself a statute and ought not to be interpreted as though it were. Regarded in its true light as a directive, to be interpreted liberally according to the occasion, this rubric which we are now considering really does no more than forbid profanation of the Sacrament.

That interpretation makes a good deal of sense historically. The relevant language did not appear in any version of the Prayer Book before 1662, and the evidence suggests that in the years immediately preceding reservation had not been a problem, but clergymen taking the consecrated bread and wine home to dinner had been.

Having disposed of the Article and the rubric, the court made a final argument based on necessity. The Prayer Book's alternative to carrying the Sacrament to the sick was to celebrate it in an abbreviated form in the sickroom. The court suggested that given the number of priests and the number of sick people in a modern urban parish, this was no longer a practical way to deal with the problem.

The author of this decision, Garth Moore, was one of the church's leading canonists, so his decision must have carried a good deal of weight. On the other hand, it was a decision of a court of first instance in the northern province, directly contrary to a decision of the highest court of the other province. How far it would have prevailed if the problem had not been solved legislatively is hard to say.

Confession had too much support in the Prayer Book and the 1604 Canons to be condemned outright. The Office for the Visitation of the Sick specifically says that the sick person "shall . . . be moved to make a special confession of his sins, if he feel his conscience burdened with any weighty matter." A form of absolution follows. There is also an Exhortation in the Communion service in which anyone who cannot quiet his conscience by private prayer is invited to "come to me, or to some other discreet and learned Minister of God's Word, and open his grief; that by the Ministry of God's holy Word he may receive the benefit of Absolution, together with ghostly counsel and advice . . . ." Finally, Canon 113 of 1604 forbids the minister to reveal any secret sin confessed to him.

On the other hand, it was hard to see support in this material for regular resort to the confessional as a form of general spiritual discipline, and Protestant sensibilities were a good deal outraged as the thought of such a discipline being inculcated in the Church of England. Victorian males seem to have been particularly upset at the prospect of their wives and daughters talking to strange clergymen about sex. They were not reassured by the appearance in 1877 of a book called *The Priest in Absolution*, which was intended for the guidance of confessors but fell into the hands of the general public.[66]

One curate, Alfred Poole, had his license lifted in 1858 because of his systematic practice of hearing confessions.[67] There was some evidence that he had asked women improper questions, and some evidence that he had brought undue pressure on people to make their confessions, but that eventually dropped out, and his unlicensing was rested ultimately on the ground that systematic hearing of confessions is bad for the church. The Court of Queen's Bench required the Archbishop of Canterbury to hold a formal hearing on appeal from the bishop's action, but, when he had done so, the Judicial Committee refused to hear an appeal from his action — saying it was not a judicial action but an exercise of discretion. Poole was the only clergyman to appear in the law reports for hearing confessions. He was vulnerable because he was a mere curate. I do not believe an incumbent could have been disciplined for hearing confessions, or even for inculcating systematic confession among his parishioners unless he was in some way scandalous or coercive.

The practice figures in the law reports also, however, in a handful of cases where a court's faculty jurisdiction has been invoked to remove confessional boxes and associated furnishings.[68] Some courts have complied on the ground that the box bespeaks a greater emphasis on confession than Anglican practice allows. In the most recent case I found on the subject (1938), the court refused to issue either a faculty to take the box out or a confirmatory faculty to leave it in.

The hearing of confessions is now governed by Canon B29 of the Canons of 1969. It is an odd document. It consists mostly of paraphrases from the 1662 Prayer Book, with its emphasis on direct confession to the Lord, and authority for hearing the confession of "any who by these means cannot quiet his own conscience." It follows this language with a prohibition against exercising "the ministry of absolution" in a parish without consent of the incumbent except in certain enumerated cases. The provision for keeping the secrets of the confessional is not included in this canon. Rather, the applicable provision from Canon 113 of 1604 is preserved from repeal. I gather that the framers of the 1969 compilation did not want to risk the political dangers of submitting a new canon on secrecy for the Royal Assent.[69] The English law of evidence is generally not at all tender with confidential communications, and there were no doubt good reasons for letting this particular sleeping dog lie.

The anointing of the sick[70] was introduced in the middle decades of the nineteenth century without, as far as I can see, any particular objection.

The biblical support for the practice (James 5:14) is too strong for
Evangelicals to oppose it on doctrinal grounds, and, since it is done
privately rather than publicly, it cannot be objected to under the Acts of
Uniformity as a liturgical observance not provided for in the Prayer Book.
The 1928 Prayer Book provided a specific office for it, and the
Convocations adopted such offices on their own authority when the book
was rejected by Parliament. It is now expressly authorized under the
Canons of 1969.

Prayers for the dead have come before the courts from time to time in
faculty proceedings over tombstones or memorials asking prayers for the
person commemorated.[71] It has been uniformly held that Article 22,
condemning the "Romish Doctrine concerning Purgatory" does not
necessarily condemn all prayers for the dead. On the other hand, courts,
as a matter of discretion, have tended to refuse permission for inscriptions
requesting such prayers. The Prayer Book liturgy, while it expresses love
for the departed, thanks for their witness, and hope to be united with them,
does not at any point intercede in their behalf. In this it contrasts with the
American version, which beseeches the Lord to "grant them continual
growth in thy love and service," and with the Alternative Service Book of
1980, which permits asking that they be granted "refreshment, light, and
peace."

Invocation of saints has also come up in faculty cases.[72] Under the
nineteenth century cases, if a saint is invoked before an image, the
invocation will constitute an abuse of the image and be ground for taking it
down. There is a 1938 case in which certain images of Our Lady were
accompanied with inscriptions asking her intercession. These were
removed before the court could pass on them, but I doubt if they would
have passed muster. An 1893 book on the legal rights of Roman Catholics
quotes a legal opinion that "Jesus, mercy; Mary, help" could not legally be
inscribed on a tomb in an Anglican churchyard.

4. Access to Sacraments — In 1874, the Reverend Flavel S. Cook fell into
a doctrinal dispute with a parishioner named Jenkins, whose views seemed
to be on the *Essays and Reviews* side. Cook finally determined that he
could not admit a person of Jenkins's views to Communion, and, when
Jenkins presented himself, Cook and his curate in fact refused him.[73]
After some efforts (inept, it seems to me) on the bishop's part to mediate
the quarrel, proceedings were brought against Cook under the Church
Discipline Act, 1840. Cook defended on the ground that the canons and
rubrics entitled him to do as he did.

Sir Robert Phillimore in the Arches court agreed. The rubric in the
Prayer Book authorizes the celebrant to repel "a notorious evil liver."
Phillimore argued that that term could not be limited to persons who lived

in a manner inconsistent with general moral principles: otherwise, even atheists could receive Communion. So he interpreted it in the light of Canon 27, which calls for repelling anyone who is a "depraver of the Book of Common Prayer," and the Exhortation in the Communion service that urges any "hinderer and slanderer of God's Word" to repent before approaching the Sacrament. Jenkins referred to the old case of *Middleton* v. *Crofts*,[74] which holds that the canons do not bind the laity, but Phillimore pointed out that this was a punitive suit against a clergyman.

The Judicial Committee reversed. Assuming, without deciding, that Canon 27 applied, they read it, like the rubric, as limited to cases where the situation of the would-be communicant is notorious in the congregation. Since Jenkins's heterodoxy was expressed only in private correspondence with Cook and with the bishop, he came under neither the rubric nor the canon. A monition issued ordering Cook to admit Jenkins to Communion, and Cook resigned rather than obey it.

This was one case where the Judicial Committee was right on history as well as on law. There was evidently some basis in medieval canon law for repelling a notorious public sinner from Communion[75] (although I have found no record of an English priest doing so), but if the facts were not notorious or the sinfulness not outrageous, the case would have to go through the court process initiated on the parish visitation. The fact that that process was now obsolete did not justify a country vicar in creating another.

In view of the result in *Jenkins* v. *Cook*, it is not surprising that a later clergyman got nowhere in trying to repel a parishioner for occasionally attending Wesleyan services.[76] He claimed she had made herself a "schismatic." Since he was one of those who refused to litigate religious questions in the Arches, insisting it was a mere lay court, he did not bring his claim before Lord Penzance in response to the parishioner's suit. Penzance, therefore, treated the case as one of entirely unexplained refusal, and punished the clergyman accordingly.

The question was litigated one more time in the case of *Banister* v. *Thompson* (1908-1912).[77] Banister had married the sister of his deceased wife, pursuant to a peculiar statute enacted in 1907 to authorize such marriages. Since the statute provided that the marriage was to be valid as a civil contract only, the Banisters' parish incumbent decided that as far as the church went they were living in sin. It followed of course that they were notorious evil livers and could be repelled from Communion. When he was brought before the Arches in a disciplinary proceeding, the incumbent made these points, and added a reference to another provision of the statute to said no clergyman should be liable to a censure after the adoption of the statute to which he would not have been liable before.

Before the statute, the Banisters would certainly have been living in sin, and he would certainly not have been liable for repelling them.

Sir Lewis Dibdin delivered a scholarly opinion, beginning by showing the tenuousness of any parish clergyman's claim to excommunicate his parishioners. The rubric about notorious evil livers is to protect public decency by excluding people whose general course of life is shocking to Christian morality. The concept of a marriage valid as a civil contract only, Dibdin pointed out, was entirely new to English law. He was not sure what to make of it, but he believed that no conceivable interpretation would make notorious evil livers of everyone involved in such a marriage. Against this background, the only possible construction of the provision protecting clergymen against censure would limit it to acts in connection with the marriage ceremony. The incumbent sought writs of prohibition against Dibdin, and lost all the way through the House of Lords.

The question of who is entitled to be married in church came up in an 1850 case.[78] A clergyman named Moorhouse James was indicted for refusing to perform a marriage on the ground that the prospective bridegroom had not been confirmed and did not intend to be. The case was thrown out on a series of technicalities, so James's substantive arguments are not altogether clear. It seems, however, that he relied on a rubric suggesting that the newly married couple receive Communion. Under another rubric, a person is not eligible for Communion until he is confirmed or ready and desirous to be. Since the groom was supposed to receive Communion at the wedding, and was ineligible to do so, it followed that he was ineligible for the wedding. This seems a tenuous argument, even though, as James pointed out, there were now alternative forms of marriage available for those who did not wish to be full-fledged Anglicans.

When the 1857 Divorce Act was before Parliament, there was some effort to put in a requirement that divorced persons choosing to remarry do so in a registry office. The proposal was rejected, evidently on theological grounds.[79] There is a text in St. Matthew's Gospel which has often been interpreted as authorizing divorce with remarriage in the case of adultery — which was the only case within the 1857 act. This text had been used ever since the seventeenth century to support private bills dissolving particular marriages, and most of the proponents of the new legislation conceived of themselves as doing no more than transferring the traditional practice from Parliament to the courts. They did not understand themselves to be meeting the needs of a pluralist society by allowing non-Anglicans to depart from Anglican teaching as to the indissolubility of marriage. The only concession in the act as finally adopted was that no clergyman could be required to perform a new marriage for the spouse whose adultery had brought about the divorce. He did, however, have to let any other clergyman in the diocese use his church for the purpose.

These provisions caused a good deal of protest, but no open defiance. Neither in the seventeenth century nor in modern times has the High Church party been of one mind on the subject of remarriage after divorce on ground of adultery. There have always been enough people of high standing in the movement (Cosin in the seventeenth century, King in the nineteenth) to accept the permissive interpretation of the text from Matthew so that reading divorced and remarried people out of the church could never become a solid High Church cause.[80]

Later legislation separating the marriage law of the state from the tradition of the church — notably the Deceased Wife's Sister Act of 1907, discussed above in connection with the *Banister* case, and the Matrimonial Causes Act, 1937, allowing divorce for reasons other than adultery — has contained broad protection for the consciences of clergymen. Such protection is implicit in the 1907 provision that no clergyman is to be liable to a censure to which he would not have been liable if the act had not passed. It is explicit in the 1937 act, which provides that no clergyman need perform a marriage for any divorced person whose former spouse is still living, nor need he allow his church to be used for such a marriage.[81]

To be sure, the parties to such a marriage cannot be repelled from Communion. They are not notorious evil livers. The teaching of the *Banister* case would seem to apply to the divorced and remarried as much as it does to people who avail themselves of the Deceased Wife's Sister Act. Churchmen have claimed, both in the media and in Convocation, that it would be within the authority of the church to adopt new rules excluding people from Communion who are not evil livers, but are involved in irregular marriages.[82] But the political and ecclesiastical obstacles to the effective exercise of any such authority have been insuperable, and are likely to remain so.

As regards the other ministrations of the church, I have already taken up the development and continued vitality of the principle that Dissenters can be buried in Anglican churchyards — and buried with Anglican rites if the survivors wish. I have also referred to the 1972 case of Bland, who did not want to baptize a child whose parents never came to church. In every situation, the cases and other materials point to the same conclusion. Although High Churchmen — and some others as well — have sought to respond to the growing pluralism and secularization by limiting the ministrations of the church to people specifically identified with its ministry and worship, the law has given them no encouragement whatever.

III. The End of Uniformity

A. Defiance.

The High Church Party, as we have seen, set little store by the courts, even the ones that were ostensibly ecclesiastical. It was a constant source of frustrated wonderment to their opponents that people so strong in their theological claims for the institutional church should be so insubmissive to its actual mandates. In fact, it took them some time to develop a plausible rationale for their intransigence. It was easy enough to arrive at an intuitive judgment that whatever judicial authority God intended His church to have did not reside in the Judicial Committee of the Privy Council, and resided still less in Lord Penzance. But it was hard to say where it resided instead, and harder to insist that it resided nowhere at all.

By the 1870s, there was a set of arguments in place, set forth in a variety of sermons, pamphlets, and open letters.[83] It ran more or less as follows:

1. Establishment is essentially a consensual relation between a particular state and a particular church.
2. As long as the relation continues, neither party can legitimately change its terms without the concurrence of the other. The assignment of ecclesiastical appeals to the Judicial Committee was illegitimate under this principle. So was the adoption of the Public Worship Regulation Act.
3. Even if the Judicial Committee were legitimate in its provenance, it would be illegitimate in its composition because laypeople cannot legitimately be given the last word on questions of doctrine or liturgy. The claim that the Judicial Committee is not deciding such questions, but merely giving effect to decisions reached by higher authorities, cannot be taken seriously. Only adherence to a particular body of theological principles can explain the departure of the Judicial Committee from the plain words of the texts it is supposed to be interpreting.
4. The illegitimate tribunal at the top poisons the whole system of ecclesiastical authority. The lower courts, even when they are not constituted under the Public Worship Regulation Act, are illegitimate because they are within the appellate jurisdiction of the Judicial Committee, and bound by its precedents. Even when the Dean of the Arches was Sir Robert Phillimore, a man of vast learning and impeccable churchmanship, commissioned in the traditional way by the archbishop of Canterbury (and, incidentally, brother-in-law of Archdeacon Denison), the appellate jurisdiction of the Judicial Committee made the rest of the system illegitimate. Furthermore, the bishops are not entitled to obedience from their

clergy if their orders come not from their own pastoral discretion, but from a supposed duty to implement the decisions of the Judicial Committee.

5. In the absence of any source of authoritative interpretation, the clergy have the right, indeed, the obligation, to interpret the formularies of the church in accordance with the dictates of their own consciences. In forming their own consciences, they should be guided by plain language and Catholic tradition.

Each point in the sequence is open to question.[84]

1. The idea of establishment as a consensual arrangement is founded on certain eighteenth century works, notably Warburton's *Alliance between Church and State*. It also fits comfortably with High Church views on ecclesiastical autonomy. But it is hard to reconcile with the historical evidence. It was only in the seventeenth century that churches began to appear on the scene with full-blown internally generated legal structures, ready to accept or reject consensual relations with the state. Anyone who has followed these volumes from the beginning will see the difficulty of assigning to the church any juridical form that the state did not give it. Sir Lewis Dibdin drew this analogy in 1883:

> A lets B a room in his (A's) house; B is a tailor, and uses the room as a workshop; B's knowledge of tailoring is not derived from A, but his power and his right to use his knowledge in A's house is entirely due to A's permission. So the power to excommunicate is inherent in the Bishops, and can be neither given nor taken away by the State; but the right to exercise it in England is conferred by the King and laws of England.

This is the doctrine that Stillingfleet was putting forth in 1659. It is also, in my opinion, the doctrine held by the Commons in 1307.

2. If it is unconstitutional for the relation between church and state to be altered by one party without the consent of the other, the Reformation itself is in jeopardy. The Convocations of the two provinces, the only bodies in England generally regarded as wielding ecclesiastical authority apart from the state, acquiesced in King Henry's proceedings only after being thoroughly intimidated, and in Queen Elizabeth's not at all.

3. Through legal analysis of the decisions in question, I have tried to show why I believe that the Judicial Committee's understanding of its role cannot be dismissed as summarily as the High Churchmen dismissed it. This is not to deny that most members of the Committee were out of sympathy with the doctrinal and liturgical

positions that the High Churchmen sought to advance. Most judges
find one side more attractive than the other in some of the cases
that come before them. My point is only that these judges were no
more swayed by their sympathies than judges generally are.

The refusal to accept what the judges claimed to be doing resulted,
I believe, from a feeling that they should have been doing something
else. Authoritative teaching, both through doctrinal statements and
through liturgical celebrations, is part of the mission of the church,
and it was unacceptable to High Churchmen that the church's
highest judicial authority should not take part in carrying that
mission out.

4. The bishops had a veto over liturgical prosecutions. In permitting
    such prosecutions, therefore, they must have exercised a pastoral
    discretion independent of the courts. In some cases, to be sure,
    they felt as a matter of pastoral discretion that the previous
    decisions of the Judicial Committee should be implemented. But as
    a general principle a good faith exercise of discretion is not
    invalidated by the reasons for exercising it. In fact, the bishops tried
    to put down liturgical violations because they desired uniformity and
    peace in their dioceses, and thought that following the lead of the
    Judicial Committee was the way to accomplish what they desired.
    Such a motive for an exercise of pastoral discretion may or may not
    be misguided, but it is hardly illegitimate.

5. The idea that parish clergymen are better equipped than lawyers to
    interpret the formularies of the church presupposes that the
    formularies are theological statements rather than legal documents.
    This is the very point at issue. Whether the formularies should be
    interpreted in the light of Catholic tradition raises the same point.
    For the lawyers on the Judicial Committee, the formularies were
    legal documents, adopted through a hard-fought political process, to
    determine who was to be accommodated within the reformed
    church structure, and to what extent. For the High Church clergy,
    the formularies were a witness to revealed truth, to be interpreted
    in accordance with what that truth is known to embrace.

In the end, the dispute seems to boil down to one between priests and
lawyers, with each party in the right by the principles of its own profession.
There is a good deal to be said for assigning to priests the task of deciding
questions of doctrine and liturgy, and just as much to be said for assigning
to lawyers the task of determining who is eligible for membership or for
office in a juridical body. It might be argued on behalf of the lawyers that
anyone dissatisfied with the terms of membership in one such body should
join another. It could be responded on behalf of the priests that this
particular body has a divine mission to proclaim God's truth to the English

nation, and one who is carrying out that mission has a divine mandate to remain a part of it. For my own part, I have no authority to adjudicate this dispute, and I shall not try to do so. Suffice it to say that neither side can be stigmatized as either ignoble or implausible.

The courts, as we have seen, outraged the High Church party about equally in what they permitted and in what they forbade. Obviously, though, it is harder to defy a permission addressed to someone else than a prohibition addressed to yourself. The High Churchmen tried to counter the judgments in the *Gorham* case and the *Essays and Reviews* case by having the offending doctrines condemned in Convocation. The condemnations were duly passed, without affecting the legal position of the clergymen involved. Bishop Phillipotts refused to institute Gorham into his living as the court ordered him to do, but the judge performed the institution himself with full legal effect. Someone suggested to Phillipotts that he send an orthodox clergyman to offer alternative ministrations to Gorham's parishioners, but Phillipotts wisely decided not to. Flavel Cook refused to administer Communion to his heterodox parishioner, Jenkins, but in the end Cook resigned his benefice and Jenkins went to Communion.

Two basic forms of defiance were always available when anyone cared to use them. One was not to appear in court when summoned; the other was to continue controversial liturgical practices when the court said to stop. The older generation of High Churchmen were reluctant to take either of these steps, but they felt they had to support their younger colleagues when the time came to do so. Pusey was upset at Bennett's refusal to appear in court and defend the Eucharistic doctrine Pusey had taught him. Denison had a good deal of a falling out with Charles Lowder, one of the most saintly of the London slum priests, over the duty of submission to the mandates of the Judicial Committee.

The proceedings that set Lowder and Denison at odds are illustrative of the generation gap that developed when the Judicial Committee first began pressing on the High Church party.[85] The occasion was a meeting in January, 1869, to protest the judgment condemning Alexander Heriot Mackonochie (who was later to be the most tragic of the victims of ritual prosecution) for various practices, especially the use of candles during the Eucharist. Denison had chaired a committee to draw up resolutions, and submitted the following:

> That this meeting does not recognize the existing Court of Final Appeal as a court qualified to declare the law of the Church of England upon either doctrine or ceremonial; that with respect to this particular judgement of the said court in *Martin* v. *Mackonochie*, the meeting finds, among other things, that the judgement disregards the Church of

England's fundamental principle of connection with and reference to the practice of the Church primitive and Catholic: nevertheless it acknowledges the duty of submitting, under protest, to the law of the land, upon that law being put in force, as far as such law is expressed in the decree of the said judgement, and until such law shall be further declared or amended.

Bennett, who had just won his doctrine case without appearing in court, moved to substitute the following for the language beginning "nevertheless:"

... therefore [this meeting] is unable to reconcile submission to the present decree with its paramount and primary duty of obedience to the church, and can only wait in patience the providence of God.

This motion lost. Lowder then moved to strike out the "nevertheless" language entirely, hoping in this way to preserve the unanimity of the meeting. Denison objected that proclaiming the illegitimacy of the court without asserting the duty of submitting to it was tantamount to saying that is should not be submitted to. As he put it later in a letter to Lowder:

... the one difference of principle between us was (and is) whether we affirm the duty of submission to the law of the land in matters which are not essential, however bad we hold the law to be; or whether we deny it .... Bennett's amendment, which negatived the principle of submission in terms, was rejected by a great majority. You then proposed and carried what is in effect the same thing.

Lowder's motion was carried, but the more conservative of the participants were not satisfied. The meeting finally settled unanimously on a waffle:

... but at the same time this meeting, feeling the great difficulty of the present case, and that there are many reasons why those who have used the ceremony or practice now condemned by the Judicial Committee of the Privy Council may be anxious to wait rather than give immediate effect to the decision now pronounced, considers that this is a matter which is best left to the individual judgement and to the circumstances of each priest who had been accustomed to use the ceremonial or practice in question.

Although everyone voted for this language, few were satisfied with it. Denison wrote Lowder later in the letter just quoted:

I will not, for one, act with men who hold their position by law, but will not submit to law.

Meanwhile, Lowder was taking part in another and smaller meeting where it was resolved:

> This meeting deems it advisable to continue the use of Altar Lights,
> leaving it to those in authority to interfere or not as they see fit.

Many of the older generation, including Denison, eventually came around
to supporting the intransigence of their younger colleagues. The pressure
of events certainly had something to do with this change of attitude: as the
battle over Ritualism grew more and more intense, it became harder and
harder to maintain a position on the sidelines. But I believe there was also
a growing awareness of a connection between Catholic liturgical practice
and Catholic Eucharistic doctrine. By 1876 — less than ten years after his
exchange with Lowder — Denison was saying not only that he would resist
interference by the courts with his liturgical practices, but also that if his
practices were forbidden by a National Synod of the church he would
resign his benefice "rather than continue to minister in the public
congregation of a church which had so betrayed its own inherited position."
He said that this was the only point on which he had ever changed his
mind.[86]

Until the adoption of the Public Worship Regulation Act, 1874, the
intransigent ritualists had to be dealt with under the Church Discipline Act,
1840. The objection to the procedures laid down by that act was evidently
that they were too cumbersome and expensive. Those under the new act
were supposed to be notably less so, and would have been had the act
passed as first introduced, but by the time Parliament was finished, the new
procedures were not much better than the old ones. Despite its
shortcomings, the new act went through because everyone expected a law
against Ritualism to be enacted at that session, and because the bishops
feared that if this one was voted down the militant Protestants in the
Parliament would put through something worse.

The act as finally enacted had a fatal flaw. Unlike its predecessor, it was
very specific about the sanctions it imposed. The clergyman guilty of illegal
practices was to be admonished to stop them. If he disobeyed, he was to
be inhibited from performing any services. If the inhibition continued for
three years, he was to be deprived. But he could not be deprived until he
had been inhibited for three years.

The potentialities for defiance in this arrangement were first exploited by
a clergyman named Arthur Tooth[87] (another aptly named litigant: a
reasonably sedate bishop spoke of chloroforming the church in order to
extract him). Tooth, a vicar in the diocese of Rochester, was proceeded
against under the 1874 act. He paid no attention to the proceedings, no
attention to the monition that issued after Lord Penzance had carefully
considered his liturgical practices and found them illegal, and no attention
to the inhibition that issued after he disobeyed the monition. Finally, when
the bishop of Rochester sought to enforce the inhibition by appointing a

curate to officiate in Tooth's stead, Tooth, along with his churchwardens and forty or fifty parishioners, excluded the curate from the church.

Under the act as written, there was now nothing to do but wait until the inhibition had been in effect for three years and Tooth could be deprived. To be sure, a man persuaded as Tooth was might pay as little attention to a deprivation as to an inhibition. But there would be other forces at work. For one thing, the police might be more willing to protect a successor incumbent against his predecessor than to protect a curate against an inhibited incumbent. Moreover, a Ritualist incumbent would be apt to have a sympathetic patron. If he left quietly after being deprived, the patron could nominate a like-minded successor. But if he resisted and the patron supported him, the bishop would get to fill the benefice after six months. Considerations of this kind were to move Mackonochie (the defendant in the candle case just discussed) to accept a judgment of deprivation a few years later.[88]

But three years is a long time. The prosecution of Tooth had been initiated by the Church Association, a group of people urgently concerned with halting Romeward tendencies in the Church of England. They could hardly be content to wait that long for their judgment to take effect. Accordingly, they turned from the 1874 act to older and more general principles of canon law, and moved Lord Penzance to set proceedings in motion for imprisoning Tooth under a writ *de contumace capiendo*. This, it will be recalled, was the writ created in 1813 to replace the ancient writ *de excommunicato capiendo*, so that the church courts could punish contempt without subjecting the offender to the spiritual consequences of excommunication. Except for the elimination of the actual excommunication, the procedure was exactly the same as it had been since 1563, and not much different from what it had been since the 1200s. The ecclesiastical court signified the contumacy into Chancery, and a writ issued requiring the sheriff to imprison the offender until he complied with the orders of the court or gave a sufficient undertaking to do so.

Lord Penzance, after carefully rejecting the argument that he lacked the powers of a traditional ecclesiastical court, held that he had no discretion when asked to use those powers against an obviously contumacious party. The process therefore took its course, and Tooth was duly lodged in the Horsemonger Lane Prison near London Bridge. "Spy" the cartoonist drew him behind bars, dressed in his clericals, standing in a nonchalant slouch, hands in pockets, and a coolly contemptuous look on his face.[89]

On paper, he was in jail for contempt of court. But in the popular mind, he was there for using lighted candles, a crucifix and a chasuble, and for celebrating the Eucharist with his back to the people. To the delight of his supporters and the acute embarrassment of his opponents, he became an instant martyr.

His martyrdom was to be a short one. With Tooth in jail, resistance to the bishop collapsed, and a curate was able to take possession of the church and hold services without incident. Since that had been the object of the proceeding, the complainants hastened to apply to the court to let Tooth out, and the court hastened to grant their application:

> This statement of facts [i.e., that the bishop's curate was now in possession] renders the course now to be taken by the Court, in my opinion, perfectly clear. There is, I am justified by the present application in thinking, no desire on the part of the promoters in the suit, and certainly none on the part of the Court, to punish Mr. Tooth, or press more hardly upon him than is necessary in order to secure that the church services should be legally performed, and as this end has been attained, there is no reason why Mr. Tooth should not be at liberty again.[90]

The complainants could have left him in jail until he paid their costs — which would have been forever — but wisely chose not to. They reserved any other options they might have for recovering costs.

But they were not to collect anything. This was the case referred to earlier in which Lord Penzance had sat in Lambeth Palace under a commission authorizing him to sit in London, Westminster, or the diocese of Rochester. The Queen's Bench Division held the whole proceeding *coram non judice*, and prohibited any further enforcement of the judgment. Tooth resigned before a new prosecution could be mounted, and spent the rest of a long life in various pastoral endeavors that did not require him to be either instituted into a benefice or licensed as a curate.[91]

Tooth was one of a number of clergymen who were prosecuted for their liturgical practices during the 1870s and 80s, and one of five who went to jail.[92] There was Purchas, who set up a stuffed dove on his altar for Pentecost. There was Mackonochie, who froze to death in a Scottish snowstorm, disoriented, some said, by the weight of his sufferings. There was Green, who spent eighteen months in jail before his three years were up and his benefice vacant — the state of his parishioners' feelings was such that the bishop did not dare send in a curate to officiate in his place. There was Lowder, who died in 1880, still not brought to court, because the Church Association could not find three parishioners willing to accuse him. The individual stories of most of these men have been elegantly narrated by P.T. Marsh in his biography of the hapless archbishop Tait, who put the 1874 act through Parliament, and spent the last few years of his life trying to put the genie back in the bottle. There is also a fine biography of

Lowder, which tells the stories of a number of his associates, and one of
Mackonochie in which his multiple prosecutions are described in detail.
All I will try to do here is supplement these and other good narratives with
an account of the major legal points that came up in the cases.

First, some of the accused clergymen tried to get the Queen's Bench
Division to issue writs of prohibition on the ground that the courts where
they were being prosecuted were not real ecclesiastical courts, and could
not exercise the traditional powers of such courts. They were encouraged
by the holding in Tooth's case that Lord Penzance should have sat where
his commission said to sit, even though the Court of Arches had always had
the power to sit anywhere in the province. They were interpreting the case
too broadly. The Queen's Bench did not actually hold that Lord Penzance's
court was not the old Court of Arches (though one of three judges said a
few words to that effect). It simply held that any court, new or old, is
subject to statutory limitations when it exercises statutory powers. After
Tooth's case, the argument, whatever form it took, that the courts involved
in these cases were not real ecclesiastical courts got nowhere in the Queen's
Bench Division, and got nowhere in the Court of Appeal and the House of
Lords when it was taken up on appeal.[93]

Other technical arguments did better.[94] Two recalcitrant clergymen,
Dale and Enraght, were let out of jail on habeas corpus because the writs
authorizing the sheriff to seize them were not opened before the justices of
the Queen's Bench in open court as an act of 1563 required. This
requirement had been adopted to make sure Elizabethan sheriffs did not
neglect their duty to enforce the processes of the church. Lord Coleridge
thought it had been repealed by an 1849 reform of the writ system called
the Petty Bag Act, but the rest of the judges thought it was still in force.
Another clergyman, Cox, was also let out on habeas corpus. Rather than
an inhibition under the 1874 act, he had defied a three month suspension
under the Church Discipline Act, 1840. He was let out because the three
months were up. The prosecutors argued that the traditional procedure
called for leaving a contumacious person in jail until he agreed to obey the
court in the future. They were right enough about the tradition, but it was
pointed out on Cox's behalf that until 1813 the imprisonment was not based
on contumacy but on excommunication. For this reason, the person in jail
could not be let out until he was absolved, and he could not be absolved
until he had repented of the behavior that had led to his excommunication,
and promised amendment for the future. These requirements were wholly
inconsistent with the elimination of excommunication from the process in
1813. The first judge to hear the case accepted Cox's argument and let him
go. The Court of Appeal reversed, holding that the 1813 statute had made
no change except the one explicitly provided for. The House of Lords

reversed the Court of Appeal on the ground that an order granting habeas corpus is not appealable. So Cox stayed out of jail.

What with one thing and another, then, the only liturgical offender whose imprisonment was upheld by the Queen's Bench Division was Green.[95] His church, in a slum district of Manchester, was in the County Palatine of Lancaster, which was not subject to the requirement that writs *de contumace capiendo* be opened before the justices of the Queen's Bench. It was Lord Penzance himself who let Green out when his three years were up. The argument that he should promise future obedience was alluded to, but the prosecution did not press it, and Lord Penzance rejected it.

The remedies provided by the 1874 act were in addition to, not instead of, the ones available under the Church Discipline Act, 1840. The older act had the advantage that it did not require a three years' wait before a refractory clergyman could be put out of his benefice. Deprivation was available for any violation of law that the court considered serious enough. As we have seen, a deprived clergyman would probably go quietly so that his successor could be chosen by a sympathetic patron instead of a hostile bishop, whereas a suspended or inhibited clergyman might well remain in place until the sheriff came for him. Accordingly, if you prosecuted under the 1840 act instead of the 1874 one, you could have your way without putting anyone in jail. This alternative would have been more expeditious if Lord Penzance had not felt some obligation to try less rigorous sanctions before imposing deprivation. But in 1881 a clergyman named Edwards (he complicated the law reports by changing his name *pendente lite* to De la Bere) was deprived under the 1840 act with so little stir that his name hardly ever appears in the history books with those of his fellow victims.[96]

Within a decade after the 1874 act, it had become apparent that no amount of litigation, however successful, would avail to restore the liturgical uniformity of an earlier time.[97] More and more young clergymen were coming to believe that orthodox Eucharistic doctrine, pastoral necessity, or both required more elaborate ceremonies. Furthermore, men who were otherwise content with the old liturgical practices began adopting the new ones as an expression of solidarity with their persecuted colleagues. At one point a list was compiled of clergymen who did not use Eucharistic vestments, but would begin doing so if the eastward position continued to be prosecuted. By the end of 1878, Archbishop Tait had begun to note similarities between the history of Ritualism in his own time and that of Methodism in the previous century, and to hope that the Ritualists would not be driven out of the church as the Methodists were. In October, 1879, he actually attended a Communion service where the priest wore vestments.

At this point the bishops gave way. They were not generally friendly to Ritualism, but they were appointed under a process calculated to exclude outspoken partisans of any kind. They tended to value peace more highly than abstract liturgical conformity, and they were apt to appreciate pastoral success, even when it was accompanied by practices they disliked. Given the general decline of religious practice and commitment, it got to seem more and more absurd to have Christians putting one another in jail over liturgical practices, or to remove a clergyman from a place where he was ministering to large devout congregations and profoundly affecting people's lives. By the late seventies, the bishops were almost routinely refusing to allow prosecutions.

The power of the bishop to veto a prosecution was challenged under both the applicable statutes, and upheld both times. The earlier and more serious challenge was under the 1840 act.[98] The test case (1879-80) involved T.T. Carter, an elderly and much beloved vicar in the diocese of Oxford. His liturgical irregularities were reported to the bishop, who refused to prosecute because in general such prosecutions did more harm than good, and in particular Carter was an old man who had most of his parish on his side. The would-be promoter brought mandamus in the Queen's Bench Division to compel the bishop to proceed.

The relevant provision of the statute said that where a clergyman is accused or suspected of violating ecclesiastical law, "it shall be lawful for the bishop . . . , on the application of any party complaining thereof, or, if he shall think fit, of his own mere motion," to initiate proceedings.

The rule of statutory interpretation in other contexts was that if a law authorized a public official to do a certain thing in a certain situation, and if there was a public interest in having him do it, then he would have to do it even though the statutory language was in terms a permission rather than a command. The prosecutors argued that the rule should be applied here, because there was a public interest in having the services of the church performed according to law. But, it was responded, the argument proved too much. To accept it would mean that every departure from the rubrics, however trivial, would have to be prosecuted at the request of anyone who cared to bring it to the bishop's attention. But mandamus is a discretionary writ, the prosecutors pointed out. The Queen's Bench could be trusted not to issue it in a trivial case. No, it was argued for the bishop, the rule that the prosecutors invoked presupposed that there was no discretion to be exercised. If anyone was to use discretion in the matter, it should be the bishop, not the Queen's Bench.

Other points were equally ambiguous. (1) The statute said that the bishop could proceed on his own motion "if he think fit." When it spoke of proceeding on someone else's application, it said nothing about thinking fit. Did it follow that the bishop had to proceed on someone else's application whether he thought fit or not? Or were the words "if he think fit" mere surplusage so that the bishop had the same powers without them as with them? (2) There was just one earlier case reported in which a court had been asked to issue a mandamus to a bishop under the act. Two judges had sat together and denied the writ. One had relied on the discretion of the bishop, the other on his own discretion. (3) Before the act was adopted, the consent of the bishop had been theoretically required to initiate a disciplinary proceeding. But in practice the consent had never been withheld.

With the law in this state, the Queen's Bench Division granted the mandamus and ordered the bishop to set the process in motion. But the Court of Appeal reversed, and the House of Lords sustained the Court of Appeal.

So it was established that the bishop could veto proceedings under the 1840 act. Under the 1874 act, that power was expressly given him. However, he was required before making his decision to consider "all the circumstances of the case," and if he decided against prosecution, he had to state his reasons. It was contended in another mandamus case (1888-91) that his consideration of the circumstances and his statement of reasons could be reviewed by the Queen's Bench Division.[99] The case involved a reredos in St. Paul's Cathedral, which was allegedly the object of idolatrous worship. The bishop stated that it was indistinguishable from a reredos that had been held lawful in an earlier case, and that litigation should not be undertaken unless absolutely necessary, because it was harmful to the church. The Queen's Bench Division, 2-1, awarded the mandamus, arguing that the bishop had not considered all the circumstances of the case, that he had considered some things that were not circumstances of the case, and that he had misinterpreted the earlier case. Again the Court of Appeal reversed and the House of Lords sustained the Court of Appeal. The bishop's discretion in deciding whether to allow a prosecution is not reviewable, and the circumstances of the case are whatever he thinks relevant.

The last prosecution of a liturgical violator under either of these acts for some years was that of Cox in 1885. His bishop, J.C. Ryle, one of the few Evangelicals to be advanced to the bench in this period, felt that a routine exercise of his veto would be tantamount to nullifying an act of Parliament, which he was not free to do. In 1892, after Cox had gone through his suspension and imprisonment, and had taken his habeas corpus proceeding through the House of Lords, the prosecutors attempted have him up again for violating the monition that had been issued at the beginning of the litigation. But Lord Penzance refused to act without a new proceeding.[100] So many years had passed, he said, that the bishop should have a new chance to exercise his veto. Presumably, the bishop did so, for no new proceeding was brought.

B. The Lincoln Judgment.[101]

With their efforts to prosecute the lower clergy frustrated by the episcopal veto, the Church Association decided to take on a bishop. The one most conspicuously associated with the revival of Catholic practices was Edward King, bishop of Lincoln, whom Gladstone had promoted to the bench in 1885. The decision to prosecute him was an odd one, for he was a saintly man, gentle and courteous in his witness to Catholic principles, and loved by churchpeople of all parties for his character and his pastoral presence. King used Eucharistic vestments in his private chapel, but when he was celebrating in a church, he followed the practice prevailing there, whatever it was. The Church Association reported to the archbishop of Canterbury a couple of occasions when King had used practices (including candles and the eastward position, but not including vestments) that had been condemned by the Judicial Committee. They demanded that the archbishop use his authority as metropolitan to hear their charges against King and make him obey the law.

Because of King's popularity, it was hard for the Association to find witnesses against him. They were accused of offering thousands of pounds to get people to come forward, but I do not believe the evidence is adequate to support so serious a charge. On the other hand, they may well have sent their own agents to attend the bishop's services for the express purpose of witnessing his practices and testifying about them, and they may well have compensated some of these agents for their time. They certainly did such things in other cases. The communicant who brought out a consecrated Host to be an exhibit in a wafer bread case must have been sent to the service for that purpose. A witness was paid two guineas a Sunday and one a weekday for attending Mackonochie's services, and the payments were included in the bill of costs submitted by the Association in one of Mackonochie's cases.[102] The archbishop evidently believed that the Association had engaged in similar tactics in King's case, for he said at the close of the proceeding:

> Although religious people whose religious feelings really suffer might rightly feel constrained to come forward as witnesses in such a case, yet it is not decent for religious persons to hire witnesses to intrude on the worship of others for purposes of espial.[103]

The archbishop to whom the Association presented its case was Tait's successor, E.W. Benson, scholar, antiquarian, and pastor, generally loved

and respected, but felt by some to be more learned than wise. He was not
sure what to do with the Association's case. There was precedent for an
archbishop hearing charges against a suffragan, but the last case had been
in 1698.[104] Benson evidently felt that it would be good for the church to
have a judgment of purely ecclesiastical provenance on the books in a
liturgical case. King's official biographer (who was too outraged at the
prosecution of his hero to be entirely trustworthy) felt that Benson, despite
his good intentions, had been led astray by

> the delightful prospect of presiding over an ecclesiastical pageant with all
> the attendant "pomp and circumstance" of legal and religious millinery —
> scarlet robes and silver maces and full-bottomed wigs — of sitting in the
> chair of St. Augustine, surrounded by comprovincial prelates, and
> solemnly passing judgment on the successor of St. Hugh.[105]

The passage is quoted from the author's own letter, published in the
Manchester *Guardian* during the preliminary phases of the proceeding. It
has to be taken with a grain of salt, but it gives some indication of the state
of feeling at the time.

Benson's response when first approached was that the would-be
prosecutors had failed to convince him that he had power to proceed, and
that he would do nothing until a higher authority instructed him that he
had such power. This was an obvious invitation to bring the case before
the Judicial Committee, and the prosecutors did so. They presented the
Committee with fairly routine English canonical material, and the
Committee, after ascertaining that nobody was going to argue the other
side, informed the archbishop that he could hear the accusation if he chose
to, left open the question whether he would have to hear it if he chose not
to, and sent the case back to him to be dealt with according to law. They
did not write an opinion. Benson then decided to hear the case, and cited
King to appear before him.

King appeared under protest, arguing that the archbishop had no
jurisdiction outside a meeting of all the bishops of the province, that
bishops were not subject to the liturgical rules he was accused of violating,
and that the rules in question were not rules of ecclesiastical law. In a
couple of preliminary hearings, Benson, sitting with five assessors (four
bishops and a vicar general later replaced by a fifth bishop), overruled the
first two objections and postponed the third to a hearing on the merits.
The finding that the word "minister" in the rubrics applied to a bishop when
he was ministering was fairly obvious. The finding that an archbishop had
jurisdiction to try his suffragans for ecclesiastical offenses was more
difficult. Benson deployed a vast array of learning from every period of
church history, and concluded:

The Court, therefore, although by an entirely different line of inquiry, has arrived at the same conclusion which was arrived at on purely legal principles by . . . the Judicial Committee . . . . The court decides that it has jurisdiction in this case, and therefore overrules the protest.[106]

Throughout the proceedings, Benson referred to himself as "the Court." Bishop Stubbs of Oxford, one of the assessors, and a historian before he was a bishop, is said to have repeated to himself over and over, "It is not a court. It is an archbishop sitting in his library."

Whatever it was, it proceeded to hear the case on the merits. The decision as it came down was almost entirely in King's favor. The practices in issue were all declared lawful except on three minor points as to which he had no trouble complying with the judgment. The Church Association appealed to the Judicial Committee, which affirmed the archbishop.

The particular practices involved in this case have all been taken up in their places. What is of interest at this point is the reasoning by which the archbishop reached a different conclusion from the Judicial Committee on several matters, and the reasoning by which the Judicial Committee accepted his doing so. It has often been supposed both then and now that the archbishop gave the Judicial Committee a real comeuppance in this case, and that the Committee completed its own discomfiture by backing off of a number of cherished positions rather than confront the archbishop. I think that overstates the case. Benson began his opinion with a statement that he had

considered with the utmost carefulness and respect the decisions which have been given in recent years upon some of the points at issue, and the elaborated reasons upon which these decisions have been based, whether by the learned judges of the diocesan and provincial courts or by the very eminent authorities before whom as Lords of the Judicial Committee of the Privy Council these matters or any of them in any form have come.[107]

Then, after referring to "conditions differing from those of former suits," and to "the researches of later students," he said:

the Court has not felt it right so to shelter itself under authority, as to evade the responsibility, or escape the labour of examining each of the points afresh, in the light of this ampler historical research, and of weighing once again all the reasons which may be advanced either for or against any of the actions now under consideration.[108]

He concluded his bow to the Judicial Committee by pointing out that in 1877 they themselves had reexamined an 1871 decision and modified its holding.

In their decision affirming the archbishop, the Judicial Committee paid great attention to the 1877 case, *Ridsdale* v. *Clifton*. They quoted at some length their predecessors' opinion in that case, and concluded

> In the present case their Lordships cannot but adopt the view expressed in *Ridsdale* v. *Clifton* as to the effect of previous decisions. Whilst fully sensible of the weight to be attached to such decisions, their Lordships are at the same time bound to examine the reasons upon which the decisions rest, and to give effect to their own view of the law.[109]

They then proceeded to examine each question independently, just as the archbishop had done.

On the merits, however, Benson really did take a different approach from the Judicial Committee. As he did with the preliminary jurisdictional decision, he supported his conclusions with a great weight of historical learning, using English material from both before and after the Reformation, together with material from other churches both eastern and western. His general approach was that practices legal at the Reformation remained legal unless some particular enactment forbade them; that practices for which there is substantial post-Reformation evidence must be presumed not have been forbidden at the Reformation; and that such changes as were made at the Reformation were intended not to impose Calvinist doctrine, but to restore the usage of the primitive church. King, in writing to his clergy, expressed "especial thankfulness . . . that the Judgment is based on independent inquiry, and that it recognizes the continuity of the English Church." This seems a fair statement both of what Benson did and of why what he did was important. The Judicial Committee, by contrast, used historical material — if they used it at all — to elucidate the meanings of particular rubrics or other enactments. Their approach was sound enough as a principle of statutory interpretation, but as a principle of liturgical development it left a good deal to be desired.

To illustrate the contrast, I will take up just one of the practices involved in the case — that of mixing water with the wine for the Eucharist. King, reviving a pre-Reformation and contemporary Roman Catholic practice, had done this at the offertory, where the rubric calls for putting bread and wine on the table. This the archbishop found unacceptable. It had been expressly required in the 1549 Prayer Book, and the requirement was eliminated in 1552:

> Although it may not be proved that everything not ordered in any particular place was prohibited, yet the express removal of so simple a direction . . . must undoubtedly be understood to mean that the mixing at that place was not to be continued.[110]

But mixing water with the wine in advance, and using a mixed cup at the service was a different matter. Benson found a wealth of material showing that this was a primitive usage, preserved in all but one or two of the eastern liturgies, and in a few western ones as well. Furthermore, he showed that the revisers of the Prayer Book were aware of the usage, and might even have intended to adopt it:

> We find therefore that to mingle the cup before service was a matter of early usage in the west, and that our revisers seeking for primitive models studied the books in which this usage is preserved. We are perhaps not wholly in the dark as to Cranmer's own view of what should be done, although too much stress must not be laid on the indication . . . . If . . . for reasons of primitive antiquity he removed the mixing from the service, it remains probable that for the same reason resting on the same early memorials of Christianity he approved the previous mixing.[111]

Benson's final word on the mixed chalice was this:

> The Court therefore concludes —
>
> I. The Church of England has, and in the 34th article declares itself to have, the same authority as any Church Western or Eastern "to ordain change and abolish ceremonies or rites of the Church, ordained only by man's authority." By and within this authority the mixing of the cup was removed from the place it had before held in the public service of the Church. It was so removed in accordance with antient, primitive and very general use of most Churches. To practise it as if it had not been removed is to disregard those precedents and this authority.
>
> II. No rule has been made to "change or abolish" the all but universal use of a mixed cup from the beginning. When it was desirable to modify the direction as to the uniform use of unleavened wafers, a rubric was enacted declaring wheat bread sufficient. Without order it seems that no person had a right to change the matter in the chalice, any more than to change the form of bread. Wine alone may have been adopted by general habit but not by law. No rule having been made, it is not within the competency of this Court to make a new rule, in fact a rubric; which it would do if it ordered that a mixed cup should not be used.
>
> The Court decides that the mixing of the wine in and as part of the service is against the law of the Church, but finds no ground for pronouncing the use of a cup mixed beforehand to be an ecclesiastical offence.[112]

Contrast this approach with Lord Halsbury's reasoning in the Judicial Committee. When he addressed himself to matters of history and symbolism, it was merely to show that they would be inconclusive even if they were relevant. His main point was that they were not relevant. For him, there were only two questions in the case: whether the mixing of water and wine was a ceremony not provided for, and whether the resulting mixture constituted "wine" within the meaning of the rubrics. To state the questions in this way was to answer them:

> Where the chalice is placed mixed upon the Holy Table, no act is done during the service, in addition to those prescribed; the acts of consecration and administration are precisely the same as if the chalice were unmixed, and the recipients may even well be ignorant whether the chalice be mixed or not. It seems to their Lordships that there is not in such a case any additional ceremony, that no ceremonial act is added to the service.[113]

And:

> It is difficult to contend that what is generally called and known as "wine" loses that character by the admixture of a little water. Wines differ in alcoholic strength, and their Lordships do not believe that any one would hesitate to apply the word "wine" to such a mixture, or that it would be an unnatural use of language to do so.[114]

The contrast between the two tribunals is similar in their treatment of the other points in issue. It is perhaps starkest in the case of the lighted candles, which the archbishop devoted fifteen pages of opinion and thirteen of appendix to justifying on historical and doctrinal grounds. Halsbury said merely that if the candles were lighted before the service started they were not an illegal ceremony because they were not a ceremony at all, and that if they were an illegal ornament the bishop was not responsible for them because it was not his church.

This ruling has sometimes been regarded as a face-saving gesture on Halsbury's part. King did not appear before the Judicial Committee, and would not have obeyed any judgment it handed down disapproving of his practices. Consequently, the argument runs, Halsbury had to find a way to salvage the prestige of his tribunal without incurring the unimaginable political consequences of provoking King to defiance. This he did by intimating that the archbishop was wrong in his elaborate treatment of candles, and at the same time finding a technical reason for leaving the erroneous decision intact. In my opinion, this argument misreads Halsbury's judgment. His intimation, as I read it, is not that Benson is probably wrong, but that he is probably right:

If the proof corresponded with the allegation in all respects, it would be matter for grave consideration how far the archbishop's elaborate exposition of the history of the question, and in particular the decision of two learned judges in 1628 and 1629, have afforded new materials for consideration . . . .[115]

Nor did Halsbury's actual decision go off on a mere technicality: in a criminal proceeding, the question whether the accused has done what he is accused of doing is of more than technical significance. Finally, the view that Halsbury was worried about the prestige of his court overestimates the importance of ecclesiastical matters in the work of the Judicial Committee. The court of last resort for a quarter of the earth and its people did not need to support its prestige by overruling archbishops on liturgical questions.

C. Diversity.

With King's exoneration, the great days of liturgical litigation were at an end. But King was not the last clergyman to be prosecuted for his liturgical practices. As far as I have been able to find from the law reports, that distinction belongs to Oliver Henly, who was deprived of his benefice by Sir Lewis Dibdin in 1909, in a proceeding brought by the bishop of Oxford under the 1840 act.[116] Henly had reserved the Sacrament, maintained a conspicuous set of regular Eucharistic devotions, refused to stop when the bishop said to, and refused to appear in court. I have not been able to find why the episcopal veto that had been routinely exercised for twenty years was not exercised in his case. In any event, there was no general change in the unwillingness of the bishops to prosecute. Conrad Noel, the socialist and medievalist vicar of Thaxted in Essex, served from 1914 to 1923 under a bishop whom he drove to the brink of apoplexy by his Eucharistic devotions, but no prosecution was brought.[117]

Bishops were a little less chary of lifting the licenses of curates whom they found violating liturgical standards.[118] Some of the Anglo-Catholic clergy lost curates in this way even though they themselves pursued their practices with impunity. In a few cases also, one as late as 1920, bishops refused to institute clergymen into benefices if they would not undertake to refrain from illegal practices. The right of a bishop to exclude a clergyman on this ground was upheld by the Queen's Bench in 1884 in a suit by the patron of the church just vacated by the long-incarcerated Green. A clergyman who refused to renounce illegal practices was not a fit incumbent. To be sure, the Queen's or King's Bench was not bound by the Judicial Committee's determination of what was illegal. But their independent determinations were not much help to the promoters of Catholic liturgical practices.

Evidently, what happened eventually in these cases was that different parishes developed different liturgical traditions, and it became customary for bishops to respect these traditions in their personnel decisions. It also became customary for parish clergy to respect parish traditions and not try to implement their own particular practices over the objections of the worshippers. A principle of broad permissiveness in liturgy as in doctrine, plus a principle of not introducing new practices or abolishing old ones without a consensus in the congregation had been talked about as a modus vivendi as early as the 1880s. By the 1920s, it had become the rule in practice. In the 1960s, it became law.[119]

One class of litigations lasted longer than the others, because any disgruntled parishioner could set it in motion without the consent of the bishop. That was faculty litigation to remove the trappings of Catholic worship from church buildings.[120] Crucifixes, images of Our Lady and of the saints, Stations of the Cross, confessionals, and the like were sporadically raided in this way up to the time of the Second World War, and a tabernacle was ordered out of a church as late as 1954 — although an aumbry for the same purpose was permitted. By the 1950s, however, the courts had become fairly permissive in faculty cases, and would not generally interfere with church furnishings unless they produced serious dissension in the congregations affected.

It is not altogether clear to me why the church courts were able to adopt this new attitude without interference by the Judicial Committee. Until 1963, that body had both the power and the duty to hear whatever appeals anyone cared to bring in such cases as this. While in recent years they have expressed reluctance to supersede the decisions of ecclesiastical authorities on ecclesiastical matters, they have always shouldered the burden manfully when required to do so.[121] Nevertheless, I do not find that any faculty case arising out of a doctrinal or liturgical controversy reached the Judicial Committee after its decision in *Liddell* v. *Westerton* in 1857. I can only guess at the reason, but what I suspect is that when the Catholic side lost one of these cases there would be no appeal, because the Catholic side did not recognize the jurisdiction of the Judicial Committee, and when the Catholic side won there would be no appeal, because the denial of a faculty to take something out of a church was a matter of discretion which there would be no hope of overturning. In 1963, as we have seen, the jurisdiction of the Judicial Committee in all cases involving doctrine or ritual — faculty cases as well as disciplinary cases — was turned over to the newly created Court of Ecclesiastical Causes Reserved. In its one decision on the subject, that court too has shown a broadly permissive attitude.

One other recourse for the defenders of Protestantism was to take the law into their own hands.[122] They often did so with considerable exuberance. I have referred to the riots that drove W. J. E. Bennett out of London in 1851. There were worse ones in 1859 and 1860 at the church of St. George in the East. Attacks on this scale became rare after 1860, when Parliament turned the disruption of religious services from an ecclesiastical offense into a misdemeanor punishable by the magistrates. In its new capacity it was both more apt to be punished and more apt to be prevented by the timely intervention of the police. Even so, a busload of rioters came to Thaxted, Essex in 1919 to disrupt Conrad Noel's midsummer procession with the Host. It took a rare combination of muscle and tact to keep them in check.

The more usual approach was to assemble a knot of people either to shout down the offending services or to walk out in the middle of them, or both. Around the turn of the century, a London tradesman named John Kensit developed this kind of disruption into something approaching an art form, and placed himself at the head of a movement to drive popish practices out of the church. He died in 1902 after (some say because of, but a jury found otherwise) being hit with a chisel thrown by a churchman who objected to his proceedings. But his son carried on in his footsteps for some years.[123]

Often, the Ritualists gave as good as they got in these encounters.[124] One rector dealt with a protest from a member of his congregation by inviting the protester to meet him outside after the service and settle the matter man to man. The rector, who had been middleweight champion of the Royal Navy before taking orders, proceeded to knock the protester down, pick him up, shake his hand, and go ahead with his liturgical program. On another occasion, the same rector stopped in the middle of a service to expel John Kensit by the scruff of the neck before going on.

Forcible expulsion cannot have been a rare experience for Kensit and his followers. Many of the clergy they were opposing were men of aristocratic background, used to having their own way, and many of their congregations were working people, used to being physical if the occasion arose. One of the few prosecutions to reach the law reports (because the magistrates' decision was appealed to a higher court) involved a would-be protester who just managed to get out one cry of "idolatry!" before being hustled out of the church. He was let off because a majority of the magistrates thought he was not the one who disrupted the service; all the disrupting was done by the people who threw him out.[125]

The prosecutions arising out of these liturgical battles raised two important legal points for the higher courts to decide. One was that the illegality of a service was not a defense to a prosecution for disrupting it.[126] The statute covered all religious services, and an illegal service was still a service. Besides, the illegality of any given service depended on obscure questions of ecclesiastical law that the magistrates could not be expected to decide.

The other interesting legal point was that a clergyman who disrupted a service was guilty of an ecclesiastical offense as well as a temporal one.[127] In January, 1900, R.C. Fillingham, a militantly Protestant vicar, evidently with a parish to match, brought forty or fifty of his parishioners to a neighboring parish's Eucharist. At the consecration, Fillingham shouted "This is idolatry! Protestants leave the house of Baal!" and led his followers out. He was convicted before the magistrates of disrupting a religious service. That conviction was held to be a conviction of an act constituting an ecclesiastical offense (i.e., brawling, under the sixteenth century statutes on the subject), and so to warrant punishment under the Clergy Discipline Act, 1892.

Fillingham's case presented something of a dilemma for the ecclesiastical judge. The only sanctions available for his offense were deprivation or suspension from his own parish, where he was evidently doing an excellent job, and one of which his parishioners generally approved:

Mr. Fillingham's suspension would involve a disturbance of the spiritual oversight of the parish . . . , and there is nothing before the Court to lead me to the conclusion that it would be desirable. It appears to me, on the contrary, that what is wanted is to secure Mr. Fillingham's closer attention to his proper duties, and to keep him from unlawful interference in the affairs of other parishes.

He was let off with a monition.

The language condemning interference in the affairs of other parishes bespeaks a growing acceptance of liturgical diversity in the church. Moderate churchpeople of all persuasions had been urging such acceptance for some time, and many of the laity had been moving the church in the same direction by voting with their feet. The Ritualist parishes in London and other metropolitan centers had always attracted worshippers from outside their territorial boundaries, as well as driving some residents to seek more congenial services elsewhere. Moving about in this way was more difficult in the country than in the city, but it was possible in some places. As we have seen, W. J. E. Bennett made explicit arrangements with his neighbors to permit parishioners to go to whatever services they liked best.

The last serious effort at coercive imposition of a uniform liturgy ran its course during the opening years of this century. While Kensit and his colleagues were at work in the back pews, Sir William Harcourt and his colleagues were at work in Parliament, introducing various draconian measures, some of which came uncomfortably close to being enacted. In 1904, the government applied the sovereign remedy for politically embarrassing issues that refuse to go away: it appointed a Royal Commission. The Commission reported in 1906.[128] One of its conclusions was that the law as it stood was too narrow to meet the needs of the church. Since no one was about to make it any broader, it seemed that the only alternative was to disregard it and let every parish go its own way. The politicians accordingly gave up trying to legislate on the subject. The Kensitites out disrupting in the field took a little longer, but they too eventually gave up.

The last case of disruption to reach the law reports (1934 — lusty singing of Protestant hymns to drown out celebrant) involved an internal dispute within a single parish.[129] The protagonists seem to have been a singularly tactless incumbent on one side and a strong minded spinster on the other. The objectors had not quite enough power or influence to keep the incumbent from having his way, but they were too numerous and too strongly identified with the parish to give up and go somewhere else. The result was a mounting frustration over many years, leading to the incident of disruption. Nothing of the kind would have happened if the incumbent's practices had commanded a consensus in the congregation. By then, any congregation where there was a consensus could do just about as it pleased without worrying about interference either legal or illegal from without.[130]

5. The Quest For Autonomy

The final item on the High Church agenda, self-government for the church, was not significantly implemented until well into the twentieth century. As we saw, Newman had urged at the start of the Tractarian movement that the leaders of the church prepare to fall back on their apostolic authority in case their temporal honors and substance should be withdrawn. This concern grew more and more urgent as the courts handed down one unacceptable decision after another, beginning with the *Gorham* case in 1850. The High Churchmen felt, rightly or wrongly (mostly, I suspect, the latter), that these decisions could be blamed on the secular provenance of the laws on which they were based, the tribunals deciding them, or both. But for most of the nineteenth century the High Churchmen had neither the theoretical insights nor the political strength to propose and have adopted institutional reforms adequate to their felt needs.

Meanwhile, much of the theory and a certain amount of the politics was being developed in Anglican churches outside England. In this chapter, we will look first at the experience of these churches with self-government, and then at the developments in the same direction in the Church of England itself.

I. The Church Abroad

As the English settled in various parts of the world, they generally took with them both their legal system and their church. But for the most part they left behind their peculiar relation between the one and the other. Accordingly, both the Judicial Committee and the bench of bishops had occasion to deal with churches in various parts of the Empire that were theologically at one with the Church of England, but juridically quite different. Their treatment of these churches sheds light on their understanding both of church polity and of establishment.

By the late eighteenth century, it was widely accepted, contrary to earlier doctrine, that it was one thing to set up a church and an entirely different thing to "establish" it. Earlier theorists had seen the church as a public institution through which the government provided the ministrations of religion in rather the same way it provided highways and police protection through other public institutions. On this theory, Dissenting congregations were private enterprises, run by people who for one reason or another chose to provide religious ministrations for themselves instead of using the ones provided by the government. The relation between public and private schools in the United States gives a fairly good analogy. As far as I can see, "The Church of England as by law established" as Bancroft used the term in the Canons of 1604[1] simply meant the church as set up by the government in the manner just described.

But Bishop William Warburton, in his famous *Alliance between Church and State*, published in 1736, took a very different approach. On his view, churches are set up by anyone who cares to set them up. Then, if the civil magistrate, looking at all the churches on the market, finds one that commands the allegiance of most of his people, he may choose to make an alliance with it for mutual benefit. An established church is one with which such an alliance has been negotiated; a Dissenting church is any other. From the time it emerged, this theory gained ground steadily. By the mid-nineteenth century, it was hardly challenged.

A corollary was that the same church could be established in one place and not in another. The Episcopal Church of Scotland, which had been in abject Dissent since the Revolution of 1688, was thus one with the established Church of England, while if the established Church of Scotland was one with any English church, it was with the Dissenting Presbyterian body. In fact, as the old Presbyterian congregations lapsed into Unitarianism, new ones were set up under trust deeds that expressly proclaimed their unity with the Church of Scotland.[2]

Well into the nineteenth century, there were some people who found it easier to be Episcopalian in England and Presbyterian in Scotland than to be members of the established church in one country and Dissenters in another.[3] Boswell was evidently quite comfortable going to the Anglican church in England and the Presbyterian in Scotland, whereas Johnson would have nothing to do with the latter. A nineteenth century archbishop of Canterbury was criticized by the *Times* for dedicating a Scottish Episcopal cathedral, because he had thereby made himself a Dissenter. At about the same time, an archbishop of York was attacked by Anglo-

Catholics for celebrating in the Church of Scotland, because he had thereby cut himself off from his own communion.

For most of the eighteenth century, official recognition of the Scottish Episcopalians was hindered by their identification with the Stuart cause.[4] The penal statutes, one enacted after each of the Stuart uprisings, did not forbid Anglican worship as such, but they required every Anglican congregation to pray for the king by name, and every minister of such a congregation to exhibit letters of orders from an English bishop. The Scottish Episcopal Church was subject to persecution because it could not meet these conditions.

In 1788, Prince Charles Edward Stuart died, leaving his tattered claim to the throne to his brother Henry, a Roman Catholic cardinal. At that point, the Scottish Episcopalians gave up on the Stuarts and began to pray for King George. In 1792, an act was passed authorizing them to meet freely as long as they signed the Thirty-Nine Articles and prayed for the king, both of which they were now willing to do.

During the period of persecution, there had grown up in Scotland a certain number of English congregations. These routinely met the statutory conditions, called themselves Church of England rather than Episcopal Church of Scotland, and operated in about the same way as Anglican congregations did on the Continent of Europe or in other places where English people lived among foreigners. When the Scottish Episcopal church was emancipated in 1792, the English bishops took the position that these congregations would be sinfully schismatical if they did not submit to the Scottish bishops and the discipline of their church. The English expatriates grumbled a good deal, but they eventually complied.

In a few of the American colonies, mainly in the South, the Church of England was organized and endowed in somewhat the same way as it was in the mother country.[5] In other colonies, it existed only as a group of independent congregations, supported partly by their members, partly by English missionary funds. The bishop of London exercised a modicum of supervision over it. Projects had been moved ever since Laud's time for providing the New World with an episcopate of its own, but every such project was thwarted by the determination of Protestant Dissenters (abetted, it is sometimes suspected, by loose living Anglican parsons in some parts of the South) to have no bishop on their side of the Atlantic. At this remove, the vehemence of the opposition seems odd, but it must be remembered that many of the colonies were founded by people who were trying to escape from the exercise of episcopal authority, and the law was not clear as to whether a bishop would bring that authority with him if he came.

With the independence of the American colonies, it became both possible and necessary for Anglicans to secure their own episcopate.[6] It required an Act of Parliament to enable a bishop to be consecrated in England without taking an oath of allegiance to the king. A suitable act was adopted in 1786, and two Americans were consecrated under it, joining a colleague who had been consecrated by Scottish bishops in Edinburgh without asking anyone's leave.

Both the 1786 act for the Americans and the 1792 act for the Scots excluded their beneficiaries and anyone deriving orders from them from officiating in England. I have not been able to learn or guess the reason for this restriction. It was anomalous, because it permanently barred a class of Anglican ministers from an Anglican ministry for which the entire residue of mankind were either eligible or capable of becoming so. A Roman Catholic or Eastern Orthodox priest, on turning Anglican, had the same rights as any other episcopally ordained clergyman. A Presbyterian or Methodist minister, or a layman, upon satisfying an English bishop of his moral and educational qualifications, could be ordained in the Church of England and placed on an equal footing with the other clergy of that church. But an Anglican clergyman ordained by an American or Scottish bishop could not become a clergyman of the Church of England whatever he did. To be eligible, he needed an episcopal ordination. By statute, the one he had received did not qualify, and by general principles of theology he could not have another. In 1840, the restriction was relaxed to the point of allowing Scots or Americans to officiate one or two days at a time with the permission of the local bishop. Finally, in 1864 an Act of Parliament made it possible for a Scottish Episcopal clergyman, on going through the proper formalities, to become a full-fledged clergyman of the Church of England. The same opportunity was made available to clergy of the American church in 1874.[7]

Meanwhile, with the episcopate in place in the newly independent states, there was less opposition to extending it to the remaining colonies.[8] A bishopric was erected by letters patent of the Crown in Nova Scotia in 1797, followed by others in other parts of the Empire as the nineteenth century progressed. The typical patent empowered the bishop to exercise authority over Anglican churches and clergy in his territory in accordance with the ecclesiastical law currently in force in England. The bishops were paid partly out of public funds (or in India out of funds of the East India Company) assigned by Parliament, partly out of colonial funds assigned by colonial legislatures, and partly out of private trust funds raised in England. In some colonies, their powers were modified in one particular or another by acts of the local legislatures. Their actions were appealable to the Judicial Committee of the Privy Council — whether as colonial appeals or as ecclesiastical appeals was not altogether clear.

But they were not bishops of the Church of England. When one of the early bishops of New Zealand vacated an English benefice to take possession of his see, the government sought to exercise the ancient royal prerogative of filling a benefice vacated by its incumbent becoming a bishop. But the courts allowed this benefice to be filled by the regular patron.[9] The incumbent's consecration made him a bishop in the Church of God, and his patent made him a bishop in New Zealand, but neither made him a bishop to whom the prerogative applied.

By the 1850s, the colonial legislatures were rapidly abolishing the privileges and revenues that they had bestowed on the church earlier in the century, and the home Parliament was on the way to abolishing the church's last remaining access to public funds. At the end of the decade, disestablishment prevailed almost everywhere in the Empire except in the United Kingdom itself, and in India, where the church remained technically established until 1927.[10] In some colonies, including Victoria on one side of the globe and Ontario on the other, the legislature empowered the church to organize itself as a voluntary association. Elsewhere, it did so on its own.

For legal principles to apply to this development, the courts had nowhere to turn except to their experience in dealing with the affairs of the Dissenting congregations that had had legal status in England since the Act of Toleration of 1688.[11] In this material could be found three governing principles. First, the courts would not intervene unless a justiciable right was at stake. Most cases for intervention involved property or emoluments, but burial rights were also justiciable. Whether other religious ministrations were was not decided.

Second, a trust for a religious body was enforceable in the same way as any other charitable trust. If the trust instrument recited that property was to be held for purposes of a certain denomination, the trustees would be required to hold it for those purposes. If the instrument called for the trustees to submit to duly constituted denominational authorities, the courts would make them submit.

Third, the individual members of a congregation impliedly agreed that their participation in its affairs should be governed by the rules of the denomination to which it belonged. This agreement would be enforced by the courts like any other contract.

To these three principles the Judicial Committee, in dealing with the colonial churches, added a fourth. That was that if a church was at one time established and its affairs regulated by law, its members and the trustees of its property would be deemed to have agreed to use the applicable legal rules among themselves when the church was disestablished or carried into a new country. This principle was used not only for the Church of England in the colonies, but also for the Roman Catholic Church in French Canada. Parliament adopted the same principle in 1869, when it disestablished the Anglican Church of Ireland:

> The present ecclesiastical law of Ireland, and the present articles,
> doctrines, rites, rules, discipline, and ordinances of the said Church, with
> and subject to such (if any) modification or alteration as . . . may be duly
> made therein according to the constitution of the said Church for the
> time being, shall be deemed to be binding on the members for the time
> being thereof in the same manner as if such members had mutually
> contracted and agreed to abide by and observe the same, and shall be
> capable of being enforced in the temporal courts in relation to any
> property which under and by virtue of this act is reserved or given to or
> taken and enjoyed by the said church or any members thereof, in the
> same manner and to the same extent as if such property had been
> expressly given, granted, or conveyed upon trust to be held, occupied,
> and enjoyed by persons who should observe and keep and be in all
> respects bound by the said ecclesiastical law, and the said articles,
> doctrines, rites, rules, discipline, and ordinances of the said church,
> subject as aforesaid; but nothing herein contained shall be construed to
> confer on any archbishop, bishop, or other ecclesiastical person any
> coercive jurisdiction whatsoever.[12]

Similar provisions were adopted in 1914 to implement the disestablishment
of the church in Wales.

The application of this last principle was affected by the rules of
evidence. A court could take judicial notice of the law as it stood at the
moment of disestablishment, because that was part of the law of the land.
But any changes after disestablishment were merely changes in private
contracts or private trusts: they would have to be proved by witnesses like
other facts. Thus, in a case out of Canada,[13] the Judicial Committee
applied the canon law as it had been in effect in French territory a hundred
years previously when France ceded Canada to Britain. The question was
whether a man could be denied burial in consecrated ground because he
had belonged to the Institut Canadien, an ecumenical society whose library
included forbidden books. The Judicial Committee found that the French
government had never allowed the canonical rules concerning books to be
enforced in its dominions. Therefore, those rules were not in force in
Canada at the last point of which the courts could take judicial notice. In
the absence of evidence that they had been put into effect among the
Roman Catholics of Canada at some later time, the court would have to
suppose that they were still inapplicable, so that no one could be denied
Roman Catholic burial for violating them.

This was the state of the law when the Anglicans of the colonies began
organizing their independent disestablished churches. The work was done
in most places with only minor dissension and confusion. But in South

Africa it produced several famous litigations and several schisms.[14] It was a combination of personalities, bad luck, and a few endowments left over from an earlier time that made the difference.

Robert Gray, the first bishop of Capetown, was the son of the bishop of Bristol whose palace was burned down by a mob after the first parliamentary reform bill was voted down by the House of Lords in 1831. Owen Chadwick characterizes him as "a moderate Tractarian and a strong Tory, . . . generous and unsubtle, . . . determined to keep heresy out of the Church of England." He was evidently upset by both the doctrinal and the liturgical decisions of the Judicial Committee, for he took care that they should have no place in the affairs of the South African church.

Gray's letters patent were issued in 1847, when there was no legislature in South Africa. Like other such patents, it gave him authority over Anglican churches and clergy, and referred to the ecclesiastical law prevailing in England. Since there was no legislature, the Crown had plenary legislative powers in the colony. Presumably, therefore, Gray had as full authority over his diocese as an English bishop had over his. This situation prevailed until 1853, when the diocese of Capetown had grown to the point that it needed to be divided. To implement the division, Gray turned in his patent, and received a new one covering a smaller diocese, but conferring metropolitan jurisdiction over the two other dioceses set up in his former territory. Patents were also issued to the bishops of these new dioceses, Natal and Grahamstown, subjecting them to the metropolitan jurisdiction of Gray and his successors at Capetown. The new bishops took oaths of canonical obedience to Gray in the same form as the oaths taken by English bishops in favor of their archbishops.

But between 1847 and 1853 the Cape Colony had been provided with a legislature. As a result, the Crown had no legislative powers when the new patents were issued. It could not give back to Gray with the new patent the authority he had surrendered with the old. Gray could no longer exercise any episcopal authority that depended on legislation.[15]

His truncated powers were first put to the test in 1856, when he decided that his diocese should have a synod consisting of clergy plus elected representatives of the laity.[16] His project accorded with recent developments elsewhere in the church. The bishops of Australia and New Zealand had been working with similar bodies since 1850 or so, and Bishop Phillpotts of Exeter had summoned a synod of his clergy in 1851 to hear and endorse his protests against the *Gorham* judgment. Before Phillpotts's proceedings, no diocesan synod had met in England for about two hundred years. It was generally supposed that such synods had been outlawed by the Act for the Submission of the Clergy under Henry VIII. Lord John Russell, however, responding to a question in Parliament, reported that

Phillpotts, although he was acting imprudently, was not acting illegally unless he purported to make canons, which he disclaimed any intention of doing.

The Reverend William Long, minister of one of the parishes in Gray's diocese, objected to Gray's proposed synod

> on the ground that it was contrary to the constitution and other laws and customs of the Church of England that such Synod should be held without the authority of the Crown or the Legislature, and that the laws likely to be made at such Synod would tend to abridge the liberty of Ministers and Members of the Church of England in the Colony . . . .[17]

The second ground suggests that Long was aware of Gray's feelings about the *Gorham* case, as well as of Phillpotts's reason for convening a synod. He refused either to participate himself or to hold an election for lay delegates from his parish. The synod met, and adopted, among other things, a procedure for summoning future synods. Three years later, when a second synod was to meet, Long again refused to participate. This time, he was in violation of a rule established in the previous synod as well as of the bishop's orders. Gray suspended him, and when he ignored the suspension, deprived him.

Long's church, built and endowed a few years previously by a fellow clergyman who retained the right to nominate the first two incumbents, was held by Gray under a trust to maintain it as a parish church with services according to the liturgy of the Church of England. Long himself held a license from Gray to officiate and have the cure of souls in the parish, subject to Gray's episcopal authority and to Gray's right to revoke the license if he should see just cause to do so. On this state of affairs, Long claimed temporal rights in his position, and sued in the temporal courts of the colony for their vindication. He lost, and appealed to the Judicial Committee, which heard his case as a colonial, not an ecclesiastical, appeal.

The Judicial Committee and the South African court were agreed that Gray had no legal authority over Long. His legal status under the 1847 patent lapsed when he turned that patent in, and the Crown had no power to revive it. The more difficult question was whether Long was subject to Gray's authority as an implied term of his contract of employment, or of the trust under which his church was held. This was the question that the South African court had decided in Gray's favor, and the one on which the Judicial Committee reversed.

Gray relied on the oath of canonical obedience taken by Long at his ordination and renewed at his installation into his church, and on the terms of Long's license authorizing the bishop to remove him if he saw just cause to do so. But the Judicial Committee insisted that these dispositions must be interpreted in the light of the general intention to set up an extension of the Church of England, and therefore that English ecclesiastical law, as far as applicable, should be read into them. In short, the contractual relation between Gray and Long should duplicate as far as possible the legal relation between a bishop and a parish incumbent in England.

With that decided, it remained only to determine whether refusing to attend synods or hold elections for them was an ecclesiastical offense in England. The Judicial Committee had no trouble saying it was not. Whether the diocesan synods that had met regularly before King Henry's time could lawfully be revived in the mid-nineteenth century was a debatable — often a hotly debated — question. Phillpotts had gotten away with his assembly more because it was not a traditional synod than because it was. Barring a criminal purpose, anyone who chooses to call a meeting may do so, and meet with anyone who chooses to come. Phillpotts's unfortunate use of the term synod was not a sufficient reason to make him an exception to this salutary rule. He did not try to punish anyone for staying away.

But whatever might be the compulsion to attend a traditional synod if one should be held, Gray's proceeding as the Judicial Committee saw it was not such a synod. The medieval synod consisted of the bishop and clergy of the diocese. There was no precedent for inviting the laity (any more than there was for limiting the clergy to elected representatives as Phillpotts had done). It followed that no English clergyman would be subject to censure for failure to cooperate in the assembling of such a body, and therefore that Long could not be subject to censure either. The Judicial Committee was willing to concede that Long had perhaps been more intransigent than he should have been:

> With the Bishop's authority in spiritual affairs, or Mr. Long's obligations *in foro conscientiae*, we have not to deal.[18]

But as regards things temporal, Long was within his rights.

The suggestion that the bishop might have a broader authority in conscience than he had in law seems, incidentally, to strike a new note. Earlier generations would have said that the bishop's authority was inherently juridical, so that if he did what he had no legal authority to do, his mandates were no more effective in conscience than they were in law.

While Gray was in the last stages of losing his litigation with Long, a new and still more unfortunate litigation was taking shape.[19] When the Capetown diocese was divided in 1853, one of the newly created sees, that of Natal, was bestowed on a learned but unimaginative Cambridge mathematician named John William Colenso. One of the projects on which Colenso embarked on taking possession of his see was the translation of the Scriptures into Zulu. While he was engaged in that project, one of his Zulu assistants flummoxed him completely by asking whether all the events narrated in the first books of the Old Testament had really happened. He found he could not in conscience say that they had. As he had been a literalist all his life, he found the realization harder to cope with than another man might have done. He wrote a book demonstrating such things as the impossibility of carrying enough food on the Ark to feed the number of animals that must have been aboard, and the numerous logistical anomalies that follow from accepting the account in Exodus of how many people participated. Having demolished the literalism in which he had formerly believed, he was not sure what if anything remained of the divine inspiration of Scripture. He concluded with a suitably sententious waffle.[20]

Many people, both in his time and in ours, felt that Colenso was belaboring a man of straw. His use of figures and measurements was made — unfairly in my opinion — the basis for disparaging allusions to his mathematical background. But Colenso was able to show in response to his critics that the opinion he was refuting was by no means rare — that Oxford and Cambridge students were still being told that every word of the Bible was of God's own dictation.

With the views he had come to hold, Colenso was in some doubt as to whether it would be right for him to continue to serve as a bishop of the Church of England. However, it occurred to him that the Henrician bishops who became heroes and martyrs of the Reformation did not abandon their sees when they ceased to believe all the tenets of Roman Catholicism. Rather, they stayed where they were and guided the church into a juster perception of the truth. He was also encouraged by the decision in the *Essays and Reviews* case. He had made considerable use of that volume in his own work, was gratified by the lenient treatment its authors received in the Arches, and was still more gratified by their exoneration by the Judicial Committee.

It was just a month after that exoneration that he was served with a citation to appear before Gray in Capetown and answer a charge of heresy. He refused to appear or to recognize the proceedings. Gray and his assessors entered a judgment finding him guilty and depriving him of his see. He appealed to the Judicial Committee — or, rather, as he put it, he sought the protection of the queen whose patent he held against proceedings purportedly under her patent to Gray. In contemplation of law, it was she who referred the case to the Judicial Committee.

Their decision was for Colenso. If, as we have seen, Gray's 1853 patent gave him no jurisdiction over a clergyman of his own diocese, *a fortiori*, it gave him no jurisdiction over a bishop of another diocese. Then, did he have authority by agreement? Colenso's patent purported to subject him to Gray and his successors as metropolitans. He accepted that patent, and took the same oath of canonical obedience that English bishops take to Canterbury or York. It was held in the *Long* case that whatever jurisdiction existed by law in England existed by consent in South Africa.

The right of a metropolitan to sit in judgment on his suffragans was less clear at the time than it was to become after Bishop King's trial before Archbishop Benson. Both parties argued the question at some length, but the Judicial Committee disposed of it with a mere *ipse dixit*:

> If, then, the Bishop of Capetown had no jurisdiction by law, did he obtain any by contract or submission on the part of the Bishop of Natal? There is nothing on which such an argument can be attempted to be put, unless it be the oath of canonical obedience taken by the Bishop of Natal to Dr. Gray as Metropolitan. The argument must be, that both parties being aware that the Bishop of Capetown had no jurisdiction or legal authority as Metropolitan, the Appellant agreed to give it to him by voluntary submission. But even if the parties intended to enter into any such agreement (of which, however, we find no trace), it was not legally competent to the Bishop of Natal to give, or to the Bishop of Capetown to accept or exercise any such jurisdiction.[21]

This language is odd, because it seems to suppose that Gray can have no claim to consensual jurisdiction except by express agreement, whereas the teaching of the *Long* case is that anyone who accepts a position in a colonial extension of the Church of England impliedly agrees to be bound by the ecclesiastical law of the mother country.

Gray had one more argument. If he had no jurisdiction, then his judgment was without legal effect and there was nothing for Colenso to appeal from. The Judicial Committee made short work of this one also. While Gray had no jurisdiction under the queen's letters patent, he had purported to exercise such jurisdiction, and it was up to the queen, with the advice of her Privy Council, to make him stop.

While all this was going on, Colenso continued publishing. *The Pentateuch and the Book of Joshua Critically Examined* came out in one volume after another, each fortified with a Preface responding to the criticism evoked by its predecessors. In a footnote in one of these Prefaces, he reached what seems to be the crux of the matter:

> Bishop Gray himself, as I conceive, has set an example of departing from the *doctrine* and the *discipline* of the Church of England in attempting to depose a bishop for saying what any Deacon would have the most perfect right and liberty to say in any Parish Church in England.[22]

Gray was determined that the baneful permissiveness foisted on the established church in England by the tribunals of the state should not be duplicated under the free and unestablished conditions prevailing in South Africa. Colenso was equally determined that the freedom of the queen's subjects in matters ecclesiastical should prevail wherever the queen's writ ran.

While the Judicial Committee sided with Colenso in this dispute, the clergy and bishops, by and large, sided with Gray.[23] The Natal clergy with a few exceptions recognized that Colenso was no longer their bishop, and participated in the election of a successor. The successor when elected could not be consecrated in England because it was illegal to consecrate a bishop in England without the queen's license, which was not forthcoming. He could not be consecrated in Scotland because the English bishops persuaded their Scottish colleagues to be cautious. But he was duly consecrated in Capetown by Gray and two other South African bishops: the Judicial Committee's decisions had put it beyond the power of the government to interfere. Once consecrated, he was recognized by all the bishops of England as their colleague in Natal. In fact, he was recognized, at least implicitly, by all the Anglican bishops in the world. The first Lambeth Conference — summoned, at least in part, for Gray's benefit — had resolved that a successor to Colenso, should one be appointed, would be recognized.

But Colenso got the cathedral at Pietermaritzburg.[24] Before the sees were divided, Gray had held the land in trust for the English church in Natal. When Colenso became the bishop of that church, he became the one entitled to use the property. Since he was still the bishop, he was still entitled to use it. The Supreme Court of Natal put Gray out of possession and the Judicial Committee affirmed. Colenso then summoned the dean, who refused to recognize him as bishop, to appear before him on a charge of disobedience, and proceeded to deprive him. The Supreme Court of Natal enforced the deprivation as warranted under English ecclesiastical law. Colenso had the same authority over the dean that the Judicial Committee had given Gray over Long.

Meanwhile, the people who were paying Colenso's salary tried to stop.[25] The Colonial Bishoprics Fund had been set up in 1841 for the purpose of providing bishops for the growing Empire. When the see of Natal was established in 1853, it was funded with an endowment of £ 10,000 out of the capital of this fund, plus an annual payment of £ 300 out of its general revenues. When Gray entered his judgment, the trustees stopped paying both the interest on the endowment (£ 362 a year) and the annual sums. Colenso sued the trustees in the Court of Chancery to have the payments restored. The trustees argued that the Judicial Committee's opinion reversing Gray's judgment had denied the authority of the Crown to create a bishopric by letters patent in a colony that had a legislature. It followed that Colenso did not have such a bishopric, and was not the kind of bishop that the trustees had envisaged when they funded him.

Lord Romilly, Master of the Rolls, rejected this argument. All the Judicial Committee had decided, he said, was that the Crown could not assign a bishop coercive jurisdiction by letters patent. The queen in her capacity as head of the Church of England could still appoint a colonial bishop, who would have the same powers over people in the colony claiming to be members or clergy of the Church of England that an English bishop would have in his diocese. The only difference would be that the colonial bishop would have to resort to the civil courts to enforce his mandates, whereas the English bishop would have a court of his own. This was not enough of a difference to keep Colenso from being the kind of bishop he was originally thought to be.

In delivering his judgment, Romilly discoursed somewhat at large on the status of the Church of England in the colonies:

> If a class of persons in one of the dependencies of the English Crown having an established Legislature, should found a church calling themselves members of the Church of *England*, they would be members of the Church of *England* — they would be bound by its doctrines, its ordinances, its rules, and its discipline, and obedience to them would be enforced by the civil tribunals of the colony over such persons; but if a class of persons should, in any colony similarly circumstanced, call themselves by any other name — such as, for instance the Church of *South Africa* — then the Court would have to inquire, as a matter of fact, upon proper evidence, what the doctrines, ordinances, and discipline of that church were; and when these were made plain, obedience to them would be enforced against all the members of that church. But the fact of calling themselves in communion with the Church of *England* would not make such a church a part of the Church of *England*, nor would it make the members of that church members of the Church of *England*. If they adopted its creed and doctrines, but repudiated a part of its rules and ordinances, they would be bound by those which they had adopted, and not by those which belonged to the Church of *England*, but which they had rejected. It would, however, be incumbent upon them fully and plainly to set forth what their rules and ordinances were, and who accepted them, in order that this might prevent doubt when the Courts of law were called upon to enforce obedience to these rules and ordinances.[26]

As Romilly used it, the distinction between a church in communion with the Church of England and the Church of England itself ran counter to one of the mainstream tenets of Anglican ecclesiology — the autonomy of national churches.[27] According to this doctrine, Anglicanism is committed to allowing the Christians of each civil community to take control of their ecclesiastical affairs and order such matters as are not of divine origin in whatever way seems expedient. When they have done this, all Christians living in or resorting to their territory should unite with them, and all Christians elsewhere should accept them: to do otherwise is to be guilty of schism. This was the principle that justified the English Reformation in the first place. It was the same principle that led the English bishops to encourage the English congregations in Scotland to submit to the Scottish bishops as soon as the latter stopped supporting the Stuarts, and the same principle that led so many Anglicans to resent the establishment of a territorial episcopate by the Roman Catholics in England.

A corollary was the relation between political and ecclesiastical independence. It went without saying that when the United States became independent of the British Crown, the Protestant Episcopal Church in the United States became independent of the Church of England. Similarly, it went without saying that the Episcopalians of the Southern states separated from their Northern brethren in 1861, and rejoined them in 1865. It followed that if New Zealand or Jamaica or Ontario or South Africa deserved its own legislature, it deserved its own ecclesiastical government. Anglican ecclesiology admits of only one Anglican church in any one territory, and that church should advance toward self-government as rapidly as the territory to which it ministers. It made sense also for that church to be called by the name of that territory. The Anglicans of South Africa had as much right to call themselves the Church of South Africa as those of England had to call themselves the Church of England. The Church of England in South Africa was a contradiction in terms.

The real issue in all this was the authority of the Judicial Committee. When Romilly referred to English ecclesiastical law, the much criticized doctrinal and liturgical decisions of that body were uppermost in his mind. By the same token, while colonial churchmen had other important theoretical and practical reasons for wanting control of their own affairs, the desire to be free of those decisions was uppermost in their minds. They were much less concerned with retention of authority by English ecclesiastics. Gray's ill-fated patent as metropolitan of Capetown would have made his decisions appealable to the archbishop of Canterbury. He made no objection to the archbishop's jurisdiction, although he was adamant in rejecting that of the Judicial Committee.

Romilly offered the colonial churchmen two alternatives. If they called themselves the Church of England, the law as laid down by the Judicial Committee would be imposed on them by colonial courts whose decisions were appealable to the same Committee. If, on the other hand, they called themselves by some other name, they could either subject themselves voluntarily to the Judicial Committee's decisions or cut themselves off from any funds or property destined for the expansion of the Church of England in their colony.

Most churches chose the first horn of this dilemma. The Anglican churches in Australia and New Zealand were called the Church of England through the 1970s; the Anglican church in Canada was called the Church of England until 1955. The choice proved to be a wise one. The theoretical subjection of these churches to the doctrinal and liturgical decisions of the Judicial Committee never came into play, because no doctrinal or liturgical questions reached the civil courts. Since the colonial churches were not established, their internal disputes reached the courts only if some temporal right turned on them. No worshipper could take a clergyman to court for wearing illegal vestments or introducing a stone altar or lighting candles.[28] Such questions could come before a bishop or an ecclesiastical tribunal, but these were not courts, and the Judicial Committee had no appellate jurisdiction over them. If a clergyman had been put out of a benefice for doctrinal error, the case would have been different: he could have litigated in the civil courts as Long did, and the civil courts would have applied the *Gorham* case and the *Essays and Reviews* case to protect him. But the colonial churches produced no Colenso outside of South Africa, and if they produced a Gorham or two, they did not produce a Phillpotts to attack him.

Meanwhile, the South African church experienced the consequences of choosing the second of Romilly's alternatives.[29] In the constitution it adopted in 1870, it took the name of the Church of the Province of South Africa. It accepted the doctrine, sacraments, and discipline set forth in the formularies of the Church of England, but added the following proviso:

> Provided . . . , that in the interpretation of the aforesaid standards and formularies the Church of this province be not held to be bound by decisions in questions of faith and doctrine or in questions of discipline relating to faith and doctrine other than those of its own ecclesiastical tribunals, or of such other tribunal as may be accepted by the provincial synod as a tribunal of appeal.

Among the clergymen who played a prominent part in the framing of this constitution was the Very Reverend Frederick Henry Williams, D.D., dean of the cathedral at Grahamstown. He continued to play a prominent part in the affairs of the Church of the Province of South Africa until 1875, when he seems to have fallen out with his bishop. In 1878, there was a dispute between him and the bishop over whether he could exclude the bishop from preaching in the cathedral. He evidently claimed, quite erroneously, that a dean had this right under English law. Proceedings ensued in the South African ecclesiastical tribunals resulting in a judgment that Williams refused to obey. The bishop then resorted to the civil courts. There, Williams took the position that he was a clergyman of the church of England occupying a building belonging to that church, and that neither he nor his building had anything to do with the church of which the plaintiff was bishop. The South African courts sustained him in that contention, and the Judicial Committee affirmed.

As the Committee saw it, the building was held on a trust to be used as a place of worship by the Church of England. No act of Williams identifying him with another church could change the terms of the trust. Therefore, unless the Church of the Province of South Africa was one with the Church of England, the bishop could not prevail:

> If . . . the plaintiff belongs to a religious body which cannot claim to be in connection with the Church of England as by law established, no contract with the defendant, or with any one else, can give him a right to use property which is settled to uses in connection with that Church.[30]

This language is followed by an interesting disclaimer:

> In conducting this examination, their Lordships do not enter into the discussions whether or not the Church of South Africa is a branch of or identical with the Church of England. What the charters of the endowment now in question require is connection with the Church of England as by law established . . . .

The notion implicit in this language that the church is one thing and the church as by law established is another is new, indeed, unique, in the annals of ecclesiology. It is as inconsistent with Warburton's notion of establishment (establishment = the bestowal of privileges on a church by the state) as it is with Bancroft's (establishment = organizing and providing for the church in a particular place). I suspect it bespeaks a certain skittishness on the part of the Committee, resulting from its constant repudiation by so many churchmen.

The Committee then sets out to determine the main question — whether the South African church has the requisite connection with the Church of England as by law established. They find the above proviso about judicial tribunals to be an insuperable obstacle. Given the circumstances of the colony, there must be a difference in polity between the two churches. But there is no reason why there cannot be "a substantial identity in their standards of faith and doctrine." The proviso indicates that the Church of South Africa explicitly and unnecessarily repudiates such an identity.

Necessarily, therefore, it is a different church from the Church of England:

> Their Lordships were strongly invited by the respondent's counsel to connect the proviso under consideration with the course of some well known controversies. There is no judicial ground for saying that it was aimed at any special practice or doctrine. But its practical effect may well be illustrated by reference to some important decisions of Her Majesty in Council. For instance, the decisions in the cases of *Gorham* v. *Bishop of Exeter* and *Williams* v. *Bishop of Salisbury*, both delivered prior to the Synod of 1870, affirm and secure the right of a clergyman of the Church of England to preach freely the doctrines which were there in question; but in the Church of South Africa, a clergyman preaching the same doctrines may find himself presented for, and found guilty of heresy. Such a reservation on the part of the Church of South Africa must tend to silence and to exclude those whom the decisions of Her Majesty in Council would protect in the Church of England.
>
> The decisions referred to form part of the constitution of the Church of England as by law established, and the Church and the tribunals which administer its laws are bound by them. That is not the case as regards the Church of South Africa. The decisions are no part of the constitution of that Church, but are expressly excluded from it. There is not the identity in standards of faith and doctrine which appears to their Lordships necessary to establish the connection required by the trusts on which the Church of St. George is settled.[31]

The upshot of this case and Colenso's cases was that there came to be a splinter group in South Africa calling itself the Church of England and occupying endowments intended for that church, but with which the real Church of England would have nothing to do. The Anglican communion worldwide recognized the Church of the Province of South Africa as their local branch, and treated the Church of England in South Africa as schismatic.[32]

When Williams and his bishop were both dead, the trustees of Grahamstown cathedral restored the building to the Church of the Province of South Africa by appointing the new bishop to be incumbent in Williams's place. The properties that Colenso took into schism with him were turned over (restored, if you prefer) to the Church of the Province of South Africa by an act of the Natal legislature in 1910, just before it was superseded by the Parliament of the new Union of South Africa. Provisos in the legislation protected the incumbents from being subjected to any doctrinal or disciplinary requirement that could not have been imposed in England.

None of these measures solved the problem of schism in South Africa. Other clergymen and congregations took advantage of the Judicial Committee's judgments to follow the course taken by Long, Colenso, and Williams, and so keep the Church of England in South Africa in a continuous if tenuous existence. Thanks to Gray's zeal for taking definite stands, the Church of the Province of South Africa was committed to a series of positions that tended to exclude a small but definite segment of Anglican thought and practice that could be reasonably comfortable with the situation in other branches of Anglicanism. With or without endowments, the Church of England in South Africa continued to attract people from this segment, and continued to receive support and encouragement from such people elsewhere, despite being officially disowned by all mainstream Anglican churches. In 1954, a retired English bishop from North Africa restored to this body the episcopate that it had lacked since Colenso died in 1883.

The South African litigations and the experience of setting up colonial churches had a profound effect on the consciousness of Anglicans in the mother country. It taught them to distinguish between ecclesiastical authority, resting on Apostolic descent, as Newman argued in the first *Tract for the Times*, and temporal authority, resting on the conditions under which a church is set up in a particular time and place. The High Churchmen had been voicing this distinction ever since the Judicial Committee began deciding cases the wrong way in 1850, but the whole episcopate became committed to it when they accepted a successor to Colenso. Eventually, as I have shown in a couple of quotations, even the Judicial Committee accepted it.

If there was an apostolic authority in the bishops, the colonial experience also brought forward a legitimate authority in the worshippers and contributors who kept the church going. In England, that authority had long been attached to the state, but it was not inherent in the state *qua* state as the sixteenth and seventeenth century Anglicans had supposed. It could and probably should be exercised by the churchgoing laity in a pluralist state — a state, that is, such as the civil societies of the colonies were from the outset, and such as the mother country had now become. The Church of England was now ready for institutions of self-government such as its daughter churches had.

II. The Growth of Self-Government

The period of institutional reform beginning in the 1830s found the church with no very promising set of institutions to exercise whatever expanded powers of self-government it ought to possess. Of the three branches recognized by political theory, the legislative was in the worst case. At least since the Restoration in 1660, whatever legislating needed to be done had been done by Parliament. In 1829, Roman Catholics were made eligible to sit in Parliament (as Protestant Dissenters had always been). The concession gravely attenuated any claim of Parliament to be the voice of the Anglican laity. At the same time, the reformed franchise and the growth of utilitarianism piled secular business on Parliament to such an extent that church legislation could often not get the floor time it required. The legislators' lack of sympathy with the concerns of the church has perhaps been exaggerated — but their preoccupation was real enough.

As we have seen, the church's own legislatures were in almost total abeyance. The Convocations of the two provinces held perfunctory or ceremonial meetings when Parliament met, but they transacted no business. No diocesan synods were held, and it was generally supposed that none could be held without a license from the Crown. The parish vestries may have retained a residual legislative power in local church matters, but they went no farther than to appoint churchwardens and vote on the hated churchrates. Like Parliament, they were open to Roman Catholics and Dissenters as fully as to Anglicans, and, except in new parishes, they had more secular than ecclesiastical business to do.

The executive branch above the parish level consisted mainly of archbishops, bishops, and archdeacons. Archbishops and bishops were appointed by the Crown. The traditional formality of election by the cathedral chapter was preserved, but the chapter was required by a statute of Henry VIII to elect the person named by the Crown and no other. If they failed to do so — it never happened — the Crown could fill the see by letters patent. Most archdeacons were appointed by their respective diocesan bishops, though a few archdeaconries were benefices in other patronage.

These prelates were probably sufficient in zeal, number, and competence to do what was traditionally expected of them — the administrative and pastoral tasks detailed in the first chapter of this volume. A modest increase in the episcopate was being called for as early as the 1830s, but the need did not become urgent until a decade or two later, as the gradual accumulation of new administrative duties under the reform legislation came to be felt, and standards of pastoral presence came to be raised under the proddings of the Victorian conscience.

The judicial power of the church was exercised mainly by a consistory court in each diocese, an appellate court in each province (the Arches Court of Canterbury and the Chancery Court of York) and the Judicial Committee of the Privy Council, which had replaced the old Court of Delegates under a statute of 1833. There were also provincial probate courts with significant jurisdiction. Lesser courts, those of the archdeacons and of certain peculiar jurisdictions, were largely moribund, although a few of them still did work.

Most of the business of these courts was concerned with the probate and matrimonial litigation that was to be taken away from them in 1857. Their judges and lawyers were learned in both civil and canon law. They had their own Inn of Court, Doctors Commons, and served the admiralty courts as well as the ecclesiastical. As we have seen, the whole apparatus had only a tenuous connection with the pastoral mission of the church. It served more as a limitation on the power of the bishops than as an exercise of it.

A. Legislative.[33]

In the early 1850s, the Canterbury Convocation resuscitated itself under its own power. It simply lingered longer and longer over its sessions, and then began appointing committees to consider matters between sessions and report back. The ground had been prepared by some years of discussion, reinforced by two notable events of 1850, the *Gorham* judgment and the restoration of the Roman Catholic hierarchy. It was widely felt that there was need for an agency to condemn people like Gorham, and widely felt — not necessarily by the same people — that there was need for an agency to resist the pope. Most government ministers and lay leaders in Parliament remained unconvinced, but the law officers of the Crown determined that there was no legal obstacle to a Convocation meeting as long as it cared to if it did not try to make canons. There was debate over whether the archbishop could prorogue a session without the consent of a majority of the bishops in attendance, but Archbishop Sumner, a mild-mannered opponent of revival, did not care to try conclusions with Bishop Wilberforce, a hard-driving supporter of it. The government could have prorogued any session at any time by means of a royal writ, but the political forces pro and con were so nicely balanced that neutrality seemed the wisest course. The government might still have interfered if the sessions had been longer or more controversial than they were, but in the first few years the meetings remained brief and the committees made useful reports on nonpartisan questions. By the end of the decade, the innocuousness of the whole process had won over most of the opponents, and the Canterbury Convocation went its own way from then on. York followed in 1861, after the death of a solidly intransigent archbishop who kept his Convocation from meeting by locking the chapter house.

Once firmly revived, the Convocations took on a wide range of concerns.[34] They monitored ecclesiastical legislation pending in

Parliament. They deplored the Ecclesiastical Commissioners, the disestablishment of the Church of Ireland, and the declaration of papal infallibility by the First Vatican Council. They adopted a Harvest Service and wondered if it would violate the Act of Uniformity to use it. They proposed legislation that did not get enacted, and opposed legislation that did. They puzzled over discipline, Ritualism, and church weddings for divorced people, just as everyone else in the church did. By condemning *Essays and Reviews* and supporting Gray against Colenso, they laid the foundation for the recognition of a set of official Anglican positions not subject to either Parliament or the courts.

Where there was real disagreement, the Convocations could not resolve it.[35] In the 1870s, the government actually authorized them to propose revisions to the Prayer Book. The results were useful in a couple of peripheral areas — a shortened daily prayer service and an alternative lectionary — but they addressed the major liturgical controversies only tentatively, ambiguously, and in a way that Parliament could never be expected to accept.

The value of the Convocations as a sounding-board for clerical opinion was impaired by their concern with juridical status. For instance, in 1859, before they could put together a protest against the new divorce law, the Lower House of Canterbury had to debate whether the objection was that it changed the law of the church without consulting Convocation, or that it set the law of the state at variance with that of the church. The purists insisted on the latter formula because only Convocation could change the law of the church. They lost on a close vote.[36] In other cases, the Convocations hesitated to propose legislation to Parliament, either because members felt that the subject was not properly Parliament's concern, or because they felt that their status would be undermined if Parliament were to amend their duly enacted proposals without consulting them. In short, their understanding of their legal position demanded that they participate directly in the legislative process, but was inimical to the negotiation and compromise required to make such participation effective. Indeed, one of the most powerful voices in the Lower House of Canterbury during the first forty years of its revival was the redoubtable and long-lived George Anthony Denison, for whom nothing religious was negotiable, and all compromise was betrayal.

Parliament as a whole was, like the government, not at all receptive to the claims of the Convocations.[37] It persisted in receiving reports on ecclesiastical matters without referring them to Convocation. There were two statutes adopted in the seventies, both involving Prayer Book revision, which the Convocations had in fact approved before they were adopted, but in one of them the reference to that approval was amended out before the bill was passed. Like their fourteenth century predecessors, the Commons of England were not disposed to be under the authority of the clergy any farther than their ancestors had been.

Part of the problem was that historically Convocation was not the church's legislature as distinguished from the state's legislature. It was the agency for the participation of the clergy, as one of the estates of the realm, in the general deliberation over public affairs. The *gravamina* and *articuli cleri* that the nineteenth century Convocations were adopting on medieval precedent were intended to be the grievances and petitions not of the church but of the clergy. To be sure, Canon 139 of the Canons of 1604 affirms that "the sacred synod of this nation in the name of Christ, and by the king's authority assembled" is "the true church of England by representation." Presumably, the two Convocations constitute the sacred synod in question: there is no other candidate. But the description is far from traditional.

The claim of the Convocations to speak for the whole church was vitiated by their composition as well as by their history.[38] The Lower House in each province consisted of the deans of all the cathedrals and some collegiate churches, all the archdeacons, one elected representative of each cathedral chapter, and two representatives elected by the beneficed clergy of each diocese in Canterbury, each archdeaconry in York. Thus, the working clergy in the parishes were inadequately represented, and the laity were not represented at all. Archbishop Tait argued that since most of the ex officio members owed their positions directly or indirectly to the government, they could be regarded as representing the laity. Those who favored lay participation in church affairs were not persuaded.

But any change in the membership of the Lower House would require either a canon or an Act of Parliament, and neither could be put through without the cooperation of the government. The government's attitude toward the whole Convocation project ranged from ambivalence to hostility, depending on who was in office. It generally seemed better, therefore, to rely on the precarious tolerance enjoyed by the bodies as historically constituted, rather than to seek the active support needed for change.

Accordingly, other expedients were developed for involving the laity in governing the church. Various private organizations were set up, including the openly partisan Church Association and English Church Union, the rather more broadly based Church Institution, and the periodic Church Congresses, which were practically an open forum for anyone who cared to attend. None of these bodies had any legal status, but they got attention through the size and fervor of their constituencies, the prestige of their leaders, the cogency of their deliberations, or some combination of the three.

Meanwhile, at the parochial and diocesan level, institutions were being developed that offered a more systematic lay involvement, though still one without legal status. As early as the 1870s, churchmen in some parishes were electing voluntary parish councils to advise incumbents who felt the need of advice that the vestries could not provide. Bills were occasionally introduced in Parliament to make such councils general and provide them with statutory powers, but nothing came of them — perhaps because their proponents had a not too well hidden agenda of checking liturgical innovation by the clergy. But voluntary councils continued to be set up, and finally, in 1897, the bishops recommended that every parish have one. At the same time, as the vestries shed their secular functions, more and more of them became vehicles for lay churchmen to advise incumbents.

Diocesan "conferences" developed during the 1870s and 80s. They were called conferences instead of synods because, unlike the traditional synods, they included elected representatives of the clergy instead of all the clergy of the diocese, and in most dioceses they included a lay element as well. The lay representatives were often elected by the parish churchwardens (or such of them as were churchmen) from among their number, although as parish councils developed they came to participate in the process in many dioceses. The constitution of the conferences varied a good deal from one diocese to another, as did the subjects with which they dealt and the importance the bishop attached to them.

By the early eighties, there were enough of these conferences in place so that a Central Council of Diocesan Conferences could claim to speak with a good deal of authority in church affairs. But this somewhat informal body was soon superseded by Houses of Laity set up by the two Convocations. Such a house met in Canterbury Province in 1886. It consisted of representatives elected by the lay members of the diocesan conferences, eight from London, six each from four other dioceses, and four each from the rest. It had power to deliberate over anything the Convocation customarily considered, excepting only matters of doctrine. A similar body was set up in York in 1892. It remained only to consolidate the two Convocations to provide a body in which both clergy and laity could meet and deliberate on behalf of the entire church. This was done with the establishment of the Representative Church Council in 1903. This body combined the Upper Houses of both Convocations into a House of Bishops, the Lower Houses into a House of Clergy, and the Houses of Laymen into one House of Laymen.

Not surprisingly, the First World War was for many people an occasion for religious reflection, and for many an occasion for new openness to institutional reform. As a result, it was possible when the war was over to put through Parliament a program for giving official status and powers to the unofficial governing apparatus that the church had been developing

over the past decades.[39] The two archbishops had appointed a committee
in 1913 that reported three years later with a detailed plan and draft
legislation to implement it. Randall Davidson, archbishop of Canterbury
and veteran of half a century of church-state encounters, kept the matter in
abeyance for the remainder of the war. His pragmatic approach caused a
good deal of frustration to the enthusiasts for immediate liberation, led by
William Temple, who was to occupy the see of Canterbury during another
war. But when the right moment came — the moment when wartime
preoccupations were over and peacetime preoccupations had not yet set in
— the combination of Temple's fervor and Davidson's pragmatism concluded
the matter with elegant success.

The plan reported out by the archbishops' committee in 1916 called for
regularizing the constitutions of the diocesan conferences and parochial
church councils, setting them up where they were not yet in place, and
assigning legislative powers to the tricameral Representative Church
Council formed in 1903. Lay representation at every level was to be based
on an electoral roll to which any baptized and confirmed member of the
Church of England could be admitted on application. The roll was to be
kept parish by parish, and eligible persons could be enrolled either where
they resided or where they habitually worshipped.

The legislative powers of the Church Council were to be exercised by
adopting "measures" with the concurrence of all three houses. Measures
were to be presented to both houses of Parliament and to an Ecclesiastical
Committee of the Privy Council. Either house could prevent a measure
from becoming law by passing a resolution within forty days disallowing it.
If it was not disallowed in this way, the Ecclesiastical Committee, if it saw
fit, could present it for the Royal Assent. On receiving that assent, it
would have the force of an Act of Parliament. The procedure was not
unlike that used in many secular regulatory schemes where delegated
legislative power was to be exercised by ministers or administrative
agencies.

Before the plan was presented to Parliament in 1919, it was amended by
changing the name of the Church Council to the National Assembly of the
Church of England, by making women eligible for election to the House of
Laity (rather than the House of Lay*men*), and by eliminating the
requirement that laypeople seeking inclusion on the electoral rolls be
confirmed.[40] Otherwise, it went before Parliament in just about the form
in which it had come out of the committee three years earlier.

Some care was required in choosing the way to present it. The
prevailing view of establishment, as we have seen, was that it is a
negotiated relation between a self-sufficient state and a self-sufficient
church. On this view, it would not do to embody the constitutions of the

various church councils in a statute, because doing so would mean that the constitution of the church was bestowed by Parliament rather than internally generated. On the other hand, Parliament could not be expected to bestow legislative powers without knowing who was going to exercise them.

The solution was to put the constitutional provisions in an appendix to identical addresses from the two Convocations to the king:

> We desire to lay before Your Majesty a recommendation agreed to by both Houses of this Convocation on the 8th day of May 1919, that, subject to the control and authority of Your Majesty and of the two Houses of Parliament, powers in regard to legislation touching matters concerning the Church of England shall be conferred on the National Assembly of the Church of England constituted in the manner set forth in the Appendix attached to this Address.

The Enabling Act presented to Parliament then simply conferred powers on the Assembly as so constituted.

The cause of self-government for the church elicited less enthusiasm in Parliament than it did in church circles. The Enabling Act had rough going in the House of Lords until Davidson saved it with a minimalist version of what it was intended to accomplish. There was no need to make an ideological case against Parliament as the church's legislature: it simply could not do the job. Davidson showed the mountain of ecclesiastical legislation that had been required to implement the great reforms of the early Victorian period, and showed how impossible it was for a twentieth-century Parliament to expend the time and effort needed to update this mass of material, let alone embark on comparable legislative efforts addressed to more recent concerns.

Thus persuaded, the Lords voted down one or two totally destructive amendments. They did, however, make a drastic alteration in the provision for turning Assembly measures into law. They did away with the role of the Privy Council in the process and increased that of Parliament. They replaced the proposed Ecclesiastical Committee of the Council with a joint committee of the two Houses of Parliament. This committee examines measures sent up from the Assembly, and reports on them to the Houses,

> stating the nature and legal effect of the measure and its views as to the expediency thereof, especially with relation to the constitutional rights of all His Majesty's subjects.

After seeing a draft of the report, the Legislative Committee of the Assembly may withdraw the measure; otherwise it goes before the Houses with the report attached. Instead of becoming law unless it is vetoed, as it would have done under the original bill, every measure must now be voted upon. Each House may vote it up or down, but may not amend it. If both Houses approve, it is submitted for the Royal Assent, and, on receiving that assent, has the force of an Act of Parliament. Davidson made no difficulty about accepting this increase in the role of Parliament in the process. Evidently, his willingness to do so disarmed any remaining opposition, for after it was passed by the Lords, the amended bill went through the Commons by a vote of 304 to 16.[41]

The scheme thus adopted continued in effect with only slight changes until 1969; in its most important features, it continues in effect today. It has evidently not lived up either to the expectations of its more enthusiastic supporters or to the forebodings of its opponents. It has probably done about what Davidson and his fellow pragmatists had in mind. Here is a somewhat rueful assessment from the 1948 biography of William Temple, leader of the enthusiasts during the years preceding the Enabling Act:

> Generally, it may be said that at the outset there was a sharp and fateful struggle between two groups in the National Church Assembly who differed widely in their conception of its policy and purpose and may be called, roughly, the legalists and the moralists. The struggle was a brief one. The legalists — of whom Sir Lewis Dibdin, the trusted adviser of Randall Davidson, will be remembered as the leader — were soon in control; the voice of the Assembly is now the voice of the administrator, not of the prophet; and so long as its constitution and time-table remain unrevised (so that, for instance, few of the laity outside the more or less leisured classes can spare the time to attend the sessions) its present tone and temper will persist. A case can be made out for the contention that the Assembly was never intended to provide a platform for the prophet — the question where exactly in the temple of the National Church a niche can be found for that sadly neglected but scripturally essential figure still awaits our answer — and if it be granted that the object of the Assembly is to reorganize the administration and finances of the Church, its members deserve credit for many useful reforms which it might have taken two generations to effect under the old system of passing church Bills through Parliament. The power in the Church remains exactly where it was before, but at least it has a constitutional sanction in the hands of the bishops, archdeacons, and "elder statesmen," who now direct the procedure and control the policy of the National Assembly of the Church of England.[42]

Measures adopted in accordance with the Enabling Act have appeared in the statute books almost every year since 1920 — sometimes only one or two, sometimes as many as eight. Of the 1,264 pages in the current (1986) Ecclesiastical Law volume of *Halsbury's Statutes*, 488 pages are Acts of

Parliament; the other 776, about 61% of the total, are measures. Most of these measures have been discussed in their places in this volume. They have obviously done important work in reforming anomalies and anachronisms and responding to new conditions. But taken in bulk they are a bit disconcerting. They have surely made the Church of England the most legislated-for ecclesial body in Christendom. It is hard not to wonder if the need for all this legislation would have been felt if there had not been such well-oiled machinery available for enacting it.[43]

Most of the time, Parliament has made little difficulty about passing the measures submitted to it. In the usual case, the Ecclesiastical Committee of the two houses examines the measure and reports it favorably. It then receives a brief, courteous, and intelligent discussion before a sparsely attended session of each house, and is sent up, often without a division, for the Royal Assent.

Occasionally, though, the church legislators have evoked a backlash in one house or the other by pursuing their utilitarian goals without sufficient regard for considerations of history or esthetics.[44] The first parliamentary veto was cast by the House of Lords in 1925, when they rejected by one vote a measure that would have reduced the ancient see of Hereford to insignificance by attaching the county of Shropshire to a new diocese of Shrewsbury. Two years later, the Commons decisively defeated a measure to tear down superfluous London churches and sell the sites. The question of what to do with "redundant" churches has continued to cause tension between the pastoral concerns of the church legislators and the architectural and historical concerns of Parliament. In 1952, it produced the only Act of Parliament regarding internal church affairs since the establishment of the Church Assembly. As recently as 1982, it resulted in one of the Pastoral Measures having some rough going in the Ecclesiastical Committee.

Other objections to measures have been more technical. For instance, several measures concerning clerical placement or tenure have been objected to because they failed to include procedural safeguards for the clergy affected. More often than not, measures open to objections of this kind are turned aside at the committee stage and do not reach the floor of Parliament. The Ecclesiastical Committee is careful to note such matters, and the church's Legislative Committee routinely withdraws a measure rather than let it go before Parliament with an unfavorable report. In any event, if the objections are merely technical or procedural, the offending measure is generally corrected, resubmitted, and passed.[45]

A few measures have raised serious doctrinal or constitutional issues for parliamentary debate. The most important of these was the measure for a new Prayer Book, which the House of Commons caused great bitterness and astonishment by voting down in 1927 and again in 1928. The debates were long (over three hundred columns of Hansard in 1928), thorough, articulate, and, above all, instructive.[46]

The prevailing arguments — those against the new Prayer Book — even if they were not irresistible, did not lack weight. The most important of them was that the Church of England was a national church, and as such accountable to the whole nation, not just to its own activist members. The broad spectrum of religious opinion, affiliation, and practice represented in the House of Commons was, therefore, better qualified to represent the affected laity than were the members of the Church Assembly, who were set apart from the general population by their more than common interest in church administration and their more than common free time to participate in it. Furthermore, the innovations were all in a Catholic direction. The machinery of the church had fallen into the hands of an obscurantist minority who would undo the Reformation, and it was up to the red-blooded Protestants in Parliament ("Play the man, Master Ridley!") to keep them from having their way. Furthermore, the innovators tended to be lawless folk. They had paid little attention to the old rules: could there be any hope of confining them within the new ones?

The main rebuttal argument was that the church had in fact spoken through its proper institutions. If any Anglican layman was not represented in the Assembly, it was his own fault for not voting when he had the chance. Establishment should be regarded as an alliance between church and state, not a general mandate for state institutions to run the church. Furthermore, the Church of England was never a merely Protestant body. It had always attempted to maintain a compromise under which people of Protestant and Catholic tendencies could live together. The proposed innovations were intended to keep that compromise in effect. If a satisfactory compromise could be adopted, all but a few extremists would live up to it.

The arguments that prevailed in 1927 and 1928 continue to be raised by a diminishing band of dissidents whenever a measure comes up that seems to call for them. The progress of ecumenism in recent years has blunted some of the concern for safeguarding the principles of the Reformation, although a few hard-core Protestants have taken up the traditional cudgels when a measure has come up that would reverse one of the great nineteenth century liturgical judgments by legalizing a practice such as stone altars or Eucharistic vestments. Recent liturgical innovations have concerned language more than doctrine, and the dissent has planted itself more on tradition than on theology. But whatever other points they make, the dissidents depend most strongly on the constitutional arguments they used in 1927 and 1928 — that they, and not the ecclesiastical legislators, are the true representatives of ordinary English churchpeople.

The last few measures that brought dissidents out in some force were the Ecclesiastical Jurisdiction Measure, 1963, which abolished the jurisdiction of the Judicial Committee over doctrinal and liturgical cases, but retained the bishop's power to veto the prosecution of such cases; the Church of England (Worship and Doctrine) Measure, 1974, which authorized the church to adopt liturgical alternatives to the Prayer Book without further resort to Parliament; and the Appointment of Bishops Measure, 1984, which would have done away with the traditional formalities accompanying the queen's appointment of a bishop.[47] The dissidents lost 182-60 in 1963 and 145-45 in 1974, but they won 32-17 in 1984. Their 1984 success was evidently due in part to the lateness of the hour — debate began at 10:40 P.M., and the division was taken at 12:21 A.M. Even so, it has been taken to indicate that the old constitutional arguments are still not dead.

The National Assembly did not supersede the two Convocations. They continued in existence, and supplied the members for the two clerical houses of the Assembly. A 1920 measure and a canon to implement it increased the representation of the working clergy in their houses, and a 1966 Act of Parliament authorized the queen to summon and dissolve the Convocations independently of her summoning and dissolution of Parliament.[48] Since measures of the National Assembly had the force of Acts of Parliament, the Convocations continued to speak for the church wherever legislation with that force was not appropriate or not politically possible. Making regulations for exchanging pulpits with non-Anglican ministers falls into the first category; making regulations for religious orders probably falls into the second. Of particular interest is the declaration by both Convocations in 1929 that they would not regard the use of the 1928 Prayer Book as "inconsistent with loyalty to the Church of England" despite its rejection by Parliament.

There is a good deal of opinion that the "acts" of Convocation, officially adopted by both houses and proclaimed by the archbishop as presiding officer, should be regarded as binding on the consciences of church members:

> An Act of Convocation is in no sense a law, but simply a rule or regulation which expresses the spiritual will of the Church in the Province; yet, for the maintenance of spiritual discipline, authority, unity, and uniformity within the fellowship of the Church it is very necessary that such rules should be recognized, known, and obeyed.[49]

This passage is interesting. To say a rule or regulation that it is very necessary to obey is in no sense a law is to make a highly debatable claim about the nature of law. There are certainly legal theorists (more often American than English, to be sure) who say that nothing is law unless a policeman or sheriff will enforce it. If they are right, then admittedly acts of Convocation are not laws. But the older, and in my opinion better, tradition is that law is primarily a set of authoritative prescriptions binding people's consciences — just what the above passage claims that acts of Convocation are.

I have no doubt that the framers of the Submission of the Clergy Act, 1534, would have thought that they had forbidden any claim of any sort to bind people's consciences without the Royal Assent.[50] Their prohibition specifically extended to any "canons, constitutions, or ordinances provincial by whatsoever name or names they may be called." Christopher St. Germain, the leading Henrician legal theorist, thought it was morally unacceptable for a churchman to regard himself as bound in conscience by an ecclesiastical enactment that the king's law made unenforceable. To do so would be "setting a conscience where none is, and regard[ing] not the law of the realm, that will discharge his conscience in this behalf."

But whatever people thought in 1534, it appears that more recent opinion will not set limits on the ability of church authorities to bind church members *in foro conscientiae*. The acts of Convocation therefore came out with a good deal of regularity during the years following the establishment of the Church Assembly, and received such respect as anyone cared to give them.[51]

With the full development of alternative devices for the central legislation of the church, there came to be four levels of such legislation in general use:

1. Measures, adopted by the three houses of the Church Assembly, approved by both houses of Parliament, and submitted for the Royal Assent. The Royal Assent is routine, since it is given or withheld on the advice of the government, and if the government opposes a measure it will not go through Commons. These measures have the force of acts of Parliament.

2. Canons, adopted by the two houses of Convocation, and submitted for the Royal Assent. These are legally binding on the clergy, and the courts, both lay and ecclesiastical, will enforce them where only clergy are involved. Under the 1736 case of *Middleton* v. *Crofts*, they do not bind the laity.[52] It was suggested in 1947 that their scope might be expanded to cover laypeople claiming the ministrations of the church, but no explicit expansion was adopted. Whether the courts would themselves make such an extension in an appropriate place remains to be seen. On some subjects, canons have been preferred to measures because it was felt that they could be more flexibly applied. On others, they have been preferred because someone's church-state doctrine rendered the subject unsuitable for consideration by Parliament. Since the government

has no chance to pass on a canon until it is submitted for the Royal Assent, that assent is not routine in the case of canons. Indeed, until the 1960s, the various governments were very chary indeed of advising it. In 1964, however, a whole new code was put through the process, replacing that of 1604.

3. Acts of Convocation, as just discussed.
4. Subordinate or delegated legislation.[53] Allowing government officials and commissions to fill in the details of an administrative scheme by making regulations has been a standard legislative technique for more than a century. We have looked at a number of statutes and measures authorizing church agencies — especially the Ecclesiastical Commissioners — to make regulations in this way. There were also a couple of measures giving such powers to the Church Assembly itself. Regulations adopted by the Assembly under such a power would have the force of a canon without requiring the Royal Assent or of a measure without requiring parliamentary approval. Some statutes limit delegated legislation by subjecting it to veto by either house of Parliament, or by requiring an Order in Council to give it effect. But the most important limit on the power to make regulations is in the detail with which the statutes assigning such power lay down the conditions for its exercise.

The most important criticism that emerged in the course of half a century of experience with this package of legislative powers was that the laity had no official part in the framing of canons or acts of Convocation. It was evidently customary to consult the Church Assembly's House of Laity before adopting either, but its role was merely advisory. The fact that the two Convocations had to deliberate separately was a lesser difficulty, but it did impair the development of uniform policies for the church. For instance, the new canons that replaced those of 1604 were adopted in 1964 in Canterbury province, but not until 1969 in York. Worse, the two Convocations never reached full agreement on the pastoral treatment of persons remarried after divorce.[54]

Accordingly, the Synodical Government Measure, 1969, provided for turning over all the powers of the two Convocations to the Church Assembly, renamed the General Synod of the Church of England.[55] Constitutional subtleties affected the structure of the measure. The General Synod was created by renaming the Church Assembly instead of replacing it, because it was thought that a new body would require a new act of Parliament, whereas a new name would not. There was not very much constitutional change to accompany the name change. The combined Upper and Lower Houses of the Convocations continued to constitute the Houses of Bishops and of Clergy. The House of Laity was elected by

deanery synods instead of diocesan conferences, thus allowing more
electors to participate. It was still felt that a general election in which all
parochial church electors could vote would be too expensive to carry out.

The membership of the General Synod was somewhat reduced from that
of the Assembly, and provision was made for all three houses to sit and
deliberate together. Final action on measures must still be voted on by
houses, but most other motions can be carried by a majority of those
present and voting, unless twenty-five of them demand a division by houses.

Certain matters of especial doctrinal or instititutional significance require
a two-thirds vote in each house. Many such matters must also be approved
by a majority of the diocesan synods before final action by the General
Synod. These requirements can be confusing to observers of the Synod,
because a proposal can move through highly publicized preliminary stages
by simple majorities, and then fail at the last minute when simple
majorities are no longer enough. It has been predicted that this is what
will happen to the recent proposal for the ordination of women priests. It
was adopted by simple majorities in the Synod, and sent to the dioceses.
When it comes back, it will have to have two-thirds majorities, which will
not be forthcoming unless some of the present opponents change their
minds.

The assignment of the Convocations' powers to the General Synod was
not accomplished by the measure itself. Since measures are equivalent to
acts of Parliament, it was felt that they could not properly alter the internal
constitution of the church. Accordingly, what the measure did was
authorize the Convocations to make the transfer by canon. The text of the
canon was set forth in a schedule to the measure.

The transfer of power does not abolish the Convocations. They continue
to exist, and meet formally in order to resolve themselves into the first two
houses of the General Synod. They retain power to meet and deliberate
separately, and may also, if they choose, retain a veto over synodical action
affecting doctrine or liturgy. I have not heard of their doing either.

The schedule establishing the powers of the General Synod lists the same
four categories of legislative action that I have listed above.[56] The division
of functions among the categories, however, has changed. Using measures
to authorize canons was a device first adopted in 1920 for reforming the
representation of the clergy in the Convocations. It was fairly rare after
that until synodical government came in; it has been in regular use since.
It would seem that if the canon is expressly authorized by a measure having
the force of an Act of Parliament, the government does not exercise further
discretion when the canon comes on for the Royal Assent: assent is
routine. This process of course blurs the distinction between canons and
delegated legislation. Like delegated legislation, the canon satisfies the
supervisory interests of the government because it is expressly authorized.

At the same time, it satisfies the ecclesiological aspirations of churchpeople because it comes from a church body.

The General Synod is also using a good deal of delegated legislation that is not by canon.[57] Powers continue to be conferred on the Church Commissioners — notably by the Pastoral Measures 1968 and 1983. Also, a great deal is being done by regulations of the General Synod itself. These regulations are sometimes authorized by measure, and sometimes by canon. In the case of the Church of England (Doctrine and Worship) Measure, 1974, there is a double delegation. The measure authorizes the General Synod to make canons authorizing itself to make regulations adopting new forms of worship. In this way, the liturgy is no longer subject either to Parliament or to the government: the regulations, as long as they are within the grant of authority, require neither parliamentary approval nor the Royal Assent. It appears that some of the parliamentary dissidents felt that by this development they had been maneuvered against their better judgment into relinquishing control over the liturgy. They mustered a good deal of support in 1981 for a proposed Act of Parliament that would have required more use of the 1662 Prayer Book than the Synod called for.

The General Synod has taken over the former role of the Convocations in making pronouncements without enforceable legal effect.[58] Subjects have included sexual ethics, political issues such as nuclear warfare and the imposition of sanctions on South Africa, and matters of internal church discipline such as church weddings for divorced persons. The Synod as such has not made any general doctrinal pronouncements, but the House of Bishops adopted a resolution in 1986 affirming that the Virgin Birth and the bodily Resurrection of Our Lord are the authentic teaching of the Church of England. This affirmation was evidently a response to the concern expressed after the elevation to the see of Durham of a man whose published views seemed inconsistent with both doctrines. It served the same purpose as the condemnation of *Essays and Reviews* by the Convocation of Canterbury in 1864.

The constitutional material attached to the 1919 Enabling Act made provision for local church bodies as well as for the National Assembly. A document called Rules for the Representation of the Laity set up a unified plan for the Assembly's House of Laity, for parochial church councils, for diocesan conferences, and for ruridecanal (i.e., covering a rural deanery) conferences where they existed.[59] The foundation of the whole scheme was the church electoral roll. The draft reported out by the 1916 committee would have made only confirmed Anglicans eligible for inclusion, but before presenting it to Parliament the Representative Church Council relaxed the requirement of confirmation. Under the rules attached to the Enabling Act, any baptized person over eighteen years of age was eligible if he or she claimed to be a member of the Church of England and did not belong to any other church not in communion with it. It is interesting to note that eligibility to be elected was more restricted than eligibility to vote. Only "communicant members" of the church could be elected (the 1916 report had a gender requirement also, but the Representative Church Council, "by a considerable majority," took it out). The term "communicant member" was interpreted to mean anyone who had received the Sacrament in the Church of England within the year preceding the election. The rule against belonging to another church was probably intended to apply here also, but it was not expressly stated: on the literal wording of the document, a Methodist who received Communion at his friends' Anglican weddings and funerals would qualify to be elected but not to vote.

There seems to have been no serious effort to limit the franchise to active churchgoers. It was perhaps felt that people who stayed away might be persuaded to come if they had a voice in church affairs. No proposal to limit the franchise to habitual attenders was put to a vote until 1987, when it got a slight majority of the laity in the General Synod, but was voted down by a similar majority of the clergy, and all but one of the bishops.[60] A communicant franchise was discussed in the Representative Church Council during the 1919 debates leading up to the Enabling Act, but it was ruled out, evidently because of the danger of insincere Communions. There was mention of the seventeenth century Corporation and Test Acts — an analogy that seems far-fetched when one compares what an insincere communicant had to gain under those acts with what he had to gain here.

In any event, narrower restrictions were eliminated out of hand, and the serious debate was over whether to require confirmation or to be content with baptism. The difference between the level of churchmanship to be expected of a baptized person who refuses to be confirmed and that to be expected of a confirmed person who refuses to receive Communion remains obscure to me. But some people took it very seriously indeed. Defeat on the issue in the Representative Church Council led Charles Gore, bishop of Oxford and noted Anglo-Catholic theologian, to resign his see.[61]

The exclusion from the franchise of persons who claimed to belong to the Church of England but belonged to other churches as well, was objected to on both historical and pastoral grounds in the 1919 debates.[62] It was argued that membership in the national church is the birthright of every Englishman who chooses to claim it, and that many good English churchmen have not hesitated to be Presbyterians in Scotland or Lutherans in Germany. Hensley Henson, the liberal bishop of Hereford, pointed out that Dissenters had not voluntarily cut themselves off from the Church of England: they were driven out by oppression in the seventeenth century and apathy in the eighteenth. On the pastoral side, it was pointed out that people were constantly drifting back and forth between the Church of England and Nonconformity, often depending on the quality of the ministrations they found in the Church of England. To require a full commitment to one church or the other could interfere with the process. It was something rather like this last argument that led to the abandonment of the one-church requirement in 1973.[63] At that time, it was pointed out that some people are ready to become Christians and participate in a local congregation, but not ready to make a denominational commitment, and that members of other churches moving into a place where there is no congregation of their own church may become valuable members of the local Anglican congregation, but not want to cut themselves off from their original identification. These arguments were of course more persuasive in the ecumenical climate of 1973 than they were in 1919.

As events fell out, the objectors to a broad franchise need not have worried. There was no great rush to get on the electoral roll.[64] Some clergymen beat the bushes to get their parishioners to sign up; more simply waited for the would-be electors to appear. In 1924, the total roll stood at ten percent of the population, a result which the editor of *Crockford* thought a majority of his readers would find disappointing. There was a wide variation among the dioceses, with 27.6 percent signed up in the rural diocese of Hereford, less than five percent in the urban dioceses of London, Birmingham, and Ripon. The number of electors has since declined along with other statistics of church participation. The ratio of electors to Easter communicants has declined slightly, from nearly 1.6:1 in 1930 to just over 1.4:1 in 1959. It appears that a substantial number of those on the rolls do not in fact vote. Mayfield, writing in 1958, agreed with the 1933 judgment of the editor of *Crockford* that the whole apparatus "was an attempt to create an interest rather than to meet a demand." The attempt has not been considered altogether successful. On the other hand, it provides a vehicle for laypeople actually interested in church affairs to give effect to their interest. That would seem to be a sufficient justification for it.

The electoral roll was kept parish by parish. Eligible members were entitled to be carried either on the roll of the parish where they lived or on that of the parish where they habitually worshipped, but until 1956 not on both. The persons on the parish roll were to meet every year, ask any questions they cared to about the running of the church, and elect their representatives to the parochial church council, the ruridecanal conference (if any), and the diocesan conference.

The number of laypeople on the parochial church council could be fixed by the annual meeting, and changed any year effective the following year.

Lay parishioners elected to diocesan or ruridecanal conferences belonged
to the parochial council ex officio. The council could, if it chose, coopt
additional members up to one-fifth of the total number. If the parish was
small enough, all the lay electors could be on the council. The incumbent,
one curate, and any churchwarden who was a communicant completed the
muster of the council. The incumbent presided.

The distribution of lay representatives to the diocesan and ruridecanal
conferences was for the diocesan conference to determine. However many
representatives were assigned to a parish, they were elected at the annual
meeting unless the diocesan conference decided that its lay members
should be elected by the lay members of the ruridecanal conferences.
Each diocesan conference could coopt up to fifteen additional laypeople to
represent teachers and students in the diocese. A similar provision for
representatives of wage earners dropped out in 1929. The lay members of
each diocesan conference constituted the diocesan electors who chose the
assigned number of members to represent the diocese in the House of
Laity.

Both diocesan and ruridecanal conferences had clerical members, some
ex officio and some elected by their colleagues. Each diocese made its
own arrangements for choosing these clergymen. The Rules for the
Representation of the Laity, as the name indicates, were silent on the
representation of the clergy. In some dioceses, the bishop occasionally
summoned a true diocesan synod in addition to the diocesan conference.
By tradition, this body consisted of all the clergy of the diocese and none of
the laity. Its role was merely to advise the bishop.[65]

At the local level as at the national, the Synodical Government Measure,
1969, made sweeping changes in terminology and modestly significant
changes in substance. The diocesan and ruridecanal conferences were
replaced by diocesan and deanery synods, and the latter were made
compulsory everywhere. The Rules for the Representation of the Laity
(renamed Church Representation Rules) were expanded to provide
complete bicameral constitutions for both sets of synods.[66] The clergy of
each deanery became the house of clergy of the deanery synod. Their
elected representatives, plus various clergy occupying diocesan, cathedral,
or university offices, became the house of clergy of the diocesan synod.
The structure of the parochial church councils was carried over pretty well
intact, but provision was made for varying their constituencies to go with
the new parochial options made available by the Pastoral Measure, 1968.

Under the new system, the lay members of the deanery synods elect both
the lay members of the diocesan synod and the representatives of the
diocese in the House of Laity. In each case, the voting is done by a voting
paper (Americans would call it a mail-in ballot). The result is a broader
franchise for the House of Laity, and a narrower one for the diocesan

synod. The person who presented the Synodical Government Measure to the House of Commons said:

> If there were plenty of money available and the Church had an extensive organisation of electoral registration and returning officers, no doubt it would be the Church's wish to have direct election from the parish up to the new synod. But, as we understand very well as parliamentarians, this is a very expensive process and thus I think that it is probably an agreeable half-way house, at any rate for the moment, that elections shall take place on a deanery as opposed to a diocesan basis, which is what they are at present with the present House of Laity.[67]

I have trouble understanding this argument. It should not be prohibitively expensive to set up a ballot box for an hour or so on consecutive Sundays, check off the parish voters as they vote, get a clergyman and a churchwarden to tally the votes, and forward the totals to a central place. Perhaps the problem is not so much counting the votes as acquainting the voters with the candidates and the issues.

The Church Representation Rules may now be amended by a two-thirds vote of each house of the General Synod.[68] Neither a parliamentary vote nor the Royal Assent is required, but each house of Parliament has a veto in the form provided for administrative regulations. The most important amendments have been ones (1973 and 1980, respectively) providing religious communities with lay and clerical representation in diocesan synods, and providing such synods with a third house consisting of the bishop, his suffragans, and anyone else in episcopal orders that he chooses to include, one (1973) allowing members of the Church of England to vote even if they belong to other churches as well, and one (1980) requiring people to receive the Sacrament three times a year instead of just once if they wish to be counted as communicant members.

Exactly what all the local bodies provided for in these constitutional documents are supposed to be doing has never been as clear as their more enthusiastic supporters would have liked. The old diocesan conferences were authorized to discuss matters relating to the church in their respective dioceses; the new synods may discuss matters relating to the Church of England without regard to place. In addition, they have accumulated by particular measures over the years a set of humdrum but very important powers regarding the personnel and property of the diocese and churches within it. We have looked at most of these powers in their proper places. They include supervising such bureaucratic bodies as the diocesan board of finance, approving schemes under the Pastoral Measure, 1983, and arranging for the periodic inspection of rectories. These are useful, indeed, vital, tasks, but it must take a more than common devotion to the church for a person to be willing to spend much time on them.

The parochial church councils when they were first set up in 1920 had no specific duties beyond advising the incumbent when their advice was sought. Evidently, the discovery that this was the case created a good deal of disappointment among parishioners who had worked for the adoption of the Enabling Act.[69] The situation was partly remedied by the Parochial Church Councils (Powers) Measure, 1921, which assigned the council all the ecclesiastical powers of the parish vestry, and all those of the churchwardens except taking care of the furniture and keeping order during services. It was also empowered to draw up the parish budget, and to administer any funds collected otherwise than through the traditional offertory collections, marriage and funeral offerings, and the like.

But the councils were persistently denied two powers that many parishioners craved. One was control over the appointment and tenure of the incumbent; the other was control over the parish liturgy. Several writers have quoted the letter written to the headquarters of the Life and Liberty Movement, the organization that did most of the lobbying for the Enabling Act, saying that the writer had been active in the Movement, that he understood that with the adoption of the Enabling Act he and his fellow parishioners could finally get rid of their parson, and the he would like to receive instructions as quickly as possible as to how to go about doing so. Alas, there was still no way.

Gradually, though, the parochial church council has gathered important (albeit not absolute) powers with respect to both the minister and the liturgy. We have seen the gradually increasing level of input under the successive patronage and incumbency measures.[70] In 1931, representatives of the council were given a limited power to disapprove a patron's choice for the incumbency. The power was strengthened in 1986. The council still has no power to get rid of an incumbent once appointed, but it can initiate an inquiry into an alleged breakdown of the pastoral relation, an inquiry which an altogether unpopular incumbent would be unlikely to get through successfully. As for liturgy, it has long been common wisdom among the clergy not to make major changes without the consent of the parishioners, and the council is the obvious vehicle for granting or withholding that consent. This common wisdom is embodied in the law regarding the Alternative Service Book (an optional replacement for the 1662 Prayer Book) and in the canon regarding vestments. Even where the law is silent, gaining the approval of the council would seem to be the obvious way for a minister to keep his liturgical innovations from precipitating a breakdown of the pastoral relation.

B. Executive.

The statutory provisions for the appointment of bishops have not changed since the sixteenth century.[71] While the theoretical threat of the dread *praemunire* was abolished by the Criminal Law Act, 1967, the cathedral chapter is still under a duty to elect the person nominated by the government, and that person must be appointed by letters patent if he is not elected. The archbishop sits to confirm the election, and still calls for objectors to come forth, although he need not and probably should not listen to them if they do. It was these formalities that would have been abolished by the ill-fated Appointment of Bishops Measure, 1984. It has been suggested that there is some residual usefulness in them. If a Crown nominee were bad enough, the chapter could vote him down or the archbishop could refuse to confirm him. Under the law, he would still be appointed, but his position among the diocesan clergy would be so undermined that he would probably withdraw. All this is highly speculative, but it was evidently enough to outweigh the interest in abolishing a harmless anachronism. After their nocturnal defeat in 1984, the proponents of abolition decided not to try again with another measure.

Meanwhile, significant changes were taking place in the manner of choosing the people whom the chapters would be ordered to elect.[72] Melbourne, who left office in 1841, was the last prime minister to make his party's strength in the House of Lords the primary concern of his episcopal appointments. As Victoria's reign progressed, more and more was being expected of a bishop both pastorally and administratively. It became harder and harder to get away with appointing an unqualified man for reasons of partisan politics. Furthermore, the Whigs did not have enough safe men with the requisite pastoral and administrative qualifications to fill all the vacancies that came up while they were in power, and the Tories had enough votes in the House of Lords so they did not have to worry about one more or less.

From the beginning of her widowhood, if not earlier, Victoria herself played a major part in choosing men for the episcopate. While constitutional conventions did not allow her either to urge the prime minister to recommend a particular candidate or to reject a recommendation on which the prime minister insisted, she could and did expect the prime minister to consult with her informally before committing himself to a particular recommendation, and to offer good reasons for any recommendation he made. She kept up a regular correspondence on church matters with the successive deans of her chapel at Windsor, and was apt to be better informed than the prime minister who was supposed to advise her.

In order to be well enough informed to satisfy the queen, prime
ministers took more and more to consulting the archbishop of Canterbury
before making recommendations. In 1891, Randall Davidson, who had
been dean of Windsor since 1883, was appointed to the see of Rochester.
The queen continued to consult him about episcopal appointments as she
had done when he was dean, and she continued to do so when he was
translated to Winchester in 1895. Edward VII, who succeeded his mother
in 1901, continued to consult Davidson as she had done. Thus, when
Davidson became archbishop of Canterbury in 1903, the two streams of
ecclesiastical input into the appointing process came together.

The practices of consultation developed in Davidson's time continued
without much change into the 1960s. Here is Guy Mayfield, writing in
1958:

> When a vacancy occurs, the Prime Minister consults with the Archbishop
> of Canterbury (and with the Archbishop of York if the vacancy is in his
> province). As a result of this consultation three or more names are put
> to the Prime Minister, who may himself have names to suggest to the
> archbishops. In either case, the archbishops make their views known to
> the Prime Minister, but only after the most searching and conscientious
> inquiries have been made. The Prime Minister for his part has a
> secretariat specially qualified to supply him with information from many
> sources about the needs of a diocese and the qualifications of possible
> nominees. (This secretariat also assists the Prime Minister and the Lord
> Chancellor in all matters of ecclesiastical patronage exercised by the
> Crown.) It would therefore be entirely misleading to say either that the
> bishops are appointed without reference to those in the Church best
> qualified to know and advise, or that the appointments are purely
> matters of State or of politics. Moreover although the Prime Minister
> makes the final choice, he does not override an archbishop's advice.
> There is reason to believe, too, that the sovereign is not necessarily
> passive in these appointments. Thus in the method of choice a final
> decision is reached only after the most exhaustive inquiry by both Church
> and State.[73]

None of these arrangements was official, or even officially acknowledged:
it was felt that an official process of consultation would detract from the
constitutional duty of the prime minister to take responsibility for the
advice he tendered the sovereign. It is very well for the sovereign to
respond to the epigram that he

Never said a foolish thing,
And never did a wise one

by pointing out that although his words are his own, his deeds are those of his ministers. But it will not do for the ministers to spread the blame farther by claiming that their deeds are those of an archbishop or an appointments secretary.[74]

But many churchpeople were dissatisfied with the process because of the unofficial character and above all the secrecy of the church's input. It came to be felt that the theoretical responsibility of the prime minister was less important that the actual responsibility of those who placed names before him. At the same time, the people who felt that the church should make its own laws naturally felt that it should choose its own bishops.

In 1976, after a couple of committee reports and a good deal of discussion, the prime minister, the leader of the Opposition, the archbishop of Canterbury, and the chairman of the House of Laity agreed on a plan for the church to "have, and be seen to have, a greater say in the process of choosing its leaders."[75] The church was to appoint a "small committee," which would present two names to the prime minister. The prime minister would then either choose one of the two or ask the committee to try again. The plan required no legislation: it was merely a statement of how the prime minister and his potential successors in both parties intended to discharge their responsibilities regarding future appointments. It was set forth in Hansard in response to a written question by a member of Parliament.

To implement the plan, the General Synod provided for a Crown Appointments Commission of twelve members: the two archbishops, three representatives each from the House of Clergy and the House of Laity, and four representatives of the "vacancy in see" committee of the diocese whose bishop is being chosen. These committees had been set up a few years previously to make representations to the prime minister concerning the diocese and its special needs.

The system thus established has accomplished its goal of giving the church a visibly larger role in the appointment process. It has made it possible for Margaret Thatcher, answering a question from a member of the House of Commons, to disclaim responsibility for the orthodoxy of her appointees:

Sir David Price asked the Prime Minister, in making recommendations for preferment within the Church of England, what account she takes of the views of candidates on doctrinal issues.

The Prime Minister: Advice on the suitability of the candidates for preferment within the Church of England is obtained in confidence from a variety of sources including, in the case of diocesan bishoprics, the Crown Appointments Commission. The Church itself is guardian of its doctrines, and before any candidate is admitted to preferment he is required, in the presence of the bishop or his commissary, to affirm his belief in the Church of England's inheritance of faith.[76]

But it has not done away with criticism. The present bishop of Durham, for instance, has been roundly attacked for his views on the Virgin Birth and the Resurrection. Indeed, there have not been lacking people to attribute a fire that occurred in York Minster shortly after his consecration there to divine displeasure at his appointment. That appointment had a good deal to do with the mistrust that led the thirty-two members of Parliament to vote for retaining the old formalities of election by the chapter and confirmation by the archbishop. It was not likely that either a chapter or an archbishop would stop an unsuitable candidate who had made it through the Crown Appointments Commission, but it was evidently felt that no straw should go ungrasped.

Queen Anne's Bounty and the Church Building Commissioners were the only agencies in place before 1833 that gave any promise of becoming part of a central church administration. They were soon joined by the Ecclesiastical Commissioners, who absorbed the Church Building Commissioners in 1856, and combined with Queen Anne's Bounty in 1948 to form the present Church Commissioners. We have considered the functions and powers of these bodies at length in an earlier chapter. The only other major central administrative agency is the Central Board of Finance, established in 1914.[77] It collects, administers, and disburses central church funds — generally contributions and legacies — that do not belong to the Church Commissioners. It also collects and disburses diocesan contributions to the annual budget of the General Synod. There are other central agencies with more limited functions, such as the Cathedral Statutes Commission that reviews cathedral statutes and adopts new ones with the consent of the bishop, the chapter, and the Privy Council, or the Redundant Churches Fund that takes care of churches no longer used for worship, but not yet put to secular uses or torn down.

At the diocesan level, the archdeacon and the bishop's secretary were the only traditional administrative officers that still had serious duties in 1833. Not long afterward, diocesan boards of education began making their appearance, although they had no statutory status until 1943. Other diocesan agencies came in during this century, mostly after the Church Assembly was available to provide for them. The main ones currently in place are:[78]

1. Diocesan Education Committees, first provided for by a measure of 1943, successors to the earlier diocesan boards of education that existed in some dioceses.

2. Diocesan Boards of Finance, established in 1914, and made official by a measure of 1925.
3. Parsonages Boards, first provided for under a 1923 measure as Dilapidation Boards.
4. Diocesan Boards of Patronage, established in 1932 to take possession of any advowsons that anyone wanted to turn over to them.
5. Pastoral Committees, set up under the Pastoral Measure, 1968, replacing Pastoral Committees set up under the Pastoral Reorganisation Measure, 1949, Reorganization Committees set up under a 1941 measure, and various ad hoc committees set up under earlier provisions for splitting and joining parishes.

Most of these agencies also have been taken up in connection with the statutes they administer.

The expansion of the church's administrative agencies has been complained of as attenuating its pastoral presence, a criticism that does not seem altogether fair. The need to keep up the buildings and the furniture, and to deploy the available personnel and resources where they will do the most good, is not going to go away. These are administrative tasks, and anyone who undertakes them becomes, for good or ill, an administrator. There is no reason to suppose that pastors would do them better, or be better pastors for having them to do.

The real problem with administrative development is more subtle, and I believe more serious, than this. It is that administrative rationalization tends to impair the internal diversity of the church. The work of Church Commissioners, Pastoral Committees, and Patronage Boards would be a lot simpler in a denomination where a minister is a minister and a service is a service. But no such denomination could claim a mission to the whole nation as the Church of England does.[79] For my own part, I find it hard to believe that the internal diversity of the church of England is in serious danger whatever administrative expedients are adopted. But the misgiving is worth keeping in mind.

C. Judicial.

The ecclesiastical court system was rationalized during the nineteenth century mainly by the good sense of the people involved in it. The more esoteric jurisdictions were allowed to fall into graceful desuetude, and the positions in the working courts were efficiently combined by a practice of placing several of them in the same hands.[80] The Public Worship Regulation Act, 1874, in what was probably its only provision that did more good than harm, provided that the main provincial courts — the Arches Court of Canterbury and the Chancery Court of York — should have the

same judge, appointed by the two archbishops with the concurrence of the
government. At the diocesan level, the bishops' willingness to appoint
judges who already held appointments in other dioceses was probably the
best way for them to make sure their courts were well served. After their
probate and matrimonial business was turned over to a lay court in 1857,
most of the diocesan courts sat only sporadically. Only by sitting in several
of them could a judge gain enough experience to be good at his job. For
similar reasons, it was not uncommon for a judge of one of these courts to
appear as advocate in another.

By the closing years of the century, the complaints about the working of
these courts were fairly familiar.[81] They centered around the
cumbersomeness of the procedure, and the submission of spiritual matters
to lay judges. The procedure had been updated somewhat by an act of
1854 authorizing the church courts to hear live evidence as the common
law courts do. But it was still forbidden to cite anyone outside the diocese
where he lived, and it was not clear that the courts could even hear legal
arguments in London, where all the lawyers and libraries were, unless the
litigants lived there also. The courts also had inadequate powers to punish
for contempt or violation of their orders. The writ *de contumace capiendo*
and the proceedings on it were simply not a modern way of securing
obedience to the orders of a modern court. The problem of lay authority
over ecclesiastical affairs is one we have taken up at length in connection
with the doctrine and liturgy cases. It was particularly felt with regard to
the hearing of appeals in those cases by the Judicial Committee of the
Privy Council. The virtual disappearance of doctrine and liturgy cases
ought to have made this less of a problem, but the anomaly remained.

A related problem was the status of the bishop in his own court. In
some dioceses it was customary for the bishop to word his patent to the
judge of his court in such a way as to reserve a right of personal
intervention.[82] Such a right was seldom exercised. When it was, it tended
to impair the legal integrity of the court without improving its theological
status very much.

These grievances, such as they were, were systematically addressed in the
Ecclesiastical Jurisdiction Measure, 1963.[83] The measure was based on a
report of an archbishops' commission appointed in 1951 to study the courts
as part of the ongoing project for revising the Canons — the project that
resulted in the adoption of the present Canons to replace those of 1604.

Under this measure, as we have seen, a normal disciplinary case, if it
gets as far as the trial stage, is heard by the diocesan chancellor with two
lay and two clerical assessors. Procedure follows that of the lay courts in
normal criminal cases. Since the chancellor must be either an ex-judge or
a barrister of seven years standing, he will presumably be familiar with that

procedure. The assessors play the part of a jury. The chancellor hears non-disciplinary cases by himself, except that the bishop, if he chooses, may reserve a personal role in faculty cases by inserting an appropriate provision in the chancellor's patent of appointment.

The measure expressly abolishes imprisonment for excommunication. It abolishes imprisonment for contumacy by repealing the 1813 legislation that created the writ *de contumace capiendo*. Instead, it gives the courts the same subpoena powers as lay courts, and empowers the High Court to punish any contempt of a church court in the same way as a contempt of the High Court itself. The measure did not create this power of the High Court. A 1932 case held that the court has inherent jurisdiction to punish contempt of any tribunal which it can control by writs of prohibition.[84]

The measure abolishes the original jurisdiction of the Arches Court of Canterbury and the Chancery Court of York. These are now exclusively appellate courts. Their joint judge has two lay and two clerical colleagues for each court. The clergymen are appointed by the prolocutor (i.e., speaker) of the Lower House of the Convocation of the province. The laymen are appointed by the chairman of the House of Laity. They must have judicial experience. The Judicial Committee of the Privy Council continues to hear appeals from the two provincial courts.

The most important innovation in this measure is the establishment of separate courts for cases involving doctrine, ritual, or ceremonial. There is created a Court of Ecclesiastical Causes Reserved, consisting of two judges or ex-judges, and three present or former diocesan bishops. They are appointed by the Crown; the measure does not say on whose advice. This court has appellate jurisdiction over all faculty cases involving doctrine, ritual, or ceremonial. It has original jurisdiction over cases of *duplex querela*. Joined by an advisory panel of eminent theologians or liturgiologists, it also has original jurisdiction over any disciplinary cases involving doctrine, ritual, or ceremonial that are not vetoed by the bishop, and that get past a preliminary inquiry by a committee of Convocation consisting of a bishop, two clergymen, and two diocesan chancellors.

Not surprisingly, the only two cases in which the court has actually sat have involved faculties.[85] In one of them, the doctrinal and liturgical issues had dropped out before the case reached the appellate level. In the other, there were other issues besides the doctrinal or liturgical ones. But it was determined that the court, once in possession of a case, may decide all relevant issues. There is no provision for sending it back to the regular appellate court.

The Judicial Committee does not hear appeals from the Court of Ecclesiastical Causes Reserved. Appeal lies to a Commission of Review, appointed ad hoc by the Crown. It must consist of two bishops with seats in the House of Lords and three Lords of Appeal — i.e., judges entitled to sit when the House of Lords acts as the final appellate court. It is expressly provided that neither the court nor the Commission of Review is bound by the past doctrinal or liturgical decisions of the Judicial Committee.

The measure also contains provisions requiring judges to be communicants; provisions abolishing odds and ends of obsolete jurisdictions, along with obsolete payments such as procurations for the archdeacon; and elaborate provisions for correcting the doctrinal, liturgical, or disciplinary offenses of bishops — replacing the tenuous tradition on which Archbishop Benson acted in the trial of Bishop King.

There is nothing impractical about this measure. It provides the church with a reasonably simple and effective court system in which we know what court has jurisdiction over what cases, and in which the cases that come up can be disposed of with pastoral wisdom and professional competence, and without unnecessary procedural complication. The criticism I raised in connection with the *Bland* case related less to defects in the judicial system than to the need for an administrative alternative. That alternative is now in place, as we have seen.

But I cannot leave the Ecclesiastical Jurisdiction Measure, 1963, without noting a certain oddity about it. It is full of antiquarian allusions. Reading it, one keeps noting which nineteenth century problems are dealt with by which sections. Here in Section 10 (1) (b) is the provision for the *Gorham* case. Here is Section 40 to take care of the accusation against Bishop King. Here is Section 45 (3) to cut loose from the old and hated decisions of the Judicial Committee, and claim for the Church of England the same liberty that the South African church was read out of its endowments for claiming. These problems were so long dormant in 1963 that one is surprised that anyone was still interested in solving them. It is the kind of surprise one feels at finding that a figure out of a dim period of history is still alive.

III. Conclusion

The attempt to bring a historical account down to the present must necessarily fail, because the present keeps turning into the past faster than anyone can write about it. It is a little like trying to jump off a moving train: there is no comfortable stopping place. Nevertheless, at this point, just short of fourteen centuries after the second introduction of Christianity into England, almost exactly eight from the beginning of the time of legal memory in English law, about four hundred fifty years after King Henry's

Reformation, three hundred after the toleration of Protestant Dissenters, two hundred after that of Roman Catholics, a little more than one hundred fifty after Keble's assize sermon, a little less than a hundred after Bishop King's trial, about seventy after the foundation of the Church Assembly, a little more than fifty after the abolition of tithe rentcharge, about twenty-five after the last reorganization of the ecclesiastical courts, and just as the latest reorganization of patronage takes effect, I must leave off. I shall close with a few general reflections on the story I have followed this distance without coming close to its end.

What is unique and characteristic about the English church-state nexus, and has been so since the sixteenth century, is a continuing consequence of the decision made then to update the medieval synthesis instead of scrapping it and building anew from first principles. The decision is in sharp contrast with both the Reformation and the Counter-Reformation on the Continent. Because of it, the privatization of religion and the secularization of the state, the two themes that were to dominate the history of church-state relations in the rest of Christendom for the next four centuries, never quite took hold in England. The national religion was to retain an integral place in the national culture, and the ministrations of the church were to continue being a public entitlement.

Because of the continuing integration of the national church in the national life, historical tensions felt elsewhere as tensions between the church and something else have been felt in England as tensions within the church. Even the tension between Catholic and Protestant understandings of Christianity has occasioned as much and as bitter (albeit not always as sanguinary) controversy within the Church of England as it has with Catholic recusants or Protestant Dissenters. Consider how the Methodists were treated as long as they claimed to be Anglicans, and how differently they were treated when they stopped. Or consider how much more obloquy Pusey attracted over the years than Newman or Manning did.

In the nineteenth century, the most important tensions between traditional church institutions and the wider society were produced by utilitarianism and religious pluralism. The national synthesis managed — after a few false starts, to be sure — to assimilate both without dislodging the church from its traditional place. Where utilitarianism in the 1820s was mounting attacks on the establishment as such, by the end of the 1830s it was a force within the establishment calling for the rationalization and redistribution of church revenues and endowments so that the church's mission could be more effectively carried out. And where in the 1840s religious pluralism was raising arguments over whether Dissenters should be made to pay for the support of the established church, by the 1870s the debate was over whether they should be permitted to receive its ministrations and participate in its government.

The aspiration to a comprehensive national synthesis has required finding places within the national church for as many different spiritual experiences and religious needs as possible. The High Church emphasis on the institutional and sacramental dimensions of Christianity, the Low Church emphasis on the personal and evangelical, and the Broad Church emphasis on the ethical have all come to be recognized and accepted within the church. There are doctrinal pronouncements at many different levels, with varying degrees of intellectual cogency or institutional authority, but there is no coercive imposition of orthodoxy:

> The characteristic of our Church is to offer to men in all its wealth and fullness the inheritance of the Catholic Church, inviting them to come and take their full share in it, but leaving them always in the last resort to decide.[86]

But the Church of England has always fought shy of compromises treating controverted issues as matters of indifference. It did not accept any of the schemes for "comprehension" proposed at the Savoy Conference of 1661, and it was chary of the South India scheme adopted in 1948. As T.S. Eliot put it in his critique of the latter scheme:

> The essential point about these extraordinary differences . . . is that we do not agree to differ. We do not say that these things do not matter . . . .

> The Church of England maintains its unity in spite of the differences, and *because* we do not agree to disagree. Each party in this Church can defend its own doctrine, in the conviction that its doctrine is the true doctrine of the Church of England.[87]

Among the things carried over from medieval times into the updated synthesis is the High Church-Erastian tension to which I have alluded so often in these volumes. The balance between these two complementary perceptions of Christendom has constantly changed, without changing the basic nature of either perception. The first decades after the Reformation saw a general triumph of the Erastianism of the medieval Commons over the High Churchmanship that had prevailed among the clergy since the Gregorian Reform. Then there was a resurgence of High Churchmanship, reaching a zenith under Laud and the Carolines. The fortunes of the two parties fluctuated during the middle years of the seventeenth century, but with the Revolution of 1688 and the departure of the Nonjurors, there was something approaching a complete ascendancy of Erastianism.

An agenda for a revived High Churchmanship was sketched out by Edmund Gibson and a few others early in the eighteenth century. It called for decency and order in the liturgy and regular reception of Communion, but not yet for the revival of Catholic practices abandoned in the course of the Reformation. It played down traditional High Church concern with the rights and duties of the Christian prince, and stressed instead the inherent authority of bishops in the apostolic succession. it claimed for the bishops and their deputies a virtually unlimited power to correct sinners and impose orthodoxy, as long as they did not attempt to visit their mandates with any temporal consequences beyond those the secular authorities saw fit to attach.

In the nineteenth century, as we have seen, concern for liturgical and Eucharistic piety led to an interest in restoring pre-Reformation doctrines and practices. The emphasis on apostolic authority led to an interest in ecclesiastical self-government, and was one of a number of forces that went into the revival of Convocation, the establishment of the Church Assembly, and the Synodical Government Measure. With the development of religious pluralism, the claim to administer pastoral correction without temporal effect turned into a claim to set conditions for church membership and exclude those who fail to qualify. The High Church agenda developed in this way was in place by the late nineteenth century, and has changed only in details since.

Needless to say, it has not been fully accepted. Rather, its encounter with the prevailing Erastianism has produced a new set of adjustments. High Church sacramental and liturgical practices have been accepted as legitimate devotional options for individuals or parishes, but have not become a norm for the church. Institutions of self-government are in place in pretty much the form High Church theorists envisaged, but whether they are to be understood in terms of High Church ecclesiology or of Erastian utility remains a matter of debate. Attempts to impose an ideological understanding of any kind on the structure have been generally rebuffed. The attempt to set conditions of membership or restrict access to the ministrations of the church has been almost entirely unsuccessful.

These adjustments have been accompanied by a general attenuation of ecclesiastical authority. The leaders of the Church of England emerged from the battles of the nineteenth century without any of the powers that support the authority of leaders in other bodies. The mainstay of any authority is a power of moral suasion attached to its mandates, a belief that it is right to obey them and wrong not to. In the Church of England, this suasion was steadily undermined by disagreement as to the legitimacy and provenance of the bodies and offices in which authority was lodged, and as to the principles on which authority should be exercised. Most authority is also supported by a power to coerce. In the Church of England, this power was undermined by the permissiveness of the courts in doctrine cases, by the successful defiance of the courts in liturgical cases, and by the trouble and expense of proceeding in disciplinary cases. Authorities in other churches, if they have no power to coerce, have at least a power to exclude. In the Church of England, as we have seen, this power has been generally denied.

Because of the severe limitations on authority in the church, conflicts have had to be resolved in other ways. Conflicts involving practice are generally compromised, and the compromises are apt to leave a good deal of scope for the contending parties to go their separate ways. Conflicts involving theory are resolved by scholarship or not at all. In the process of not being resolved, they are apt to elicit non-binding authoritative pronouncements that reinforce the claim of one side or the other to carry the authentic tradition of the church, but do nothing to dissuade or unchurch the opposite side. I have referred in that connection to the 1987 pronouncement of the General Synod on sexual ethics, the 1986 pronouncement of the House of Bishops on the bodily Resurrection and the Virgin Birth, and the condemnation of *Essays and Reviews* by Canterbury Convocation in 1864.

For upholders of the Catholic tradition, the attenuation of authority presents a paradox, which Bishop G.K.A. Bell of Chichester pointed out in a charge to his clergy in 1937:

> *Ecclesia Anglicana* has inherited the Catholic ideal. But . . . the practice of many Anglican local assemblies is Congregationalist. The adoption outside the Roman Catholic Church of practices used by authority within the Roman Catholic Church does not of itself make "Catholic" worship. It lacks the primary requisite of due authorization.[88]

The paradox was an old one when Bell wrote, and it is no less striking today.

Because of its profound historical and cultural roots, the Anglican synthesis continues to survive internal shocks that would tear any other organization apart. In one crisis after another, people have ringingly predicted that the failure to decide the question of the moment their way will wreck the establishment, drive great numbers of Anglicans into schism, or both. They have always been wrong. In each case, there have been a few scattered withdrawals — often of prominent churchmen to be sure — and a few scattered rumblings about disestablishment, and all has gone on as before.

The fact is that serious Anglicans are deeply reluctant to leave their church. Their associations with it are deeper psychologically than any of the issues that might lead them to part company. This is not to say that they will sacrifice personal integrity or theological conviction in order to remain. But they will be receptive to solutions that avoid so radical a choice. Because of the convoluted institutional patterns of the church, it is usually possible to find such a solution. As Eliot pointed out in the passage quoted above, it is very possible for a dispute to end with each side convinced that its own position is authentic mainstream Anglicanism, and its opponent's a mere tolerated aberration.

Many Anglicans are content with such an accommodation not only because they are reluctant to leave, but also because they are reluctant to put other people out. Respect for genuine Christian commitment has a way of jumping party lines even in the midst of bitter debate. And even where that respect is lacking, Anglicans have common historical and cultural bonds that do not depend on theological or liturgical agreement. They may be unwilling to disown their fellow Anglicans in the same way family members are unwilling to disown an erring relative.

As I write in the summer of 1988, the three most divisive issues facing the old synthesis seem to be the residual church identification of people who are not active churchgoers, the stand, if any, of the church on sexual ethics, and the ordination of women — not necessarily in that order.

The problem I have called residual identification is the most ubiquitous of the three, and the one that cuts deepest philosophically and theologically. It pits an Erastian understanding of the church as the religious aspect of a historical and cultural community against a High Church understanding of the church as a distinct community gathered out of the wider society and set apart through a personal appropriation of the Christian message. The issue thus defined was obscured in earlier centuries by a perception (not always warranted by the facts) that the community defined by history and culture and the community defined by personal decision consisted of pretty much the same people. The nominal adherent who is baptized, married, and buried in a church he does not otherwise frequent has, I think, a longer history than is sometimes supposed, but he has only recently come to play a large part in institutional debate. Is his tenuous identification with the church worth preserving, and, if so, at what cost to those more fully involved?

This question underlies a good many others that we have had occasion to consider. It appears at its most virulent in the debate over liturgical reform. One side sees the Alternative Service Book (not altogether fairly) as a sell-out of an important historical and spiritual heritage, and complains of

a determination on the part of bishops and clergy, to say nothing of the lay ecclesiastical politicians, to turn their backs on responsible outside opinion and behave as if they were a congregation of saints who had no need to notice the vulgar and the damned.[89]

The other side, meanwhile, points out (again, not altogether fairly) that many of the opposition did not attend the Prayer Book services they were so anxious to preserve, and suggests that

> The crux of the matter . . . was whether the primary purpose of the liturgy was the preservation of great literature from the past or whether it was to be the vehicle of living faith for the present.[90]

The same questions and the same alignment of parties turn up when the question of "redundant" churches is raised, or the question of what to do about the tourists who flock to stare at churches where they do not worship.[91] On one side are the people who would like to tear down or secularize all churches not needed for active congregations, sell the sites, and use the money where it will do the most pastoral and evangelical good. They would like to treat superfluous Communion vessels and art works the same way. On the other side are people who see the village church as an essential source of local identification, and the tourist sites as an opportunity to expose the wider society to the ancestral faith. The issues thus raised have given the church some hard times in Parliament, as we have seen. They have also been debated at length in the General Synod, and have occasioned some agitation for removing the church's exemption from legislation governing other historic buildings.

The High Church vision of a congregation set apart by personal decision has made a good many clergymen impatient with their legal duty to administer rites of passage to people who do not attend services. We have seen how Mr. Bland occasioned the only reported case under the 1963 disciplinary machinery by taking a stand on what he called indiscriminate infant baptism. Other clergy do not go as far as Bland did, but they do try to use the rites to get people more involved in the life of the church. One of the 1969 canons authorizes a minister to "delay," but not refuse, to baptize a child "for the purpose of preparing or instructing the parents or guardians or godparents."[92] I suspect that these efforts at preparation and instruction are deterring some parents from having their children baptized. It has been noted that the number of infant baptisms in the Church of England per thousand live births fell from 554 in 1960 to 347 in 1982.

It is generally supposed that a parish incumbent has an obligation to perform marriages for his parishioners even if they are not Anglicans, or even if they are not baptized. On the other hand, if the couple has no aspiration to Christian marriage as generally understood, it is hard to see what trouble the incumbent could get into for refusing. The precedents, all from 1850 or earlier, make it very doubtful that he would be held either civilly or criminally liable in a lay court,[93] and prosecution in a church court is discretionary with the bishop. The bishop has no less an authority than Randall Davidson to support him in refusing to declare that it is the duty of a parish priest to use this quite distinctly Christian service with a Christian declaration of a dogmatic kind at its centre for the marriage of one who, however earnest and excellent his religious life, is not prepared to declare himself a member of the Church of Christ.

In parliamentary debates over the measures of the General Synod, opponents have consistently grounded themselves on a traditional Erastian view of a broadly comprehensive church, and have stressed the narrowness of the constituencies represented in the General Synod. The defenders of the Synod, instead of reminding their opponents of the practical concerns and democratic aspirations that led to the original adoption of the Enabling Act, have tended to raise High Church claims that the decisions of duly constituted ecclesiastical authorities on internal church affairs are not to be challenged by the organs of the state. The resulting contention has been perceived as highly divisive, and threats of disestablishment have in fact been raised on both sides. But it is doubtful that either side would have the power to bring about so radical a result, even if it had the will. While the parliamentarians talk of representing a broad constituency of the nation, they are in fact a pretty small minority of the House of Commons. Even if the whole House has the right to speak for the Anglican laity (it is probably too busy to do so), it is not clear that this group does. As for the General Synod, a number of writers have questioned its authority to speak even for the convinced and active churchgoing minority of the nation. The desire to attend meetings is not at all necessarily felt by the same people as the desire to attend church. And even those who do attend may not have the time to inform themselves well enough to exercise a judgment independent of the church insiders who set their agenda and staff their committees. There are some signs that the High Church party are backing off from the extreme positions they have sometimes taken. Their decision not to reintroduce the Appointment of Bishops Measure after its defeat in 1984 is such a sign.

Turning to another divisive issue, sexual ethics, we find that the broad doctrinal permissiveness that has prevailed at least since Gorham's time has only recently begun to be felt in this area of the church's witness. The development has been resisted. As one member of the General Synod put it during an inconclusive debate on the subject:

For goodness' sake, let us have some honesty about this. You can have a pluralism of dogmatic theology as much as you like, but you cannot have a pluralism in sex ethics because in this matter people know what we are talking about.[94]

Nevertheless, a plurality of attitudes has been coming in. A more or less official marriage preparation pamphlet has taken a fairly offhand view of the possibility that parties have already established a sexual relationship, and various committees have urged a permissive attitude toward homosexual practices. As the editor of *Crockford* put it in 1982:

> While it is obvious that the Church will always prefer sex within marriage, and will be right to do so, it seems to be likely that before long there will be a more public and reasoned discussion about the degrees of disapproval of the various widespread forms of other sexual activity. Nowadays, consciences vary.[95]

In 1987, the General Synod adopted a statement affirming the divine ideal of sex in marriage, stating that fornication and adultery are sins against this ideal "to be met by a call to repentance and the exercise of compassion," and that homosexual genital acts also fall short of this ideal.[96] An amendment to insert the words "casual and promiscuous" in front of the words "homosexual genital acts" was defeated by the bishops 5-14 and the clergy 82-138, though the laity voted 136-84 in favor of it. An amendment stating that homosexual genital acts also are to be met with a call to repentance and the exercise of compassion was adopted without a division. A stronger measure, that would have required "Christian leaders . . . to be exemplary in all spheres of morality, including sexual morality, as a condition of being appointed to or remaining in office," was proposed and rejected, evidently because it was felt as a rebuke to the bishops for not enforcing a stricter discipline on the clergy. Given the nuances of individual cases and the elaborate procedures required by the governing legislation, the bishops were probably being as strict as they could reasonably be asked to be.

Despite the growing permissiveness, I have no doubt that a clergyman involved in a non-marital sexual relation, whether with a woman or with a man, would be found by the courts to be guilty of "conduct unbecoming the character of a clerk in holy orders," and so subject to discipline if his bishop chose to prosecute. Furthermore, in most parishes, if his conduct became generally known, it would probably occasion a "serious breakdown of the pastoral relationship," subjecting him to removal.[97]

Whether the courts would still regard an unmarried cohabiting couple or a stable homosexual couple as "notorious evil livers" subject to exclusion from lay Communion is more problematical. In theory, such a couple could produce an embarrassing update of *Jenkins* v. *Cook* by presenting themselves to a priest who would refuse them, and then taking their case to court. But such a couple would be more apt to seek out a congregation where they would be accepted, one where they were not known, or one where the priest was not in the habit of repelling would-be communicants on moral grounds.

In short, it would seem that proponents of traditional sexual standards can appeal to a clear if non-binding statement from the General Synod, together with unrepealed if not strictly enforced principles of law to support their claim that theirs is the authentic Anglican position. At the same time, proponents and practitioners of sexual permissiveness, although not officially vindicated, will be let alone, and can point to the unofficial character of any condemnation applied to them. In the Anglican tradition, this state of affairs is probably the best either side can expect.

Of all potentially divisive issues, the ordination of women has had the most publicity, and has occasioned the most vigorous discussion both in and out of the church. As we have seen, a measure to authorize women priests has gone out to the diocesan synods, and will eventually work its way back to the General Synod for final adoption. Opponents still hope that it will not get the necessary two-thirds majorities in the three houses when it returns; some may even hope that one or the other of the houses of Parliament will veto it if it gets past the General Synod. But there is little doubt in my mind that it or some other provision to the same effect will eventually become law. Admitting women to the priesthood accords with the general pattern of updating the old synthesis, and the theological objections are not clear enough to stand permanently in its way.

The stated objections sound for the most part in ecclesiology rather than sacramental theology. A declaration on the subject, signed by more than a hundred bishops from different parts of the Anglican Communion, states:

> We do not consider that the churches of the Anglican Communion have authority to change the historic tradition of the Church that the Christian ministerial priesthood is male.[98]

According to this declaration, the ordination (or purported ordination, if you prefer) of women will impair "the wider unity of the Church" — i.e., the developing ecumenical relations with Roman Catholics and Eastern Orthodox, who have both expressed official concern at the prospect. It will deprive Anglicans of the "commonly accepted ministry" that is one of the few elements of cohesion in the midst of their prevailing diversity. It is not to be done without a "clear ecumenical consensus."

Underlying these objections, but seldom articulated among them, is the fear of encumbering the church with a spurious Eucharist. What if it is not merely inexpedient to ordain women to the priesthood? What if it is impossible? What if, as one American bishop put it, a woman can no more be a priest than she can be a father? If the rite of ordination cannot make her a priest, then the bread and wine she offers will not be the Sacrament.

The Catholic tradition is not to take chances with the validity of the sacraments:

> All that has been said so far about doubt and how to resolve it holds good only for purely juridical effects, which depend on the will of the lawgiver, or for moral effects, whose formal value depends on the good will of the subject. When we examine effects of an ontological order, we must proceed quite differently. If an act has a physical or quasi-physical effect, as the sacraments do, it will or will not produce that effect depending on whether or not the conditions are fulfilled. It follows that when a necessary or quasi-necessary sacrament is in issue, we resolve our doubts by taking the path of maximum certainty. Otherwise we run the risk of making an act invalid when it is of the utmost importance that it be valid.[99]

This passage, translated from a standard Roman Catholic canonical work, seems to overlook the common teaching that a sacrament received in good faith will not fail of its spiritual effect even if the conditions for its ontological effect are not fulfilled. Nevertheless, it remains the common Catholic understanding of how to proceed in such cases.

As matters stand, the sacramental ministrations of a woman cannot rise to the level of certainty that this criterion requires. For most Anglo-Catholics, that level of certainty cannot be achieved without the "clear ecumenical consensus" referred to in the declaration quoted above. Anglo-Catholic tradition has commonly looked to such a consensus as the source of authoritative teaching in the church — rather as traditional Roman Catholics (and some Anglo-Catholics as well) look to the pope.

But there is another Anglican tradition, the one expressed in the Preface to the 1789 American Prayer Book:

> that, in every Church, what cannot be clearly determined to belong to Doctrine must be referred to Discipline; and therefore, by common consent and authority, may be altered, abridged, enlarged, amended, or otherwise disposed of, as may seem most convenient for the edification of the people "according to the various exigency of times and occasions."[100]

The exclusion of women from the priesthood can no more be clearly determined to belong to doctrine than their ordination can be shown to be certainly valid. Thus, the two traditions are in a direct conflict which no authority within Anglicanism can resolve.

Even so, I do not think that this is the rock on which the ever-precarious Anglican synthesis will finally break apart.[101] It is not likely that anyone will find the ministrations of women, even if they are sacramentally invalid, any more unacceptable than John Kensit or R. C. Fillingham found the

Anglo-Catholic services that they set out with such determination to disrupt. If adequate provision is made — as indeed it has been in the measure now pending — to see that anyone who does not believe a woman can be a priest has access to the priestly ministrations of a man, I see no reason why the Church of England should lose any more adherents on account of this crisis than it has on account of the various crises of the past.

For two centuries and perhaps more, the privatization of religion and the secularization of society have been regarded in most of Christendom as the one effective solution to the problem presented by religious pluralism in a free democratic society. But in our time, there is more than one indication that the traditional solution is coming unstuck. More and more Christians are encountering aspects of public life on which they believe fidelity to the Gospel requires them and their churches to take a stand. In our time, therefore, more than ever, all Christendom has much to learn from the experience of the English nation and the English national church. For they have never accepted the privatization of religion or the secularization of society as necessary concomitants to freedom and pluralism, but have devoted great love and great technical skill to providing an alternative.

It is a remarkably resilient alternative, as we have seen. Over the past century, it has survived the loss of the liturgical uniformity on which it was once thought to depend. I have just predicted that it will survive the loss of the "commonly accepted ministry" to which the opponents of women's ordination appeal. If it comes to that, I predict that it will survive even disestablishment, just as it survived the loss of those political privileges whose passing Keble lamented in his Assize Sermon of 1833. The Anglican synthesis is what it is because of a historical and cultural identification that goes back to the earliest times. It will remain what it is as long as that identification endures.

This special character of the Anglican synthesis continues to have important pastoral consequences. In the first place, it assures the church of a place in public affairs. To be sure, that place has often been used merely to attach divine cachet to a current secular agenda. Sometimes, though, it has made possible a Christian challenge to prevailing assumptions about war, politics, or economics. Either way, it supports a continuing recognition of Christian principles as relevant to public debate. The claim that such principles require a particular course of action can be accepted or rejected, but it cannot be ignored.

On an individual level, people's enduring historical and cultural identification with the church has led the church itself to conceive its mission more in terms of deepening the involvement of its peripheral members than in terms of gathering new members in. Guy Mayfield refers to "a steady movement from the circumference towards the centre,"[102] and it is with this movement in mind that personnel and resources continue to be distributed with a view toward serving the whole population rather than ministering to those most anxious to be ministered to. Those who favor the theology of a gathered church have tended in one way or another to write off the Anglican periphery, but the church is still a long way from redefining its mission in accordance with their views.

There is a certain discouragement that attaches in this day and age to a pastoral mission understood as embracing the whole population, or at least those members of the whole population who are residually identified with the church. Statistics of baptisms, Easter Communions or average Sunday attendance are constantly being laid alongside general demographic figures, and found sadly wanting. Locally, also, an active parish with a well-filled church may be considered unsuccessful because it reaches so small a percentage of the overall population. The 1964 Paul Report on *The Deployment and Payment of the Clergy* notes that "the size of the congregation in densely populated areas can mask the failure of impact on the parish as a whole," and speaks of a parish "drifting to hopelessness about the pastoral outreach and beginning to die or turn inwards and live only in terms of the actual gathered congregation."[103]

To my mind, there is less cause for discouragement here than is often supposed. The Second Vatican Council, with its Constitution *Gaudium et Spes* on the Church in the Modern World, has brought into new prominence an understanding of the church's mission that does not measure success or failure in terms of attendance figures:

> The joys and the hopes, the griefs and the anxieties of the men of this age, especially those who are poor or in any way afflicted, these too are the joys, and hopes, the griefs and anxieties of the followers of Christ. Indeed, nothing genuinely human fails to raise an echo in their hearts .... That is why this community realizes that it is truly and intimately linked with mankind and its history.[104]

If the ecclesiology stated in this document gains a place in Anglican thought, it cannot fail to give new support to the traditional aspiration of the Church of England to be the church of the whole English nation.

Especially, it can give a deeper significance to the historical and cultural identification that so many people feel who are not active worshippers. If we take the claim of *Gaudium et Spes* seriously, peripheral identification with the church is not a mere accident of history and culture; it is the human condition. It is not a consequence of indiscriminate infant baptism; it is a consequence of being born into a world whose redemption the church proclaims.

On this understanding, the gathered church is a sign to the wider society. To the state, "she is at once a sign and a safeguard of the transcendence of the human person." To the individual, "the Church is 'the universal sacrament of salvation,' simultaneously manifesting and exercising the mystery of God's love for man." The state, by maintaining a residual establishment, and the people, by claiming nominal membership in the church and approaching it for their rites of passage, are recognizing and accepting the presence of that sign among them. In the long history of England, that presence, that recognition, that acceptance, have had a profound and salutary effect.

Please God, they will continue to do so.

Citations

Cases, statutes, measures and statutory instruments are cited in accordance with the forms generally used in legal writing. I have striven for uniformity in my abbreviations of the old reports, but I am not sure I have achieved it. Acts of Parliament and Church Assembly measures were cited by regnal year until 1962. Now they are cited by calendar year only. I have attributed the Jacobean canons that were in force until 1969 to 1604 instead of 1603 because 1604 was when they were promulgated. The canons that superseded them were adopted for Canterbury Province in 1964, but were not adopted for York Province until 1969, so I have attributed them to the latter year. Both sets are cited by year and canon number.

I have tried to put dates on cited materials, even when it has been impossible to do so with pinpoint accuracy. Accordingly, unless my sources give me a different year, I have assigned anything happening in a regnal year to the calendar year in which that regnal year began. And I have assigned undated material in a compilation that appears to be in chronological order to a year between the years of the dated material preceding and following it.

Abbreviated citations are:

Acts of Conv.   *Acts of the Convocations of Canterbury and York 1921-1970* (London, S.P.C.K., 1971).

Addison   W.G. Addison, *Religious Equality in Modern England, 1714-1914* (London, S.P.C.K., 1944).

Anno. B.C.P.   J.H. Blunt, *The Annotated Book of Common Prayer* (rev. ed. New York, 1889).

Archdeaconry of Chichester	*The Archdeaconry of Chichester,* ed. Johnstone (Sussex R.S., lxix, 1949).
Bell, *Davidson*	G.K.A. Bell, *Randall Davidson, Archbishop of Canterbury* (2 vols., New York, 1935).
Bentley	J. Bentley, *Ritualism and Politics in Victorian Britain* (Oxford, 1978).
Best	G.F.A. Best, *Temporal Pillars* (Cambridge, 1964)
Bodl.	material in the Bodleian Library, cited by call number.
Boyle	W.R.A. Boyle, *A Practical Treatise on the Law of Charities* (London, 1833).
Brodrick and Fremantle	G. Brodrick and W. Fremantle, *A Collection of the Judgments of the Judicial Committee of the Privy Council in Ecclesiastical Cases Relating to Doctrine and Discipline* (London, 1865).
Brose	O.J. Brose, *Church and Parliament* (Stanford, 1959).
Burn	R. Burn, *Ecclesiastical Law* (2 vols., London, 1763).
"Canterbury Visitations"	"Visitations of the Archdeacon of Canterbury," *Archaeologia Cantiana*, xxv, 11, xxvi, 17, xxvii, 213, ed. Hussey (1903-5).
Chadwick	O. Chadwick, *The Victorian Church* (2d ed., 2 vols., London, 1970-72).
Co. Inst.	Coke's *Institutes*, cited by number and original pagination.
Crockford	*Crockford's Clerical Directory*, cited by year and page.
Cr. Pref.	*Crockford Prefaces, The Editor Looks Back* (Oxford and London, 1947).
Curtis and Boultwood	S. Curtis and M. Boultwood, *An Introductory History of English Education since 1800* (London, 1960).
D.N.B.	*Dictionary of National Biography*, cited by person.
Denison Letters	G.A. Denison, *Fifty Years at East Brent, The Letters of George Anthony Denison, 1845-1896* (New York, 1902).

Ellsworth, *Lowder*	L.E. Ellsworth, *Charles Lowder and the Ritualist Movement* (London, 1982).
Eng. Pres.	G.C. Bolam et al., *The English Presbyterians* (London, 1968).
Eng. Hist. Doc.	*English Historical Documents*, various volumes and dates.
Eng. Hist. Rev.	*English Historical Review*
Flindall	*The Church of England, 1815-1948: A Documentary History*, ed. R.P. Flindall (London, S.P.C.K., 1972).
Foss	E. Foss, *The Judges of England* (9 vols., London, 1848-64).
G.S.	General Synod papers and committee reports, cited by number.
Gibson	E. Gibson, *Codex Juris Ecclesiastici Anglicani* (London, 1713) cited by title and chapter.
Gibson, *First Charge*	E. Gibson, *First Charge to the London Clergy* (London, 1744).
Gibson, *Visitations*	E. Gibson, *Visitations Parochial and General* (London, 1717).
Groves, *Noel*	R. Groves, *Conrad Noel and the Thaxted Movement* (New York, 1968).
Halévy	E. Halévy, *History of the English People in the Nineteenth Century*, tr. Watkin (paperback ed., 5 vols., London, 1961).
Halsbury	*Halsbury's Laws of England*, 4th ed. "Ecclesiastical Law" in vol. xiv if no other article is referred to.
Halsbury (3rd)	*Halsbury's Laws of England*, 3d ed. "Ecclesiastical Law" in vol. xiii if no other article is referred to.
Hansard	The various series of parliamentary debates are so cited regardless of their official title. The volumes before 1803 are cited as *Parl Hist*, later ones by series number.
Hart	A.T. Hart, *The Country Priest in English History* (London, 1959).

Holdsworth W.S. Holdsworth, *A History of English Law* (various editions).

Holmes *Elizabethan Casuistry*, ed. P.J. Holmes (Cath. Record Soc., lxvii, 1981).

Iremonger, *Temple* F.A. Iremonger, *William Temple* (abr. ed., London, 1963).

Kemp E.W. Kemp, *Counsel and Consent* (London, 1961).

Kemp, *Kirk* E.W. Kemp, *Kenneth Escott Kirk* (London, 1959).

L.Q. Rev. *Law Quarterly Review*

Lilly and Wallis W.S. Lilly and J.E.P. Wallis, *A Manual of the Law Specially Affecting Catholics* (London, 1893).

Macaulay T.B. Macaulay, *Speeches on Politics and Literature*, London, Everyman's Lib., 1909).

Marsh P.T. Marsh, *The Victorian Church in Decline: Archbishop Tait and the Church of England* (London, 1969).

Mathieson W.L. Mathieson, *English Church Reform, 1815-1840* (London, 1928).

Mayfield G. Mayfield, *The Church of England* (London, 1958).

Mayfield, *Like Nothing* G. Mayfield, *Like Nothing on Earth* (London, 1965).

McClatchey D. McClatchey, *Oxfordshire Clergy, 1777-1869* (Oxford, 1960).

Newsom G. Newsom, *Faculty Jurisdiction in the Church of England* (London, 1988).

Nias *J.C.S. Nias, Gorham and the Bishop of Exeter* (London, S.P.C.K., 1951).

1916 Report *Report of the Archbishops' Committee on Church and State* (London, S.P.C.K., 1918). For the 1916 attribution, see Bell, *Davidson*, 959.

O.D.P. Oxford Diocesan Papers. I consulted them in the Bodleian Library, but I am told that they are now in the Oxfordshire Record Office. I have cited them by call number and folio.

Owen	D. Owen, *English Philanthropy, 1660-1960* (Cambridge, 1964).
Paul Report	L. Paul, *The Deployment and Payment of the Clergy* (Westminster, 1964).
Phil.	R. Phillimore, *Ecclesiastical Law,* 2d ed., W.G.F. Phillimore (2 vols., London, 1895).
Pitt	V. Pitt, *The Church Commissioners for England* (Prism Pamphlet No. 36, late 1960s, no date).
P.P. Eng.	English Parliamentary Papers, cited by year, volume, and page.
Port	M.H. Port, *Six Hundred New Churches* (London, 1961).
Ret. App.	*Return of All Appeals in Causes of Doctrine or Discipline made to the High Court of Delegates*, P.P. Eng., 1867-68, lvii, 75. Cited by case number.
Reuters	Reuters dispatch of the date cited.
Russell, *King*	G.W.E. Russell, *Edward King, Bishop of Lincoln* (London, 1912).
Spec. Dioc. Linc.	*Speculum Diocesis Lincolniensis 1705-1723*, ed. Cole (Lincoln Record Soc., iv, 1913).
Stubbs	W. Stubbs, *Visitation Charges* (London, 1904).
Sykes	N. Sykes, *Church and State in England in the XVIIIth Century* (Cambridge, 1934).
Sykes, *From Sheldon*	N. Sykes, *From Sheldon to Secker* (Cambridge, 1959).
Tate	W.E. Tate, *The Parish Chest* (Cambridge, 1960).
Thompson	K. Thompson, *Bureaucracy and Church Reform* (Oxford, 1970).
V.C.H.	*Victoria County History*, followed by abbreviation of county.
Vol. I	R.E. Rodes, *Ecclesiastical Administration in Medieval England* (Notre Dame, 1977).
Vol. II	R.E. Rodes, *Lay Authority and Reformation in the English Church* (Notre Dame, 1982).

Welsby   P.A. Welsby, *A History of the Church of England,*
                    1945-1980 (London, 1984).

Whiting   C.E. Whiting, *Studies in English Puritanism* (London,
                    1931).

Woodforde   J. Woodforde, *Diary, 1758-1802,* various editions,
                    cited by date of entry.

Notes

1: The Quiet Time

1. On the convoluted politics surrounding the juridical simplicity, see R. Bosher, *The Making of the Restoration Church Settlement* (Westminster, 1951), 143-217. Bishop Skinner's patent to his chancellor, bound into O.D.P., d. 106, is dated 18 December, 1660, in the twelfth year of the king, and the nineteenth of the bishop. On Skinner's career during the Interregnum, see Sykes, *From Sheldon*, 8. It appears, though, that Sykes is mistaken in saying that Skinner "died in his little bishopric." He was translated to Worcester in 1663, and died there in 1670. *D.N.B.*, Skinner. I owe the point about episcopal and capitular lands to a lecture by G. V. Bennett on January 29, 1970.

2. See A. Whiteman, "The Reestablishment of the Church of England, 1660-1663," *Trans. of the Royal Hist. Soc.* (5th ser.), v (1955), 111. A new archdeacon of Canterbury was appointed on July 12, 1660. "Canterbury Visitations," xxv, 19.

3. Bosher, *supra*, note 1 at 199-204.

4. 13 Car. 2, St. 1, c. 12 (1661) repealed the limitations placed on ecclesiastical jurisdiction by 16 Car. 1, c. 11 and c. 27 (1640), except for continuing the abolition of the High Commission and the *ex officio* oath. The new Act of Uniformity was 13-4 Car. 2, c. 4 (1662).

5. R. Usher, *The Reconstruction of the English Church* (New York, 1910), ii, 266, characterized as "Usher's notorious phrase" by Christopher Hill in *Economic Problems of the Church* (Oxford, 1956), 349.

6. 13 Car. 2, St. 1, c. 12, §§ 2, 3 (1661).

7. For Coke's attack on the High Commission, see Vol. II, 207-11. The statute abolishing it is 16 Car. 1, c. 11 (1640).

8. In vol. ii of his *Works* (1709). For the date of first publication, see D.N.B.

9. *Duties and Rights of Parochial Clergy (Ecclesiastical Cases, Part I)* (1698), *Works*, iii (1709); *D.N.B.*

10. *A Discourse Concerning the Power of Excommunication in a Christian Church*, *Works*, ii (1709); *Ecclesiastical Cases, Part II*, *Works*, iii, 741 (1709); *The Unreasonableness of a New Separation*, Id., 937; *A Vindication of Their Majesties Authority to Fill the Sees of the Deprived Bishops*, Id., 959.

11. *Rotuli Parliamentorum*, i, 219a (London, 1783), quoted in the preamble to the
Statute of Provisors, 25 Edw. 3, St. 6 (1350). See Vol. II, 1-3 and *passim*.   12.
Stillingfleet, *supra*, Note 10; C. Burges, *No Sacrilege nor Sin to Alienate or Purchase
Cathedral Lands*, Bodl. Pamph. c. 112 (27) (London, 1660); C. Hill, *Economic
Problems of the Church* (Oxford, 1956), 164-66.

13. For a forerunner of Davis, see the anonymous pamphlet, *Pulpit Conceptions,
Popular Deceptions*, Bodl. D. 118 (1) (1662), evidently occasioned by the Savoy
Conference. I do not find any theoretical articulation of the principle of uniformity
before the Restoration.

14. J. Tottle, *A Charge Relative to the Articles* (Oxford, 1772); Sykes, 383;
Halévy, i, 392. But see *Bishop* v. *Stone*, 1 Hag. Con. 424, 161 Eng. Rep. 604 (Con.
London, 1808), where a clergyman convicted of preaching contrary to the Articles is
told it is not enough to promise not to do it again. He must expressly recant the
offending doctrine.

15. Vol. II, 87-94, 108-10. For examples of how the royal supremacy was
understood in the period we are now considering, see J. Tombes, *A Serious
Consideration of the Oath of the King's Supremacy*, Bodl. Pamph. c. 112 (26) (1660);
Anon., *A Second Defense of the Church of England*, Bodl. Pamph. 228 (19) (London,
1698); *Anon.*, *The Politicks of the High Church*, Bodl. Pamph. 260 (6) (London,
1705); P. Middleton, *A Dissertation Upon the Power of the Church* (London, 1733);
and the epistle dedicatory to George III in Burn, i. For a modern treatment of the
subject, see G. Every, *The High Church Party*, 1688-1718 (London, 1956).

16. Sir Lewis Dibdin attributes the revival of this doctrine to Gladstone. Dibdin,
Church Courts (London, 1881); *Establishment in England* (London, 1932), 51-2. He
refers to *Remarks on the Royal Supremacy* (1850, 2d ed., 1865), a pamphlet elicited
by the *Gorham* case.

17. See note 10, *supra*.

18. For another statement of this view, see *Anon.*, *A Second Defense of the
Church of England*, Bodl. Pamph 228 (19) (London, 1698).

19. Gibson's theory was developed in his introduction to the Codex. Gibson, p.
xxiii. It is rejected from the High Church side in Middleton, *supra*, note 15.
Stillingfleet's rejection is found in Chapter 1 of Discourse 2 of his *Ecclesiastical
Cases, Part II, Works*, iii (1709), 763. The view in his *A Discourse Concerning the
Power of Excommunication in a Christian Church, Works*, ii (1709) is somewhat
different.

20. On Foster's biography, see the entries in *D.N.B.*, and in Foss.

21. Sykes, *From Sheldon*, c. 2, pp. 36-67.

22. In fact, in 1853, when the question came up anew, the law officers of the
Crown accepted Atterbury's position. Kemp, 183.

23. Kemp, 172; Best, 45-6, 60. The statutes referred to in this paragraph are:
Probate: 22-3 Car. 2, c. 10 (1671); 4 Will. & Mar., c. 2 (1692); Marriage: 7-8 Will.
3, c. 35 (1696); 26 Geo. 2, c. 33 (1753); 21 Geo. 3, c. 53 (1781); Vicarages: 29
Car. 2, c. 8 (1677); Curacies: 12 Anne, St. 2, c. 6 (1713); Cathedral statutes: 6
Anne, c. 21 (1707); Parishes: 1 Geo. 1, St. 2, c. 23 (1714); 6 Geo. 2, c. 21 (1733);
21 Geo. 3, c. 71 (1781); Church courts: 27 Geo. 3, c. 44 (1787); 53 Geo. 3, c. 127
(1813); 10 Geo. 4, c. 53 (1829).

24. On necessary legislation that did not get adopted, see Sykes, *From Sheldon*, 56-7, 222. The introduction of church legislation into Parliament was also impaired by the fear of churchmen that it would receive hostile treatment. Id. at 202-3.

25. Id., c. 6, pp. 188-204.

26. *Ecclesiastical Cases, Part II*, Discourse I, *Works*, iii (1709), 742.

27. *Anon.*, 1 Freem. 289, 89 Eng. Rep. 209 (1677). *Accord: Anon.*, 11 Mod. 413, 88 Eng. Rep. 1121 (1728); *Wilson* v. *M'Math*, 3 Phil. Ecc. 67, 161 Eng. Rep. 1260, *prohibition denied*, 3 B. & Ald. 650, 106 Eng. Rep. 650 (1819).

28. *Wentworth* v. *Collins*, 2 Ld. Raym. 850, 92 Eng. Rep. 68 (1702).

29. *Cranden* v. *Walden*, 3 Lev. 17, 83 Eng. Rep. 554 (1682).

30. 1 Sid. 217, 82 Eng. Rep. 1066. Other reports are *Slader* v. *Smallbrook*, 1 Lev. 138, 83 Eng. Rep. 337; *Smallbrook* v. *Slader*, 1 Keble 731, 762, 83 Eng. Rep. 1211, 1230; *Smallbrook* v. *Slaughter*, 1 Keble 721, 83 Eng. Rep. 1206. The 1618 case referred to in text is *Searle* v. *Williams*, Hobart 288, 80 Eng. Rep. 433, discussed at length at pp. 216-17, *infra*. It held that a clergyman who had been granted benefit of clergy for an offense could not be deprived for it. Cases along the same lines as *Slater* are *Philips's Case*, 1 Sid. 169, 82 Eng. Rep. 1037 (1663) (general pardon does not prevent deprivation for simony), and *Townsend* v. *Thorpe*, 2 Ld. Raym. 1508, 92 Eng. Rep. 479 (1726); *Newcomb & Higgs*, Fitz-G. 190, 94 Eng. Rep. 714 (1731), both involving parish clerks.

31. 2 Add. 405, 414, 162 Eng. Rep. 343, 347 (Arches, 1825), *consultation awarded*, 5 B. & C. 399, 108 Eng. Rep. 149 (1826), *affirmed*, 2 Bligh N.S. 65, 4 Eng. Rep. 1055 (H.L. 1828), *further proceedings*, 2 Hag. Ecc. 456, 162 Eng. Rep. 921 (Arches 1829), *affirmed*, 2 Hag. Ecc. 663, 162 Eng. Rep. 991 (Delegates 1830).

32. Bibliographical references to Gibson and Burn will be found under their names in the Table of Citations. Burn's work appears in multiple editions, the last put out by Sir Robert Phillimore in 1842. Later, Phillimore incorporated a good deal of Burn's prose into his own treatise, where it continued through the second edition put out by his son, Sir Walter G.F. Phillimore, in 1895. Ayliffe's work is *Parergon Juris Canonici Anglicani* (London, 1726).

33. *Patten* v. *Castleman*, 1 Lee 387, 161 Eng. Rep. 143 (Arches 1753); *Harris* v. *Buller*, 1 Hag. Con. 463n, 161 Eng. Rep. 618n (Arches 1798).

34. The cases referred to in this paragraph are *Sollers* v. *Lawrence*, Willes 414, 125 Eng. Rep. 1243 (1743); *Middleton* v. *Crofts*, 2 Atk. 650, 26 Eng. Rep. 788 (1736); *More* v. *More*, 2 Atk. 158, 26 Eng. Rep. 499 (Ch. 1741). Note that although the 1604 canons did not bind the laity, the medieval canon law, insofar as it was still in force, bound clergy and laity alike. *Matthews* v. *Burdet*, 2 Salk. 412, 672, 3 Id. 318, 91 Eng. Rep. 357, 571, 846 (1702).

35. The cases of Jewish marriages are *Lindo* v. *Belisario*, 1 Hag. Con. 215, 161 Eng. Rep. 530 (Con. London 1795) *affirmed*, 1 Hag. Con. (App.) 7, 161 Eng. Rep. 636 (Arches 1796), and *Goldsmid* v. *Bromer*, 1 Hag. Con. 323, 161 Eng. Rep. 568 (Con. London 1798). Sir William Scott struggled mightily to inform himself of the applicable Jewish law, consulting treatises and experts tendered by the parties, and sending questions to the local rabbinical court. It is interesting to speculate whether Scott would have excommunicated the parties if they had been guilty of contempt. The place referred to in text where the court insists it is administering law, not

theology is *Kemp* v. *Wickes*, 3 Phil. Ecc. 263, 277, 161 Eng. Rep. 1320, 1324 (Arches 1809).

36. *Anon.*, 11 Mod. 46, 88 Eng. Rep. 874 (1705); O.D.P., d. 106, ff. 32-43 (1733). See O.D.P., c. 653, ff. 158-60 (1756) for a plan to refer to Doctors' Commons a jurisdictional dispute between the diocesan chancellor and the archdeacon's surrogate. See also *Jones* v. *Bishop of Llandaff*, 4 Mod. 27, 87 Eng. Rep. 242 (1691), 12 Mod. 47, 88 Eng. Rep. 1156 (1693), holding that a bishop cannot deprive his chancellor for incompetence. But see *Beswick* v. *Ashton*, Ret. App. #88 (1685-6), where the allegations against a clergyman are so scandalous that the consistory court sends the case for the personal decision of the bishop.

37. *Bishop of Lincoln* v. *Smith*, 1 Ventris 3, 86 Eng. Rep. 3 (1668). *Sheffield* v. *Archbishop of Canterbury*, 2 Show. K.B. 146, 89 Eng. Rep. 849 (1681) (archbishop cannot proceed in Arches court to recover legacy because it is his own court) seems contrary, but it appears to have been disregarded. *Ex parte Medwin*, 1 El. & Bl. 610, 118 Eng. Rep. 566 (1853) relied on *Smith*, and made the analogy of the royal courts explicit.

38. G. Bennett, *White Kennett* (London, 1957), 216-19. On the Lincoln peculiars, see Archbishop Secker's letter to his successor in the see of Oxford, O.D.P., c. 654, f. 35 (1761), and the correspondence between the two bishops in O.D.P., c. 655, *passim*, (1800-01), especially the bishop of Lincoln's statement, f. 56, that litigation between bishops or chapters "at the present moment is not to be desired." O.D.P., c. 652 (1743-49), ff. 83-4 seems to be referring to the same dispute. Id., ff. 113-15 is an example of the bishop washing his hands of a case. The parishioners claim a custom of dining at the rector's expense on certain days, and the bishop tells them to go to court if they cannot reach an agreement. O.D.P., c. 654, ff. 73-4 (1774) has a case sent for counsel's opinion — whether trees can be cut down in the churchyard, and the wood be sold for chancel repairs.

39. O.D.P., c. 655, ff. 73-96 (1800-01) (drunken curate); O.D.P., c. 656, ff. 16, 49-50 (1802-3) (incestuous parishioner); O.D.P., c. 660, ff 99-100 (1812) (farmer).

40. O.D.P., c. 655, ff. 172-74 (1801), O.D.P., c. 656, ff. 66-9 (1803).

41. The ecclesiastical courts handled all the probate and matrimonial business in the system until 1857, when it was transferred to a new court by 20-1 Vic. c. 77, 85. This predominantly secular business tended to overshadow the strictly ecclesiastical concerns of bench and bar. For instance, *The Clerk's Instructor in the Ecclesiastical Courts* (Dublin, 1766), a form book, has 254 pages dealing with probate and marriage, six dealing with admiralty (which used the same lawyers, but not the same courts), and 81 dealing with other ecclesiastical matters.

42. *Hodgkins* v. *Corbet*, 1 Strange 545, 93 Eng. Rep. 690 (1722); *Lockey* v. *Dangerfield*, 2 Strange 1100, 93 Eng. Rep. 1057 (1739); "Defamation," Burn, i, 476. On the earlier history of jurisdiction over defamation, see Vol. II, 204-6; R. Helmholz, "Introduction," *Select Cases on Defamation* (Selden Soc. ci, 1985), pp. xli-xlvii. It was generally thought that words actionable at common law were not actionable in the ecclesiastical courts. *Anon.*, 1 Freeman 296, 89 Eng. Rep. 214 (1678). At the same time, the eighteenth century judges, unlike the Elizabethans, would not allow the church courts to correct for "mere words of heat." Ibid. So there was not much left for the church courts except accusations of specific sexual

irregularities. *Anon.*, 1 Freeman 295, 89 Eng. Rep. 214 (1678). In *Baker* v. *Pierce*, Holt K.B. 655, 90 Eng. Rep. 1262 (1703), Chief Justice Holt ruled that any words tending to take away a man's reputation would be actionable at common law. Had this ruling been followed completely, there would presumably have been no church defamation cases at all.

43. *R.* v. *March*, 1 Sid. 101, 82 Eng. Rep. 995 (1663) (forcible entry); *Beckwith* v. *Harding*, 1 B. & Ald. 509, 106 Eng. Rep. 187 (1818)(monument). Incumbency could also be tried in actions for trespass based on the taking of tithe, *Brown* v. *Mugg*, Holt K.B. 136, 90 Eng. Rep. 974 (1699), or on intrusion into the benefice, *Phillips* v. *Crawley*, 1 Freeman 83, 89 Eng. Rep. 61 (1673), or in ejectment, *Watson* v. *Fletcher*, 8 B. & C. 27, 108 Eng. Rep. 952 (1828).

44. Dilapidation: *Jones* v. *Hill*, 3 Lev. 268, 83 Eng. Rep. 683 (1685); *Kingford* v. *Lloyd*, 1 Lutw. 117, 125 Eng. Rep. 62 (1695); "Dilapidation," Burn, i, 491. Sacrament: *Henley* v. *Burstow*, 1 Keble 946, 83 Eng. Rep. 1335 (1666). Pew: *Cross* v. *Salter*, 3 T.R. 638, 100 Eng. Rep. 777 (1790). Family vault: *Bryan* v. *Whistler*, 8 B. & C. 287, 108 Eng. Rep. 1050 (1828). See also *Phillibrown* v. *Ryland*, 2 Ld. Raym. 1389, 92 Eng. Rep. 404 (1724), where the court considers, but does not decide, whether an action on the case lies for exclusion from a parish vestry. *Beaurain* v. *Scott*, 3 Camp. 387, 170 Eng. Rep. 1420 (N.P. 1813) holds an ecclesiastical judge liable in an action on the case for wrongful excommunication. This decision, rendered by Lord Ellenborough at nisi prius, was not appealed. The right it recognized was qualified almost into extinction by the King's Bench in *Ackerley* v. *Parkinson*, 3 M. & S. 411, 105 Eng. Rep. 665 (1815). Halsbury, 699n seems to overstate the possibility of being held liable.

45. G. Palmer, *Law of Restitution* (Boston, 1978), i, 6-9. *Quantum meruit:* *Pierson* v. *Atkinson*, 1 Freeman 70, 89 Eng. Rep. 52 (1672) (curate); *Birch* v. *Wood*, 2 Salk. 505, 91 Eng. Rep. 432 (1697) (ditto); *Pitts* v. *Evans*, 2 Str. 1012, 93 Eng. Rep. 1063 (parish clerk). Money had and received: *Garnett* v. *Gordon*, 1 M. & S. 205, 105 Eng. Rep. 77 (1813) (canons); *Sellon* v. *Parry*, 5 Burr. 2762, 98 Eng. Rep. 450 (1771) (incumbent of mother church against incumbent of new church); cf. *R.* v. *Bishop of Durham*, 1 Burr. 564, 97 Eng. Rep. 451 (1758) (refers canon to common law action, presumably this one). Churchwardens: *Styrrop* v. *Stoakes*, 12 Mod. 10, 88 Eng. Rep. 1130 (1690) (account); Phil., ii, 1488 (chancery bill).

46. Tithe: *Nicholas* v. *Elliot*, Bunbury 19, 145 Eng. Rep. 580 (Exch. 1717); *Warden and Minor Canons of St. Paul's* v. *Dean of St. Paul's*, 4 Prince 64, 147 Eng. Rep. 395 (Exch. 1817); *Evans* v. *George*, 12 Prince 64, 147 Eng. Rep. 660 (Exch. 1823); Best, 66. Easter offering: *Laurence* v. *Jones*, Bunbury 173, 145 Eng. Rep. 637 (Exch. 1724); *Edgerton* v. *Still*, Bunbury 198, 145 Eng. Rep. 646 (Exch. 1725); *Carthew* v. *Edwards*, Amb. 72, 27 Eng. Rep. 43 (Exch. 1749). On the general development of Exchequer jurisdiction through fictitious debts to the king, see Holdsworth, i, 240-41.

47. Tithe on enclosure: *Cholmley* v. *Attorney General*, 7 Brown 34, 3 Eng. Rep. 23 (H.L. 1737). Other tithe cases: *Yateman* v. *Cox*, 2 Brown 191, 1 Eng. Rep. 879 (H.L. 1774); *Stockwell* v. *Terry*, 1 Ves. Sen. 116, 27 Eng. Rep. 927 (Ch. 1748); but see *Clare Hall* v. *Orwin*, Dickens 456, 21 Eng. Rep. 347 (Ch. 1772) (bill between rector and vicar over tithes will be dismissed in favor of church court when both are

spiritual persons). Nominations: *Herbert* v. *Dean and Chapter of Westminster*, 1 P. Wms. 773, 24 Eng. Rep. 608 (Ch. 1721); *Dixon* v. *Kershaw*, Amb. 529, 27 Eng. Rep. 341 (Ch. 1766). Patronage agreement: *Attorney General* v. *Marquis of Stafford*, 3 Ves. Jr. 78, 30 Eng. Rep. 903 (Ch. 1796). Other patronage cases sorted out rights to present as between trustee and settlor's heirs, *Athington* v. *Coverly*, 2 Eq. Cas. Abr. 518, 22 Eng. Rep. 437 (Ch. 1733), or between mortgagor and mortgagee, *Thexton* v. *Betts*, 2 Freeman 87, 22 Eng. Rep. 1075 (Ch. 1683); *Gardiner* v. *Griffith*, 2 P. Wms. 404, 24 Eng. Rep. 787 (Ch. 1726); *Robinson* v. *Jago*, Bunbury 130, 145 Eng. Rep. 621 (Ch. 1733). Chancery would also enforce the augmentation of a vicarage, *Attorney General* v. *Brereton*, 2 Ves. Sen. 425, 28 Eng. Rep. 272 (Ch. 1752), or require a lay impropriater to endow a curate where there was no vicar, *Bonsey* v. *Lee*, 1 Vern. 247, 23 Eng. Rep. 445 (Ch. 1682). It would entertain a patron's suit to enjoin a parson from wasting the glebe, *Bradly* v. *Stratchy* Barn. C. 399, 27 Eng. Rep. 695 (Ch. 1740). But it would not entertain a bill to enjoin the collection of an improperly assessed churchrate, *Dunn* v. *Coats*, 2 Eq. Cas. Abr. 629, 22 Eng. Rep. 528 (Ch. 1734), or a bill *quia timet* to cancel a presentation obtained by fraud, *M'Namara* v. _____, 5 Ves. Jr. 824, 31 Eng. Rep. 878 (Ch. 1801).

48. Churchwardens: *Churchwardens of Northampton's Case*, Carthew 118, 90 Eng. Rep. 673 (1689); *R.* v. *Rice*, 5 Mod. 325, 87 Eng. Rep. 684 (1695). It is not clear how the question of proper election was to be tried. The court in *Anon.*, 1 Ventris 267, 86 Eng. Rep. 179 (1675) was evidently prepared to try it in the mandamus proceeding. But in *R.* v. *Commissary of the Bishop of Winchester*, 7 East 572, 102 Eng. Rep. 222 (1801), it was tried on a feigned issue, and in *R.* v. *Harris*, 1 Blackw. 430, 96 Eng. Rep. 245 (1763), Lord Mansfield ordered both rival claimants to be sworn, presumably leaving them to pursue their claims in any other proceeding they wished. The same was done in the ecclesiastical judge case, *R.* v. *Ward*, 2 Strange 893, 93 Eng. Rep. 922 (1731), where the churchwarden cases were extensively discussed. Parish Clerk: *R.* v. *Warren*, 1 Cowp. 370, 98 Eng. Rep. 1135 (1776). Prebend: *R.* v. *Dean and Chapter of Norwich*, 1 Strange 160, 93 Eng. Rep. 447 (1718); *Clarke* v. *Bishop of Sarum*, 2 Strange 1082, 93 Eng. Rep. 1046 (1738). Vestry meeting: *R.* v. *Churchwardens of St. Margaret and St. John*, 4 M. & S. 250, 105 Eng. Rep. 827 (1815); *contra*, *Anon.*, 2 Strange 685, 93 Eng. Rep. 783 (1725). Mandamus was also available to determine who was properly elected to a curacy, *R.* v. *Blooer*, 2 Burr. 1043, 97 Eng. Rep. 697 (1760), or even to a Dissenting pastorate, *R.* v. *Barker*, 3 Burr. 1264, 97 Eng. Rep. 823 (1760). But if the position was a canonical benefice, the parties would be left to normal patronage remedies. *R.* v. *Bishop of Chester*, 1 T.R. 395, 99 Eng. Rep. 1158 (1786) (overruling *pro tanto Clarke* v. *Bishop of Sarum*, supra); *R.* v. *Marquis of Stafford*, 3 T.R. 647, 100 Eng. Rep. 782 (1790). Mandamus always required a showing of a legal right. Thus, it could not be used to gain admission to an unendowed lectureship, *Case of Lecturer of St. Anne's Westminster*, 2 Strange 1192, 93 Eng. Rep. 1121 (1743), or even an endowed one if the endowment was not immemorial, *R.* v. *Bishop of Exeter*, 2 East 461, 102 Eng. Rep. 445 (1802). Nor could it be used to obtain admission as an advocate or proctor in an ecclesiastical court. *R.* v. *Oxenden*, 1 Show. K.B. 216, 261, 89 Eng. Rep. 545, 560 (1690); *R.* v. *Archbishop of Canterbury*, 8 East 212, 103 Eng. Rep. 323 (1807).

49. *R.* v. *Bishop of Lichfield and Coventry*, 2 Strange 1023, 93 Eng. Rep. 1008 (1736); *R.* v. *Archbishop of York*, 6 T.R. 490, 101 Eng. Rep. 664 (1795); *R.* v. *Archbishop of Canterbury and Bishop of London*, 13 East 419, 15 East 117, 104 Eng. Rep. 433, 789 (1811-12).

50. Feigned issues were used in *Austin* v. *Gervas*, 2 Barn. K.B. 242, 94 Eng. Rep. 475 (1733) (right to be parish clerk); *Barnard* v. *Garnons*, 7 Brown 105, 3 Eng. Rep. 69 (H.L. 1797) (right to tithe); *R.* v. *Commissary of the Bishop of Winchester*, 7 East 572, 102 Eng. Rep. 222 (1801) (election of churchwarden); *Golding* v. *Fenn*, 7 B. & C. 764, 108 Eng. Rep. 909 (1828) (legality of select vestry). The Gaming Act, 1845, 8-9 Vic. c. 109, §§18-19 made wagering contracts unenforceable, and replaced the fictitious bet with a simple reference of a designated issue from one court to the other for trial.

51. *Shotter* v. *Friend*, 3 Mod. 283, 87 Eng. Rep. 188 (1689).

52. *Turton* v. *Reignolds*, 12 Mod. 433, 88 Eng. Rep. 1431 (1699). In what appears to be the same case, 12 Mod. 420, 88 Eng. Rep. 1423, Holt, C.J. is reported to have said that anyone who preaches in the parish church without the parson's consent is a trespasser.

53. Pews: *Jacob* v. *Dallow*, 7 Mod. 8, 87 Eng. Rep. 1060 (1702); *Byerly* v. *Windus*, 5 B. & C. 1, 108 Eng. Rep. 1 (1826). Burial fees: *Andrews* v. *Symson*, 3 Keble 523, 527, 84 Eng. Rep. 857, 859 (1675). Court offices: *Sharrock* v. *Bourchier*, Raym. Sir T. 88, 83 Eng. Rep. 48 (1663); *Jones* v. *Bishop of Llandaff*, 4 Mod. 27, 87 Eng. Rep. 242 (1690). Interpretation of cathedral statutes: "Deans and Chapters," Burn, i, 440, 466-67. Dissolution of marriage: *Wortley* v. *Watkinson*, 2 Lev. 254, 83 Eng. Rep. 544 (1679); *Collet's Case*, Jones T., 213, 84 Eng. Rep. 1223, S.C., *Collet* v. *Collet*, Skinner 37, 90 Eng. Rep. 18 (K.B., 1682); *Harris* v. *Hicks*, 2 Salk. 548, 91 Eng. Rep. 463 (1693).

54. The intestacy case is *Smith* v. *Tracy*, 1 Freeman 288, 89 Eng. Rep. 208 (1676), applying 22-3 Car. 2, c. 10 (1671). The main marriage cases are *Harrison* v. *Burwell*, Vaughan 206, 124 Eng. Rep. 1039 (1668); *Watkinson* v. *Mergatron*, Raym. Sir T. 464, 83 Eng. Rep. 243 S.C. *Murgatroyd* v. *Watkinson*, Jones T. 191, 84 Eng. Rep. 121 (1682); *Wortley* v. *Watkinson*, 2 Lev. 254, 83 Eng. Rep. 544, (1679); *Hill* v. *Good*, 1 Mod. 254, 86 Eng. Rep. 863 (1696); *Denny* v. *Ashwell*, 1 Strange 53, 93 Eng. Rep. 380 (1716). The relevant language was from 32 Hen. 8, c. 38 (1540): "No reservation or prohibition, God's law excepting, shall trouble or impeach any marriage without the levitical degrees, and no person shall be admitted in the spiritual court to any process, plea or allegation to the contrary." In *Harrison*, the court concluded that under this language a proceeding to invalidate a marriage that was neither within the Levitical degrees nor forbidden by God's law (evidently prescinding from the question whether the Levitical degrees are part of God's law) would have to be prohibited at the outset. But in *Hill*, involving a marriage to a deceased wife's sister, and in *Denny*, involving marriage to a deceased wife's sister's daughter, the courts were willing to rely on canonical tradition to interpret God's law. *Man's Case*, Cro. Eliz. 228, 78 Eng. Rep. 484, 4 Leonard 16, 74 Eng. Rep. 697 (1591) is ambiguous on the point.

55. 1 Freeman 282, 89 Eng. Rep. 203.

56. *Anon.*, 1 Freeman 287, 89 Eng. Rep. 207 (1675); cf. *Parker* v. *Williams*, 1

Sid. 100, 82 Eng. Rep. 995 (1663) (court splits on prohibition in dilapidation case where defendant claims incumbency under statute).

57. Admission and discipline: *R.* v. *Oxenden*, 1 Show. K.B. 216, 261, 89 Eng. Rep. 545, 560 (1690); *R.* v. *Archbishop of Canterbury*, 8 East 212, 103 Eng. Rep. 323 (1807). Fees: *Johnson* v. *Oxenden*, 4 Mod. 255, 87 Eng. Rep. 30 (1692); *Davies* v. *Williams*, Bunbury 170, 145 Eng. Rep. 636 (Exch. 1724); cf. *Ballard* v. *Gerrard*, 12 Mod. 608, 88 Eng. Rep. 1553 (1700) (registrar); *Pearson* v. *Campion*, 2 Dougl. 629, 99 Eng. Rep. 399 (1781) (apparitor). Vague pleading: *Anon.*, 1 Freeman 286, 89 Eng. Rep. 206 (1675). This concession evidently obtained only where there was a customary form of pleading. See *Anon.*, 1 Freeman 285, 89 Eng. Rep. 206 (1674); "Child-birth," Burn, i, 228, 230. Foreclosure of improperly presented rights: *Asgill* v. *Hunt*, 10 Mod. 440, 88 Eng. Rep. 800 (1718); *Owen* v. *Hughes*, Fortescue 198, 92 Eng. Rep. 817 (1720); cf. *Dr. Bows* v. *Jurat*, 10 Mod. 440, 88 Eng. Rep. 800 (1718); *Stephenson* v. *Sands*, Fitz-G. 191, 94 Eng. Rep. 714 (1731); *Darby* v. *Cosens*, 1 T.R. 552, 99 Eng. Rep. 1247 (1787), all cases that would not have been prohibited if the lay court had been satisfied that the ecclesiastical judgment was on procedural grounds. Self incrimination: *Symes* v. *Symes*, 2 Burr. 814, 97 Eng. Rep. 576, S.C. *Sims* v. *Sims*, 2 Kenyon 537, 96 Eng. Rep. 1271 (1759). *Ex officio* proceeding: *Anon.*, 1 Freeman 290, 89 Eng. Rep. 210 (1677); *Grove* v. *Elliott*, 2 Ventris 40, 86 Eng. Rep. 296 (1670); but cf. Anon., 1 Freeman 283, 89 Eng. Rep. 204 (1674).

58. The marriage case referred to in text is *DaCosta* v. *Villareal*, 2 Strange 961, 93 Eng. Rep. 968 (1734). Other cases giving *res judicata* effect to ecclesiastical judgments are *Phillips* v. *Crawley*, 1 Freeman 83, 89 Eng. Rep. 61 (1673); *Wyndham* v. *Bowen*, Sayer 141, 96 Eng. Rep. 831 (1754); *Clews* v. *Bathurst*, 2 Strange 960, 93 Eng. Rep. 968 (1734). For the earlier law, see, Vol. II, 22, 211-12.

59. Gibson, t. 4, c. 6; *Anon.*, *Considerations for the Better Establishment of the Church of England* (London, 1701), c. 4. The 1813 statute is 53 Geo. 3, c. 127. The process is described in Vol. II, 58, 212-13.

60. 2 Co. Inst. *623.

61. The leading case is *R.* v. *Fowler*, 1 Ld. Raym. 618, 91 Eng. Rep. 1313, 1 Salk. 350, 91 Eng. Rep. 306 (1700). See also *R.* v. *Eyre*, 2 Strange 1067, 93 Eng. Rep. 1036 (1736). Other cases are discussed in *R.* v. *Payton*, 7 T.R. 154, 101 Eng. Rep. 906 (1797), and in "Excommunication," Burn, i, 545, 554-56.

62. Vol. II, 197-200.

63. *E.g.*, *Weekes* v. *Trussel*, 1 Sid. 181, 82 Eng. Rep. 1044 (1664); *Pawly* v. *Wiseman*, 3 Keble 614, 84 Eng. Rep. 910 (1676); *Burdeaux* v. *Lancaster*, 12 Mod. 172, 88 Eng. Rep. 1242 (1696); *Paxton* v. *Wright*, 2 Kenyon 15, 96 Eng. Rep. 1091, S.C. *Paxton* v. *Knight*, 1 Burr. 314, 97 Eng. Rep. 328 (1757) (costs).

64. *E.g.*, *Juxon* v. *Lord Byron*, 2 Lev. 64, 83 Eng. Rep. 451 (1672); *Gould* v. *Gapper*, 3 East 473, 5 East 345, 102 Eng. Rep. 678, 1102 (1803-4); *Pawly* v. *Wiseman*, *supra*, note 63 (dissent).

65. *E.g.*, *Selby* v. *Bank*, 12 Mod. 497, 88 Eng. Rep. 1473 (1700); *Bishop of Ely* v. *Bentley*, 2 Brown 220, 1 Eng. Rep. 898 (H.L. 1732); *Bishop of Ely* v. *Gibbons*, 4 Hag. Ecc. 157, 162 Eng. Rep. 1405 (Arches 1833). The selective procedure is also referred to in *Banister* v. *Hopton*, 10 Mod. 12, 88 Eng. Rep. 602 (1710); *Hart* v.

Marsh, 5 Ad. & E. 591, 111 Eng. Rep. 1289 (1836).

66. *Full* v. *Hutchins*, 2 Cowp. 422, 98 Eng. Rep. 1165 (1776).

67. *Oldman* v. *Rightson*, 12 Mod. 326, 88 Eng. Rep. 1355 (1698) (delay); *Smith* v. *Wallet*, 1 Ld. Raym. 587, 91 Eng. Rep. 1293 (1700) (surmise notoriously false); cf. *Burdet* v. *Newell*, 2 Ld. Raym. 1211, 92 Eng. Rep. 299 (1705) (plaintiff ordered to support surmise with affidavit, case dismissed on his failure to do so).

68. *Bishop of Ely* v. *Bentley*, 2 Brown 220, 1 Eng. Rep. 898 (H.L. 1732) (article by article); *Hart* v. *Marsh*, 5 A. & E. 591, 111 Eng. Rep. 1289 (1836) (no prohibition after judgment); *contra*, *R.* v. *Reeves*, W. Kel. 197, 25 Eng. Rep. 566 (K.B. 1734). *Banister* v. *Hopton*, 10 Mod. 12, 88 Eng. Rep. 602 (1710) seems more like *Hart* than like *Reeves*.

69. *Banister* v. *Hopton, supra*, note 68; *Churchwardens of Market Bosworth* v. *Rector of same*, 1 Ld. Raym. 436, 91 Eng. Rep. 1189 (1697); *Full* v. *Hutchins, supra*, note 66; *Patten* v. *Castleman*, 1 Lee, 387, 161 Eng. Rep. 143 (Arches 1753) (ecclesiastical court will try custom according to common law rules).

70. The post-Restoration rule is stated in *Full* v. *Hutchins*, 2 Cowp. 422, 98 Eng. Rep. 1165 (1776). It is adumbrated in *Juxon* v. *Lord Byron*, 2 Lev. 64, 83 Eng. Rep. 451 (1672), and *Carter* v. *Crawley*, Raym. Sir T. 496, 83 Eng. Rep. 259 (1680). Coke's understanding of the law is set forth in his answer to the twentieth of Bancroft's *Articuli Cleri* of 1606, 2 Co. Inst. *613-14, and applied in *Porter and Rochester's Case*, 13 Co. Rep. 4, 77 Eng. Rep. 1416 (1609). The two alternative approaches elicit disagreement among the judges in *Parker* v. *Williams*, 1 Sid. 100, 82 Eng. Rep. 995 (1663) and in *Pawley* v. *Wiseman*, 3 Keble 614, 84 Eng. Rep. 910 (1676).

71. The cases referred to in this paragraph are *Galizard* v. *Rigault*, 2 Salk. 552, 91 Eng. Rep. 467, Holt 597, 90 Eng. Rep. 1230, S.C., *Gallisand* v. *Rigaud*, 2 Ld. Raym. 809, 92 Eng. Rep. 40; *Rigaut* v. *Gallisard*, 7 Mod. 76, 87 Eng. Rep. 1106 (1702) (solicitation of chastity); *Nash* v. *Nash*, 1 Hag. Con. 139, 161 Eng. Rep. 503 (Con. London 1790) (bigamy); *Campbell* v. *Aldrich*, 2 Wils. K.B. 79, 95 Eng. Rep. 697 (1757) (clandestine marriage). *Campbell* indicated that a temporal conviction might be required before the deprivation proceeding could be undertaken, but *Taylor* v. *Morley*, 1 Curt. 470, 163 Eng. Rep. 165 (Arches 1837) finally decided otherwise. *Townsend* v. *Thorpe*, 2 Ld. Raym. 1508, 92 Eng. Rep. 479 (1726) and *Newcomb* v. *Higgs*, Fitz-G. 190, 94 Eng. Rep. 714 (1731) allowed a parish clerk to be deprived for felonious conduct directly related to his fitness for his position, even though he had not been convicted of the felony. For later material on this problem, see pp. 212-25, *infra*, especially the discussion on p. 217 of *Matter of A.B.*, 11 P.D. 56 (Ch. York 1886).

72. *Walker's Case*, 1 Freeman 62, 89 Eng. Rep. 52 (1672). Cf. *Boyle* v. *Boyle*, Comberbach 72, 90 Eng. Rep. 350 (1688) (jactitation suit prohibited as inconsistent with facts found in bigamy prosecution).

73. "Courts," Burn, i, 409, 426.

74. Bishop King: *Archdeaconry of Chichester*, 146-49. Gibson: *Visitations*. Printed forms: O.D.P., c. 19 (1816), c. 37 (1817), c. 273 (1842). The form used in 1857, O.D.P., c. 276, has no inquiries about morals.

75. The records referred to in this paragraph are: *Archdeaconry of Chichester*,

127-end; "Canterbury Visitations"; O.D.P., d. 708, ff. 75, 76, 82; *Spec. Dioc. Linc.*; Oxford Archdeaconry Papers c. 27, c. 28; O.D.P., c. 2139 (note especially f. 64, saying that few courts were held by the chancellor or his surrogate after July 1758 — before that, they were fairly regular); Woodforde, February 3 and 7, 1768, cf. November 17, 1794. See Ollard, "Introduction" *Archbishop Herring's Visitation Returns*, i (Yorks. Archaeol. Assoc. R.S. lxxi, 1928), p. xxi.

76. O.D.P., c. 656, ff. 66-9 (1803). Nineteenth century penances are referred to in Tate, 148 and Chadwick, i, 489. I have lost my source for the story of the railroad sightseers. The absence of an effective penitential system is lamented in Chambers, "Decay of Discipline," in *Ecclesiastical Reform*, ed. Shipley (London, 1873).

77. Gibson, *Visitations*.

78. 13 Car. 2, St. 1, c. 12, § 4 (1661). On the practice before 1640, see W.H. Hale, *Precedents and Proceedings in Criminal Causes, 1475-1640* (London, 1847).

79. Gibson, t. 42. See *Nosworthy* v. *Wainwright*, Ret. App. #114 (1703) (layman presented for suspicion of adultery, ordered to beg pardon for the scandal; excommunication for refusing to do so reversed).

80. "Fees," Burn, i, 559; "Stamps," Burn, ii, 349. For parish authorities dropping or trying to drop cases on account of expense, see O.D.P., c. 655, ff. 175-76, c. 656, ff. 49-50.

81. O.D.P., c 652, ff. 170-71 (1757); *Spec. Dioc. Linc.*, 180, 181-2.

82. Vol. II, 181-82; "Penance," Burn, ii, 142; Gibson, t. 46, c. 3; Sykes, *From Sheldon*, 189. Compare the two chancellors' commissions in O.D.P., d. 106, ff. 30-33, 48-50. The first one (1737) contains a general authorization to commute penances, whereas the second (1742) expressly requires prior resort to the bishop.

83. *E.g.*, O.D.P., c. 2139, f. 17, c. 653, ff. 170-71 (1757); *Spec. Dioc. Linc.*, 181 ("one woman for Bastardy stood in *Albis* through the Pious sentence and Prudent care and conduct of your Venerable Chancellour . . . . She performed her Penance with great signs of Repentance, and being very Poor, the Chancellour forgave her all his fees"), 183 (all 1721).

84. Id. 181 ("the Court keeps us in the Dark about all such matters"), 181-82. But see Id. 182 ("Our Chancellor . . . is a worthy Gentleman, and I daresay would scorn to suffer anything of that nature . . . .") (all 1721).

85. Gibson, t. 42, c. 7; Gibson, *Visitations*; "Visitation," Burn, ii, 481, 491-92. See the Oxford cases, *supra*, note 80, and O.D.P., c. 2139, f. 17, a churchrate case. In a few cases, the prosecution would be carried on by an aggrieved party. *E.g.*, *Chamberlayne* v. *Hewetson*, Ret. App. #100 (1693) (adultery prosecution by wronged spouse); *Blackiston* v. *Bernard, Blew* v. *Bernard*, Ret. App. #163-64 (1744) (prosecution of widow for cohabitation maintained by persons who will recover certain property if she remarries).

86. The process of dealing with contumacy is documented in Anon., *The Clerk's Instructor in the Ecclesiastical Courts* (Dublin, 1766), 26-30. See also "Excommunication," Burn, i, 545, 548-49; 1604, c. 65, 85.

87. O.D.P., c. 2139.

88. On common fame as a basis for prosecution, see 1604, c. 115; "Visitation," Burn, ii, 481, 489-90; *Robson* v. *White*, Ret. App. #57 (1669). In this batch of

cases, an accused who denied the fact but admitted to the bad reputation was treated the same as one who denied both.

89. The other proctor, one Beaver, shows up instead of Bilstone on February 5, 1743. Both appear in the act books, Oxford Archdeaconry Papers, c. 27, and figure occasionally in the bishop's correspondence, *e.g.*, O.D.P., c. c. 653, f. 123 (1756) (Beaver); Id., ff. 158-60 (1756) (Bilstone).

90. *Spec. Dioc. Linc.*, 181-2. See also, Id., 180.

91. See the 1842 return from All Saints, Oxford in O.D.P., c. 273. I owe the point about the effect of the Declaration of Indulgence and the Toleration Act to lectures by G.V. Bennett on February 12 and 19, 1970. As to the effect of temporal penalties, see Gibson, *First Charge*. F.D. Price suggests also that enclosures gave local landowners so much power as employers that they no longer needed the processes of the church to enforce social discipline in the countryside.

92. On the duty to present, see 1604 c. 26, 109-12, 117. The prohibition case referred to in text is *Selby's Case*, 1 Freeman 298, 89 Eng. Rep. 216 (1680). Cf. *Anon.*, 1 Freeman 290, 89 Eng. Rep. 210 (1677) (presentment, even if made under compulsion, may be processed).

93. 1604 c. 119. O.D.P., c. 27 has a set of printed articles from 1816 telling the churchwardens that unless they mark the form they are swearing that the buildings are in good repair, the cure well served, and none of the parishioners known to be guilty of incest, adultery, fornication, or other notorious crime presentable by the ecclesiastical laws. O.D.P., c. 37 has articles from 1817 that go back to the questionnaire form. But many churchwardens ignored the questions and scrawled "all well" across the whole sheet. One set was more verbose but equally vague: "that all are at all times exempt from suspicion with regard to every one of these improprieties we cannot aver, or say that any are notoriously guilty." The 1672 cases referred to in text are Anon., 1 Ventris 126, 86 Eng. Rep. 87, and Anon., 1 Ventris 114, 86 Eng. Rep. 78. The expedient of swearing to present whatever was presentable was evidently worked out between the judges and the ecclesiastical lawyers in a set of conferences described in *Dominus Rex and Pratt*, 3 Keble 205, 84 Eng. Rep. 678 (1674). Gibson's view of the subject appears in *Visitations*, 64ff.

94. 1604 c. 113.

95. Phil. ii, 956-57.

96. Tate, 213-20; Peyton, "Introduction", *Minutes of Proceedings in Quarter Sessions, Kesteven, 1675-95* (L.R.S., xxv, 1931), p. cix. The case of the man who already had a wife is in O.D.P., c. 655, ff. 145-46 (1801).

97. E.g., O.D.P., c. 656, ff. 179-80 (1804).

98. O.D.P., c. 2139, ff. 11, 17 and *passim*. The 1757 letter is O.D.P., c. 653, ff. 170-71.

99. *Blunt* v. *Park Lane Hotel, Ltd.*, [1942] 2 K.B. 253 is the most fully stated of several cases holding that the prospect of ecclesiastical correction is not serious enough to constitute a reason for not answering relevant interrogatories concerning sexual relations. Halsbury, 143-4, n. 10 gathers the rest of the cases. The author argues that the Ecclesiastical Jurisdiction Measure, 1963, while it does not abolish the church's criminal jurisdiction over the laity, abolishes every proceeding by which it may be exercised. I am not sure he is right. While § 69 seems to have the effect he

claims § 6(e) would seem to have the opposite effect. See also § 83(2)(f), preserving the visitatorial jurisdiction of the archdeacon. Of course, since there is no possibility of the jurisdiction being invoked, the question of whether it still exists is purely academic.

100. *Hutchinson* v. *Brooksbank*, 3 Lev. 376, 83 Eng. Rep. 738 (1693); *Wigmore's Case*, Holt 460, 90 Eng. Rep. 1153 (1706); *Haydon* v. *Gould*, 1 Salk 119, 91 Eng. Rep. 113 (Delegates, 1711); "Marriage," Burn, ii, 1, 29-30. In *Orchard* v. *Cobb*, Ret. App. #98 (1692), an invalidly married couple was separated at the suit of a third person. The possibility of bringing a similar proceeding was discussed in O.D.P., c. 656, f. 16 (1802), and Sir Robert Phillimore actually entertained one in 1856. Phil. 1040. On clergy who perform clandestine marriages, see note 71, *supra*. The church's control over the ceremony was ended by 6-7 Will. 4, c. 85 (1836), the jurisdiction of the church courts over marriage cases by 20-1 Vic., c. 85 (1857).

101. Tate, 148. The church defamation proceeding was abolished by 18-9 Vic., c. 41 (1855).

102. See O.D.P. b. 68 and d. 708 *passim*; *Archdeaconry of Chichester*, *passim*; "Canterbury Visitations," *passim*.

103. Peyton, "Introduction," *Minutes of Proceedings in Quarter Sessions, Kesteven, 1674-95* (L.R.S., xxv, 1931), pp. cxiv-cxxx. Occasionally, though, fines were imposed. See the cases in the index to the above work under Church, absence from; Conventicles; Sacrament, not receiving; Sunday, profanation of; Recusancy. Examples of the common law courts throwing cases out on technicalities include *R.* v. *Sedan*, 3 Keble 575, 84 Eng. Rep. 887 (1675); *Anon.*, 1 Freeman 285, 89 Eng. Rep. 206 (1674). For a truly inspired piece of pettifogging on behalf of religious freedom, see *Anon.*, *A Letter from a Justice of the Peace to a Counsellor at Law Concerning Conventicles with the Counsellors Reply*, Bodl. Pamph. c. 148 (15) (no date).

104. O.D.P., c. 430 has the returns to an inquiry put out by Bishop Fell of Oxford in 1682 to all his parish incumbents asking which parishioners did not come to church and why. O.D.P., b. 68, ff. 9-10 has Fell's notes for this or some other similar inquiry, and indicates that he is planning to single out someone for prosecution as an example to the others. The 1682 returns, however, indicate that pastoral approaches are uppermost in the bishop's mind. The 1662-63 visitation questionnaire in *Archdeaconry of Chichester*, 146-49 inquires whether the minister endeavors to convert recusants. Compare O.D.P., c. 432, questionnaires of 1767 and 1780 on papists — before they became legal. The bishop urges his clergy "that the Inquiry may be conducted with all the good will due from us to Fellow Subjects and Professors of Christianity." The clergy were often less tolerant than the bishops. See O.D.P., c. 430, ff. 17, 21, 31. As late as 1803, a parish incumbent was trying to get his bishop to stop the building of a Methodist meeting house in his parish. O.D.P., c. 656, f. 131.

105. *Britton* v. *Standish*, 6 Mod. 188, 87 Eng. Rep. 943 (1704).

106. Lecture by G.V. Bennett, February 19, 1970.

107. H. Prideaux, *Directions to Churchwardens* (Norwich, 1701). To the same effect is "Publick Worship," Burn, ii, 250, 251.

108. *Stanfield* v. *Sterne*, Ret. App. #165 (1749). The absentee defended by showing she had already been fined by the justices of the peace.

109. Lectures by G.V. Bennett, February 12 and 19, 1970.

110. Best, 55-6, 62-70; McClatchey, 98-122.

111. Mortgages and trusts: see note 47, *supra*. 1708 statute: 7 Anne, c. 18; see "Usurpation," Burn, ii, 499, 500. Bishop honoring equitable interest in advowson: *Athington* v. *Coverly*, 2 Eq. Ca. Abr. 518, 22 Eng. Rep. 437 (Ch. 1733); *Attorney General* v. *Bishop of Lichfield*, 5 Vesey Jr. 825, 31 Eng. Rep. 828 (Ch. 1801).

112. *R.* v. *Archbishop of York*, 3 Lev. 9, 83 Eng. Rep. 551 (1681); *R.* v. *Paget*, 3 Lev. 205, 83 Eng. Rep. 652 (1684); *R.* v. *Bishop of Norwich*, 3 Lev. 337, 83 Eng. Rep. 718 (1691); *R.* v. *Trussel*, 1 Sid. 329, 82 Eng. Rep. 1137 (1667); *Phillips* v. *Crawley*, 1 Freeman 83, 89 Eng. Rep. 61 (1673) Compare Vol. II, 145-47, 215-16. The consequences of these doctrines were mitigated by 1 Will. and Mar., c. 16 (1688) for third parties dealing in good faith with simonists.

113. Best, 58, quoting Jane Austen's *Sense and Sensibility*; McClatchey, 4.

114. Deathbed: *Barret* v. *Glubb*, 2 W. Bl. 1052, 96 Eng. Rep. 619 (1776); *Fox* v. *Bishop of Chester*, 6 Bing. 1, 130 Eng. Rep. 1180 (H.L. 1829). Induction: *Bishop of Lincoln* v. *Whitehead and Wolferstan*, 1 W. Bl. 491, 96 Eng. Rep. 284 (1764).

115. The 1713 statute is 13 Anne, c. 11 (sometimes called 12 Anne, St. 2, c. 12). The right of a clergyman to present himself to a living in his own gift was not definitively established until *Walsh* v. *Bishop of Lincoln*, L.R. 10 C.P. 518 (1875). "Benefice," Burn, i, 96, 103 says that self-presentation is illegal, but a clerical patron can request the bishop to admit him. The correspondence in O.D.P., c. 660, ff. 158-63 (1813) seems to arise from such a request.

116. "Benefice," Burn, i, 96, 103-4. The fact that every dispensation from the archbishop of Canterbury required £ 6 worth of stamps may have encouraged people not to bother. "Dispensation," Burn, i, 494, 499.

117. He cannot retire on a pension. Until the Incumbents Resignation Act, 1871, 34-5 Vic., c. 44, such a pension was regarded as simoniacal, since it constituted a financial inducement to resign the benefice. "Resignation," Burn, ii, 314-17; *Young* v. *Jones*, 3 Dougl. 98, 99 Eng. Rep. 558 (1782).

118. Best, 53-9.

119. *Anon.*, 12 Mod. 505, 88 Eng. Rep. 1479 (1701); *Hilliard* v. *Stapleton*, 1 Eq. Ca. Abr. 87, 21 Eng. Rep. 898 (Ch. 1701); *Peele* v. *Com' Carliol'*, 1 Str. 227, 93 Eng. Rep. 487 (1719); *Grey* v. *Hesketh*, Amb. 268, 27 Eng. Rep. 178 (Ch. 1755). Attacks by churchmen include Degge, *Parsons Law* (London, 1676), c. 5; Stillingfleet, *A Discourse Concerning Bonds of Resignation* (*Works*, iii, 713); Gibson, *First Charge*; "Simony," Burn, ii, 334, 340-42. For the earlier material, see Vol. II, 235-36.

120. *Hesketh* v. *Gray*, Sayer 184, 96 Eng. Rep. 846 (1755); cf. *Steeper* v. *Carver*, 2 Eq. Ca. Abr. 183, 22 Eng. Rep. 157 (Ch. 1708).

121. Legitimate use: *Anon.*, 12 Mod. 505, 88 Eng. Rep. 1479 (1701); *Hawkins* v. *Turner*, Prec. Ch. 513, 24 Eng. Rep. 230 (Ch. 1719). Illegitimate use: *Hilliard* v. *Stapleton*, 1 Eq. Ca. Abr. 87, 21 Eng. Rep. 898 (Ch. 1801); *Durston* v. *Sandys*, 1 Vern. 412, 23 Eng. Rep. 562 (Ch. 1683); *Peele* v. *Com' Carliol'*, 1 Str. 227, 93 Eng. Rep. 487 (1719). Cf. O.D.P., c. 651, f. 27 (1736), regarding a presentment to "hold the benefice."

122. *Bishop of London* v. *Ffytche*, 2 Brown 211, 1 Eng. Rep. 892 (H.L. 1783).

The number of bishops in the majority is stated in Best, 57n. Holdsworth, i, 376 has thirteen bishops and five lay peers. See *ibid.* and Beven, "The Appellate Jurisdiction of the House of Lords," *L.Q.Rev.*, xvii (1901) 357, 367-68 for criticisms — ill taken, in my opinion — of the decision. Lord Kenyon in 1790 was still hoping for the House to change its mind. *Bagshaw* v. *Bossley*, 4 T.R. 79, 100 Eng. Rep. 904 (1790).

123. *Bagshaw* v. *Bossley, supra*; *Partridge* v. *Whiston*, 4 T.R. 358, 100 Eng. Rep. 1063 (1791). Other cases are collected and discussed in *Fletcher* v. *Sondes*, *infra*.

124. 3 Bing. 499, 130 Eng. Rep. 606 (H.L. 1826). A subsidiary argument on the prevailing side was that there was no way to assure the presentment of the person named in the bond, and therefore no adequate distinction between this case and *Ffytche*. 7-8 Geo. 4, c. 25, moved on the spot, validated existing bonds. Thereupon, 9 Geo. 4, c. 94 was adopted validating future bonds under the conditions stated in text. It remained the law until Benefices Act, 1898 (Amendment) Measure, 1923, 14-5 Geo. 5, No. 1, § 5. In the actual case, the incumbent's victory was a hollow one. He was put out of the benefice for simony and the presentment devolved upon the king under 31 Eliz. 1, c. 6 (1589). The king presented the man in whose favor the bond had been made. *Watson* v. *Fletcher*, 8 B. & C. 27, 108 Eng. Rep. 952 (1828).

125. Best, 29, 232-33; Kennett, *Case of Impropriations* (London, 1704). 17 Car. 2, c. 3, § 7 (1665) exempted such donations from the mortmain laws. For examples of such donations, see O.D.P., c. 650, f. 7; d. 708, f. 132 (1685); c. 653, f. 58 (1752).

126. Voluntary endowment by impropriator: *Perne* v. *Oldfield*, 2 Chan. Cas. 19, 22 Eng. Rep. 826 (Ch. 1679) (to allow removal of curate would "lay a foundation for simony forever"). Endowment by Queen Anne's Bounty: 1 Geo. 1, St. 2, c. 10 (1714). Crown: *Bonsey* v. *Lee*, 1 Vern. 247, 23 Eng. Rep. 445 (Ch. 1683).

127. *Walwyn* v. *Awberry*, 1 Mod. 258, 2 Mod. 254, 86 Eng. Rep. 866, 1057 (1677) S.C. *Walwin* v. *Auberry*, 2 Ventr. 35, 86 Eng. Rep. 293; S.C. *Anon.*, 3 Keble 829, 84 Eng. Rep. 1037. The reports are confusing. The one in Keble indicates that the sequestration was upheld. The one in Ventris says it was rejected because the impropriation is lay property and therefore the church court has no jurisdiction. But the one in Modern Reports indicates that the church court can enforce the obligation by issuing a monition and enforcing it by the standard process of excommunication and *significavit*. The last view was the one that utimately prevailed. See the discussion in *Wickhambrook P.C.C.* v. *Croxford*, [1935] 2 K.B. 417 (C.A.). Gibson's argument, t. 9, c. 5, that since the impropriator had all the obligations of the former religious house he should be just as subject to sequestration as the religious house was seems to confound substance with procedure. The Chancel Repairs Act, 1932, 22-3 Geo. 5, c. 20 replaced the ecclesiastical proceeding with a secular proceeding to recover the cost of repairs as an ordinary debt. Most (but not quite all) obligations of lay impropriators to repair chancels were done away with when tithe rentcharge was abolished in 1936, as we shall see when we take up that subject at p. 103, *infra*.

128. Waste: *Bradly* v. *Stratchy*, Barn. C. 399, 27 Eng. Rep. 695 (Ch. 1740). Preaching: *Duke of Portland* v. *Bingham*, 1 Hag. Con. 156, 161 Eng. Rep. 509 (Con.

London 1792) (unsuccessful proceeding as patron); Ret. App. #181 (1795) (successful promotion as parishioner). Seats: *Clifford* v. *Wicks*, 1 B. & Ald. 509, 106 Eng. Rep. 187 (1818); *Jarratt* v. *Steele*, 3 Phil. Ecc. 167, 161 Eng. Rep. 457 (Con. London 1820). Burial vault: *Rich* v. *Bushnell*, 4 Hag. Ecc. 164, 162 Eng. Rep. 1407 (Arches 1827). Later cases established that the impropriator could not lock the vicar and churchwardens out of the chancel, *Griffin* v. *Dighton*, 5 B. & S. 93, 122 Eng. Rep. 767 (1864), but that he could in some cases pasture his sheep in the churchyard. *Greenslade* v. *Darby*, L.R. 3 Q.B. 421 (1868).

129. On churchwardens generally, see Prideaux, *Directions to Churchwardens* (1st ed., Norwich, 1701, through 8th ed., by Tyrwhitt, London, 1830); "Churchwardens," Burn, i, 283; Vol. II, *passim*; *Haw* v. *Blanner*, 2 Keble 125, 84 Eng. Rep. 79 (1666); *Hutchins* v. *Denziloe*, 1 Hag. Con. 169, 181, 161 Eng. Rep. 514, 519 (Con. London 1792).

130. 1604, c. 89. Theoretically, they were to agree on two names; the provision for each to choose one was to apply only if they failed to reach agreement. As a practical matter, it was simpler for each to choose one at the outset. The cases referred to in this paragraph are: *Anon.*, 1 Ventr. 267, 86 Eng. Rep. 179 (1675) (custom prevails over canon); *Churchwardens of Northampton's Case*, Carth. 118, 90 Eng. Rep. 673 (1690) (absent custom, parishioners choose both); *Hubbard* v. *Penrice*, 2 Str. 1246, 93 Eng. Rep. 1159 (1746) (absent custom, canon applies).

131. *R.* v. *Rice*, 5 Mod. 325, 87 Eng. Rep. 684 (1696) (not to pass on fitness); *Anon.*, 1 Ventr. 126, 86 Eng. Rep. 87 (1671) (not to pass on right to elect); *Williams* v. *Vaughan*, 1 W. Bl. 28, 96 Eng. Rep. 15 (1748) (ditto); *R.* v. *White*, 8 Mod. 325, 88 Eng. Rep. 233, 2 Ld. Raym. 1380, 92 Eng. Rep. 399 (1724) (*non fuit electus* is not a good return to alternative writ of mandamus to swear in churchwarden); *R.* v. *Harwood*, 8 Mod. 380, 88 Eng. Rep. 270, 2 Ld. Raym. 1405, 92 Eng. Rep. 414 (1724) (ditto in Mod.; not finally decided according to Lord Raymond, who thought the return was good and *White* wrongly decided); *R.* v. *Harris*, 1 W. Bl. 430, 96 Eng. Rep. 245 (1763) (swear both applicants); *R.* v. *Commissary of the Bishop of Winchester*, 7 East 572, 103 Eng. Rep. 222 (1806) (feigned issue); cf. *R.* v. *Dawbeny*, 2 Strange 1196, 93 Eng. Rep. 1123 (1744) (*quo warranto* does not lie for office of churchwarden).

132. *Anthony* v. *Seger*, 1 Hag. Con. 9, 161 Eng. Rep. 457 (Con. London 1789). The court argues that it is the duty of the ordinary not to accept an ineligible person, and that duty persists unless a contrary writ actually issues.

133. The 1682 incident is referred to in O.D.P., c. 430, ff. 2-3. The right to appoint a deputy was established for Protestant Dissenters by 1 Will. & Mar., c. 18, §§ 5, 8 (1688) and for Roman Catholics by 31 Geo. 3, c. 32, § 7 (1791). Generally, any eligible person was required to serve if appointed. *Castle* v. *Richardson*, 2 Strange 715, 93 Eng. Rep. 802 (1726); *Cooper* v. *Allnutt*, 3 Phil. 165, 161 Eng. Rep. 1289 (1820). The non-churchgoing churchwarden played a considerable role in some of the nineteenth century litigations. *E.g.*, *Ritchings* v. *Cordingley*, L.R. 3 A. & E. 113 (Arches 1868). See the return from Summer Town in O.D.P., c. 273 (1848), where the churchwarden making the return could not say if order was kept in church, because he was seldom there. It would seem that the secular duties of churchwardens plus the opportunity to block churchrates and oppose polish innovations kept non-

Anglicans interested in the office for some time.

134. The 1691 case: *Styrrop* v. *Stoakes*, 12 Mod. 9, 88 Eng. Rep. 1130. Cases holding that church court can require churchwardens to account: *Wainwright* v. *Bagshaw*, Cun. 34, 94 Eng. Rep. 1045 (1734); *Hooper* v. *Leach*, 3 Dougl. 434, 99 Eng. Rep. 735 (1784). Cases, besides the last two, holding that church court cannot examine churchwardens' accounts: *Adams* v. *Rush*, 2 Strange 1133, 93 Eng. Rep. 1083 (1740); *Snowden* v. *Herring*, Bun. 289, 145 Eng. Rep. 677 (1730); *Nutkins* v. *Robinson*, Bun. 246, 145 Eng. Rep. 662 (Ex. 1727); *Lyman* v. *Goulty*, 3 T.R. 3, 100 Eng. Rep. 424 (1789). Parishioners sue in church court after disallowing account: *Lewis* v. *James*, 1 Lee 611, 161 Eng. Rep. 224 (Arches 1755). Note that while the church court could not examine accounts, it could require the return of church property. *Welcome* v. *Lake*, 2 Keble 22, 84 Eng. Rep. 14 (1666).

135. "Parish Clerk," Burn, ii, 135; Vol. II, 222-23; 1604, c. 91; *Austin* v. *Gervas*, 2 Barn. K.B. 242, 94 Eng. Rep. 475 (1733) (rival claimants); *Peak* v. *Bourne*, 2 Strange 942, 93 Eng. Rep. 956 (1733) (deputy). On parish clerks generally, see S. and B. Webb, *History of English Local Government* (1906), 32-4.

136. *Anon.*, 12 Mod. 583, 88 Eng. Rep. 1535 (1701); *Pollard* v. *Awker*, 12 Mod. 260, 88 Eng. Rep. 1307 (1699); *Pitts* v. *Evans*, 2 Strange 1108, 93 Eng. Rep. 1063 (1739).

137. The cases referred to in this and the following paragraph are: *Candict and Plomer's Case*, Godb. 163, 78 Eng. Rep. 99 (1610); *Gaudyes Case*, 2 B. & G. 38, 123 Eng. Rep. 802 (1609); *Townsend* v. *Thorpe*, 2 Ld Raym. 1508, 92 Eng. Rep. 479 (1726); *Peak* v. *Bourne*, 2 Strange 942, 93 Eng. Rep. 956 (1733); *Newcomb* v. *Higgs*, Fitz-G. 190, 94 Eng. Rep. 714 (1731); *Barton* v. *Ashton*, 1 Lee 350, 460, 533, 161 Eng. Rep. 129, 170, 197 (Arches 1753-54); *R.* v. *Warren*, 1 Cowp. 370, 98 Eng. Rep. 1135 (1776); *Tarrant* v. *Haxby*, 1 Burr. 564, 97 Eng. Rep. 355 (1757).

138. *R.* ex rel. *Harris* v. *Smith*, 5 Q.B. 614, 114 Eng. Rep. 1381 (1844); Lecturers and Parish Clerks Act, 1844, 7-8 Vic., c. 59.

139. On the vestry generally, see "Vestry," Burn, ii, 477; Tate, 13-4. The case establishing the right of the incumbent to preside is *Wilson* v. *M'Math*, 3 Phil. Ecc. 67, 161 Eng. Rep. 1260, *proh. denied*, 3 B. & A. 650, 106 Eng. Rep. 650 (1819). J. Toulmin Smith, *The Parish* (London, 1854), c. 6, disagrees with the decision, arguing that the vestry was always a secular agency, and the minister presided over it simply because he could read. Mandamus to make the churchwardens summon a vestry was denied in *Anon.*, 2 Strange 685, 93 Eng. Rep. 783 (1725). It was granted in *R.* v. *Churchwardens of St. Margaret and St. John*, 4 M. & S. 249, 105 Eng. Rep. 827 (1815), but the case rested on a statute, 10 Anne, c. 11, § 24 (1711), specifying exactly when the meeting was to be held and what notice was to be given. In any event, mandamus was too expensive for regular use. *Dawe* v. *Williams*, 2 Add. 130, 162 Eng. Rep. 243 (Arches 1824) (parishioner guilty of offense when he interrupts service to call vestry meeting after churchwardens have failed to do so). Churchwardens' accounts are dealt with in note 134, *supra*. For other points made in this paragraph, see *Francis* v. *Steward*, 5 Q.B. 984, 114 Eng. Rep. 1519 (1844) (prohibition against proceeding to coerce vestry); *Hoile* v. *Scales*, 2 Hag. Ecc. 564, 162 Eng. Rep. 958 (Con. London 1829) (brawling); *Palmer* v. *Tijou*, 2 Add. 196, 162 Eng. Rep. 266 (Canterbury Pecul. Ct. 1824) (ditto); *Stutter* v. *Freston*, 1 Strange

52, 93 Eng. Rep. 379 (1716) (bishop cannot appoint churchwardens).   140. The cases referred to in this paragraph are *Jones* v. *Bishop of Llandaff*, 4 Mod. 27, 87 Eng. Rep. 242 (1691); *Anon.*, 11 Mod. 46, 88 Eng. Rep. 874 (1705); *Trelawny* v. *Bishop of Winchester*, 1 Burr, 218, 97 Eng. Rep. 281 (1757). See also *Sharrock* v. *Bourchier*, Raym. Sir T. 88, 83 Eng. Rep. 48 (1664) (litigation over right to freehold office must be in lay court). For later developments, see pp. 226-29, *infra*.

141. See, generally, "Peculiar,", Burn, ii, 135; *Wrighton* v. *Brown*, 3 Lev. 211, 83 Eng. Rep. 655 (1685). See O.D.P., c. 652, f. 36 (1744) on the problem of confirmation in the Dorchester peculiar. For various stages in a long-running dispute or cluster of disputes involving Lincoln College, the Dean and Chapter of Lincoln, and various bishops of Lincoln, see O.D.P., c. 651, ff. 62-5 (1739), 139-44 (1742); c. 652, ff. 83-4 (1745); c. 654, ff. 35 (1751), 85-6 (1786), 124 (1790); c. 655, ff. 56, 60, and *passim*. A proposed bill to abolish peculiars is referred to on f. 56. The Pluralities Act, 1838, 1-2 Vic., c. 106, § 108, and the Church Discipline Act, 1840, 3-4 Vic., c. 86, § 2 gave diocesan bishops authority over peculiars for purposes of those acts. The Ecclesiastical Jurisdiction Act, 1847, 10-11 Vic., c. 98 (an annual act, renewed every year until made permanent in 1922) gives all bishops uniform jurisdiction throughout their dioceses.

142. "Cathedrals," Burn, i, 199; "Colleges," Burn, i, 307; "Deans and Chapters," Burn, i, 440. The Exeter College case is *Philips* v. *Bury*, Skin. 447, 90 Eng. Rep. 198 (K.B. and H.L. 1692-94). On Richard Bentley, the embattled master of Trinity College, see *D.N.B.*, Bentley; *R.* v. *University of Cambridge*, 2 Ld. Raym. 1334, 92 Eng. Rep. 370 (1723); *Bishop of Ely* v. *Bentley*, 2 Brown 220, 1 Eng. Rep. 898 (H.L. 1732). Mandamus cases: *R.* v. *Dean and Chapter of Trinity Chapel*, 8 Mod. 27, 88 Eng. Rep. 21 (1721); *Clarke* v. *Bishop of Salisbury*, 2 Strange 1082, 93 Eng. Rep. 1046 (1738); *R.* v. *Bishop of Chester*, 1 Wils. K.B. 206, 95 Eng. Rep. 577 (1748); *R.* v. *Bishop of Ely*, 2 T.R. 287, 100 Eng. Rep. 156 (1788). *Phillips* v. *Bury*, *supra*, was an ejectment case. The 1707 statute referred to in text is 6 Anne, c. 21. The difficulties to which it responded, and those to which it gave rise, are described in Burn, i, 458-70.

143. Protection in church courts: *Cranden* v. *Walden*, 3 Lev. 17, 83 Eng. Rep. 554 (1681); *Yates* v. *Lodge*, 3 Lev. 19, 83 Eng. Rep. 555 (1681); *Gouch* v. *Buxton*, 11 Mod. 77, 88 Eng. Rep. 904 (1706), *but see Coxeter* v. *Parsons*, 2 Salk. 692, 91 Eng. Rep. 586 (1698). In lay court: See dictum in *Coxeter*, and the lengthy discussion in *Gallwey* v. *Marshall*, 9 Ex. 294, 156 Eng. Rep. 126 (Ex. 1853). Modern law; *Carter-Ruck on Libel and Slander* (London, 1985), 79.

144. Vol. II, 86, 95; 6 Geo. 4, c. 25 (1825); 7-8 Geo. 4, c. 28 (1827).

145. "Sequestration," Burn, ii, 329. The process was not available for a share in common funds, as in a cathedral chapter. *Mosely* v. *Warburton*, 1 Ld. Raym. 265, 91 Eng. Rep. 1073 (1698). In *Berry* v. *Wheeler*, 1 Sid. 91, 82 Eng. Rep. 989 (1662), a creditor was allowed to sue out a writ of *elegit* on a rectory; I cannot reconcile this case with anything I know about the law as it stood either before or since. There were other alternatives to sequestration, though. O.D.P., c. 655, ff. 103-5 (1800) shows a vicar who sold annuities payable out of his benefice income. O.D.P., c. 664, ff. 98-9 shows one who mortgaged his income. Id., ff. 46-66 shows one who left the country with his bishop's permission, and turned his whole benefice

over to his creditors. The transfer seems inconsistent with *Arbuckle* v. *Cowan*, 3 B. & C. 322, 127 Eng. Rep. 177 (1803).

146. Recreation: Hart, 85-98; W. Addison, *The English Country Parson* (London, 1947), 140-49. Justices of the Peace: McClatchey, 178-201; O.D.P., c. 431, f. 18 (1767):

> My Lord, If the beneficed Clergy, who have a competent income, would reside in their Parishes, throw away their cards, forbear to act in the Commissions of the Peace, which Commission infatuates them with a pride as senseless as that of Lucifer, and confine themselves to their proper business, they would cease to be despised by the Laity; and might then have it in their power to infuse into their Parishioners a rational and well-grounded abhorrence of Popery, with a true sense of Christian morality.

The horse dealer case is O.D.P., c. 664, ff. 67-8. Until 1869, only traders could be discharged in bankruptcy.

147. 21 Hen. 8, c. 13 (1529); 43 Geo. 3, c. 84 (1803); *Ex parte Meymot*, 1 Atk. 196, 26 Eng. Rep. 127 (Ch. 1747) (debts held binding); *Frogmorton* ex dem. *Fleming* v. *Scott*, 2 East 466, 102 Eng. Rep. 447 (1802) (lease held void); *Morris* v. *Preston*, 7 Ves. Jr. 597, 32 Eng. Rep. 220 (Ch. 1802) (ditto).

148. "Privileges and Restraints of the Clergy," Burn, ii, 224, 237.

149. Gibson, *Visitations*.

150. "Fees," Burn, i, 559; 1604, c. 135. Whitgift's table is printed in Burn, i, 562-64. The fees to be taken by practitioners in Doctors Commons were settled by a jury on November 19, 1734, according to Burn, i, 565-66. Burn cannot have meant a jury in the common understanding of the term; I have not been able to learn or guess what he did mean. The Ecclesiastical Courts Act, 1829, 10 Geo. 4, c. 53, began the series of modern statutes on the subject.

151. *Anderson* v. *Walker*, 3 Salk. 86, 91 Eng. Rep. 708, 2 Lutw. 1030, 125 Eng. Rep. 573 (1691) (custom triable in lay court); *Thompson* v. *Davenport*, 3 Salk. 86, 91 Eng. Rep. 708, 2 Lutw. 1030, 125 Eng. Rep. 573 (1701) (ditto); *Burdeaux* v. *Lancaster*, 12 Mod. 172, 88 Eng. Rep. 1242 (1697) (no work no pay); *Richards* v. *Dovey*, Willes 414, 125 Eng. Rep. 1352 (1746-47) (ditto); *Patten* v. *Castleman*, 1 Lee 387, 161 Eng. Rep. 143 (Arches 1753) (ditto).

152. Vol. II, 231; Boyle, 61ff; "Mortmain," Burn, ii, 72. The statutes concerning licenses referred to in text are 17 Car. 2, c. 3 (1665); 2-3 Anne, c. 11 (1703); 7-8 Will. 3, c. 37 (1696). It was the Bill of Rights, 1 Will. & Mar., Sess. 2, c. 2 (1689) that was regarded as abolishing the royal licensing power. Actually, though, the mortmain license was not a dispensation from the operation of a general law, it was a waiver of a property right. See Vol. II, 46.

153. 9 Geo. 2, c. 36 (1736); Boyle, 69ff; Best, 103-9. Exemption of Queen Anne's Bounty: 43 Geo. 3, c. 107 (1803); Exemption of new churches: 43 Geo. 3, c. 108 (1803). The effects of this act were largely mitigated by the Mortmain and Charitable Uses Act, 1868, 51-2 Vic., c. 42, but it was not finally repealed until the Charities Act, 1960, 8-9 Eliz. 2, c. 58, § 38. On American survivals, see "Wills," *Corpus Juris Secundum*, xciv, § 109.

154. O.D.P., c. 655, ff. 108-9. See Sykes, 90-91 where notice of a parliamentary election was being given in one part of a church while confirmation was being held in

another. 19 Geo. 2, c. 21 (1745), against swearing, called for reading the whole text in church four times a year. It was repealed by 4 Geo. 4, c. 31 (1823). Other acts are referred to in the Parish Notices Act, 1837, 7 Will. 4 and 1 Vic., c. 45 (1837), where the posting of notices is substituted for reading or announcement during services.

155. "Midwives," Burn, ii, 47; "Physicians," Burn, ii, 150. Some licenses are recorded in the register books in O.D.P., e. 14-25, and the power to grant such licenses was included in the 1733 arbitration between the archdeacon of Oxford and the diocesan chancellor over their respective jurisdictions. O.D.P., c. 266, ff. 34-43. *Benskin* v. *Cripes*, Rolle Abr. 286 (1633) held that the church courts had no jurisdiction over the offense of practicing midwifery without a license. Nevertheless, unlicensed surgeons and midwives appear occasionally in the disciplinary records during the late seventeenth century: e.g., O.D.P., d. 708, ff. 88, 114; "Canterbury Visitations", xxv, 19, 40; xxvi, 38 (1662); *Archdeaconry of Chichester*, 124-49, *passim*. I find no later ones. 3 Hen. 8, c. 11 (1511) required a license from the bishop to practice medicine or surgery. 14-15 Hen. 8, c. 5 (1522-23) required examination by the Royal College of Physicians or else a degree from Oxford or Cambridge to practice medicine. The later statute made no mention of surgery, nor did it say whether its requirement of an examination superseded the earlier requirement of a license or merely set a condition that had to be met before the license would issue. The situation just before the beginning of Victoria's reign is described in *Collins* v. *Carnegie*, 1 A. & E. 694, 110 Eng. Rep. 1323 (K.B. 1834). The Henrician statutes were superseded, although not formally repealed, by the Medical Act, 1858, 21-2 Vic., c. 90, which set up a modern register of physicians and surgeons. There was no statutory regulation of midwifery until the Midwives Act, 1902, 2 Edw. 7, c. 17. The archbishop of Canterbury still has power to award medical degrees, but his degree confers no right to be registered as a physician or surgeon. See Bell, *Davidson*, 1030-34.

156. Vol. II, 170; "Register Book," Burn, ii, 296; Tate, 43-82. On the right to inspect, see *Anon. (Dormer* v. *Ekyns)*, 2 Barn. K.B. 269, 94 Eng. Rep. 493 (1733). On reports by Dissenters, see Burn, ii, 297; 52 Geo. 3, c. 146 (1812).

157. Tax: 5-6 Will. & Mar., c. 21 (1693-94); 6-7 Will. & Mar., c. 6 (1694); 7-8 Will. 3, c. 35 (1695); Tate, 48-49. Burial in woollen: 18-9 Car. 2, c. 4 (1666); 30 Car. 2, c. 3 (1678); 54 Geo. 3, c. 108 (1813-14); Tate, 66-9. Tate quotes Pope's famous lines on the subject, *Moral Essays*, Ep. I, lines 246-51.

158. O.D.P., c. 655, ff. 172-74.

159. See Sykes, 41-91 on the political role of the bishops, and Id., 91-105 on the division of their time between the capital and their dioceses.

160. Archdeacons generally: Sykes, *From Sheldon*, 196-98. Suffragans: Sykes, 141-42. Rural Deans: "Deans and Chapters," Burn, i, 440, 476. For the epithet "oculus episcopi," see Gibson, t. 42, c. 8; "Archdeacon," Burn, i, 66, 69. Gibson as archdeacon: *Visitations*. As bishop: *First Charge*. Matters figuring in correspondence between the archdeacon of Oxford and his bishop included the building of a new church, O.D.P., c. 654. ff. 27-31 (1758), the repair of an old one, O.D.P., c. 660, ff. 183-84 (1813), a spurious title for ordination, Id., ff. 22-23 (1812), and an upcoming archidiaconal visitation, O.D.P., c. 653, f. 75 (1752).

161. A couple of commissions to chancellors are recorded in O.D.P., d. 106, ff. 30-3 (1737), 48-50 (1742). *Spec. Dioc. Linc.*, 181 (1721) has praise from a parish minister for the diocesan chancellor's handling of a bastardy case (quoted *supra*, note 83). Examples of correspondence between the bishop of Oxford and his chancellor include O.D.P., c. 651, ff. 113-16 (1741); c. 652, ff. 6-7 (1743); c. 655, ff. 164-69 (1801-2); c. 656. ff. 66-9 (1803). See also O.D.P., c. 651, ff. 14-17 (1738), where the bishop uses his chancellor's position to avoid taking the blame for not accommodating the redoubtable duchess of Marlborough in a pew case. Examples of advice to the bishop from his secretary include O.D.P., c. 652, f. 40 (1744); c. 653, f. 123 (1755); c. 654, ff. 126-29 (1790). On the chaplains, see Sykes, 106-10.

162. The following treatment of visitation, where not otherwise documented, is based on Sykes, 115-46. See also O.D.P., c. 652, ff. 67-68, 73-74 (1745), a report, evidently from the chancellor, on a visitation he has conducted for the bishop.

163. Gibson, *First Charge* is an example.

164. Gibson, *Visitations* is an example. On drafting a surrogate preacher, see "Visitation," Burn, ii, 481, 485-86.

165. 1604, c. 137. O.D.P., d. 19 (1679), e. 3 (1666-72), e. 7 (1704-6) are examples of books in which the different documents are listed and checked off. O.D.P., c. 653, ff. 25-28 (1750) has a sharp rebuke from the bishop for a clergyman who attended a meeting of the land tax appeal board to which he belonged instead of the visitation held at the same time. O.D.P., c. 652, f. 40 (1744) has a letter, perhaps from the bishop's secretary, advising him that clergy who fail to show up when they are supposed to should be cited to appear at the next stop. On procurations, see "Visitation," Burn, ii, 481, 492-95.

166. O.D.P., b. 18, b. 68, c. 19, c. 37, and c. 239 are examples. The quotation in this paragraph is from c. 37, f. 107. Other examples are "Canterbury Visitations"; *Archdeaconry of Chichester*.

167. Examples include: *Eng. Hist. Doc.*, x, 369-74; O.D.P., c. 432, d. 554, d. 565, d. 581.

168. Examples include O.D.P., b. 68, c. 327, d. 19, d. 708, d. 759, d. 760, e. 3, e. 7.

169. Woodforde, 10 June, 1777.

170. The examples mentioned in text are: Transported husband: O.D.P., c. 656, ff. 37-38 (1802). Low company: O.D.P., c. 655, ff. 147-48 (1801). Reading of services: O.D.P., c. 654, f. 80 (1780). Parishioners eating: O.D.P., c. 652, ff. 113-15 (1745). Family vault: O.D.P., c. 660, ff. 123-30 (1813). Close inquiry: O.D.P., c. 652, ff. 87-89 (1745). Excuses for nonresidence: O.D.P., c. 651, ff. 58-61 (1739); c. 652, f. 101 (1745); c. 656, ff. 99-103 (1805); c. 660, ff. 95-98 (1812). Curates and stipends: See notes 191-202 and accompanying text, *infra*. New church: O.D.P., c. 651, ff. 113-16 (1741); c. 652, ff. 27-31 (1758); cf. c. 266, ff. 67-70 (1751) (chapel); c. 653, ff. 125-28 (gallery). Rectory: O.D.P., c. 266, ff. 2-5 (1689); d. 106, ff. 139-40 (1692); c. 654, ff. 85-86 (1786). Quarrels: O.D.P., c. 651, f. 44 (1739); c. 654, ff. 87-104 (1787). Fist fight: O.D.P., c. 655, ff. 177-79 (1801). Law: O.D.P., c. 654, ff. 42-54 (1763).

171. E.g., O.D.P., d. 106, ff. 139-40 (1692); c. 266, ff. 2-5 (1689). Inquiry by the archdeacon was evidently an alternative. E.g., O.D.P., c. 654, ff. 27-31 (1758).

172. See note 232, *infra*.

173. This account of ordination, where not otherwise documented, is based on Sykes, 96-115; "Ordination," Burn, ii, 103.

174. O.D.P., c. 187 (1767-68), c. 194 (1777), c. 204 (1787-88), c. 208 (1796-97) contain documents submitted by ordinands. O.D.P., c. 941 has examination papers beginning in 1827. Forgery of the necessary documents would be a problem. E.g., O.D.P., c. 654, ff. 263-66 (1800).

175. Act of Uniformity, 1662, 14 Car. 2, c. 4, § 10. *Hill* v. *Boomer*, 2 Show. K.B. 53, 89 Eng. Rep. 788 (1679) established that the question of ordination should be tried in an ecclesiastical court and not by a jury. Presumably, this kept a Presbyterian from taking advantage of the sympathy of the local populace, and kept and unordained Anglican from getting by on his reputation.

176. E.g., O.D.P., c. 651, f. 27 (1738).

177. Sykes, 199-203. The quotation is from O.D.P., c. 660, ff. 144-47 (1813). It seems that the person involved succeeded in getting ordained in time despite the unwillingness of the bishop of Oxford to accommodate him. Id., f. 196.

178. Gibson, *First Charge*, 62-3; O.D.P., c. 656, ff. 108-9, 112 (1805), c. 660, ff. 22-3, 108 (1812). Most of O.D.P., c. 663 (1816-29) is taken up with the case of a pluralist vicar who presents an ignorant candidate for ordination so he can have a cheap curate. See especially ff. 30-2, 35-6. *Martyn* v. *Hind*, 1 Dougl. 142, 99 Eng. Rep. 94 (1779) holds that a rector's promise of a curacy as a title for ordination is a lay contract enforceable by the curate.

179. *Bishop of Exeter* v. *Hele*, Shower 88, 1 Eng. Rep. 61 (H.L. 1693); *R.* v. *Bishop of Hereford*, 1 Comyns 357, 92 Eng. Rep. 1110 (1720); cf. *M'Namara* v. _____, 5 Vesey Jr. 824, 31 Eng. Rep. 878 (Ch. 1801). These seem to overrule *Specot's Case*, 5 Co. Rep. 57a, 77 Eng. Rep. 141 (1590). The later nineteenth century cases seem to return to the *Specot* doctrine. *Bishop of Exeter* v. *Marshall*, L.R. 3 H.L. 17 (1867); *Willis* v. *Bishop of Oxford*, 2 P.D. 192 (Arches 1877).

180. *R.* v. *Archbishop of Canterbury and Bishop of London*, 13 East 419, 15 East 117, 104 Eng. Rep. 433, 784 (1811-12).

181. Sykes, 220. In some cases, examination of would-be pluralists was stricter. Id., 217-19; cf. O.D.P., c. 651, ff. 85-86 (1740). On curates, note that the nomination papers in O.D.P., c. 83 do not include evidence of the qualifications of the nominees.

182. The following discussion, where not otherwise documented, is based on Sykes, 214-20; "Plurality," Burn, ii, 154; "Residence," Burn, ii, 299; McClatchey, 30-69.

183. The excuses for pluralism were mainly financial. See *Spec. Dioc. Linc.*, xvi-xvii. Pluralism, of course, provided an excuse for nonresidence on all but one of the plural benefices. On other excuses, see Id., xiv, and the following from the Oxford correspondence: Incumbent cannot afford the hospitality expected of him: O.D.P., c. 650, ff. 32-7. Health, liberty, and worldly affairs: O.D.P., c. 651, ff. 58-61 (1739). Wife refuses to live in parish: O.D.P., c. 652, f. 101 (1749). Unfit house: O.D.P., c. 655, ff. 150-58 (1801). Incumbent cannot get tenant to leave vicarage: O.D.P., c. 656, ff. 87-88 (1803). Incumbent has not the heart to make his aged and infirm mother move: Id., ff. 95-103 (1805). Incumbent cannot educate his daughter

adequately in parish: O.D.P., c. 660, ff. 34-51 (1812). House too small, intended only to accommodate curate on Saturday night: Id., ff. 95-98 (1812).

184. *Brown* v. *Mugg*, Holt K.B. 136, 90 Eng. Rep. 974 (1700); *R.* v. *Bishop of Lichfield and Coventry and Clive*, 2 W. Bl. 969, 96 Eng. Rep. 571 (1775); *Apperley* v. *Bishop of Hereford*, 9 Bing. 681, 131 Eng. Rep. 769 (1833); *Alston* v. *Atlay*, 7 A. & E. 289, 112 Eng. Rep. 480 (Exch. Ch. 1837).

185. The applicable canon is 1604, c. 41. The two month rule is in Burn, ii, 163; Burn says it is a proviso habitually included in dispensations. McClatchey, 47-67 shows 32 pluralists with and 29 without dispensations in 1793, 19 with and 51 without in 1825.

186. 21 Hen. 8, c. 13, §§ 9-25 (1529). See Vol. II, 77-78, 215, 234.

187. *Jones* v. *Gegg*, 7 Mod. 374, 87 Eng. Rep. 1300 (1741). Gibson, *First Charge* seems to require a dispensation.

188. 21 Hen. 8, c. 13, §§ 26-33 (1529), amended by 28 Hen. 8, c. 13 (1536). See Vol. II, 77-78. Burn's suggestion is in Burn, ii, 303.

189. Halévy, i, 440-45; 43 Geo. 3, c. 84 (1803); 57 Geo. 3, c. 99 (1817). For later material, see pp. 199-203, *infra*. I have found only two reported cases under the Henrician statute, *Bevan* v. *Williams*, 3 T.R. 635n, 100 Eng. Rep. 775n (1776), and *Wilkinson* v. *Allot*, 2 Cowp. 429, 98 Eng. Rep. 1169 (1776). Perhaps other cases did not involve reportable legal issues.

190. 13 Eliz. 1, c. 20 (1571), temporary, kept in force by periodic renewals until made perpetual by 3 Car. 1, c. 4 (1627). See *Riler* v. *Cosen*, 2 Lee 189, 161 Eng. Rep. 143 (Arches 1753) (tithe action by lessee dismissed because lessor nonresident); *Frogmorton* ex dem. *Fleming* v. *Scott*, 2 East 466, 102 Eng. Rep. 447 (1802) (nonresident may avoid his own lease; ironically, the action, in ejectment, was based on a fictitious lease from the same nonresident).

191. E.g., O.D.P., c. 651, ff. 58-61 (1739) (note that in this case the churchwardens supported the incumbent's wish not to reside); c. 652, ff. 16-23 (1750); c. 655, ff. 136-44, 150-58 (1801); c. 660, ff. 57-67, 133-34, 158-63 (1812-13).

192. O.D.P., c. 655, ff. 111-16 (1800).

193. Great Chesterford is a few miles south of Cambridge, Swyncombe a somewhat longer distance southeast of Oxford. With a ruler and an atlas, I make the distance about 65 miles in a straight line. In a letter just previous to the one quoted, Marshall expressed trust that "your Lordship's goodness will prevent the distance between them being any objection." The bishop did not gainsay him.

194. Sykes, 238-50.

195. O.D.P., c. 651, ff. 40-41 (1739).

196. Sykes, 209. I checked a particular time and place in *Spec. Dioc. Linc.*, Manlake Deanery in 1721. I found twenty churches and one chapel, and seventeen clergy. Of these, two were beneficed in the deanery, but served, if at all, elsewhere. One was beneficed elsewhere and served in the deanery as a curate. One was beneficed in one church of the deanery, but hired a curate for that church and served another. Of the others, six served two cures, seven served one. Particularly complicated arrangements from the Oxford papers include O.D.P., c. 653, ff. 16-23 (1750) and c. 655, ff. 106-7 (1800). Particularly strenuous ones include O.D.P., c.

654, ff. 196-97 (1749), where a rector gets £ 29/7/2 out of his total income of £ 150 from a parish with twelve parishioners whom he must ride twenty miles to serve, and c. 660, ff. 26-27 (1812), where a man who earned £ 130 a year from two benefices and a curacy walked twelve miles every Sunday to serve them all. On the availability of university clergymen, see O.D.P., c. 653, ff. 67, 70, 71, 83 (1752), where a neighboring incumbent claims he can do the job better than a commuter from Oxford, and c. 660, ff. 22-23 (1812), where the archdeacon tells the bishop that there is no need for a curate in an Oxford city church because university men are always available. On complaints by parishioners, see O.D.P., c. 655, ff. 150-58 (1801) (curate serves four churches); c. 663, ff. 24-29 (three churches). Note that 1604, c. 48 forbids serving more than one cure on the same day without special permission from the bishop.

197. Curate for nonresident incumbent: 1604, c. 47; Vol. II, 125; O.D.P., c. 655, ff. 136-44 (1801). Curate for chapel of ease: O.D.P., c. 650, f. 25 (1682). Where a curacy was funded by Queen Anne's Bounty, it became a benefice under 1 Geo. 1, St. 2, c. 10 (1714), so that the bishop could fill it for lapse if the incumbent failed to nominate to it. If it was funded in some other way, the attorney general could enforce it as a charity, and stop the incumbent from serving it in person. *Attorney General* v. *Brereton*, 2 Vesey Sr. 425, 28 Eng. Rep. 272 (Ch. 1752). Curate for resident incumbent: O.D.P., c. 654, f. 80 (1780) (incumbent's preaching "so wild, disjointed, and unbecoming that the gravest persons in the church could not refrain from laughing"); c. 663, *passim* (case of Stevens, the blind vicar, 1820s); 57 Geo. 3, c. 99 (1817); *Capel* v. *Child*, 2 Cr. & J. 558, 149 Eng. Rep 235 (Exch. 1832). On the medieval situation, see Vol. I, 162. There were evidently so many priests during most of the medieval period that having at least one full time in each parish was not a problem. J. R. H. Moorman, *Church Life in England in the Thirteenth Century* (Cambridge, 1946), 55.

198. Sykes, 206-11. The statutes referred to in text are 13 Anne, c. 11 (sometimes cited as 12 Anne, St, 2, c. 12) (1713); 36 Geo. 3, c. 83 (1796); 57 Geo. 3, c. 99 (1817). Multiple curates: O.D.P., c. 663, ff. 24-29 (1827); c. 664, f. 27 (1829). Use of parsonage: O.D.P., c. 654, ff. 156-58 (1797); c. 655, ff. 64-68 (1800). Mortgage: O.D.P., c. 664, ff. 98-99 (1830). Some statistics on curates' stipends are compiled in *Spec. Dioc. Linc.*, xvi-xvii.

199. *R.* v. *Bishop of Peterborough*, 3 B. & C. 46, 107 Eng. Rep. 652 (1824); "Curates," Burn, i, 427, 434-35. O.D.P., e. 29 (1777-1811), *passim*, contains curates' licenses with stipends specified. See O.D.P., c. 651, ff. 72-73 (1740) for a contretemps that ensued when the incumbent balked at the stipend specified in his curate's license.

200. Queen Anne's Bounty: 1 Geo. 1, St. 2, c. 10 (1714); *R.* v. *Bishop of Chester*, 1 T.R. 395, 99 Eng. Rep. 1158 (1786). Other perpetual curacy: "Curates," Burn, i, 427, 436-37; *Perne* v. *Oldfield*, 2 Chan. Cas. 19, 22 Eng. Rep. 826 (Ch. 1679); *Attorney General* v. *Brereton*, 2 Vesey Sr. 425, 28 Eng. Rep. 272 (Ch. 1752); *but see Farnworth* v. *Bishop of Chester*, 4 B. & C. 555, 107 Eng. Rep. 1166 (1825). Nomination for life ineffective: *Price* v. *Pratt*, Bunbury 272, 145 Eng. Rep. 671 (Exch. 1729). Title: *Martyn* v. *Hind*, 1 Dougl. 142, 99 Eng. Rep. 94 (1779); O.D.P., c. 654, ff. 87-104 (1787); O.D.P., c. 656, ff. 108-9, 112 (1805).

201. 1604, c. 48 required a license. The seventh of Archbishop Wake's instructions to his suffragans (1716), printed in Burn, ii, 122-23, called for enforcing the canon, and Gibson, at least, announced his intention to do so. *First Charge.* See also O.D.P., c. 653, ff. 26-28 (1750), where the bishop reprimands a rector whose curate is not licensed. On more lenient bishops, see Sykes, 210, where Archbishop Secker refers to the cost of the stamp duties as an excuse for not licensing curates. On the tenure conferred by the license, see O.D.P., c. 653, ff. 163-67 (1756), c. 656, ff. 160-74 (1804). The vicar who preferred not to license his curate appears in O.D.P., c. 655, ff. 183-86 (1801). On incumbents returning to reside, compare O.D.P., c. 655, ff. 103-5 (1800), where the curate is licensed, with ff. 177-79 (1801), where he is not.

202. On the medieval canon, see "Curates," Burn, i, 427, 436-37; Vol. I, 117n. In *Martyn* v. *Hind*, 2 Cowp. 437, 98 Eng. Rep. 1174 (1776), an earlier stage of the case cited in note 200, *supra*, Lord Mansfield held that a rector who gave a curate his title for orders was estopped to take advantage of his lack of a license. There is an odd case in O.D.P., c. 655, ff. 73-96 (1800), in which a curate resists dismissal on the ground he is *not* licensed. Cases where the bishop patches things up, or tries to, include O.D.P., c. 651, ff. 72-73 (1740); c. 654, ff. 42-54 (1763); ff. 87-104 (1787); c. 656. ff. 181-82, 185-88 (1804).

203. The cases referred to in this paragraph are: A: O.D.P., c. 656. ff. 87-88 (1805); B: O.D.P., c. 663, ff. 12-13 (1826); C: O.D.P., c. 655, ff. 170-71 (1801); D: O.D.P., c. 652, f. 142 (1749); E and F: O.D.P., c. 651, f. 44 (1739) (a letter of thanks from one of the parties: the arbitration had evidently already taken place); G: O.D.P., c. 652, ff. 46-8 (1749); H: O.D.P., c. 266, f. 54 (1753); I: O.D.P., c. 656, f. 131 (1805); J: O.D.P., c. 653, ff. 115-17, 136-38 (1754).

204. *E.g.*, *Hutchins* v. *Denziloe*, 1 Hag. Con. 169, 161 Eng. Rep. 514 (Con. London 1792); O.D.P., c. 656, ff. 181-82, 185-88 (1804). Among the proceedings before the Court of Delegates, I have found two doctrinal cases, *Jones* v. *Pusey*, Ret. App. #118 (1704); *Havard* v. *Evanson*, Ret. App. #173 (1777), and one church ornament case, involving a stained glass window, *Pierson* v. *Gell*, Ret. App. #171 (1762). I also found one doctrinal case in the London Consistory Court, *Bishop* v. *Stone*, 1 Hag. Con. 424, 161 Eng. Rep. 604 (1808).

205. 7-8 Will. 3, c. 35 (1696) created a secular penalty. *Middleton* v. *Crofts*, 2 Atk. 650, 26 Eng. Rep. 788 (K.B. 1736) held that the canonical penalty could not be imposed on the laity, thereby leaving much of the field to the secular statute. 26 Geo. 2, c. 33 (1753) made clandestine marriages invalid as well as increasing the penalty for performing them. But bishops still had occasionally to deal with misguided clerics who violated the law, *e.g.*, O.D.P., c. 656, ff. 104-5, 110-11 (1805), as well as parish officers who encouraged clandestine marriages for the sake of the poor rates, e.g., O.D.P., c. 655, ff. 145-46, 175-76 (1801). See also O.D.P., c. 653, ff. 110-11 (1753), involving a license issued on a false oath. On hedge priests and "Fleet" marriages, see Sykes, 221, and pp. 116-18, *infra*.

206. Service chaplain: O.D.P., c. 655, ff. 103-5 (1800). Horse dealer: O.D.P., c. 664, ff. 67-68 (1830). Man £ 600 in debt: O.D.P., c. 660, ff. 26-27 (1812). Poor law settlement: *R.* v. *Inhabitants of Wantage*, 2 East. 65, 102 Eng. Rep. 293 (1801) (settlement denied). See also O.D.P., c. 664, ff. 98-99 (1835), where a man

mortgaged all but £ 10 of his income and Id., ff. 46-66 (1830), where a man left the country on account of his debts, and left his creditors to take possession of his benefice.

207. Incumbent complains of curate: O.D.P., c. 655, ff. 73-96 (1800-01). Curate complains of incumbent: O.D.P., c. 654, ff. 156-58 (1797). Letters from parishioners: Id., f. 80 (1780); c. 655 ff. 150-58 (1801); c. 652; ff. 129-35 (1756). Presentment by churchwardens: O.D.P., c. 239, ff. 196-203 (1829); "Canterbury Visitations," xxvii, 221 (1679); Id., 229 (1685). Copy of complaint to person complained of: O.D.P., c. 653, f. 157 (1829). Gist of charge: O.D.P., c. 655, ff. 147-48 (1801); Id., ff. 73-96 (1800). Investigation without stating grounds: O.D.P., c. 652, ff. 87-89 (1745); c. 655, ff. 177-79 (1801). Exhortation: O.D.P., c. 654, ff. 87-104 (1787); c. 655, ff. 147-48 (1801); c. 660 ff. 57-67 (1812). New job: O.D.P., c. 654, ff. 87-104 (1787). Reprimand: O.D.P., c. 653, ff. 25-28 (1750); c. 653, ff. 30-32 (1827). Promise of improvement: O.D.P., c. 651, ff. 40-41 (1739).

208. Incontinence: *Rich* v. *Gerald and Loder*, 1 Hag. Ecc. (App.) 8, 162 Eng. Rep. 763, Ret. App. #94 (1690); *R.* v. *Bishop of Chester*, 1 Wils. K.B. 206, 95 Eng. Rep. 577 (1748) (no warning necessary). Drunkenness: O.D.P., c. 655, ff. 164-69 (1801-2). Failure to obey monition to reside: *Jones* v. *Gegg*, 7 Mod. 374, 87 Eng. Rep. 1300 (K.B. 1741). Effect of general pardon: *Brereton* v. *Lane*, Ret. App. #121 (1707). Neglect of duty: *Pullen* v. *Clewer*, 1 Hag. Ecc. (App.) 2, 162 Eng. Rep. 760, Ret. App. #79 (1682). Simony: *R.* v. *Archbishop of York*, 3 Lev. 9, 83 Eng. Rep. 551 (1681); *Philips's Case*, 1 Sid. 169, 82 Eng. Rep. 1037 (1663) (general pardon not applicable). The statute referred to is 31 Eliz. 1, c. 6 (1589). Churchwardens or a private promoter might set the disciplinary process in motion where the bishop might not have done so on his own. *Bennett* v. *Bonaker*, 2 Hag. Ecc. 24, Eng. Rep. 773 (Arches 1824) (churchwardens); *Duke of Portland* v. *Bingham*, Ret. App. #181 (1795) (private promoter). I have already taken up the financial obstacles to any such proceeding.

209. *Hill* v. *Boomer*, 2 Show. K.B. 53, 89 Eng. Rep. 788 (1679). See also the discussion of *Slater* v. *Smallbrooke*, *supra*, note 30. On the medieval law, see *Corpus Juris Canonici*, c. 14, I, 6 in VI°; Vol. I, 83-84.

210. Lecturers: Act of Uniformity, 1662, 14 Car. 2, c. 4, §§ 15-17; "Lecturer," Burn, i, 659. Curates and preachers: 1604, c. 48-49; Vol. II, 120, 123-24. Chancellor's license will not do: *Smith* v. *Lovegrove*, 2 Lee 162, 161 Eng. Rep. 299 (Arches 1755); O.D.P., c. 652, ff. 15-18 (1743). License from chapter will not do: *Herbert* v. *Dean and Chapter of Westminster*, Fortescue 345, 92 Eng. Rep.. 883 (1720). Bishop may not determine right to position: *R.* v. *Churchwardens of St. Bartholomew's*, 3 Salk. 87, 91 Eng. Rep. 709 (1700) (prohibition granted); *but see Trapp.* v. *Finlay*, Ret. App. #130 (1712). Bishop may determine fitness: *R.* v. *Churchwardens of St. Bartholomew's*, *supra*; *R.* v. *Archbishop of Canterbury and Bishop of London*, 13 East 419, 15 East 117, 104 Eng. Rep. 433, 789 (1811-12).

211. On licenses to preach, see "Publick Worship," Burn, ii, 250, 279. On curates, see note 201, *supra*. *Gates* v. *Chambers*, 2 Add. 177, 162 Eng. Rep. 259 (Arches 1824) indicates that for occasional filling-in no license is required.

212. *Finch* v. *Harris*, 12 Mod. 640, 88 Eng. Rep. 1573 (1701) (donative; incumbent cannot be deprived, but other censures can be imposed); *R.* v. *Wroughton*,

3 Burr. 1682, 97 Eng. Rep. 1045 (1765) (invitation of incumbent; removed by force); *Trebec* v. *Keith*, 2 Atk. 498, 26 Eng. Rep. 700 (Ch. 1742) (secular arm; no help from Toleration Act).

213. Trespasser: *Anon.*, 12 Mod. 420, 88 Eng. Rep. 1423 (1699), S.C. *Turton* v. *Reignolds*, 12 Mod. 433, 88 Eng. Rep. 1431. Bishop cannot be compelled: *R.* v. *Bishop of London*, 1 T.R. 331, 99 Eng. Rep. 1123 (1786); *R.* v. *Bishop of Exeter*, 2 East 461, 102 Eng. Rep. 445 (1802). Bishop will not license without incumbent's consent: O.D.P., c. 652, ff. 163-67 (1756). Once licensed, may stay on. Ibid. See also *R.* v. *Field*, 4 T.R. 125, 100 Eng. Rep. 930 (1791) (rector cannot be required to admit lecturer); *R.* v. *Bathurst*, 1 W. Bl. 210, 96 Eng. Rep. 115 (1760) (vicar may change time of popular lecture); *Clinton* v. *Hatchard*, 1 Add. 94, 162 Eng. Rep. 34 (Commissary of Dean and Chapter of Westminster 1822) (parishioners guilty of brawling for trying to introduce lecturer over objections of incumbent).

214. "Chapel," Burn, i, 213; *Carr* v. *Marsh*, 2 Phil. Ecc. 198, 161 Eng. Rep. 1188 (Arches 1814). Private chapel: *Moysey* v. *Hillcoat*, 2 Hag. Ecc. 30, 162 Eng. Rep. 775 (Arches 1828); *Anno B.C.P.*, 399. Chapel of ease; *Attorney General* v. *Brereton*, 2 Vesey Sr. 425, 28 Eng. Rep. 272 (Ch. 1752); *Dixon* v. *Kershaw*, Amb. 529, 27 Eng. Rep. 341 (Ch. 1766); *Farnworth* v. *Bishop of Chester*, 4 B. & C. 555, 107 Eng. Rep. 1166 (1825); O.D.P., c. 650 f. 25 (1682); c. 663 f. 41 (1827).

215. There is a complete set of documents and consents in O.D.P., c. 266, ff. 67-70 (1761). The requirements are discussed in *Dixon* v. *Kershaw*, Amb. 529, 27 Eng. Rep. 272 (Ch. 1766); *R.* v. *Bishop of Exeter*, 2 East 461, 102 Eng. Rep. 445 (1802); *Moysey* v. *Hillcoat*, 2 Hag, Ecc. 30, 162 Eng. Rep. 775 (Arches 1828). *Dixon* is the case where the parishioners had been choosing the lecturer for ninety years.

216. Vol. I, 125, 180; 1604, c. 71. *Pace me ipso*, Vol. II, 153.

217. "Church," Burn, i, 231. Magistrates: O.D.P., c. 655, ff. 108-9 (1800) ("Answered expressing my disapprobation and that it was the Duty of the Church Wardens to prevent it."). Encroachments: *Quilter* v. *Newton*, Carthew 152, 90 Eng. Rep. 693 (1690); *Pew* v. *Cresswell*, 2 Str. 1012, 93 Eng. Rep. 1002 (1735).

218. The statute of Edward VI referred to in text is 5-6 Edw. 6, c. 4 (1551-52), repealed as to lay offenders by Ecclesiastical Courts Jurisdiction Act, 1860, 23-4 Vic., c. 32. The 1702 case is *Wenmouth* v. *Collins*, 2 Ld. Raym. 850, 92 Eng. Rep. 68. See also *Ex parte Williams*, 4 B. & C. 314, 107 Eng. Rep. 1076 (1828); *Hutchins* v. *Denziloe*, 1 Hag. Con. 169, 161 Eng. Rep. 514 (Con. London 1792) on the relation between the statute and the traditional canon law. Vestry meetings: *Hoile* v. *Scales*, 2 Hag. Ecc. 564, 162 Eng. Rep. 958 (Con. London 1829); *Palmer* v. *Tijou*, 2 Add. 196, 162 Eng. Rep. 266 (Canterbury Pecul. 1824); *Lee* v. *Mathews*, 3 Hag. Ecc. 169, 162 Eng. Rep. 1119 (Arches 1830). Visitation: *Taylor* v. *Morley*, 1 Curt. 470, 163 Eng. Rep. 165 (Arches 1837). Abuse of pulpit: *Cox* v. *Gooday*, 1 Hag. Con. 138, 161 Eng. Rep. 694 (Con. London 1810); *Newbery* v. *Goodwin*, 1 Phil. Ecc. 282, 161 Eng. Rep. 985 (Arches 1811); Vol. II, 128. Decorum in services: *Dawe* v. *Williams*, 2 Add. 130, 162 Eng. Rep. 243 (Arches 1824).

219. See Vol. II, 134, 234, and material cited there.

220. From a leaflet "A Free Church and no Favour," (London, Free and Open Church Association, 1875).

221. See generally, "Church," Burn, i, 230, 254-59. On seating by class, see the

plan of a proposed new church in O.D.P., c. 654, f. 37 (1763). Duty of churchwardens: *Walter* v. *Gunner*, 1 Hag. Con. 315, 161 Eng. Rep. 565 (Con. London 1798); *Fuller* v. *Lane*, 2 Add. 419, 162 Eng. Rep. 348 (Arches 1825). Common law proceeding against disturber: *Buxton* v. *Bateman*, 1 Sid. 88, 82 Eng. Rep. 987 (1662); *Cross* v. *Salter*, 3 T.R. 638, 100 Eng. Rep. 777 (1790). Ecclesiastical proceeding: *Wyllie* v. *Mott*, 1 Hag. Ecc. 28, 162 Eng. Rep. 495 (Arches 1827). It appears, however, that equitable relief was not available. *Baker* v. *Child*, 2 Vern. 226, 23 Eng. Rep. 746 (Ch. 1691). On the superior rights of the ordinary, see *Greatchery* v. *Beardsley*, 2 Lev. 240, 83 Eng. Rep. 537 (1679); *Langley* v. *Chute*, Raym. Sir T. 246, 83 Eng. Rep. 126 (1679); *Presgrave* v. *Churchwardens of Shrewsbury*, 1 Salk. 167, 91 Eng. Rep. 154 (1704). On the scope of faculties and other appropriations, see *Anon.*, 12 Mod. 554, 88 Eng. Rep. 1514 (1701), and general discussion in *Walter* and *Fuller*, *supra*, and the bishop's apologies to the Duchess of Marlborough in O.D.P., c. 651, ff. 14-19 (1738). On the changing criteria for issuing faculties, compare O.D.P., c. 105 (late seventeenth and early eighteenth centuries) with O.D.P., b. 20 (1754-1850).

222. *Swetnam* v. *Archer*, 8 Mod. 338, 88 Eng. Rep. 241, Fort. 346, 93 Eng. Rep. 884 (1724). In this case, the ecclesiastical proceeding was prohibited because it was inconsistent with a claim to a customary right. An ecclesiastical proceeding to enforce a customary right was also prohibitable, since the trial of custom belonged in the lay court. *Paxton* v. *Wright*, 2 Kenyon 15, 96 Eng. Rep. 1091 (1757); *Byerley* v. *Windus*, 5 B. & C. 1, 108 Eng. Rep. 1 (1826). Usually, you established a custom by showing that you or your ancestors had repaired the seat in question. But if you or your ancestors had built the aisle or chapel in which the seat was situated, you did not have to show repairs. *Buxton* v. *Bateman*, 1 Sid. 88, 82 Eng. Rep. 987 (1662). Also, the standard of proof was less rigorous if you were suing someone who sat in your seat than if you were litigating with the ordinary or the churchwardens. Ibid. Gibson's concern about parishioners prescribing against the ordinary is expressed in Gibson, t. 9, c. 4, and Burn, i, 255. It rests on two cases: *Brabin* v. *Trediman*, 2 Rolle 24, 81 Eng. Rep. 634 (1618), and *Colebach* v. *Baldwyn*, 2 Lutw. 1032, 125 Eng. Rep. 574 (1692). But in *Colebach* there was no specific grant by the ordinary in issue, and in *Brabin* there was an alternative ground for holding the ordinary's grant to be unlawful — it was to the grantee and his heirs, and the heir was not a parishioner. See the other report, *Brabin and Tradum's Case*, Popham 140, 79 Eng. Rep. 1241. *Langley* v. *Chute*, Raym. Sir T. 246, 83 Eng. Rep. 126 (1679) and *Presgrave* v. *Churchwardens of Shrewsbury*, 1 Salk. 167, 91 Eng. Rep. 154 (1704) are both clear that the ordinary's powers cannot be prescribed against. *Brabin* was cited to the court in *Langley*, and caused one of the three judges to dissent. But the cases are distinguishable, because the ordinary's action in *Langley* annexed the disputed pew to a house in the parish rather than granting it to a non-parishioner.

223. *Walter* v. *Gunner*, 1 Hag. Con. 315, 161 Eng. Rep. 565 (Con. London 1798).

224. Since the proprietary chapel was an innovation and had no legal status, the bishop could withhold or revoke a license for any reason or no reason at all. *Hodgson* v. *Dillon*, 2 Curt. 388, 163 Eng. Rep. 488 (Con. London 1840).

225. On this and the following two paragraphs, see generally "Church," Burn, i,

231, 263-65. Authority of incumbent where no faculty: O.D.P., c. 653, ff. 115-17,
136-38 (1754); *Seager* v. *Bowle*, 1 Add. 541, 162 Eng. Rep. 191, Ret. App. #186
(Delegates 1823); *Bryan* v. *Whistler*, 8 B. & C. 287, 108 Eng. Rep. 1050 (1828)
(vault). Churchwardens: *Beckwith* v. *Harding*, 1 B. & Adl. 509, 106 Eng. Rep. 187
(1818). Faculty cases: *Cart* v. *Marsh*, 2 Str. 1080, 93 Eng. Rep. 1044 (1738)
(appeal); *Bulwer* v. *Hase*, 3 East 216, 102 Eng. Rep. 580 (1803) (incumbent has no
veto); *Rich* v. *Bushnell*, 4 Hag. Ecc. 164, 162 Eng. Rep. 1407 (Arches 1827) (ditto);
O.D.P., c. 651, ff. 113-16 (1742) (correspondence between chancellor and bishop).

226. "Church," Burn, i, 231, 247-53. Statistics: "Canterbury Visitations" shows
13 entries regarding the fabric from 1660 through 1699, none thereafter.
Archdeaconry of Chichester shows 27 from the 1660s. Out of 188 churchwardens'
returns between 1784 and 1817 in O.D.P., c. 37, I find only six complaints of the
state of repair of the church. Examples of churchwardens' reports of dilapidations
include O.D.P., d. 708, ff. 67, 82 (1685). On archdeacons' reports, see Gibson,
Visitations; "Canterbury Visitations," xxvii, 221 (1679), and Id., xxv, 40, where the
archdeacon's official and the churchwardens inspected the church together. Cf.
O.D.P., c. 652, ff. 67-68 (1745) (chancellor reports to bishop). On churchrates, see
note 239, *infra*. On voluntary collections and repairs by local landowners, see Sykes
232-33 and the failure of the fund drive referred to in O.D.P., c. 654, ff. 27-31
(1763). On making a lay impropriator repair the chancel, see note 127, *supra*.

227. On parsonages generally, see "Dilapidations," Burn, i, 486; McClatchey, 19-
23; Hart, 135-39. On the condition of the parsonage as an excuse for nonresidence,
see Best, 204-5; *Spec. Dioc. Linc.*, xiv, xvi; O.D.P., c. 655, ff. 150-58 (1801); c.
656, ff. 95-98 (1812). In *Wilkinson* v. *Allot*, 2 Cowp. 429, 98 Eng. Rep. 1169
(1776), Lord Mansfield said that the incumbent must reside within the parish even if
the actual parsonage is not suitable. See the further development of this subject in
pp. 203-7, *infra*. Suits by incumbents against their predecessors include *Sand's Case*,
Skinner 122, 90 Eng. Rep. 57 (1683) in the ecclesiastical court, *Jones* v. *Hill*, 3 Lev.
268, 83 Eng. Rep. 683 (1690), and *Wise* v. *Metcalfe*, 10 B. & C. 298, 109 Eng. Rep.
461 (1829) in the lay court. A person who lost in the lay court could not try again in
the ecclesiastical. *Okes* v. *Ange*, 3 Lev. 413, 83 Eng. Rep. 757 (1695). A curate
could proceed in the lay court but not in the ecclesiastical. *Pawley* v. *Wiseman*, 3
Keble 614, 84 Eng. Rep. 910 (1676). On commissioners, see *Sollers* v. *Lawrence*,
Willes 414, 125 Eng. Rep. 1243 (1743); O.D.P., c. 266, ff. 2-5 (1689); d. 106, ff.
139-40 (1692); c. 653, ff. 35-36 (1750); c. 660, ff. 34-51 (1812). See O.D.P., c.
654, ff. 85-86 (1786); c. 660, ff. 34-51 (1812), 131 (1813) for correspondence
regarding funds for repairs. The statutes referred to in text are 17 Geo. 3, c. 53
(1777) (referred to in the above correspondence as "Gilbert's Act"); 21 Geo. 3, c. 66
(1781); 43 Geo. 3, c. 107 (1803); 57 Geo. 3, c. 99 (1817); 7 Geo. 4, c. 66 (1826).

228. The role of the incumbent in administering local charities is dealt with in
McClatchey, 123-31. For examples of schools in church, see "Canterbury
Visitations," xxv, 35 (1686); O.D.P., c. 239, ff. 196-203 (1829). The library statute
is 7 Anne, c. 14 (1709). On the enforcement of charities by the attorney general, see
Attorney General v. *Ruper*, 2 P. Wms. 126, 24 Eng. Rep. 667 (Ch. 1722); *Attorney
General* v. *Gardner*, Barn. C. 483, 27 Eng. Rep. 729 (Ch. 1741); *Attorney General*
v. *Bishop of Lichfield*, 5 Vesey Jr. 825, 31 Eng. Rep. 878 (Ch. 1801). For examples

of visitation inquiries and reports, see *Archdeaconry of Chichester*, 146–49 (1662-63); "Canterbury Visitations," xxv, 30 (1679); O.D.P., d. 708, ff. 58, 103, 115 (1685); O.D.P., d. 759, f. 85 (1759). For correspondence, see O.D.P., c. 651, ff. 22-25 (1738); f. 29 (1739); f. 54 (1739); ff. 121-25 (1742); d. 760, ff. 8, 10 (1774).

229. "Schools," Burn, i, 319; 1604, c. 77, 79, 137; Vol. II, 55, 151, 233. The points made in this paragraph are established in *Cox's Case*, 1 P. Wms. 28, 24 Eng. Rep. 281 (1700) (grammar school only); *Belcham* v. *Barnardiston*, 1 P. Wms. 32n, 24 Eng. Rep. 282n (1698-99) (lay schoolmaster); *Matthews* v. *Burdet*, 2 Salk. 412, 672, 3 Salk. 318, 91 Eng. Rep. 357, 571, 846 (1701) (founder's statutes). The bishop's general licensing power and his power to inquire into the moral and intellectual qualifications of the would-be licensee are upheld in *Matthews*, and in *R.* v. *Bishop of Lichfield and Coventry*, 2 Str. 1023, 93 Eng. Rep. 1008 (1736); *R.* v. *Archbishop of York*, 6 T.R. 490, 101 Eng. Rep. 664 (1795). Visitation reports on schoolmasters include O.D.P., b. 68, f. 6 (1679); "Canterbury Visitations," xxv, 30 (1679); O.D.P., d. 708, ff. 64, 68 (1685) ("In Horton there is one Henry Kemp a schoolmaster who comes not to church. q. whether licensed."). The 1779 statute referred to in text is 19 Geo. 3, c. 44.

230. For the Elizabethan and Henrician statutes on leases and alienations, see Vol. II, 225-29. The statutory adjustments referred to in text include 5 Geo. 3, c. 17 (1765), allowing tithes and incorporeal hereditaments to be leased on the same terms as land, 39-40 Geo. 3, c. 41 (1800), allowing land to be leased in parcels, 41 Geo. 3, c. 109 (1801), allowing twenty-one year leases of allotments given on enclosure, and 55 Geo. 3, c. 147 (1815), allowing exchanges generally with the consent of patron and ordinary. On private enclosure bills, see Best, 64; McClatchey, 98-122. It appears that enclosures were usually by agreement until around 1720, usually by private bill thereafter. T.E. Scrutton, *Commons and Common Fields* (Cambridge, 1887), 130 ff. For a case invalidating an enclosure agreement because the king, as patron, had not acquiesced, see *Cholmley* v. *Attorney General*, 7 Brown 34, 3 Eng. Rep. 23 (H.L. 1767). In O.D.P., b. 68, ff. 13-14 (1774) an incumbent complains of an enclosure effected without his consent, which he cannot afford to take to court.

231. "Glebe Lands," Burn, i, 585, 587-88. O.D.P., b. 111, deed #9 (1784) is an example of such an agreement. It had the consent of the bishop and the patron, but, as it was before the 1815 statute, it would have been open to attack.

232. O.D.P., d. 106, ff. 132-37 (1691) is an example of an exchange approved by a commission on enclosure of a parish. O.D.P., c. 266 has several other examples. Lost lands are inquired for in the visitation papers in *Archdeaconry of Chichester*, 146-49. Among episcopal complaints and exhortations are O.D.P., d. 760, f. 9 (1771) ("Church Land let for 1/3 of the Value."); Best, 99n ("Glebe lands have been blended with temporal Estates: and Pretenses set up, that only such a yearly Rent, far inferior to the real Value, is payable from them." — Bishop Secker to his clergy, 1750); O.D.P., d. 759, f. 85 (1759) ("a Terrier wanted" underlined). In the visitations from the 1660s in *Archdeaconry of Chichester*, I find two parishes reporting the lack of a terrier. 1604, c. 87 requires every parish to have one. "Terrier," Burn, ii, 367, 368-72 sets forth in full Burn's own terrier for his vicarage of Orton in Westmoreland. It is signed by the churchwardens and principal inhabitants as well as by Burn as vicar. It recites that it has been compiled by

direction of the bishop, and has been exhibited before the chancellor of the diocese. Other terriers are discussed in Tate, 125-33. Best, 100 points out that the compiling of these records provoked a good deal of resentment: "It was the kind of precaution that no layman in his right mind neglected to take, but what was prudence in a layman became, of course, avarice in a parson, and could not be judged on its merits."

233. The flooded lands case is *R.* v. *Commissioners of the Nene Outfall*, 9 B. & C. 874, 109 Eng. Rep. 461 (1829). The status of tithe as a personal obligation was also reflected in the discussion and even occasional collection of tithe on wages and other personal income. Best, 99; "Tithes," Burn, ii, 373, 436-39. There was a case as late as 1833 of a man being held liable to pay fourpence in the pound on his wages, and being imprisoned by the justices of the peace for not doing so. P.P. Eng., 1833, xxvii, 497. See also *Weekes* v. *Trussel*, 1 Sid. 181, 82 Eng. Rep. 1044 (1664), which seems to indicate that the obligation to set out tithes dies with the person who should have done it. W. Bohun, *Law of Tithes* (3d ed., London, 1744), 159 says an executor must pay out of the assets of the estate, but he shows no authority. Even if the executor is liable, Bohun doubts if the heir is. On the part played by tithes in private enclosure bills, see McClatchey, 104-7. In the enclosure agreement in O.D.P., d. 106, ff. 132-37 (1690), the rector was given an annual sum in lieu of all tithes from the patron. He was free to abandon the agreement at any time, but could not go back to it once he had done so. Presumably, that was a sufficient incentive to keep the agreement in force.

234. "Tithe," Burn, ii, 373, 388-97; W. Bohun, *Law of Tithes* (3d ed., London, 1744), 200-52. The 1571 statute is 13 Eliz. 1, c. 10. For an additional example of a *modus* disallowed as too rank, see *Smith* v. *Roocliff*, Bunbury 20, 145 Eng. Rep. 580 (Exch. 1717) (one shilling in the pound, either of rent or of the value of the land). The above authorities distinguish a composition from a *modus* according to whether it arises by agreement or by custom. In my opinion, they are not quite accurate. While it is true that a *modus* could arise by custom and a composition could not, I believe that was a consequence of the difference between them, rather than the difference itself. The real difference was that a *modus* was a "way of tithing," a replacement for the mathematical tenth by something equivalent but easier to compute, whereas a composition was an agreement by the titheholder to forego tithe in exchange for some other consideration.

235. E.g., Gibson, *First Charge*. Gibson also refers to a proposed bill that would have finalized prescriptive loss of tithe by requiring the plaintiff in every tithe case to show that he had collected tithe within a specified number of years. The 1696 statute referred to in text is 7-8 Will. 3, c. 6. Secker's address to his clergy is referred to in Best, 99.

236. See O.D.P., c. 663, ff. 12-3 (1826), where a rector seeks his bishop's advice as to whether he should seek an augmentation from Queen Anne's Bounty or try to collect the tithes he is entitled to. That some incumbents opted for more tithe is indicated by Best, 62-67.

237. The statutes in question were 32 Hen. 8, c. 28 (1540); 1 Eliz. 1, c. 19 (1559); 13 Eliz. 1, c. 10, 20 (1571); 18 Eliz. 1, c. 11 (1576); 1 Jac. 1, c. 3 (1603); 5 Geo. 3, c. 17 (1765); 39-40 Geo. 3, c. 41 (1800). On the earlier ones, see Vol. II,

225-29. On the easygoing attitudes of clerical landlords, see Best, 101.

238. Mortuaries: "Mortuary," Burn , ii, 80; *Oldham* v. *Rightson*, 12 Mod. 326, 88 Eng. Rep. 1355 (1699). Easter offerings: *Carthew* v. *Edwards*, Amb. 72, 27 Eng. Rep. 43 (Exch. 1749); *Edgerton* v. *Still*, Bunbury 198, 145 Eng. Rep. 646 (Exch. 1725); *Lawrence* v. *Jones*, Bunbury 173, 145 Eng. Rep. 637 (Exch. 1724); *Fuller* v. *Say*, Willes 629, 125 Eng. Rep. 1356 (1747). Procurations: "Visitation," Burn, ii, 481, 492-95; *Sanderson* v. *Clagget*, 1 Str. 421, 93 Eng. Rep. 609 (1720) J. Stephens, *Procurations, Synodals and Pentecostals* (London, 1661); O.D.P., c. 653, f. 39 (1750). Customary fees: *Andrews* v. *Symson*, 3 Keble 523, 527, 84 Eng. Rep. 857, 859 (1675); *Burdeaux* v. *Lancaster*, 12 Mod. 172, 88 Eng. Rep. 1242 (1697); *Naylor* v. *Scott*, 1 Barn. K.B. 159, 94 Eng. Rep. 110, 2 Ld. Raym. 1558, 92 Eng. Rep. 510 (1729); *Richards* v. *Dovey*, Willes 621, 125 Eng. Rep. 1352 (1746-47); *Patten* v. *Castleman*, 1 Lee 387, 161 Eng. Rep. 143 (Arches 1743). On the medieval understanding of these points, see Vol. I, 46-48.

239. "Church," Burn, i, 231, 268-75. The 1813 statute authorizing the collection of small sums before the justices of the peace is 53 Geo. 3, c. 127. Cases referred to in text are *Hawkins* v. *Rouse*, Holt K.B. 139, 90 Eng. Rep. 975, 1. Ld. Raym. 59, 91 Eng. Rep. 934, 1 Salk. 166, 91 Eng. Rep. 153 (1695) (chancel); *Moyle* v. *Churchwardens of St. Clement's*, 1 Freeman 299, 89 Eng. Rep. 217 (1681) (heavy rate and splendid reconstruction); *Rogers* v. *Davenant*, 1 Mod. 194, 2 Mod. 8, 86 Eng. Rep. 823, 852, 910 (1674-77) (bishop cannot make rate). There is dictum in *Thursfield* v. *Jones*, 1 Ventr. 367, 86 Eng. Rep. 236 (1683) to the effect that the churchwardens may make a rate if the parishioners refuse to do so, but that view was rejected later, as we shall see. "Churchwardens," Burn, i, 283, 294 refers to the case of *Nicholson* v. *Masters*, 2 Eq. Ca. Abr. 203, 22 Eng. Rep. 173 (Ch. 1714), in which the Court of Chancery ordered ninety parishioners to reimburse the churchwardens for money previously spent to repair the church. This too was contrary to later authority. If the churchwardens themselves refused to have a rate made, mandamus would lie under some circumstances to make them call a meeting, *R.* v. *Churchwardens of St. Margaret and St. John's*, 4 M. & S. 249, 105 Eng. Rep. 827 (1815), but not to make them make the rate. *R.* v. *Churchwardens of St. Peter's*, 5 T.R. 364, 101 Eng. Rep. 203 (1793). The monition issued to the churchwardens in *Maynard* v. *Brand*, 3 Phil. Ecc. 501, 161 Eng. Rep. 1397 (Con. London 1821) could probably not have been enforced. Nor could the order in "Canterbury Visitations," xxv, 20 (1694).

240. On the Feoffees for Impropriations, see C. Hill, *Economic Problems of the Church* (Oxford, 1956), 245-74. On the Trustees for Augmentations, see *Acts and Ordinances of the Interregnum* (London, H.M.S.O., 1911), i, 879 (1646), ii, 81, 142 (1649); 14 Car. 2, c. 25 (1662).

241. The following discussion of Queen Anne's Bounty, where not otherwise documented, is based on Best, 78-136, 209-38, and A. Savidge, *The Foundation and Early Years of Queen Anne's Bounty* (London, 1955). The basic statutes are 2-3 Anne, c. 20 (1703) and 1 Geo. 1, St. 2, c. 10 (1714). The 1707 statute exempting poor benefices is 5 Anne, c. 24. On the earlier history of First Fruits and Tenths, see Vol. II, 82-83.

242. O.D.P., c. 652, f. 135. I have found several other places where Queen

Anne's Bounty figures in the Oxford episcopal correspondence, including c. 653, f. 58 (1753) and c. 663, ff. 12-13 (1826), where possible approaches to the Bounty are discussed, c. 660, ff. 171-72 (1813), where a proposed augmentation is withdrawn when it turns out that the incumbent has a higher income than he claims to have, d. 106, ff. 50-53 (1750), where the Bounty is one party to an augmentation agreement, and c. 660, f. 195, where commissioners are appointed to buy land with Bounty money for the augmentation of a living.

243. The statutes for borrowing money are 17 Geo. 3, c. 53 (1777); 43 Geo. 3, c. 107 (1803); 5 Geo. 4, c. 89 (1824). Those on coal duties are 9 Anne, c. 22 (1710) and 1 Geo. 1, St. 2, c. 23 (1714). Examples of implementing local acts are 2 Geo. 2, c. x (1729); 3 Geo. 2, c. xvii, xxxiii (1730); 6 Geo. 2, c. xi, xxi (1733). See *Sellon* v. *Parry*, 5 Burr. 2762, 98 Eng. Rep. 450 (1771) for a case interpreting such an act.

244. 58 Geo. 3, c. 45 (1818); 59 Geo. 3, c. 134 (1819); 3 Geo. 4, c. 72 (1822); 5 Geo. 4, c. 103 (1824). See Port.

245. See notes 213-15 and accompanying text, *supra*. The 1714 legislation referred to in text is 1 Geo. 1, St. 2, c. 10.

246. E.g., 29 Geo. 3, c. *11* (1789). See *Sellon* v. *Parry*, 5 Burr. 2762, 98 Eng. Rep. 450 (1771); *Shirt* v. *Carr*, 2 Brown 173, 1 Eng. Rep. 868 (H.L. 1817) for protection of existing rights under such acts.

247. 1-2 Will. 4, c. 38 (1831). The 1824 act referred to above is 5 Geo. 4, c. 103.

2: The Rise of Religious Pluralism

1. This section, where not otherwise documented, is based on Holmes. The book is short and well indexed, so I have given specific references only where I have quoted it.

2. P. Hughes, *The Reformation in England*, ii (London, 1954), 110-11. On Mary's household, see id., 108n.

3. W.P.M. Kennedy, *Elizabethan Episcopal Administration* (London and Milwaukee, 1924), i, pp. cxvi-cxvii, clxv-cc; P. Hughes, *The Reformation in England* iii (London, 1955), 247-52, 249-60.

4. Holmes, 76.

5. The four quotations following are from Holmes, 77, 95, 77, and 96, respectively. For the attributions, see Holmes, 8-9.

6. The first two quotations are from Holmes, 118, the third from Holmes, 75.

7. 1604, c. 1, 110, 114.

8. E.g., *Anon.*, *A Learned Discourse of Ecclesiastical Government* (London, 1584), Bodl. Gold. 8° C 24 Th; P. Hughes, *The Reformation in England*, iii (London, 1955), 170-71, 180-84; Vol. II, 155-57. There was some intellectual continuity between the medieval Lollards and the post-Reformation Separatists, but evidently no significant institutional continuity. A.G. Dickens, *The English Reformation* (revised ed., London, 1967), 46-62.

9. *Acts and Ordinances of the Interregnum*, i, 749-57 (1645), 1188-1215 (1648), ii, 1462 (1660); *Eng. Pres.*, 43-6; C. Hill, *The Century of Revolution* (Edinburgh, 1961), 165.

10. Ibid.; Whiting, 31. The commissions are set up in *Acts and Ordinances of the Interregnum*, ii, 855-58, 968-90.

11. R. Bosher, *The Making of the Restoration Settlement* (Westminster, 1951), 143-277. The statute is 14 Car. 2, c. 4.

12. Whiting, 1-42.

13. Whiting, 82-132 (Baptists), 186-232 (Quakers).

14. Whiting, 25-26, 43-81. Whiting indicates that the Presbyterians continued to hope for accommodation within the Church of England.

15. O.D.P., c. 430. The first three quotations are from f. 3, the fourth from f. 17.

16. Whiting, 319-20. See also id., 19 (Dissenting ministers as lay communicants in Church of England).

17. *Britton* v. *Standish*, 6 Mod. 188, 190, 87 Eng. Rep. 943, 944 (1704); cf. *Burdet* v. *Newell*, 2 Ld. Raym. 1211, 92 Eng. Rep. 299 (1705).

18. Anglican violating formulas: *Bishop* v. *Stone*, 1 Hag. Con. 424, 161 Eng. Rep. 604 (Con. London 1808). Services without permission: *Trebec* v. *Keith*, 2 Atk. 498, 26 Eng. Rep. 700 (Ch. 1742); *Carr* v. *Marsh*, 2 Phil. Ecc. 198, 161 Eng. Rep. 1118 (Arches 1814). Services in Dissenting congregation: *Barnes* v. *Shore*, 8 Q.B. 640 115 Eng. Rep. 1013 (1846); *Bishop of St. Albans* v. *Fillingham*, [1906] P. 163 (Arches). Dissenter ministering in Anglican church: *R.* v. *Wroughton*, 3 Burr. 1683, 97 Eng. Rep. 1045 (1765); *but see* Whiting, 33.

19. Enforcement of trust: *Atty. Gen.* v. *Hickman*, W. Kel. 34, 25 Eng. Rep. 482 (Ch. 1732); *Atty. Gen.* v. *Cock*, 2 Vesey Sr. 273, 28 Eng. Rep. 177, 545 (Ch. 1751); *R.* v. *Barker*, 3 Burr. 1264, 97 Eng. Rep. 823 (1762). Document interpreted: *Waller* v. *Childs*, Amb. 524, 27 Eng. Rep. 338 (Ch. 1765); *Atty. Gen.* v. *Clapham*, 4 DeG. M. & G. 591, 43 Eng. Rep. 638 (Ch. 1855). Presumed intent of founders: *Atty. Gen.* v. *Pearson*, 3 Mer. 353, 36 Eng. Rep. 135 (ch. 1817); *Atty. Gen.* v. *Molland*, Younge 632, 159 Eng. Rep. 1114 (1832); *Shore* v. *Wilson*, 9 Cl. & Fin. 355, 8 Eng. Rep. 450 (H.L. 1842); see note 34 and accompanying text, *infra*.

20. Eng. Pres. 174-249 (reading somewhat between the lines); "Congregationalism," and "Presbyterianism" in *Encyclopedia Britannica* (3d ed.).

21. See the discussion in *Atty. Gen.* v. *Murdoch*, 1 DeG. M. & G. 86, 42 Eng. Rep. 484 (Ch. 1852); Chadwick, i, 398-99.

22. This account of Methodism, where not otherwise documented, is based on *A History of the Methodist Church in Great Britain* (ed. R. Davies and G. Rupp), i (London, 1965), especially chapters II, VI, VII, and IX.

23. B. Williams, *The Whig Supremacy, 1714-1760* (Oxford, 1939), 92-93.

24. See *R.* v. *Denbigh Justices*, 14 East. 284, 104 Eng. Rep. 610 (1811), holding that the language of the Toleration Act, protecting anyone in holy orders or pretended holy orders, or the preacher or teacher of a Dissenting congregation, would not protect an unordained preacher without a settled congregation. The case does not say that the person involved was a Methodist circuit rider, but it would seem likely that he was. Halévy, i, 431-32.

25. Anon. (attributed to Gibson, I am not sure by whom), *Observations upon the Conduct and Behaviour of the Methodists* (no date). Preaching licenses and restrictions on those lacking them: 1604, c. 49-52, 66-67. Ministry in private houses: 1604, c. 71. Conventicle Act: 22 Car. 2, c. 1 (1670). There was also the Act of Uniformity, 14 Car. 2, c. 4, § 10 (1662), which imposed a fine of up to £ 100 on anyone lacking priestly orders conferred by a bishop if he presumed to celebrate the Eucharist.

26. See Wesley's *Journal*, entry for 3 November, 1787. See O.D.P., d. 760, ff. 4, 10 for cases where Methodists had taken out licenses as Independents as early as the 1760s.

27. E.g., *R.* v. *Bathurst*, 1 W. Bl. 210, 96 Eng. Rep. 115 (1760); *R.* v. *Wroughton*, 3 Burr. 1683, 97 Eng. Rep. 1045 (1765).

28. A friend told me some years ago that this was the case in the village where she grew up. See *Swayne* v. *Benson*, 6 T.L.R. 7 (Arches 1889) (Anglican cannot be repelled from Communion for attending Wesleyan services). See the discussion at pp. 350-51, *infra* concerning the adoption and elimination of the rule excluding members of more than one church from the Church of England electoral rolls.

29. 13 Car. 2, St. 2, c. 1 (1661); 25 Car. 2, c. 2 (1673), repealed by 9 Geo. 4, c. 17 (1828). On hypocritical Communions to comply with these acts, see Addison, 11n; E. Carpenter, *The Protestant Bishop* (London, 1956), 192-93. The Occasional Conformity Act was 10 Anne, c. 2 (1711), repealed by 5 Geo. 1, c. 4 (1719). On its provenance and effect, see Sykes, *From Sheldon*, 97-102.

30. E.g., W. W. Jackson, *Reform or Revolution in the National Church?* (Oxford, 1917). See pp. 350-51, *infra*, for discussion of this exclusion. *Trapp* v. *Finlay*, Ret. App. #130 (1712) dealt with the question whether Dissenters' votes should be counted in electing a parish lecturer. The Delegates, reversing the Arches, decided not. Cases involving non-Anglicans in liturgical disputes, include *Ritchings* v. *Cordingly*, L.R. 3 A. & E. 113 (Arches 1868) (a reluctant churchwarden) and *Ex parte Edwards*, L.R. 9 Ch. 138 (1873) (a Congregationalist with no official status).

31. Roman Catholic Relief Acts: 31 Geo. 3, c. 32 (1791); 10 Geo. 4, c. 7 (1829). Some of the more horrendous penalties had already been repealed by 18 Geo. 3, c. 60 (1778) Quakers' oaths: 7-8 Will. 3, c. 24 (1696); 1 Geo. 1, st. 1, c. 6 (1714). Moravian Brethren: 22 Geo. 2, c. 30 (1749). These did not extend to allowing their beneficiaries to be witnesses in a criminal case. Not until 1861 was this disability removed. 24-25 Vic., c. 66. Finally, in 1888, 51-52 Vic., c. 46, affirmations were put on the same footing as oaths for everyone. The 1767 case referred to in text is *Harrison* v. *Evans*, 3 Brown 465, 1 Eng. Rep. 1437 (H.L. 1767). Earlier cases include *Major & Probi Homines de Guldeford* v. *Clarke*, 2 Ventris 247, 86 Eng. Rep. 420 (1690), going the same way, and *R. & R.* v. *Larwood*, 1 Salk. 168, 91 Eng. Rep. 155 (1694), going the other way. The City of London had made £ 15,000 between 1742 and 1767 by the practice involved in these cases. Addison, 12; B. Williams, *The Whig Supremacy, 1714-1760* (Oxford, 1939), 69.

32. Compulsory church attendance was imposed by 1 Eliz. 1, c. 2 (1559), and mitigated by the Act of Toleration, 1 Will. & Mar., c. 18, § 16 (1688) only as to people attending services allowed by that act. P.P. Eng. 1842, xxxiii, 573 reports a prosecution in 1844 for nonattendance. Mathieson, 161n indicates that many

prosecutions for nonattendance were really for drunkenness. The penalty (but not the duty) was abolished by 9-10 Vic., c. 59 (1846). *Taylor* v. *Timson*, 20 Q.B.D. 671 (1888) (everyone has a right to attend church because everyone has a duty to do so). The Blasphemy Act was 9-10 Will. 3, c. 32 (1697). Unitarians were exempted from it by 53 Geo. 3, c. 160 (1813), and it was finally repealed by 1967, c. 58. "Criminal Law and Procedure," Halsbury (3d), x, at 662n says that there had never been a prosecution under it. The Religious Disabilities Act, 1846, 9-10 Vic., c. 59, placed Jewish congregations on the same footing as Protestant Dissenting congregations.

33. *Da Costa* v. *De Pas*, Amb. 228, 27 Eng. Rep. 150 (1754). Private masses and Roman Catholic religious orders: Lilly and Wallis, 135-50; Roman Catholic Relief Act, 1926, 16-17 Geo. 5, c. 55. The courts were generally astute to get around these restrictions before they were finally done away with. *R.* v. *Kennedy*, 86 L.T. (N.S.) 753 (K.B.D. 1902); *In re Greene*, [1914] 1 I.R. 305; *In re Smith*, [1914] 1 Ch. 937.

34. *Eng. Pres.*, 218-53; *Atty. Gen.* v. *Pearson*, 3 Mer. 353, 36 Eng. Rep. 135 (Ch. 1817); Ibid., 7 Sim. 290, 58 Eng. Rep. 848 (Ch. 1835). Another case went to the House of Lords, which decided the same way in 1842. *Shore* v. *Wilson*, 9 Cl. & Fin. 355, 8 Eng. Rep. 450. The Nonconformists Chapels Act, 1844, 7-8 Vic., c. 45, provided that anything done for twenty-five years preceding litigation, and not contrary to express provisions in the trust documents, would be conclusively presumed to be lawful. See *Atty. Gen.* v. *Bunce*, L.R. 6 Eq. 563 (1868) for a case applying this act. The parliamentary debates leading up to it evoked a fine speech from Macaulay. Macaulay, 240.

35. *R.* v. *Carlile*, 1 St. Tr. (N.S.) 1033 (1821); *R.* v. *Hetherington*, 4 St. Tr. (N.S.) 563 (1841); *Shore* v. *Wilson*, 9 Cl. & Fin. 355, 8 Eng. Rep. 450 (H.L. 1842); *R.* v. *Lemon*, [1979] All E. R. 898 (H.L.); *Bowman* v. *Secular Society*, [1917] A.C. 406 (H.L.) Other cases are gathered and discussed in *Bowman*. On the *Lemon* case, see Welsby, 204.

36. The statutes referred to in this paragraph are 9 Geo. 4, c. 17 (1828); Roman Catholic Relief Act, 1829, 10 Geo. 4, c. 7; Jews Relief Act, 1858, 21-22 Vic., c. 49. It appears that the Declaration against Transubstantiation still had to be taken by anyone not professing Roman Catholicism until its final abolition by 30-31 Vic., c. 62 (1867). Presumably, some members of Eastern Orthodox churches might have been excluded by it, as well as some followers of the developing Anglo-Catholic movement. On the situation of the Jews before 1858, see H.S.O. Henriques, *The Jews and the English Law* (Oxford, 1908). Several earlier bills for their relief passed the Commons, but were defeated in the Lords. One of Macaulay's most notable speeches was delivered in 1833 in support of such a bill. Macaulay, 85.

37. *Clarke* v. *Bradlaugh*, 7 Q.B.D. 38 (1881), *rev'd on other grounds*, 8 A.C. 354 (H.L. 1883); *Bradlaugh* v. *Gossett*, 12 Q.B.D. 271 (1884). The statute solving the problem is 51-52 Vic., c. 46 (1888). An earlier act, 24-25 Vic., c. 66 (1861), applied only to judicial proceedings, although Bradlaugh made an ingenious argument for applying it to his situation.

38. This paragraph is based on Port. The funding statutes were 58 Geo. 3, c. 45 (1818), amended, 59 Geo. 3, c. 124 (1819) and 5 Geo. 4, c. 103 (1824). The Commissioners were abolished under 19-20 Vic., c. 55 (1856).

39. 5-6 Will. 4, c. 76 (1835); Chadwick, i, 108-12; *R.* v. *Mayor etc. of Liverpool*, 8 Ad. & E. 175, 112 Eng. Rep. 804 (1838) (enforcement of stipend).

40. *Atty. Gen.* v. *Aspinall*, 2 My. & Cr. 612, 40 Eng. Rep. 773 (Ch. 1837).

41. 58 Geo. 3, c. 45, § 34 (1818); 3 Geo. 4, c. 72 (1822); 36-7 Vic., c. 50 (1873); 45-6 Vic., c. 21 (1882).

42. See *Anon.*, *Some Observations on the Illegal and Unconstitutional Character of the Ecclesiastical Commissioners by a Layman* (Oxford, 1838) for a defense of tithe along these lines.

43. "Tithes," Burn, ii, 373, 439-42, 495.

44. A.G. Little, "Personal Tithes," *Eng. Hist. Rev.*, 1x (1945), 67; P.P. Eng. 1833, xxvii, 497. The flooded land case is *R.* v. *Commissioners of the Nene Outfall*, 9 B. & C. 874, 109 Eng. Rep. 325 (1829).

45. Vol. II, 81-2.

46. Holmes, 58. Cf. Holmes, 25 on lands charged with repair of churches. The avoidance of persecution was another ground for paying tithes. Holmes, 22-23, 96-98, 101-2. But this ground also depends on tithe not being regarded as direct support for heretical worship. Holmes, 22. On the Quakers' attitude, see Whiting, 135. The statutes for collecting from them were 7-8 Will. 3, c. 34 (1696); 1 Geo. 1, St. 2, c. 6 (1714); 5-6 Will. 4, c. 71 (1835). On Ireland, see Chadwick, i, 49-51.

47. Mathieson, 20-1. The story of the cabbages is in Hansard, 3d ser., xxviii, 478-79 (1835).

48. 6-7 Will. 4, c. 71. Some tithes had already been commuted or swapped for additional glebe under enclosure acts for individual villages. McClatchey, 104-17.

49. The apportionment provided for in § 55 seems to determine conclusively not only who pays how much, but also "to whom and in what right the same shall be respectively payable." "Awards" fixing the total amount for the parish are subject to judicial review under § 46, but apportionments seem not to be. I find the apportionment sections and their finality hard to reconcile with § 71, which provides that claims to tithe rentcharge shall be litigated in the same way as claims to the former tithes. See *Clarke* v. *Yonge*, 5 Beav. 523, 49 Eng. Rep. 680 (Rolls 1842); *Edwards* v. *Bunbury*, 3 Q.B. 885, 114 Eng. Rep. 748 (1842); *R.* v. *Tithe Comm'rs*, 15 Q.B. 620, 117 Eng. Rep. 594 (1850), all holding that disputed rights to tithe cannot be reviewed under § 46. Cf. *Walker* v. *Bentley*, 9 Hare 629, 68 Eng. Rep. 665 (V.C. 1852), which seems to preclude using either § 46 or § 71 where the commissioners, erroneously believing the land and the tithe were in the same hands, authorized a merger extinguishing the tithe rentcharge.

50. *Bailey* v. *Badham*, 30 Ch.D. 84 (1885). But the Statute of Limitations on "rent" applied. *Asplen* v. *Pullen*, [1917] 1 K.B. 187 (1916).

51. *Lanchbury* v. *Bode*, [1898] 2 Ch. 120. But cf. *In re Alms Corn Charity*, [1901] 2 Ch. 750 (charity charged on tithe). On use of tithe for poor relief compare J. Toulmin Smith, *The Parish* (London, 1854), c. 1, with "Tithes," Church Defense Institution Leaflet No. 18 (1880s or '90s — no date).

52. Best 465-79; The 1891 Act referred to in text is 54-55 Vic., c. 8.

53. 26 Geo. 5 and 1 Edw. 8, c. 43.

54. Finance Act, 1977, c. 36, § 56.

55. *Cr. Pref.* 178, 192. Mayfield, 86 refers to an average loss of income of

18½ % from the 1936 act.

56. *General Synod Proceedings*, xiii, 201-23 (1982); G.S. 515 (1981); *Chivers and Sons, Ltd.* v. *Sec. of State for Air*, [1955] Ch. 585; Halsbury, 590. The bill must be rendered before, not after, the repairs are made. Compare *Morley* v. *Leachcraft*, [1896] P. 92 (Con. Southwell) with *Neville* v. *Kirby*, [1898] P. 160 (Arches). The obligation of incumbent rectors to repair chancels was abolished by Ecclesiastical Dilapidations Measure, 1923, 14-15 Geo. 5, No. 3, § 52, which also provided for the commutation by agreement of obligations of lay rectors, cathedrals, universities and other non-incumbents. The Chancel Repairs Act, 1932, 22 Geo. 5, c. 20 transferred jurisdiction to enforce remaining liabilities from the ecclesiastical courts to the county courts.

57. Vol. II, 219-20; 37 Hen. 8 c. 12 (1545); Phil. 1223-31; *Watson* v. *All Saints*, 46 L.T. (N.S.) 201 (Q.B.D. 1882); *Proprietors of Hay's Wharf* v. *Trustees of St. Olave's Rectory Rate*, 25 T.L.R. 648 (K.B.D. 1909); *London County Council* v. *St. Botolph Churchwardens*, [1914] 2 K.B. 660 (C.A.); 10-11 Geo. 6, c. xxxi (1947); Corn Rents Act, 1963, c. 14.

58. Ecclesiastical Jurisdiction Measure, 1963, No. 1, § 82(3); Halsbury, x, 660; R. v. *Hall*, L.R. 1 Q.B. 632 (1866); *R.* v. *Kidd*, 16 L.T. 203 (1866).

59. 59 Geo. 3, c. 134 § 14; *R.* v. *Churchwardens of St. Michael*, 5 Ad. & E. 603, 111 Eng. Rep. 1293 (1836) (mandamus).

60. *Chesterton* v. *Farlar*, 1 Curt. 345, 163 Eng. Rep. 118 (Con. London 1836, Arches 1837, P.C. 1838); Ibid.; 7 Ad. & E. 713, 112 Eng. Rep. 638 (1838); *Ellis* v. *Griffin*, 2 Curt 673, 163 Eng. Rep. 546 (Arches 1841); *R.* v. *Churchwardens of Dursley*, 5 Ad. & E. 10, 111 Eng. Rep. 1070 (K.B. 1835).

61. Open vestries: *Phillibrown* v. *Ryland*, 2 Ld. Raym. 1389, 92 Eng. Rep. 404 (1724); *Ranson* v. *Campkin*, 2 Rob. Ecc. 370, 163 Eng. Rep. 1348 (Arches 1851); *White* v. *Steele*, 12 C.B. (N.S.) 383, 142 Eng. Rep. 1191 (1862); 58 Geo. 3, c. 59 § 3 (1818). Select vestries : Phil. 1500-3; 1-2 Will. 4, c. 60 (1831); 18-19 Vic., c. 120 (1855); 19-20 Vic., c. 112 (1856); *Lockburn* v. *Harvey*, 2 B. & Ad. 796, 109 Eng. Rep. 1338 (1831); Cf. *Carter* v. *Cropley*, 8 DeG. M. & G. 680, 44 Eng. Rep. 552 (Ch. 1857) (right of parishioners to elect incumbent remains with old vestry).

62. *R.* v. *Churchwardens of St. Michael's*, 5 Ad. & E. 603, 111 Eng. Rep. 1293 (1836); cf. *R.* v. *Churchwardens of St. Peter's*, 5 T.R. 364, 101 Eng. Rep. 203 (1793), where no statute applied.

63. C. Drew, *Early Parochial Organisation in England* (London, 1954), *passim*. The interdict suggestion is in W. H. Hale, *Precedents in Causes of Office against Churchwardens* (London, 1841). Lord North's dictum is in *Rogers* v. *Davenant*, 1 Mod. 194, 236, 2 Mod. 8, 86 Eng. Rep. 823, 852, 910 (1675). A monition was issued to the parishioners in *Fielding* v. *Standen*, 2 Curt. 663, 163 Eng. Rep. 543 (Arches 1841), but there was nothing said on how it was to be enforced.

64. *Greenwood* v. *Graves*, 4 Hag. Ecc. 77, 162 Eng. Rep. 1376 (Delegates, 1832); *Cooper* v. *Wickham*, 2 Curt. 303, 163 Eng. Rep. 420 (Arches 1839); cf. *Fry and Greata* v. *Treasure*, 2 Moo. P.C. N.S. 539, 15 Eng. Rep. 1003 (1865) (one churchwarden cannot sue for churchrate without the other).

65. *Steward* v. *Francis*, 3 Curt. 209, 163 Eng. Rep. 705 (Arches 1843), *prohibition granted, Francis* v. *Steward*, 5 Q.B. 984, 114 Eng. Rep. 1519 (1844).

The quotations are from 5 Q.B. at 996-97, 114 Eng. Rep. at 1523-24.

66. The Braintree cases described in text are *Veley* v. *Burder*, 1 Curt. 372, 163 Eng. Rep. 127 (Con. London 1837), *prohibition granted*, *Burder* v. *Veley*, 12 Ad. & E. 233, 113 Eng. Rep. 801 (1840), *affirmed*, 12 Ad. & E. 265, 113 Eng. Rep. 813 (Exch. Ch. 1841); *Veley* v. *Gosling*, 3 Curt. 254, 163 Eng. Rep. 720 (Con. London 1842 and Arches 1843), *prohibition denied*, *Gosling* v. *Veley*, 7 Q.B. 406, 115 Eng. Rep. 542 (1847), *affirmed*, 12 Q.B. 328, 116 Eng. Rep. 891 (Exch. Ch. 1850), *reversed*, 4 H.L.C. 679, 10 Eng. Rep. 627 (1852-53). The quotations are from 3 Curt. at 254, 163 Eng. Rep. at 720; 3 Curt. at 255-56, 163 Eng. Rep. at 720; 4 H.L.C. at 681, 10 Eng. Rep. at 628. For background, see Chadwick, i, 155-58.

67. I am indebted to Mr. Alan McQuade of Braintree for providing me with references to several works of local history including his own *A Brief History of the Parish Church of St. Michael Braintree* (1980). The handsome response to the subscription drive is described in a work by J.W. Kenworthy, vicar from 1883 to 1910. An interesting postscript is provided by W.F. Quin, *A History of Braintree & Bocking* (1981), 119, describing a testimonial banquet where Samuel Courtland, the industrialist who led the opposition to the rate, was presented with a piece of plate worth 700 guineas.

68. Hansard, 3d ser., xxxvi, 1207ff (1837); W.H. Hale, *Abolition of Church Rates* (London, 1859) (charge to the clergy of the archdeaconry); *Chronicle of Convocation*, 1859-65, 192-218 (Lower House, 1860).

69. R. Aitken, *Hints, Suggestions and Reasons for the Provisional Adjustment of the Church Rate* (London, 1859).

70. Chadwick, i, 146-47; Halévy, iii, 166-67; Hansard, 3d ser., xxv, 28 (1834), xxxvi, 1207 (1837).

71. 31-32 Vic., c. 109. On voluntary churchrates, see Chadwick, ii, 195-96; W.L. Dale, *The Law of the Parish Church* (London, 1967), 65. A questionnaire put out by the Bishop of Oxford in 1878, O.D.P., c. 344, shows a number of parishes using voluntary churchrates.

72. *Rippin* v. *Bastin*, L.R. 2 A.&E. 19 (Arches 1869); *Bell* v. *Bassett*, 47 L.T. (N.S.) 19 (Q.B.D. 1882); *Watson* v. *All Saints*, 46 L.T. (N.S.) 201 (Q.B.D. 1882); *R.* v. *Vestry of St. Marylebone*, [1895] 1 Q.B. 771 (C.A.); *Proprietors of Hay's Wharf* v. *Trustees of St. Olave's Rectory Rate*, 25 T.L.R. 648 (K.B.D 1909); *London County Council* v. *St. Botolph Churchwardens*, [1914] 2 K.B. 660 (C.A.).

73. *R.* v. *Lee*, 4 Q.B.D. 75 (1878); cf. *Plumstead Board of Works* v. *Ecclesiastical Commissioners*, [1891] 2 Q.B. 361. The statute in the *Lee* case was 18-19 Vic., c. 122 (1855).

74. On the historical question, see C. Drew, *Early Parochial Organisation in England* (London, 1954); S. and B. Webb, *English Local Government*, i (London, 1906); J. Toulmin Smith, *The Parish* (London, 1854); H.M. Cam, "The Community of the Vill" in *Medieval Studies Presented to Rose Graham* (Oxford, 1950). On the power of the incumbent over the vestry, see *Wilson* v. *M'Math*, 3 Phil. Ecc. 67, 161 Eng. Rep. 1260, *prohibition denied*, 3 B. & Ald. 650, 106 Eng. Rep. 650 (1819); *R.* v. *D'Oyley*, 12 Ad. & E. 233, 113 Eng. Rep. 801 (1840), and on the duties of churchwardens, *R.* v. *Inhabitants of Wix*, 2 B. & Ad. 197, 109 Eng. Rep. 1117 (1831).

75. S. and B. Webb, *English Local Government*, i (London, 1906); J. Toulmin Smith, *The Parish* (London, 1854); Chadwick, ii, 193-202. Cases sorting out the distinction between ecclesiastical and secular parishes include *R. v. Overseers of Kingswinford*, 3 El. & Bl. 687, 118 Eng. Rep. 1299 (1854); *Jones v. Hayworth*, Tristram 47 (Con. London 1881); *Fuller v. Alford*, 10 Q.B.D. 418 (1883); *R. v. Peters*, 6 El. & Bl. 225, 119 Eng. Rep. 848 (1856). See also *St. Anne's Faculty Case*, [1901] P. 73, where secular and ecclesiastical vestries advocate different sides in a question of church furnishing. On highway districts, see Tate, 247-48; on the poor law, R. A. Soloway, *Prelates and People* (London, 1969), 160-92.

76. 18-19 Vic., c. 120, clarified by 19-20 Vic., c. 112, §§ 1-3 (1856).

77. The enactments referred to in this and the following paragraph are 56-57 Vic., c. 73, § 6 (1894); 62-63 Vic., c. 14, § 23 (1899); Local Government Act, 1933, 23-24 Geo. 5, c. 43, § 269 (effective June 1, 1934); Parochial Church Councils (Powers) Measure, 1921, 11-12 Geo. 5, No. 1.

78. J. Dukemenier and S. Johanson, *Family Wealth Transactions* (Boston, 1978) 10-11. This is by no means the only explanation on the market, but I find it more persuasive than the common alternatives: (1) that there was a tacit agreement between the two sets of judges because the churchmen had a body of substantive law available and the lay judges did not. F. Pollock and F. W. Maitland, *The History of English Law Before the Time of Edward I* (Cambridge 1898), ii, 332, and (2) that churchmen "have more knowledge of what is for the profit and benefit of the soul of the testator." "Wills," Burn, ii, 503, 602. The alternatives are not entirely incompatible. M. Sheehan, *The Will in Medieval England* (Toronto, 1963), 166 offers a persuasive synthesis. The Wills Act, 7 Will 4 & 1 Vic., c. 26 (1837) did away with most nuncupative wills.

79. Chapter 1, note 35, *supra*.

80. 20-21 Vic., c. 77, 85. On divorce *a vinculo*, see P.P. Eng. 1852-53, xl, 249. The distribution of the property of Doctors Commons raised interesting questions concerning the nature of corporate personality. Holdsworth, xii, 49. Phil. 638 indicates that the new matrimonial courts should inherit the ancient responsibility of the bishop to try questions of marriage or bastardy arising incidentally in common law proceedings. Actually, though, that form of trial was dying out, and such questions were routinely tried by jury. Phil. 1070 refers to an ecclesiastical jurisdiction to separate invalidly married couples. Sir Robert Phillimore himself decided such a case in 1856 and indicated that he would be willing to do so again despite the 1857 statute.

81. The exceptions referred to in this paragraph are provided in 7-8 Will. 3, c. 6, 34 (1696); 1 Geo. 1, St. 2, c. 6 (1714); 53 Geo. 3, c. 127 §§ 4-7 (1813); 5-6 Will. 4, c. 74 (1835). On what constitutes an uncontested claim, see *R. v. Kidd*, 16 L.T. 203 (1867); *R. v. Sandford*, 30 L.T. 601 (1874).

82. See note 56 *supra*.

83. 18-19 Vic., c. 41; Slander of Women Act, 1891, 54-55 Vic., c. 51.

84. *Hoile v. Scales*, 2 Hag. Ecc. 564, 162 Eng. Rep. 958 (Con. London 1829); *Palmer v. Tijou*, 2 Add. 196, 162 Eng. Rep. 266 (Cant. Pecul. Ct. 1824); 13-14 Vic., c. 57 (1850).

85. Ecclesiastical Courts Jurisdiction Act, 1860, 23-24 Vic., c. 32. In fact, this act did not create the secular offense of disturbing religious worship. 1 Mar. sess. 2,

c. 3 (1553) did that as to the established church, and the Toleration Act, 1 Will. &
Mar., c 18, § 15 (1688) did it for all lawful worship. These statutes, expressly saved
from repeal by § 6 of the 1860 act, would seem sufficient by themselves, but they
seem to have been overlooked. The 1832 Royal Commission on the Ecclesiastical
Courts, P.P. Eng. 1831-2, xxiv, 1, on which this and much other legislation was
based, does not mention them. See pp. 61-62. And no one challenged Sir George
Lewis's assertion in the Commons when this bill was introduced that there was no
secular remedy then in existence. Hansard, 3d Ser., clvii, 1807. Bishop Phillpotts
was aware of the 1553 act, but pointed out that the police had been unwilling to
enforce it during the riots at a London church in the previous year. Hansard, 3d.
ser., clviii, 1078.

86. 1604, c. 62-63; 7-8 Will. 3, c. 35 (1696); 10 Anne, c. 19 (1711).

87. "Marriage," Burn ii, 1, 29-30. T.A. Lacey, *Marriage in Church and State*,
(Revised ed., London, 1947), 167-8; J. Jackson, *The Formation and Annulment of
Marriage* (2d ed. London, 1969), 14-18. The authorities are exhaustively collected
and analyzed in *R. v. Millis*, 10 Clark & F. 534, 8 Eng. Rep. 844 (H.L. 1843-44), a
case out of Ireland, where the law was the same as it had been in England a century
before. The case was a prosecution for bigamy where the first marriage of the
accused was before a Presbyterian minister. The Irish courts acquitted him on the
ground that that marriage was invalid. The judges unanimously advised the Law
Lords to affirm and the Lords did so by an equal division (2-2). The case occupies
374 pages of Clark and Finnally's Reports. Some of the applicable cases are cited in
Chapter 1, n. 100 supra.

88. J. Jackson, *The Formation and Annulment of Marriage* (2d ed. London, 1969),
61-63; B. Williams, *The Whig Supremacy, 1714-1760* (Oxford, 1939) 131. It is
curious how the belief in the effectiveness of these marriages survived the 1753
legislation abolishing them. Such a belief figures in *Wuthering Heights* (1847), and in
Sherlock Holmes's "Adventure of the Solitary Cyclist" (1895). To be sure, in the
latter case, there is reference to a license, but only a special license from the
Archbishop of Canterbury would validate a marriage not performed in church.

89. 26 Geo. 2, c. 33.

90. Hansard, *Parl. Hist.*, xv, 12-86.

91. J. Bossy, *The English Catholic Community 1570-1850* (N.Y. 1976) 136-40. J.
Aveling, *Catholic Recusancy in the City of York 1558-1791* (London, C.R.S. 1970)
118; J. Williams, *Catholic Recusancy in Wiltshire 1660-1791* (London, C.R.S. 1968)
65-66; Chadwick ii, 143.

92. W.H. Hale, *Remarks on Two Bills* (London, 1836).

93. The discussion of Russell's 1834 bill appears in Hansard, 3d ser., xxi, 776-89;
that of Peel's 1835 bill in Hansard, 3d ser., xxvi, 1073-1118; that of the successful
1836 bill in Hansard, 3d ser., xxxi, 367-85; xxxiv, 1021-40. See also Mathieson,
102, 124-26 on all three bills.

94. 6-7 Will. 4, c. 85.

95. 6-7 Will. 4, c. 86, § 31 (1836), *Prager* v. *Prager*, 108 L.T. 734 (P. 1913).
Jews were subject to the requirements of Jewish law only if they chose a Jewish
ceremony. They were as free as anyone else to follow other forms.

96. The Registrar General's annual reports were published as submitted. The

results of the 1851 census are gathered and discussed in B. Coleman, *The Church of England in the Mid-Nineteenth Century*, (London 1980). I computed the percentages myself.

97. Phil 632-34; *Bryant* v. *Foot*, L.R. 3 Q.B. 497 (Exch. Ch. 1868). Nor could the rites be withheld to collect the fee.

98. The letter is printed in Lilly and Wallis, 191-95. Other problems mentioned include the difficulty of uneducated people understanding the registration process, the difficulty of finding people in poor parishes who qualify as "householders" under the act, the obstacles to a ceremony validating an Anglican marriage under Roman Catholic canon law, and the inability of the registration process to uncover sources of invalidity.

99. 61-62 Vic., c. 58.

100. 6-7 Will. 4, c. 86. On the origin of parish registers, see Tate, 43 ff; "Register book," Burn ii, 296. The quote is on p. 297. The statutes are 5-6 Will. & Mar., c. 21 (1693-94); 6 & 7 Will. & Mar., c. 6 (1694); 7-8 Will. 3, c. 35 (1695). While the tax imposed by these statutes was temporary, the registration requirements appear to have endured until a general repeal of obsolete revenue acts in 33-34 Vic., c. 99 (1870). 52 Geo. 3, c. 146 (1812), which Phil., 497, regards as superseding the earlier acts, although it does not repeal them, provides for the registration of baptisms, marriages and burials only if they take place according to Anglican rites.

101. W.H. Hale, *Remarks on Two Bills* (London, 1836); O. Shipley, "Church and State" in *Ecclesiastical Reform* (ed. Shipley, London, 1873); Hansard, 3d ser., xxxv, 82.

102. McClatchey, 123-64; Chapter 1, notes 228-29, *supra*; 1604, c. 77-79. The Incumbents and Churchwardens (Trustees) Measure, 1964, No. 2, provided for turning most property of these trusts over to a central diocesan agency, but leaving the incumbent and churchwardens a role in the distribution of the benefits.

103. The five following quotations from *The Warden* appear on pages 5-6, 125-26, 126, 71-72 and 73-75 of the Everyman's Library edition (London, 1958). *The Warden* appeared in 1852, and purported to describe the situation as it had existed "a few years since."

104. Anon., *The Black Book or Corruption Unmasked* (London, 1820); Anon., *Extraordinary Black Book* (London, 1831); Boyle 182-90. The 1609 case referred to is *Case of Thetford School*, 8 Co. Rep. 130b, 77 Eng. Rep., 671. The evasion was articulated by Lord Brougham in *Atty. Gen.* v. *Smythies*, 2 Russ. & M. 746, 39 Eng. Rep. 568 (Ch. 1833).

105. The figures are from *Atty. Gen.* v. *Brentwood School*, 1 My. & K. 374, 39 Eng. Rep. 273 (Ch. 1833). The situation in *Atty. Gen.* v. *St. Cross Hospital*, 17 Beav. 435, 51 Eng. Rep. 1103 (Rolls 1853) was probably worse. See G.F.A. Best, "The Road to Hiram's Hospital," *Victorian Studies* (1961), 135. Owen, 196. See also *Atty. Gen.* v. *Dulwich Coll.*, 4 Beav. 255, 49 Eng. Rep. 337 (Rolls 1841), and *Atty. Gen.* v. *Pretyman*, 4 Beav. 462, 49 Eng. Rep. (Rolls 1841), where the warden leased lands of a charity at £ 32 a year, and pocketed entry fines of as much as £ 9000.

106. *Atty. Gen.* v. *Whitely*, 11 Ves. Jr. 241, 32 Eng. Rep. 1080 (Ch. 1805); *Atty. Gen.* v. *Earl of Mansfield*, 2 Russ. 501, 521-24, 39 Eng. Rep. 423, 431-32 (Ch.

1826); Owen, 248-49; Boyle, 155-66. In *Whitely*, Lord Eldon commented both on the inutility of the classical curriculum and the resulting increase in the salary of the clergyman in charge, but was unwilling to vary the founder's intent on that ground. The transformation of the Brentwood school is referred to in *Atty. Gen.* v. *Brentwood School*, 1 My. & K. 374, 392-93, 39 Eng. Rep. 723, 730 (Ch. 1833).

107. A.W. Scott, *The Law of Trusts*, § 399.4; Boyle, 155-69.

108. Leach's decision is *Atty. Gen.* v. *Brentwood School*, 1 My. & K. 374, 39 Eng. Rep. 273 (Ch. 1833), Brougham's is *Atty. Gen.* v. *Smythies*, 2 Ross & M. 746, 39 Eng. Rep. 568 (Ch. 1833), reversing a decision by Leach. O. Tudor, *The Law of Charitable Trusts* (1867), 51-2, tries to reconcile the two cases, but I think he takes undue liberties with them in order to do so. Boyle, 190, thinks they are irreconcilable. As to Leach's reputation, see Foss.

109. Owen 84-87; On attitudes toward the poor, see B. Williams, *The Whig Supremacy, 1714-1760*, 124-26 (Oxford 1939). On the 1601 Act, 43 Eliz. 1, c. 4, see Vol. II, 231-33.

110. Owen 182-208, 247-329; *Eng. Hist. Doc.*, xii(1), 899-911. The statutes referred to in this and the next two paragraphs are: 3-4 Vic., c. 77 (1840) (gingerly permission); Charitable Trusts Act, 1853, 16-17 Vic., c. 167; Endowed Schools Act, 1869, 32-33 Vic., c. 56; Charitable Trusts Act, 1860, 23-24 Vic., c. 136; Endowed Schools Act, 1874, 37-38 Vic., c. 87. For an example of an act adopting an elaborate scheme developed by the Commission, see 20-21 Vic., c. 84 (1857).

111. *In the Matter of the Norwich Charities*, 2 My. & Cr. 275, 40 Eng. Rep. 645 (Ch. 1837).

112. *Atty. Gen.* v. *Haberdashers Co.*, 19 Beav. 385, 52 Eng. Rep. 399 (Rolls 1854). The 1860 act provided explicitly that no one could be removed from the governing body of a charity on account of his religion. This evidently did not repeal the earlier provision for preserving the preferential status of the Church of England, but it bespoke a cautious application of it.

113. *Atty. Gen.* v. *Calvert*, 23 Beav. 248, 53 Eng. Rep. 97 (Rolls 1857); *Atty. Gen.* v. *Haberdashers Co.*, 19 Beav. 385, 52 Eng. Rep. 399 (Rolls 1854) (Jacobean foundation — compare *Atty. Gen.* v. *Sherborne Grammar School*, 18 Beav. 256, 52 Eng. Rep. 101 (Rolls 1854) involving a foundation of Edward VI); *In re Perry Almshouses*, [1898] 1 Ch. 391.

114. *Supra*, note 113. The quote is from 23 Beav. at 257-8, 53 Eng. Rep. at 101.

115. Cf. *Atty. Gen.* v. *Cullum*, 1 Y. & C.C.C. 411, 62 Eng. Rep. 948 (Ch. 1842). The exemption of Dissenters' children from religious instruction was made statutory by 23-24 Vic., c. 11 (1860).

116. The cases referred to in this paragraph are *Atty. Gen.* v. *Haberdashers Co.*, 19 Beav. 385, 52 Eng. Rep. 399 (Rolls 1854); *Baker* v. *Lee*, 8 H.L.C. 495, 11 Eng. Rep. 522 (1860); *Atty. Gen.* v. *St. John's Hospital, Bath*, 2 Ch.D. 554 (1876).

117. 8 H.L.C. at 499, 11 Eng. Rep. at 524.

118. 8 H.L.C. at 505, 11 Eng. Rep. at 526.

119. *Atty. Gen.* v. *Calvert*, 23 Beav. 248, 260-61, 53 Eng. Rep. 97, 102 (Rolls 1857).

120. 23 Beav. at 261, 53 Eng. Rep. at 102.

121. *In re Perry Almshouses*, [1898] 1 Ch. 391.

122. 56-57 Vic., c. 73. On the problems of separating secular from ecclesiastical charities, see Chadwick ii, 197-98.

123. Addison, 108-13, 141-44; Oxford University Act, 1854, 17-18 Vic., c. 81; Cambridge University Act, 1856, 19-20 Vic., c. 88; Universities Tests Act, 1871, 34-35 Vic., c. 26; Universities of Oxford and Cambridge Act, 1877, 40-41 Vic., c. 48. The report of the Royal Commission leading up to this course of legislation, P.P. Eng. 1852, xxii, is excerpted in *Eng. Hist. Doc.*, xii(1), 875-91. For additional background, see Mathieson, 104-8. The 1871 act applied also to the university founded at Durham in 1832.

124. See Matthieson, 104n; Addison, 112.

125. *Eng. Hist. Doc.*, xii(1), 875, 885-87.

126. The work of the commissioners is collected in *Statutes of the Commissioners under the Universities Act 1877* (Oxford, 1883). Their exceptions for Christ Church were not as broad as some people would have liked, *Corp. of the Sons of the Clergy v. Christ Church, Oxford*, 42 Ch. D., 624 (C.A. 1889) (commission may abolish restriction of scholarship to future clergy).

127. The commissioners also had no power to alter endowments less than fifty years old. See § 13 of the 1877 act. The question of what was an existing college was not always easy to determine. See *R. v. Hertford College*, 3 Q.B.D. 693 (C. A. 1878). Mr. F. D. Price has kindly supplied me with the later constitutional history of Keble College. It appears that the peculiar constitution of Keble was an obstacle to its achievement of full status as a constituent college of the university. A series of constitutional changes between 1930 and 1952 brought Keble into line with the other colleges, and in the process eliminated its explicitly Anglican identification. Mr. Price tells me he was "the last fellow of Keble to be admitted to office (in 1949) under the pre-1952 statutes, and thus the last Fellow of an Oxford College to have to conform to medieval tradition in making a declaration of faith before admission."

128. The following account of the education laws, where not otherwise documented, is based on Halévy, iii, 104-16, 221-24, iv, 174-76, v, 139-45, vi, 64-9, 71-3; Lilly & Wallis 106-34; Chadwick i, 336-46; Macaulay, 349-69; Brose, 181-206; Curtis and Boultwood, 54-103, 162-209; *Eng. Hist. Doc.* xii(1), 891-99, 911-15; Addison 129-44.

129. See O.D.P., c. 273 (1848) (Cuxham) for parishioners using a visitation questionnaire to complain of the lack of a school. By contrast, see O.D.P., c. 239 ff. 196-203 (1829) (St. Ebbe's), where parishioners complain that the incumbent is holding school in their pews.

130. *Eng. Hist. Doc.* xii(1), 363-64, taken from the minutes of the Wesleyan Conference at Sheffield on 26 July, 1843. The relevant provision of the 1833 Factory Act is 3-4 Will. 4, c. 103, §§ 20-23.

131. Macaulay, 349, 357-58.

132. *Eng. Hist. Doc.* xii(1), 854-58. For arrangements with the British and Foreign Society, see id., 858-59. Archdeacon G.A. Denison of whom we shall see more in later chapters, was an articulate opponent of all compromise, G.A. Denison, *Notes of my Life 1805-1878* (Oxford and London, 1878); *Denison Letters*, 6, 9-10, 14-18, 31-32, 37-41, 93-94; *Chronicle of Convocation 1866*, 30-57, 69-103. For more moderate Anglican views, see J.M. Monk, *Charge to the Clergy of Gloucester*

and Bristol (1847); W.H. Hale, *Charge to the Clergy of the Archdeaconry of London* (1847).

133. 33-34 Vic., c. 75.

134. Lilly and Wallis, 112.

135. The statutes referred to in this paragraph are Elementary Education Act, 1876, 39-40 Vic., c. 79 and Elementary Education Act, 1891, 54-55 Vic., c. 56.

136. § 23 of the act envisages sharing of time. See *National Society* v. *School Board of London*, L.R. 18 Eq. 608, 621 (1874). Tait encouraged hard bargaining on this matter. Marsh, 79.

137. National Society has no standing: *National Society* v. *School Board of London*, L.R. 18 Eq. 608 (1874). Intent to transfer: *In re Burnham National School*, L.R. 17 Eq. 241 (1873). Cy-près: *Glamorgan County Council* v. *Price*, [1912] 1 Ch. 667, [1914] A.C. 20.

138. 2 Edw. 7, c.42. the Board of Education referred to in this paragraph was established by the Board of Education Act, 1899, 62-63, Vic., c. 33. Besides the functions of the Department of Education, it took over those of the Charity Commissioners regarding schools.

139. *Atty. Gen.* v. *West Riding of Yorks. County Council* [1907] A.C. 29 (H.L.).

140. *Blencowe* v. *Northants County Council* [1907] 1 Ch. 504 upheld a requirement that secular instructions begin at 9:45 every day, and allowed the County Council to close down a Church of England school whose managers refused to stop taking children to 11:00 services on saints' days. The case of the teacher who became a Methodist is *Smith* v. *Macnally* [1912] 1 Ch. 816.

141. Education Act, 1944, 7-8 Geo. 6, c. 31. §§ 25-30 deal with religious education and corporate worship. On the church's response to the act, see Welsby, 18-24; Kemp, *Kirk*, 115-22. The Education Reform Act, 1988, c. 40 creates a new category of "grant-maintained" schools. §§ 84-88 make alternative provisions for religious education and worship in these schools. They are not much different from the alternatives available under the 1944 act. Which alternative applies depends partly on the wishes of the parents, partly on the status of the school before it adopted the new status. The 1988 act also makes explicit that the nondenominational syllabus and corporate worship are to be "broadly Christian" except where concentrations of non-Christian pupils make other provisions appropriate.

142. Curtis and Boultwood, 410-14 summarizes the conclusions of the 1963 Newsom Report regarding education under these syllabi. The problems are not small, but it does not seem that denominationalism figures prominently among them.

143. *Chronicle of Convocation 1870*, Appendix 2.

144. Best, 153-61.

145. *R.* v. *Stewart*, 12 A. & E. 773, 113 Eng. Rep. 1007 (Q.B. 1840). On the right to be buried in the churchyard, see Phil., 653. Church of England (Miscellaneous Provisions) Measure, 1976, No. 3, § 6 extends the right to everyone on a parish electoral roll. The right does not embrace burial in any particular part of the churchyard, *Ex parte Blackmore*, 1 B. & Ad. 120, 109 Eng. Rep. 732 (K.B. 1830), nor to any unusual mode of sepulture. *R.* v. *Coleridge*, 2 B. Ald. 806, 106 Eng. Rep. 559 (K.B. 1819) (iron coffin — preliminary to the famous case of *Gilbert* v. *Buzzard*, 2 Hag. Con. 333, 161 Eng. Rep. 761, 3 Phil. Ecc. 335, 161 Eng. Rep.

1342 (Con. London 1820)). The exceptions to the right are laid down by 1604, c. 68, and by the first rubric at the head of the Prayer Book burial service. It is not clear whether they are exceptions to the right to be buried in the churchyard at all (as they were in earlier times), or merely to the right to be buried with the Prayer Book liturgy. 4 Geo. 4, c. 52 (1823) provided for burial of suicides in the churchyard, but expressly preserved the existing rule as to the service. In *R.* v. *Taylor*, Phil. 653n, a 1721 case not found in the regular law reports, a lay court seems to have ordered the burial of an unbaptized person in the churchyard, but refused to order the service to be used because that was a matter for the church courts. On the other points made in this paragraph, see *R.* v. *Sharpe*, Dears & B. 160, 169 Eng. Rep. 959 (C.C.R. 1857) (disinterment for burial in churchyard); *R.* v. *Price*, 12 Q.B.D. 247 (1884) (burning). It is worth noting in the *Price* case that the defendant claimed to be a druid, and that the judge was Virginia Woolf's uncle.

146. In *Doe d. Thompson* v. *Pitcher*, 3 M. & S. 407, 105 Eng. Rep. 663 (K.B. 1815) a Quaker graveyard was held to be a charity.

147. *Kemp.* v. *Wickes*, 3 Phil. Ecc. 263, 161 Eng. Rep. 1320 (Arches 1809); *Mastin* v. *Escott*, 2 Curt. 692, 163 Eng. Rep. 553 (Arches 1841), *affirmed*, 4 Moo. P.C. 104, 13 Eng. Rep. 241; *Titchmarsh* v. *Chapman*, 3 Curt. 840, 163 Eng. Rep. 920 (Arches 1844). The rubric referred to in these cases is the first one at the head of the Prayer Book burial service. 1604, c. 68 also excludes excommunicates, but is limited by *Middleton* v. *Crofts*, 2 Atk. 650, 26 Eng. Rep. 788 (1736) as were 1604, c. 2-12, the ones invoked to excommunicate Dissenters. The 1813 statute referred to is 53 Geo. 3, c. 127. The incumbent could refuse to let Dissenters be buried in the church or in a family vault with their Anglican relatives. O.D.P., c. 653, ff. 115-17, 136-38 (1754).

148. Dissenters' practice: Addison, 64; Fees: Phil., 673-78. Dissenters grievances: *Anon.*, *On the Law Relating to Burials* (Cardiff, 1876). Anglican objection to the indiscriminate use of the service: T.L. Vogan, *Use of the Burial Service as Required by Law* (London, 1864); E.J. Randolph, *Reasons for Altering Certain Expressions in the Burial Service* (London, 1864); W. Pound, *Alterations in the Burial Service Superseded* (London, 1864); *Anon.*, *The Burial Service Question* (London, 1863); C.S. Grueber, *A Letter* (London, 1863). In *Cooper* v. *Dodd*, 2 Rob. Ecc. 270, 163 Eng. Rep. 1314 (Arches 1850), the suspension provided for in 1604, c. 68 was imposed on an incumbent for refusing to bury a man who had apparently died drunk. Marsh, 253 and Addison, 118 are evidently referring to this case. In *Re Todd*, 3 Notes of Cases 1, Supp. (Bishop of Exeter in person, 1844), the incumbent omitted the language of the service expressing hope for the final state of the decedent, and was roundly castigated by Bishop Phillpotts for doing so:

> To assert for the priesthood a right to judge in every case of the final state of the deceased would be to claim a power of the Keys, above that to which papal Rome ever dared to aspire, and which this reformed Church, while it maintains the just authority of its priests for edification, not for destruction, hath always most strongly repudiated.

Anno. B.C.P., 476-77 suggests that some incumbents were willing to omit the service on request at the burial of Roman Catholics and Dissenters.

149. *Keet* v. *Smith*, 1 P.D. 73 (P.C. 1876) (Reverend); *Breeks* v. *Wolfrey*, 1 Curt.

880, 163 Eng. Rep. 304 (1838) (prayer for deceased); *Pearson* v. *Stead* [1903] P. 66
(ditto — inscription rejected as a matter of discretion); Lilly and Wallis, 62n (Jesus
mercy, Mary help).

150. The basic scheme was adopted for London in 15-16 Vic., c. 85 (1852), and
extended to the rest of the country by 16-17 Vic., c. 134 (1853). Various refinement
were introduced by 18-19 Vic., c. 128 (1855). The whole series is cited in *Halsbury*,
iv, 28n. On referring to the Home Secretary duties assigned by statute to "one of her
Majesty's principal secretaries of state," see Holdsworth, xiv, 112-13.

151. *Preston Corp.* v. *Pyke* [1929] 2 Ch. 338; Lilly and Wallis, 60.

152. *Day* v. *Peacock*, 18 C.B. (N.S.) 701, 144 Eng. Rep. 620 (1865); *Wood* v.
Headingley Burial Board, [1892] 1 Q.B. 713; *Gell* v. *Mayor etc. of Birmingham*, 10
L.T. (N.S.) 497 (Q.B. 1864); *Hornby* v. *Toxeth Park Burial Board*, 31 Beav. 52, 54
Eng. Rep. 1056 (Rolls 1862); *Burial Board of St. Margaret's, Rochester* v.
Thompson, 34 L.J. C.P. 213 (1871); *Stewart* v. *West Derby Burial Board*, 34 Ch. D.,
314 (1886). On fees generally, see *Winstanley* v. *N. Manchester Overseers*, [1910]
A.C. 7 (H.L.); Phil. 673-84. On control by the burial board over monuments, see
Lilly and Wallis, 61, complaining of a board that refused to allow in a Catholic
section of its burial ground an inscription requesting prayers for the soul of the
deceased. There was evidently no legal recourse against such a decision.

153. Burial Laws Amendment Act, 1880, 43-44 Vic., c. 41, referred to in some of
the cases as Osborne Morgan's Act. See Addison, 118-21; Marsh, 256-63.

154. Cemeteries Clauses Act, 1847, 10-11 Vic., c. 65 (1847) contains provisions to
be incorporated by reference in private bills. It is also incorporated in the Public
Health (Interments) Act, 1879. §§ 27-31 of the 1847 Act provide for appointment of
chaplains; §§ 52-57 for paying the incumbent "such sums, if any, as shall be
prescribed for that purpose in the special act."

155. 63-64 Vic., c. 15. The report of the select committee appears in P.P. Eng.
1898, viii, 259.

156. *Williams* v. *Briton Ferry Burial Board*, [1905] 2 K.B. 565 (C.A.).

157. 1972, c. 70, § 214 and Schedule 26; Local Authorities Cemeteries Order,
1977, Statutory Instrument 1977 No. 204 (note especially § 17 regarding the right and
duty of the parish incumbent); Ecclesiastical Fees Measure, 1962, 10-11 Eliz. 2 No.
1.

158. Burial Act, 1855, 18-19 Vic., c. 128, § 18; Local Government Act 1972, c.
70, § 216 provides that a parochial church council is responsible for a closed
churchyard, but may require the local government authority to take over the
responsibility. On removal of remains, see *Rector etc. of St. Mary-at-Hill* v.
Parishioners of Same, [1892] P. 394 (Con. London).

159. *Vicar and Churchwardens of St. Mary Abbots* v. *Inhabitants and Parishioners
of Same*, Tristram 17 (Con. London 1873); *St. George in the East Faculty Case*, 1
P.D. 311, Tristram 38 (Con. London 1876); *Vicar and Churchwardens of St. Botolph*
v. *Parishioners of Same*, [1892] P. 161 (Con. London per Tristram); *Re Plumstead
Burial Ground*, [1895] P. 225 (Con. Rochester per Dibdin). In *In re Biddeford
Parish*, [1900] P. 314 (Con. Exeter and Arches), Dibdin adhered, albeit reluctantly,
to his earlier position, and was reversed.

160. *Adlam* v. *Colthurst*, 36 L.J. Ec. 14, L.R. 2 A. & E. 30 (Arches 1867).

161. 47-48 Vic., c. 72. On what the act does and does not permit, see, e.g., *Bermondsey Borough Council* v. *Mortimer*, [1926] P. 87 (Con. Southwark); *Re St. Luke, Chelsea*, [1976] Fam. 295 (Con. London). Other statutes referred to in this paragraph are Town and Country Planning Act, 1944, 7-8 Geo. 6, c. 47, and its successor now in place, Town and Country Planning Act, 1971, c. 78, especially § 128; Open Spaces Act, 1906, 6 Edw. 7, c. 25, especially § 11; Pastoral Measure, 1983, No. 1. Section 30 of that measure (following 1968, No. 1 § 30) allows burial grounds to be built on after fifty years disuse, or sooner if no relatives object. A statute, 1981, c. 18 makes the same provision for non-Anglican grounds.

162. Statutory Instrument 1950 No. 792, Reg. 10.

163. Marsh, 32; Macaulay, 271-83.

164. Dibdin, *Establishment in England* (London 1932), 11. To the same effect is *The Church and the Law of Nullity of Marriage* (London, S.P.C.K., 1955), the report of an archiepiscopal commission.

3: Value for Money

1. In connection with the following account, see Brose, 38, 208-15; Halévy, iii, 152-66.

2. Macaulay, 288-89. Macaulay said this in 1845 to contrast the Church of England with the Church of Ireland, which he was for disestablishing because its ministrations were unacceptable to the great majority of the Irish people. The Irish church was in fact disestablished for that reason in 1869, as the Anglican church in Wales was, for similar reasons, in 1920. Since all the other arguments were the same for Ireland and Wales as they were for England, the fate of establishment in those two countries indicates that the utilitarian argument was decisive for England.

3. *Rotuli Parliamentorum* (London, 1783), i, 219a, quoted in the preamble to the Statute of Provisors, 25 Edw. 3, St. 6 (1350).

4. The following statistics are compiled from the reports in P.P. Eng., 1835, xxii, and P.P. Eng., 1836, xxxvi, 1-78. My figures regarding bishops agree with those in Best, 545. My other figures differ slightly from those, evidently compiled from the same source, in C.K.F. Brown, *A History of the English Clergy 1800-1900* (London, 1953), 16, 32n, and in Mathieson, 112. The *Black Book* referred to in the next paragraph (London, 1820) was followed by the *Extraordinary Black Book* (London, 1831). It appears that one John Wade (1788-1875), an otherwise undistinguished writer on legal subjects, was the author of both books. *D.N.B.*, Wade. His statistics were exaggerated. Chadwick, i, 33-4; Mathieson, 25, 62-3. Bentham, *Church of Englandism* (London, 1818) is a more exuberant — and more wildly idiosyncratic — statement of similar principles.

5. Examples: Anon., "Royal and Parliamentary Ecclesiastical Commissions" *British Critic*, xxiii (1838), 455 (attributed to Pusey: Brose, 145-46); W. J. Aislabie, *A letter to Lord John Russell*, Bodl. 38.615 (London 1838) (particularly noteworthy for suggesting to Lord John that the Russell family had already despoiled the church enough in Henry VIII's time); W. L. Bowles, *A Final Defence of Rights of Patronage*

in Deans and Chapters (London, 1838); Anon., *Observation on the Illegal and Unconstitutional Character of the Ecclesiastical Commissioners by a Layman* (Oxford, 1838) (the peers analogy); S. Smith, *Second Letter to Archdeacon Singleton* (London, 1838); H. Manning, *The Principles of the Ecclesiastical Commission Examined* (London, 1836).

6. Best, 277, 298; 6-7 Will. 4, c. 77 (1836). Some of these changes were foreshadowed by the Irish Church Temporalities Act, 3-4 Will. 4, c. 37 (1833).

7. Ecclesiastical Commissioners Act, 1840, 3-4 Vic., c. 113.

8. See H. Humble "Cathedrals and Chapters" in *Ecclesiastical Reform*, ed. O. Shipley (London, 1873) for a statement of one set of ideals for a cathedral chapter.

9. One pamphlet argued that bestowing nonresidentiary canonries on underpaid parish incumbents would meet the legitimate objections to cathedral establishments without any need for legislation. C.A. Moysey, *Suggestions* . . . (London, 1838).

10. But see *Gleaves* v. *Parfitt*, 7 C.B. (N.S.) 838, 141 Eng. Rep. 1045 (1860) (individual liability for dilapidations).

11. These figures appear in §66. There was debate over whether the discretion given the Commissioners in §52 permitted them to increase these figures. They decided they did. Best, 438-40.

12. Best, 312-17.

13. Ecclesiastical Commissioners Act, 1860, 23-24 Vic., c. 124.

14. Episcopal Endowments and Stipends Measure, 1943, 6-7 Geo. 6, No. 2; Mayfield, 38.

15. Ecclesiastical Commissioners Act, 1850, 13-14 Vic., c. 94, §§20, 24.

16. Best, 453-60. The agreements referred to in text were provided for by Ecclesiastical Commission Act, 1868, 31-32 Vic., c. 114, but some had been made earlier. See, for instance, *V.C.H., Wilts*, iii, 203-4 on the arrangements with Salisbury Cathedral. The chapter turned over its endowments in 1861, and received annual cash payments until 1875, when new endowments were provided. The final pooling was provided for by Cathedrals Measure, 1931, 21-22 Geo. 5, No. 7.

17. Cathedrals Act, 1864, 27-28 Vic., c. 70; Cathedrals Measure, 1931, 21-22 Geo. 5, No. 7.

18. Holdsworth, xiii, 234, xiv, 133; Halévy, iii, 98-129, 210-24. The statutes referred to in this paragraph are 1 Geo. 3, c. 1 (1760); 27 Geo. 3, c. 13 (1787); 52 Geo. 3, c. 11 (1812); 7 Will. 4 & 1 Vic., c. 46 (1837).

19. *Administrative Reform of the Church* (London, S.P.C.K., 1918) (report of archbishops' commission); H. Maynard Smith, *Administrative Reform* (London, S.P.C.K., 1919) (a dissenting view that shrewdly analyzes the prevailing one).

20. This section, where not otherwise documented, is based on Best, 369-94.

21. Ecclesiastical Commissioners Act, 1850, 13-14 Vic., c. 94. Murray's tenure before his downfall was protected under 3-4 Vic., c. 113, §91. He rehabilitated himself in Australia, and was a leader of the Sydney bar when he died in 1865. Best, 392.

22. Compare the definitions in the *Oxford English Dictionary and the Merriam-Webster Third International Dictionary* with those in *Black's Law Dictionary* and the *Oxford Companion to Law*.

23. Ecclesiastical Leasing Act, 1842, 5-6 Vic., c. 108. Minor canons, unlike

other corporations, were excluded.

24. *Doe d. Brammall* v. *Collinge*, 7 C.B. 939, 137 Eng. Rep. 372 (1849).

25. Best, 376-77.

26. See Bentley, 23 on the Denison family. The archdeacon thought Evelyn was an "excellent landlord" as well as "eminently a just man." *Denison Letters*, 129.

27. 14-15 Vic., c. 104.

28. 21-22 Vic., c. 57.

29. The 1858 act is remarkably lacking in legislative history. Hansard records no debate on it, and the select committee that reported negatively on what seems to be the same bill, P.P. Eng., 1857, ix, 265, recorded neither its evidence nor the reasons for its recommendation.

30. This section, where not otherwise documented, is based on Best, *passim*; Mayfield, 85-97.

31. Mayfield, 86; See *General Synod Reports*, v, (1974), 544-45, where a speaker, opposing the centralization of glebe, refers to clergymen working their land as "the first worker-priests we ever had." Against this material must be set the example of the Oxfordshire incumbent in *Rice* v. *Bishop of Oxford*, [1917] P. 181, whose agrarian pursuits contributed to a charge of neglect of duty against him.

32. Ecclesiastical Leasing Act, 1842, 5-6 Vic., c. 108; Ecclesiastical Leases Act, 1842, 5-6 Vic., c. 27.

33. *Jenkins* v. *Green*, 28 Beav. 87, 54 Eng. Rep. 299 (Rolls 1859), *affirmed*, *Green* v. *Jenkins*, 1 De G. F. & J. 454, 45 Eng. Rep. 435 (Ct. App. in Ch. 1860). The suggestion referred to in text comes from the lower court opinion in this case. The act is another with no significant legislative history.

34. 51-52 Vic., c. 20. On the Land Commissioners, see 14-15 Vic., c. 53 (1851); 52-53 Vic., c. 30 (1889); 9-10 Geo. 5, c. 91 (1919).

35. Mayfield, 86. The 1976 transfer was effected by Endowments and Glebe Measure, 1976, No. 4. For the debate on that measure, see *General Synod Reports*, v, 530-55.

36. Mayfield, 135-38; Best, 499-512, 547-57. The table in Best, 554-55 shows that securities provided about one-seventh of the income of the Ecclesiastical Commissioners in 1900, one-fourth in 1912, and a little more than half in 1934. Pitt, 10-11 shows that more liberal investment policies raised the Church Commissioners' income from £ 7,000,000 in 1949 to £ 21,000,000 in 1967. On the investment powers of fiduciaries generally, see G. W. Keeton and L.A. Sheridan, *The Law of Trusts* (10th ed., London, 1974), 246-57. Separate portfolios for individual benefices were pooled in some cases under the Ecclesiastical Commissioners (Powers) Measure, 1938, 1-2 Geo. 6, No. 4, in the rest under the Benefices (Stabilization of Incomes) Measure, 1951, 14-15 Geo. 6, No. 5. Investment of church funds was specifically regulated under Church Funds Investment Measure, 1958, 6-7 Eliz. 2, No. 1.

37. See pp. 101-3, *supra*. Mayfield, 86 reports an immediate, pre-inflation loss of 18½% from this substitution.

38. Welsby, 30; Mayfield, 90-91; *Paul Report*, 118. Parochial church councils were established by Parochial Church Councils (Powers) Measure, 1921, 11-12 Geo. 5, No. 1, diocesan stipends funds by Reorganization Areas Measure, 1944, 7-8 Geo. 6, No. 1, § 30 for some dioceses, by Pastoral Reorganization Measure, 1949, 12-14

Geo. 6, No. 3, § 11 for the rest.

39. *Paul Report*, 117-24. Pastoral Reorganization Measure, 1949, 12-14 Geo. 6, No. 3, §12 provided for diversion of some excess endowment income to the diocesan stipends fund, but it seems to have had little effect. *Paul Report*, 115.

40. Mayfield, 92-93.

41. Ecclesiastical Commissioners (Provision for Unbeneficed Clergy) Measure, 1928, 18-19 Geo. 5, No. 1.

42. 1976, No. 4.

43. The legislative provisions referred to in this paragraph are Ecclesiastical Commissioners Act, 1840, 3-4 Vic., c. 113, § 67; Pastoral Reorganisation Measure, 1949, 12-14 Geo. 6, No. 3, § 11; Diocesan Stipends Funds Measure, 1953, 1-2 Eliz. 2, No. 2; Endowments and Glebe Measure, 1976, No. 4, §8. On the practice of the Commissioners just before the 1976 measure, see Mayfield, 104-5; Pitt, 9.

44. *Paul Report*, 186-91; Welsby, 131-39; *Crockford*, 1976, xiii-xv.

45. Best, 480-98; Pitt, 14-17. Mayfield, *Like Nothing*, 93-97. The quote is from Pitt, 15. A motion to make the Church Commissioners divest themselves of their South African investments was debated in the General Synod in 1986 without coming to a vote. *General Synod Reports* xvii, 988-1013.

46. Church Building Act, 1831, 1-2 Will. 4, c. 38. The parochial status of these churches was limited by §10. Marriages were not authorized in them until the Church Building (Banns and Marriages) Act, 1844, 7-8 Vic., c. 56. The ecclesiastical court had to entertain a collateral attack on the status of the church if the statutory requirements were not met. *Williams* v. *Brown*, 1 Curt. 54, 163 Eng. Rep. 19 (Con. London 1838) ; *R.* v. *Bishop of London*, 1 Will., Woll. & H. 151 (1838). The demographic restrictions of the 1831 act were eliminated by Church Building Act, 1851, 14-15 Vic., c. 97, § 7.

47. 6-7 Vic., c. 37 (1843); 19-20 Vic., c. 104 (1856).

48. 19-20 Vic., c. 104, § 6 (1856). In some cases, the Church Building Commissioners enabled Peel districts to charge pew rents by making them nominal grants and thus bringing them under the other set of statutes. Port, 117-18.

49. Best, 408-10. Compare W.H. Jones, *A Letter to the Right Honorable the Visct. Palmerston, K.G., K.C.B.* (London, 1857) on the loss of fees to the mother church. Jones argued that the parochial rights of the Peel district were concurrent with, not exclusive of, those of the mother church. Although the statutes were not crystal clear on the point, his view was consistently rejected. *Cardinall* v. *Molyneaux*, 4 De G. F. & J. 117, 45 Eng. Rep. 1128 (Ch. 1861). It appeared in a new and ingenious form — that the new parish was for ecclesiastical purposes and marriage is not an ecclesiastical purpose — in *Fuller* v. *Alford*, 10 Q.B.D. 418 (1883), and was still rejected. On compensation to the incumbent of the mother church, see *King* v. *Alston*, 12 Q.B. 971, 116 Eng. Rep. 1134 (1848) (where incumbent of mother church is given two-thirds of surplice fees in new church, he has no complaint if incumbent of new church collects no fees). Another interesting case on fee divisions is *Day* v. *Peacock*, 18 C.B. (N.S.) 701, 144 Eng. Rep. 620 (1865) (where new parish has no burial ground, incumbent is not entitled to fees for burial of parishioners in Burial Board ground).

50. Church Building Commissioners (Transfer of Powers) Act, 1856, 19-20 Vic.,

c. 55; New Parishes Measure, 1943, 6-7 Geo. 6, No. 1. Where a parish was divided by a private act, it was difficult to bring it under the general legislation because a general law is held not to repeal a private act not specially mentioned. *Fitzgerald* v. *Champneys*, 2 J. & H. 31, 70 Eng. Rep. 958 (Ch. 1861). Cf. *Fitzgerald* v. *Fitzpatric*, 33 L.J. Ch. 670 (1864) (transformation of proprietary chapel into new parish voids rights of incumbent of mother church).

51. 31-32 Vic., c. 177 (1868). Perpetual curacies were created by Queen Anne's Bounty Act, 1714, 1 Geo. 1, St. 2, c. 10, § 4.

52. "Union," Burn ii, 495. The applicable statutes are 37 Hen. 8, c. 21 (1545) and 17 Car. 2, c. 3 (1665). The leading case upholding the power outside the statute is *Austin* v. *Twyne*, Cro. Eliz. 500, 78 Eng. Rep. 750 (1595). It appears that two benefices permanently united become one for all purposes, *Robinson* v. *Marquis of Bristol*, 11 C.B. 241, 138 Eng. Rep. 464 (Exch. Ch. 1852), but not if they were united only for the life of the incumbent. *Daniel* v. *Morton*, 16 Q.B. 197, 117 Eng. Rep. 854 (1850) (incumbent of united benefices is nonresident on one of them).

53. 1-2 Vic., c. 106, § 16.

54. Pluralities Act, 1850, 13-14 Vic., c. 98.

55. Union of Benefices Act, 1860, 23-24 Vic., c. 142.

56. 9-10 Geo. 5, c. 98.

57. Union of Benefices Measure, 1923, 14-15 Geo. 5, No. 2.

58. *In re Benefices of Great Massingham and Little Massingham*, [1931] A.C. 328 (P.C.); *In re Union of Benefices of Westoe and South Shields St. Hilda*, [1939] A.C. 269 (P.C.). Cf. *In re Benefices of Edburton and Poynings*, [1934] A.C. 115 (P.C.) (where bishop's approval of scheme provided for transfer of income from united parishes, it was no approval at all, and Commissioners had no jurisdiction).

59. Union of Benefices (Amendment) Measure, 1936, 26 Geo. 5 and 1 Edw. 8, No. 2.

60. 7-8 Geo. 6, No. 1, patterned on 7-8 Geo. 6, c. 47 (1944) and 38-39 Vic., c. 36 (1875).

61. See pp. 339 and 352, *infra*.

62. 12-14 Geo. 6, No. 3. The Judicial Committee's departure from the *Westoe* criteria is in *Re Union of Whippingham and East Cowes Benefices*, [1954] A.C. 245 (P.C.). The parliamentary objections referred to appear in Hansard, 5th Ser., clxiii, 1056-57.

63. 1968, No. 1, replaced by 1983, No. 1. P. Crowe, *Pastoral Reorganization* (London, S.P.C.K., 1971) contains a good discussion of the 1968 measure and its background.

64. The Judicial Committee has power to hear these appeals de novo, but in fact accords almost conclusive weight to decisions properly emerging from the process. *Parochial Church Council of Little Leigh* v. *Church Commissioners*, [1960] 1 W.L.R. 567 (P.C.) (under 1949 measure); *Elphick* v. *Church Commissioners*, [1974] A.C. 562 (P.C.); *Hargreaves* v. *Church Commissioners*, [1983] 2 A.C. 457 (P.C.).

65. Welsby, 38-41.

66. § 61. The brewery case is *In re Ecclesiastical Commissioners and New City of London Brewery Company's Contract*, [1895] 1 Ch. 702. The eighteenth century material is discussed in Phil., 1399, following Gibson. On secularization under

Henry VIII, see Vol. II, 80-81. A form of deconsecration service, previously adopted by the two archbishops, was approved by Canterbury Convocation in 1950. *Acts of Conv.*, 116. The use of secularized church buildings was inconclusively debated in the General Synod in 1972 and 1973 *General Synod Reports*, iii, 442ff, iv, 196-218, 344-53. The main issue was whether use for non-Christian worship was better or worse than total secularization. "I find it a little distressing to think that there should be a cocktail bar where the altar stood, a water closet where the font was, and baths in the belfry." Id., iii, 450. In 1983, a motion to allow use for non-Christian worship was narrowly defeated. Id., xiv, 133-57.

67. 47-48 Vic., c. 72. See p. 146 *supra*.

68. Demolition of churches under the Pastoral Measure is not subject to the statutory limitations on demolition of other historic buildings. Redundant Churches and Other Religious Buildings Act, 1969, c. 22. It was evidently assumed that historical concerns would be as safe in the hands of the Church Commissioners as in those of the regular planning authorities — an assumption vigorously and persuasively attacked in *Country Life*, Aug. 21, 1986, p. 566. There is also a more general exemption from the historic preservation laws of buildings in current use for public worship. Town and Country Planning Act, 1971, c. 78, §§ 56(1)(a), 58(2)(a). This exemption may be limited by an order under § 58AA, added by the Housing and Planning Act, 1986, c. 63. These general provisions extend to churches of all denominations. *Attorney General* v. *Howard United Reformed Church Trustees*, [1976] A.C. 363 (H.L.). But they do not permit demolition because a church about to be demolished is not currently used for worship. Ibid. But a church can be razed to ground level if worship will still be held in the crypt. *Re St. Lukes, Cheetham*, [1978] Fam. 144 (Con. Manchester).

69. City of London (Guild Churches) Act, 1952, 15-16 Geo. 6 & 1 Eliz. 2, c. xxxviii.

70. Welsby, 253-54.

71. Ibid.; *General Synod Reports*, viii, 278-88 (1977); G.S. 316 (1977).

72. 1-2 Vic., c. 106 §§ 75-102. For an example of an objection to this legislation on freedom of contract grounds, see W. J. Aislabie, *A Letter to Lord John Russell* (London, 1838, Bodl. 38.615). Sydney Smith's understanding of the applicable principles of honor is quoted from the *Edinburgh Review* of 1808 in Best, 207-8. See *Fraser* v. *Denison*, 57 L.L.Q.B. (N.S.) 550 (1888), holding that despite this legislation, it is for the court, not the bishop, to determine money damages for failure of an incumbent to provide his curate with board and lodging as promised.

73. 1-2 Vic., c. 106, § 98. Hearing: *R.* v. *Archbishop of Canterbury*, 1 El. & El. 545, 120 Eng. Rep. 1014 (1859). Privy Council: *Poole* v. *Bishop of London*, 14 Moo. P.C. 262, 15 Eng. Rep. 304 (1862). Proprietary chapel: *Sedgwick* v. *Bishop of Manchester*, 38 L.J. Eccl. 30 (Abp. of York, 1869). Chaplain: *R.* v. *Visitors of Middlesex Asylum*, 2 Q.B. 433, 144 Eng. Rep. 171 (1842). See also *R.* v. *Bishop of Liverpool*, 20 T.L.R. 485 (1904) (bishop has more scope in denying license than in revoking it); *In re National Insurance Act*, 1911, [1912] 2 Ch. 563 (curate is not employee).

74. For the previous law, see Chapter 1, note 197 and accompanying text, *supra*.

75. 34-35 Vic., c. 35 (1871); 48-49 Vic., c. 54 (1885); 61-62 Vic., c. 48 (1898);

16-17 Geo. 5, No. 8 (1926). Cf. *Lawrence* v. *Edwards*, [1891] 1 Ch. 144 (despite sequestration of rectory, rector, not curate, appoints parish clerk).

76. *Cr. Pref.*, 62-63.

77. *Rice* v. *Bishop of Oxford*, [1917] P. 181; *Huntly* v. *Bishop of Norwich*, [1931] P. 210. The court provided for consisted of one judge to interpret the law and determine the facts, and the archbishop of the province to pronounce sentence.

78. 8-9 Geo. 6, No. 3 (1945); 10-11 Geo. 6, No. 1 (1947) See pp. 220-22, *infra*.

79. Chadwick, i, 449-50; C. Whitefoord, *Letter to the Church Pastoral Aid Society* (London, 1841); *Cr. Pref.*, 204.

80. Ecclesiastical Commissioners (Provision for Unbeneficed Clergy) Measure, 1928, 18-19 Geo. 5, No. 1. Other legislation referred to in this paragraph is Endowments and Glebe Measure, 1976, No. 4, § 8; 14-15 Geo. 5, No. 2, § 18 (1923); 1968, No. 1, §§ 26, 38(g). The Pastoral Measure, 1983, No. 1, makes no provision for assistant curates, evidently preferring a more flexibly structured team ministry. § 20.

81. Best, 436-37. On peers of Scotland, see Peerage Act, 1963, c. 48, § 4.

82. 10-11 Vic., c. 108 (1847). There was evidently some fear that a bishop without a seat in the Lords would be a dangerous precedent. J. Kaye, *Letter to the Archbishop of Canterbury* (London, 1838).

83. 13-14 Vic., c. 94, § 15; Best 437.

84. 38-39 Vic., c. 34. The legislation referred to in the next paragraph is 39-40 Vic., c. 54 (1876) (Truro); 41-42 Vic., c. 68 (1878) (four sees). All the dioceses founded under those and later statutes or measures are listed with dates in Halsbury 219-20. For background on some of these, see Bell, *Davidson*, i, 644-46; Iremonger, *Temple*, 130-33; P. Jagger, The Formation of the Diocese of Newcastle," In *A Social History of the Diocese of Newcastle* ed. Pickering (1981), 24-52. A measure of the Church Assembly to erect a new bishopric at Shrewsbury was defeated 61-60 in the House of Lords in 1926, evidently because of its effect on the ancient see of Hereford. *Cr. Pref.* 62, 160.

85. Vol. I, 104. For an example of a medieval commission to an Irish bishop, see *The Register of Henry Chichele, Archbishop of Canterbury, 1414-1443*, ed. Jacob, iv (Canterbury and York Soc. xlvii, 1947), 78. For the term suffragan, see *O.E.D.* I cannot agree with the derivation offered by Phil. 76, following "Bishop," Burn, i, 137, 178.

86. 26 Hen. 8, c. 14.

87. Phil. 76-80; Sykes, *From Sheldon*, 193-94 (quoting Gibson); Colonial Bishops Act, 1852, 15-16 Vic., c. 52.

88. Episcopal Endowments and Stipends Measure, 1943, 6-7 Geo. 6, No. 2, § 5(a).

89. Suffragans Nomination Act, 1888, 51-52 Vic., c. 56; Halsbury, 239n; Welsby, 248-52.

90. Kemp, *Kirk*, 90-91.

91. 1978, No. 1.

92. G.S. 287 (1977) and *General Synod Reports*, vii, 544, 547 are all I could find on the question, and it is not a lot.

93. 3-4 Vic., c. 113, §§ 41, 42, 44; Best, 326-28.

94. 5-6 Will. 4, c. 76, § 139 (1835); 26-27 Vic., c. 120 (1863); 19-20 Vic., c. 50 (1856).

95. Best, 412. Church Discipline Act, 1840, 3-4 Vic. § 24 and Public Worship Regulation Act, 1874, 37-38 Vic., c. 85, § 16 substitute the archbishop for the bishop where the accused holds preferment in the bishop's gift; Church Discipline Act, 1892, 55-56 Vic., c. 32 does not. See § 10(3).

96. Chadwick, i, 449-50; Mathieson, 1-3; R. Mainwaring, *From Controversy to Co-Existence* (Cambridge, 1985), 101-2. On the Feoffees for Impropriations, see C. Hill, *Economic Problems of the Church* (Oxford, 1956), 245-74.

97. *Hunter* v. *Attorney General*, [1899] A.C. 309 (H.L.); *In re Church Patronage Trust*, [1904] 2 Ch. 643 (C.A.); cf. P.P. Eng., 1874, vii, 369-70.

98. Chapter 1, notes 114-15, *supra*.

99. *Young* v. *Jones*, 3 Dougl. 98, 99 Eng. Rep. 558 (1782); Incumbents Resignation Act, 1871, 34-35 Vic., c. 44.

100. *Sweet* v. *Meredith*, 6 L.T. (N.S.) 413 (Ch. 1862). The device is mentioned by J.B. Lee, a professional bishops' secretary, in P.P. Eng., 1874, vii, 347-49.

101. P.P. Eng., 1874, vii, 425 (per Rev. Lord S.G. Osborne). On the lawyers' advice, see Id., 324-27 (per R.J. Phillimore). Osborne believed that the lawyers were mistaken, but that the fear of costs kept the bishops from taking a stand. Id., 425-26, 433.

102. Hansard, 3d Ser., cccxi, 678, 680; Chadwick, ii, 209.

103. *Lee* v. *Merest*, 39 L.J. Eccl. 53 (Arches, 1869). The quoted passages from Workman's letters appear on p. 57. Osborne's testimony on the subject is in P.P. Eng., 1874, vii, 427-28. Workman appears in J. Foster, *Alumni Oxoniensis 1715-1886*. He was born Rawlins. He matriculated at Brasenose in 1845 at age 18. He changed his name in 1848 and died in 1880. *Crockford* for 1879 lists him with an address but no job history. Lambeth Palace has no record of any disciplinary proceeding against him. Merest appears in J. Venn, *Alumni Cantabrigiensis, Pt. II, 1752-1900*, iv. He was born in 1821, matriculated at Peterhouse, 1841, graduated and ordained 1846, occupied two curacies and two incumbencies before coming to Upton-Snodsbury. He died in poverty in 1887. He appears in *Crockford* for 1879 as not responding to the editors' inquiries. According to Osborne's testimony, he had already acquired an unsavory reputation before coming to Upton-Snodsbury. The Hereford and Worcester Record Office were kind enough to supply me with a newspaper account of the libel case, dated March 13, 1869. That account indicates that there was a trust fund set up at some point in the transactions involving the living: "Prosecutor [i.e., Workman] seemed to think he was entitled to derive pecuniary advantage from the purchase and sale of the living for the defendant [i.e., Merest], and the defendant seemed to be of opinion — probably rightly advised — that the prosecutor being in the position of trustee could not in law or equity be so entitled." The nature of the exposure that Merest threatened in order to coerce Workman into seeing his view of the trust was not made public. It appears that the letters drafted by Workman for Merest to send to the bishop are not in the episcopal correspondence in the Hereford and Worcester Record Office. I am grateful to Mr. Robin Whittaker for checking the files for me. V.C.H. Worcester, iv, 212 shows Merest buying the advowson direct from O'Donnell, and does not include Workman

in its list of patrons of Upton-Snodsbury. There are bound volumes of the *Church and School Gazette* in the Bodleian. Each issue devotes a large page or more to small print listings of benefices available for purchase or exchange. The list is preceded by a statement praising the service provided and warning of the trouble one can get into by working with less competent agents. About the time of the Merest controversy, wording was added defending the legitimacy of the service offered and disapproving of references to Simon Magus in connection with it. It is worth noting in passing that Thomas Tristram, later to become an important ecclesiastical judge, appeared in the Arches for Workman and tried unsuccessfully to avoid having Workman's title deed to the advowson put into evidence.

104. Hansard, 3d Ser., cccxi, 687.

105. P.P. Eng., 1874, vii, 301. Note especially 347-49 on accepting new preferment as an alternative to resignation, and 352, where it is stated that the case of *Bishop of Exeter* v. *Marshall*, L.R. 3 H.L. 17 (1866), discussed below, arose because the bishop suspected a presentee of simony. On donatives, see also *Lowe* v. *Bishop of Chester*, 10 Q.B.D. 407 (1883).

106. *Whish* v. *Hesse*, 3 Hag. Ecc. 659, 162 Eng. Rep. 1299 (Arches 1831); *Beneficed Clerk* v. *Lee*, [1897] A.C. 266 (P.C.). The 1589 statute is 31 Eliz. 1, c. 6.

107. *Apperley* v. *Bishop of Hereford*, 9 Bing. 681, 131 Eng. Rep. 769 (1833).

108. *Bishop of Exeter* v. *Marshall*, L.R. 3 H.L. 17 (1866). The case arose in a lay court in a patronage case (*quare impedit*). In *Willis* v. *Bishop of Oxford*, 2 P.D. 192 (Arches 1877) (*duplex querela*), the church court followed it for the sake of uniformity. The 1604 canon involved in the case was c. 48, requiring a testimonial from the bishop of the diocese from which the presentee came. The 1693 precedent is *Bishop of Exeter* v. *Hele*, Shower 88, 1 Eng. Rep. 61 (H.L.), discussed in Chapter 1, note 179 and accompanying text, *supra*.

109. P.P. Eng. 1874, vii, 300 (committee report), Id., ii, 31 (bill); P.P. Eng. 1886, i, 485 (bill); P.P. Eng. 1896, i, 117, 133 (bill); Benefices Act, 1898, 61-2 Vic., c. 48. The 1886 bill is discussed in Hansard, 3d ser., cccxi, 678, 1027, 1227, cccxii, 336, 1127. Stubbs takes it up in his 1886 charge to the clergy of Chester, Stubbs, 9-11. I do not find in the bill as printed all the provisions he refers to. An 1893 bill is referred to in Stubbs, 224, an 1896 one in Stubbs, 263.

110. Mayfield, *Like Nothing*, 81-82; *Crockford*, 1976, xii "The public declaration against simony is no longer demanded by the law (possibly because no ecclesiastical position is now worth a bribe)."

111. Benefices Act, 1898 (Amendment) Measure, 1923, 14-15 Geo. 5, No. 1.

112. Benefices (Diocesan Boards of Patronage) Measure, 1932, 22-23 Geo. 5, No. 1.

113. Benefices (Exercise of Rights of Presentation) Measure, 1931, 21-22 Geo. 5, No. 3; Mayfield, 46.

114. The 1886 bill is in P.P. Eng. 1886, i, 485. Liturgical controversies evidently affected the transfer of advowsons again in the 1920s. Mayfield, 45. It would seem that Benefices (Purchase of Rights of Patronage) Measure, 1933, 23 Geo. 5, No. 1, empowering the parochial church council to purchase at an arbitrated price any advowson that had been sold since 1898 except as part of a landed estate, was intended to keep patronage trusts from controlling advowsons of parishes whose

churchmanship differed from their own. *Cr. Pref.* 125-27. Dr. William Evershed in his not yet published thesis, *Party and Patronage in the Church of England 1800-1945: A Study of Patronage Trusts and Patronage Reform* (1985), argues persuasively that the problem was much less serious than it was made out to be, and that such problem as there was resulted from the 1923 measure, *supra*, note 111, because it required people to sell their advowsons immediately or run the risk of not being able to sell them at all. I am grateful to Dr. Evershed for giving me the benefit of his thinking and research on this and other aspects of patronage.

115. Stubbs, 39-40.

116. *R.* v. *Archbishop of Canterbury, ex parte Morant*, [1944] K.B. 282 (C.A.). But note that this non-judicial process applied only where the parochial church council had rejected the patron's candidate. In other cases, the bishop's refusal of a presentee remained subject to judicial review — under common law or general canon law where the refusal was on a ground of doctrine or ritual; under the 1898 act in other cases. On withdrawal of an earlier version, see *Church Assembly Reports*, xii, 213 (1931). The objections are stated in *Cr. Pref.*, 94. The measure finally passed differed from the one withdrawn by giving the final say to the bishop and the archbishop rather than to a board. The board was retained with a different composition, and reduced to an advisory role.

117. *E.g.*, H.M. Smith, *Administrative Reform* (London, S.P.C.K., 1919); Mayfield, *Like Nothing*, 60, 81-82; *Paul Report*, 109.

118. Patronage (Benefices) Measure, 1986, No. 3.

119. Welsby, 252-53.

120. *R.* v. *Archbishop of Canterbury, ex parte Morant*, [1944] K.B. 282 (C.A.).

121. *Paul Report*, 197-200.

122. Mayfield, *Like Nothing*, 81-82.

123. *Paul Report*, 286.

124. 1-2 Vic., c. 106 (1838); 3-4 Vic., c. 86 (1840).

125. Vol. I, 73-88; Vol. II, 77-78, 125; 4th Lateran, c. 29, c. 28, X, III, 5; 21 Hen. 8, c. 13 (1529); 1604, c. 41. On the King James Bible, see D. Daiches, *The King James Version of the English Bible* (Chicago, 1941), 65-68.

126. McClatchey, 57-67.

127. Hansard, 3d ser., xlii, 916-18 (1838), cx, 1083-85 (1850).

128. Hansard, 3d ser., xlii, 915.

129. *Storie* v. *Bishop of Winchester*, 17 C.B. 653, 139 Eng. Rep. 1232 (1836).

130. *Burder* v. *Mavor*, 1 Rob. Ecc. 614, 163 Eng. Rep. 1154 (Arches 1848).

131. McClatchey, 57-69.

132. Pluralities Act, 1850, 13-14 Vic., c. 98. Later legislation referred to in this paragraph is Pluralities Acts Amendment Act, 1885, 48-49 Vic., c. 54; Pluralities Measure, 1930, 20-21 Geo. 5, No. 7.

133. Hansard, 3d ser. cx, 1081-89 (1850).

134. 1-2 Vic., c. 106, § 85 (1838) provided that the curate for a nonresident was to have £80 or the full value of the benefice, whichever was greater. See O.D.P., c. 308 for a case from the late 1850s involving this provision.

135. Pastoral Measure, 1983, No. 1, § 85 states the present law on pluralities.

136. 43 Geo. 3, c. 84 (1803); 57 Geo. 3, c. 99 (1817); Cf. 21 Hen. 8, c. 16

(1529). See Chapter 1, note 189, *supra*.

137. *Ex parte Bartlett*, 12 Q.B. 488, 116 Eng. Rep. 950 (1848). *Contra; Butler and Goodales Case*, 6 Co. Rep. 21b, 77 Eng. Rep. 285 (1598).

138. *Capel* v. *Child*, 2 Cr. & J. 558, 149 Eng. Rep. 235 (Exch. 1832). The other cases referred to in this paragraph are *Cooper* v. *Wandsworth Board of Works*, 14 C.B. (N.S.) 180, 143 Eng. Rep. 414 (1863); *Painter* v. *Liverpool Gas Works*, 3 Ad. & E. 432, 111 Eng. Rep. 478 (1836); *R.* v. *Archbishop of Canterbury*, 1 El. & El. 545, 120 Eng. Rep. 1014 (1859). In *R.* v. *Cambridge University*, 1 Str. 557, 567, 93 Eng. Rep. 698, 704 (1722), it is said that *audi alteram partem* is a principle that God Himself follows, as is shown by His interrogation of Adam and Eve after they ate the fruit. But the principle applies only where the action in question is in some way judicial. *R.* v. *Archbishop of Canterbury, ex parte Morant*, [1944] K.B. 282 (C.A.).

139. *Bonaker* v. *Evans*, 16 Q.B. 162, 117 Eng. Rep. 840 (Ex. Ch. 1850).

140. *Bartlett* v. *Kirwood*, 2 E. & B. 771, 118 Eng. Rep. 956 (1853).

141. *Sharpe* v. *Bluck*, 10 Q.B. 280, 116 Eng. Rep. 109 (1847). Other litigations involving Bluck are *Bluck* v. *Rackham*, 1 Rob. Ecc. 367, 163 Eng. Rep. 1069 (Arches 1845), *affirmed*, 5 Moo. P.C. 305, 13 Eng. Rep. 508 (1846), *prohibition denied*, 9 Q.B. 690, 115 Eng. Rep. 1439 (1846), a successful proceeding to collect statutory penalties for nonresidence, and *Bluck* v. *Hodgson*, 5 Notes of Cases 167 (1847), where Bluck resisted an attempt to build him a parsonage. It appears that the benefice involved in these proceedings was worth more than £ 1000 a year. The Sequestration Act, 1849 is 12-13 Vic., c. 67.

142. *Canning* v. *Dr. Newman*, 2 Brownl. & Golds. 54, 123 Eng. Rep. 811 (1610). For Bonaker's early experience in his parish, see *Bennett* v. *Bonaker*, 2 Hag. Ecc. 25, 3 Hag. Ecc. 17, 163 Eng. Rep. 773, 1066 (Arches 1828-29). It appears that the vicarage was ruinous in 1817 when Bonaker came, but that he had made some effort to repair it. The duty of the incumbent to keep his house in repair was an old one. Vol. I, 96.

143. This doctrine had been laid down by Lord Mansfield in *Wilkinson* v. *Allott*, 2 Cowp. 429, 98 Eng. Rep. 1169 (1776).

144. *Rickard* v. *Graham*, [1910] 1 Ch. 722. On statutory protection for tenants, see *Bishop of Gloucester* v. *Cunnington*, [1943] K.B. 101 (C.A.).

145. *Boyd* v. *Barker*, 4 Drewry 582, 583-84, 62 Eng. Rep. 223, 224 (Ch. 1859).

146. 34-5 Vic., c. 43.

147. Ecclesiastical Dilapidations Measure, 1923, 14-15 Geo. 5, No. 3.

148. *Cr. Pref.* 106 (1931).

149. Phil. 1125-43, 1264-80.

150. 1972, No. 2.

151. Medieval procedure: Vol. I, 96. Mid-eighteenth century: "Sequestration," Burn, ii, 329, 330. Sheriff must name benefice: *R.* v. *Powell*, 1 M. & W. 321, 150 Eng. Rep. 456 (Exch. 1836). Account to lay court: *Dawson* v. *Symonds*, 12 Q.B. 830, 116 Eng. Rep. 1082 (1848); *Morris* v. *Phelps*, 4 Ex. 495, 154 Eng. Rep. 1480 (Exch. 1850). Cf. *Baylis* v. *Bishop of Lincoln*, [1913] 1 Ch. 127 (C.A.) (bishop liable for money paid to sequestrator by mistake). A court of equity could use the sequestration process to enforce an order to pay money. *Allen* v. *Williams*, 1 Sm. & Giff. 455, 65 Eng. Rep. 478 (Ch. 1854). But it could not impose a receiver on the

benefice unless it was one without cure. *Hawkins* v. *Gathercole*, 6 de G. M. & G. 1,
43 Eng. Rep. 1129 (Ch. 1855); *Grenfell* v. *Dean and Chapter of Windsor*, 2 Beav.
544, 48 Eng. Rep. 1292 (Rolls 1840).

152. *Ex parte Meymot*, 1 Atk. 196, 26 Eng. Rep. 127 (Ch. 1747); *Arbuckle* v.
Cowtan, 3 Bos. & Pul. 321, 127 Eng. Rep. 177 (1803); 7 Geo. 4, c. 57, § 28.

153. *Ex parte Chick, in re Meredith*, 11 Ch.D. 731 (C.A. 1879); *Lawrence* v.
Adams, 75 L.T. 410 (Ch. 1896).

154. *Lawrence* v. *Edwards*, [1891] 1 Ch. 144; Sequestration Act, 1871, 34-35
Vic., c. 45.

155. 24-25 Vic. c. 134, § 135 (1861); 34-35 Vic., c. 45 (1871).

156. 1-2 Vic., c. 106, § 110 (1838); *Bunter* v. *Cresswell*, 14 Q.B. 825, 117 Eng.
Rep. 317 (1850); *In re Thackenham Sequestration Moneys*, L.R. 12 Eq. 494 (1871).

157. 61-2 Vic., c. 48, § 10.

158. It would seem that the definition of the employment relation in Attachment of
Earnings Act, 1971, c. 32, §§ 6(2), 24(1)(a) is broad enough to include the relation
between an incumbent and the Church Commissioners, the diocesan stipends fund or
the parochial church council. But I find no cases on the question.

159. 1-2 Vic., c. 106, §§ 28-31 (1838). The 1817 act was 57 Geo. 3, c. 99, the
Henrician one 21 Hen. 8, c. 13 (1529). The case referred to in text is *Hall* v.
Franklin, 3 M. & W. 260, 150 Eng. Rep. 1141 (Exch. 1838). The retroactive
validation referred to in the next paragraph is 1-2 Vic., c. 10. The 1841 act referred
to is 4-5 Vic., c. 14. For an ingenious but unsuccessful attempt to avoid the
application of this language, see *Lewis* v. *Bright*, 4 El. & Bl. 917, 119 Eng. Rep. 341
(1855).

160. *Rice* v. *Bishop of Oxford*, [1917] P. 181 (Court under Benefices Act, 1898).
The medieval case referred to is in *Visitations of Religious Houses*, iii (Lincoln
Record Soc., xxi, 1929), ed. Thompson, 119-27 (1441). Rice was found guilty of
neglect, and a curate was imposed. The medieval chaplain was made to swear that he
would behave properly in the future.

161. 1-2 Vic., c. 106, § 28. For the earlier material, see Chapter 1, note 147 and
accompanying text, *supra*.

162. 1964, No. 6, § 11. Cf. 1969, c. C28.

163. 1604, c. 75; Phil. 840-41 (hunting). I have found no post-Reformation
English material on shows and dances, but c. 3, D. XXIII and c. 19, D. XXXIV of
Gratian would seem to have remained in force.

164. Chadwick, i, 444-45.

165. Mathieson, 7. Phillpotts: Hart, 93-94; W. Addison, *The English Country
Parson*, (London, 1947), 142. Wilberforce: O.D.P. d. 550, ff. 90 (Berks. licenses),
152 (Oxon. hunters, news clipping), 156 (ball); McClatchey, 230.

166. 1969, c. C26(2). The Bab Ballad appears on p. 69 of an edition published in
Cambridge, Mass. in 1970.

167. 3-4 Vic., c. 86.

168. Neither the bishop nor the provincial court was limited to the case found in
the commission's report. *Simpson* v. *Flamank*, L.R. 1 P.C. 463 (1867); *Sheppard* v.
Bennett (First Appeal), L.R. 4 P.C. 350 (1870). Even after the commission was
appointed, the bishop could send letters of request without waiting for it to report.

Sanders v. *Head*, 3 Curt. 32, 163 Eng. Rep. 645 (Arches 1842).

169. 1532 Statute: 23 Hen. 8, c. 9. Under this statute, the provincial court may have had some discretion about whether to accept letters of request. It had none under the 1840 act. *Sheppard* v. *Phillimore and Bennett*, L.R. 2 P.C. 450 (1869). Bishop did not have to initiate proceedings: *Julius* v. *Bishop of Oxford*, 5 A.C. 214 (H.L. 1880). Could not drop case after commission convened: *R. ex rel. Ditcher v. Archbishop of Canterbury*, 6 El. & Bl. 547, 119 Eng. Rep. 968 (1856). Secretary as complainant: *R.* v. *Bishop of St. Albans*, 9 Q.B.D. 454 (1882).

170. Commission limited to acts within diocese: *Homer and Bloomer* v. *Jones*, 9 Jur. 167 (1845). Lincolnshire rector: *Edwards* v. *Moss*, 20 L.T. (N.S.) 834 (P.C. 1869). Cf. *Voysey* v. *Noble*, L.R. 3 P.C. 357 (1870), a doctrinal case against a Yorkshire vicar based on a publication in London. The bishop of London appointed a commission and the archbishop of York sent letters of request to his own court based on the commission's report.

171. *Ex parte Denison*, 4 El. & Bl. 293, 119 Eng. Rep. 113 (1854); *R.* v. *Dodson*, 7 El. & Bl. 315, 119 Eng. Rep. 1264 (1857); *Ditcher* v. *Denison*, 11 Moo. P.C. 324, 14 Eng. Rep. 718 (1857).

172. *Bishop of Hereford* v. *T_____n*, 2 Rob. Ecc. 595, 163 Eng. Rep. 1425 (Arches 1853); *Ditcher* v. *Denison*, Deane 334, 164 Eng. Rep. 594 (Arches 1857), *affirmed*, 11 Moo. P.C. 324, 14 Eng. Rep. 718 (1857).

173. *Edwards* v. *Moss*, 20 L.T. (N.N.) 834 (P.C. 1869). Ecclesiastical Jurisdiction Measure, 1963, No. 1, § 16 provides expressly that where the "offence consists of a series of acts or omissions," only the last of them need occur within the period of limitations. On refusing a presentee, see *Marriner* v. *Bishop of Bath and Wells*, [1893] P. 145 (Arches 1876).

174. Vol. II, 178-80.

175. Chapter 1, notes 77-79 and accompanying text, *supra*.

176. *Burder* v. _____, 3 Curt. 822, 163 Eng. Rep. 914, 4 Notes of Cases 483 (Arches 1844); *Dean of Jersey* v. *Rector of* _____, 3 Moo. P.C. 229, 13 Eng. Rep. 97 (1840).

177. *Borough* v. *Collins*, 15 P.D. 81 (Arches 1890).

178. The commission in *In re Monckton*, 3 Notes of Cases lv Supp. (Comm. of Inq. 1845) was headed by Stephen Lushington. It reported prima facie evidence that the conduct of the accused had been degrading to a minister and had brought grave scandal on the church. Whether this conduct could have been prosecuted is questionable. The parties submitted to the bishop's judgment.

179. Vol. I, 138-39; Vol. II, 31-33, 86-87; 18 Eliz. 1, c. 7 (1576).

180. Hobart 288, 80 Eng. Rep. 433 (1618).

181. 7 Geo. 4, c. 28 (1826).

182. *Matter of A.B.*, 11 P.D. 56 (Ch. York 1886).

183. "Buggery" was made a capital offense by 25 Hen. 8, c. 6 (1533), and remained so until 24-25 Vic., c. 100 § 61 (1861), which provided for imprisonment instead. Homosexual acts in private between consenting adults were made non-criminal by Sexual Offences Act, 1967, c. 60, § 1.

184. *Bishop of Ely* v. *Close*, [1913] P. 184 (Arches).

185. 55-56 Vic., c. 32.

186. The appellate court could take new evidence and make its own determination of the facts. *Chesney* v. *Newsholme*, [1908] P. 301 (Ch. York); *Wakeford* v. *Bishop of Lincoln*, [1921] A.C. 813 (P.C.).

187. *Bishop of Ely* v. *Close*, [1913] P. 184 (Arches).

188. The quoted language is in § 2, the definitions referred to are in § 11, and the canons referred to are 1604, c. 75, 109.

189. *Sweet* v. *Young*, [1902] P. 37 (Con. Rochester); *Fitzmaurice* v. *Hesketh*, [1904] A.C. 266 (P.C.); *Moore* v. *Bishop of Oxford*, [1904] A.C. 283 (P.C.).

190. *Bishop of Rochester* v. *Harris*, [1893] P. 137 (Con. Rochester); *Bowman* v. *Lax*, [1910] P. 300 (Ch. York).

191. 10-11 Geo. 6, No. 1. The 1945 measure is 8-9 Geo. 6, No. 3. The earlier legislation is cited, *supra*, note 75.

192. *Rice* v. *Bishop of Oxford*, [1917] P. 181. Under the 1926 measure, see *Huntley* v. *Bishop of Norwich*, [1931] P. 210.

193. Phil., 840 n; notes 186-92, *supra*; *Cr. Pref.*, 135; *Bland* v. *Archdeacon of Cheltenham*, [1972] Fam. 157, 162 (Arches). P.P. Eng. 1846, xxxii, 3 indicates twenty-six proceedings so far under the 1840 act, including seven for incontinence, four involving doctrine or ritual, four for improper marriages or officiating without licenses, three for brawling, carousing, or fighting, one for nonresidence, the rest unspecified.

194. 1963, No. 1.

195. § 55. *Sweet* v. *Bishop of Ely*, [1902] 2 Ch. 508 held that separation on a ground created since 1892 could not be made the basis for automatic deprivation under the 1892 act. Ecclesiastical Jurisdiction (Amendment) Measure, 1974, No. 2 made the amendment referred to in this paragraph.

196. § 14(1).

197. See *Bland* v. *Archdeacon of Cheltenham*, [1972] Fam. 157 (Arches), discussed below; Halsbury, 762-63.

198. Hansard, 4th ser. iii, 1622 (1892).

199. *Bland* v. *Archdeacon of Cheltenham*, [1972] Fam. 157 (Arches).

200. 1977, No. 1. The quotations are from §§ 9(1) and 6(1). *General Synod Reports*, viii, 720-40 has a debate on an earlier version of this measure with considerable discussion of the *Bland* case. It was reported that the case cost £20,000 in legal fees, and a bishop stated that the 1963 measure would probably never be used again in such a case (p. 726).

201. See Welsby, 227-29 for the progress of this term from a separate opinion in a Royal Commission report of 1956 to an ecclesiastical report ten years later (*Putting Asunder: A Divorce Law for Contemporary Society*), to Divorce Reform Act, 1969, c. 55.

202. Mayfield, 40-42.

203. *General Synod Reports*, vii, 4, 1190; G.S. 289x, ¶28; Hansard, 5th Ser. cmxxxiv, 513-18 (1977). Another objection was the absence of an adequate hearing for the incumbent.

204. Ecclesiastical Commissioners Act, 1840, 3-4 Vic., c.113, §§ 22, 51; Ecclesiastical Commissioners Act, 1841, 4-5 Vic., c. 39, § 7.

205. Episcopal Endowments and Stipends Measure, 1943, 6-7 Geo. 6, No. 2, § 5;

Mayfield, 101.

206. Ecclesiastical Courts Act, 1829, 10 Geo. 4, c. 53; Ecclesiastical Fees Act, 1867, 30-31 Vic., c. 135; Ecclesiastical Officers Remuneration Measure, 1939, 2-3 Geo. 6, No. 2; Ecclesiastical Fees Measure, 1962, 10-11 Eliz. 2, No. 1. Other provisions are cited in the repealing schedule to the 1962 measure.

207. Ecclesiastical Jurisdiction Act, 1847, 10-11 Vic., c. 98, § 9. Ecclesiastical Fees Act, 1875, 38-39 Vic., c. 76 made similar provision for other offices. 6-7 Will. 4, c. 67 (1836) had given similar warning to future holders of cathedral preferment. The earlier law on freehold offices is discussed at p. 43, *supra*.

208. *R.* v. *Bishop of Gloucester*, 2 B. & Ad. 158, 109 Eng. Rep. 1102 (1831); *Pickering* v. *Bishop of Ely*, 2 Y. & C.C.C. 249, 63 Eng. Rep. 109 (Ch. 1843).

209. The following discussion, where not otherwise documented, is based on W.L. Dale, *The Law of the Parish Church* (3d ed., London, 1957), 27-31, 55-59. For earlier material, see Vol. II, 162-64, 222-23. It is traditional to derive the term "sidesman" from "synodsman," but the *Oxford English Dictionary* says there is no foundation for doing so.

210. Parochial Church Councils (Powers) Measure, 1921, 11-12 Geo. 5, No. 1, § 13. Churchwardens (Appointment and Resignation) Measure, 1964, No. 3, now in force, is to the same effect.

211. The Act of Toleration, 1 Will. & Mar., c. 18 (1688) allowed a Dissenter who had scruples against being a churchwarden to appoint a deputy. In *Adey* v. *Theobald*, 1 Curt. 446, 163 Eng. Rep. 157 (Archdeacon of London 1836), a Quaker who had scruples against appointing a deputy (*qui facit per alium facit per se*) was held to be totally exempt. For an example of a ritual case involving a churchwarden who was no communicant of any church, and very reluctant to assume the office, see *Ritchings* v. *Cordingley*, L.R. 3 A. & E. 113 (Arches 1868). The current provision on the subject is Churchwardens (Appointment and Resignation) Measure, 1964, No. 3, § 1(3).

212. Parochial Church Councils (Powers) Measure, 1921, 11-12 Geo. 5, No. 1, § 4(1) (ii). Charitable trusts held by churchwardens were transferred to the diocese (to hold on the same trusts) by Incumbents and Churchwardens (Trusts) Measure, 1964, No. 2. On keeping order in church, see *Burton* v. *Henson*, 10 M. & W. 105, 152 Eng. Rep. 401 (Exch. 1842); *Asher* v. *Calcraft*, 18 Q.B.D. 607 (1887) (illegal to resist them when they enforce seating assignment); *Taylor* v. *Timson*, 20 Q.B.D. 671 (1888) (they may not keep parishioners out). On illegal ornaments: *Ritchings* v. *Cordingley*, L.R. 3 A. & E. 113 (Arches 1868). On changing the interior: *Dewdney* v. *Good*, 7 Jurist N.S. 637 (Arches 1861) On taking the collection: *Cope* v. *Barber*, L.R. 7 C.P. 393 (1872). W.L. Dale, *The Law of the Parish Church* (3d ed. London, 1957), 74-75 points out that the churchwardens no longer have funds to discharge whatever responsibility they retain for objects used in worship. It would seem, therefore, that those responsibilities, insofar as they cost money, now belong to the parochial church council.

213. On the tenure of the parish clerk, see *R.* v. *Neale*, 3 Nev. & M. M.C. 108, 4 Nev. & M. K.B. 868 (1835) (Mandamus to reinstate clerk fired by incumbent for drunkenness). Occasionally, the office was valuable. In *Nichols* v. *Davis*, L.R. 4 C.P. 80 (1868), it appeared that a clerk had purported to sell his office for £ 1900

(the office was held non-assignable, and the sale was held to be a delegation). Among his emoluments was 9d for every marriage by banns in the city of Manchester. On the sexton's position, see *R*. v. *Vicar and Churchwardens of Dymock*, [1915] 1 K.B. 147, which sorted out the highly ambiguous authorities and held that a sexton has the burden of proving that the custom in a particular parish is to give him life tenure. I believe that in most places it was supposed that the custom obtained. See the entry for Faringdon in O.D.P., c. 276 (1857). The 1844 act referred to in this paragraph in 7-8 Vic., c. 59.

214. Parochial Church Councils (Powers) Measure, 1921, 11-12 Geo. 5, No. 1, § 6(iii); 1969, c. E3.

215. *R*. v. *Vicar, etc. of St. Stephens*, 14 L.J. Q.B. 34 (1844); *Wyndham* v. *Cole*, 1 P.D. 130 (Arches 1875); 1969, c. B20(2).

216. *Acts of Conv.*, 43-64; Mayfield, 66-67; Deaconesses and Lay Ministry Measure, 1972, No. 4; 1969, c. D1-D3, E3-E8. On the difference between women deacons and deaconesses, see G.S. 549 and *General Synod Reports*, xiii, 919-51. Deacons (Ordination of Women) Measure, 1986, No. 1, §§ 1(2), 2 envisages phasing out the order of deaconess, and newly ordaining any deaconesses who wish to become deacons. Some of these ministries carry the statutory rights of employees. *Barthorpe* v. *Exeter Diocesan Board of Finance*, [1979] I.C.R. 900 (Employment Appeals Tribunal).

217. Pp. 67-68, *supra*; Phil. 1424-50; *Asher* v. *Calcraft*, 18 Q.B.D. 607 (1887); *Taylor* v. *Timson*, 20 Q.B.D. 671 (1888); *Claverly Faculty Case*, [1909] P. 195 (Con. Hereford); 1969, c. F7.

218. Phil. 1424; *St. Saviour Faculty Case*, [1898] P. 217 (Comm. Canterbury).

219. Notes 46-50 and accompanying text, *supra*. These statutes deal specifically with pew rents as follows: 58 Geo. 3, c. 45, §§ 62-63, 75, 77-79 (1818); 58 Geo. 3, c. 154, §§ 26-27 (1818); 1-2 Will. 4, c. 38, § 4 (1831); 14-15 Vic., c. 97, § 1 (1851); 19-20 Vic., c. 104, §§ 5-8 (1856); 32-33 Vic., c. 74, §§ 3-4 (1869).

220. Port, 117-18, 120.

221. P.P. Eng., 1857-58, ix; Anon., *Free and Open Churches—Facts and Opinions from Five Hundred Parishes in Town and Country* (London, Free and Open Church Ass'n, 1876); *The Free and Open Church Movement — An Appeal* (same, 1875); Chadwick, i, 520-22; *Ex parte Medwin*, 1 El. & Bl. 610, 118 Eng. Rep. 566 (1853) (man sent by bishop); *Dewdney* v. *Good*, 7 Jurist N.S. 637 (Arches 1861). Cf. *Randell* v. *Dixon*, 38 Ch.D. 213 (1888) (trust for incumbent as long as church seats free).

222. Chadwick, i, 329-30.

223. *Bexley Faculty Case*, Trist. 172 (Comm. Canterbury 1879); *Claverly Faculty Case*, [1909] P. 195 (Con. Hereford); *Re St. Mary's, Banbury*, [1986] Fam. 24 (Con. Oxford), [1987] Fam. 136 (Arches).

224. Phil. 419-20, 1969, c. F13(3); *Rugg* v. *Kingsmill*, L.R. 2 P.C. 59, 66-67 (1868) (standard of review in Judicial Committee); *In re St. Gregory's, Tredington*, [1972] Fam. 236 (Arches) (standard of review in provincial court). Note that the faculty proceeding is not conclusive as to the legality of the proposed alteration, and would not prevent other proceedings to stop it. *London County Council* v. *Dundas*, [1904] P. 1.

225. Member of Parliament: *Vincent* v. *Eyton*, [1897] P. 1 (Con. London). Rented room: *Kensit* v. *Rector and Churchwardens of St. Ethelburga*, [1900] P. 80 (Con. London). Measure: Faculty Jurisdiction Measure, 1938, 1-2 Geo. 6, No. 6, revised, Faculty Jurisdiction Measure, 1964, No. 5. Air Minister: *Re St. Ethelburga's Abberton*, [1962] P. 10 (Arches). Cf. *Lee* v. *Fagg*, L.R. 6 P.C. 38 (1873); *Noble* v. *Reast* [1904] P. 34 (Con. York), both holding that a bishop's secretary, as such, has no standing.

226. *Ritchings* v. *Cordingley*, L.R. 3 A. & E. 113 (Arches 1868): 1-2 Geo. 6, No. 6, § 3 (1938); 1964, No. 5, § 5; *In re St. Mary's, Balham*, [1978] 1 All E.R. 993 (Con. Southwark). If church furnishings are sold without a faculty, the buyer gets no title. *In re St. Mary's, Barton-upon-Humber*, [1987] Fam. 41 (Con. Lincoln). A person making unauthorized alterations could at one time be found guilty of an ecclesiastical offense, and condemned in costs. *Walter* v. *Mountague*, 1 Curt. 251, 163 Eng. Rep. 85 (Con. London 1836). No other sanction (except the obsolete one of penance) was available against a layman. Since the Ecclesiastical Jurisdiction Measure, 1963, it is doubtful whether any proceeding can be taken against a layman for an ecclesiastical offense. See Chapter 1, note 99, *supra*. I suppose a clergyman could still be punished for making changes without a faculty.

227. Contempt: *Lee* v. *Vicar and Churchwardens of Herne*, Trist. 217 (Comm. Canterbury 1842). Chancery proceeding: *Cardinall* v. *Molyneux*; 4 de G. F. & J. 117, 45 Eng. Rep. 1128 (Ch. 1861); cf. *Marriott* v. *Tarpley*, 9 Sim. 278, 59 Eng. Rep. 365 (Ch. 1838) (Churchwardens enjoined); Phil. 1422; Halsbury (3d), 419; Halsbury (4th) 298 (hints in a note at continuing jurisdiction). The Chancery Court cannot require the restoration of the status quo once the illegal alterations have been made. *Batten* v. *Gedye*, 41 Ch.D. 507 (1889).

228. Uniform design: *In re St. Nicholas's, Baddesley Ensor*, [1983] Fam. 1 (Con. Birmingham). Color photographs: *Re St. Mark's, Haydock*, [1981] 1 W.L.R. 1164 (Con. Liverpool). List of mourners: *Re St. Mark's, Haydock (No. 2)*, [1981] 1 W.L.R. 1167 (Con. Liverpool).

229. Flower offerings: *Evans* v. *Dodson*, Trist. 26 (Con. London 1874). Baby Jesus in bath: *Re St. Edward the Confessor, Mottingham*, [1983] 1 W.L.R. 364 (Con. Southwark). Regimental Colors: *Vincent* v. *Eyton*, [1897] P. 1 (Con. London 1896); cf. S. Paget and J. Crum, *Francis Paget* (London 1912), 159. Black Madonna: *In re St. Michael and All Angels, Great Torrington*, [1985] Fam. 81 (Ct. of Ecc. Cases Res.). Tablets: *Re St. Nicholas, Brockenhurst*, [1978] Fam. 157 (Con. Winchester). Electric candles: *In re St. Andrew's, Dearnley*, [1981] Fam. 50 (Con. Manchester).

230. Choir: *Sergeant* v. *Dale*, Trist. 33 (Con. London 1875). The verse is from J. Betjeman, *Collected Poems* (Boston, 1971), 3. See also O.D.P., d. 178, f. 308 (entry in bishop's notebook for Iffley, 1856): "the parishioners move to complete the restoration of their church which done in 1843 . . . without a particle of real Ecclesiastical taste, and hideous in parts." Tottenham: *Vicar and Churchwardens of Tottenham* v. *Venn*, L.R. 4 A. & E. 221 (Con. London 1874). Secular medievalism: *St. Augustine Faculty Case*, L. R. 4 P.D. 112, Trist. 60 (Con. London 1877). Pimlico: *Vicar and Churchwardens of St. Barnabas, Pimlico* v. *Bowran*, L.R. 4 A. & E. 207, Trist. 1 (Con. London 1873).

231. Stubbs, 78. The entry from the bishop's notebook quoted in note 230, *supra*,

suggests an attempt to bypass the courts. On judicial deference to the bishop's wishes, see *St. Ethelburga Faculty Case*, Trist. 69 (Con London 1878). The bishop, in his patent to his chancellor, may reserve the right to intervene in these cases, and a few bishops still do so. *R.* v. *Tristram*, [1902] 1 K.B. 816; Ecclesiastical Jurisdiction Measure, 1963, No. 1, § 46(1). But in *Re St. Mary's Barnes*, [1982] 1 All E.R. 456, 458 (Con. Southwark), the bishop's intervention was characterized by his chancellor as "very considerable folly." Newsom, 11 says that no one invited to be a chancellor should accept a patent with such a restriction.

232. *Bishop of St. Davids* v. *De Rutzen*, 4 L.T. (N.S.) 90 (Arches 1861). On a fairly typical patronal restoration of the period, see R. Gill "Priest and Patron in a Northumberland Parish" in *A Social History of the Diocese of Newcastle 1882-1982*, ed. Pickering (1981), 146, 150. On the effect of the abolition of compulsory churchrates, see Chadwick, ii, 199.

233. E.g., *In re Holy Innocents, Fallowfield*, [1982] Fam. 136 (Con. Manchester); *Re All Saints, Whitstable*, [1984] 1 W.L.R. 1164 (Comm. Canterbury) (six months trial); *Re St. Matthews, Wimbledon*, [1985] 3 All E.R. 670 (Con. Southwark); *In re St. Mary's, Banbury*, [1986] Fam. 24 (Con. Oxford), [1987] Fam. 136 (Arches).

234. 1969, c. F16.

235. [1980] Fam. 89 (Con. Winchester).

236. *Hawkes* v. *Jones*, Trist. 222 (Con. Hereford 1887); *Re St. Agnes's, Toxteth Park*, [1985] 1 W.L.R. 641 (Con. Liverpool). Under Faculty Jurisdiction Measure, 1964, No. 5, § 12(1)(d) an existing heating system may be altered on an archdeacon's certificate, but putting in a new one still requires a faculty.

237. In addition to the *Toxteth Park* case, *supra*, note 236, see *In re St. Mary's, Gilston*, [1967] P. 125 (Con. St. Albans); *In re St. Mary's, Westwell*, [1968] 1 W.L.R. 513 (Comm. Canterbury); *In re St. Gregory's, Tredington*, [1972] Fam. 236 (Arches 1970); *In re St. Helen's, Brant Broughton*, [1974] Fam. 16 (Arches 1972); *In re St. Mary's, Broadwater*, [1976] Fam. 222 (Con. Chicester); *In re St. Andrews, Thornhaugh*, [1976] Fam. 230 (Con. Peterborough); *In re St. Andrews, Heddington*, [1978] Fam. 121 (Con. Salisbury); *In re St. Mary le Bow*, [1984] 1 W.L.R. 1363 (Con. London). On the problems of security and insurance, see also G.S. 91 (1972), 44; G.S. 505 (1981); *General Synod Reports*, iii (1972), 588-93.

238. Lay rector: General Synod Legal Advisory Commission, *Reports*, 20-21; *Parker* v. *Leach*, L.R. 1 P.C. 312 (1867) (seat); *Greenslade* v. *Darby*, L.R. 3 Q.B. 421 (1868) (sheep); *Griffin* v. *Dighton*, 5 B. & S. 93, 122 Eng. Rep. 767 (1864) (no general control). Incumbent: *R.* v. *Lee*, 4 Q.B.D. 75 (1878) (dangerous building); *Winstanley* v. *N. Manchester Overseers*, [1910] A.C. 7 (H.L.) (rates); *Hilcoat* v. *Archbishops of Canterbury and York*, 10 C.B. 327, 138 Eng. Rep. 132 (1850) (valuation of incumbent's interest on compulsory purchase).

239. *Churton* v. *Frewen*, L.R. 2 Eq. 634 (1866); *Chapman* v. *Jones*, L.R. 4 Exch. 273 (1869); *Duke of Norfolk* v. *Arbuthnot*, 4 C.P.D. 290, *affirmed*, 5 C.P.D. 390 (C.A. 1880); *Sutton* v. *Bowden*, [1913] 1 Ch. 518. The prohibition of non-Anglican worship may now be relaxed by an agreement under the Sharing of Church Buildings Act, 1969, c. 38.

240. *Churton* v. *Frewen*, L.R. 2 Eq. 634 (1866); *Vicar and Churchwardens of Peckham* v. *Geary*, Trist. 189 (Con. London 1889); Halsbury (3d), 414, citing *Ex*

parte St. Pancras M.B.C., 53 T.L.R. 456 (1937); Halsbury (4th), 725.

241. *Walker* v. *Clyde*, 10 C.B. (N.S.) 382. 142 Eng. Rep. 500 (1861); *In re Escot Church*, [1979] Fam. 125 (Con. Exeter).

242. *In re St. Andrew's, Thornhaugh*, [1976] Fam. 230 (Con. Peterborough); *Corven's Case*, 12 Co. Rep. 105, 77 Eng. Rep. 1380 (1612); *Frances* v. *Ley*, Cro. Jac. 367, 79 Eng. Rep. 314 (1615); *Lady de Wyche's Case*, Y.B. 9 Edw. 4, 14 (1469); Phil. 691-92; Halsbury (3d), 389; Halsbury (4th), 581.

243. *In re St. Mary's, Broadwater*, [1976] Fam. 222 (Con. Chichester).

244. 1964, No. 5.

245. *In re St. Andrews, Thornhaugh*, [1976] Fam. 230 (Con. Peterborough); cf. *In re St. Mary's, Broadwater*, [1976] Fam. 222 (Con Chichester) (title). Administration of Estates Act, 1925, 15 Geo. 5, c. 23, §§ 45, 52 abolishes primogeniture only as to property devisable by will.

246. *Paul Report*, 23.

247. Mayfield, *Like Nothing*, 205.

4: Sion's War

Note: There are a number of books whose influence on this account has been too pervasive for specific reference. These include Halévy; Marsh; Chadwick; Bentley; C. Dawson, *The Spirit of the Oxford Movement* (New York, 1933); C.P.S. Clarke, "The Genesis of the Movement," in *Northern Catholicism*, ed. N.P. Williams and C. Harris (London, 1933), 1; W.J. Sparrow Simpson, "The Revival from 1845-1933," in Id., 36; and D. Bowen, *The Idea of the Victorian Church* (Montreal, 1968). Some of these I have not cited at all in the notes; others I have cited, but not in all the places I have drawn on them.

1. S. Gaselee "The Aesthetic Side of the Oxford Movement," in *Northern Catholicism*, ed. N.P. Williams and C. Harris (London, 1933), 423, 424; Marsh, 112.

2. Flindall, 105-13 reproduces both the dean's letter and Russell's reply.

3. *Eng. Hist. Doc.*, xii(i), 339-40.

4. G. Battiscombe, *John Keble* (London, 1963), 11; G. A. Denison, *Notes of My Life 1805-1878* (Oxford and London, 1878). R. Griffin, *John Keble, Saint of Anglicanism* (Macon, Ga., 1987), 19 says, however, that there is no "scholarly evidence" that Keble learned Catholic doctrines from his father, or even that his father held such doctrines.

5. Flindell, 80-91; Froude, Remains (London and Derby, 1838-39). Tract Ninety is excerpted in *Eng. Hist. Doc.*, xii(1), 346-50.

6. Chadwick ii, 308-25.

7. 1 Eliz. 1, c.1, § 36 (1559); *Case of Heresy*, 12 Co. Rep. 56, 77 Eng. Rep. 1335 (1601); 29 Car. 2, c.9 (1677); Phil., 842.

8. *Pelling* v. *Whiston*, 1 Comyns 199, 92 Eng. Rep. 1033 (1709); *Proceedings against William Whiston*, 15 St. Tr. 703 (1711); *Bishop* v. *Stone*, 1 Hag. Con. 424,

433n, 161 Eng. Rep. 604, 607n (1808).

9. *Pusey* v. *Jowett*, 1 New Rep. 488 (V. C. Oxon. 1863); *R.* v. *Chancellor etc. of the University of Cambridge*, 6 T.R. 89, 101 Eng. Rep. 451 (1794) (Frend); Chadwick, i, 207-11 (Ward). *See also* Flindell, 148-51 regarding the dismissal of F.D. Maurice from his professorship at King's College, London. I believe that if Maurice had gone to court he would have won.

10. *R.* v. *Archbishop of Canterbury*, 11 Q.B. 481, 116 Eng. Rep. 557 (1848); *R.* v. *Archbishop of Canterbury*, [1905] 1 K.B. 504 (C.A.). For ecclesiastical proceedings in the first case, see *Re Hampden*, 5 Notes of Cases (Supp.) 9. For background on the second, see G.L. Prestige, *The Life of Charles Gore* (London, 1935), 230-37.

11. *Kensit* v. *Dean and Chapter of St. Paul's*, [1905] 2 K.B. 249.

12. 1 Edw. 6, c. 1 (1547) (Eucharist); Act of Uniformity, 1548, 2-3 Edw. 6, c. 1, § 3 (Prayer Book), both repealed by Statute Law Repeals Act, 1969, c. 52; *Caudrey's Case*, 5 Co. Rep. 1, 77 Eng. Rep. 1 (1606).

13. 13 Eliz. 1, c. 12, § 2 (1571), repealed, Ecclesiastical Jurisdiction Measure, 1963, No. 1, § 87 and Sch. 5.

14. Vol. II, 168-69; Clerical Subscription Act, 1865, 28-29 Vic., c.122 (the quoted language appears in § 1); Church of England (Worship and Doctrine) Measure, 1974, No. 3, § 2. The declaration now in use appears in 1969, c. C15, added in 1975 pursuant to the authorization in the 1974 measure.

15. Chadwick, i, 528-33. Chadwick indicates that until the courts decided that respectful skepticism was not blasphemy (I presume he refers to *Shore* v. *Wilson*, 9 Cl. & Fin. 335, 8 Eng. Rep. 450 (H.L. 1842)) the fear of prosecution under the blasphemy laws inhibited the translation of German critical scholarship into English.

16. The material in the next few paragraphs is expanded and documented at pp. 276-90, *infra*.

17. 1585: *Synodalia*, ed. E. Cardwell (Oxford, 1842), i, 142; 1604, c. 95; *Hutton's Case*, Hobart 15, 80 Eng. Rep. 166 (1615) (a description of the proceeding that does not use the name); *Gorham* v. *Bishop of Exeter*, 2 Rob. Ecc. 1, 18, 163 Eng. Rep. 1221, 1228 (Arches 1849); "Double Quarrel," Burn, i, 536; Codex Juris Canonici (1918), c. 274(1); I. Churchill, *Canterbury Administration* (London, 1933), i, 351.

18. *Walsh* v. *Bishop of Lincoln*, L.R. 4 A. & E. 242 (Arches 1874).

19. 37-38 Vic., c. 85. The political background is treated in Marsh, 158-92. Bentley is primarily devoted to this act with its origins and consequences.

20. *Hudson* v. *Tooth*, 3 Q.B.D. 46 (1877). The ill-fated commission in this case followed a form adopted by Order in Council in 1875. Form 13, 1 P.D. 21. Another of the first prosecutions was thrown out by the Court of Arches because the representation was not served soon enough on the defendant. *Howard* v. *Bodington*, 2 P.D. 203 (Arches, 1877).

21. Marsh, 229.

22. The Committee was created by 3-4 Will. 4, c. 41 (1833), and heard ecclesiastical cases by virtue of 2-3 Will. 4, c. 92 (1832). *See* W. Finlason, *History, Constitution and Character of the Judicial Committee of the Privy Council* (London, 1878) for a good statement of the objections to this tribunal; see L. Dibdin, *Church*

Courts (London, 1881) for a good defense of it. See also the Introductions to Broderick and Fremantle, one by Bishop (soon to be Archbishop) Tait. I am not persuaded by the argument of D. Bowen, *The Idea of the Victorian Church* (Montreal, 1968), 90-96 that the objectionable decisions of the Judicial Committee were attributable to the lack of canonical learning among the common law judges who sat.

23. Mathieson, 156.

24. Appellate Jurisdiction Act, 1876, 39-40 Vic., c. 59.

25. *Gorham* v. *Bishop of Exeter*, Brodrick and Fremantle 65, 97 (P.C. 1850). On the maxim, see Nias, 75.

26. *Sanders* v. *Head*, 3 Curt. 32, 163 Eng. Rep. 645 (Arches 1842), 4 Moo. P.C. 186, 13 Eng. Rep. 273 (1842), 3 Curt. 565, 163 Eng. Rep. 827 (Arches 1843), Brodrick and Fremantle 30.

27. *Hodgson* v. *Oakeley*, 1 Rob. Ecc. 322, 163 Eng. Rep. 1053 (Arches 1845). The quote is from 1 Rob. Ecc. 353, 163 Eng. Rep. 1064. For Oakeley's later career, see *D.N.B.*

28. *Heath* v. *Burder*, 15 Moo. P.C. 1, 15 Eng. Rep. 394, Brodrick and Fremantle, 212 (1862); *Voysey* v. *Noble*, 7 Moore (N.S.) 167, 17 Eng. Rep. 65 (P.C. 1871).

29. *Ex parte Denison*, 4 El. & Bl. 293, 119 Eng. Rep. 113 (1854); *R.* ex rel. *Ditcher* v. *Archbishop of Canterbury*, 6 El. & Bl. 547, 119 Eng. Rep. 968 (1856); *R.* v. *Judge of Arches Court*, 7 El. & Bl. 315, 119 Eng. Rep. 264 (1857); *Ditcher* v. *Denison*, Deane 334, 164 Eng. Rep. 594 (Arches 1857), 11 Moo. P.C. 324, 14 Eng. Rep. 718, Brodrick and Fremantle, 156 (1858); Chadwick, i, 491-95. The Latin quote is from St. Thomas Aquinas's Corpus Christi sequence, *Lauda Sion. The Penguin Book of Latin Verse*, ed. F. Brittain (1962), 252 translates it: "The righteous and the wicked receive him alike, but with the unlike destiny of life or death. It is death for the wicked, life for the righteous. See how unlike the end is of a like reception."

30. *Denison Letters*, 66.

31. G.A. Denison, *Notes of My Life 1805-1878* (Oxford and London, 1879), 167. See also *Denison Letters*, 382, his last published letter, dated 10th March 1896: "Public position troubles me much — there is so little of principle and so much of compromise in it. After a long life of the first, and none of the second, I cannot welcome the second, or find any comfort in it or any room for comfort."

32. *Sheppard* v. *Bennett*, L.R. 2 A. & E. 335 (Arches 1868), L.R. 2 P.C. 450 (1869), 21 L.T. 650 (P.C. 1869), L.R. 4 P.C. 350 (1870), L.R. 3 A. & E. 167 (Arches 1870), L.R. 4 P.C. 371 (1871-72); Chadwick, i, 301-3, ii, 314-16; Marsh, 114, P.P. Eng., xx, 816. Bennett gained good will in Frome by opposing churchrates. Chadwick, i, 152. A more serious set of riots occurred at the church of St. George in the East in 1859 and 1860. Chadwick, ii, 499-501.

33. E.B. Pusey, *Unlaw* (Oxford and London, 1881); H.P. Liddon, *Life of Edward Bouverie Pusey* (1897), iv, 215ff. The quote from Phillimore appears at L.R. 3 A. & E. 281. On the English Church Union and the Church Association, see Marsh 124-25.

34. Nias; *Gorham* v. *Bishop of Exeter*, 2 Rob. Ecc. 1, 163 Eng. Rep. 1221 (Arches 1849), Brodrick and Fremantle 64 (P.C. 1850).

35. He also sought writs of prohibition out of the three common law courts, arguing that 24 Hen. 8, c. 12, § 9 (1532) precluded an appeal from the Arches to the Judicial Committee. That provision called for an appeal to Convocation in cases touching the king, and Gorham's vicarage was in the gift of the queen. The courts held, however, that that statute had applied only to certain types of cases, and that it was superseded by 25 Hen. 8, c. 19, § 4 (1533), which provided for appeals to the King in Chancery, and for the appointment of commissioners (later the Court of Delegates) to hear the appeals. *Gorham* v. *Bishop of Exeter*, 15 Q.B. 52, 117 Eng. Rep. 377 (1850), 10 C.B. 101, 138 Eng. Rep. 41 (1850), 5 Ex. 630, 155 Eng. Rep. 276 (1850).

36. E.B. Pusey, *Unlaw* (Oxford and London, 1881); W. J. Sparrow Simpson, *The History of the Anglo-Catholic Revival from 1845* (London, 1932), 55.

37. *Bishop of Salisbury* v. *Williams*, 1 New Rep. 196 (Arches 1862); *Fendall* v. *Wilson*, 1 New Rep. 213 (Arches 1862); *Williams* v. *Bishop of Salisbury*, 2 Moore (N.S.) 375, 15 Eng. Rep. 943, Brodrick and Fremantle 247 (P.C. 1863); *Pusey* v. *Jowett*, 1 New Rep. 488 (V.C. Oxon. 1863); Chadwick, ii, 75-90. The quotations in the following paragraph are from 1 New Rep. 214 and 215.

38. Brodrick and Fremantle at 281. Lushington had rejected as too vague an article attacking the general tendency of Williams's work. 1 New Rep. at 212.

39. Temple: Phil., 42-47. Gore: *R.* v. *Archbishop of Canterbury*, [1909] 2 K.B. 503. Bland: *Bland* v. *Archdeacon of Cheltenham*, [1972] Fam. 157.

40. 1969, c. C15, added in 1975 pursuant to authority contained in Church of England (Worship and Doctrine) Measure, 1974, No. 3, § 2; Ecclesiastical Jurisdiction Measure, 1963, No.1, § 14(2); Welsby, 234-35.

41. Bishop (later Archbishop) Tait makes a persuasive case for this forebearance in Brodrick and Fremantle xvii-xix. See Welsby, 235-39 for an example of the gradual purging of doctrine by scholarship.

42. *Faulkner* v. *Litchfield*, 1 Rob. Ecc. 185, 163 Eng. Rep. 1007 (Arches 1845); *Liddell* v. *Westerton*, Brodrick and Fremantle 117 (P.C. 1857); *Liddell* v. *Beal*, 14 Moo. P.C. 1, 15 Eng. Rep. 206 (1860); Chadwick, i, 221. The following discussion applies only to altars more or less newly introduced. it appears that, at least by 1910, stone altars surviving from medieval times were left alone. *Rector etc. of Hayes* v. *Fulford*, [1910] P. 18, 21 (Con. London).

43. 59 Geo. 3, c. 134, § 6 (1819); 2-3 Will. 4, c. 61, § 1 (1832) Church Building Act, 1845, 8-9 Vic., c. 70, § 9 uses "communion table." But it does not amend the earlier acts.

44. *Liddell* v. *Westerton*, Brodrick and Fremantle 117 at 148 and 152 (P.C. 1857).

45. Holy Table Measure, 1964, No. 4, 1969, c. F2. The 1964 measure was repealed by Church of England (Worship and Doctrine) Measure, 1974, No. 3. It was presumably thought that canon F2 was within the authority conferred by the 1974 measure, though the wording does not seem all that clear.

46. *In re St. Stephen's, Walbrook*, [1987] Fam. 146 (Con. London and Ct. of Ecc. Causes Res.) The quote is on p. 169.

47. See Halsbury, 506-9, where all the cases are cited. The most important ones are *Liddell* v. *Westerton*, Brodrick and Fremantle 117 (P.C. 1857); *Liddell* v. *Beal*, 14 Moo. P.C. 1, 15 Eng. Rep. 206 (1860); *Boyd* v. *Phillpotts*, L.R. 4 A. & E. 297

(Arches 1874), L.R. 6 P.C. 435 (1875); *Durst* v. *Masters*, 1 P.D. 373 (P.C. 1876); *Ridsdale* v. *Clifton*, 1 P.D. 316 (Arches 1876), 1 P.D. 383 (P.C. 1876), 2 P.D. 276 (P.C. 1877). See also *St. Augustine Faculty Case*, Tristram 60 (Con. London 1877); *St. Ethelburga Faculty Case*, Tristram 69 (Con. London 1878); *Re Church of St. John*, Tristram 67 (Con. London 1888) for cases showing how the court exercised discretion where proposed objects were reminiscent of Roman Catholic practice although not strictly illegal.

48. *Martin* v. *Mackonochie*, L.R. 2 P.C. 365 (1868); *Read* v. *Bishop of Lincoln*, [1891] P. 9 (Abp. of Canterbury).

49. *Vicar and Churchwardens of St. Barnabas, Pimlico* v. *Bowran*, L.R. 4 A. & E. 207, Tristram 1 (Con. London 1873). The church and its altar were involved in *Liddell* v. *Westerton*, Brodrick and Fremantle 117 (P.C. 1857).

50. E.g., *Davey* v. *Hinde*, [1901] P. 95 (Con. Chichester) (per Tristram, Ch.); *Vincent* v. *Rector and Churchwardens of St. Magnus the Martyr*, [1925] P. 1 (Arches); *Rector and Churchwardens of Capel St. Mary* v. *Packard*, [1927] P. 289 (Arches); *Re St. Mary's Tyne Dock*, [1954] P. 369 (Con. Durham).

51. The two main cases on Eucharistic vestments are *Hebbert* v. *Purchas*, L.R. 3 P.C. 605, 664, L.R. 4 P.C. 301 (1870-71) and *Ridsdale* v. *Clifton*, 2 P.D. 276 (P.C. 1877). The proponents of the vestments were especially outraged because the interpretation of the rubric in these cases seemed inconsistent with the one adopted in *Liddell* v. *Westerton*, Brodrick and Fremantle 117 (P.C. 1857). Among the numerous polemical statements in favor of the vestments, see M. MacColl, *Lawlessness, Sacerdotalism and Ritualism* (London, 1875), 44-145. The applicable Acts of Uniformity are 1 Eliz. 1, c. 2 (1559) and 14 Car. 2, c. 4 (1662) Parker's Advertisements are published in *Visitation Articles and Injunctions*, ed. W.J. Frere, iii (1910), 171-80. On their provenence and effect, see Vol. II, 165. On Elizabeth's attitude, see W.P. Haugaard, *Elizabeth and the English Reformation* (Cambridge, 1968), 225-26.

52. S. Butler, *Hudibras* (1663), lines 1-6.

53. Dean Stanley of Westminster did point out in Convocation that the proponents of the vestments were relying on statutes to avoid the clear provision of the 1604 canon. *Convocation Chronicle 1866*, 175-79. On the abrogation of canonical rules by contrary custom, see Van Hove, "Coûtume," *Dictionnaire de Droit Canonique*, iv (Paris, 1949), 731.

54. They were legalized by Vestures of Ministers Measure, 1964, No. 7, and 1969, c. B8. The measure, like the Holy Table Measure, 1964, No. 4, was repealed by Church of England (Worship and Doctrine) Measure, 1974, No. 3, leaving the canon in place. In *Gore-Booth* v. *Bishop of Manchester*, [1920] 2 K.B. 412, the King's Bench rejected the decisions of the Privy Council, applied the plain meaning rule to the ornaments rubric, and held the vestments legal. The question was whether a bishop could exclude a presentee to a benefice on the ground that he intended to use the vestments if admitted. Evidently, he could not. But there were other grounds available and the bishop won his case.

55. The cases on the eastward position are *Hebbert* v. *Purchas*, L.R. 3 P.C. 605, 664, L.R. 4 P.C. 301 (1871); *Ridsdale* v. *Clifton*, 2 P.D. 276 (P.C. 1877); *Read* v. *Bishop of Lincoln*, [1891] P. 9 (Abp. of Canterbury), [1892] A.C. 644 (P.C.). The

westward position — the one currently common in Roman Catholic churches — was authorized experimentally by the Upper House of Canterbury Convocation in 1954 *Acts of Conv.*, 116-17.

56. See Stubbs, 159, "We were vexed with the sight of the clergyman lolling with his arms on a great table-cushion and hitching the sacred vessels about at the full length of his arms, long or short, during the most solemn parts of the service."

57. Russell, *King*, 195.

58. *Hebbert* v. *Purchas*, L.R. 3 P.C. 605 (1871). On the rubric, see *Anno. B.C.P.* 398-99. 1969, c. B17 seems to authorize wafer bread.

59. *Ridsdale* v. *Clifton*, 2 P.D. 276 (P.C. 1877).

60. Marsh, 231-32. The accused clergyman, R. W. Enraght, figured prominently in the law reports, as we shall see. But the proceeding in which he was convicted before Lord Penzance is not reported, so we cannot tell what use, if any, Penzance made of the exhibit. A witness before the Royal Commission on Ecclesiastical Discipline (1904-6) brought in a Host that he had received as Communion, and was dismissed with a rebuke. P.P.Eng., 1906, xxxiii, 1113.

61. These practices are all dealt with in Halsbury (3d) 339-44. The main cases are *Martin* v. *Mackonochie*, L.R. 2 A. & E. 116 (Arches 1868), L.R. 2 P.C. 365 (1868); *Elphinstone* v. *Purchas*, L.R. 3 A. & E. 66 (Arches 1870); *Hebbert* v. *Purchas*, L. R. 3 P.C. 605 (1871); *Read* v. *Bishop of Lincoln*, [1891] P. 9 (Abp. of Canterbury), [1892] A.C. 644 (P.C.). The quoted provision of the Act of Uniformity is 1 Eliz. 1, c. 2, § 2 (1559). The provision for hymns out of the Bible is 2-3 Edw. 6, c. 1, § 7 (1548), incorporated by reference fairly clearly in 14 Car. 2, c. 4, § 20 (1662), less clearly by 1 Eliz. 1, c. 2, § 1 (1559).

62. 1964, No. 4; 1964, No. 7; 1965, No. 1; 1974, No. 3; 1969, c. B1-B5, B8.

63. W. J. Sparrow Simpson, *The History of the Anglo-Catholic Revival from 1845* (London, 1933), 253-66; Bell, Davidson, ii, 795-815; *Anno. B.C.P.*, 472-73. The 1909 disciplinary case is *Bishop of Oxford* v. *Henly*, [1907] P. 88, [1909] P. 319 (Arches). Among faculty cases are *Kensit* v. *Rector and Churchwardens of St. Ethelburga*, [1900] P. 80 (Con. London); *Davey* v. *Hinde*, [1901] P. 95, [1903] P. 221 (Con. Chichester); *Rector and Churchwardens of Capel St. Mary* v. *Packard*, [1927] P. 289 (Arches); *Roffe-Silvester* v. *King* [1939] P. 64 (Arches). Later material, legislative (such as it is) and judicial, is analyzed in Newsom, 130-33, and in Halsbury 509-10, 521-22. The rubric relied on to legalize the practice now appears in *Alternative Service Book*, 1980, 144, 150, 198. The wording is not irresistably compelling: "Any consecrated bread and wine which is not required for purposes of communion is consumed at the end of the distribution or after the service." In *In re St. Peter and St. Paul, Leckhampton*, [1968] P. 495 (Con. Gloucester), the court (Garth Moore, another of whose decisions is discussed below, pp. 287-88) interpreted "for purposes of communion," to include purposes of communion outside the service. This interpretation does make sense, since Communion within the service has already taken place, so that there would be no need to keep bread and wine for that purpose. 1969, c. B37 is ambiguous on whether the sick can be communicated from the reserved Sacrament. It says that the priest shall "minister" the Communion to the sick person. That term appeared in the 1559 Prayer Book, but the later Elizabethans took it to mean "celebrate," and it was

replaced by the latter term in 1662. W.P.M. Kennedy, *Law and Custom of Reservation 1547-1661* (Cambridge, 1929).

64. *In re Lapford (Devon) Parish Church*, [1955] P. 205, 214 (Arches 1954).

65. *Rector and Churchwardens of Bishopwearmouth* v. *Adey*, [1958] 3 All E. R. 441. Both quotations appear on p. 444.

66. Bentley, 30-35; Ellsworth, *Lowder*, 138-44; Marsh, 233-34. The book is elusive bibliographically. In the copy I found in the Pusey House library, Part I bears an 1869 date, Part II no date at all. To a modern reader it appears totally innocuous.

67. *R. v. Archbishop of Canterbury*, 1 El. & Bl. 545, 120 Eng. Rep. 1014 (1859); *Poole* v. *Bishop of London*, 5 Jur. (N.S.) 522 (Abp. of Canterbury 1859); *Poole* v. *Bishop of London*, 14 Moo. P.C. 262, 15 Eng. Rep. 304 (1862). I found Poole in *Crockford* for 1900. It appears that he served as Keble's curate in 1858, as a schoolmaster from 1859 to 1861, and had parishes of his own from 1861 on.

68. Thomas Tristram in *Davey* v. *Hinde*, [1901] P. 95 (Con. Chichester) held confessional boxes to be illegal and ordered them removed. In *Bradford* v. *Fry*, 4 P.D. 93 (Con. Rochester and Arches 1878), the court ordered a confessional removed because it had been introduced without a faculty — it did not pass on legality. The 1938 case was *Roffe-Silvester* v. *King*, [1939] P. 64, 94-95 (Arches). *In re St. Mary, Tyne Dock*, [1954] P. 369 (Con. Durham) involved a table and chair used for hearing confessions.

69. *Convocation Chronicle*, October 10, 1966, 246-53. On privileged professional communications generally, see *Phipson on Evidence* (13th ed. London, 1982) § 15-09. It appears that while the courts are reluctant to recognize across-the-board privileges, they will claim a good deal of discretion in not making people testify.

70. Chadwick, ii, 325n; *Acts of Conv.*, 84-98; 1969, c. B47.

71. *Breeks* v. *Wolfrey*, 1 Curt. 880, 163 Eng. Rep. 304 (Arches 1838); *Egerton* v. *All of Odd Rode*, [1894] P. 15; *Pearson* v. *Stead*, [1903] P. 66; *Dupuis* v. *Parishioners of Ogbourne St. George*, [1941] P. 119; *Anno. B.C.P.*, 380; *B.C.P. (U.S.) 1789*, 74-75; *Alternative Service Book, 1980*, 184.

72. The earlier material is summarized and applied by Sir Lewis Dibdin in *Vincent* v. *Rector and Churchwardens of St. Magnus the Martyr*, [1925] P.1 (Arches). The 1938 case referred to in text is *Roffe-Silvester* v. *King*, [1939] P. 64, 93-4 (Arches). The legal opinion appears in Lilly and Wallis, 62n.

73. *Jenkins* v. *Cook*, L.R. 4 A. & E. 463 (Arches 1875), 1 P.D. 80 (P.C. 1876); F. Cook, *Three Sermons* (1876); *Denison Letters*, 186-88.

74. 2 Atk. 650, 26 Eng. Rep. 788 (1736).

75. Iung, "Communion," *Dictionnaire de Droit Canonique*, iii (Paris, 1942), 1098, 1115-16.

76. *Swayne* v. *Benson*, 6 T.L.R. 7 (Arches 1889).

77. [1908] P.362, *prohibition denied*, *R.* v. *Dibdin*, [1910] P.57 (K.B. & C.A.), *affirmed*, *Thompson* v. *Dibdin*, [1912] A.C. 533 (H.L.); 7 Edw. 7, c. 47 (1907); Bell, *Davidson*, 555-57. S. Paget and J.M.C. Crum, *Francis Paget, Bishop of Oxford* (London, 1912), 234-35.

78. *R.* v. *James*, 2 Den. 1, 169 Eng. Rep. 393 (C.C. Res. 1850).

79. T.A. Lacy and R.C. Mortimer, *Marriage in Church and State* (London, 1947), 162-63, 179-85; Chadwick, i, 481-84. The Statute is Matrimonial Causes Act,

1857, 20-21 Vic, c. 85.

80. See Stubbs 249-58. Cosin: Lacey, *supra*, note 79 at 162. King: Russell, *King*, 279-80. Some of the prevailing confusion is reflected in the Convocation discussion of whether discretionary licenses dispensing from banns should be issued to divorced people. *Convocation Chronicle 1869*, 54-79; *Convocation Chronicle 1871*, 390-97.

81. 1 Edw. 8 and 1 Geo. 6, c. 57, § 12. 1965, c.72, § 8(2), now in force, is to the same effect. *General Synod Reports*, iii, 75-116 (1972), though it waffles a good deal, seems to accept church marriages for divorced persons, at least in some cases. For further discussion of this question, see Welsby, 226-32. As to marriage with a deceased wife's sister, the law of the church would seem no longer to differ from that of the state. 1969, c. B31.

82. *Church and Marriage* (Report of Joint Committee of the Convocations of Canterbury and York, 1935); Kemp, *Kirk*, 136-49; *Acts of Conv.*, 117-24. The same claim was made in Parliament when expanded divorce legislation was first brought up. Bell, *Davidson*, 991-1002. Resolutions were adopted by York Convocation in 1938, Canterbury Convocation in 1955 leaving it to the discretion of the bishop whether to admit divorced and remarried persons to Communion. In view of *Banister*, they would not have been enforceable against any clergyman or would-be communicant who chose to disregard them. They were repealed in 1982. *General Synod Reports*, xiii, 606-10.

83. Examples include: E.G. Wood, "Ecclesiastical Suits" in *Eccelsiastical Reform*, ed. O. Shipley (London, 1873), c. 6; M. MacColl, *Lawlessness, Sacerdotalism, and Ritualism* (London, 1875); A.H. Mackonochie, *First Principles versus Erastianism* (London, 1876); Anon., *The Disobedience of the Clergy* (London, 1876); C.L. Wood (the future Viscount Halifax), *Address to the English Church Union* (London, 1877); W. Finlason, *History, Constitution and Character of the Judicial Committee of the Privy Council* (London, 1878); C.L. Wood, *The Just Limits of Comprehension in the National Church* (London, 1878); R. W. Enraght, *My Ordination Oaths* (Birmingham and London, 1880); C. Adams, *The Church and the Law* (Rugby, 1881); E.B. Pusey, *Unlaw* (Oxford and London, 1881).

84. The best formulation of these arguments, to my mind, is that of Sir Lewis Dibdin in *Church Courts* (London, 1881), and in *Establishment in England* (London, 1932). The quote is from pp. 133-34 of the latter book, reprinting an article from the *Quarterly Review* for October, 1883. A similar analogy was drawn by John Selden in the time of James I. A.G. Dickens, *The English Reformation* (revised ed. London, 1967), 412. On Warburton, see p. 318, *infra*; on Stillingfleet and the 1307 Commons, see pp. 2-4, *supra*.

85. Ellsworth, *Lowder*, 94-99.

86. Denison, *Notes of My Life 1805-1878* (Oxford and London, 1879).

87. *Hudson* v. *Tooth*, 2 P.D. 125 (Arches 1876); 3 Q.B.D. 46 (1877). The episcopal pun is quoted at Bentley, 101.

88. Ellsworth, *Lowder*, 171.

89. The cartoon is reproduced facing Marsh, 226. It is rather differently described in M. Reynolds, *Martyr of Ritualism* (London, 1965), 203-4.

90. *Hudson* v. *Tooth*, 2 P.D. 125, 140 (Arches 1876).

91. Marsh, 229. In 1919, already eighty years old, he appeared at Thaxted, Essex, in support of Conrad Noel. Groves, *Noel*, 235.

92. The other four who went to jail are Dale, Enraght, Cox, and Green, all discussed below. Purchas's dove is mentioned in Marsh, 118. The biographies mentioned in this paragraph are Marsh, Ellsworth, *Lowder*, and M. Reynolds, *Martyr of Ritualism* (London, 1965) (Mackonochie).

93. *Dale's Case, Enraghts' Case*, 6 Q.B.D. 376 (Q.B.D. and C.A., 1881); *Enraght* v. *Lord Penzance*, 7 A.C. 240 (H.L. 1882); *Re Green*, 7 Q.B.D. 273 (1881); *Green* v. *Lord Penzance*, 6 A.C. 657 (H.L. 1881). Other unsuccessful technical arguments were raised in *Combe* v. *De la Bere*, 22 Ch. D. 316 (Ch. Div. and C.A. 1881-2) where Lord Penzance had sat in Westminster Palace, a royal peculiar exempt from the jurisdiction of his court, and *R.* v. *Lord Penzance*, 3 T.L.R. 579 (C.A. 1887), where Lord Penzance, sitting as the Chancery Court of York, had written out a judgment in London and sent it to a surrogate to read at York.

94. Dale's and Enraght's cases are cited *supra*, note 93. See also *Serjeant* v. *Dale*, 2 Q.B.D. 558 (1877), an earlier stage where the prosecution failed because the bishop was patron of Dale's benefice. The 1563 act, 5 Eliz. 1, c. 23, is discussed in Vol. II, p. 213. The Petty Bag Act is 12-13 Vic., c. 109. Cox's habeas corpus cases are *Ex parte Cox*, 19 Q.B.D. 307, 20 Q.B.D. 1 (Q.B.D. and C.A. 1887); *Cox* v. *Hakes*, 15 A.C. 506 (H.L. 1890). Cox was also involved in *R.* v. *Lord Penzance*, *supra*, note 93.

95. *Re Green*, 7 Q.B.D. 273 (1881); *Green* v. *Lord Penzance*, 7 A.C. 240 (H.L. 1882); *Dean* v. *Green*, 8 P.D. 79 (Ch. York 1882).

96. *Ex parte Edwards*, L.R. 9 Ch. 138 (1873); *Combe* v. *Edwards*, L.R. 4 A. & E. 390 (Arches 1874), 3 P.D. 103 (Arches 1878); *Combe* v. *De la Bere*, 6 P.D. 157 (Arches 1881); *Combe* v. *De la Bere*, 22 Ch. D. 316 (Ch. Div. and C.A. 1881-82).

97. Ellsworth, *Lowder*, 115; Marsh, 240-41.

98. *R.* v. *Bishop of Oxford*, 4 Q.B.D. 245, 525 (Q.B.D. and C.A. 1879); *Julius* v. *Bishop of Oxford*, 5 A.C. 214 (H.L. 1880).

99. *Allcroft* v. *Bishop of London*, 23 Q.B.D. 414 (1888), 24 Q.B.D. 213 (1889) (C.A.), [1891] 2 Q.B. 48; [1891] A.C. 666 (H.L.).

100. *Hakes* v. *Cox* [1892] P. 110 (Ch. York).

101. *Ex parte Read*, 13 P.D. 221 (P.C. 1888); *Read* v. *Bishop of Lincoln*, 14 P.D. 88, 148 (Abp. of Canterbury 1889), [1891] P. 9 (Abp. of Canterbury, [1892] A.C. 644 (P.C.); Russell, *King*, 132-210 and *passim*.

102. On wafer bread, see note 60 and accompanying text *supra*. The payment in Mackonochie's case is referred to in S.C. Carpenter, *Church and People, 1789-1889* (London, 1933), 243n. Carpenter shows it as part of the bill of costs submitted by the plaintiff, but does not make it clear that it was allowed by the court. I would be somewhat surprised if it was.

103. [1891] P. at 94.

104. *Bishop of St. David's* v. *Lucy*, 1 Salk. 134, 91 Eng. Rep. 126, 1 Ld Raym, 447, 539, 91 Eng. Rep. 1197, 1260, 12 Mod. 237, 88 Eng. Rep. 1287 (1698).

105. Russell, *King*, 171.

106. 14 P.D. at 129. The Stubbs quote appears in Russell, *King*, 177.

107. [1891] P. at 20.

108. [1891] P. at 20-21.

109. [1892] A.C. at 655. *Ridsdale* v. *Clifton* is 2 P.D. 276 (P.C. 1877). The earlier decision from which it departed is *Hebbert* v. *Purchas*, L.R. 3 P.C. 664 (1871).

110. [1891] P. at 22.

111. [1891] P. at 27. On the development of the mixed chalice in the eastern churches, see R. Taft, *The Great Entrance* (Rome, 1975).

112. [1891] P. at 29-30.

113. [1892] A.C. at 657.

114. [1892] A.C. at 656.

115. [1892] A.C. at 656-57.

116. *Bishop of Oxford* v. *Henly*, [1907] P. 88, [1909] P. 319 (Arches). I am indebted to the Rev. Robert G. Rhodes of Wolverton, Bucks, and his parishioner, Mrs. Susan Pedley, for providing me with background information on this case. It is noticed in the *Wolverton Express* for November 9, 1906, September 3, 1907, and August 13, 1909. It is recounted at length in S.F. Markham, *The Nineteen Hundreds* (1951), 56-59. Henly became a Roman Catholic shortly after these proceedings. Markham says it was in 1913, but the last edition of *Crockford* in which he appears is 1910. The copy in Pusey House library has "Rome" handwritten in red beside his name. Two court cases later than Henly's (1920) are mentioned in Bell, *Davidson*, 1024-26, but I have not found them in the law reports.

117. Groves, *Noel*, 219-42 and *passim*.

118. Curates: See Poole's case, *supra* note 67; Ellsworth, *Lowder*, 159-60, 229-34. Would-be incumbents: *Heywood* v. *Bishop of Manchester*, 12 Q.B.D. 404 (1884); *Gore-Booth* v. *Bishop of Manchester*, [1920] 2 K.B. 412. Other cases are referred to in Chadwick, ii, 358n. Another case, *sui generis*, is that of Father Dolling, Bell, *Davidson*, 263-80, where the bishop's control over the licensing of a chapel gave him control over the practices of the chaplain.

119. Vestures of Ministers Measure, 1964, No. 7, § 2; Prayer Book (Alternative and Other Services) Measure, 1965, No. 1, § 3 both provide for input from the parochial church council before changes are made. 1969, c. B3, B8 make similar provisions.

120. E.g., *Kensit* v. *Rector and Churchwardens of St. Ethelburga*, [1900] P. 80 (Con. London); *Davey* v. *Hinde*, [1901] P. 95, [1903] P. 221 (Con. Chichester); *Rector and Churchwardens of Capel St. Mary* v. *Packard*, [1927] P. 289 (Arches); *Roffe-Silvester* v. *King*, [1939] P. 64 (Arches). The 1954 tabernacle case is *In re St. Mary, Tyne Dock* [1954] P. 369 (Con. Durham). The different treatment of different receptacles for the reserved Sacrament is rationalized as well as it can be in *In re Lapford (Devon) Parish Church*, [1954] P. 416 (Con. Exeter), *affirmed* [1955] P. 205 (Arches). See also Newsom, 132-33. On general permissiveness since 1950, see Newsom, 115.

121. See the discussion in *Hargreaves* v. *Church Commissioners*, [1983] 2 A.C. 457 (P.C.) and *Elphick* v. *Church Commissioners*, [1974] A.C. 562 (P.C.). The Ecclesiastical Jurisdiction Measure, 1963, No. 1, § 8 preserves the jurisdiction of the Judicial Committee in faculty cases not involving doctrine or ritual. Newsom, 82, says that there has been no faculty case of any kind in the Judicial Committee since

1928. The Court of Ecclesiastical Causes Reserved has heard two cases, *In re St. Michael and All Angels, Great Torrington*, [1985] Fam. 81 and *In re St. Stephen's Walbrook*, [1987] Fam. 146. The latter case is discussed in note 46 and accompanying text, *supra*. The former case, as finally decided, did not involve a question of doctrine or ritual, but was retained by the court under § 10(3) of the 1963 measure.

122. On the riots at St. George's, see Chadwick, ii, 498-501; Ellsworth, *Lowder*, 49-54. The act of Parliament referred to is 23-24 Vic. c. 32 (1860). The incident at Thaxted in 1919 is described in Groves, *Noel*, 221-28.

123. *D.N.B.* Kensit. Kensit was also the successful plaintiff in the faculty case of *Kensit* v. *Rector and Churchwardens of St. Ethelburga*, [1900] P. 80 (Con. London). It was his son whose conviction for brawling was upheld in *Kensit* v. *Dean and Chapter of St. Paul's* [1905] 2 K.B. 249.

124. The ex-boxer appears in Groves, *Noel*, 191. On the social status of the Ritualist clergy, see Bentley, 12-25.

125. *Jones* v. *Catterall*, 18 T.L.R. 367 (K.B.D. 1902).

126. *Matthews* v. *King*, [1934] 1 K.B. 505.

127. *Girt* v. *Fillingham*, [1901] P. 176 (Con. St. Albans). Fillingham got in more trouble a few years later for holding a purported ordination in a Dissenting chapel. *Bishop of St. Albans* v. *Fillingham*, [1906] P. 163 (Arches).

128. P.P. Eng. 1906, xxxiii, xxxiv.

129. *Matthews* v. *King*, [1934] 1 K.B. 505. This is the same dispute that led to the faculty case of *Roffe-Silvester* v. *King*, [1939] P. 64, discussed above. See notes 68 and 72 and accompanying text, *supra*.

130. See G.K.A. Bell, *Common Order in Christ's Church* (1937), 37: "*Ecclesia Anglicana* has inherited the Catholic ideal. But . . . the practice of many Anglican local assemblies is Congregationalist."

5: The Quest For Autonomy

1. 1604, c. 3.

2. *Atty. Gen.* v. *Murdock*, 1 De G. M. & G. 86, 42 Eng. Rep. 484 (Ch. 1852); Chadwick i, 399.

3. Chadwick, i, 398-99. Boswell: *The Life of Samuel Johnson*, 26 October, 1769; *Journey to the Hebrides*, 7 November, 1773. Archbishop of Canterbury: W. Perry, *The Oxford Movement in Scotland* (Cambridge, 1933), 87. Archbishop of York: *D.N.B.*, Thomson; Chambers, "Decay of Discipline," in *Ecclesiastical Reform*, ed. O. Shipley (London, 1873).

4. On the history of the Episcopal Church of Scotland, see J.P. Lawson, *History of the Scottish Episcopal Church from the Revolution to the Present Time*, (Edinburgh, 1843) Phil., 1760-68; E. Carpenter, *The Protestant Bishop* (London, 1956), 301-21; *1916 Report*, 100-110; *Correspondence between his Grace the Duke of Argyll and the Right Reverend W.J. Trower, Bishop of Glasgow and Galloway* (Glasgow, 1849); *A Remonstrance Addressed to Archibald Campbell, Esq., by the Right Reverend W.J.*

Trower D.D., Bishop of Glasgow and Galloway, (Glasgow, 1849), (both in Pusey House bound pamphlets, vol. xc). The statutes referred to in text are 1 Geo. 1, c. 29 (1718); 19 Geo. 2, c. 38 (1745); 21 Geo. 2, c. 34 (1747); 32 Geo. 3, c. 63 (1792). On the English congregations in Scotland, see Boswell, *Journey to the Hebrides,* 1. Johnson analogized Anglicans in Scotland to Christians among Turks. Id., 21 August, 1773.

    5. E. Carpenter, *The Protestant Bishop* (London, 1956), 250-80; A.P. Stokes, *Church and State in the United States* (N.Y. 1950), i, 222-44.

    6. Stokes, *supra,* note 5 at 273-85. The 1786 Statute is 26 Geo. 3, c. 84.

    7. 3-4 Vic. c. 33 (1840); 27-28 Vic., c. 94 (1864); 37-38 Vic., c. 77 (1874). *Innes* v. *Beddoe,* 13 T.L.R. 466 (Q.B.D. 1897).

    8. *1916 Report,* 94-100, 120-77; *Bowerbank* v. *Bishop of Jamaica,* 2 Moo. P.C. 449, 12 Eng. Rep. 1077 (1838-39).

    9. *R.* v. *Eton College,* 8 El. & Bl. 610, 120 Eng. Rep. 228 (1857).

    10. India: *1916 Report,* 94-98, Phil., 1794-1801; Indian Church Measure, 1927, 17-18 Geo. 5, No. 1; Indian Church Act, 1927, 17-18 Geo. 5, c. 40. Victoria: *1916 Report,* 149. Ontario: Id., 127; 19-20 Vic., c. 121 (Canada 1856); 22 Vic., c. 139 (Canada 1859).

    11. Halsbury, 157-63.

    12. 32-33 Vic., c. 42, § 20 (1869); cf. Welsh Church Act, 1914, 4-5 Geo. 5, c. 91, § 3. See *Aldenham* v. *Archbishop of Armagh,* 33 T.L.R. 208 (Ch. 1917), holding that disestablishment did not affect the continuity of the office of Archbishop of Armagh or his title of Primate of all Ireland.

    13. *Brown* v. *Curé de Montréal,* L.R. 6 P.C. 157 (1874).

    14. The following account, where not otherwise documented, is based on Chadwick, ii, 90-95; A.O.J. Cockshut, *Anglican Attitudes* (London, 1959), 88-120.

    15. Cf. 15-16 Vic., c. 88 (1852), preventing the same problem in New Zealand.

    16. *Long* v. *Bishop of Capetown,* 1 Moore (N.S.) 411, 15 Eng. Rep. 756 (P.C. 1863). On synods, see R. Giles, *Constitutional History of the Australian Church* (London, 1929), 81, 98; *1916 Report,* 145 (Australia), 158 (New Zealand); Kemp. 179-80 (Exeter); "Synod," Burn, ii, 365, (supposed effect of Henry's statute); Flindall, 141-44 (Russell).

    17. 1 Moore (N.S.) at 419, 15 Eng. Rep. at 759.

    18. 1 Moore (N.S.) at 462, 15 Eng. Rep. at 775.

    19. *In re Lord Bishop of Natal,* 3 Moore (N.S.) 115, 16 Eng. Rep. 43 (1864).

    20. J.W. Colenso, *The Pentateuch and the Book of Joshua Critically Examined* (7 vols., London, 1862-79), i, pp. ix-xiii.

    21. 3 Moore (N.S.) at 155, 16 Eng. Rep. at 58.

    22. Colenso, *supra,* note 20 at v, p. xxv n.

    23. *Convocation Chronicle,* 1866, 296-99, Id., 1868, 1349, 1397.

    24. *Bishop of Capetown* v. *Bishop of Natal,* 6 Moore (N.S.) 203, 16 Eng. Rep. 702 (1869); *Bishop of Natal* v. *Green,* 18 L.T. 112 (S.C. Natal 1868).

    25. *Bishop of Natal* v. *Gladstone,* L.R. 3 Eq. 1 (Rolls 1866).

    26. L.R. 3 Eq. at 37. To somewhat similar effect, see W.H. Hale, *An Inquiry into the Legal History of the Supremacy of the Crown* (London, 1867).

    27. J.H.B. Masterman, *The Rights and Responsibilities of National Churches*

(Cambridge, 1908).

28. See *Forbes* v. *Eden*, L.R. 1 Sc. and Div. 568 (H.L. 1867), (question of liturgy of Episcopal Church of Scotland is not justiciable).

29. *Merriman* v. *Williams*, 7 A.C. 484 (P.C. 1882). The proviso is quoted on pp. 508-9.

30. 7 A.C. at 506 and 507.

31. 7 A.C. at 510.

32. On the subsequent history of the schismatic Church of England in South Africa, see A. Ive, *The Church of England in South Africa; A Study of its History, Principles and Status* (Capetown, 1966); *1916 Report*, 177 (Natal legislature); *In re The Colonial Bishoprics Fund*, 1841, [1935] 1 Ch. 148 (funds turned over to bishops of the main South African church through doctrine of cy près); *Crockford*, 1956, viii (restoration of episcopate).

33. The following account, where not otherwise documented, is based on Kemp, 165-231; Chadwick, i, 309-24, ii, 359-65; Thompson, 91-128, 156-21.

34. Pending legislation: *Convocation Chronicle*, 1870, App. 6. Ecclesiastical Commissioners: Id., 1859-65, 272. Ireland: Id., 1869, 54-71; Id., 1870, 298-304. Pope: Id., 1871, 118-43. Harvest service: Id., 1870, App. 5. Proposed legislation: Marsh, 216-17, 269-71; *Convocation Chronicle*, 1859-65, 224. Opposed legislation: Id., 1433; Id., 1866, 30-57, 69-103, 216. Discipline: Id., 1872, App. Ritualism: Id., 1866, 155-59, 175-79. Divorce: Id., 1869, App. 2; Id., 1871, 390-97. *Essays and Reviews*: Id., 1859-65, 1655-83; Colenso: see note 23, *supra*.

35. Marsh, 209-17; see the doggerel on the subject in *Denison Letters*, 179.

36. *Convocation Chronicle*, 1859-65, 40-53; Marsh, 109.

37. Chadwick, ii, 361; Marsh 102-06; *Convocation Chronicle*, 1872, App. The statutes referred to in this paragraph are Prayer Book (Tables of Lessons) Act, 1871, 34-35 Vic., c. 37, and Act of Uniformity Amendment Act, 1872, 35-36 Vic., c. 35. The reference to Convocation was taken out of the 1871 act, Marsh, 105-6, but left in the 1872 act over considerable objection, Marsh, 109. Fourteenth-century Commons: *Rotuli Parliamentorum* (London, 1783), iii, 141 (1382): Il n'estoit mie lour entent d'estre justifiez, ne obliger lour ne lours successours as Prelats plus q lours auncestres n'ont este en temps passez.

38. A Smethurst, *Convocation of Canterbury* (London, 1949), 61-6; Halévy, iv, 360-61; *Cr. Pref.*, 5. On Tait, see Thompson, 120-21.

39. The following account is based on *1916 Report*; Bell, *Davidson*, 956-80; Iremonger, *Temple*, 93-124, Thompson, 156-78.

40. *Representative Church Council Proceedings*, 1919, 108-120 (women), 165-207 (franchise).

41. Church of England Assembly (Powers) Act, 1919, 9-10 Geo. 5, c. 76.

42. Iremonger, *Temple*, 123-24.

43. See *Crockford*, 1979, xix-xx.

44. Shrewsbury diocese: *Church Assembly Reports*, vii (1926), 168; *Cr. Pref.*, 160. London Churches: *Church Assembly Reports*, viii (1927), p. i; *Cr. Pref.*, 63. 1952 Act: City of London (Guild Churches) Act, 1952, 15-16 Geo. 6 and 1 Eliz. 2, c. xxxviii, amended and extended by 8-9 Eliz. 2, c. xxx (1960). Pastoral Measure: F. Field, "The Church of England and Parliament: a Tense Partnership," in *Church*

and Politics Today, ed. G. Moyser (Edinburgh, 1985), 55, 66-70. I have not included the Sharing of Church Buildings Act, 1969, c. 38 among acts regarding internal church affairs, because it deals with other churches besides the Church of England.

45. E.g. *Cr. Pref.* 13-14; *Church Assembly Reports*, x (1929), 302, xii (1931), 213, xxxviii (1958), 399; *General Synod Reports*, viii (1977), 672-74, xvi (1985), 410.

46. Bell, *Davidson*, 1340-58; Hansard (5th Ser.) ccxi, 2531-2655 (1927), ccxviii, 1003-1324 (1928). The reference to Master Ridley playing the man was made by a Mr. Wedgwood at col. 1263.

47. 1963: Hansard (5th ser), dclxxxi, 344-404. 1974: Id., dccclxxxii, 1567-1698. 1984: Id. (6th Ser.), lxiv, 126-44; Field, *supra*, note 44, at 70-72.

48. Convocation of the Clergy Measure, 1920, 10-11 Geo. 5, No. 1; Church of England (Convocations) Act, 1966, c. 2. The 1929 declaraton referred to in this paragraph is printed in *Acts of Conv.*, 65-67.

49. A. Smethurst, *Convocation of Canterbury* (London, 1949), 37.

50. 25 Hen. 8, c. 19 (1533). C. St. Germain, *A Dialogue between a Doctor of Divinity and a Student of the Laws of England* (*Doctor and Student*) (various editions), Dialogue II, c. 26. See Vol. II, 76.

51. The whole set, from the establishment of the Church Assembly to that of the General Synod, is collected in *Acts of Conv.*

52. *Middleton* v. *Crofts*, 2 Atk. 650, 26 Eng. Rep. 788 (1736). 1947 suggestion: Canon Law Commission, *The Canon Law of the Church of England* (London, 1947), proposed canon 9. See *Convocation Chronicle*, 1961, 477, where a provision requiring parochial church councils to pay for bread and wine for Communion is deleted from a proposed canon because the law officers of the Crown cannot advise the Royal Assent for any canon imposing new duties on laypeople. The code of canons put through Canterbury Convocation in 1964 is generally referred to as the Canons of 1969 because the York Convocation did not adopt them until 1969.

53. Provision for delegated legislation is made in New Dioceses (Transitional Provisions) Measure, 1927, 17-18 Geo. 5, No. 3; Clergy Pensions Measure, 1961, 9-10 Eliz 2, No. 3, § 46; Cathedrals Measure, 1963, No. 2, § 3; 1969, c. B 12, Par. 3. On delegated legislation generally, see G. Wilson, *Cases and Materials on Constitutional and Administrative Law* (Cambridge, 1966), 208-38.

54. *Acts of Conv.*, 117-22.

55. Synodical Government Measure, 1969, No. 2. On the concerns leading up to the measure, see the report, *Synodical Government in the Church of England* (London, 1966). Further constitutional material appears in Synodical Government (Special Majorities) Measure, 1971, No. 1, in 1969, c. H1-H3, and in the Standing Orders of the General Synod. Church of England (Worship and Doctrine) Measure, 1974, No. 3, § 3 requires a two-thirds majority for the canons on doctrine and liturgy authorized by that measure.

56. Synodical Government Measure, 1969, No. 2, Sch. 2, § 6. Examples of measures authorizing canons include Convocation of the Clergy Measure, 1920, 10-11 Geo. 5, No. 1; Admission to Holy Communion Measure, 1972, No. 1; Deaconesses and Lay Ministry Measure, 1972, No. 4; Church of England (Worship and Doctrine)

Measure, 1974, No. 3; Church of England (Miscellaneous Provisions) Measure, 1976, No. 3.

57. Church Commissioners: Pastoral Measure, 1983, No 1; Clergy Pensions Measure, 1961, 9-10 Eliz. 2, No. 3, § 10; Endowments and Glebe Measure, 1976, No. 4, § 4. Other agencies: Cathedrals Measure, 1976, No. 1; Ecclesisstial Fees Measure, 1962, 10-11 Eliz. 2, No. 1. General Synod Regulations: Clergy Pensions (Amendment) Measure, 1972, No. 5, § 6; Incumbents (Vacation of Beneficies) Measure, 1977, No. 1, § 18. Double delegation: Church of England (Worship and Doctrine) Measure, 1974, No. 3, § 1(1). 1969, c. B2 and B4A provide for regulations as authorized. For dissidents in Parliament, see Field, *supra*, note 44 at 55-66.

58. Sexual ethics: *General Synod Reports*, xviii, 913-56 (1987). Nuclear warfare: J. Elford, "The Church and Nuclear Defence Policy," in *Church and Politics Today*, ed. G. Moyser (Edinburgh, 1985), 176; Reuters, 10 February, 1983. South Africa: *General Synod Reports*, xvii, 988-1013 (1986) Reuters, 7 July, 1986. Weddings: *General Synod Reports*, xiii, 606-10 (1982), xv, 289-362 (1984). 1986 resolution: Reuters, 6 June, 1986; to similar effect, Reuters, 11 October, 1984. *Essays and Reviews*: Chadwick, ii, 83; *Convocation Chronicle, 1859-65*, 1655-83, 1830.

59. The Rules for the Representation of the Laity were printed as a Schedule to the Constitution attached to the Enabling Act, 9-10 Geo. 5, c. 76 (1919). For their original form, see *1916 Report*, 80-90. Debates in the Representative Church Council: Gender: *Proceedings*, 108-20. Confirmation and Communion requirements; Id., 165-207. Meaning of "communicant member:" Halsbury (3d), 52.

60. *General Synod Reports*, xviii, 593-611.

61. G.L. Prestige, *The Life of Charles Gore* (London, 1935), 422; Bell, *Davidson*, 971.

62. *Representative Church Council Proceedings*, 209-14.

63. *General Synod Reports*, iv., 143-57.

64. *Cr. Pref.*, 40-41; Mayfield, 57-59. I have compiled the ratios from figures given in Mayfield, 58, 197 and *Paul Report*, 20. The quote is from *Cr. Pref.*, 133. The representation of each diocese in the House of Laity was originally to be based on population, *1916 Report*, 86. It was quickly changed to be based on the number of electors. *Representative Church Council Proceedings*, 224-25.

65. *Acts of Conv.*, 1-3.

66. Synodical Government Measure, 1969, No. 2, Sch. 3.

67. Hansard (5th Ser) dcclxxxvii (1969), 1779.

68. Synodical Government Measure, 1969, No. 2, § 7. The amendments referred to in this paragraph appear in S.I. 1973/1865 and S.I. 1980/178.

69. Iremonger, *Temple*, 119-22. The letter about getting rid of the person is quoted on p. 120. The 1921 measure is 11-2 Geo. 5, No. 1.

70. See pp. 191-93, *supra* on patronage and p. 224 on incumbency. On liturgical changes, see Church of England (Worship and Doctrine) Measure, 1974, No. 3, § 1(3). 1969, c. B8 makes similar provisions regarding Eucharistic vestments, as did the Vestures of Ministers Measure, 1964, No. 7, which it replaced. A "breakdown of the pastoral relationship" is referred to in Incumbents (Vacation of Benefices) Measure, 1977, No. 1. The term would seem to apply to the liturgical dispute

chronicled in *Matthews* v. *King*, [1934] 1 K.B. 505 and *Roffe-Silvester* v. *King*, [1939] P. 64.

71. Appointment of Bishops Act, 1533, 25 Hen. 8, c. 20. Criminal Law Act, 1967, c. 58, Sch. 4 repealed all statutory provisions imposing *praemunire*. On objections to a bishop-elect, see *R.* v. *Archbishop of Canterbury*, [1902] 2 K.B. 503. The arguments against abolishing the old rule appear in Hansard (6th ser), lxiv (1984), 126-44.

72. Chadwick, i, 121-26, 226-30, 234-36, 468-76, ii, 328-42; Bell, *Davidson*, 162-81, 1236-53.

73. Mayfield, 36.

74. Bell, *Davidson*, 1246 has a striking anecdote told by Gladstone of Melbourne. It appears that Melbourne was attacked by the archbishop of Canterbury in the House of Lords for an ecclesiastical appointment that the archbishop himself had recommended. Melbourne did not bring up the recommendation because he believed he must take sole reponsibility for the advice he gave the Crown. As given, the anecdote cannot be true. It refers to Hampden's appointment to the see of Hereford, which was made by Russell, not Melbourne. Melbourne did advise the earlier appointment of Hampden to the Regius Prefessorship of Divinity at Oxford, but the archbishop did not recommend it. Chadwick, i, 113-14, 117-18. Charles II's response to the Earl of Rochester's epigram is quoted, without attribution, in J.M. and M. J. Cohen, *The Penguin Dictionary of Quotations* (1977), 106:6.

75. Hansard, (5th Ser.), cmxix (1976); 940-1036; Welsby, 223-24; *General Synod Reports*, vii, 752-61 (1976).

76. Hansard (6th Ser.), lxiii (1984), 494. For a critique of the process as filling the episcopate with bland centrists instead of securing representation of different parties, see *Crockford*, 1988, 72-75. On the fire in York Minster, see D. Holloway, *The Church of England, Where is it Going?* (Eastbourne, 1985) 8, 212-13.

77. Halsbury (3d) 59-60; Thompson, 188. On central agencies generally, see Id. 179-211. On the Church Commissioners, see Pitt. The Cathedral Statutes Commission was created by Cathedrals Measure, 1976, No. 1. It replaces a temporary commission created by Cathedrals Measure, 1963, No. 2. The Redundant Churches Fund was created by Pastoral Measure, 1968, No. 1, § 45, and continued by Pastoral Measure, 1983, No. 1, § 44. An interesting case regarding central church agencies is *In re Barnes*, [1930] 2 Ch. 80 (1922), holding that a gift to the Church of England, *simpliciter* is charitable, and goes to the Central Board of Finance.

78. Mayfield, 106-8. Particular agencies were established as follows: Diocesan Education Committees: Diocesan Education Committees Measure, 1943, 6-7 Geo. 6, No. 3, replaced by Diocesan Education Committees Measure, 1955, 4-5 Eliz. 2, No. 1. Further revision is in progress. *General Synod Reports*, xviii, 119-40 (1987). Diocesan Board of Finance: Diocesan Boards of Finance Measure, 1925, 15-16 Geo. 5, No. 3. Parsonages Boards: Repair of Benefice Buildings Measure, 1972, No. 2. The former Diocesan Dilapidations Boards were established by Ecclesiastical Dilapidations Measure, 1923, 14-15 Geo. 5, No. 3. Diocesan Boards of Patronage: Benefices (Diocesan Boards of Patronage) Measure, 1932, 22-23 Geo. 5, No. 1. Pastoral Committees: Pastoral Measure, 1983, No. 1, §§ 1-2; Pastoral Measure,

1968, No. 1, §§ 1-2; Pastoral Reorganisation Measure, 1949, § 1; Diocesan Reorganisation Committees Measure, 1941, 4-5 Geo. 6, No. 1. I have not included in this list the Diocesan Advisory Committees set up by Faculty Jurisdiction Measure, 1964, No. 5, §§ 13, because their role is purely advisory.

79. See Thompson, 212-43 on the distinction between *ecclesia* and denomination.

80. The title page of Tristram's report (London, 1893) shows him as holding the diocesan courts of London, Hereford, Ripon, Wakefield, and Canterbury. The title page of Newsom shows the author as chancellor of London, Bath and Wells, and St. Albans. Public Worship Regulation Act, 1874, 37-38 Vic., c 85, § 7 combined the judgeships of the provincial courts. Ecclesiastical Jurisdiction Measure, 1963, No. 1, § 3 maintained the combination, but assigns four additional judges to each court who need not be appointed to both. Id., § 2A, added by Ecclesiastical Judges and Legal Officers Measure, 1976, No. 2, authorizes the House of Bishops of the General Synod to limit the number of judgeships one person can hold. No such limit has been adopted. Newsom, 9n. For an example of a judge of one court acting as advocate in another, see *Re St. Mary, Tyne Dock*, [1954] P. 369 (Con. Durham), where Garth Moore acted as advocate and *Re St. Peter, St. Helier*, [1951] P. 303 (Con. Southwark), a similar case where he acted as judge.

81. The grievances are effectively assembled in the Lloyd-Jacob Report (so called after the chairman of the commission that adopted it), *The Ecclesiastical Courts* (London, 1954). The power to hear live evidence was conferred by Ecclessiastical Courts Act, 1854, 17-8 Vic., c. 47. On hearing arguments in London, see *Noble* v. *Ahier*, 11 P.D. 158 (Ch. York 1886), upholding the practice. But in the case, Lord Penzance relied on a rule made under authority of Church Discipline Act, 1840, 3-4 Vic., c. 86, § 13. If the proceeding had not been under that act, the result might have been different.

82. See Chapter 3, note 231, *supra*.

83. 1963, No. 1. The Commission's report is the Lloyd-Jacob report cited in note 81, *supra*.

84. *R.* v. *Editor, Printers and Publishers of the Daily Herald, ex parte Bishop of Norwich*, [1932] 2 K.B. 402. The Ecclesiastical Jurisdiction Measure, 1963, No. 1, § 81 provides for contempt. § 82(4) abolishes imprisonment for excommunication.

85. *Re St. Michael and All Angels, Great Torrington*, [1985] Fam. 81; *Re St. Stephen's Walbrook*, [1987] Fam. 146.

86. Mayfield, 189, Quoting William Temple's first visitation charge as archbishop of York.

87. Eliot, *Reunion by Destruction* (Council for the Defence of Church Principles Pamph. 7, no date, evidently mid-1940s), 16-17.

88. Bell, *Common Order in Christs' Church* (1937), 37.

89. C. H. Sisson, "A Warning to the Church," in *No Alternative*, ed. D. Martin and P. Mullen (Oxford, 1981), 226, 228-29.

90. Welsby, 241-42.

91. Redundant churches: Chapter 3, note 68, *supra*; *Paul Report*, 69. Tourism: *General Synod Reports*, xii, 1049-76 (1981); G. S. 505 (1981).

92. 1969, c. B22. The statistic is from *Crockford*, 1988, 68.

93. Halsbury (3d), 353, note(b). The quotation is from Bell, *Davidson*, 1203.

94. *General Synod Reports*, x, 1048 (1979).

95. Premarital sex: Reuters, 9 January, 1984. Homosexuality: Welsby, 205-6. The quotation is from *Crockford*, 1982, 71.

96. *General Synod Reports*, xviii, 913-56 (1987).

97. On discipline of the clergy, see pp. 221-25, *supra*. On exclusion of laypeople from the sacraments, see pp. 290-93, *supra*.

98. *Aambit, The Newsletter of the Association for Apostolic Ministry*, No. 3, July, 1988.

99. R. Naz, "Doute," *Dictionnaire de Droit Canonique*, iv (Paris, 1949), 1437, 1441 (my translation). On the relation between spiritual and ontological effects, see my "On Validity and Invalidity of Sacraments," *Theological Studies*, xlii (1981), 580.

100. This language appears in the first paragraph of the Preface. While it is common Anglican doctrine, I have not been able to find an English source for it.

101. The *New York Times* for October 1, 1989, reports a statement unanimously adopted by the House of Bishops of the American Episcopal Church, which the leader of the traditionalist wing described as creating "an atmosphere . . . in which we can actually go forward together without compromising our beliefs." Ms. Judy Bliven, secretary to the bishop of Northern Indiana, was kind enough to provide me with a copy. The statement characterizes opposition to the ordination of women as "a recognized theological position" consistent with being "loyal members of the family," and calls for "pastoral sensitivity" to those who cannot accept the priestly ministrations of a woman. We may suppose that this is code for making available the ministrations of a man.

102. Mayfield, 57.

103. *Paul Report*, 77.

104. *Gaudium et Spes*, ¶ 1. The quotations in the next paragraph are from ¶ 76 and ¶ 45.

Index

Note: A date not otherwise explained after a person's name is that of the case or event in which the person figured. I have used such dates only where I could not find dates of birth and death in standard biographical material.

Note: These Tables include all the cases, statutes, measures, and canons mentioned individually in text, but not those mentioned only in the notes. A few of the more important statutes are included in the main Index and cross-referenced here.

Table of Cases

Table of Statutes

Table of Measures

495

Table of Canons